Legal Risk Management, Governance and Compliance

A Guide to Best Practice from Leading Experts

Consulting Editors **Stuart Weinstein** and **Charles Wild**

Consulting editors
Stuart Weinstein, Charles Wild

Publisher
Sian O'Neill

Commissioning editor
Katherine Cowdrey

Editor
Carolyn Boyle

Production
Russell Anderson

Publishing directors
Guy Davis, Tony Harriss, Mark Lamb

Legal Risk Management, Governance and Compliance:
A Guide to Best Practice from Leading Experts
is published by
Globe Law and Business
Globe Business Publishing Ltd
New Hibernia House
Winchester Walk
London SE1 9AG
United Kingdom
Tel +44 20 7234 0606
Fax +44 20 7234 0808
Web www.globelawandbusiness.com

Printed and bound by CPI Group (UK) Ltd, Croydon, CR0 4YY

ISBN 9781905783946

Legal Risk Management, Governance and Compliance: A Guide to Best Practice from Leading Experts
© 2013 Globe Business Publishing Ltd

DISCLAIMER
This publication is intended as a general guide only. The information and opinions which it contains are not intended to be a comprehensive study, nor to provide legal advice, and should not be treated as a substitute for legal advice concerning particular situations. Legal advice should always be sought before taking any action based on the information provided. The publishers bear no responsibility for any errors or omissions contained herein.

Table of contents

Foreword ——————— 7
Lord David Gold

Preface ——————— 9
Stuart Weinstein
Charles Wild
University of Hertfordshire

Part I: Legal risk management

Developing the right formula — 11
for successful legal risk
management, governance
and compliance
Stuart Weinstein
Charles Wild
University of Hertfordshire

The transformation of ———— 45
general counsel: setting the
strategic legal agenda
Constance E Bagley
Yale University
Mark Roellig
Massachusetts Mutual Life Insurance
Company

Using alternative dispute ——— 67
resolution as a tool for
containing legal risk
Wolf Juergen von Kumberg
Northrop Grumman
Stuart Weinstein
Charles Wild
University of Hertfordshire

Legal risk management ———— 111
and governance in the
financial world
Boris Georg Hallik
DekaBank

Part II: Governance

An international overview ——— 125
of board structures
Jan M Eickelberg
Peter Ries
Berlin School of Economics and Law

Sarbanes-Oxley requirements — 145
and the implementation of US
corporate governance controls –
an overview for non-US corporates
Zabihollah Rezaee
University of Memphis

Risk management and the ——— 165
board of directors: lessons
to be learned from UBS
Roger Barker
Institute of Directors
Stuart Weinstein
Charles Wild
University of Hertfordshire

Understanding the role of ——— 187
the independent director in
family-controlled listed enterprises
Richard L Narva
Narva & Company LLC

Corporate social _____ 201
responsibility
    Richard Smerdon
    CHH Corporate Governance Handbook

'Tone at the top' and _____ 219
corporate governance
    Peter Giblin
    Cass Business School

Part III: Compliance

Bribery and corruption

The Foreign Corrupt _____ 229
Practices Act: compliance to
protect business clients globally
    Aaron Schildhaus
    Law Offices of Aaron Schildhaus

The rising tide of a new _____ 247
international phenomenon:
carbon-copy prosecutions
    Andrew S Boutros
    United States Attorney's Office
    for the Northern District of Illinois
    T Markus Funk
    Perkins Coie LLP

The Bribery Act 2010 _____ 273
    Paul Feldberg
    Willkie Farr & Gallagher LLP
    Ian Leist QC
    Fulcrum Chambers LLP

Health, safety and environment

Issues relating to health, _____ 295
safety and environment
practice
    Jon Cooper
    Bond Pearce LLP

Human resources

Human resources issues _____ 315
for managers
    Marjorie Hurwitz Bremner
    Berg Kaprow Lewis LLP
    Thushara Polpitiye
    Astute HR Ltd

Information systems

Data privacy: data transfers, _____ 351
offshoring and the cloud
    Hazel Grant
    Mark Watts
    Bristows

Corporate information _____ 377
risk management
    Rita Esen
    University of Northumbria

International risks

Managing legal risks _____ 393
in China
    Fang Ma
    University of Hertfordshire

Process management controls

Third parties, agents and _____ 409
supply chain due diligence
    David Curran
    Risk Readiness Corporation
    Wolf Juergen von Kumberg
    Northrop Grumman
    Peter Mancusi
    Weber Shandwick

Implementing compliance _____ 419
management systems: an
organisational learning process
    Lutz-Ulrich Haack
    German Graduate School of
    Management and Law, Heilbronn
    Robert Nothhelfer
    Former head of GRC Lidl
    International
    University of Freiburg, Asperg

Regulated industries –
the financial sector

European debt capital _____ 431
markets regulation in the
context of retail market risks
    Ferdinando Bruno
    University of Lugano, Switzerland

Fraud within the _____ 453
banking sector
    Nikolay Dobrev
    University of Liverpool

About the authors _____ 469

Foreword

Lord David Gold

The Bribery Act 2010, which came into force on July 1 2011, was a wake-up call to British businesspeople, particularly those engaged in international business. Until then, many had perhaps not thought that certain business practices, such as the making of facilitation payments, might be unlawful. The Bribery Act removed any doubts about that and the business community realised that unlawful activities abroad could more readily be prosecuted in the United Kingdom. The Bribery Act also introduced a new corporate offence of failing to prevent bribery, which has effectively required companies to review their procedures and practices to ensure that they are doing enough to avoid problems arising. Additionally, high-profile corporate scandals involving compliance failures have put companies on high alert.

Companies determined to put their house in order must demonstrate that they have in place systems and controls designed to reduce the risks. That is just the start, though. Companies must also properly train their staff and ensure that communication within the organisation is effective. Most organisations will today have a code of conduct setting out their values. There must be no doubt to all that management is determined that the business will be run in an ethical way, that inappropriate behaviour is unacceptable and that wrongdoers will be disciplined. Whistleblowers should be encouraged and staff must not fear retaliation if they report inappropriate conduct.

The pressure on management to ensure that the business operates in a compliant way is great. Although a sizeable industry has emerged where professional firms can provide help, managers must be permanently on their guard against things going wrong and cannot rely on their advisers always to be on the scene to deal with the issues. They must take responsibility and do their best to reduce risk to a minimum.

In this book, Stuart Weinstein and Charles Wild have continued their successful blend of legal practice with legal academia in writing and putting together considerable material that will provide valuable assistance to those within companies who have to deal with issues of compliance and governance. First, they identify the risks and regulatory issues that concern companies today. Second, they provide practical advice as to how these issues can properly be managed and risks reduced. The true worth of this work is that it provides practical assistance to those responsible for delivering good governance. The editors have assembled an impressive team of contributors from around the globe to provide real-world insights into risk management and governance, together with cutting-edge research in the field. The book will be useful for any manager seeking comprehensive guidance as to how day-to-day risk, governance or compliance issues should be managed.

In August 2010 the Department of Justice, Washington DC, appointed Lord Gold as corporate monitor of BAE Systems, to review its response to the implementation of recommendations made by Lord Woolf following his inquiry into the company. This role continues until the end of August 2013. In January 2013 Lord Gold was appointed by Rolls-Royce plc to review its governance and compliance. In March 2013 Lord Gold took up the role of non-executive chairman of Proven Limited, a global investigations firm which is part of the Good Governance Group.

Lord Gold entered the House of Lords as a Conservative working peer in February 2011 and in March 2011 established a disputes strategy consultancy, David Gold & Associates LLP.

Lord Gold is a governor of the London School of Economics, serving on its finance committee, and is also an accredited CEDR mediator.

Until February 2011 Lord Gold was a litigation partner at Herbert Smith, having qualified at the firm in 1975. He became head of the litigation division in 2003 and senior partner in 2005, and left the firm in 2011.

Preface

Stuart Weinstein
Charles Wild

The ascendancy of the general counsel, coupled with the critical role that other lawyers employed in-house within companies, government and the non-profit sector play in these organisations, is quite rightly regarded as one of the most significant changes to take place in the practice of law over the past quarter-century. As Ben Heineman[1] has noted, the general counsel is now seen as the go-to person to advise the chief executive and the board of directors on the most pressing legal and ethical enterprise-threatening issues facing a company.

While this shift has gained recognition within the United States, being incorporated into the curricula of leading law schools and business and management schools such as Harvard, Columbia, Stanford and Yale, the University of Hertfordshire's School of Law remains the first to offer such a course ("Legal Risk Management, Governance and Compliance") within the United Kingdom.[2] As such, this text comes at a critical juncture in the recognition and acceptance of this area as a significant part of both legal education and practice at a national and international level.

This text not only reflects an extensive body of multi-jurisdictional research from leading academics, but also draws upon a wealth of invaluable experience from practitioners across the globe. The book offers in-house legal and compliance managers a wealth of strategic and operational advice, as well as legal guidance on a myriad of issues that such an individual might face on a day-to-day basis; in short, it is a unique text from a unique group of contributors.[3] Contributions from such a wide range of disciplines as accountancy, business, computer forensics, corporate governance, law, management and regulatory fields, coupled with input from leading legal practitioners and managers in allied fields of law such as compliance, corporate governance, human resources and risk management, ensure that cutting-edge practitioner guidance on best practice in legal risk management, governance and compliance is at the heart of this work. Underpinning this text is also the acknowledgement that legal decisions are never isolated from the commercial, ethical, operational risk, political or reputational concerns that inform them.

---

1   Former general counsel at General Electric.
2   The course draws upon Stuart Weinstein's pre-academic career as general counsel at Daewoo in Korea and the United States, and introduces participants to the analytical framework and methodology which general counsel and other trusted legal advisers in business use in order to manage legal risk and compliance, and ultimately lead the legal governance function of the organisations that they advise.
3   The consulting editors would like to thank Thomas Pearson for involving them in *Legal Week*'s Corporate Governance & Risk Forum, which has not only become a successful annual conference since its launch in 2011, but also provided a forum to meet a number of the contributors to this work.

We are extremely grateful to everyone who has contributed to this project. We are also grateful to Lord David Gold for his willingness to write the foreword to this text. Lord Gold is an excellent example of someone who offers those hard-to-quantify skill sets that leading trusted legal advisers bring to bear on enterprise-threatening legal risk management issues.

Finally, the editors would like to thank Katherine Cowdrey, the commissioning editor at Globe Law and Business, for her continued encouragement, support and patience during the writing and editorial processes of this text.

Stuart Weinstein is associate dean (research and enterprise) at the University of Hertfordshire School of Law, Hatfield, Hertfordshire. Before joining the university, he worked as general counsel to Korean multinational Daewoo in Seoul, Republic of Korea, and Los Angeles. Mr Weinstein is co-author with Charles Wild of Smith & Keenan's English Law *(17th ed, Pearson 2013) and* Smith & Keenan's Company Law *(16th ed, Pearson 2013). In addition to his various research and writing projects, Mr Weinstein remains active in practice as a solicitor of the Superior Courts of England and Wales advising companies, governmental entities and non-profit organisations on aspects of legal risk management, governance and compliance. He is admitted to practise law in the US jurisdictions of California, District of Columbia and New York.*

Mr Weinstein earned his BA (honours) in the history of ideas from Williams College, Williamstown, Massachusetts, his JD from Columbia Law School, New York City, where he was a Harlan Fiske Stone scholar and an MBA with commendation from the University of Hertfordshire Business School, and he was selected to be a Fulbright scholar grantee. Mr Weinstein also serves as vice chair of the Bar Standards Board's Education and Training Committee.

Charles Wild is professor of legal education and dean of the University of Hertfordshire School of Law, where he teaches company law, corporate governance and risk management. He is the co-author with Stuart Weinstein of Smith & Keenan's English Law *(17th ed, Pearson 2013) and* Smith & Keenan's Company Law *(16th ed, Pearson 2013). Dr Wild holds a PhD in law from the University of Sheffield, an MBA (distinction) from the University of Hertfordshire Business School, an LLM in international and commercial law from the University of Sheffield (distinction), together with a number of other qualifications including a BSc (hons) in economics from University College, London. Dr Wild is also a member of the Education and Training (Standard Setting) Committee at the Law Society of Scotland.*

Developing the right formula for successful legal risk management, governance and compliance

Stuart Weinstein
Charles Wild
University of Hertfordshire

In this chapter, we explore how effective legal risk management and compliance is now a central component of sound governance in the public, private and non-profit sectors. The premise for this chapter is that an effective compliance regime is a key competition differentiator for an organisation. With the spectacular failures of Lehman Brothers, AIG, Northern Rock, RBS and HBOS/Lloyds TSB, the Toyota recall crisis, the BP Deepwater Horizon oil spill, the Siemens corruption scandal, the BAE bribery scandal, the TEPCO/Fukushima Nuclear Power Station failure, the Wal-Mart-Mexico bribery scandal, and the *News of the World* phone hacking scandal, we will consider how the corporate governance debate has moved from corporate social responsibility to organisational responsibility and accountability.

1. The Triple A formula

Philip Bramwell, Group General Counsel at BAE Systems plc, has spoken of the need for organisations to develop the 'AAA formula' for successful legal risk management and compliance, consisting of appreciation, architecture and assurance.[1] An organisation must have a keen appreciation of the environment it operates in and how it might be affected by increased regulatory burden. The company must also have architecture in place beyond internal controls in response to promulgated rules and standards.

Consider the architecture in place for publicly traded companies and the role of the audit function. While an external audit of a public company is a given for finance, a similar external audit should take place for non-financial matters in order to provide greater assurance to shareholders and stakeholders.[2] At the heart of this recognition is the need to provide greater assurance that an organisation's failure to meet the increased burden of regulation and standards can result in an irrecoverable loss of brand goodwill and reputation.

---

1 Remarks of Philip Bramwell, The Lawyer Governance Risk and Compliance Congress, June 8 2011, Brighton, available at: www.thelawyersummits.com/grc/summit_programmePopup.asp (accessed April 5 2013).
2 *Ibid.*

Imagine what a compliance audit of Wal-Mart would have revealed. According to the New York Times, in seeking to dominate the Mexican retail market, Wal-Mart de Mexico undertook a major bribery campaign in Mexico, which included payments to zoning and municipal officials all over Mexico to permit prompt building of its stores.[3] The *New York Times* alleged that after being made aware of this illegal conduct in its Mexico subsidiary, Wal-Mart's leaders ordered that the internal investigation be shut down after a protracted struggle between the company's public stance on ethics and morality and its relentless desire for increased growth in new markets: "Confronted with evidence of corruption in Mexico, top Wal-Mart executives focused more on damage control than on rooting out wrongdoing."[4] One of the ironies uncovered by the *New York Times'* investigation was that Wal-Mart gave primary responsibility for investigation of the bribery allegations to the Wal-Mart de Mexico general counsel. It is alleged that this individual had authorised the bribes in the first place!

2. Behavioural modification

The authors of this chapter suggest that compliance alone must never be the means to an end. The right formula for legal risk management and compliance requires a far more subtle balancing of the 'carrot-stick' approach than is normally used in compliance-driven regimes. For example, the regulatory regime provided by the Sarbanes-Oxley Act of 2002 – widely derided as too process-based and too 'tick-box' in its approach – did not prevent a number of prominent corporate failures that grew out of dubious accounting practices (eg, AIG (General Re) and Lehman Brothers (Repo 105)), indicating that a rigorous emphasis on tick-box compliance rather than an evaluative approach to legal risk management is not effective.

In the global business place, companies face a remarkable array of new and often contradictory laws and regulations. High-profile corporate scandals involving compliance failures show that the loss of reputation can have a significant, if not fatal, effect on a company. For instance, recent scandals in the banking industry such as those at UBS and Goldman Sachs have resulted in clients abandoning the private banking industry in favour of other investments. "Millions in assets that would have gone to investment portfolios run by wealth managers have already been driven elsewhere", says Cath Tillotson, managing partner at Scorpio Partnership, which researches the wealth management industry, "with London property, private equity and gold among the main beneficiaries".[5]

International companies recognise this and invest heavily in implementing internal mechanisms and controls, including sophisticated information technology (IT) systems designed to detect and prevent compliance breaches. For instance, research undertaken by the IBM Almaden Research Centre and the University of

---

3   David Barstow, "Vast Mexico Bribery Case Hushed Up by Wal-Mart after Top Level Struggle", *New York Times*, April 21 2012, available at: http://www.nytimes.com/2012/04/22/business/at-wal-mart-in-mexico-a-bribe-inquiry-silenced.html?pagewanted=all (accessed 9 April 2013).

4   *Ibid.*

5   Chris Vellacott and Sinead Cruise, "UBS Faces Fight to Uphold Reputation among Super-rich", Reuters, December 20 2012, available at: http://uk.reuters.com/article/2012/12/20/uk-ubs-reputation-idUKBRE8BJ0S320121220 (accessed February 26 2013).

Stuttgart suggests that the use of database technology can play an important role compliance with the internal controls provisions of Sections 302 and 404 of the Sarbanes-Oxley Act.[6] The research proposes the use of workflow modelling, compliance auditing and online analytical tools to automate many internal control functions.[7]

However, no matter how good or technically innovative, such systems and controls cannot succeed without the development of a strong compliance culture that is supported by executives, managers, employees, contractors and business partners all at levels.

As David Gebler, an expert on ethics and risk management in corporate culture, asks: "What leader would not want to foster a culture of compliance?"[8] Gebler argues that a company cannot achieve compliance without first addressing the behavioural issues in its culture that impact the ability and the desire to be compliant.[9]

A Freshfields Bruckkhaus Deringer (Freshfields) study bears out Gebler's observations, namely that behavioural crises are the most deadly to companies. The law firm commissioned a study of the impact of 78 major global corporate crises since 2007 and divided them into four categories:

- behavioural – crises triggered by reports of the illegal or questionable conduct of the company in general or by specific employees, such as anti-competitive conduct or money laundering;
- operational – crises that seriously impair the company's ability to function properly, for example, major accidents or asset seizures;
- corporate – crises that affect the corporate and financial well-being of the organisation, including liquidity issues or material litigation; and
- informational – crises that seriously affect the company's IT infrastructure or electronic systems, such as customer data loss or theft of commercial secrets.[10]

The 2012 Freshfields' study found that, of the above crises, only behavioural crises result in share price falls of 50 per cent or more on day one,[11] that is, such crises frighten the market the most. As such, what is the role of the general counsel and/or the chief compliance officer in inspiring proper corporate behaviour to avoid such disaster?

At the heart of this compliance culture is the internal legal and compliance adviser. This chapter is designed to explore the issues facing the internal legal and compliance adviser and to offer readers an appreciation for the issues involved in the development and management of a sophisticated legal risk management and compliance operation suitable for a company operating in a cross-border business environment or dependent on a global supply chain for its operations.

---

6   Rakesh Agrawal, Christopher Johnson, Jerry Kiernan (IBM Almaden Research Centre) and Frank Leymann (University of Stuttgart), "Taming Compliance with Sarbanes-Oxley Internal Controls using Database Technology", available at: www.almaden.ibm.com/cs/projects/iis/hdb/Publications/papers/ICDE06SOX_CR.pdf (accessed February 26 2013).

7   *Ibid.*

8   David Gebler, "Creating a Culture of Compliance", Ark Group, 2011, available at: www.ark-group.com/Downloads/Culture-of-compliance-TOC.pdf (accessed 25 February 2013).

9   *Ibid.*

10   Freshfields Bruckhaus Derringer, "Crisis Management: Prepare for the Unexpected", available at: www.freshfields.com/en/insights/crisis_management/ (accessed February 27 2013).

11   *Ibid.*

3.   The lawyer as legal risk manager

Crucial to the survival and profitability of a business, the effectiveness of a governmental agency or the responsiveness of a non-profit organisation to its constituent stakeholders is that it must be proactive in identifying and managing legal risk. The organisation must have a keen understanding of the key elements of legal risk management, legal governance and compliance, and must evaluate their impact on its effective operation and strategic planning.

One need only look at the situation of BP today to understand the complexities of legal risk management. In March 2012, BP reached a $7.8 billion settlement with 110,000 Gulf of Mexico businesses and individuals over the Deepwater Horizon oil spill, but it still faces a $18 billion civil claim against it from the US government and the various states that have suffered damages as a result of the oil spill.[12] This is on top of a criminal settlement with the US Department of Justice for $4 billion, which is the largest environmental penalty paid in US history.[13]

Rupert Bondy, general counsel at BP, has earned a solid reputation for his work in managing the legal risk crisis at BP: "[Bondy] has sat squarely in the driving seat of the company's risk management strategy, effectively steering its emergency response from the beginning of the incident through to the eventual financial settlement", according to *Legal Business*.[14] *Legal Business* reports that "the consensus is that few in-house lawyers could have responded so assuredly to what former White House energy adviser Carol Browner called the 'worst environmental disaster the US has faced'".[15] This is all the more impressive when one considers that at the time of his appointment as BP general counsel in 2007, Mr Bondy's expertise was not in energy but in pharmaceuticals, where he had worked for 13 years with SmithKline Beecham (later GlaxoSmithKline).

Melanie Hatton, an in-house lawyer working for Latitude, offers the following definition for legal risk: "the risk to a business of an event occurring which brings about a legal consequence impacting the business".[16] Legal risk management involves identifying issues such as legal liability and compliance failure, mitigation and the balancing of risk in all its forms. The definition arises out of the concept of governance, risk management and compliance, an offshoot of legislation such as the Sarbanes-Oxley Act.[17] It involves legal advisers pointing out where and how things can and might go wrong, appreciating the extent of any negative impact if problems

---

12   James Quinn and Richard Blacken, "US to Press On with $18bn BP Lawsuit Despite Settlement", *Daily Telegraph*, February 26 2012, available at: www.telegraph.co.uk/finance/newsbysector/energy/oilandgas/9121264/US-to-press-on-with-18bn-BP-lawsuit-despite-settlement.html (accessed February 26 2013).

13   Julie Cart, "Greed Caused BP's Gulf Oil Spill, Lawyers Argue", *Los Angeles Times*, February 25 2013, available at: www.latimes.com/news/nationworld/nation/la-na-bp-trial-20130226,0,7288349.story (accessed February 27 2013).

14   Legal Business, GC Power List 2013 (posted 2012), available at: www.legalbusiness.co.uk/index.php/global-counsel/698-rupert-bondy-bp-energy (accessed February 27 2013).

15   *Ibid.*

16   Melanie Hatton, "5 Steps to Legal Risk Management", In-House Lawyer – A Commentary From an In-House Lawyer Who's Experimenting With How Lawyers Can Use Social Media for Best Effect, available at: http://in-house-lawyer.blogspot.co.uk/2010/02/5-steps-to-legal-risk-management.html (accessed February 26 2013).

17   Linda Musthaler and Brian Musthaler, Governance, Risk Management and Compliance and What it Means to You, *Network World*, May 7 2007, available at: www.networkworld.com/newsletters/techexec/2007/0507techexec1.html (accessed February 27 2013).

arise, devising plans to cope with threats, and putting in place strategies to deal with the risks either before or after their occurrence. Legal governance is generally accepted as the establishment, execution and interpretation of processes and rules put in place by company legal departments in order to ensure a smoothly run legal department and company.[18]

As early as 2003, Andrew Whittaker (then general counsel for the UK's financial regulator, the Financial Services Authority, and now group general counsel of Lloyds Banking Group) identified the trend for in-house lawyers to play a greater role in risk management activity in financial institutions:

> The role of lawyers is changing. Traditionally, we have been advisers, helping our clients to understand the law. We also have been implementers, achieving goals for our clients by drafting legal instruments or conducting litigation. Increasingly, many of us, particularly in-house lawyers, are taking on a role as legal risk managers.[19]

Whittaker stresses that the role of lawyers as risk managers must involve the broad strategic aspects of legal risk management and not just focus on more isolated operational aspects such as negotiating exclusion clauses in a particular contract for the sales team: "The key point about the relationship with the risk management function is that it enables lawyers to set out to identify and tackle an organisation's overall legal risk, not simply specific manifestations of it arising in particular cases or transactions, important though they may be."[20]

A 2013 Berwin Leighton Paisner study[21] (BLP Study) carried out by RSG Consulting[22] on behalf of the law firm indicates that the old-fashioned way of managing legal risk by relying on the experience of senior in-house lawyers and external counsel has, since the recent financial crisis, given way to the introduction of greater process management in the mitigation of legal risk escalating issues and integrating with the risk management frameworks and risk culture of the broader business. This is especially true in highly regulated sectors, such as utilities and financial institutions, where a more process-based approach to risk exists and legal risk management has become as process-based as credit decision-making might be in the finance department.

This thinking is in line with current practice followed in the United States, as evidenced by the promulgation and use of a legal risk management planning matrix developed by the Association of Corporate Counsel.[23] In assessing legal risk management practices, the association breaks down a number of strategic areas to be

---

18 Jonathan Konkle, "Legal Risk Management Requires a Corporate Strategy, Mindset and Commitment", DCIG, January 9 2008, available at: www.dcig.com/2008/01/interview-with-stephen-whetstone-pt1.html (accessed February 27 2013).

19 Andrew S Whittaker, "Lawyers as Risk Managers", *Butterworths Journal of International Banking and Financial Law*, January 2003, pp. 5-7, available at: www.ibanet.org/Document/Default.aspx?Document Uid...4655... (accessed February 27 2013).

20 *Ibid*.

21 Berwin Leighton Paisner, "Managing Legal Risks Effectively – An Evolving Approach", January 22 2013, available at: www.legalweeklaw.com/abstract/managing-legal-risk-effectively-insights-counsel-15691 (BLP Study) (accessed March 8 2013).

22 http://rsgconsulting.com/.

23 Association of Corporate Counsel, ACC Value Challenge Tool Kit Resource (September 2008), "How to Assess Legal Risk Management Practices", available at: www.acc.com/advocacy/valuechallenge/toolkit/ loader.cfm?csModule=security/getfile&pageid=38926 (accessed March 9 2013).

incorporated in the matrix, including:

- law department leadership;
- outside counsel participation;
- business partner legal risk awareness;
- legal risk management coordination;
- identifying legal risks;
- project legal risk management;
- reporting to senior management; and
- law department legal risk performance management.

The degree to which such plans are implemented – from 'not at all' to 'fully in place' – is assessed for each category, which is broken down into a 37-item checklist.

Developing a checklist such as that developed by the Association of Corporate Counsel is the starting point for using process as a tool to support legal risk management. However, this alone is never enough. Matthew Whalley, client knowledge manager at Berwin Leighton Paisner, writes that:

> ... the landscape has changed and in-house counsel should position themselves as proactive legal risk management as opposed to a reactive advisery role. In risk parlance, the in-house legal team is a 'second line of defence' – an unglamorous description of our profession, but an uncomfortable fact that many in private practice should remember.[24]

The BLP Study used the responses of the general counsel it surveyed to group the key indicators of a robust approach to legal risk management into five categories (processes, knowledge and communications, structure, culture, and individuals). For instance, a robust and clearly identified approach to legal management is indicated by the business having a clear knowledge and understanding of risk, a culture of 'doing the right thing', a highly structured and well-run legal and other risk functions managed by individuals widely acknowledged within the organisation to be of high quality. The BLP Study also identified the various levels of maturity of risk management frameworks. Nearly all those surveyed noted significant improvements in the quality of their risk management systems over the past couple of years; however, equally so, each general counsel surveyed identified the steps and processes they needed to take within their own department to progress further up the legal risk management maturity model outlined below.

In developing a spectrum for legal risk management maturity, ranging from 'next generation', which has risk-driven recruitment, strategic risk mitigation projects, emerging risk reporting, dedicated legal risk managers and independent legal risk assurance, to 'ad hoc', where no formal legal risk management programme exists and risk decisions are made principally on an event-driven basis with no formal reporting, the BLP Study identified two 'in between' states along the continuum from ad hoc to next generation: those organisations that can be said to have a 'mature' management approach that is characterised by systematised recording of

---

24   Matthew Whalley, "The Second Line of Defence – In-house Counsel and Risk Management", *Legal Week*, January 25 2013, available at: www.legalweek.com/legal-week/analysis/2237798/the-second-line-of-defence-inhouse-counsel-and-risk-management (accessed March 9 2013).

legal risks, tactical risk mitigation projects, a legal function aligned with business objectives, quantitative reporting of organisational exposure and assigned responsibilities; and those characterised by a 'developing' approach where there are policies in place, legal risks are discussed with business teams and the company engages in *ad hoc* risk mitigation projects.

In moving up this maturity scale, the BLP Study identified certain essential key aspects, including language, ownership, risk ratings, process and a forward-looking approach. An example of such maturity is a company that defines legal risk and its technicalities in simpler, non-technical terms that are easily understood by business people. In-house legal teams also have a role to play. They must understand how risk exposure sits within the entity and be comfortable operating in this framework. Of course, ultimately the responsibility for overall risk management process lies with the business, but within this picture legal risk management responsibility is owned by the legal department. "Getting under the skin of their business", according to the BLP Study is seen as the legal department's role, whether this means inviting itself to meetings or working with C-level executives. The BLP Study suggests that, today, one of the legal department's critical responsibilities is the proactive measurement and assessment of risk. It is thought best that legal risk measurement follows operational approaches to risk rating, provided that such risk rating processes are sufficiently robust and forward-looking to be of value in the legal arena, where risks may develop over longer timescales. Critical to this process is that risk rating is realistic and not merely a tick-box checking exercise.

The BLP Study sees process improvements as essential to the legal risk management effort because as risk management becomes more complex, supporting processes and systems become essential. Concepts such as risk registers, control rating reports, risk portfolio reports, board reporting and escalation procedures all must be factored into the overarching framework of legal risk management. While it is seen that the key value the legal function adds in a corporate setting is the identification of potential risk before any issues become crystallised, this is not so easy to do if the legal department does not look outside its own business, and even outside the industry, for equivalent warning signs or changes that could impact on specific business units. Greater thought must be given to 'unlikely but plausible' events and the 'unthinkable', even in the legal department. The BLP Study identified five specific factors that would make implementing enterprise-wide legal risk management easier. Lawyers must develop better links with operational risk and audit teams to gain a better sense of the risk appetite of the company. This can only be done through adequate resourcing of the legal function. In short, if the lawyers are too bogged down in the day-to-day process of 'putting out fires', they cannot adequately consider the broader strategic issues that give rise to better legal risk management. Developing a sound legal risk framework is essential; merely adapting what other companies in the same industry do without further reflection will be insufficient. Every entity is different and will have different risks. While it goes without saying that lawyers who work with businesses must understand the business and the industry they are working in, they must also be given the time to learn how properly to evaluate and use the legal risk management tools and processes they have put in place to help them better quantify legal risk.

It must be noted that fewer than half of the general counsel surveyed said that they were able to quantify the value of risk management or had taken a fact-based approach.[25] Where fact-based approaches are employed, many general counsel use standard likelihood versus impact matrices to assign a scale to risks, in which individual risks are then scored and given traffic light ratings of red, amber or green for all purposes.[26] A clear desire on the part of these counsel to have risk assessments that are three-dimensional in nature, taking into account the timeframe in which a risk is likely to occur, was considered most helpful. Finally, many of those surveyed felt that reputational risk should be considered alongside and equal to financial risk in the light of recent reputational risk failings.[27]

Melanie Hatton offers her own five steps to better legal risk management. These may be more applicable to smaller companies where a single in-house lawyer carries on the legal function on his or her own, with limited recourse to outside counsel. Her advice starts with the importance of the legal audit function. Regular legal audits where the legal team works closely with the business management team to analyse risks, prioritise them and anticipate future legal needs of the company are essential. In Hatton's view, such audits form the basis of a "corporate memory", which will be useful for future due diligence exercises and the storage of key management data. It will also be of value to the compliance and legal risk management functions going forward. Her second priority is the importance of education: the company's lawyer must communicate the message of legal risk management throughout the company, and at all levels. Getting the word out at all levels is important as risks generally do not emerge in the C-level suite but much further down the hierarchy, for example, on the shop floor, at the retail level or in the supply chain. As such, if legal risk management is not seen and heard across the company, people will not think it is a resource that has relevance to their work. Training sessions can be used to get the message out that it is a proactive not reactive task. For Hatton, these training sessions can be a good precursor to rolling out new legal risk management strategies and schemes.

Hatton points out the reality that legal risk is not freestanding but should be conjoined to financial, reputational, operational, political, regulatory and tax risks. This conjoining of legal risk with other risk management issues in a company often presents challenges to those new to the role of in-house counsel in that the risk-averse nature of law firm practice is often at odds with the entrepreneurial acceptance of risks in a successful business. It is this working together with other departments on risk management issues and with individuals at all levels of the company which will anticipate the success of the introduction of any new compliance and governance policies that in-house counsel will be involved with at the company.

Hatton points out that the involvement of in-house counsel in daily operations "always proves to be the most fertile ground for legal input" in that "an abundance of legal consequences can be found in supply, manufacturing and distribution

---

25   BLP Study 2013, note 21 above.
26   *Ibid.*
27   For more information on reputation risk management and the related problems, see Jonathan Copulsky, *Brand Resilience: Managing Risk and Recovery in a High-Speed World*, Palgrave Macmillan, 2011.

chains, protection of intellectual property rights, brand protection (online and offline), pending and threatened litigation, product liability, sales and marketing practice, insurance, property matters, employment and HR practice, industry regulation as well as company secretarial, board and shareholder matters".[28] As such, it is important for legal counsel to maintain good working relationships with colleagues operating in each of these areas and to be seen as part of the team, and not an obstacle, to achieving operational outputs and objectives.

Hatton's final observation on managing legal risk in a company today is that legal departments are expected to do this with fewer resources available than in the past due to tougher economic conditions. Whether it is pressure to reduce head count or to reduce spending on outside legal advice, in-house lawyers are expected to deliver more with less. As such, a core skill of today's in-house lawyer is his or her ability to manage the risks in this more intense climate by better clarifying the role of the legal function within the business, demonstrating added value, and selecting, managing and getting the most out of their internal and external legal resource.[29]

Hatton's suggestions clearly indicate that the model for in-house legal risk management in a modern, non-hierarchical corporate entity is to be fully involved with the day-to-day activities of the organisation rather than isolating itself in a specialised environment. It must be seen to be heard and cannot hide behind its professional rank or status to remove itself from operational involvement and supervision.

Hatton emphasises the need for a "legal audit". This concept is not new.[30] Andrew J Sherman, partner with US law firm Dickstein Shapiro Morin and Oshinsky LLP, identifies a legal audit as involving a company's management team meeting with corporate counsel in order to discuss strategic plans and objectives, review key documents and records, and analyse and identify the current and projected legal needs of the company.[31] According to Sherman, this will provide the basis for an ongoing legal compliance and prevention programme in order to ensure that the company's goals, structure and ongoing operations are consistent with the latest developments in business and corporate law. It can also help managers to identify the legal issues triggered by changes in strategies, goals or objectives, and plan for the resulting legal tasks. Each company will have different needs to be identified. The legal audit may be performed on a periodic basis as part of an ongoing compliance programme or may be carried out in connection with a specific event or transaction, for example, a merger or sale of assets. Additionally, there are more specialised legal audits that will take place more often in specialised areas such as in the tax, employment, government contracts, franchising or environmental law fields, which may operate on a different schedule from the enterprise-wide legal audit.

---

28 Hatton, note 16 above.
29 Ibid.
30 See Louis M Brown, "Legal Audit", 38 S Cal L Rev 431 (1964-5); Louis M Brown, "Introducing a Legal Audit Manual: Procedure and Substance (Part One)", 2 Preventive L Rep 162 (1983-4); and Louis M Brown, Richard Kuner and Anne Kandel, The Legal Audit: Corporate Internal Investigation, Clark Boardman Callaghan, 2005-12.
31 Andrew J Sherman, "The Legal Audit: A Reality Check for Entrepreneurial Companies", Entrepreneurship Resource Centre, 2013, available at: www.entrepreneurship.org/en/resource-center/the-legal-audit-a-reality-check-for-entrepreneurial-companies.aspx.

Roger S McCormick,[32] Director of the Law and Financial Markets Project at the London School of Economics (an academic with a long career as a financial services lawyer in the City of London), writes that the expectation that in-house lawyers will be legal risk managers from the outset is not without problems. McCormick suggests that the traditional position of the in-house lawyer as employee needs consideration: "A degree of independence, perhaps quite a considerable degree, would seem to be essential if the in-house lawyer is to be able to perform the role effectively."[33] Without suggesting what particular structure is needed to ensure this independence, McCormick acknowledges that "although perfection may not be achievable (and seeking to achieve it may be counter-productive if it results in lawyers losing the necessary 'feel' for the dynamics of the business that employs them) it seems prudent to adopt the habit of checking at regular intervals that the independence of the function is not being eroded".[34]

Professor Edward A Dauer does not see what we term here as legal risk management as a new concept, considering it to be the modern-day version of what is referred to in the United States as preventive law[35] and in Europe as proactive law.[36] Proactive law borrows considerably from preventive law. While preventive law looks at matters mainly from a lawyer's viewpoint, focusing on the prevention of legal risks and disputes, proactive law has an emphasis on securing success and making it possible to achieve the desired goals in a specific situation.[37] Dauer cites Professor Louis M Brown, who pioneered preventive law as a discipline: "In curative law, it is essential for the lawyer to predict what a court will do. In preventive law, it is essential to predict what people will do."[38]

---

32   See Roger S McCormick, *Legal Risk in the Financial Markets*, Oxford University Press, 2010.
33   Roger S McCormick, "The Management of Legal Risk By Financial Institutions in the Context of Basel II, Part 2", 19(9) *Journal of International Banking & Financial Law* (JIBFL) 354 (2004).
34   *Ibid.*
35   "The premise of preventive law is that the legal profession can better serve clients by investing resources in consultation and planning rather than relying on litigation as the primary means of addressing legal problems. This theory recognizes that while litigation is sometimes necessary to address past wrongs, the fact that one ends up in an adversarial proceeding may be evidence of a lack of planning or communication. By applying foresight, lawyers may limit the frequency and scope of future legal problems", quoting the National Centre for Preventive Law website, available at: www.preventivelawyer.org/main/default.asp?pid=brown_program.htm (accessed February 28 2013).
36   "Traditionally, the focus in the legal field has been on the past. Legal research has been mainly concerned with failures – shortcomings, delays, and failures to comply with the law. The focus of the proactive approach is different; it is on the future. Being proactive is the opposite of being reactive or passive. The approach specifically called Proactive Law emerged in Finland in the 1990s. In response to a need to further develop practical methods and legal theories in this emerging field, the Nordic School of Proactive Law was established in 2004. The word proactive implies acting in anticipation, taking control, and self-initiation. These elements are all part of the Proactive Law approach, which differentiates two further aspects of proactivity: one being the promotive dimension (promoting what is desirable; encouraging good behaviour) and the other being the preventive dimension (preventing what is not desirable, keeping legal risks from materialising)", quoting the European Economic and Social Committee (EESC), adopted in its Opinion, *The proactive law approach: a further step towards better regulation at EU level (Ref CESE 1905/2008) (MS doc)* at its plenary session on December 3 2008.
37   See the European Economic and Social Committee (EESC), Opinion *The proactive law approach: a further step towards better regulation at EU level (Ref CESE 1905/2008) (MS doc)* (December 3 2008) at 5.5. The EESC is a consultative body of the European Union. See more at: www.eesc.europa.eu/?i=portal.en.the-committee#sthash.C9IY4Fy6.dpuf (accessed April 5 2013).
38   Edward A Dauer, "The Role of Culture in Legal Risk Management", in *A Proactive Approach*, Scandinavian Studies in Law vol. 49, Peter Wahlgren ed., 2006.

4.   Legal versus compliance

Compliance can be described as anticipating, identifying and resolving regulatory and ethical risks, and redesigning systems to improve compliance. As early as 2005, banks in particular were made aware of the importance of compliance "starting at the top":

> Compliance starts at the top. It will be most effective in a corporate culture that emphasises standards of honesty and integrity and in which the board of directors and senior management lead by example ... Failure to consider the impact of its actions on its shareholders, customers, employees and the markets may result in significant adverse publicity and reputational damage, even if no law has been broken.[39]

The Basel Committee defines compliance risk as the risk of legal or regulatory sanctions, material financial loss, or loss to reputation an entity may suffer as a result of its failure to comply with laws, regulations, rules, related self-regulatory organisation standards, and codes of conduct applicable to its activities.[40]

For effective legal risk management and compliance, legal and compliance managers must have in-depth knowledge of the business and societal risks, awareness and insight into regulation and regulatory changes, and an understanding of the impact of regulation on an organisation. Once the risks have been identified and appropriate regulatory challenges ascertained, these managers must develop, implement and communicate policies, and put appropriate controls in place.

It is the drawing of this linkage between regulation and the formulation of sound policies related to risks and controls at all relevant levels of the organisation and the implementation of procedures to support such policies that is often the most difficult task facing a legal risk manager. When contemplating this challenge, one can only think of the adage of Prime Minister Harold Macmillan when asked what a prime minister most feared: "Events, dear boy, events."[41]

Under the Sarbanes-Oxley Act, US publicly listed companies must conduct a review of the effectiveness of their risk management and internal control systems, covering all material controls, including financial, operational and compliance controls.

In the United Kingdom, the Corporate Governance Code[42] and the Financial Reporting Council's Guidance on Audit Committees[43] (both September 2012) envisage the need for an internal audit function and suggest that senior management and the board may require objective assurance and advice on risk and control covering specialist areas such as regulatory and legal compliance. This has given rise

---

39   Basel Committee on Banking Supervision, "Compliance and the Compliance Function in Banks", April 2005, available at: www.bis.org/publ/bcbs113.pdf (accessed February 27 2013).

40   *Ibid.*

41   Robert Harris, "As Macmillan Never Said: That's Enough Quotations", *Daily Telegraph*, June 4 2002, available at: www.telegraph.co.uk/comment/personal-view/3577416/As-Macmillan-never-said-thats-enough-quotations.html (accessed February 27 2013).

42   All companies with a premium listing of equity shares in the United Kingdom are required under the Listing Rules to report on how they have applied the UK Corporate Governance Code in their annual report and accounts. The relevant section of the Listing Rules can be found at: http://fsahandbook.info/FSA/html/handbook/LR/9/8. (accessed February 28 2013).

43   http://www.frc.org.uk/Our-Work/Publications/Corporate-Governance/Guidance-on-Audit-Committees-September-2012.aspx (accessed April 9 28 2013).

to the position of chief compliance officer, whose role is increasingly being seen as separate and different from that of general counsel.[44]

The chief compliance officer is seen as the 'go to' person responsible for supervising and managing compliance issues within an organisation. The concept proliferated as a result of the call by Commissioner Cynthia A Glassman of the US Securities and Exchange Commission (SEC) in 2002 for companies to appoint a "corporate responsibility officer":

He or she should have sufficient seniority and authority to take the actions necessary under the circumstances. To assess whether your corporate responsibility officer meets this requirement, ask yourself if the person would be able to address the worst-case scenario.

The position should have the full support of the CEO and senior management, both in theory and in practice. The corporate responsibility officer should have access and provide regular reports to senior management ...

Although regular board reports on compliance and controls seem advisable, even if they do not occur regularly, the corporate responsibility officer should have the ability to report directly to the board (for example, to the audit committee chairman) on matters of significant import to the company or matters involving misconduct by senior management.

In addition, the responsible officer should have sufficient time and adequate resources to implement the company's corporate responsibility programme in an effective manner. The best written code of ethics will be worthless if the company starves the budget of the officer who has to implement it.[45]

By 2004, Commissioner Glassman had started to speak of a chief compliance officer instead of a chief responsibility officer. Thus, in an address to the Securities Industries Association (now the Securities and Financial Markets Association) Compliance & Legal Division's 35th Annual Seminar, she set out the case for companies to have both a strong compliance programme and a chief compliance officer in place.[46]

Having identified the role and function of the chief compliance officer, a question for many companies in the United States is whether this should be a separate role or be undertaken by the company's general counsel.[47] Ben Heineman, former General Electric Company senior vice president-general counsel, has identified three broad organisational options:

- the chief compliance officer is independent of the general counsel and chief financial officer (CFO) and reports directly to the chief executive officer (CEO) and board;
- the general counsel is also the chief compliance officer; or
- the chief compliance officer reports to the general counsel and the CFO, and

---

44   See Stuart Weinstein, "Analysis: Separating Out Legal and Compliance Functions – The View from America", *Legal Week*, November 10 2011, Incisive Media Limited.

45   SEC Commissioner Cynthia A Glassman, Speech, Sarbanes-Oxley and the Idea of "Good" Governance, September 27 2002, available at: www.sec.gov/news/speech/spch586.htm (accessed February 28 2013).

46   SEC Commissioner Cynthia A Glassman, Speech, Remarks at the SIA Compliance & Legal Division's 35th Annual Seminar, March 23 2004, available at: www.sec.gov/news/speech/spch032304cag.htm (accessed February 28 2013).

47   Catherine Dunn, "General Counsel, Chief Compliance Officer or Both", *Corporate Counsel*, March 29 2012, available at: www.law.com/corporatecounsel/PubArticleCC.jsp?id=1202547254471&General_ Counsel_Chief_Compliance_Officer____or_Both (accessed March 1 2013).

deals primarily with the process of compliance across all substantive subject matter areas.[48]

Heineman favours the last option because it "builds on the vital need in a corporation for a strong, broad-gauged GC [general counsel] while avoiding significant organisational overlap and confusion and because it focuses the chief compliance officer on critical process management, uniformity and rigour across the corporation".[49] Heineman still believes this is the correct position and goes further: "But, the idea that a CCO [chief compliance officer] is more independent than the GC or CFO is wrong. All serve at will. All have financial benefits that vest in the future. The key in all three jobs is to maintain that guardian role and the necessary independence to speak out about what is right for the company."[50]

In contrast to Heineman's view, some organisations have chosen to separate the chief compliance officer function from that of the general counsel. This viewpoint is supported by research showing that companies which had combined the two roles, when subject to a US government investigation, separated the dual role if their ethics and compliance programmes were brought into question. The investigations referred to were healthcare fraud cases – Tenet, WellCare and Pfizer. Pfizer now requires its chief compliance officer to report directly to the CEO rather than to the general counsel.

Donna Boehme, the principal of Compliance Strategists LLC, writes that:

> ... legal has a separate and distinct mandate from compliance, and the two mandates will differ on any given day, week, or time of crisis (eg, when there are differences between how legal and compliance want to treat internal whistleblowers).[51]

In these circumstances, Boehme posits that legal and compliance must be equal partners and that they provide different skills. Boehme warns:

> Many companies that have placed the CCO under the thumb of the GC, and have viewed compliance purely through a legal prism, have paid a steep price for that misstep. Just ask Tenet Healthcare, Pfizer, Hewlett-Packard, and now Wal-Mart about that one.[52]

For Boehme, the Wal-Mart case is the perfect example why the chief compliance officer role needs a proper structure, position and reporting line: "At least one respected former general counsel [Ben Heineman] is arguing that the CCO should report to the general counsel as a 'process integrator' and legal 'lieutenant'. Wal-Mart is just the latest example of why this doesn't work."[53]

---

48 Ben Heineman, Jr, "Don't Divorce the GC and Compliance Officer", The Harvard Law School Forum on Corporate Governance and Financial Regulation, December 26 2010, available at: http://blogs. law.harvard.edu/corpgov/2010/12/26/don%E2%80%99t-divorce-the-gc-and-compliance-officer/ (accessed March 1 2013).

49 Ibid.

50 Ben Heineman, Jr, "Can the Marriage of the GC and the Compliance Officer Last?", Corporate Counsel, March 30 2012, available at: www.law.harvard.edu/programs/corp_gov/articles/Heineman_CorpCon_03-30-12.pdf (accessed March 1 2013).

51 Donna Boehme, "The Real Happy Marriage between the GC and the Compliance Officer", Corporate Counsel, May 2 2012, available at: www.law.com/corporatecounsel/PubArticleCC.jsp?id=120255 0879126 &thepage=2 (accessed March 22 2013).

52 Ibid.

53 Donna Boehme, "Opinion: An Independent CCO could have Saved Wal-Mart's Hide", Agenda, May 21 2012, available at: www.compliancestrategists.org/wp-content/uploads/2012/09/May-21-2012-Agenda-PDF-Download.pdf (accessed March 22 2013).

Much of the case for an independent chief compliance officer operating separately and apart from the general counsel stems from the healthcare industry in the United States, where emerging best practices and changes in the business environment mitigate towards this in supporting the board of directors' compliance oversight role. In 1998, the Office of the Inspector General of the US Department of Health and Human Services set out the following guidance for various segments of the healthcare industry:

> *The OIG believes that there is some risk to establishing an independent compliance function if that function is subordinate to the hospital's general counsel, or comptroller or similar hospital financial officer. Freestanding compliance functions help to ensure independent and objective legal reviews and financial analyses of the institution's compliance efforts and activities. By separating the compliance function from the key management positions of general counsel or chief hospital financial officer (where the size and structure of the hospital make this a feasible option), a system of checks and balances is established to more effectively achieve the goals of the compliance program.*[54]

The Office of the Inspector General sees the role of the compliance department in a hospital as being separate and distinct from that of general counsel. In the 2005 OIG Supplemental Compliance Programme Guidance for Hospitals issued by the Department of Health and Human Services, the office suggested that hospitals ask the following questions when reviewing the effectiveness of their compliance operations:

- Is the relationship between the compliance function and the general counsel function appropriate to achieve the purpose of each?
- Does the compliance officer have direct access to the governing body, the president or CEO, all senior management, and legal counsel?
- Does the compliance officer have independent authority to retain outside legal counsel?[55]

This view confirms the opinion expressed in a September 5 2003 letter to Tenet Healthcare Corporation from US Senator Charles Grassley (R-IA), who observed that: "Apparently, neither Tenet nor (its General Counsel) saw any conflict in her wearing two hats as Tenet's General Counsel and Chief Compliance Officer ... It doesn't take a pig farmer from Iowa to smell the stench of conflict in that arrangement."[56] A dual-role general counsel/chief compliance officer or a reporting line through the legal department simply does not meet the standard of care required for bringing forward an ambitious, broad and complex compliance programme in a large organisation. An appropriate reporting structure, access to top management and the board, and the resources to enable compliance to discharge its function is essential. A 2013 survey of

---

54   Office of the Inspector General, Department of Health and Human Services, OIG Compliance Programme Guidance for Hospitals, February 23 1998 (see 63 FR 8987 (February 23 1998)), available at: https://oig.hhs.gov/authorities/docs/cpghosp.pdf (accessed March 22 2013).

55   Office of the Inspector General, Department of Health and Human Services, OIG Supplemental Compliance Programme Guidance for Hospitals, January 31 2005 (see 70 FR 4858 (January 31 2005)), available at: https://oig.hhs.gov/fraud/docs/complianceguidance/012705HospSupplemental Guidance.pdf (accessed March 20 2013).

56   United States Senator Chuck Grassley, Press Release, September 8 2003, "Grassley Investigates Tenet Healthcare's Use of Federal Tax Dollars", available at: www.grassley.senate.gov/releases/2003/p03r09-08.htm (accessed March 22 2013).

chief compliance officers by the Society of Corporate Compliance and Ethics supports this view. One person surveyed said: "The great majority of GC's do not have the background, worldview, and experience to be, or be in a position to veto/filter, the chief compliance officer."[57] Another indicated that because of the defensive outlook general counsel have: "Compliance should be independent of Legal to ensure that information flow is not interrupted or 'spun'."[58]

Michael W Peregrine and Joshua T Buchman of McDermott Will & Emory, Chicago, suggest that the US government has provided enough guidance to inform leadership decisions on designing the appropriate relationship between the general counsel and chief compliance officer in hospitals and healthcare-related organisations.[59] They suggest the end goal is to achieve a "conflict-free management structure" that facilitates the board's ability to exercise oversight of the organisation's legal/compliance profile. In looking at the function of the two posts, clear differences emerge. The American Bar Association (ABA) view is that the general counsel should have primary responsibility for assuring the implementation of an effective legal compliance system under the board's oversight.[60] Counsel's ethical responsibility is to the corporation, not to its constituents (eg, officers, directors, other agents) with whom he may communicate in connection with representing the corporation.[61] By contrast, the chief compliance officer is perceived as a neutral fact-finder, expected to perform duties that transcend the practice of law, with specific responsibility for uncovering legal or ethical misconduct within the organisation.[62]

The US government mindset on the need for separation of the general counsel and chief compliance officer roles is demonstrated by the Corporate Integrity Agreement entered into between the Office of the Inspector General, the Department of Health and Human Services and Pfizer Inc on August 31 2009[63] as part of the record $2.3 billion payment Pfizer made to settle federal charges that one of its subsidiaries had illegally marketed a painkiller, Bextra. Pfizer indicated that its general counsel would no longer oversee the drug company's ethics and compliance programme.[64] Instead, it agreed that a chief compliance officer, independent from

---

57 Donna Boehme, "Making the CCO an Independent Voice in the C-Suite, The Compliance Strategist", *Corporate Counsel*, March 19 2013, available at: www.compliancestrategists.org/wp-content/uploads/2012/09/Making-the-CCO-an-Independent-Voice-in-the-C-Suite.pdf (accessed March 24 2013).

58 *Ibid*.

59 Michael W Peregrine and Joshua T Buchman, "Managing the General Counsel/Compliance Officer Relationship", AHLA Connections, October 2011, 34-39, 34, available at: www.mwe.com/info/pubs/Analysis_Oct20111.pdf (accessed March 23 2013).

60 ABA Task Force Report on Corporate Responsibility, 59 Bus Law 145, at 155 n. 43 (2003) (ABA Task Force Report). "If the corporation has no General Counsel, it should identify and designate a lawyer or law firm to act as General Counsel": *ibid*, at 161 n. 63.

61 ABA Model Rules of Professional Conduct, Rule 1.13(a).

62 Erica Salmon-Byrne and Jodie Frederickson, "The Business Case for Creating a Standalone Chief Compliance Position", *Ethisphere*, May 25 2010, available at: www.fairfaxco.us/docs/separation_of_gc_and_cco.pdf (accessed March 25 2013).

63 Corporate Integrity Agreement between Office of the Inspector General, Department of Health and Human Services, and Pfizer Inc, August 31 2009, available at: https://oig.hhs.gov/fraud/cia/agreements/pfizer_inc.pdf (accessed March 25 2013).

64 Amy Miller, "$2.3bm Pfizer Settlement Strips Legal Team of Compliance Brief", legalweek.com (September 11 2009), available at: www.legalweek.com/legal-week/news/1533237/usd2-3bn-pfizer-settlement-strips-legal-team-compliance-brief (accessed April 5 2013).

the general counsel, will be responsible for developing and implementing policies, procedures and practices designed to ensure compliance in healthcare programmes and with the agreement. The chief compliance officer is required to be a member of Pfizer's senior management, reporting in directly to the CEO and providing reports to the audit committee of the board of directors. Most importantly, under the terms of the agreement, the chief compliance officer must not be subordinate to or report to the general counsel or the CFO. Chief counsel for the Office of the Inspector General Lewis Morris stated that this mandate was intended to "eliminate conflicts of interest, and prevent Pfizer's in-house lawyers from reviewing or editing reports required by the agreement".[65] According to Morris, "the lawyers tell you whether you can do something, and compliance tells you whether you should – Pfizer's upper management should hear both arguments".[66]

These trends, from the healthcare sector, of a compliance function separate and independent from the legal function appears to be the current position in the financial services industry. "In quick succession, Goldman Sachs, HSBC, Barclays, and JPMorgan Chase have all taken their CCOs out from under the thumb of their general counsel and bolstered the role's positioning, empowerment, and resources."[67] Antony Jenkins, CEO of Barclays Bank plc, in announcing Project Transform to address the shortcomings identified as a result of the bank's LIBOR scandal, has indicated that all compliance officers across the bank will report to him directly and will operate separately from regional managers.[68] In response to the JP Morgan Chase 2012 chief investment office trading loss, JP Morgan's chief compliance officer now reports directly to the two chief operating officers rather than through the general counsel.[69] The new regulatory approach characterised by compliance work that is far more technical in approach and discipline-specific (eg, anti-money laundering, environmental protection) raises questions about the role of in-house counsel in implementing and overseeing compliance mechanisms inside the corporation. One of the few empirical studies in this area has identified the fact that most general counsel see their legal risk function as a responsibility to be the 'gatekeeper' of the company they worked for, namely preventing them getting involved in illegal conduct and guarding the reputation of their company.[70]

E Norman Veasey, former chief justice of the Delaware Supreme Court, and Christine DiGuglielmo take the view that the general counsel has a responsibility,

---

65   Salmon-Byrne and Frederickson, note 62 above, at 5.

66   *Ibid.*

67   Donna Boehme, "Big Banks Giving the CCO a Seat at the Table", *Corporate Counsel*, March 1 2013, available at: www.law.com/corporatecounsel/PubArticleCC.jsp?id=1202590410783&Big_Banks_Giving_the_CCO_a_ Seat_at_the_Table (accessed March 22 2013).

68   Paul Waldie, "'We get it', New Barclays Chief Says as Unveils Major Overhaul, Job Cuts", *The Globe and Mail*, February 12 2013, available at: www.theglobeandmail.com/report-on-business/international-business/european-business/we-get-it-new-barclays-chief-says-as-he-unveils-major-overhaul-job-cuts/article8480377/ (accessed March 22 2013).

69   Jessica Silver-Greenberg, "Amid a Shake-Up, JP Morgan's Risk Officer Takes a Leave", Deal Book, *New York Times*, January 25 2013, available at: http://dealbook.nytimes.com/2013/01/25/top-jpmorgan-executive-takes-temporary-leave-amid-reshuffling/ (accessed March 23 2013).

70   Tanina Rostain, "General Counsel in the Age of Compliance: Preliminary Findings and New Research Questions", 21 Geo J Legal Ethics 465-90 (2008), available at: http://lawweb.usc.edu/centers/scip/ participants/documents/RostaingeneralcounselintheageFIN.pdf (accessed March 25 2013).

either directly or by working in conjunction with other compliance-oriented executives in the company, to ensure that the company has effective compliance systems and to monitor these on an ongoing basis.[71] In addition, they note that many companies will have a chief compliance officer in place to help the board effectively monitor compliance and who may report to the general counsel, the CFO, the CEO or the audit committee of the board.[72] However, regardless of the formal reporting structure, Veasey and DiGuglielmo conclude that the general counsel and the compliance function should be closely linked and coordinated in most cases.[73]

Sven Erik Holmes, vice chair of legal and compliance for KPMG and a former US federal judge, warns against this separation of the chief compliance officer and general counsel functions: "Although it is debatable whether such separation creates a better governance model, one thing is clear: separation of the roles can have negative consequences, such as siloing and turf wars, if the responsibilities of the two positions are not clearly defined."[74] Holmes points to differences in how the general counsel and chief compliance officer see their roles: the general counsel is charged with defending and preserving the legal position of the company while the chief compliance officer has to take a more conciliatory approach ("mistakes have been made, lessons have been learned") to the same problem.[75]

In defining the general counsel/chief compliance officer relationship, an organisation must consider objective structuring issues such as

- whether the general counsel/chief compliance officer positions should be separated and held by different persons, or combined and held by the same person;
- the specific job description for each position, noting the areas of appropriate overlap and avoiding gaps in coverage;
- relevant reporting relationships to corporate officers and to the board;
- preservation of the attorney-client privilege;
- the impact of the Rules of Professional Responsibility; and
- communication and coordination between the two positions.[76]

Equally important are the more subjective structuring issues that may arise given the different skill sets required for the positions and their different roles – particularly the interpersonal relationship between the general counsel and the chief compliance officer.

The US legal regime provides other advantages to having a compliance programme in place. For instance, the 2012 US Federal Sentencing Guidelines Manual, Chapter 8, makes it clear that if a corporation has a qualifying compliance

---

71   E Norman Veasey and Christine T DiGuglielmo, *Indispensable Counsel: The Chief Legal Officer in the New Reality*, Oxford University Press, United States, 2012, p. 148.
72   *Ibid.*
73   *Ibid.*
74   Sven Erik Holmes, "Insights from Sven Erik Holmes: Establishing and Maintaining the Right Relationship between the General Counsel and the Chief Compliance Officer", Association of Corporate Counsel, 2011, available at: www.acc.com/_cs_upload/vl/membersonly/Article/1276964_2.pdf (accessed March 1 2013).
75   *Ibid.*
76   Peregrine and Buchman, note 59 above, at 34.

and ethics programme in place it will reduce an organisation's guidelines culpability score. In fact, the existence of an effective compliance and ethics programme in accord with the guidelines will determine the threshold question of whether a corporation is to be prosecuted in the first place (USSG, Section 8C2.5 (f)(3)(C)). The guidelines also explain what reasonable steps can be taken to respond appropriately after criminal conduct is suspected, for example, using outside counsel to ensure adequate assessment and implementation of any modifications to the organisation's compliance and ethics programme (USSG, Section 8B2.1, App. Note 6.)

Notwithstanding the existence of an effective compliance and ethics programme, an organisation will not benefit if high-level personnel were involved with or should have known about the criminal conduct. However, if four conditions are met as stated in the guidelines, an organisation can still be credited for having an effective compliance and ethics programme – even where high-level personnel were involved with or should have known about the criminal conduct at issue (USSG, Section 8C2.5 (f)(3)(C)).

5.   Defining what is legal risk

Many commentators on law department management speak of 'legal risk' as if it is an absolute term with a self-evident meaning. Of course, this is not the case. McCormick suggests that legal risk can be broken down into its functional elements (just as the Basel Committee on Banking Supervision (Basel Committee) has done with the definition of 'operational risk'), namely identification, assessment, monitoring and control/mitigation.[77] McCormick notes that for any of these functions to be effective legal risk must be appropriately defined: "Opinions may differ as to whether certain risks are properly to be regarded as legal risk (for example, in relation to risks on the borderline with political risk or fraud), but one would expect, over time, a consensus of opinion to develop as to what legal risk generally means."[78] Of course, as with all other definitions, McCormick emphasises that no one definition will fit all institutions. For instance, certain kinds of legal risk are so unlikely to affect a particular organisation that McCormick notes that an organisation may feel it appropriate to discount the particular concern when formulating its risk management policies and procedures.[79]

The Basel Committee paper of February 2003 on "Sound Practices for the Management and Supervision of Operational Risk" (Basel Committee Operational Risk Paper)[80] incorporated into the Basel Capital Accord (Basel II)[81] requires banks to assess their overall risk, including legal risk as a form of operational risk, to ensure that management is exercising sound judgment and setting aside adequate capital.

77   Roger S McCormick, "The Management of Legal Risk by Financial Institutions in the Context of 'Basel II', Part 1", 8 JIBFL 304 (2004).

78   Ibid.

79   Ibid.

80   Bank for International Settlements, Basel Committee on Banking Supervision, "Sound Practices for the Management and Supervision of Operational Risk" (Basel Committee Operational Risk Paper), February 2003, available at: www.bis.org/publ/bcbs96.pdf (accessed March 4 2013).

81   Bank for International Settlements, "Basel II: International Convergence of Capital Measurement and Capital Standards: A Revised Framework – Comprehensive Version", June 2006, available at: www.bis.org/publ/bcbs128.htm (accessed March 4 2013).

The intention behind Basel II was to reduce the probability of consumer loss or market disruption as a result of prudential failure.

The effect was limited. In response to the deficiencies in financial regulation revealed by the late-2000s financial crisis, Basel III has been developed,[82] which is a series of amendments to the existing Basel II framework to come into effect by 2018. While there have been a number of changes to the operational risk management approaches set out in Basel II, the definition of legal risk remains unchanged and informs our discussion herein.

Even though operational risk is broadly defined in the Basel Committee Operational Risk Paper, it does include legal risk, a concept for which no definition has been provided (although a footnote to the reference to legal risk in Basel II states that "legal risk includes, but is not limited to, exposures to fines, penalties, or punitive damages resulting from supervisory actions, as well as private settlements").[83]

Janet Terblanché, a leading South African legal and compliance expert, suggests that the Basel Committee definitions of operational risk, legal risk and compliance risk might not be adequate for countries with a common law system.[84] Looking at the current Basel Committee definition of operational risk ("the risk of loss resulting from inadequate or failed internal processes, people and systems, or from external events"[85]), Terblanché notes that the definitions of legal risk and compliance risk might be interpreted differently in civil law and common law jurisdictions. In civil law systems, the law consists only of legislation, and the Basel definition of compliance risk would include legal risk and vice versa; however, in common law and/or mixed legal systems which include case law precedent as well as indigenous law elements, this Basel notion of compliance with legislation thereby excludes large areas of the law.[86]

The International Bar Association Working Party on Legal Risk[87] has suggested the following definition (IBA Definition), with the caveat that it can only be read with the accompanying notes (Notes), which affect how it should be interpreted:

Legal risk is the risk of loss to an institution which is primarily caused by:

- a defective transaction; or
- a claim (including a defence to a claim or a counterclaim) being made or some other event occurring which results in a liability for the institution or other loss (for example, as a result of the termination of a contract) or;

---

82   See more generally John Thirlwell, "Risk and Regulation: Basel III and operational risk: the missing piece?", available at: www.johnthirlwell.co.uk/FS_Focus.pdf (accessed March 8 2013).

83   Basel Committee Operational Risk Paper, note 80 above, para. 644, p. 144.

84   Janet Terblanché, "Basel's Risk Definitions Open to Interpretation in Common-law Countries", *Operational Risk & Regulation*, May 24 2012, available at: www.risk.net/operational-risk-and-regulation/feature/2178751/basels-risk-definitions-interpretation-common-law-countries (accessed March 4 2013).

85   Bank for International Settlements, Basel Committee on Banking Supervision, "Principles for the Sound Management of Operational Risk", June 2011, updates the Basel Committee Operational Risk Paper, February 2003, note 80 above, available at: www.bis.org/publ/bcbsca07.pdf (accessed March 4 2013).

86   Terblanché, note 84 above.

87   See Hugh S Pigott, "Editorial – Legal Risk", *Butterworths Journal of International Banking and Financial Law*, pp. 3-4, available at: www.ibanet.org/Document/Default.aspx?DocumentUid...9BE5... (accessed March 4 2013);

- failing to take appropriate measures to protect assets (for example, intellectual property) owned by the institution; or
- change in law.[88]

The Notes refer to the consultation paper of July 1 2003 issued by the EU Commission Services which contains a 'Working Document' that sets out proposed risk-based capital requirements for financial institutions.[89] Article 106 of the Working Document states that: "Operational risk is the risk of loss resulting from inadequate or failed internal processes, people and systems or from external events, including legal risk."[90] The Notes suggest that a legal risk taken deliberately by an organisation fully aware of the circumstances and based on sound analysis does not fall within this Article 106 definition. The Working Document does not offer any definition of legal risk. The Notes point out that the definition offered "should not be regarded as prescriptive" in that institutions may have to adapt the definition to fit their own particular purposes, management structure and the regulatory environment within which they operate.[91] The Notes also offer further guidance on the "distinction between claims which reflect a risk that has been anticipated (but nevertheless deliberately taken) and claims which come as a genuine 'surprise' such as those that arise from wilful or reckless behaviour (including fraud)".[92] While the former may be regarded as legal risks, the latter cannot be regarded as such.

Moreover, the Notes distinguish between risk of loss caused by contractual commitments to pay money, such as indemnities or guarantees, which are voluntarily contracted into and those caused by a breach of contract.[93] Normally, a breach of contract should not be seen as a legal risk but rather as an operational risk. However, where there are extremely complex contractual arrangements that might give rise to technical breach simply on the grounds that the contract is hard to administrate in those circumstances, it could be considered as falling within the category of legal risk rather than financial risk.[94] One example of this is a complicated debt covenant contained in a loan agreement that may be breached for a short period of time even though the entity is materially meeting its debt obligations as they come due.

The Notes also suggest that there may be situations with "strong political overtones" which should not be considered an example of legal risk but rather an example of political risk combined with legal risk. For instance, the risk of asset seizures in emerging markets is to be seen as a political risk not a legal risk. However, it may be argued that the risk of political interference with the judicial process may be legal risk.[95]

---

88   International Bar Association Working Party on Legal Risk, "Suggested Definition of Legal Risk", February 2004, available at: www.federalreserve.gov/SECRS/2005/August/20050818/OP-1189/OP-1189_2_1.pdf (accessed March 23 2013), pp.13-16.

89   European Commission Internal Market DG, "Review of Capital Requirements for Banks and Investment Firms", Commission Services Third Consultation Paper, Working Document, July 1 2003, available at: http://images.to.camcom.it/f/tofinanza/DU/DU_66.pdf (accessed March 23 2013).

90   *Ibid.*, Article 106.

91   Note 88 above, Notes 2 and 3.

92   *Ibid*, Note 4.

93   *Ibid*, Note 5.

94   *Ibid.*

The Notes[96] discuss the risk of change in law, for example, when a statute is passed or a case decision is reached. However, it must also be noted that a change in law can be a political risk rather than a legal risk. For instance, while it may be relatively straightforward to categorise the change in law that might result from Parliament enacting the Financial Services Act 2012 or the outcome of *Federal Trade Commission v. Watson Pharmaceuticals Inc et al.*, US Supreme Court, No. 12-416 (the pay for delay drugs case) currently before the US Supreme Court, there are situations which are less clear. For instance, is the German government's decision to stop all nuclear power production by 2022 a risk of change of law or a political risk? The IBA Definition refers to a non-exclusive list of defective transactions that exemplify what it refers to in subpart (a), including those which are defectively structured, those which are void or unenforceable in whole or in material part, those entered into on the basis of misleading or false representations, due diligence or lack of disclosure of material facts or circumstances, those where there is a misunderstanding of the effect of one or more transactions on certain rights involved between the parties, those entered into with ineffective or unfair dispute resolution mechanisms, those which have been entered into inadvertently (a contract by accident not by intent of the parties), and those transactions entered into with defective security arrangements (such as an unperfected lien). The risk of a defective transaction includes any trust arising from such a defective transaction or any assignment of a contract, right or obligation under such a defective transaction.[97]

McCormick further examines the specific role of the legal department in risk management and offers a number of insightful questions that should be considered when assessing the individuals in a company responsible for management of legal risk, for example: What is the role of the in-house lawyer? Does he have final decision-making authority or if he disagrees with the business people is the decision escalated to a business person for final decision? Is the in-house lawyer's recommendation or advice likely to be covered by privilege if litigation arises? How can the in-house lawyer be sure his or her advice is being followed? What confidence can the in-house lawyer have in the internal fact-gathering processes that he must rely on when giving legal advice? What is to be made of the role of an in-house lawyer who sits on internal management committees that make business decisions as opposed to providing pure legal advice only? Finally, are there areas where, if the in-house lawyer finds issues of regulatory non-compliance, he can exercise her discretion to remedy these problems rather than be mandated by law to whistle-blow on his or her employer?[98]

McCormick points to fairly obvious indicators, such as the remark of Bill Lytton, the senior vice president and general counsel of Tyco, that: "it is a warning sign if there is a meeting going on and, as a lawyer, you are not allowed to go. There should

---

95   *Ibid*, Note 6.
96   *Ibid*, Note 7.
97   Roger McCormick, "The Management of Legal Risk by Financial Institutions", Draft Discussion Paper, February 2004, available at: www.federalreserve.gov/SECRS/2005/August/20050818/OP-1189/OP-1189_2_1.pdf (accessed March 5 2013).
98   McCormick, note 33 above.

be no meeting which a general counsel cannot go to – especially now, when general counsel are recognised as having more of a central part in management decisions than before."[99] In-house lawyers must have sufficient independence within the organisational structure to allow a rigorous approach to the relevant procedures (whether this amounts to whistle-blowing in more extreme situations or not).[100]

It is also important that the lawyers have access to the necessary information, for example, Parmalat's former general counsel was powerless to prevent widespread fraud because of a lack of proper reporting lines. The lead counsel to Parmalat's administrator, Mr Bruno Cova, observed that:

> ... there was a legal department in Parmalat with perfectly good lawyers – but they were not given the opportunity to understand what was going on ... before a general counsel accepts a job in any company, he must make sure that he reports directly to the Chief Executive or the Chairman. All other lawyers within the company should report to the general counsel so that the general counsel can understand what is going on. Parmalat did not have those reporting lines. Lawyers only reported to the operation they were working for, and so the general counsel was not put in the situation where he could help.[101]

The Financial Services Authority (FSA) has identified a number of issues of particular concern for legal risk managers working in financial institutions with respect to conflicts of interest and non-standard transactions.[102] In the case of non-standard transactions, the FSA suggests that best practice means that policies and procedures are put in place for managing transactions subject to heightened legal and reputational risk covering the full transaction life cycle and the establishment of clear roles and responsibilities between the front office, control functions and senior management proportionate to the nature, scale and complexity of the firm's business.[103]

The FSA has compiled a non-exhaustive list of transaction characteristics for the identification and escalation of non-standard transactions ('red flags') that it has found to be commonly used among firms, including:

- transactions where a material objective is to achieve a particular accounting or financial disclosure treatment, including instances where the accounting treatment may be unclear or the proposed treatment may not reflect the economic substance of the transaction;
- transactions designed to achieve a particular tax treatment, especially if there is no significant economic substance apart from the tax treatment;
- transactions designed to achieve a particular regulatory or legal treatment, or as to which, in the view of lawyers advising the firm, there is material uncertainty about the intended legal or regulatory treatment;

---

99   McCormick, note 97 above.
100 McCormick, note 97 above.
101 Rachel Rothwell, "Parmalat Lawyers 'Kept in the Dark' Claims Counsel", *Law Society Gazette*, March 5 2004, available at: www.lawgazette.co.uk/news/parmalat-lawyers-amp145kept-darkamp146-claims-counsel (accessed March 6 2013).
102 Hector Sants, CEO, FSA, Letter to Senior Management Responsibilities, "Conflicts of Interest and Non-Standard Transactions", November 10 2005, available at: www.fsa.gov.uk/pubs/ceo/senior_management.pdf (accessed March 6 2013).
103 *Ibid.*

- transactions where the firm is asked to act in an 'accommodation' role, that is, without contributing economic substance to the transaction;
- transactions with self-referencing features;
- excessive or high profitability for the firm (relative to the risk), or non-transparent profits/fee structure for the firm;
- year-end transactions where the firm believes the intended purpose of the transaction is to achieve a favourable accounting treatment;
- transactions with substantively offsetting legs, or circular transfers of risk;
- transactions with highly complex structures or cash flow profiles, especially if the purpose, economic substance and risks of such structures are not transparent;
- transactions with undocumented leg(s);
- derivatives-based financings;
- transactions with significant non-transparent leverage;
- off-market transactions;
- 'barter' transactions;
- connection to politically exposed persons or particular 'risky' countries;
- heightened conflicts of interest;
- suitability issues; and
- a catch-all clause for any other transaction that could cause adverse publicity for the firm, or damage client relationships.[104]

In 2006 (before the financial crisis), McCormick suggested that Sants' letter was essential reading for legal risk managers, noting that it is striking that, in the context of non-standard transactions, legal and reputational risk are considered together, virtually in the same breath.[105] Emphasising this point again in 2011 (after the financial crisis), McCormick in a letter to the editor of the Financial Times again warned that investment banking houses still do not fully understand the management of legal risk in the context of the complicated transactions these banks engage in on a regular basis:

This has three principal facets: change in law risk; adverse claims risk; and documentation risk, the risk of failing to appreciate the impact of what you are signing. It is a risk that has generally been overlooked and underappreciated by the regulators and the regulated, which is surprising – given its close relationship with reputational risk and political risk.[106]

McCormick concludes his letter by suggesting that it is time for legal risk management to be given more prominence in the lexicon of bank corporate governance.

---

104   See appendix to the Sants letter of 10 November 2005, note 102 above.
105   Roger S McCormick, "Legal Risk Management Red Flags and Risk Scenarios", 2 JIBFL 51 (2006). See also M Solinas, "Review: Roger McCormick, Legal Risk in the Financial Markets, Oxford University Press, 2nd edn, 2010", 16(1) *Edinburgh Law Review* 139-40 (2012).
106   Roger S McCormick, Letter to the Editor, "Temptation to Cut Legal Corners is a Threat to Markets", *Financial Times*, February 7 2011, available at: www.ft.com/cms/s/0/22cacbee-3258-11e0-a820-00144feabdc0.html#axzz2MoLXauVj (accessed March 6 2013).

6.   What is legal governance?

Legal governance refers to the establishment, execution and interpretation of processes and rules put in place by corporate legal departments in order to ensure a smoothly run legal department and corporation.[107] It is often difficult to define a smooth-running legal department; however, an examination of the contemporary views of the general counsel will provide a better understanding of the role of in-house legal counsel as a whole and their role in corporate legal governance. An observation must be made here – please distinguish corporate governance from legal governance. Generally, corporate governance is seen as the set of processes, customs, policies, laws and institutions affecting the way a corporation (or company) is directed, administered or controlled, while legal governance is more narrowly defined to concern itself with the operation of the legal function within an entity.

The law firm Allen & Overy, in an online publication, maps out some of the legal governance problems faced by British general counsel which have resonance across a wide range of industries:

GCs are already adapting and responding to the increasing expectations of them. There can be no substitute for well thought-out, diligent compliance. Systemising the management of legal risk is key, as is connecting with the business. Only by being fully attuned to the business will GCs be able to spot the indications that all is not as it should be ...

Increasingly, the onus is on businesses to initiate an investigation when things appear to have gone awry and to demonstrate that swift, pro-active measures have been taken to root out and expose wrong-doing. In the US standard practice requires the GC to bring in an independent law firm and a team of forensic accountants to conduct the investigation.

So what does the future hold for the GC of a UK PLC? They will become more like their American counterpart, sitting right at the heart of the business, in a high-profile role, increasingly independent and having very significant influence. It'll undoubtedly also be better paid. The trade off? Tomorrow's GC will become the guardian of ethics, culture and values, whilst shouldering more responsibility than ever before. Some may see it as a bitter-sweet proposition.[108]

Transatlantic differences in the role of the general counsel are not surprising. For instance, in the investigation of cartel behaviour by the European Commission (EC), the European general counsel's role is complicated by the current rule that when participating in investigations by the EC, he is not entitled to claim privilege for advice given.[109] On September 14 2010, the Court of Justice of the European Union (CJEU) dismissed an appeal brought by Akzo Nobel Chemicals Ltd and Akcros Chemicals Ltd against a judgment of the General Court, and confirmed that legal

---

107   Konkle, note 18 above.

108   Allen & Overy, "Risky Business – General Counsel Forums – 'Risky Business' – Did you expect when you were appointed General Counsel that you might find yourself being interviewed by the police or some other enforcement agency?", April 7 2010, available at: www.allenovery.com/publications/en-gb/Pages/'Risky-business'—General-Counsel-Forums.aspx (accessed March 6 2013).

109   http://eur-lex.europa.eu/LexUriServ/LexUriServ.do?uri=CELEX:62007J0550:EN.html (accessed March 5 2013).

professional privilege does not apply to communications between a company and its in-house lawyers in the context of European Union (EU) antitrust investigations (*Akzo Nobel Chemicals Ltd and Akcros Chemicals Ltd v Commission* (Case C-550/07 P) [2010]).[110] The CJEU concluded this on the basis that in-house lawyers are not sufficiently independent of their employers – they are too closely tied economically to their employers and unable to ignore their employers' commercial strategies. In such circumstances, the CJEU concluded that in-house lawyers are less able than external lawyers to deal with conflicts between their professional obligations and the aims of their client.

While any legal advice on competition law given by an in-house lawyer will not be protected from disclosure to the EC, the ruling does not affect the scope of privilege as a matter of law in England and Wales.[111] Under English law, the advice of in-house lawyers continues to enjoy ostensibly the same protection as the advice given by a lawyer in private practice. In-house lawyers will have to decide whether to instruct external lawyers based on a range of factors relevant to their business. The fact that any legal advice given by an external lawyer would be protected by legal professional privilege in any EU competition law investigation should be borne in mind. Interestingly, advice given by an in-house lawyer orally rather than in writing would not be discoverable by the EC unless it has been committed to writing (eg, through repetition in an email). However, the EC may make requests for "all necessary information" under Article 18 of the Modernisation Regulation,[112] and this might conceivably require a client to disclose the facts of in-house legal advice given orally.

An important consideration is how the general counsel function fits within the overall strategic functioning of the company. Some general counsel report that in some organisations there is greater pressure than ever to transfer commercial risk to their in-house legal teams by encouraging the general counsel or his or her team to involve themselves in commercial decisions. This approach can be problematic in that it could distract in-house counsel from focusing on the appropriate risks involved by paying too much attention to the possibility of reward for the entity as a role (and possible performance-related pay for themselves as well). A survey of the compensation packages of the top 100 highest paid US general counsel whose salaries are disclosed publicly (eg, through securities filings) indicates that almost all receive performance-related pay compensation well in excess of their basic salary.[113]

Can the possibility of earning performance-related pay cloud a general counsel's judgment? The authors cannot say, but it is worth noting as a cautionary tale what happened to Mark A Belnick. Although exonerated of any criminal wrongdoing by a jury on charges that he stole millions of dollars from Tyco International in the form of unauthorised bonuses and loans and that he failed to disclose the payments, Mr

---

110   *Ibid*.
111   Law Society, "The Akzo Nobel Case – Frequently Asked Questions", September 14 2010, available at: http://international.lawsociety.org.uk/node/9955 (accessed March 6 2013).
112   http://eu.altalex.com/content/modernisation-regulation (accessed March 6 2013).
113   Corporate Counsel, "The 2011 GC Compensation Survey", available at: www.law.com/corporatecounsel/ PubArticleCC.jsp?id=1202499548177&slreturn=20130208045817 (accessed March 6 2013).

Belnick's fall from when he became mesmerised by the meteoric wealth possibilities the role of being general counsel at Dennis Kozlowski's Tyco presented.[114]

As well as understanding the strategy and objectives of the business, the general counsel must also be able be an effective public communicator. Corporate crises often have significant legal implications (eg, employee misconduct, a hostile takeover or an environmental disaster), and reputation management has moved to the forefront of corporate consciousness. As such, the general counsel must be involved in the forefront of any well-thought-out public relations strategy designed to help a firm handle such a crisis, communicate its message to stakeholders and duly emerge with limited damage and sometimes possibly an enhanced reputation.1[15]

Christopher Reynolds, group vice president, general counsel and secretary for legal services at Toyota Motor Sales in the United States, notes that the general counsel or corporate secretary should have a well-nourished relationship with the PR group so that legal can impact on the PR strategy when necessary, such as a pointing out a securities law issue involved in the timing of a press release: "Showing that you are adding value to other functions of the company is one of the critical roles of a good legal department."[116] Essential for success in this role is the internal goodwill built up by the legal department before a crisis arrives so that legal is trusted to be active the crisis centre ("dealmaker, not dealbreaker"), an ability to fashion messages in such a way that they do not sound like lawyer-speak (eg, avoid, "it depends on what the meaning of the word 'is' is") and, finally, avoid issuing statements that can generate their own legal crises by imprecision or implying matters unintentionally.[117]

KPMG commissioned the GC Survey 2012 to find out how much progress general counsel are making as business decision-makers and the challenges they face in this growing role by examining information gathered from across 32 countries, from 320 corporate counsels, from across sectors and in both mature and high-growth economies. The survey indicated increased involvement by general counsel in commercial decisions that reduced corporate rate and a major concern over the exponentially increasing burden posed by regulatory and compliance workloads worldwide.[118]

The survey indicates that although general counsel are making significant progress in playing a bigger role in their companies, they still have some way to go to realise their full potential as business leaders in that there is a gap between the

---

114 Jonathan D Glater, "Jury Finds Ex-Tyco Lawyer Not Guilty of All Charges", *New York Times*, July 16 2004, available at: www.nytimes.com/2004/07/16/business/jury-finds-ex-tyco-lawyer-not-guilty-of-all-charges. html?pagewanted=all&src=pm www.nytimes.com/20s04/07/16/business/jury-finds-ex-tyco-lawyer-not-guilty-of-all-charges.html?pagewanted=all&src=pm (accessed April 9 2013).

115 Aarti Maharaj, "The General Counsel's Role in Creating a Successful PR Strategy", Corporate Secretary, Governance, Risk and Compliance, November 14 2011, available at: www.corporatesecretary.com/articles/corporate-secretary-week/12059/general-counsels-role-creating-successful-pr-strategy/ (accessed April 5 2013).

116 *Ibid.*

117 For more on the pre-eminence of risk reputation in corporate culture today, see Deloitte, "A Risk Intelligent View of Reputation – An Outside-in Perspective", Risk Intelligence Series, Issue 22, 2011, available at: www.deloitte.com/assets/Dcom-UnitedStates/Local%20Assets/Documents/IMOs/Governance%20and%20Risk%20Management/us_grm_risk%20intelligentviewofreputation_091511.pdf (accessed March 8 2013).

118 KPMG, "KPMG Global General Counsel Survey 2012", available at: www.kpmg.com/BE/en/IssuesAndInsights/ArticlesPublications/Pages/General-counsel-survey.aspx (accessed March 9 2013).

beneficial impact that they can have and their actual involvement in strategic decision-making.[119] The report concludes that the influence of the general counsel in the C-Suite is growing, but that changes in governance, processes and attitudes need further change.

The idea of the general counsel sitting on the board of directors (a situation identified as being the case in 38% of the global companies surveyed by KPMG) is not popular in the United States, where the general counsel is seen as the company's police officer. In today's modern US corporations, the general counsel will often hold potentially conflicting roles – one as the corporation's chief legal officer and the other as a member of the executive management team.[120] This dual role must be evaluated to determine whether the general counsel having a seat at the strategic management table benefits the corporation or hinders the general counsel's role as the corporate police officer:

The general counsel faces ethical and practical considerations when working with the independent chair or lead independent director of the board regarding risk oversight issues. The management team expects the general counsel to be an advocate for management's strategies and business plans. On the other hand, the lead director expects candid and frank disclosure of risks and potential problems.

The corporation benefits from a culture where senior managers will freely share concerns with the general counsel, as the lawyer for the company. However, to the extent the general counsel is viewed as the "policeman," executives may be reluctant to be candid.[121]

Given the complexity of the general counsel role and the important connection of the role to maximising shareholder wealth, the board of directors will need to implement methods to ensure that the general counsel meets his or her primary duty as the corporation's chief legal officer. These efforts may be hampered by regulations and/or professional obligations outside the realm of the board's control, which may further limit the general counsel's actions.

Nancie Lataille and Gabriella Kilby conducted interviews with senior members of the legal function in leading Canadian organisations in order to identify best recruitment and staff retention practices common to legal departments in a broad cross-section of companies in a wide range of industries.[122] Rather than embracing a narrow focus on the technical aspects of their role, the general counsel interviewed see the calibre and composition of their legal department staff as the key to success. They indicate that a significant portion of their time is devoted to human capital issues along with business issues:

---

119   *Ibid.*

120   Zina Kiryakos, "The Modern Role of the General Counsel as Corporate Lawyer & Business Executive", *Illinois Business Law Journal*, April 7 2010, available at: www.law.illinois.edu/bljournal/post/2010/04/07/THE-MODERN-ROLE-OF-THE-GENERAL-COUNSEL-AS-CORPORATE-LAWYER-BUSINESS-EXECUTIVE.aspx (accessed March 7 2013).

121   Gardner Davis, "Regulatory: The Evolving Role of the General Counsel", February 23 2011, available at: www.insidecounsel.com/2011/02/23/regulatory-the-evolving-role-of-the-general-counsel- (accessed March 10 2013).

122   Nancie Lataille and Gabriella Kilby, "The Legal Function Transformed: Best Practices of Today's General Counsel", The Korn/Ferry Institute, 2008, available at: www.kornferryinstitute.com/files/pdf1/LegalGeneralCounsel-WP-Web.pdf (accessed March 9 2013).

To meet the needs of a changing function, GCs seek lawyers who are flexible rather than focused on one specialisation. They want team players, lawyers who want to contribute to the organisation through productive collaboration rather than as an individual. Strong business judgment and the ability to assume a counsellor role are essential. Like the general counsel, legal staff members must learn how to deliver a message to others in the company and clients, accomplished individuals who do not respond well to edicts. Talent must be proactive, possess a strong level of self-awareness and be appropriately ambitious.[123]

Joost Maes, an executive search consultant with Egon Zehnder, a firm heavily involved in recruiting general counsel to multinational corporations, identifies some of the prominent forces bearing on the general counsel role today which make this an increasingly difficult role to fill – the right candidate must meet the full set of new and complex competencies necessary to perform the role:

Legal norms for governing the globalized world are lacking. National laws do not necessarily provide an answer to all of the legal questions that can arise in a global marketplace, nor do international organisations always have the authority and credibility to impose and enforce rules. In addition, the laws of different countries may sometimes conflict. Absence of rules, however, does not mean absence of law. A company's GC must be able to provide guidance in those areas where the norms are not yet clear.

No single person can fully understand the complex environment in which today's company acts: the associated risks, the maze of national and international laws and regulations, and the company's detailed operating conditions in locations around the globe. The GC must therefore be capable of leading and, where necessary, creating a competent and cohesive legal team. The skills required include the ability to recruit, retain, and evaluate people. They also include the ability to collaborate, to motivate teams, and to establish trust. And they include the ability to manage a far-flung function in a multi-cultural and multi-lingual context. Few potential candidates possess this range of competencies, especially since the legal field tends to reward technical proficiency rather than business or leadership skills. Legal education also focuses largely on technical skills, not leadership; and law graduates tend to be experts in the legal system of only one nation. Given these limitations, a GC who can build a strong team is all the more necessary.[124]

7. The general counsel and the board: separating the company secretary role

One trend to note in the United Kingdom is that there is increasing separation of the function of general counsel and company secretary. An examination of the top 100 companies ranked by market capitalisation listed on the London Stock Exchange (FTSE) shows that in just over 40% of the companies, the role of general counsel and company secretary is combined, while the other 60 % have different individuals

---

123   *Ibid.*
124   Joost Maes, "Finding Your Next General Counsel: Understanding the Demands of the New Role", Egon Zehnder International, 2013, available at: www.egonzehnder.com/global/practices/functionalpractices/legalprofessionals/article/id/83700229 (accessed March 10 2013).

filling the two roles. Ian J Maurice of Egon Zehnder notes that, undoubtedly, there is a move towards a separation of the roles.[125]

One might ask why in these times of increasing complexity companies would want to separate out the two roles. An immediate answer is that the burden of regulation has increased so much that it is no longer practical to keep the two roles separate. Maurice points out that when the two roles are combined in one individual, the general counsel/company secretary is only one of two people in the organisation – the other is the head of internal audit – who have a direct reporting relationship to two senior individuals within the organisation.

The dynamic is illustrated in Table 1.

Table 1: Reporting structure for general counsel and company secretary

General counsel	Reports to the chief executive and acts as the senior legal officer of the organisation serving on the executive committee.
Company secretary	Responsibilities are to the board and the reporting line is to the chairman.

A question that is now being asked in many FTSE companies is the one that Maurice posits, namely whether in times of increasing complexity "it is reasonable to expect one individual to have the breadth of skills to be able to fulfil these tasks".[126] Since under the Companies Act 2006, the role of company secretary remains mandatory for public companies, the company secretary has an important role to play in corporate governance and company administration.[127] Private companies are no longer required to appoint a company secretary.[128]

The decision to combine the general counsel and secretarial roles will often be a matter of the size and the type of industry in which a company operates. For instance, smaller companies may have only a company secretary and no in-house legal staff. By contrast, large, highly regulated companies may find it beneficial to separate out the two functions. Tesco plc has Jonathan Lloyd as its company secretary and Adrian Morris as its group general counsel.[129] Another example is GlaxoSmithKline plc, which employs Simon Bicknell as its senior vice president governance, ethics and assurance and Dan Troy as senior vice president and general counsel.[130] By contrast, in the United States, the general counsel and corporate

---

125   Ian J Maurice, "General Counsel and Company Secretary: To Combine or Not Combine", Egon Zehnder International, 2011, available at: www.egonzehnder.com/leadership-insights/legal-professionals/general-counsel-and-company-secretary-to-combine-or-not-to-combine.html (accessed March 10 2013).

126   *Ibid.*

127   Companies Act 2006, Section 271.

128   *Ibid*, Section 270.

129   Tesco plc website, available at: www.tescoplc.com/index.asp?pageid=172 (accessed March 10 2013).

130   GlaxoSmithKline plc website, available at: www.gsk.com/about-us/corporate-executive-team.html (accessed March 11 2013).

secretary roles tend to be combined and remain as such or managed by the general counsel's office. For instance, Brad Smith is Microsoft Corporation's general counsel and executive vice president, legal and corporate affairs and is also its corporate secretary and chief compliance officer.[131] At the insurance company Allstate, Mary J McGinn is secretary and deputy general counsel and reports in to Susan L Lees, the executive vice president and general counsel.[132]

One lost benefit of separating out the roles is that if the general counsel is not the company secretary, he will not automatically take part in board-level discussions on risk management. Part of the general counsel's role is to make informed judgments regarding risk across the business. Usually, this is done working closely with internal audit, a function which in turn reports to the CFO/CEO as well as to the chairman of the audit committee. If the general counsel is not serving as company secretary and so is not on the board, there will be only one route to the board for raising risk concerns, namely through the audit committee, whereas in the past there was a second route through the general counsel into the board.[133]

All of this raises the question of what the degree of involvement of the general counsel in meetings of the board and its committees should be. Jörg Thierfelder of Egon Zehnder International notes that the:

... degree of involvement of the general counsel in meetings of the board and its committees has risen continually in recent years. This trend is now stronger also in Europe, where general counsel have significantly more often become members of the executive management team, thereby interacting regularly and closely with the board. Besides offering legal expertise and advising on risk exposure, liability, compliance, and governance, these general counsel take a broader view that encompasses the company's reputation and integrity.[134]

This thinking is in line with the view expressed by prominent general counsel such as Ben Heineman namely that general counsel are responsible for both the legal and ethical tone of the company they serve. As such, general counsel must assist the board in setting the 'tone at the top' and leveraging their authority to establish the right legal and compliance culture at the company. At the same time, the general counsel's duty is: "to take an active role in counselling the board on how legal and regulatory environments can be used to a company's strategic advantage. This constructive engagement today is fundamentally influencing the role of the GC with the board – a factor that boards, in many instances, may not even be aware of yet."[135]

8.   Internal and external investigations

Sandra Leung, now senior vice president, general counsel and corporate secretary of Bristol-Myers Squibb Company, is an example of a general counsel who has had to

---

131   Microsoft Corporation website. Available at www.microsoft.com/en-us/news/exec/bradsmith/ (accessed March 11 2013).
132   Allstate website, available at: www.allstatenewsroom.com/channels/Senior-Leadership-Team/releases/susan-lees (accessed March 11 2013).
133   Maurice, note 125 above.
134   Jörg Thierfelder, "The General Counsel and the Board", Egon Zehnder International, 2011, available at: www.egonzehnder.com/files/the_general_counsel_and_the_board.pdf (accessed March 10 2013).
135   Ibid.

help navigate her company through a number of very complex crises, all of which involved both internal and external investigations:

> [She] was promoted to interim general counsel of Bristol-Myers Squibb during a late-night phone call in September 2006 [she joined the company in 1992 after working at New York District Attorney's Office]. It was two months after the FBI had raided the pharmaceutical company's Manhattan offices while investigating a collusion involving its top-selling drug, Plavix. At the urging of the company's government-appointed monitor – implemented the previous year, after a $2 billion accounting scandal – its CEO and general counsel had just stepped down.[136]

Once a crisis hits, a general counsel's first role is to start investigating immediately to understand what has occurred. "You need to understand what it is that happened", Tom Campbell, a partner at Pillsbury Winthrop Shaw Putnam, says. "The general counsel needs to lead the crisis-management team, most often in coordination with a very senior executive so that you have both the management and legal sides of the equation."[137] According to Sandra Leung, a critical aspect of the general counsel's role in the investigation is to focus on integrity: "You must make sure that the facts are known and not let emotions or subjectivity get in the way ... People will look to you and will open up to you if they know you're someone they can trust. It's important to have that reputation within the company before the crisis happens – to be known as a person who will do the right thing and the type of person people can go to for advice."[138]

Dramatic changes in the law with respect to criminal and civil liability have made the task of responding to a corporate wrongdoing an even more complex affair. For instance, an allegation of accounting impropriety or securities violation may give rise to investigations and actions in the United States by the SEC, the US Department of Justice and the US State attorney generals as well as the plaintiffs' class action bar. Often, general counsel have to deal with all of these government and private matters simultaneously while also ensuring that audits and investigations are conducted quickly yet thoroughly. It is this dealing simultaneously with internal and external investigations that can be the most taxing of times for general counsel.

Barry Donnelly and Iain Mackie of Macfarlanes LLP suggest that the first step will be to assemble the investigation team, including internal and/or external counsel, a member of the senior management team, a member of compliance and a representative from the internal audit team (where appropriate).[139] If assets need to be traced or recovered, the services of a forensic accountant may also be required; it will often be necessary to search for, preserve and review large amounts of digital data and forensic IT experts can be instructed to help with this process.[140]

---

136   Kristen Marcum, "The Decider", Super Lawyers, Corporate Counsel Edition, January 2010, available at: www.superlawyers.com/new-york-metro/article/The-Decider-/f6a5c760-e891-4c92-8950-fefa4029dd77.html (accessed March 10 2013).

137   Ashley Post, "The GC's Guide to Corporate Crises', Inside Counsel, January 28 2013, available at: www.insidecounsel.com/2013/01/28/the-gcs-guide-to-corporate-crises?t=corporate-crime (accessed March 10 2013).

138   Ibid.

139   Barry Donnelly and Iain Mackie, "Internal Investigations: What You Need to Know", The In-House Lawyer.co.uk, September 10 2012, available at: www.inhouselawyer.co.uk/index.php/litigation-a-dispute-resolution/9944-internal-investigations-what-you-need-to-know (accessed March 10 2013).

140   Ibid.

It is obvious that no member of the investigation team should have been involved in the events that gave rise to the investigation, because the team must be, and must be seen to be, completely independent. This was one of the most glaring errors in the internal investigation undertaken by Wal-Mart into the Wal-Mart de Mexico bribery scandal. Wal-Mart's top lawyer arranged to ship the internal investigators' files on the case to the general counsel of Wal-Mart de Mexico – a remarkable choice since the same general counsel was alleged to have authorized bribes. The general counsel promptly exonerated his fellow Wal-Mart de Mexico executives.[141]

A regulator will not be satisfied with the quality of the investigation if individuals subject to or somehow involved with the original events are involved in the investigation. For this reason, it is often preferable to instruct external, rather than internal, counsel because their input may be seen as being more objective. In the United States, this is seen as best practice for a variety of reasons:

The Association of Corporate Counsel profiled leading practices for the use of outside counsel in conducting internal investigations, and the results revealed that as a general rule, two factors drove such a practice: the need for independent and impartial inquiries whose methods and results were beyond government reproach, and the desire for the concomitant confidentiality afforded by the attorney-client and work product privileges.[142]

Finally, Donnelly and Mackie suggest that due to the amount of time and energy that will need to be devoted to an investigation, members of the team from within the business will probably need to be relieved of other duties.[143] They point to the fact that an under-resourced investigation is likely to make slow progress, while a quick response will help a business to get to the root of the problem efficiently and, where relevant, persuade a regulator that the systems and controls in place are in fact robust and indicative of the company taking such matters seriously?

9.   Conclusions

In examining how different companies meet the challenge of developing the right formula for successful legal risk management and compliance within their legal governance structures, it becomes apparent that one approach does not fit all. Each company will have developed its own model over time that works for it, taking into account the industry within which it works, the regulation it is subject to, the country it operates in and the personalities in the executive suite. Having said that, certain characteristics become clear – an emphasis on creating problem-solving, active engagement in all aspects of operations and strategy, and a desire to be the 'eyes and ears' on all compliance issues characterise the modern legal function in a corporate structure.

As where in the past the work of the in-house legal department was a largely

---

141   David Barstow, "Vast Mexico Bribery Case Hushed Up By Wal-Mart After Top Level Struggle", *New York Times*, April 21 2012, available at: www.nytimes.com/2012/04/22/business/at-wal-mart-in-mexico-a-bribe-inquiry-silenced.html?pagewanted=all&_r=0#h (accessed March 10 2013).

142   McGrath & Grace, Ltd, "Why Use Independent Counsel – Independent Counsel: A Best Practice", available at: www.mcgrathgrace.com/areas-of-investigation/8.html (accessed March 10 2013).

143   Donnelly and Mackie, note 139 above.

reactive affair, the modern general counsel must take a proactive stance, often relying on processes and real-time data to ensure the robustness of the compliance function they are involved with. Even in those cases where compliance is separated from legal, the influence of legal into compliance matters will be felt decisively. Finally, there is the 'tone at top' issue to consider. Leaders in the general counsel role such as Ben Heineman, Sandra Leung and Rupert Bondy, who are seen as both legal and ethical advisers to the companies they work for, add real value to the bottom line of the companies that cannot be quantified but can help a company get through some very difficult periods. In short, while we have not identified a single formula for success in legal risk management, the authors note with some satisfaction that today, in many companies there are many different formulas producing success in legal risk management.

The transformation of general counsel: setting the strategic legal agenda

Constance E Bagley
Yale University
Mark Roellig
Massachusetts Mutual Life Insurance Company

1.   Introduction

The evolving role of general counsel worldwide reflects the ever-expanding duties owed by businesses, not only to their home country but also to the countries in which they do business. Failure to comply with the law may lead to the demise of a firm and the imprisonment of its responsible managers. Enron and WorldCom collapsed in the wake of massive accounting fraud, and their executives were sentenced to prison.

More recently, lawmakers and regulators criticised banks for selling billions of dollars of faulty subprime mortgages and mortgage-backed securities. The investment bank Goldman Sachs paid $550 million to settle allegations by the US Securities and Exchange Commission that it had engaged in fraud when it failed to disclose that a counterparty that had a long position in derivative securities, whose value was based on the value of a basket of mortgage-backed securities, had hand-selected the underlying mortgages.[1] In September 2012, Bank of America Corporation agreed to pay $2.43 billion to settle a class action brought by investors who were allegedly misled about the bank's acquisition of Merrill Lynch & Company.[2] Less than a week later, the attorney general of New York State brought a civil action against JPMorgan Chase & Co, in which he alleged that its Bear Stearns unit had engaged in massive fraud, resulting in losses of over $22 billion.[3]

These scandals have not been limited to the United States. Standard Chartered Bank in the United Kingdom paid $340 million to settle claims that it broke US money laundering laws.[4] In 2012, Barclays' chief executive officer (CEO) lost his job after regulators found that the bank had attempted to manipulate the London interbank offered rate (Libor), which is the reference rate for everything from student loans to commercial paper.[5] The bank paid $450 million in government fines.[6] Swiss bank UBS AG paid US, UK and Swiss regulators approximately $1.5 billion in fines

1   Sewell Chan and Louise Story, *Goldman Pays $550 Million to Settle Fraud Case*, NY Times, July 16 2010, at A1.
2   Jean Eaglesham and Dan Fitzpatrick, *JPMorgan Sued on Mortgage Bonds*, Wall St J, October 2 2012, at A1.
3   *Ibid*.
4   Liz Rappaport, *Bank Settles Iran Money Case*, Wall St J, August 15 2012, at A1.
5   Josh Gallu, Howard Mustoe, Svenja O'Donnell and Roben Farzad, *The Libor Scandal Claims Its First CEO*, Bloomberg Bus Wk, July 3 2012, at A1.
6   Mark Scott, *Testifying in Britain, Volcker Questions Bank Innovation*, NY Times, October 18 2012, at B5.

and penalties to settle similar claims.

The general counsel of a business firm:

> ... is sometimes viewed as the "ethics police person", who catches inappropriate activities and institutes corrective actions to bring the rule-breaker into compliance with corporate governance standards. The GC is also a key member of the committees that examine the adequacy of internal controls and compliance with regulatory rules. Thus, the GC occupies an important position for establishing and maintaining governance procedures within the firm.[7]

General counsel also play a "multiplicity of [other] roles",[8] including manager of the legal department, legal adviser, transaction engineer,[9] negotiator, arbitrator, legal educator, crisis manager and strategic planner.[10] They are "the 'Swiss army knife' of the legal profession".[11]

In this chapter, we explore the evolving role of the general counsel in the United States and elsewhere. We then suggest ways that chief legal officers can not only keep their corporate client out of trouble, but also be strategic partners, actively helping the company to create and capture value and marshal resources while managing both legal and business risk. Indeed, we submit that general counsel can be more effective drivers of compliant corporate behaviour if they are strategic partners with the non-lawyer managers and encourage managers to take an active role in legal matters – that is, to be legally astute.

2. "Where were the lawyers?"

After the collapse of Enron and WorldCom, Judge Stanley Sporkin, former head of the Department of Enforcement at the Securities and Exchange Commission, famously asked: "Where were the lawyers?"[12] In an effort to ensure that lawyers protected public investors by playing a "gatekeeper role", Congress passed the Sarbanes-Oxley Act of 2002.[13] Among other things, the act required general counsel to report to the CEO certain material violations of law or breaches of fiduciary duty. The act further required general counsel to report such acts to the audit committee if he was not satisfied with the CEO's response. Although the SEC ultimately backed down on a more controversial proposal, which would have required general counsel to notify the SEC if a publicly traded company failed to correct misleading disclosures, regulators and scholars continued to debate exactly what responsibilities in-house lawyers owe the public.

Jagolinzer, Larcker and Taylor found that publicly traded firms that required the

---

7   Alan D Jagolinzer, David F Larcker and Daniel J Taylor, *Corporate Governance and the Information Content of Insider Trades*, 49(5) J Accounting res 1249 (2011).

8   E Norman Veasey and Christine T DiGuglielmo, *The Tensions, Stresses, and Professional Responsibilities of the Lawyer for the Corporation*, 62 BUS L 1, 5 (2006).

9   Ronald J Gilson, *Value Creation by Business Lawyers: Legal Skills and Asset Pricing*, 94 Yale LJ 239 (1984).

10   Sarah Helene Duggin, *The Pivotal Role of the General Counsel in Promoting Corporate Integrity and Professional Responsibility*, 51 St Louis U LJ 989 (2007).

11   Omari Scott Simmons, *The Under-Examination of In-House Counsel*, 11 Transactions: Tenn J Bus L 145, 146 (2009).

12   Egon Guttman and Stanley Sporkin, *The Evolving Legal and Ethical Role of the Corporate Attorney After the Sarbanes-Oxley Act of 2002*, 52 AM U L REV 639, 641 (2003).

13   Sung Hui Kim, *The Banality of Fraud: Re-Situating the Inside Counsel as Gatekeeper*, 74 Fordham L Rev 983, 985-986 (2005).

general counsel to approve trades by insiders during trading blackout windows (which restrict insider trading immediately before earnings releases) had fewer atypical profitable trades based on non-public information than those that did not: "Thus, when given the authority, it appears the general counsel can effectively limit the extent to which corporate insiders use their private information to extract rents from shareholders".[14] In other words, notwithstanding the temptation "to seek to please the corporate officials with whom they deal rather than to focus on the long-term interest of their client, the corporation",[15] general counsel do not just rubber stamp such trades. This study supports Gilson's assertion that in-house counsel may be the lawyers best positioned to act as private gatekeepers.[16]

The emphasis that the Sarbanes-Oxley Act put on the role of inside counsel as gatekeeper, or what Nelson and Nielsen call 'cop',[17] made it more difficult for the general counsel to be an active participant in creating value. A lawyer seen primarily as a cop may be excluded from key conversations and decisions, on the assumption that "it is better to ask for forgiveness than for permission". Unfortunately, the later a lawyer is brought into the planning of a transaction, the more likely it is that the lawyer will have to advise "no". Business managers may anticipate this, and provide counsel with a biased set of facts in hopes of improving the likelihood of a "yes" answer. Under either scenario, proceeding with the initial plan may not be the best approach for the enterprise.

This is why, as we discuss later in the chapter, legally astute top management teams take a proactive approach to legal matters. They bring counsel in early to assist not only in assessing legal risk but also in creating a strategy and a plan of execution that maximises realisable value while eliminating any unnecessary legal or business risks. Each member accepts responsibility for the ethical and legal conduct of business as well as for the firm's overall economic success. When strategically astute lawyers and legally astute non-lawyers work together, they are more likely to develop workable solutions than either the lawyers or the business managers acting alone.

3. A brief history of the general counsel transformation in the United States

The role of general counsel within large US corporations has evolved considerably from the late 19th century to the present, undergoing both rises and falls in its power and prominence. Today, the position is one of great prestige. (We call this the 'general counsel transformation'.) In-house counsel have not been held in such high esteem since the early 20th century.

Before the 1930s, general counsel served both legal and business functions, "were held in high repute", and "their sage counsel was regularly sought" by corporate management.[18] The position's high remuneration levels further emphasised this high

---

14   *Ibid.*
15   American Bar Association, Recommendations of the American Bar Association Task Force on Corporate Responsibility (March 31 2003), available at www.abanet.org/media/corpgovpdf.
16   Ronald J Gilson, *The Devolution of the Legal Profession: A Demand Side Perspective*, 49 Md L Rev 869, 915 (1990).
17   Robert Nelson and Laura Beth Nielsen, *Cops, Counsel, and Entrepreneurs: Constructing the Role of Inside Counsel in Large Corporations*, 34 Law & Soc'y Rev 457 (2000).
18   Carl D Liggio, Sr, *A Look at the Role of Corporate Counsel: Back to the Future—Or Is It the Past?*, 44 Ariz L Rev 621, 621 (2002).

status: counsel received roughly 65% of the CEO's salary and often were among the corporation's three highest paid officers.[19] For example, in post-Civil War America, general counsel positions at railroad companies were considered the most prestigious within the legal profession, attracting even federal judges.[20]

However, from the 1940s, there was a steady decline in the power and prominence of the general counsel position due to the rise of large outside law firms serving corporations' increasingly complex legal needs.[21] General counsel evolved into a "relatively minor management figure, stereotypically, a lawyer from the corporation's principal outside law firm who had not quite made the grade as partner".[22] The position handled "corporate housekeeping" matters, and acted as liaison to the outside legal firm.[23] Further contributing to the position's decline was the rise in status of those with master's degrees in business administration (MBA), of the new "wunderkinds of the business community".[24]

The high costs associated with switching between firms[25] gave outside counsel substantial bargaining power against their corporate clientele.[26] Because elite law firms were not able or willing to adjust their fee structures, corporations began to seek other, more favourable avenues to satisfy their legal needs, ultimately substituting inside counsel for outside counsel.[27] John Coffee explained:

> The participant in this drama who gained the most from this transition was the in-house general counsel, who now became as much a general manager of legal services as an actual counselor to management. For his or her own self-interested reasons, the general counsel typically did not want competition from outside counsel. He or she wanted to be the primary conduit of legal advice to management and hence sought to discourage any long-term, continuing relationship between senior management and outside counsel. As much from this reason as to encourage price competition, the in-house counsel moved legal business around, thereby assuring his or her own monopolistic position as the supplier of legal advice to senior management. What shifted then was not the relative number of insider versus outside counsel, but the balance of power between them.[28]

Robert Rosen called this shift the inside counsel's "age of enlightenment".[29] As he explained: "No longer lacking resolution and courage, inside counsel exercise their own powers with advice from, but not at the direction of, outside counsel".[30]

The American Corporate Counsel Association was established in 1980.[31] It was

---

19   *Ibid.*
20   Debora A DeMott, *The Discrete Roles of General Counsel*, 74 Fordham L Rev 955, 958-959 (2005).
21   *Ibid.*
22   Abram Chayes and Antonia H Chayes, *Corporate Counsel and the Elite Law Firm*, 37 Stan L Rev 277, 277 (1985).
23   *Ibid.*
24   Liggio, note 18 above, at 621.
25   Gilson, note 16 above, at 915.
26   Robert Eli Rosen, *The Inside Counsel Movement, Professional Judgment and Organizational Representation*, 64 IND LJ 479, 508-509 (1989).
27   *Ibid.*, at 505.
28   John C Coffee Jr, *Gatekeepers: The Professions And Corporate Governance* 224 (2006).
29   Rosen, note 26 above, at 488.
30   *Ibid.*
31   Chayes and Chayes, note 22 above, at 514.

"expressly designed to create a new identity for the lawyers formerly known as 'house counsel'".[32] By the 1980s, general counsel performed increasingly diverse and nuanced roles:

> They managed and reviewed the legal services provided to corporate clients by outside counsel; they regularly supplied routine legal services and, on some occasions, directly handled complex transactions and even litigation; they counselled clients and their constituents on regulatory requirements; and they created compliance programs.[33]

According to the association, general counsel should:

- maintain a broader awareness of 'big picture' implications;
- manage an unfiltered flow of information throughout the corporation;
- provide frank and candid counsel to the CEO; and
- espouse a risk assessments approach.[34]

Perhaps the best known example of the high-status general counsel was General Electric's Benjamin Heineman, Jr. A former managing partner at the prestigious law firm Sidley & Austin, Heineman served as general counsel of General Electric from 1989 until 2006.[35] He built within General Electric an internal team of 1,000 lawyers, which in many respects mirrored the experts and specialists found in a top outside firm. Today, the general counsel of a major corporation in the United States is likely to be a former partner of a prestigious outside firm (eg, Dan Cooperman was a partner at Bingham McCutchen before becoming general counsel of Oracle then Apple) or a lawyer of a comparable calibre (eg, Paul Dacier, the general counsel at EMC Corporation, is the incoming president of the Boston Bar Association). As the type of work done by in-house departments became increasingly sophisticated and high profile, the status of in-house lawyers further increased.

This new breed of general counsel reduced the overall legal costs and fees paid to outside firms and expanded resources for the in-house legal function by stressing the need to introduce price competition to keep down legal costs. They actively managed the enterprise's overall legal function, including deciding what work to do in-house and by whom (eg, by using internal non-attorney professionals wherever possible), questioning costs (such as having junior associates accompany a partner at depositions), and putting work out to bid among a variety of firms or alternative legal service providers.

Although the shift did reduce legal costs and fees, it had another effect that has remained largely unexamined in the literature. By setting firms against each other, general counsel eliminated what had been strong ties between executives and directors in the corporation and the firm's outside counsel. Some general counsel go

32 David B Wilkins, *Is the In-House Counsel Movement Going Global? A Preliminary Assessment of the Role of Internal Counsel in Emerging Economies (Symposium: The Changing Role and Nature of In-House and General Counsel)*, 251 Wis L Rev 251, 277 (2012).
33 Mary C Daly, The Cultural, Ethical, and Legal Challenges in Lawyering for a Global Organization: The Role of the General Counsel, 46 Emory L J 1057, 1061-1062 (1997).
34 Constance E Bagley, *Winning legally: How Managers can use the Law to Create Value, Marshal Resources, and Manage Risk* 232 (2005).
35 David B Wilkins, *Team of Rivals? Toward a New Model of the Corporate Attorney-Client Relationship*, 78 Fordham L Rev 2067, 2081 (2010).

so far as to insist that one of their lawyers is involved in any conversation between an outside lawyer and a member of the management team. The insertion of in-house counsel between managers and the firm's outside lawyers has had several effects. First, to the extent that mixed questions of business and law are discussed with the general counsel, the outside lawyer may lose some of the nuance that would be picked up on if the communication was more direct. Perhaps more importantly, the distribution of a corporation's work over a variety of outside law firms eliminated the presence of an individual external lawyer capable of acting as a trusted adviser or consigliere to the corporation.

Historically, the senior partner in the outside firm that did most of the corporation's work served as the consigliere. That partner often attended all board meetings and established professional and social ties with the top management team. As a result, that lawyer understood the broad range of business activities with which the firm was engaged and often had a better sense of when a particular transaction might create undue financial or reputational risks than a lawyer brought in to handle a one-off matter. The final effect of this process of putting out legal work for bid was that, over time, the provision of legal services became more of a commodity than a trusted relationship. This is what happened in the accounting world when, before the Sarbanes-Oxley Act, companies paid relatively low fees for their audits, prompting the big accounting firms to augment their audit income with higher-priced consulting services. Reducing the role of outside counsel to a commodity gave them less incentive to develop firm-specific knowledge about their corporate clients.

In addition, the shift in power to in-house counsel prompted concerns that general counsel were becoming overly susceptible to forces that decreased independence. Nelson and Nielsen reported increased entrepreneurialism among modern lawyers, with:

> ... corporate counsel ... adapt[ing] their images and lawyering styles to the prerogatives of contemporary management. Accordingly, inside lawyers limit their gatekeeping functions, emphasize their dedication to managerial objectives, and defer to management's judgments about legal risk.[36]

Donald Langevoort argued that general counsel became too "comfortable" in their roles and may "too readily [have engaged in] ... a process of collective rationalization" where "objectivity [or cognitive independence] is predictably diminished".[37] This comfort level and lack of objectivity may cause a corporation to assume unacceptable legal risks,[38] as arguably happened at Enron, Arthur Andersen, Google, Symbol Technologies, Rite Aid, Inso, Warnaco, Computer Associates International, Gemstar-TV Guide and Tyco.[39] Responding to many instances of blatant illegality, Congress enacted the Sarbanes-Oxley Act, which "essentially deputized a public corporation's CLO [chief legal officer] as a gatekeeper of ... national securities markets".[40]

---

36   Nelson and Nielsen, note 17 above, at 457.
37   Donald C Langevoort, *Getting (Too) Comfortable: In-house Lawyers, Enterprise Risk, and the Financial Crisis,* 2012 WIS L REV 493, 495 (2012).
38   *Ibid.*
39   Kim, note 13 above.
40   *Ibid.*

4. Relationship with the top management team and the board: cop, counsel or strategic partner?

A key challenge for general counsel is how to negotiate not only the relationship with outside counsel but also the relationship with the CEO and the board of directors, especially the audit committee. Nelson and Nielsen divided lawyers into three categories: cop, counsel and entrepreneur.[41] A cop is primarily concerned with policing the conduct of business clients. Cops "interact with business people almost exclusively through legal gatekeeping functions, such as approving contracts, imposing and implementing compliance programs, and responding to legal questions".[42] Counsel not only give advice on the law but also more broadly advise on the potential, ethical and reputational effects of a proposed course of action.[43] Arguably, every lawyer should take such factors into account because, as the American Bar Association points out, ethical, political and social concerns inform not only what laws are enacted, but how laws are interpreted and applied over time.[44] As Victor Tettmar, the managing partner of Bond Pearce, put it, general counsel should be the "guardian of moral capital".[45]

What Nelson and Nielson call the entrepreneur is a lawyer who recognises that "law can itself be a source of profits, an instrument to be used aggressively in the marketplace, or the mechanism through which major transactions are executed".[46] As noted above, the entrepreneurial lawyer plays a more limited gatekeeping role than either the cop or counsel, which may lead to undue risk-taking by the firm. For example, over 30% of the firms subject to civil or criminal investigations for illegal accounting of backdated stock options fired their general counsel.

We believe that general counsel should be both a trusted counsellor and a participant in value creation and capture, or what we call a 'strategic partner'. A strategic partner understands that his or her role goes beyond keeping the corporation out of trouble; it extends to participating in the creation and capture of firm value. Support for this proposition is found in a recent KPMG survey of 320 general counsel:

> Our survey has shown how GC's role is changing, to be a more strategic business adviser and barometer for the business. Boards expect GC to be commercially aware and to combine this awareness with their legal knowledge and experience.[47]

However, unlike Nelson and Neilsen's entrepreneurial lawyer, who adapts to the prerogatives of the top management team, a true strategic partner never forgets that he has an overriding professional duty to promote compliance with both the letter and the spirit of the law. As an officer of the court, an attorney may not participate

---

41   Nelson and Nielsen, note 17 above, at 463-466.
42   *Ibid.*, at 463.
43   *Ibid.*, at 464.
44   American Bar Association, Model Rules Of Professional Conduct, Model Comments to Rule 2.1 (2002).
45   Rebecca Lowe, *Compliant Counsel*, 18(2) In-House Perspective 13, 14 (April 2012). As former Yale Law School dean Anthony T Kronman explained, a true counsellor at law has the wisdom to offer deliberative advice about not just the means for attaining the client's goals but also the ends themselves. Anthony T Kronman, *The Lost Lawyer; Failing Ideals of the Legal Profession* (1995).
46   Nelson and Nielsen, note 17 above, at 466.
47   KPMG International Cooperative, *Beyond the Law: KPMG's Global Study of How General Counsel are Turning Risk to Advantage* 1, 53 (2012) (on file with the authors).

in defrauding a judge or regulatory body. As Dan Cooperman, Stanford Law School professor and former general counsel at Oracle and Apple, put it:

> There is a professional duty not to be complicit in a criminal act, so if you believe that the corporation is violating the law, you really have no choice but to resign.[48]

This role is not unlike that of a chief financial officer, who also has an obligation to ensure that the reported financial results fairly reflect the overall results of the corporation, despite any pressure from line business leaders or the CEO to be overly aggressive. Of course, every business leader has an obligation to ensure that the enterprise does not make irrational business decisions (including breaking the law), and should address any decision that could fall within this area.

4.1 Relationship with the top management team

The development of an organisational structure for any corporation is highly context-specific, and no one structure constitutes a panacea.[49] In order to be a strategic partner, the general counsel ought to be a member of the top management team. A 2001 survey conducted by the American Corporate Counsel Association found that 61.4% of general counsel report to the CEO, 15.3% report to the president and 12.7% report to another executive (roughly 7% report to the chief financial officer).[50] Simmons and Dinnage assert: "The general counsel must report to the board of directors or, at least, the CEO. Anything less than this will inhibit the functioning of the value-creation attributes that are vital to in-house counsel effectiveness."[51] We believe that the preferable structure is for the general counsel to report to the CEO, with the clear understanding that the general counsel has not only the power, but also the responsibility, to report any potentially illegal acts to the audit committee of the board.[52] We use the term 'chief legal officer' to refer to general counsel who are part of a top management team, that is, part of the so-called C-suite. (As discussed further below, building a strategically astute legal department also requires the chief legal officer to select the best structure for the legal department, appropriately to marshal and use human resources, and to develop legal strategies and tactics that drive business success.)

A chief legal officer may play a more strategic role as a member of the top management team, but he may lose some objectivity in the process. If an individual has been actively involved in creating a certain strategy or plan of execution, it is unrealistic to expect that person to be an objective critic of that strategy or plan. For this reason, if a chief legal officer acts as a strategic partner, an independent chief compliance officer or chief risk officer should be available to vet all courses of action to ensure legality. This officer may report to the chief legal officer for routine matters,

---

48   Lowe, note 45 above, at 15.
49   Rosen, note 26 above, at 499.
50   Susan Hackett, *Inside Out: An Examination of Demographic Trends in the In-House Profession*, 44 Ariz L Rev 609, 612 (2002).
51   Omari Scott Simmons and James D Dinnage, *Innkeepers: A Unifying Theory of the In-House Counsel Role*, 41 Seton Hall L Rev 77, 146 (2011).
52   Depending on an entity's governance structure, the independent directors or the full board may assume the role of supervision and assess the reports from the general counsel and other control functions. However, for the purposes of this chapter, we will refer to the most common structure for publicly traded US companies, in which the audit committee assumes the role.

but should have a direct reporting relationship to the audit committee as well. For example, at MassMutual, the chief compliance officer reports functionally to the chairperson of the audit committee, with administrative and informational (as defined by resolution) reporting to the general counsel.

Often, in highly regulated industries, the chief risk officer will report directly to the board or a committee from the board. For example, Andrea Bonime-Blanc, senior vice president of Global Corporate Responsibility & Risk Management at software company Verint Systems, reports to the chair of the audit committee. However, she also has a dotted line relationship with the chief legal officer.[53] She reports that many companies in Europe use this structure and notes that "in any case where there has been a settlement or successful prosecution by the government, the pharmaceutical industry has had to agree that the compliance piece is taken out of legal."[54] Similarly, John Wotton, president of the Law Society of England and Wales, argues that the roles of general counsel and chief compliance officer should be split, especially in regulated sectors.[55]

In contrast, the American Bar Association Task Force on Corporate Responsibility recommended that the general counsel of publicly traded firms "have primary responsibility for assuring the implementation of an effective legal compliance system under the oversight of the board of directors"; that general counsel's selection, retention and compensation be approved by the board; and that general counsel report regularly to a committee of independent directors.[56] The report also recommended that independent directors "make it clear to the general counsel (and to the CEO and other senior management) that such reporting would be expected to cover actual or potential material violations of law, breaches of fiduciary duty, and other 'substantial legal concerns'".[57]

One way to reconcile these approaches is to follow the recommendation of the Office of Inspector General of the Department of Health and Human Services in its 2004 guidance, An Integrated Approach to Corporate Compliance,[58] namely that firms are best served by separating the roles of general counsel and chief compliance officer but that "the positions complement each other in helping ensure corporate compliance".[59] The office further recommends that healthcare organisations "provide adequate means for the general counsel to bring legal compliance issues to the attention of the board where necessary".[60]

We recommend that the audit committee select the chief compliance officer/chief risk officer, with non-binding advice from the general counsel, and

---

53   Lowe, note 45 above, at 15.
54   Lowe, note 45 above. See also authorities cited in William W Horton, *Serving Two (or More) Masters: Professional Responsibility Challenges for Today's In-House Healthcare Counsel*, 3 J Health Life Sci L 187, 196 n 9 (January 2010).
55   Horton, note 54 above.
56   American Bar Association Task Force on Corporate Responsibility, *Report of the American Bar Association Task Force on Corporate Responsibility*, 59 BUS L 145, 161 (November 2003).
57   Horton, note 54 above, at 194.
58   US Department of Health and Human Services and American Health Lawyers Association, *An Integrated Approach to Corporate Compliance – A Resource for Health Care Organization Boards of Directors* (2004).
59   Horton, note 54 above, at 196.
60   *Ibid*, at 196-197.

determine his or her performance and prospects. In a lot of ways, this arrangement reflects the role of the internal auditing team in many companies. The chief compliance or risk officer reports not just to the chief financial officer or general counsel, but also directly to the audit committee.

Some scholars argue that too much attention has been paid to concerns about the independence of general counsel, what Usha Rodrigues calls a fetishization of independence.[61] Simmons and Dinnage argue that this short-sightedness ignores other value contributed by general counsel that may even outweigh the "risk and probabilities associated with conflicts".[62] They assert that the critical factor is not "independence per se, but rather a shared understanding between corporate management and in-house counsel as to the latter's role". We agree.

A possible middle ground is to have the general counsel report to the CEO but require the CEO to share with the board (or a board committee) in advance any decisions around the hiring, compensation and termination of the general counsel. In addition, the general counsel should have direct access to the board and regularly meet independently (that is, without the CEO or chief financial officer present) with the board (or a board committee).

Whatever the reporting structure, a lawyer cannot be a true strategic partner unless the top management team itself is legally astute – that is, has the ability to communicate effectively with counsel and to work together to solve complex problems.[63] We turn to that managerial capability next.

5. Building the legally astute top management team

Much of the legal literature on the role of general counsel has focused on the agency problems that may occur when general counsel reports directly to another corporate officer, such as the chief financial officer or CEO. There has been far less discussion of what changes should be made in the perspectives and experience of the other members of the top management team if the chief legal officer is to be a strategic partner in value creation and capture. The basic premise of this section is that managers who view the law purely as a constraint, something to comply with and react to rather than to use proactively, will miss opportunities to use the law and the legal system to increase the value created by the firm and the share of that value captured by that firm.[64] Moreover, even if the general counsel is a member of the top management team, he is chief legal officer in name only if the team itself is not legally astute.

Legal astuteness requires

- a set of value-laden attitudes,
- a proactive approach,
- the exercise of informed judgment and
- context-specific knowledge of the law and the application of legal tools.[65]

---

61   Usha Rodrigues, *The Fetishization of Independence*, 33 J Corp L 447, 447 (2008): "Current rules thus over-rely on independence, transforming an essentially negative quality – lack of ties to the corporation – into an end in itself, and thereby fetishizing independence."
62   Simmons and Dinnage, note 51 above, at 90-92.
63   Constance E Bagley, Winning Legally: *The Value of Legal Astuteness*, 33 Acad Mgt Rev 378 (2008).
64   *Ibid.*, at 378-379. See also Constance E Bagley, *What's Law Got to Do with It?: Integrating Law and Strategy*, 47 Am Bus L J 587, 588 (2010).

Legally astute managers call on their lawyers to play an active role in formulating the corporate strategy as a whole, rather than just being technical consultants brought in when the firm is confronted with a legal problem. As Marshall Clinard and Peter Yeger stated: "Business corporations do not have legal problems. They have business problems where legal considerations may be more or less important, depending on the specific circumstances."[66] For example, when the CEO of EMC Corporation asked the general counsel whether EMC should buy VMWare, a developer of cutting-edge virtualization software that was embroiled in patent litigation with Microsoft, Paul Dacier responded: "Can you afford not to?" Dacier was not being cavalier about the legal risks; he also understood the business imperatives.

By actively engaging the other members of the team in a proactive manner, a chief legal officer can help to devise strategies and plans that advance the corporation's interests without taking unreasonable legal risk or violating societal expectations. Al Spies, the chief financial officer of US West, used to say: "I have no use for lawyers who talk in the third person. This is not about what you can do; this is about what we can do." Similarly, the senior vice president of legal affairs at PepsiCo, David Andrews, stressed to his lawyers the importance of getting close to the client by working closely with the managers of the business units. He established the PepsiCo Legal Academy in 2003, at which the top 30 PepsiCo lawyers had the opportunity to meet with Indra Nooyi, the company's president and chief financial officer, and others to discuss the company's strategy, financial performance and accounting controls. Nooyi, who subsequently became CEO of PepsiCo, encouraged the PepsiCo lawyers to use both their legal expertise and their business judgement when working with managers, stating: "We can't afford this separation of church and state."[67] She encouraged the lawyers to speak up if a manager proposed a business deal that did not make good business sense, instead of just focusing on preparing the perfect legal documentation for a flawed deal.

Counsel has to earn the respect of the non-lawyers on the top management team by learning enough about the company's business and strategy to make a creative contribution to setting strategy and developing the best plans to execute it. This means that legal advice needs to be business-oriented and should help managers address business opportunities and threats in a legally permissible, effective and efficient manner. Both internal and external counsel must be able to translate legal cases, statutes, regulations, briefs, memoranda and legal jargon into understandable business communications, terms and concepts. Similarly, internal counsel must be able to transmit the business facts, alternatives and objectives to external counsel in a manner that makes it possible for the outside lawyers to provide valuable advice and counsel.

By the same token, the non-lawyers on the top management team need to learn enough about the legal aspects of the business to enable them to engage in meaningful conversations with counsel about the pros and cons of various courses

---

65   Bagley, note 63 above.
66   Marshall G Clinard and Peter C Yeager, *Corporate Crime* 20 (1980).
67   Quoted in Bagley, note 34 above, at 227.

of action. Thus, legal literacy is key. Law affects each of the five forces that Michael Porter identified as being determinants of the attractiveness of an industry: buyer power, supplier power, the threat posed by current competitors, the availability of substitutes and the threat of new entrants.[68] For example, a patent can differentiate a product, create barriers to entry and eliminate substitutes, thereby making it more likely a buyer will pay a premium price. Government regulation can create barriers to entry and allow firms to operate as de jure monopolies. (This was the case in the US telecommunications arena until the 1980s and remains the case under many cable television franchise agreements.)

Law may impose a chance of a negative monetary return if legal requirements are not met. For example, Kodak was required to shut down its instant camera and film business when it was found to have violated Polaroid's patents.[69] In late 2012, Wal-Mart was under investigation for alleged violations of US and international anti-bribery laws (including the Foreign Corrupt Practices Act) in several of the corporation's most important markets.[70]

Donald Langevoort describes the legal groupthink (schema) that is present in all organisations. It is imperative that general counsel openly discuss with the top management team ways that they can actively (and not passively) avoid "cognitive co-dependency" and "collective rationalisation" so the general counsel has the "professional independence" required for the most effective execution of his or her duties.[71] One of the most challenging roles of a general counsel is to have the courage and foresight to respond to the assertion, "Everyone else does it this way", with "But we don't"; then to shift the dialogue to a discussion of how the firm might otherwise accomplish the business objectives with less risk.

Legally astute managers practise strategic compliance management and view the costs of compliance as an investment, not an expense. By following this 10-step programme, managers can promote legal compliance as a source of strategic advantage:

- Start with ethics and start at the top;
- Understand duties and recognise risks;
- Implement appropriate controls and processes;
- Prevent securities fraud;
- Compete hard but fairly;
- Look for opportunities to convert constraints into opportunities;
- Help shape the rules of the game;
- Play it safe;
- Educate all employees and distribute written policies; and
- Be prepared to deal with compliance failures.[72]

---

68   Michael E Porter, *Competitive Strategy: Techniques For Analyzing Industries And Competitors* 3-33 (1980). See also G Richard Shell, *Make The Rules Or Your Rivals Will* (2004).
69   Ben Dobbin, *Kodak Patent Sale could Save Photography Company from Bankruptcy*, Huffington Post, October 30 2011.
70   Stephanie Clifford and David Barstow, *Wal-Mart Takes a Broader Look at Bribery Cases*, NY TIMES, November 16 2012, at A1.
71   Langevoort, note 37 above, at 496, 499.
72   Adapted from Constance E Bagley, Winning Legally: How to use the Law to Create Value, Marshal Resources, and Manage Risk 47-50 (2005).

Under certain circumstances, a firm can create competitive advantage by going beyond what the law requires. At a time when the Food and Drug Administration was considering requiring firms to label their products to show the amount of trans fats they contained, PepsiCo's Frito Lay division stopped using hydrogenated oils in its potato chips and other snacks, then obtained Food and Drug Administration approval to label its products prominently as having zero trans-fats.

Rather than passively awaiting regulatory change, managers can actively work to influence the legislators and administrative agencies responsible for shaping the structure of an industry. As Michael Porter aptly put it, because a regulatory change may affect an industry's structure:

> ... a company must ask itself, "Are there any government actions on the horizon that may influence some elements of the structure of my industry? If so, what does the change do for my relative strategic position, and how can I prepare to deal with it effectively now?"[73]

For example, while other diesel engine manufacturers were fighting more stringent Environmental Protection Agency emissions standards for diesel engines, Cummins Inc. successfully lobbied the agency to set tougher standards. This allowed Cummings to capture the value of the research and development it had funded to make its engines more environmentally efficient. Indeed, proactive environmental strategies can offer competitive advantage, but only when firms replace the mindset of reducing pollution to meet government end-pipe restrictions with the search for ways to use environmentally friendly processes to create value.[74]

Law affects every activity in the value chain, from the structure of the firm to the management of human resources, the deployment of technology and procurement. Law helps determine not only the value of firm resources, but also:

- the allocation of firm resources among stakeholders;
- the environment in which resources are converted into products;
- the marshalling of human and financial resources and physical assets; and
- the uniqueness of resources.

Legally astute top management teams can

- use formal contracts to complement trust-building and other forms of relational governance to reduce transaction costs and strengthen relationships;
- protect and enhance the realisable value of knowledge assets and other firm resources;
- use legal tools to create valuable options; and
- as discussed above, practice strategic compliance management.[75]

For example, brand association trademarks, such as slogans, packing colours,

---

73   Porter, note 68 above, at 183-84.
74   Chad Nehrt, *Maintainability of First Mover Advantages when Environmental Regulations Differ Between Countries*, 23 Acad Mgt Rev 77 (1998).
75   Bagley, note 34 above, at 47-50.

scents and shapes, increase cash flow and decrease the variability of that cash flow.[76] Apple Inc. successfully trademarked the shape of its iPod music player[77] and negotiated licences to sell copyrighted music.

There are degrees of legal astuteness.[78] We submit that a general counsel cannot be an effective strategic partner unless the top management team has the requisite degree of legal astuteness. Accordingly, general counsel should promote the degree of legal astuteness best suited to the corporation. Some of the factors that determine this include industry type, countries of operation and source of competitive advantage (eg, price or product differentiation).

6. Building the strategically astute legal team

In addition to being an active member of a legally astute top management team who participates in the development of the overall corporate strategy, the chief legal officer must take three additional steps to build a strategically astute legal team. First, he must choose the best structure for the legal department given the firm's competitive position and strategy. Second, he must decide how to marshal and allocate human resources, both within and outside the company. Finally, he must work with the legal team to develop legal strategies and tactics that will help drive business success (see Figure 1).

Figure 1: Building the strategically astute legal team

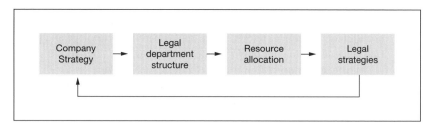

6.1 Structure of the legal department

The best structure for a company's legal department depends on the firm's strategy. One form does not fit all. The legal department may be centralised, decentralised or physically located to meet the business needs. In a highly decentralised corporate structure, such as General Electric, MassMutual and United Technologies, it makes sense for significant business units to have their own dedicated legal resources. In a business that is focused on integrating its various offerings, as is common in the telecommunications sector, a more centralised legal structure is appropriate. A firm with strategies focused around customer segments may organise its legal staff by customer segment. If subsidiaries or business units have headquarters in several locations, it may be necessary to locate the legal staff who support them at those

---

76   Alexander Krasnikiov, Saurabah Mishra and David Orozco, *Evaluating the Financial Impact of Branding Using Trademark: A Framework and Empirical Evidence*, 73 J MKTG 154-161 (2009).
77   David Orozco and James Conley, *Shape of Things to Come*, WALL ST J, MAY 12, 2008.
78   Bagley, note 63 above, at 384.

locations. In a decentralised structure, certain areas of legal expertise not unique to the strategies of each business may be best handled on a centralised basis (eg, tax, employee benefit plans and litigation). Regardless of the strategy or structure, generally it is necessary to have some form of corporate overlay at the parent company to address governance issues.

It is important to integrate the legal department into some overall organisational reporting structure. The board should be able to rely on the chief legal officer to handle legal issues and matters throughout the enterprise. Board members will also expect the general counsel to transmit information in a consistent and uninhibited manner. Enhanced clarity, confidence and supervision will be achieved if the responsibilities of the chief legal officer, the supervisory role of the board and information flows are documented and discussed fully with the full board. At MassMutual, the audit committee reviews and approves the charters of all of the control functions (eg, law, risk, finance, compliance and internal audit), so it has a clear understanding of the roles and responsibilities of the various legal organisations within the enterprise and their reporting obligations.

An integrated legal structure allows all the legal teams within the enterprise to work together by facilitating the sharing of knowledge, offering opportunities for the assignment of the best legal personnel to the most important areas, and promoting the development and training of the entire legal team. For example, despite having a decentralised legal group, many law departments are managed as one organisation (with hard-line reporting to the chief legal officer) to ensure the best deployment of resources; attorneys move to and from different subsidiaries and locations as part of learning the business and their career development.

6.2 Resourcing and staffing

After determining structure, the chief legal officer must address resources and staffing. The resourcing issue is not simple. The chief legal officer must decide what should be done in-house, what should be done with external resources and, in both situations, by whom. To do so, he will need to determine the effective billing rates for in-house counsel by calculating what each lawyer would have to bill to cover the internal cost. The decision to use internal or external resources should be based not only on economics, but also on the quality of work needed for the risk involved. If a particular legal activity is recurrent within the business or requires a high level of understanding of the business and its strategy, it is probably better done by the in-house legal team. Generally, for large corporations, more than 50% of the legal spend should be internal; for some industries this may be as high as 90%. Henry H Hopkins, vice president and chief legal counsel at investment manager T Rowe Price, reports that 90% of the firm's legal work is performed by in-house lawyers, who "probably have more expertise in specific functions, like registration statements and mutual funds, than outside attorneys because we do it all of the time".[79]

If the work is within the ambit of the internal legal team, the chief legal officer must decide which aspects should be undertaken by lawyers and which can be

---

79   Janet Stidman Eveleth, *New Day Dawning in Corporate Law*, MD BAR J 16, 20 (January/February 2004).

carried out by non-lawyer professionals under the direction of the lawyers. Because very little of what attorneys learned in law school or at a law firm is necessary to handle unique repetitive legal issues, much of this work can more efficiently be assigned to non-lawyer professionals. At Fisher Scientific, essentially all of the SEC reporting was handled by experienced paralegals, who kept up-to-date with the applicable rules and law and undertook the reporting obligations in a faster, more efficient way than most attorneys.

If the legal activity is unique to a particular jurisdiction, or information about how other clients are addressing the issue may be valuable, or the matter requires specific narrow expertise or a high degree of variable resources, it may best be handled by external resources. Henry Hopkins of T Rowe Price relies on outside counsel for non-routine matters, such as major litigation. When vice president, general counsel and corporate secretary of Constellation Energy Group, Kathleen Chagnon, faces issues common to the utility industry, she hires outside law firms that represent other utilities facing similar issues.[80] She also uses outside counsel to handle IP matters because her firm has few trademarks and patents, and for major acquisitions "because we don't have the back office, like large law firms, and these are paper and time-intensive".[81] If external resources are used, the chief legal officer will need to decide which firm or alternative provider should be retained, what the fee structure should be, and who in the firm or other provider should be assigned to the matter.

Regardless of the team that is assembled, one of the core competencies of a chief legal officer is the ability to establish the objectives of the overall internal/external team, to determine the resources needed and to match the resources to the objective. Henry Hopkins of T Rowe Price Associates prioritises projects and constantly monitors the work of his team, meeting regularly with each in-house lawyer to obtain progress reports.[82]

6.3   Developing the legal strategy

Unlike in a law firm, which generally is selling advice measured on a time basis, in-house attorneys add value by providing business results. Thus, an important skill is the ability to analyse the value and economic impact of legal advice and options. In addition, effective in-house counsel must exercise informed judgment to evaluate and weigh multiple inputs and accurately assess the likely impacts of any particular decision, and to decide how much time and effort to expend on a particular issue. For issues with minimal impact or risk, a quick response will often be most valuable to the business. Other issues, especially those involving enterprise risk, will require a more detailed critical analysis. Finally, the correct 'legal' answer may not always be the best answer for the business if it has significant stakeholder, public policy or other implications.

Failure to meet societal expectations will result in stricter and often more costly

---

80   *Ibid.*
81   *Ibid.*
82   *Ibid.*

regulation. Examples include the Foreign Corrupt Practices Act of 1977, the Dodd-Frank Wall Street Reform and Consumer Protection Act of 2010, and the stricter international banking rules imposed by the Basel Committee on Banking Supervision and the Financial Stability Board.[83] Even if new laws and stricter regulations are not enacted, regulators and consumers may respond negatively to questionable business practices.

Consider the life insurance industry. A life insurance policy, which is the contract between the insurer and the policy owner, clearly requires the beneficiary to give notice and proof of the insured's death to obtain the death benefit. Thus, historically, filing the claim was the trigger that activated an insurer's policy obligations. Many of the same companies that sell life insurance also sell annuities, which once annuitized continue to pay out until the annuitant dies. Insurance companies have an economic interest in tracking annuitized policies on a real-time basis so they do not overpay annuitants, but they may not have the same interest in tracking the deaths of insureds. Certain companies began checking public records for deaths of annuitants, but not for deaths of their life insureds, essentially using the public records on an asymmetric basis. Despite the legal argument that a life insurance contract clearly requires the beneficiary to provide notice of death, public policy scrutiny occurs in a different way. Seeing beyond the letter of the law, companies with strategically astute law groups recommended that their clients track and act on the death information symmetrically. This approach positioned those companies well in the media and with insurance commissioners and attorneys general, as they began to question these asymmetric industry practices. Similarly, although it was profitable and legal for big employers, such as Wal-Mart, to buy so-called pauper policies payable to the employer in the event of the death of non-key employees, such as janitors, once the practice became known, the employers faced media outrage that damaged their reputations, especially among average consumers, who likened the practice to having a lord obtain a life insurance policy on a serf.[84]

It is critical that the legal staff work closely with the subsidiaries, business units and corporate units as the lawyers develop their strategies and set objectives. This ensures the two-way flow of information between the legal team and the business. Just as the chief legal officer provides value by being a part of the top management team, in-house lawyers add their greatest value when they are closest to the business and involved in the strategic and business decisions of the business and corporate units.

Thus, the chief legal officer of a strategically astute legal team must employ a different type of lawyer from many of those who may succeed in private practice or government. Lawyers are generally trained in law schools and law firms to provide detailed, accurate and high-quality advice to clients, and they typically work autonomously or in small, established groups.[85] To be strategically astute, an in-

---

83   Brooke Masters, *Banks Face More Regulation over Risk*, Fin Times, November 25 2012.
84   See, eg, article available at http://consumerist.com/2007/07/03/walmart-took-secret-life-insurance-policies-out-on-employees-collected-after-their-death/.
85   David M Love III and Mark Roellig, *So You Want to Be a General Counsel? How to Maximize Your Chances for Such an Opportunity*, Association of Corporate Counsel Docket 9 (January/February 2012).

house lawyer must have an interest in the company's business and in management generally. Such a foundation allows strategic in-house lawyers to combine legal, business and situational information and to work with the business partners to find alternatives and opportunities, rather than just focusing on the problems and obstacles. An MBA, or at least some financial and accounting skill, is helpful because such a business grounding helps lawyers identify what additional business information might exist or should be obtained to make a better decision.

As well as having strong business skills, in-house counsel must earn and retain the trust of the non-lawyer managers by providing honest and candid advice. Like defensive medicine (eg, ordering excessive tests to guard against malpractice claims), overstating legal risk is neither ethical nor effective. Although it is true that few lawyers are ever sued in connection with a deal that never happens, playing the role of the 'Dr No' of the organisation increases the likelihood that managers will not seek legal advice in the first place. Instead, the best in-house counsel have the ability to articulate complex legal concepts in clear ways that managers can understand, so the concepts can be factored into a rational decision-making process.[86] Thus, the ability to interact with, listen to, communicate with and influence business partners is critical. In-house attorneys need to build trusting relationships while they operate both horizontally through the legal department and vertically through the various business units.

To be effective, in-house lawyers must be team players who can effectively participate in or lead teams, often without structural authority, to bring the correct information to bear or to bring the decision-makers together. Having the ability to develop and work with diverse teams effectively and to listen to and understand conflicting views improves the likelihood that various perspectives will be integrated, leading to better decision-making processes and outcomes.

In addition to having a mix of legal, business and interpersonal expertise, the most valuable in-house lawyers are proactive – they see issues before others do and can often convert seeming constraints into opportunities for value creation and capture. In short, they are not content solely to provide a legal answer. The challenge is to move the organisation from the reactive ("What is the answer to this legal question?") to the proactive ("What can we do to advance the business or reduce legal and business risks?"). There is a need to 'see around corners'. As Kathleen Chagnon put it:

> As in-house counsel, you function more as a strategic partner [with the executive management], identifying and spotting issues that need to be brought to the attention of commercial people, often before they are even aware that there are issues … .You study all facets of the company's operations so that its management may be more proactive when addressing this type of legal risk in the future.[87]

Similarly, in the KPMG survey of general counsel: "A number of general counsel commented that predicting risks before they arose was key to success. The role is moving from one of a 'fire-fighting' and reacting to events to being more strategic

---

86 See generally Gilson, note 9 above.
87 Eveleth, note 78 above, at 18.

and proactively anticipating risks at an earlier stage." The survey also quoted a company president who stated that the purpose of the legal department is to "anticipate and protect us from potential risk because the world is changing and creates more risk. GC should make us aware of what we should be doing and tell us this in a straightforward manner, not in complex legal language".[88]

The Nordic School of Proactive Law takes a similar approach: "In addition to avoiding disputes, litigation and other hazards, Proactive Law seeks ways to use the law to create value, strengthen relationships and manage risk."[89] The European Economic and Social Committee embraced this approach when it opined that setting "the desired goals" and selecting "the most appropriate mix of means to achieve them requires involving stakeholders early, aligning objectives, creating a shared vision, and building support and guidance for successful implementation from early on."[90]

Yet, high-quality, responsive and proactive legal advice is just the ticket to entry. To be strategically astute, lawyers not only need to anticipate and identify the risks and challenges that may occur, but must also spend time and energy to develop strategies to assist the business in creating a sustainable competitive advantage as the legal and business environment evolves. They must fully understand each business objective, which flows from the overall business strategy, and develop specific legal strategies and tactics to advance these objectives. When aligned with the unique strategic direction of the business, legal strategies help to create a differentiation that can maintain a successful and sustainable business strategy. For example, a company may have a strategy to extend a particular product line, which will require that it expand into a particular jurisdiction; a corresponding legal/regulatory strategy would be to work to change the laws in that jurisdiction to provide favourable regulatory or tax treatment for such an expansion. It is also important to recognise that legal rules are not static and to ask which laws, regulations or case law can be changed to the advantage of the business.

At US West, the legal team brought a legal action to relieve the company from regulations that had required major incumbent telecommunications companies to obtain customer approval before using their customers' records and personal information to market their services. In contrast, new competitors and carriers in other related businesses could market new services (including telephony) to their existing customers without restriction. The court ruled that the regulations violated US West's right to free speech under the First Amendment of the US Constitution. This ruling gave US West a legal competitive advantage for its marketing efforts as it competed with new entrants and other carriers.[91] Similarly, US West brought a successful action against the United States to declare unconstitutional, as a violation of free speech, the cable cross-ownership ban that prohibited telecommunication

---

88   See KPMG, note 47 above, at 10.
89   George J. Siedel and Helena Haapio, *Using Proactive Law for Competitive Advantage*, 47 AM BUS LJ 641, 657 (2010).
90   Opinion of the European Economic and Social Committee, "The Proactive Law Approach: A Further Step Towards Better Regulation at EU Level", 2009 O.J. (C 175) § 1.6.
91   *US West, Inc. v FCC*, 182 F 3d 1224 (10th Cir 1999).

companies from providing video services. This decision opened new markets and opportunities to US West, enabling it to compete with cable and broadcast companies on an equal footing.[92]

To further the business objectives, in-house lawyers need not only the requisite legal and business skills, but also the ability to suggest innovative legal strategies and tactics. Frequently, these strategies do not start at the highest level in the legal organisation – the lawyer nearest to the issues often has the best ideas and solutions. After the lawyers agree on the proposed legal strategies and tactics, the legal organisation should discuss them with the business leaders, asking such questions as: "What are your thoughts? What have we missed? Do these strategies and tactics align with what you are attempting to accomplish?" Such a discussion on the development of the legal strategies and tactics helps to change the company culture and the business leaders' perspective of the lawyers: "You mean you are here to actually assist me in meeting my objectives?"

After reaching an agreement on the legal strategies and tactics with the business leaders, the chief legal officer should assign specific, observable, measurable and time-bound tasks to both in-house and outside counsel. It is not enough to promise, "We will do high-quality legal work". Instead, it is necessary to evaluate the proposed strategies and tactics to eliminate any conflicts or overlaps and to ensure that the proper teams and individuals are working on each particular strategy or tactic. The chief legal officer should delegate the execution of legal strategies and tactics to teams within the legal organisation, who will then be responsible for further delegating them to specific individuals. As a result, when a lawyer or non-lawyer professional is working on a particular legal tactic, he will know which legal strategy it supports, what business objective it furthers and how it advances the company's overall success. By transforming firm-wide and legal department objectives into individual objectives, the process ensures that performance is appropriately measured and rewarded and, as needed, efforts and resources are redirected.

7. Export of the US model

The transformation in the status and responsibilities of general counsel and their in-house legal team is most advanced in the United States, but it has also taken root elsewhere. Reflecting and reinforcing this trend, the Association of Corporate Counsel dropped 'American' from its name in 2003 and now has members from over 75 countries.[93]

In the United Kingdom, "a number of top UK companies boast large and sophisticated in-house legal teams".[94] But because general counsel face obstacles unique to their own societal contexts, it is naïve to assume that the US model will spread abroad in the same, or even in a similar, form that it has in the United States. As David Wilkins argues:

---

92   *US West, Inc. v United States*, 855 F Supp 1184 (WD Wash), aff'd, 48 F 3d 1092 (9th Cir 1994), vacated and remanded after being rendered moot by the Telecommunications Act of 1996, 516 US 1155 (1996).
93   Association of Corporate Counsel, History of ACC, www.acc.com/aboutacc/history/index.cfm (accessed November 25 2012).
94   Wilkins, note 32 above, at 255.

In many European countries, for example, "employed" lawyers were prohibited from being members of the bar and were required to surrender their law licenses if they joined an in-house legal department. Even in common law jurisdictions such as the United Kingdom where in-house counsel did not suffer from any of these formal restrictions, these positions remained relatively low status throughout the 1990s.[95]

Some challenges are more formidable than others. Of particular concern is the refusal of the Court of Justice of the European Union to extend attorney-client privilege to communications between in-house counsel and the corporation.[96] However, no challenge is insurmountable, as Professor Wilkins explains:

Notwithstanding the absence of the kind of similarities in legal structure (unlike the United Kingdom, both China and Brazil are civil law jurisdictions), political accountability (the state plays a much larger role in the economy in all three BIC countries [Brazil, India and China] than in the United Kingdom and most of Europe), regional coordination (there is no equivalent of the European Union pushing harmonization), and cultural affinity (even India has not had particularly close connections to the United States for much of its history) that arguably facilitated the migration of the American mode of the production of law to the United Kingdom and Europe, we have nevertheless seen the development of many large US-style law firms in each of the BIC countries.[97]

As companies in emerging countries such as these "seek to capture the shift in economic globalization toward emerging markets",[98] they "will [most likely] look to the model of in-house counsel currently employed by the established Western companies with whom they are competing for guidance about how to set up their own internal counsel".[99] Indeed, much of the reason why such countries have emerged as key players in the global economy is that they each espoused certain regulatory reforms that more developed countries, such as the United States, held as fundamental.[100] As more capital has flowed to these countries, and their firms have increased their interaction with firms based in more economically established countries, the general counsel transformation has spread.[101] The increasing number of lawyers around the world who receive a legal education in the United States, where the general counsel transformation is most advanced and successful, contributes to this trend.[102]

8.   Conclusion

The general counsel transformation in the United States and elsewhere reflects a complex and evolving web of business and legal goals situated in increasingly competitive global markets. The rise in power and prominence of the general counsel over the second half of the 20th century precipitated unprecedented occupational

---

95	*Ibid.*, at 262-64.
96	AM&S Case (155/79), May18 1982, paras 21, 24, [1982] ECR 1610, 1611.
97	Wilkins, note 32 above, at 264-265.
98	*Ibid.*, at 273.
99	*Ibid.*
100	*Ibid.*
101	*Ibid.*
102	*Ibid.*, at 275.

obstacles, including the challenge of maintaining professional objectivity over business decisions in which the general counsel actively participated. In the wake of the large corporate scandals that accompanied this rise, federal law put pressure on in-house counsel to act as gatekeepers to protect the public. This deputisation prompted corporations to reprioritise compliance, sometimes at the expense of legitimate value creation and capture.

Of Nelson and Nielsen's three lawyer types, the entrepreneurial lawyer is closest to our proposed role of chief legal officer as strategic partner. However, unlike the entrepreneurial lawyer, who adapts to the prerogatives of the top management team, a strategic partner maintains the professional independence necessary for success by never forgetting that he has a overriding duty to promote compliance with both the letter and the spirit of the law. However, a strategic partner understands that his or her role goes beyond keeping the corporation out of trouble. By assuming a more active role in setting both the business and the legal agenda and by promoting the degree of top management team legal astuteness most appropriate to the firm, a strategic partner actively participates in the creation and capture of firm value. To be effective, the chief legal officer must understand the corporate strategy and translate it into identifiable and measurable outputs, including selecting the structure of the legal department, allocating resources and staff, and establishing the legal strategies and objectives. Strategic partners encourage both the in-house lawyers and non-lawyer managers to be proactive, and thus able to influence resource allocations and to convert seeming constraints into opportunities to create value for all constituencies.

Because being an active member of the top management team may impact on the chief legal officer's objectivity, we submit that there should be an independent chief compliance officer or chief risk officer, who vets all courses of action to ensure legal and corporate compliance. This officer may report to the chief legal officer for routine matters, but he should have a direct reporting relationship to the audit committee as well.

General counsel must never forget the duties inherent in the office. If, despite their lawyers' best efforts, the corporation persists in engaging in illegal or ignoble practices, it is far better for counsel to resign from the company than to be complicit in wrongful conduct. Although not always possible, such clashes should be avoided. Often, the best outcomes are achievable only when there is a relationship of trust, confidence and respect between and among the lawyers, the non-lawyer managers and the board members. When dealing with conflict, legal and business leaders should keep trying to reframe issues and refine tactics until they are satisfied that the firm's legitimate business objective of 'winning' in the marketplace is being advanced in an effective, legal and above-board manner. We submit that corporations managed by legally astute top management teams and advised by strategically astute counsel will be better positioned to achieve sustained competitive advantage than those lacking either capability.

The authors gratefully acknowledge the excellent research assistance provided by Yale research assistant Gianmarco Massameno.

Using alternative dispute resolution as a tool for containing legal risk

Wolf Juergen von Kumberg
Northrop Grumman
Stuart Weinstein
Charles Wild
University of Hertfordshire

1. Introduction and hypothetical examples

In this chapter, we examine how legal departments use conciliation, mediation and arbitration as a tool to contain legal risk. Not every dispute will be suitable for these tools, but the authors believe that the majority of employment and commercial disputes businesses face can successfully and efficiently be resolved through one of these forms of alternative dispute resolution (ADR). Moreover, they believe that the use of ADR as a means to settle disputes is one way in which an internal in-house legal function can show problem-solving commercial judgment and reduce company exposure to the uncertainty of litigation in many jurisdictions.

1.1 Hypothetical examples

(a) Example A

Michael is the manager of a jewellery outlet which is part of a large, nationwide chain. Mary is one of the store's employees. Michael fired Mary following a row about mixed-up orders. By accident, Mary had mixed up two customers' orders and they had left "horrible" tweets on the company's twitter account telling the world how bad the service was at Michael's store. Michael is furious with Mary and the two have an argument. Mary becomes belligerent and Michael asks her to leave the premises. Later, the company's human resources department sends Mary notice of termination. Mary calls the Advisery, Conciliation and Arbitration Service (ACAS) for advice on going to a tribunal for unfair dismissal. She speaks to an ACAS conciliator, who suggests that she considers conciliation. ACAS then contacts Michael, who says there is nothing to conciliate. Mary brings a tribunal claim for unfair dismissal.

(b) Example B

The same scenario as Example A except that the day after Michael asks Mary to leave the premises he contacts human resources and the manager tells Michael about the potential for workplace mediation to resolve this dispute and get Mary and Michael back working together in an effective manner. Both Michael and Mary agree to workplace mediation and, after spending an afternoon with a skill workplace mediator, they agree to a plan to resolve their differences and continue to work together. Problem solved.

(c) Example C

For 10 years, your company has been dealing with a manufacturer that has been supplying you high-quality kitchen appliances which you include in the production of luxury specification kitchens. Recently, the company moved its manufacturing plant from Italy to China, and there have been some problems with timely delivery of appliances for your kitchen installations and a number of quality control issues with the products manufactured in China. While you have reservations about the manufacturing plant being moved from Italy to China (this move is not seen as attractive to your high-net-worth clientele), it is still a strong drawing point that the products are Italian designed and the manufacturer gives you good credit terms, which helps you to keep your borrowing costs low. Your sales team has visited the factory in China several times to review the situation, but has not achieved a satisfactory outcome, and the Italian corporate headquarters has not addressed the issue because it has larger customers with bigger problems. You want to keep the commercial relationship going but you are concerned that filing a legal action will bring unwarranted publicity about the quality of the appliances you have already installed in your customers' luxury kitchens.

(d) Example D

You are the in-house counsel for a major multinational firm and your company is suing its local business partner in the courts of Country X. Your local legal adviser tells you that you will lose the case at trial because of the political influence Country X's government has on the courts, but that you can expect the judgment to be overturned on appeal because Country X's appellate courts are generally reliable.

(e) Example E

The Canadian Motor Vehicle Arbitration Plan[1] is a voluntary ADR programme where eligible disputes between automobile manufacturers and their customers can be resolved through arbitration. An agreement for arbitration provides for arbitration before an impartial arbitrator, who will listen to both sides of the case, weigh the evidence and make a decision that is final and binding on both parties. The arbitrator decides all questions of fact, law, procedure and evidence that arise in the case.

(f) Example F

Your company has successfully won an arbitration held in France. The award was made in Paris, so the seat of the award is France. France is a contracting state to the New York Convention and therefore the award can be enforced internationally as a New York Convention award. You now wish to enforce the award in Brazil. In order to be enforced in Brazil, the French arbitral award must first be recognised by the

---

1   Available at: www.camvap.ca/wp-content/uploads/CAMVAP_Agreement_Arbitration_2011.pdf (accessed 29 March 2013).

Superior Tribunal of Justice, the highest court in Brazil for non-constitutional matters. As long as the requirements of the New York Convention and the Arbitration Law are satisfied and enforcement of the award would not be contrary to national sovereignty or public policy, the successful party in a foreign arbitration can be confident that the award will be recognised in Brazil.[2]

(g) Example G

A foreign entity and a Chinese company enter into a contract with English and Chinese versions. The English version says the administering arbitration centre is the Singapore International Arbitration Centre while the Chinese version names another arbitration centre. A further provision says that both language versions have equal effect.[3]

2. Why lawsuits do not settle quickly

Often, one of the immediate problems a general counsel will face is that the first time he hears of a problem is when an action has been filed, perhaps when a member of the press phones to ask for a comment about a lawsuit that has been filed in another country. At this point, already some of the damage has been done because the dispute is now a news item and it may have a negative effect on your ability to put forward a solution. So how does a general counsel prevent such situations from happening?

First, it is not always possible to prevent legal actions. Sometimes a statute of limitation may run unless an action is followed; in this circumstance it may be anticipated. However, in most situations where there is a breakdown of communication with the other party's business people or counsel, this may give rise to such a circumstance. For instance, if strongly worded letters have been exchanged between the parties, unless some other, 'last chance' solution is offered (eg, conciliation, mediation or arbitration), it is natural that the next step will be the filing of papers.

Sometimes, general counsel may be reluctant to explore ADR at any early stage of litigation because they fear being seen within their company as weak, or externally as a pushover or an easy mark for future litigants. In some situations the general counsel will let an action progress until the other side provides a realistic legal basis for their claim. This is not the case with the usual contract breach cases or commercial disputes.

In the United States, where contingency fee action cases are commonplace, the plaintiff's lawyer has an incentive to do as little as possible until the eve of trial, at which point he has the greatest leverage to force a settlement. In the interim, the general counsel will be learning of the strengths and weaknesses of the case, having

---

2   Fabiana Videira Lopes, The recognition of foreign arbitral awards in Brazil, May 17 2010, DLA Piper website. Available at: www.dlapiper.com/the-recognition-of-foreign-arbitral-awards-in-brazil/ (accessed March 30 2013).

3   Arvin Lee, Singapore overview of arbitrations involving Chinese parties, 2012. Available at: www.siac.org.sg/index.php?option=com_content&view=article&id=418:siacs-experience-administering-arbitrations-involving-chinese-parties&catid=56:articles&Itemid=171 (accessed March 30 2013).

used the plaintiff's deposition to gauge its credibility. More importantly, the general counsel can use this time to evaluate the skill of the plaintiff's lawyers in comparison with your company and its formidable team of external legal advisers.

In some cases it is impossible to quantify damages at the outset or to assign a value to a claim, for example, "he sexually harassed me", "my boss belittled me" or "my career ended when I blew the whistle". Here, both sides need time to establish the facts and assess their impact before the quantum of damages can be set. In certain situations, it may be impossible to focus the business people on settling a case rather than more pressing matters, or if deeply emotional issues and personalities are involved.

3.   Three tips on managing litigation in-house

Before examining ADR, we would like to suggest three tips gathered from expertise gained over the years defending companies against lawsuits.

First, when faced with a lawsuit, the first step should be to check whether you are covered by your insurance policies, such as products liability, fraud and theft, directors' and officers' liability, premises liability, employees and workers compensation, umbrella coverage, maritime insurance, aviation. Depending on the insurance you have, you may need to notify your insurance carrier and tender the claim to it to defend. Often, the insurer will appoint a firm of lawyers (one of its panel counsel) to represent your company in the defence of the action.

You should consult a specialist insurance lawyer rather than try to evaluate the terms of the insurance contract yourself or rely on your internal insurance expert or insurance broker. The specialist will look at, for example, the Lloyds of London insurance provisions to see what immediate and long-term help you are entitled to under the terms of your insurance policy. General counsel will not be able to provide the same specialist expertise.

Second, it is important to use local counsel when litigating. This may not be such an important issue with international litigations, since many countries have restrictive requirements on non-licensed practitioners appearing in their courts (eg, Korea, Japan, India and Israel). However, in national actions, it may be tempting to assume that a large, national firm of lawyers can handle everything. The *Texaco v Pennzoil*[4] case from 1987, where Joe Jamail, the legendary trial lawyer for Texas-based Pennzoil, skilfully was able to use regional bias to his advantage in winning a $10.5 billion Houston jury verdict against New York-based Texaco is such an example.[5] However, bear in mind the advantages of local counsel – when the national lawyers leave at the end of the working day, their local-based opponent may be playing golf with the judge at the country club!

The *Texaco* result is not unusual. In November 1996, a jury in Jackson, Mississippi awarded a local funeral home owner $500 million in damages from the Loewen Group, a Canada-based corporation with more than 700 funeral homes and 109 cemeteries in

---

4   729 S W 2d 768 (Tex App 1987).
5   See Robert M Lloyd, *Pennzoil v Texaco*, Twenty Years After: Lessons for Business Lawyers, 6 [2005] Transactions: The Tennessee Journal of Business Law 321 at 324. Available at: http://trace.tennessee.edu/cgi/viewcontent.cgi?article=1073&context=transactions (accessed April 24 2013).

the United States, in a claim that the foreign corporation had tried to put him out of business.[6] Mr Loewen, chief executive of the Loewen Group, said to his investors: "I had at least a dozen lawyers – not one of them flagged the danger of a Southern jury."[7] These results might not have happened after *BMW of North America, Inc v Gore*,[8] where the US Supreme Court limited punitive damages under the due process clause of the Fourteenth Amendment, and *State Farm Mutual Automobile Insurance Co v Campbell*,[9] in which the US Supreme Court applied the *BMW of North America v Gore* factors to conclude that the due process clause usually limits punitive damage awards to less than 10 times the size of the compensatory damages awarded. Nonetheless, the comment of former US Speaker of the House of Representatives the late Thomas P ('Tip') O'Neill, Jr on politics, namely that "all politics is local", is also true for law – all law is local.

The third tip before moving into the discussion of ADR is that if the law firm that handled the case was not victorious at trial, do not use it for the appeal. Instead, find and appoint the best appellate attorney in that jurisdiction. The issues an appellate specialist will consider to raise on appeal when looking at a trial record are quite different from the issues that trial counsel may have considered important, and you need a fresh and dispassionate view.

4. What do we mean by ADR?

ADR[10] includes dispute resolution processes and techniques that act as a means for disagreeing parties to come to an agreement outside of litigation. It is a collective term for the ways that parties can settle disputes, with (or without) the help of a third party. This is ADR within the broadest sense of the meaning and what we refer to here in this discussion. However, what is meant by ADR is not always clear. For instance, the Commission of the European Communities (EC), *Green paper on alternative dispute resolution in civil and commercial law*,[11] defines alternative methods of dispute resolution as "out-of-court dispute resolution processes conducted by a neutral third party excluding arbitration proper".[12] The Green Paper distinguished those ADR mechanisms that are conducted by the court or entrusted by the court to a third party ("ADRs in the context of judicial proceedings") and ADRs used by the parties to a dispute through an out-of-court procedure ("conventional ADRs"). The EC also excludes the following procedures:

- expert opinions, which are not a method of dispute resolution, but a procedure involving recourse to an expert in support, for example, of a judicial or arbitration procedure;

---

6   Nina Bernstein, "Brash Funeral Chain Meets Its Match in Old South", *New York Times*, January 27 1996. Available at: www.nytimes.com/1996/01/27/us/brash-funeral-chain-meets-its-match-in-oldsouth.html? pagewanted=all&src=pm (accessed March 27 2013).

7   *Ibid.*

8   517 US 559 (1996).

9   538 US 408 (2003).

10   In Australia, ADR is sometimes referred to as external dispute resolution (EDR). See, for instance, Australian Securities & Investment Commission, Information Sheet 114, December 13 2010. Available at: www.asic.gov.au/asic/pdflib.nsf/LookupByFileName/What_is_EDR_and_how_can_it_help_me_0114. pdf/$file/What_is_EDR_and_how_can_it_help_me_0114.pdf (accessed March 27 2013).

11   COM/2002/0196 final, April 19 2002 ('Green Paper'). Available at: http://eur-lex.europa.eu/ LexUriServ/LexUriServ.do?uri=COM:2002:0196:FIN:EN:PDF (accessed March 27 2013).

12   *Ibid*, at 6.

- complaint handling systems made available to consumers by professionals as these are procedures not conducted by third parties but by one of the parties to the dispute; and
- automated negotiation systems which do not involve any human intervention, which are offered by providers of information technology services and are not considered to be dispute resolution procedures conducted by third parties but technical instruments designed to facilitate direct negotiations between the parties to the dispute.

The EC sees arbitration as closer to a quasi-judicial procedure than to an ADR as arbitrators' awards replace judicial decisions. Arbitration is the subject of some legislative instruments in the Member States (see eg, the Arbitration Act 1996[13] for England and Wales, and Northern Ireland) and at international level, such as the 1958 New York Convention on the recognition and enforcement of foreign arbitration decisions (New York Convention),[14] or, within the framework of the Council of Europe, the 1966 European Convention providing a Uniform Law on Arbitration.[15]

A second distinction which the EC makes is between the different conventional ADRs. Following certain ADR procedures, the third party or parties responsible for the procedure can be called upon to take a decision that is binding for one party or to make a recommendation to the parties which they are free to follow or not. In other ADR procedures, the third parties do not formally adopt a position on the possible means of resolving the dispute but simply help the parties to come to an agreement.[16] The approaches commonly used in national practice and legislation (ie, mediation and conciliation) are examples of the latter.

The European Judicial Network in civil and commercial matters, which was set up by the Council under the Decision of May 28 2001 and began operating on December 1 2002 with the aim of simplifying judicial cooperation between the Member States, characterises ADR (following the Green Paper format above) based on the role of the third party involved. For instance, if the third party helps the parties come to an agreement without formally expressing an opinion on any of the possible solutions to the dispute, this ADR process is 'conciliation' or 'mediation'. The European Judicial Network notes that the parties are invited to open or resume a dialogue and avoid confrontation, they themselves choose the technique for settling the dispute and they play a particularly active role in trying themselves to find the solution that suits them best.[17] The point stressed of mediation and conciliation is that these methods provide an opportunity to go beyond the purely legal position and reach a personalised solution that matches the real nature of the dispute. This consensus-based approach will increase the likelihood that once the parties have settled their dispute, they will be able to maintain normal business or personal relations.

---

13   www.legislation.gov.uk/ukpga/1996/23/section/2?view=extent (accessed March 27 2013).
14   www.uncitral.org/uncitral/en/uncitral_texts/arbitration/NYConvention.html (accessed March 27 2013)
15   http://conventions.coe.int/Treaty/en/Treaties/Html/056.htm (accessed March 27 2013).
16   See note 11 above.
17   http://ec.europa.eu/civiljustice/adr/adr_gen_en.htm (last updated November 4 2009) (accessed March 27 2013).

In other cases, it is the third party that suggests a solution to the parties, particularly in consumer disputes – a strong feature of the ADR process is that the third party produces the solution or makes a recommendation that the parties are then free to accept or not. Sometimes the third party takes a decision that is binding on the tradesperson or the professional person. For example, this is the case with the 'ombudsman' set up in certain businesses such as banking and insurance. The ombudsman's decisions are binding on firms taking part in the scheme. If the consumer is not satisfied with the decision, he can take his or her case to court. In England and Wales, this is the structure followed by the new Legal Ombudsman set up by the Office for Legal Complaints under the Legal Services Act 2007.[18]

The other common ADR scenario we will consider in this chapter is more similar to a court procedure. The third party is called an 'arbitrator' and takes a decision to settle the dispute. The decision, which is binding on both parties to the dispute, may be taken following the rules of law (classic arbitration) or on an equitable basis (amicable arbitration). The arbitrator's award has the status of an enforceable decision, which means that the settled dispute cannot be taken to court. As discussed above, because arbitration involves a decision made by a third party binding on both parties to the dispute, it is viewed by many as not being a form of ADR but rather an imposed private judicial solution to the parties' dispute.

In England and Wales, since the introduction of Lord Woolf's reforms around 15 years ago,[19] there has been a clear sense that going to court was not always the best or most appropriate route and that greater emphasis could and should be placed on taking action before applying to court. The reforms encouraged the early settlement of disputes through a combination of pre-action protocols, active case management by the courts, and cost penalties for parties who unreasonably refused to attempt negotiation or to consider ADR. The introduction in 1999 of the Civil Procedure Rules (CPR) and the pre-action protocols[20] gave some improvement in this area. The pre-action protocols provide that the court may take into account the conduct of either the claimant or defendant in failing to pursue ADR when determining costs: "The courts take the view that litigation should be a last resort, and that claims should not be issued prematurely when a settlement is still actively being explored."

5. Conciliation – last chance to resolve employment disputes

Conciliation is more common in labour and employment disputes. Example A above (see 1.1(a)) is an example of a situation where conciliation might have worked to resolve an employment dispute without recourse to an employment tribunal.

A conciliator appointed by the parties will meet with each of the parties separately to try to resolve their differences. Some of the steps taken by the conciliator will aim to lower tension and rhetoric between the parties, and to

---

18   Legal Ombudsman website, www.legalombudsman.org.uk/aboutus/index.html (accessed March 27 2013).

19   The Right Honourable Lord Woolf, Master of the Rolls, Access to Justice Final Report, July 1996. Available at: http://webarchive.nationalarchives.gov.uk/+/www.dca.gov.uk/civil/final/index.htm (accessed March 28 2013).

20   Civil Procedure Rules 1998, SI 1998/3132. Available at: www.legislation.gov.uk/uksi/1998/3132/contents/made (accessed March 28 2013).

improve communications between them by reopening channels, offering some interpretation of issues that may need further consideration, giving technical assistance where needed, tabling potential solutions and structuring a negotiated settlement. A conciliator will work best moving between the parties before the lawyers are called in. The conciliator should be seen as the last clear chance an employer might have before an employee brings a tribunal claim against it.

In employer-employee disputes, neither the manager nor the employee will wish to be the first to concede; however, also they are unlikely to wish to undertake testifying at an employment tribunal and being subject to cross-examination.

In the UK, if a tribunal claim has been (or, in some cases, could be) made, conciliation through ACAS[21] is offered to both sides with the aim of settling the matter without the need to attend a hearing. The conciliation process is voluntary. Although similar to mediation, the term conciliation is used when an employee is making, or could make, a specific complaint against his or her employer to an employment tribunal. It is unlike arbitration because the conciliator has no authority to seek evidence or call witnesses, or to make decisions or awards. ACAS also offers conciliation services in instances where an ongoing dispute exists between an employer and a union, if the parties think that such negotiation might avert a strike or resolve an ongoing dispute that involves more than one employee.

Another difference between conciliation and mediation is that the conciliator seeks concessions from the parties whereas a mediator will try to guide the discussion in such a way to optimise the parties' needs and wants, taking feelings into account and reframing representations. Perhaps the best thing about conciliation is that the parties never face off against each other in the presence of the conciliator. This is especially important if the work relationship between the parties is critical to the entity.

In the United Kingdom, an early conciliation procedure is to be introduced in April 2014. Under the scheme, persons wishing to lodge an employment tribunal claim must first notify ACAS, which will have up to a month to attempt to resolve the dispute.[22] This is being introduced as a result of the success of the pre-claim conciliation service currently run by ACAS. Statistics for 2011/12 indicate that 78% of the pre-claim conciliation cases dealt with by ACAS did not go on to become an employment tribunal claim.[23] When staff and management time and legal costs are factored in, employers save on average £2,700 by using pre-claim conciliation compared with resolving a dispute once an employment tribunal claim has been made.[24]

---

21   The Advisery, Conciliation and Arbitration Service (ACAS) in the United Kingdom performs a similar service to the Federal Mediation & Conciliation Service (FMCS) in the United States.

22   See the current position set forth in the Guidance Note, Conciliation in cases that could be the subject of employment tribunal proceedings after 6 April 2009. Available at: www.acas.org.uk/ media/pdf/4/d/Conciliation_and_tribunals.pdf (accessed March 27 2013). See also the proposed Enterprise and Regulatory Reform Bill (laid in Parliament May 2012). Available at: http://services .parliament.uk/bills/2012-13/enterpriseandregulatoryreform.html (accessed March 27 2013).

23   ACAS, ACAS Early Conciliation – launching in 2014, undated. Available at: www.acas.org.uk/index.aspx? articleid=4028 (accessed March 27 2013).

24   Ibid.

So why does conciliation work? Industrial relations expert Professor Linda Dickens suggests that "conciliation officers bring 'realism' to bear, helping shape the desire to settle by conveying information about the nature of tribunal hearings, decision-making and outcomes".[25] Conciliation involves marshalling and channelling pressures towards settlement (or withdrawal) that are present in the system.[26] Many potential claimants are less keen to pursue a claim when told of the relatively low success rates they face, and that the average level of compensation in a successful case is around £5,000 for an unfair dismissal, and that they may face a large bill for costs if they lose an adversarial hearing. The academic literature suggests that the risk of having to pay the other side's legal costs if they lose their case this appears to weigh particularly heavy with claimants when considering whether to proceed to a hearing (although in practice such cost awards are rare).[27]

Conciliation works best when a dispute is tackled early on, before the opposing parties become too set in their views and damaged by their argument. According to Ron Woods, assistant individual conciliation director at ACAS: "PCCs [pre claim conciliations] can give both sides a chance to step back and consider the other party's position, to see that it's in both their interests to get over this dispute, if only they can ditch the emotional baggage."[28] Wood also notes that: "interestingly, now [that] the [PCC] scheme has been rolled out, we're finding that the proportion going on to tribunal is smaller. About one third end up making a claim, a lot of these are where the employer flatly refuses to talk."[29] When faced with an expensive and lengthy discrimination case brought by an employee, most employers will not pass up the opportunity for conciliation.

6. Workplace mediation

Example B above (see 1.1(b)) is a good example of the use of workplace mediation as a tool to resolve employment disputes. Workplace mediation involves employees at a workplace sitting down with a mediator who then tries to resolve the issues of conflict so that the working relationship can be restored to productivity. Workplace mediation can take place between employees at the same level, between a manager and one of the employees he manages, or in any other context where there is internal discord. There may be tensions in a workplace between workers of different ages, ethnicity, race, nationality, gender, sexual orientation or social class that might be resolvable through this technique. Alleged instances of harassment or bullying (eg, not-so-harmless banter, discourteous conduct or rudeness) can be addressed informally and the underlying tensions that these symptoms evidence can be examined in a safe and confidential environment, identifying mutual solutions and agreements which will

25 Linda Dickens, The role of conciliation in the employment tribunal, November 30 2012. Available at: www2.warwick.ac.uk/fac/soc/wbs/research/irru/publications/recentconf/ld_-_conciliation_in_ets.pdf (accessed March 27 2013).
26 *Ibid.*
27 *Ibid.*
28 Jill Insley, Employment tribunal? Try pre-claims conciliation at ACAS first, *Guardian*, March 27 2010. Available at: www.guardian.co.uk/money/2010/mar/27/pre-claims-conciliation-acas (accessed March 28 2013).
29 *Ibid.*

restore respectful, professional working relationships. With harassment or bullying, people want certain behaviour or language to change and would rather explore positive solutions through mediation than follow the route of formal investigation or grievance, especially if they need the working relationship to continue.

An experienced workplace mediator can bridge the gaps and issues that exist on both sides. If the mediation is not successful, the more formal workplace procedure can continue. However, the workplace mediation and its process remain confidential. The mediator will not report to managers or the human resources department and none of the participants are under a duty to disclose anything. There are different ways of running a workplace mediation session. One experienced workplace mediator has said that when the two sides come together each will be given time at the start to have a say about what has occurred: "It typically gets very emotional. I encourage them to lay out as much as they can about their feelings and what is prompting their own behaviour. In even five or 10 minutes, you can get a lot of stuff out, and then there's a palpable sense of relief."[30] Another mediator speaks of the importance of anger in these sessions: "Anger is a cover-all emotion. It always comes from something underneath – hurt, for example … what we're trying to do is enable people to express that underlying emotion, because that often leads to a breakthrough."[31]

The mediator's task is to find a solution while keeping the dialogue respectful and allowing each side to have their say in a manner such that a true dialogue is possible. One of the tenets of workplace mediation is that if either of the parties (or the mediator) feels unsafe in the mediation process due to the conduct of one of the participants, the mediator may take a time out or end the process. It may not be easy for a manager to recognise or admit that there is a conflict in his or her department which he is unable to resolve. At this point, the human resources manager may suggest workplace mediation to restore morale and productivity in the department. Different workplace mediators will have different ground rules as to how they proceed – some will want pre-mediation, one-on-one meetings with the parties beforehand; others may want telephonic interviews; some may want a follow-up call to the individuals involved to see that what was agreed at mediation has been acted on – so when a workplace mediator contracts with the human resources department, the variables and costs involved may range from mediator to mediator. In any case, a company must bear in mind the costs arising from not engaging in workplace mediation against the cost of hiring the mediator.

7.   Mediation – when a party wishes to maintain the commercial relationship

The late Theodore Kheel, who was New York's pre-eminent labour mediator and arbitrator from the 1950s to the 1980s, once described the process of reaching agreement through mediation as follows: "It is like sculpting an elephant. You chip away everything that doesn't look like an elephant, and what's left is an elephant.

---

30   Louise Tickle, Mediation in the workplace: Can't we talk about this?, *Guardian*, October 31 2009. Available at: www.guardian.co.uk/money/2009/oct/31/mediation-in-the-workplace (accessed March 29 2013).

31   *Ibid.*

When you're trying to get a ... contract, you do the same thing. You chip away everything that doesn't belong in the agreement, and what is left is the agreement."

8. The European Code of Conduct for Mediators and the Mediation Directive

The European Code of Conduct for Mediators[32] defines mediation as any structured process, however named or referred to, whereby two or more parties to a dispute attempt by themselves, on a voluntary basis, to reach an agreement on the settlement of their dispute with the assistance of a third person – the 'mediator'. The code must also be read in conjunction with Directive 2008/52/EC of the European Parliament and of the Council of 21 May 2008 on certain aspects of mediation in civil and commercial matters[33] (Mediation Directive). The directive is designed to promote amicable dispute resolution and applies to cross-border disputes in civil and commercial matters, with the exception of revenue, customs or administrative matters or the liability of the state for acts or omissions in the exercise of state authority. It does not apply in Denmark. The directive provides that Member States should authorise the courts to suggest mediation to the litigants; however, without compelling them to use it.

Although, generally, agreements reached through mediation are more likely to be implemented voluntarily, the directive requires Member States to establish a procedure whereby an agreement may, at the request of the parties, be confirmed in a judgment, decision or authentic act by a court or public authority. This is to allow for mutual recognition and enforcement throughout the European Union of agreements reached through mediation. The conditions by which such mediation agreements should be enforced must be the same conditions as those established for the recognition and enforcement of court decisions in civil and commercial matters and in matrimonial matters and matters of parental responsibility. Also, Member States are required to ensure that the parties are not prevented from initiating judicial proceedings or arbitration following mediation due to the expiry of the prescription periods. Neither mediators nor those involved in the mediation process are compelled to give evidence in judicial proceedings regarding information obtained during the mediation process. The directive provides only two circumstances where this may be ignored: (1) where necessary for overriding considerations of public policy, particularly to protect the physical integrity of a person; and (2) where disclosure of the content of the agreement resulting from mediation is necessary in order to implement or enforce that agreement. Member States are also required to encourage the training of mediators, as well as the development and application of voluntary codes of conduct for the profession.

The code sets out a number of principles to which individual mediators may voluntarily decide to commit themselves, under their own responsibility, and may be used by mediators involved in all kinds of mediation in civil and commercial matters. Similarly, it encourages organisations providing mediation services to make

---

32   http://ec.europa.eu/civiljustice/adr/adr_ec_code_conduct_en.pdf (2004).
33   http://eur-lex.europa.eu/LexUriServ/LexUriServ.do?uri=CELEX:32008L0052:EN:NOT (2008).

such a commitment by asking mediators acting for their organisation to respect the code. Adherence to the code is without prejudice to national legislation or rules regulating individual professions. The code emphasises that mediators must be competent and knowledgeable in the process of mediation. Mediators must always provide the parties with complete information on the fees they will charge and they must not agree to act in a mediation before the principles of their remuneration have been accepted by all parties concerned.

Under the code, the mediator's independence and impartiality is paramount. Thus, if there are any circumstances that may, or may be seen to, affect a mediator's independence or give rise to a conflict of interests, the mediator must disclose those circumstances to the parties before acting or continuing to act. In such cases, the mediator may only agree to act or continue to act if he is certain of being able to carry out the mediation completely impartiality and the parties explicitly consent. The duty to disclose is a continuing obligation throughout the process of mediation. Under the code, mediators must always act, and endeavour to be seen to act, with impartiality towards the parties and must be committed to serve all parties equally in the mediation.

The code requires mediators to ensure that the parties to the mediation understand the mediation process and the role of the mediator and the parties in it. In addition to ensuring that all parties have adequate opportunities to be involved in the process, the mediator must inform the parties, and may terminate the mediation, if the settlement that is being reached appears to be unenforceable or illegal (having regard to the circumstances of the case and the competence of the mediator for making such an assessment) or the mediator considers that continuing the mediation is unlikely to result in a settlement. Under the code, at the end of the process, the mediator must take all appropriate measures to ensure that the agreement has been reached through the informed consent of all parties, and that all parties understand the terms of the agreement. Finally, the mediator must keep confidential all information arising out of or in connection with the mediation, including the fact that the mediation is to take place or has taken place, unless compelled by law or grounds of public policy to disclose it. Any information disclosed in confidence to mediators by one of the parties must not be disclosed to the other parties without permission, unless compelled by law.

9.   English case law on mediation

In *Dunnett v Railtrack plc*, the Court of Appeal held that a party to an appeal cannot ignore the court's recommendation that mediation should be attempted without providing an explanation.[34] Brooke LJ pointed out:

> *Skilled mediators are now able to achieve results satisfactory to both parties in many cases which are quite beyond the power of lawyers and courts to achieve. This court has knowledge of cases where intense feelings have arisen, for instance in relation to clinical negligence claims. But when the parties are brought together on neutral soil with a skilled mediator to help them resolve their differences, it may very well be that the mediator is able to achieve a result by which the parties shake hands at the end and feel*

---

34   *Dunnett v Railtrack plc* [2002] EWCA Civ 303.

that they have gone away having settled the dispute on terms with which they are happy to live. A mediator may be able to provide solutions which are beyond the powers of the court to provide.[35]

In *Halsey v Milton Keynes General NHS Trust*,[36] Dyson LJ made clear that the court had no power to order the parties to participate in the mediation process, and identified a number of factors which could be considered as justification for a refusal to mediate when determining whether a party that had been successful in litigation should not be awarded costs. The factors (now known as the Halsey factors) to determine whether a party has unreasonably refused ADR will include (but are not limited to):

- the nature of the dispute;
- the merits of the case;
- the extent to which other settlement methods have been attempted;
- whether the costs of the ADR would be disproportionately high;
- whether any delay in setting up and attending the ADR would have been prejudicial; and
- whether the ADR had a reasonable prospect of success.

Lord Justice Dyson said:

We recognise that mediation has a number of advantages over the court process. It is usually less expensive than litigation which goes all the way to judgment, although it should not be overlooked that most cases are settled by negotiation in the ordinary way. Mediation provides litigants with a wider range of solutions than those that are available in litigation: for example, an apology; an explanation; the continuation of an existing professional or business relationship perhaps on new terms; and an agreement by one party to do something without any existing legal obligation to do so.[37]

In *Burchell v Bullard*,[38] the Court of Appeal applied the *Halsey* factors and determined that under the circumstances of the case it was unreasonable behaviour for the householders to fail to mediate the case. The case arose out of a building dispute from August 2000 where the builder had issued proceedings for approximately £18,000 and the defendants counterclaimed for a sum over £100,000. Following the trial, the builder was awarded £18,327 and the owners were awarded £14,373 on their counterclaim. The case resulted in costs of approximately £185,000. The court felt that this kind of dispute lent itself to ADR and that the merits of the case favoured mediation. The home owners had declined to mediate. Nonetheless, despite the unreasonable behaviour of the householders, no costs sanction was imposed as the offer to mediate had been made in 2001, when "the law had not become as clear and developed as it is now ...".[39]

Ward LJ said:

The court has given its stamp of approval to mediation and it is now the legal profession

---

35   *Ibid*, at [14].
36   [2004] EWCA Civ 576.
37   *Ibid*, at [15].
38   [2005] EWCA Civ 358.
39   *Ibid*, at [42], Ward LJ.

which must become fully aware of and acknowledge its value. The profession can no longer with impunity shrug aside reasonable requests to mediate. The parties cannot ignore a proper request to mediate simply because it was made before the claim was issued. With court fees escalating, it may be folly to do so.[40]

10. Mediation – win-win versus win-lose

Example C above (see 1.1(c)) is a good example of the type of dispute that a company should mediate. If there is a long-standing commercial relationship and the parties have a history of working together, it makes sense for the parties to try to resolve a problem in their relationship in a manner that does not escalate into expensive litigation. The facts of the dispute in Example C suggest a solution – the case goes to manufacturing standards and shipping schedules, both of which can be resolved in the context of a commercial mediation. For instance, the appointment of quality control inspector at the factory in China or an expediting service to ensure that the goods are shipped on time could resolve the dispute satisfactory, with a discounted price on future orders to compensate the luxury kitchen manufacturer for past problems. Mediation puts the kitchen supplier and the appliance manufacturer immediately in control of the outcome of their dispute without the costs of litigation procedures.

In the scenario described, neither company may benefit from having a court determine issues of law or construction which may be essential to the future trading relations of the parties.

What may be the proper legal result may not be the best for business on either side. Mediation will not be appropriate:

- if one of the parties to a dispute wants the court to resolve a point of law which arises from time to time and binding precedent would be useful such a case is not appropriate for mediation;
- if there are allegations of fraud or other commercially disreputable conduct by one of the parties. In these circumstances mediation might not work. A workable solution will not be possible if the parties no longer trust each other; or
- in cases where injunctive or other relief is essential to protect the position of a party.

In the dispute described, it would be sensible to bring in a trained mediator early in the dispute resolution process to help reach a resolution before spending resources on pre-trial court litigation. A solution that the parties could work out between themselves will be as good as a judicial decision binding the parties. In the context of Example C, all the court could do is to issue an order for damages – it could not

---

40   *Ibid*, at [43]. See *Rolf v De Guerin* [2011] EWCA 78 where the Court of Appeal in another household construction claim (Part 36 offer in the amount of £14,000) made an order of no costs where refusal to mediate by Mr Guerian (builder) was unreasonable. Rix LJ, at [48]: "Nevertheless, in my judgment, the facts of this case disclose that negotiation and/or mediation would have had reasonable prospects of success. The spurned offers to enter into settlement negotiations or mediation were unreasonable and ought to bear materially on the outcome of the court's discretion, particularly in this class of case."

impose a solution on the parties that would keep the relationship between them economically productive. If the parties choose the right mediator and work towards a commercially productive solution, they can produce a win-win outcome for all, whereas the court can only impose a win-lose solution on them that may benefit neither party.

11. *Halsey* – the game changer – the risk of refusing mediation

Halsey v Milton Keynes General NHS Trust[41] is of particular value to general counsel considering a decision to refuse to engage in ADR such as mediation. In evaluating the merits of the case, the *Halsey* factors suggest that the fact that a party reasonably believes that it has a strong case is relevant to the question whether it has acted reasonably in refusing ADR. As the Court of Appeal notes, if the position were otherwise, there would be considerable scope for a claimant to use the threat of costs sanctions to extract a settlement from the defendant, even where the claim is without merit:

> *Large organisations, especially public bodies, are vulnerable to pressure from claimants who, having weak cases, invite mediation as a tactical ploy. They calculate that such a defendant may at least make a nuisance-value offer to buy off the cost of a mediation and the risk of being penalised in costs for refusing a mediation even if ultimately successful.*[42]

A clear-cut case where an organisation could refuse mediation is where a party would have succeeded in an application for summary judgment under CPR 24.2, but for some reason did not make such an application. However, in a borderline case scenario, the fact that a party refused to agree to ADR because it thought that it would win will be given little or no weight by the court when considering whether the refusal to agree to ADR was reasonable. The courts see borderline cases as likely to be suitable for ADR unless there are significant countervailing factors. Dyson LJ notes in Halsey: "The fact that a party unreasonably believes that his case is watertight is no justification for refusing mediation. But the fact that a party reasonably believes that he has a watertight case may well be sufficient justification for a refusal to mediate."[43]

In Halsey, the court gives special weight to the value of mediation separate from other attempts to settle a case. This is worth considering if general counsel considers that settlement overtures without attempting mediation may protect against being ordered to pay costs for unreasonable refusal to mediate:

> *The fact that settlement offers have already been made, but rejected, is a relevant factor. It may show that one party is making efforts to settle, and that the other party has unrealistic views of the merits of the case. But it is also right to point out that mediation often succeeds where previous attempts to settle have failed.*[44]

A party may refuse to participate in mediation if the costs would be disproportionately high. This is particularly true if, on a realistic assessment, the

---

41   [2004] EWCA Civ 576.
42   *Ibid*, at [18].
43   *Ibid*, at [20] (emphasis of Dyson LJ).
44   *Ibid*.

sums at stake in the litigation are comparatively smaller. General counsel are advised in these circumstances to consider that:

- mediation can sometimes be at least as expensive as a day in court;
- parties will often have legal representation before the mediator; and
- the mediator's fees will usually be borne equally by the parties regardless of the outcome (although the costs of a mediation may be the subject of a costs order by the court after a trial).

If mediation is suggested at a late stage, acceptance of it may have the effect of delaying the trial of the action, which may be relevant to take into account in deciding whether a refusal to agree to ADR was unreasonable.

Since the prospects of a successful mediation cannot be predicted with confidence, the possibility of the ultimately successful party being required to incur the costs of an abortive mediation is a relevant factor that may be taken into account in deciding whether the successful party acted unreasonably in refusing to agree to ADR. Additionally, a burden is placed on the unsuccessful party to show that there was a reasonable prospect that mediation would have been successful. However, this is a lower standard than having to prove that mediation would in fact have succeeded.[45]

If a successful party refuses to agree to ADR despite the court's encouragement, court will take this factor into account when deciding whether the refusal was unreasonable. The stronger the encouragement from the bench, the easier it will be for the unsuccessful party to discharge the burden of showing that the successful party's refusal was unreasonable.

12. Who will be the mediator?

The late Theodore Kheel, New York's pre-eminent labour mediator and arbitrator from the 1950s to the 1980s, once explained the secret to his success:

> The essence of mediation is getting information. The dirtiest question you can ask in bargaining is "What will you settle for?" If you ask that question, you ought to resign, but that's the question you must have an answer to. You get it by asking every question except that. What's left over is the answer.[46]

One factor that can make a significant difference is the skill of the mediator selected. This is not straightforward. Each mediator will offer different skills. Once the parties have agreed to mediation, they must decide what they wish to accomplish from it. Some mediators will suggest options to move the parties closer towards agreement while others will resist offering their own views, leaving the parties to take responsibility for producing a solution. If the parties hold unequal power, the selection of the mediator will be a key issue. The right mediator, for example, a retired judge, may help redress this balance of power more effectively than other mediators. However, some judges are so used to deciding between parties that they may not move proposals between the parties sufficiently to produce a settlement.

---

45   *Ibid*, at [28], Dyson LJ.
46   Steven Greenhouse, Theodore W Kheel, Labor Mediator, Dies at 96, *New York Times*, November 14 2010. Available at: www.nytimes.com/2010/11/15/nyregion/15kheel.html?pagewanted=all&_r=1& (accessed 29 March 2013).

Mediators work either independently or as a member of a particular panel of mediators. For sophisticated commercial work, the mediators will be affiliated with a panel, so, generally, using a panel and referral is the safest option. If the industry or dispute is in a specialised field, a mediator who has appropriate expertise should be sought. For instance, if the dispute is on the quality or efficiency of HVAC in a new building, a mediator who is or was an engineer in this field might be useful; if the case is one involving interpretation of insurance contracts, perhaps appoint a mediator who is a retired judge or a lawyer with expertise in this area.

However, the selection of mediator will often set the tone for the mediation. Bear in mind that business people and the lawyers that represent them may behave differently when mediating before a distinguished judge or a former justice minister than they would before someone that they consider to be their peer. Authority (whether used consciously or unconsciously) has its own issues to deal with and can factor into the overall ease or difficulty of resolving a dispute. For instance, in some cases that are highly emotive or subjective evidence-based, a former judge who has handled such cases in court might be a safer choice than someone who has not had this experience.

After considering the reputation of potential mediators, the next step should be to talk to those shortlisted, in person or by phone. Usually, the parties' lawyers will do this together over the phone to select the most suitable mediator from a shortlist of about three. If possible, it is better to meet prospective mediators in person rather than speak to them by phone as their interviewing skills, verbal and nonverbal communication, ability to listen, ability to define and clarify issues, problem-solving ability and empathy are easier to evaluate in a meeting (which you will have to pay for) than in a 15-minute phone conversation.

In complex cases or those with multiple parties, it may be preferable to appoint a team of two mediators to work together in tandem, provided they can work together effectively as a team. Such a team, dealing with perhaps four parties, makes more sense, especially if the two mediators have a dynamic for working with each other. The problem of a single mediator with numerous parties reminds at least one co-author of his experiences growing up in the United States, watching professional wrestling tag team wrestling on the television – whenever the referee was busy with one member of a wrestling duo, the other member of the same team was performing a dastardly act upon the wrestler from the other side lying helpless on the mat!

After considering the personality and style of the mediator, you have to think about all the issues covered in the European Code of Conduct for Mediators, such as ethics, confidentiality, logistics and cost. With logistics, to the extent it is possible, schedule the mediation to be a full day, away from mobile phones and so on, in a comfortable setting. Mediations should start early in the day. One does not want to spend thousands of dollars to arrange a mediation to begin at 2pm only to have one side getting impatient at 5:30pm because it has to catch a 7:30pm flight. Generally, mediations should only take one day, but if this is not possible in a complex case appropriate ground rules should be set. A mediator does not want a whole day's worth of work to be upset by second-guessing from an executive not present at the mediation and not party to the dynamics of negotiation at the scene.

13. International Mediation Institution (IMI)

IMI is a charitable foundation established in The Hague in 2007 to certify mediators and promote mediation worldwide as a profession. Funded by both mediation institutions and users of mediation services, its board of directors consists of representatives of mediation institutions and of users of mediation services, chaired by a user, an advisory council chaired by Lord Woolf, and an independent standards commission.[47] In 2008, IMI launched its mediator certification scheme, under which individual mediators may become IMI-certified by qualifying with an educational, training, service provider or professional institution that offers a programme meeting certain criteria set by the independent standards commission. In addition to being qualified in this way, mediators must provide an online profile with IMI that includes an independently prepared digest containing feedback on their performance as a mediator from users (disputants and their professional representatives). In this way, the mediator's ongoing competency is assessed and validated by the community they serve. The IMI website[48] is open to anyone looking for an IMI-certified mediator worldwide. It provides background and specialisation information on each mediator in addition to their objective feedback digest. Northrop Grumman has added language to its international disputes that allow for parties to consult the IMI profiles and feedback when selecting a mediator. See Appendix A.

14. Authority to negotiate and settlement

It is critical that each party's business representative comes to the mediation with authority to settle the case that day. If one of the parties lacks authority to settle on the day, there is no point in the mediation. Often, the chief executive will give its party authority to settle up to X amount – if it is over X amount then authority must be given by the chief executive by phone. This can work so long as the person outside the room is reachable. If the chief executive cannot be reached, the mediation and settlement may collapse.

The non-availability of the executive with final authority may be used to negotiate down the other side at the last minute ("I can give you a $100,000 today, but I may not get you a $125,000 because this is over my authority and the chief executive is on a flight to Ohio"), and an astute mediator will require both sides to produce valid and binding powers of attorney authorising them to settle the case in dispute or to call off the mediation. Such powers of attorney will encourage the parties to reach an agreement on the day.

The memorandum setting out the settlement reached must be drafted and signed by all the parties and their legal representatives before they leave the mediation meeting. It is never appropriate to leave this until a later date. Although the parties' lawyers may wish to draft the mutual release and the stipulation to withdraw the case (with or without prejudice), the settlement should be drafted by the mediator, in a one or two-page memorandum that the legal representatives can transform into a full release at a later stage.

---

47 One of the co-authors of this chapter, Wolf Juergen von Kumberg, was the 2008 chair of IMI and currently serves on its board of directors.
48 http://imimediation.org/home.

The mediator's memorandum is important. It confirms what was agreed between the parties, if this is disputed at a later stage and the mediator is compelled to testify.

15. Why arbitrate?

Arbitration has been criticised as being as expensive, inefficient and uncertain as litigation in court. So why do people arbitrate? Three scenarios offered by US lawyers Alan Dabdoub and Trey Cox[49] match the co-authors' experience as to when arbitration should be used:

- jurisdictional quagmires;
- consumer arbitration; and
- international disputes.

Example D above (see 1.1(d)) provides an example of jurisdictional complications that a skilled general counsel prefers to avoid. This was the advice that one of the chapter's co-authors received when his company faced an action in one of the Commonwealth of Independent States (CIS) that make up the former Soviet Union. The solution to this difficult situation was to agree to arbitrate before the Arbitration Institute of Stockholm Chamber of Commerce in English, to be governed by the substantive law of the CIS country involved. At the time, Stockholm was one of the few places that had expertise in handling commercial disputes with CIS countries because it had been central to trade arbitration with the former Soviet Union since 1917. The clause set out at note 50 below (modified for use today)[50] took the foreign multinational out of the courts of the former CIS country involved but gave the local party the assurance that its substantive law would apply. Ideally, the multinational would have preferred the law of a jurisdiction other than that of the particular CIS country, but this was the best arrangement it was able to negotiate under the circumstances. In depoliticising the dispute by having it heard in Stockholm under the auspices of a retired judge or an academic from that country known for their independence and integrity, the problem could be avoided. Incidentally, in negotiating this provision the company never gave away the real reason why it wanted the arbitration to be held in Stockholm – to do so would have been offensive and could have cost the company the entire deal.

Jurisdictional issues may also arise in the United States, particularly since companies are attracted by the high punitive damages awarded by civil juries in the US court system. In the experience of one of the co-authors of this chapter, who

---

49 Alan Dabdoub and Trey Cox, Litigation: When, why and how arbitration can help obtain better results at lower costs – Don't listen to the critics – Arbitration can be a useful tool, *Corporate Counsel*, November 22 2012. Available at: www.insidecounsel.com/2012/11/22/litigation-when-why-and-how-arbitration-can-help-o (accessed March 30 2013).

50 "Any dispute, controversy or claim arising out of or in connection with this contract, or the breach, termination or invalidity thereof, shall be finally settled by arbitration administered by the Arbitration Institute of the Stockholm Chamber of Commerce (the "SCC"). The Rules for Expedited Arbitrations shall apply, unless the SCC in its discretion determines, taking into account the complexity of the case, the amount in dispute and other circumstances, that the Arbitration Rules shall apply. In the latter case, the SCC shall also decide whether the Arbitral Tribunal shall be composed of one or three arbitrators. The seat of arbitration shall be SCC. The language to be used in the arbitral proceedings shall be English. This contract shall be governed by the substantive law of Country X."

served as general counsel for a major multinational for several years, the US court system is best avoided by foreign-based companies, and also out-of-state defendants defending themselves in state courts. Earlier in the chapter, we examined some of the difficulties that out-of-state and foreign defendants faced when dealing, respectively, with a Texas and a Mississippi jury. While an arbitration clause would not have helped Texaco because Texaco was not a party to the contract between Pennzoil and Getty Oil, it could have helped Raymond Loewen in Hinds County, Mississippi. Dabdoub and Cox suggest that arbitration clauses are useful in the United States to avoid expensive motion practice over whether a particular court and/or venue is the most appropriate place in which to require a defendant to fight an action.[51] By agreeing to an arbitration clause in advance, the parties "understand where the dispute is going to be heard from the outset and can more quickly get to the crux of the issues. And that saves time and money".[52]

Example E (see 1.1(e)) is a good example of a successful consumer arbitration programme that works for both manufacturers and consumers to resolve automobile warranty claims arising out of alleged defectively manufactured new motor vehicles in a fast, cost-effective way that preserves customer good will. While the example given is a Canadian one, the US Supreme Court has consistently found consumer arbitration contracts legally enforceable. In Doctor's Associates, Inc v Casarotto,[53] the Supreme Court endorsed a contractual approach to arbitration law requiring lower courts to apply contract law principles when determining whether arbitration agreements are unconscionable. In *AT&T Mobility v Concepcion*,[54] the Supreme Court held that the Federal Arbitration Act pre-empts state laws and allows parties contractually to waiver their class action rights. The case allows businesses to use standard-form contracts to forbid consumers claiming fraud from banding together in a single arbitration or class action court. According to Brian T Fitzpatrick, a law professor at Vanderbilt University: "The decision basically lets companies escape class actions, so long as they do so by means of arbitration agreements ... This is a game-changer for businesses. It's one of the most important and favourable cases for businesses in a very long time."[55] On February 27 2013, the US Supreme Court heard oral arguments in *American Express Co v Italian Colours Restaurant*,[56] where the issue is whether plaintiffs may avoid arbitration agreements that require individualised rather than class arbitration by arguing that they cannot "effectively vindicate" their federal claims under the antitrust laws without the use of class proceedings. A decision is expected late June 2013.

The Federal Arbitration Act[57] provides for judicial facilitation of private dispute resolution through arbitration. It applies in both state courts and federal courts[58] where the transaction contemplated by the parties "involves" interstate commerce

---

51   Dabdoub and Cox, note 49 above.
52   *Ibid.*
53   517 US 681 (1996).
54   584 F 3d 849 (2011).
55   Adam Liptak, Supreme Court allows contracts that prohibit class-action arbitration, *New York Times*, April 27 2011. Available at: www.nytimes.com/2011/04/28/business/28bizcourt.html?_r=0 (accessed March 29 2013).
56   Docket File 12-133. Available at: www.supremecourt.gov/Search.aspx?FileName=/docketfiles/12-133.htm (accessed March 29 2013).
57   Pub L 68-401, 43 Stat 883, enacted February 12 192, 59 USC, Section 1 *et seq.*

and is based on the US Constitution's commerce clause powers given the Congress. Contractually based compulsory binding arbitration results in an arbitration award which may be entered by an arbitrator or arbitration panel. The parties to arbitration give up the right to an appeal on substantive grounds to a court and are required to arbitrate instead of going to court. Once an award is entered by an arbitrator or arbitration panel, it must be confirmed in a court of law. Once confirmed, the award is reduced to an enforceable judgment, which may be enforced by the winning party in court, like any other judgment. Under the Federal Arbitration Act, awards must be confirmed within one year; any objection to an award must be challenged by the losing party within three months. An arbitration agreement may be entered in advance of the actual dispute (prospectively) or by disputing parties once a dispute has arisen (after the fact). In *Hall Street Associates, LLC v Mattel, Inc*,[59] the US Supreme Court held that the grounds for judicial review specified in the Federal Arbitration Act may not be expanded even if the parties to the arbitration agreement agree to allow such expanded review of the decision.

16.   Is arbitration cheaper? Probably not

Dabdoub and Cox presented the result of a comparative study that a company undertook to assess whether its US arbitration programme with employees lowered litigation costs and yielded better results than litigation (19 single-plaintiff cases in the United States were studied, of which nine were resolved through arbitration and 10 were resolved in court). "The big-picture takeaway is that arbitration is not a panacea to lowering litigation costs. The study, in a nutshell, shows that arbitration costs rival those of litigation."[60] However, in the few arbitration cases that were more costly, it is clear that a lot of the costs incurred could have been avoided by crafting arbitration provisions with cost in mind, for example, employing one arbitrator rather than a panel of three arbitrators. The arbitration cases were not necessarily faster to resolve (in the study, the median case took 19 months to litigate but 21 months to arbitrate). One author, writing in the New York State Bar Association Journal, suggested that the cost of the arbitrators' fees makes litigation the less expensive alternative for resolving commercial disputes.[61] Thus, if arbitration is not cheaper and faster, why do some companies still prefer it? "Choice – the opportunity to tailor procedures to business goals and priorities – is the fundamental advantage of arbitration over litigation", according to Professor Stipanowich.[62] The freedom to choose and the key resulting differences between contract-based arbitration and

---

58   *Southland Corp v Keating*, 465 US 1 (1984).

59   552 US 576 (2008).

60   Alan Dabdoub and Trey Cox, Which costs less? Arbitration or litigation, December 6 2012, *Inside Counsel*. Available at: www.insidecounsel.com/2012/12/06/which-costs-less-arbitration-or-litigation?t=litigation (accessed March 30 2013).

61   Edna Sussman, Why arbitrate? The benefits and the savings, *New York State Bar Association Journal*, October 2009, pp. 20-4, note 2, citing Ronald J Offenkrantz, Arbitrating commercial issues: Do you really know the out-of pocket costs? NY St BJ, July/August 2009, p. 30. Available at: www.sussmanadr.com/docs/why%20arbitrate%20NYSBA%20Journal%20Oct%2009-.pdf (accessed March 31 2013).

62   Thomas Stipanowich, Arbitration and choice: Taking charge of the 'new litigation', 7 *DePaul Business & Commercial Law Journal*, April 2 2009; Pepperdine University Legal Studies Research Paper 2009/16, 402, 454. Available at SSRN: http://ssrn.com/abstract=1372291 (accessed March 31 2013).

court trial explain why most business users prefer arbitration for resolving commercial disputes.[63]

17. New York Convention – 'Concrete jungle where arbitral dreams are made'

In the international context, arbitration allows for more flexible procedures, such as those that can be agreed between the parties. The ability to arbitrate a dispute under a mixed-procedural structure incorporating the best of both common and civil law systems[64] or allowing for multi-lingual proceedings is something domestic courts cannot accommodate. It also affords the parties the use of expert arbitrators with subject-matter expertise of the issues before them. The finality of awards is very critical to the attractiveness of arbitration processes. For instance, a construction project can continue very quickly to completion once a key point of dispute between the parties is resolved. Arbitration also affords neutrality, whether this means taking a case out of a jurisdictional dispute or the use of arbitrators from a variety of nationalities not involved in the dispute between the parties. Moreover, arbitration affords confidentiality in that the specifics of the disputes, whether they involve trade secrets, executive compensation agreements or cutting-edge technology, will not be made public. Similarly, an arbitral award does not create case law precedent, which can be damaging to the parties to the dispute as well at the industry they are involved in. Finally, an arbitral award is far easier to enforce internationally than national court judgments. For instance, as there is no convention or treaty providing for the reciprocal enforcement of judgments between the United States and the United Kingdom, a US judgment cannot be enforced in the UK by execution but only as a debt for which UK proceedings must issue. This raises issues that the English court will have to deal with separately from the US court, such as whether:

- there was proper jurisdiction in the United States;
- the US judgment was for a definite sum;
- the US judgment was final and conclusive;
- the US judgment was obtained by fraud;
- the US judgment is not enforceable because it is contrary to UK public policy (eg, English courts will not enforce punitive award damages in the United Kingdom); and
- the judgment in the United States does not offend natural or substantive judgment.[65]

---

63   *Ibid.*
64   The International Bar Association Rules on the Taking of Evidence in International Commercial Arbitration, May 29 2010, do not adopt all the common law jurisdictions' broad disclosure procedures (eg, discovery), nor do they follow entirely the civil law in eliminating the ability to engage in some disclosure-related practices. Nonetheless, many in the arbitration field believe the rules mitigate more towards US-style discovery in an arbitration. Available at: www.int-bar.org/images/downloads/ IBA%20rules%20on%20the%20taking%20of%20Evidence.pdf (accessed March 31 2013). See also the International Bar Association Guidelines on Conflicts of Interest in International Arbitration (22 May 2004). Available at: www.siac.org.sg/images/stories/ documents/ guides/guides-conflicts.pdf? phpMyAdmin=OP8vu698vunuzJZYZoW2%2CoDB3yb (accessed March 31 2013).
65   See Taylor Wessing, Enforcement of US judgments in England, 2010. Available at: www.taylorwessing.com/uploads/tx_siruplawyermanagement/Enforcing_US_judgments_in_UK.pdf (accessed March 30 2013).

Example F above (see 1.1(f)) shows how arbitration is especially beneficial in international commerce because of the existence of the Convention on the Recognition and Enforcement of Foreign Arbitral Awards, which was adopted by a United Nations diplomatic conference on June 10 1958 and entered into force on June 7 1959 (the New York Convention). A convention is an instrument that is binding under international law on states and other entities with treaty-making capacity that choose to become a party to that instrument. In general, departures from a convention are only permitted if the convention allows reservations to be taken to its provisions.[66] In today's global economy, the New York Convention makes foreign arbitral awards enforceable in signatory countries and eliminates inconsistent results from multiple international lawsuits over the same matter. Today, approximately 148 nations have ratified the New York Convention, which requires courts of contracting states to give effect to private agreements to arbitrate and to recognise and enforce arbitration awards made in other contracting states. The convention applies to arbitrations which are not considered as domestic awards in the state where recognition and enforcement is sought, provided that the arbitration agreement satisfies the requirements of Article II (1) and (2), which include among other things that the agreement to arbitrate must be in writing.

The New York Convention deals with the recognition and enforcement of foreign arbitral awards and the referral by a court to arbitration.[67] Here, we examine, first, the recognition and enforcement of foreign arbitral awards and, secondly, referral by a court to arbitration. Article III sets out the general obligation for a court to recognise and enforce an arbitral award made in the territory of another contracting state as binding and to enforce it in accordance with those rules of procedure. Under Article IV, a party seeking to enforce a foreign award must supply to the court (a) the arbitral award and (b) the arbitration agreement. Article V allows the party against whom enforcement is sought to object to the enforcement by submitting proof of one of the grounds for refusal of enforcement provided in Article V(1). Alternatively, the court may on its own motion refuse to enforce the arbitration award for reasons of public policy as provided in Article V(2). Article VI provides that if the award is subject to an action for setting aside in the country of origin, the foreign court where enforcement of the award is being sought may adjourn its decision on enforcement. Under the "more favourable right" provision of Article VII(1), a party seeking enforcement may base its request for enforcement of the arbitral award on the court's domestic law on enforcement of foreign awards, on a bilateral treaty or on a multilateral treaty other than the New York Convention that is in force and in effect in the country where enforcement is sought. Article II (3) of the New York Convention provides that a court of a contracting state when seized of a matter in respect of which the parties have made an arbitration agreement must at the request of one of the parties refer the matter to arbitration unless the agreement itself to

---

66   UNCITRAL website, www.uncitral.org/uncitral/en/uncitral_texts/arbitration_faq.html (accessed 31 March 2013).

67   See Professor Jan Van Der Berg's website, www.newyorkconvention.org/ (accessed March 29 2013) for more information. Alternatively, refer to the UNCITRAL website: www.newyorkconvention 1958.org/index.php (accessed March 29 2013).

arbitrate is in and of itself invalid.

For a successful claimant to enforce its arbitral award, the award must not be impaired by any of the grounds for refusal of enforcement laid down in Article V:

(i) *the agreement containing the arbitration clause is not valid;*

(ii) *the party against whom the award is invoked was not given proper notice of the appointment of the arbitrator or of the arbitration proceedings, or was otherwise unable to present his case;*

(iii) *the award deals with a difference not contemplated or not falling within the terms of submission to arbitration or it contains decisions on matters beyond the scope of the submission;*

(iv) *the composition of the arbitral authority or the procedure is not in accordance with the agreement of the parties or the law of the country where the arbitration took place;*

(v) *the award has not yet become binding on the parties or has been set aside or suspended by a competent authority of the country under whose law the award was made;*

(vi) *the subject matter of the dispute is not capable of resolution by arbitration; or*

(vii) *the recognition or enforcement of the award would be contrary to public policy.*

Unlike the other grounds, grounds (vi) and (vii) may be invoked by the court before which enforcement is sought on its own motion. The controversy surrounding the public policy exception is that it is incapable of being precisely determined and it varies from one state to another. This situation can lead to an award not being contrary to the public policy of the state of the seat although it is contrary to the public policy of the enforcement state.[68]

In England, enforcement of an arbitral award depends on where the award was granted, with the process for enforcement applicable in any particular case dependent on the seat of arbitration and the arbitration rules that apply. Arbitral awards can be enforced under:

(i) *the Arbitration Act 1996;*

(ii) *the New York Convention;*

(iii) *the Geneva Convention 1927;*

(iv) *the Administration of Justice Act 1920 and the Foreign Judgments (Reciprocal Enforcement) Act 1933; and*

(v) *the common law.*[69]

There may be other treaties and agreements governing the enforcement of an arbitral award (see preceding paragraph), but this is beyond the scope of this chapter.

18.   The Arbitration Act 1996 and related case law

The Arbitration Act 1996[70] consolidated modern English arbitration law and procedure in statute and also made a number of substantive changes. Under Section 1(b) of the act, most commercial disputes are capable of being arbitrated if the parties

68   Obinna Ozumba, Enforcement of arbitral awards: Does the public policy exception create inconsistency?, 2009. Available at: http://www.dundee.ac.uk/cepmlp/car/html/car13_abstracts1.php (accessed 24 April 2013).

69   Pinsent Masons, Advice Note: Enforcing international arbitration awards in England and Wales, 2009. Available at: www.pinsentmasons.com/PDF/EnforcingInternationalArbitrationAwards.pdf (accessed March 20 2013).

70   www.legislation.gov.uk/ukpga/1996/23/data.pdf (accessed April 14 2013).

agree to that form of dispute resolution. Where the courts are concerned that the arbitral process may breach one of the party's statutory rights, it is not possible to submit the dispute to arbitration as the sole means of deciding the dispute.[71] The act applies to all arbitrations, the legal seat of which is in England and Wales or Northern Ireland. Scotland is not covered under the act.

In *Sulamerica v Enesa Engenharia*,[72] the Court of Appeal was asked to determine the law applicable to an arbitration agreement contained in two construction all risk policies. The law of the insurance policies was Brazilian, and the court confirmed that the law of the arbitration clause is legally distinct from the contract of which it forms a part. On the facts, the court upheld the High Court's decision that the law of the seat of the arbitration (which was English law) should apply in this case and set out a test by which to ascertain the relevant law.

Certain provisions of the Arbitration Act 1996 will be applicable if the place of arbitration is outside England, Wales and Northern Ireland or if no place has been designated or determined (Section 3 of the act defines both) in the arbitration agreement. The provisions included are:

- stay of legal proceedings (Sections 9-11);
- enforcement of awards (Section 66);
- securing of the attendance of witnesses (Section 43); and
- the court's powers in support of arbitral proceedings (Section 44).

The provisions of Part I of the Arbitration Act 1996 apply to all arbitrations conducted under an arbitration agreement. Part II of the act deals with consumer arbitrations and arbitrations conducted on a statutory basis to which Part I of the act does not apply. Part III deals with the recognition and enforcement of foreign awards and Part IV contains general provisions. The act's three guiding principles are fairness, party autonomy and non-intervention by the courts. Section 5 stipulates that the arbitration agreement must be made in writing, which is broadly interpreted. A reference in a main agreement to a separate written arbitration clause or to a document containing an arbitration clause constitutes an arbitration agreement if the reference makes that clause part of the main agreement (Section 6(2)). Under Section 7, the arbitration agreement must be treated as separate from the main commercial agreement into which it has been incorporated and the arbitration clause therefore survives the invalidity, non-existence or ineffectiveness of the main agreement.

Schedule 1 to the act lists the mandatory provisions of Part I, which include:

- the duty of the court to stay its proceedings;
- the power of the court to extend time limits;
- the power of the court to remove an arbitrator;
- the joint and several liability of parties to arbitrators for fees and expenses;
- the immunity of arbitrators;
- objections to the arbitral tribunal's jurisdiction;
- the general duties of the arbitral tribunal;

---

71   *Clyde & Co LLP v Bates Van Winkelhof* [2011] EWHC 668 (QB) (employment).
72   [2012] EWCA Civ 638.

- the general duties of the parties;
- the enforcement of an award;
- the challenges to the award; and
- the immunity of arbitral institutions.

All other provisions of Part I are not mandatory. If the parties do not make arrangements different from the non-mandatory provisions of Part I, the non-mandatory provisions form a set of 'model rules' to apply in the absence of any express agreement on a point by the parties. However, the parties are free to deviate from the model rules by adopting the procedural rules laid down by an arbitral institution or another body. Where the parties incorporate institutional rules into their arbitration agreement, such as those of an arbitral institution or another body, the Arbitration Act 1996 provides that this amounts to parties making their own arrangements and displaces non-mandatory provisions in circumstances where the arbitration rules are contrary to any such provisions.

To the extent an arbitration agreement contains a choice of law provision, that provision will be respected by the English courts. C v D[73] involved the parties' incorporation of the Bermuda Form "where the striking feature of the form is that it requires the parties to arbitrate in London but provides for the proper law of the insurance contract to be the internal laws of New York".[74] This choice was respected. Where the parties choose England as the seat of the arbitration, they will be taken to have agreed that the English courts will have exclusive jurisdiction of the arbitration and the mandatory provisions of the Arbitration Act 1996 will apply. Most notably, Sections 67 and 68 (lack of jurisdiction and serious irregularity) will apply.[75] In *Petrochemical Industries Co (KSC) v Dow Chemical Co*,[76] the Commercial Court confirmed the high bar that must be met before an English court will accept a challenge to a London arbitral award under Section 68.

Section 15(1) of the act provides that the parties are free to agree on the number of arbitrators as well as whether there is to be a chair or umpire. Where there is an arbitral agreement determining the number of arbitrators as an even number, it shall be understood as requiring the additional appointment of a chair, unless the parties agree otherwise. If there is no agreement on the number of arbitrators, the arbitral tribunal shall consist of a sole arbitrator. If the parties have agreed that there is to be a chair or umpire, they are free to agree on his or her role. If there is no agreement on this role, the following default rules apply:

- the chair's role (Arbitration Act 1996, Section 20(3) and (4)): decisions, orders and awards shall be made by all or a majority of the arbitrators (including the chair) and the view of the chair shall prevail in relation to a decision, order or award, in respect of which there is neither unanimity nor a majority;
- the umpire's role (Arbitration Act 1996, Section 21(3) and (4)): the default position is that the umpire shall attend the arbitral proceedings and be

---

73   [2007] EWCA Civ 1282.
74   *Ibid*, at [1], Longmore LJ.
75   *Ibid*, at [13].
76   [2012] EWHC 2739 (Comm), October 11 2012.

supplied with the same documents and other materials as supplied to the other arbitrators, with decisions being made by the arbitrators unless and until they cannot agree, in which case the umpire shall replace the arbitral tribunal and make decisions, orders and awards as if he were sole arbitrator.

Normally, the arbitration agreement will set the procedure for appointing the arbitral tribunal. However, if the parties do not do this, the default procedures for appointment of the arbitral panel are given in Section 16 et seq of the Arbitration Act 1996. Section 23 provides the circumstance when the authority of an arbitrator can be revoked. Section 27 covers the procedure for the appointment of substitute arbitrators if an arbitrator ceases to hold office (whether due to resignation, removal or death) and the parties have not agreed whether, and if so how, the vacancy is to be filled. Section 28 makes express provision for the parties' liability to the arbitrators for fees and expenses. Section 29 provides that arbitrators enjoy immunity from claims unless they act in bad faith.

The arbitral tribunal is given authority to rule on its own jurisdiction and determine which, if any, of the disputes referred to arbitration are within the scope of the arbitration agreement under Section 30. Section 31 mandates that any objection to the substantive jurisdiction of the arbitral tribunal that a party may have must be raised at the earliest possible stage in the proceedings. This section must be read with Section 73, which provides that the right to object to the arbitral tribunal's lack of substantive jurisdiction may be lost if the objection is not made at the earliest opportunity. Section 33(1) provides that the arbitral tribunal shall act fairly and impartially, shall give each party the right to be heard and shall adopt procedures that are suitable for a particular case to avoid unnecessary delay or expense. Under Section 40, the parties have a general duty to do everything necessary for the proper and expeditious conduct of the arbitral proceedings and, corresponding to the duties imposed on the arbitral tribunal by Section 33, a duty to comply with the arbitral tribunal's directions without delay. Section 34 sets out a non-exhaustive list of the procedural issues to be determined by the arbitral tribunal, including the power to impose expedited procedures or dispense with discovery procedures normally found in arbitral hearings.

Under Section 48, the arbitral tribunal may make a declaration on any matter to be determined in the arbitral proceedings or order the payment of a sum of money in any currency. The arbitral tribunal also has the same powers as the courts to grant a permanent injunction, to order specific performance of a contract or to order the rectification, cancellation, or setting aside of a deed or other document. Express provision for the allocation of the costs of the arbitration as between the parties is given in Sections 59 to 65. An award of costs generally follows the event, but there is discretion to take other relevant factors into account. The powers of the court in relation to arbitral proceedings are limited to the enforcement of peremptory orders made by the arbitral tribunal (Section 42), securing the attendance of witness (Section 43), making preservation orders in relation to evidence and assets (Section 44) and the determination of preliminary points of law (Section 45). Section 44 is not mandatory and the parties may agree that the courts shall have wider powers than those set out in the section.

Section 9 provides that, on application by a party to an arbitration agreement against whom court proceedings are brought in regard to the same matter, the court must grant a stay of the court proceedings unless satisfied that the arbitration agreement is null and void, inoperative or incapable of being performed. The courts will enforce arbitration agreements strictly, as was the case in *Fiona Trust & Holding Corporation v Yuri Privalov*.[77] This case concluded that a dispute under contracts induced by bribery and then rescinded because of the bribery can (and should be) determined by arbitration in the context of a common form of arbitration clause. Section 12 of the Arbitration Act 1996 gives the court in certain limited circumstances the power to extend the time for starting arbitral proceedings.

Awards can be appealed on points of law only after permission has been granted by the court or by the agreement of the parties. Section 69(3) of the act provides that leave to appeal shall be given only if the court is satisfied that:

- the determination of the question will substantially affect the rights of one or more of the parties;
- the question is one which the arbitral tribunal was asked to determine;
- on the basis of the findings of fact in the award, the decision of the arbitral tribunal on the question is obviously wrong;
- on the basis of the findings of fact in the award, the question is one of general public importance and the decision of the arbitral tribunal is at least open to serious doubt; or
- that despite the agreement of the parties to resolve the matter by arbitration, it is just and proper in all the circumstances for the court to determine the question.

Section 69(7) provides that the court may either confirm the award, vary the award, remit the award to the arbitral tribunal for reconsideration in whole or in part, or set the award aside in whole or in part.

The right of parties to appeal on points of law can be excluded by agreement between the parties, either in the arbitration agreement or at a later stage. It is also automatically waived under the arbitration rules of both the International Chamber of Commerce (Article 28.6 of the International Chamber of Commerce) and the London Court of International Arbitration (Article 26.9 of the London Court of International Arbitration Rules). Parties who elect to use ad hoc arbitration rules such as the UNCITRAL Rules should note that such rules do not expressly exclude rights of appeal. *Shell Egypt West Manzala GmbH, Shell Egypt West Qantara GmbH v Dana Gas Egypt Limited (formerly Centurion Petroleum Corporation)* is instructive on this point.[78]

Domestic awards may be enforced with the permission of the court as if they were court judgments (Arbitration Act 1996, Section 66). Permission shall only be refused if the person against whom the award is to be enforced shows that the arbitral tribunal lacked substantive jurisdiction to make the award.

In *West Tankers Inc v Allianz SPA and another*,[79] the Court of Appeal (Tolson LJ)

---

77   [2007] APP LR 01/24.
78   [2009] EWHC 2097 (Comm).
79   [2012] EWCA Civ 27. See www.bailii.org/ew/cases/EWCA/Civ/2012/27.html (accessed March 29 2013).

favoured a broader interpretation of Section 66, stressing that the stipulation therein for awards to be enforced in the same manner as a court judgment to the same effect refers to any means of giving judicial force to an award, and not just the normal forms of execution of a judgment. Thus, the declaratory nature of the award given in the case was not a bar to its enforcement by the courts in an appropriate case. The *West Tankers* Court of Appeal ruling is one of a number of rulings involving the same parties that have been heard both in England[80] and at the European Court of Justice of the European Union dealing with different countries taking court action consistent with the Brussels Regulation[81] in the context of arbitration.

Sections 100 to 104 of the Arbitration Act 1996 govern the recognition and enforcement of New York Convention awards. Under Section 104, enforcement may be refused if the party against whom it is to be enforced proves one or more of the following:

- incapacity of a party to the arbitration agreement;
- invalidity of the arbitration agreement;
- lack of due notice or opportunity to present its case;
- lack of substantive jurisdiction of the arbitral tribunal;
- irregularity in the composition of the arbitral tribunal or conduct of the arbitral proceedings;
- award not binding on parties, set aside or suspended;
- the subject matter of the arbitration is not capable of settlement by arbitration; or
- recognition and enforcement of the award would be contrary to public policy.

The UK Supreme Court's decision in *Dallah Real Estate & Tourism Holding Co v Pakistan*[82] is an example of an arbitral tribunal's decision on jurisdiction being re-examined for the purposes of considering enforcement under the New York Convention.

In *Jivraj v Hashwani*,[83] the UK Supreme Court ruled that, considering EU labour law cases and the purpose of discrimination legislation, it was legitimate for the parties to an arbitration to stipulate that the arbitrator selected be a member of a particular religion (here the Ismaili faith).

The Arbitration Act 1996 does not examine the confidentiality of the arbitration process or its findings. Instead, this was an issue that remains to be addressed on a case-by-case basis. However, in *Ali Shipping Corporation v Shipyard Trogir*,[84] the Court of Appeal held that confidentiality of the arbitral process was implied by law. In this case, a party was seeking disclosure of arbitration documents relating to prior arbitration proceedings in support of a plea of issue estoppel in a new arbitration. Issue estoppel prevents an issue that has already been litigated and decided on the

---

80   [2007] UKHL 4.
81   Regulation 44/2001/EC.
82   [2010] UKSC 46.
83   [2011] UKSC 40.
84   [1998] 1 Lloyd's Rep 643.

merits from being re-litigated. The party against disclosure of the documents belonged to the same group of companies as the party involved in the first arbitration. The Court of Appeal held that the duty of confidentiality ought to be implied by law, subject to defined exceptions of the general rule. The exceptions include where disclosure is authorised by implied or express consent of the parties to the first award; where a court order orders disclosure for the purposes of a later court action; when necessary to protect the legitimate interest for instance to found a cause of action against a third party; and where public interest requires disclosure.

19.   United Nations Commission on International Trade Law (UNCITRAL)[85]

UNCITRAL, the core legal body of the UN system in the field of international trade law, plays a significant role in the field of international arbitration. According to UNCITRAL,[86] the UNCITRAL Model Law on International Commercial Arbitration (1985) is an example of a how a model law form can be adapted to the subject matter under consideration and to the degree of flexibility sought by the drafters. This model law, which may be described as a procedural instrument, provides a discrete set of interdependent articles. It is recommended that, in adopting this model law, very few amendments or changes are made. As a rule, relatively few deviations from its text have been made by states adopting enacting legislation, suggesting that the procedures it establishes are widely accepted and understood as forming a coherent basis for international commercial arbitration.

The full list of UNCITRAL's texts and their current status[87] with respect to international commercial arbitration and conciliation are as follows:

- 2012 – Recommendations to assist arbitral institutions and other interested bodies with regard to arbitration under the UNCITRAL Arbitration Rules (as revised in 2010);
- 2010 – UNCITRAL Arbitration Rules (as revised in 2010);
- 2006 – Recommendation regarding the interpretation of Article II (2), and Article VII (1), of the Convention on the Recognition and Enforcement of Foreign Arbitral Awards (New York, 1958);
- 2002 – UNCITRAL Model Law on International Commercial Conciliation;
- 1996 – UNCITRAL Notes on Organising Arbitral Proceedings;
- 1985 – UNCITRAL Model Law on International Commercial Arbitration (amended in 2006);[88]
- 1982 – Recommendations to assist arbitral institutions and other interested bodies with regard to arbitrations under the UNCITRAL Arbitration Rules;
- 1980 – UNCITRAL Conciliation Rules;

---

85   www.uncitral.org/uncitral/en/index.html (accessed April 1 2013).
86   UNCITRAL, A Guide to UNCITRAL, 2013. Available at: www.uncitral.org/pdf/english/texts/general/12-57491-Guide-to-UNCITRAL-e.pdf (accessed March 31 2013).
87   www.uncitral.org/uncitral/en/uncitral_texts/arbitration.html (accessed March 31 2013).
88   www.uncitral.org/pdf/english/texts/arbitration/ml-arb/07-86998_Ebook.pdf (accessed March 31 2013). However, there may be other uniform laws on international arbitration which may be the subject of an international convention, most specifically, the Council of Europe, European Convention on International Arbitration (Strasbourg, January 20 1966). Available at: http://conventions.coe.int/Treaty/en/Treaties/Html/056.htm (accessed March 31 2013).

- 1976 – UNCITRAL Arbitration Rules; and
- 1958 – Convention on the Recognition and Enforcement of Foreign Arbitral Awards – the New York Convention.

19.1 UNCITRAL Model Law on International Commercial Arbitration[89]

The UNCITRAL Model Law on International Commercial Arbitration provides a template that law-makers in national governments can adopt as part of their domestic legislation on arbitration.[90] On the other hand, the UNCITRAL Arbitration Rules are selected by parties either as part of their contract or after a dispute arises, to govern the conduct of an arbitration intended to resolve a dispute or disputes between themselves.[91] The model law is directed at states, while the arbitration rules are directed at potential (or actual) parties to a dispute – in other words:

- UNCITRAL legislative texts, such as conventions, model laws, and legislative guides, may be adopted by states through the enactment of domestic legislation;
- UNCITRAL non-legislative texts, such as the UNCITRAL Arbitration Rules, can be used by parties to international trade contracts;
- legislative texts include the UNCITRAL Model Law on International Commercial Arbitration and the UNCITRAL Model Law on International Commercial Conciliation; and
- non-legislative texts include the UNCITRAL Arbitration Rules, the UNCITRAL Conciliation Rules and the UNCITRAL Notes on Organizing Arbitral Proceedings.[92]

19.2 UNCITRAL Arbitration Rules (as revised on August 15 2010)[93]

One key point to note is that a reference in a dispute settlement clause to the UNCITRAL Arbitration Rules or (in a frequent, but inaccurate formulation) to 'UNCITRAL arbitration' or any other provision to the same effect means that the parties agree that an existing or future dispute should be settled in arbitral proceedings conducted in accordance with the UNCITRAL Arbitration Rules.[94] Although UNCITRAL and its Secretariat have prepared legislative and contractual provisions and rules relating to international commercial arbitration and conciliation, they do not act as an arbitral tribunal, administer arbitration proceedings or otherwise perform any function related to individual arbitration proceedings, or any other system of public or private dispute settlement.[95]

The UNCITRAL Arbitration Rules provide a comprehensive set of procedural rules upon which parties may agree for the conduct of arbitral proceedings arising out of their commercial relationship. The rules are widely used in ad hoc arbitrations as well

---

89 http://www.uncitral.org/uncitral/en/uncitral_texts/arbitration/1985Model_arbitration.html (accessed 24 April 2013).

90 www.uncitral.org/uncitral/en/uncitral_texts/arbitration_faq.html (accessed March 31 2013).

91 *Ibid.*

92 *Ibid.*

93 www.uncitral.org/pdf/english/texts/arbitration/arb-rules-revised/arb-rules-revised-2010-e.pdf (accessed March 31 2013).

94 *Ibid.*

95 *Ibid.*

as in administered arbitrations.[96] The rules cover all aspects of the arbitral process, providing a model arbitration clause, setting out procedural rules regarding the appointment of arbitrators and the conduct of arbitral proceedings, and establishing rules in relation to the form, effect and interpretation of the award.[97]

20. International commercial arbitration centres

International commercial arbitration takes place under the auspices of several major international institutions and rule-making bodies. The most significant ones are discussed below.

20.1 International Court of Arbitration of the International Chamber of Commerce (ICC)[98]

There are no restrictions on who can use ICC arbitration or who can act as arbitrators. Since its inception in 1923, the ICC has administered more than 19,000 cases involving parties and arbitrators from some 180 countries. Parties using arbitration have a choice between designating an institution, such as the ICC, to administer the arbitration or proceeding *ad hoc* outside an institutional framework.

In ad hoc cases, the arbitration will be administered by the arbitrators themselves. Should problems arise in constituting the arbitral tribunal, the parties may require the assistance of a state court or the ICC as appointing authority, if so empowered by an arbitration clause or a subsequent agreement between the parties. To provide this service, the ICC applies a special set of rules, the Rules of ICC as Appointing Authority (in force from January 1 2004), designed for use both in proceedings under UNCITRAL Arbitration Rules and in other ad hoc proceedings

The ICC Rules of Arbitration (ICC Rules) are used worldwide to resolve business disputes through arbitration. The current ICC Rules came into force on January 1 2012 and define and regulate the conduct of cases submitted to the ICC. Commonly known as the ICC Rules, the rules of arbitration govern the conduct of ICC arbitration proceedings from start to finish. They regulate the filing of claims, the constitution of arbitral tribunals, the conduct of proceedings, the rendering of decisions and the determination of costs. While offering security and predictability, the ICC Rules also accommodate any preferences parties in dispute might have with respect to certain aspects of the proceedings, such as the choice of arbitrators, and the place, and the language, of the arbitration. In all matters that are not expressly provided for in the ICC Rules, courts and arbitral tribunals will follow the rules and attempt to provide an enforceable award. The ICC is the only body authorised to administer arbitrations under the ICC Rules.

20.2 JAMS International[99]

JAMS, the premier mediation and arbitration provider in the United States, combined with ADR Centre in Italy to form JAMS International in 2011.

---

96   *Ibid.*
97   *Ibid.*
98   www.iccwbo.org/products-and-services/arbitration-and-adr/arbitration/ (accessed March 31 2013).
99   www.jamsinternational.com/ (accessed March 30 2013).

Headquartered in London, JAMS International provides mediation and arbitration of cross-border and domestic disputes. Some non-US parties have expressed concern that if they agree to a US-based arbitration, they risk US-style discovery and other unwanted practices of US courts, hence, JAMS and JAMS International have adopted the Efficiency Guidelines for the Pre-Hearing Phase of International Arbitrations. The guidelines are designed to assure parties around the world that an international arbitration before JAMS or JAMS International will follow more efficient internationally accepted standards and practices rather than domestic practice in the United States.[100] The guidelines include having the JAMS International arbitrator develop a specialised protocol for pre-hearing disclosure for a case, taking into account the applicable rules, industry norms and the expectations and preferences of the parties and counsel. JAMS International/JAMS arbitrators are drawn from the highest ranks of the legal profession, including retired judges. The JAMS International Arbitration Rules (effective August 2011) are used where parties have agreed in writing to arbitrate disputes under them or have provided for arbitration of an international dispute by JAMS or JAMS International as in effect at the date of commencement of the arbitration subject to whatever modifications the parties may adopt in writing. A dispute that is subject to the JAMS International Rules may be administered by JAMS or JAMS International, as requested by the parties or as determined by JAMS or JAMS International.

20.3 International Centre for Dispute Resolution of the American Arbitration Association (ICDR)[101]

Established in 1996, the International Centre for Dispute Resolution (ICDR) is the international division of the American Arbitration Association. One of the unique aspects of the ICDR is its emphasis on party choice where feasible, such as the ability to file under a number of sets of procedural rules and to choose where a dispute is heard. ICDR procedures also encourage party input in selecting the appropriate arbitrator or mediator. The UNCITRAL-based rules of the ICDR have been advanced with a variety of rule and procedural amendments that set it apart from other institutions. For instance, Article 37 of the International Centre for Dispute Resolution International Arbitration Rules (ICDR Rules) provides a procedure for the granting of emergency arbitral relief. Hence, a party is able to apply to an emergency arbitrator appointed by ICDR for emergency interim relief before the appointment of an arbitrator or tribunal to adjudicate the merits of the dispute.[102] For more on the adoption by other arbitration organisations of similar emergency relief, see the report of Chaffetz Lindsey LLP.[103]

---

100   www.jamsinternational.com/rules-procedures/international-arbitration-guidelines (accessed March 30 2013).
101   www.adr.org/aaa/faces/aoe/icdr (accessed April 24 2013).
102   Guillaume Lemenez and Paul Quigley, "The ICDR's emergency arbitrator procedure in action, Part I: A look at the empirical data, 63(3) Disp Resol J 60–9 (August/October 2008). Available at: www.adr.org/cs/idcplg?IdcService=GET_FILE&dDocName ... (accessed March 31 2013).
103   Chaffetz Lindsey LLP, Changing the rules – Emergency measures of protection: Creeping consensus or a passing fancy, 2011 spring meeting, ABA Section of International Law. Available at: www.chaffetzlindsey.com/wp-content/uploads/2011/04/00070460.PDF (accessed March 31 2013).

The ICDR requires arbitrators to manage arbitration proceedings in a way that achieves a simpler, less expensive and more expeditious process through compliance with the ICDR Guidelines for Arbitrators Concerning Exchanges of Information.[104] The ICDR Rules apply where parties have agreed in writing to arbitrate disputes under them or have provided for arbitration of an international dispute by the ICDR or the American Arbitration Association without designating particular rules, subject to whatever modifications the parties may adopt in writing.[105] The ICDR Rules govern the arbitration, except that, where any such rule is in conflict with any provision of the law applicable to the arbitration from which the parties cannot derogate, that provision shall prevail. Finally, the ICDR Rules specify the duties and responsibilities of the ICDR acting as administrator for the arbitration.

20.4 London Court of International Arbitration (LCIA)[106]

The LCIA dates back to the 19th century and was designed to be a tribunal for the arbitration of domestic and, in particular, transnational commercial disputes arising within the ambit of the City of London. The current arbitration rules of the LCIA were promulgated in 1998 and are currently under review. They are designed to combine the best features of the civil and common law systems, including, in particular, maximum flexibility for parties and tribunals to agree on procedural matters. Parties to LCIA arbitration may be from any geographical location and the parties are free to agree the seat, or legal place of the arbitration. Parties adopting, or adapting, the LCIA's recommended clauses will specify the seat in their contract, but if they fail to do so, Article 16.1 of the rules provides for a London default seat. However, if one or more of the parties wishes to argue for an alternative seat, the LCIA court will decide the issue. Hearings may be held in any location convenient to the parties and the tribunal, irrespective of the chosen seat. The LCIA's charges, and the fees charged by the tribunals it appoints, are not based on the sums in issue. The LCIA is of the view that a very substantial monetary claim (and/or counterclaim) does not necessarily mean a technically or legally complex case and that arbitration costs should be based on time actually spent by the administrator and the arbitrators. A non-refundable registration fee is payable on filing the request for arbitration. Thereafter, hourly rates are applied both by the LCIA and by its arbitrators, with part of the LCIA's charges calculated by reference to the tribunal's fees. The LCIA sets a maximum hourly rate, at or below which the arbitrators it appoints must (other than in exceptional cases) set their fees.

20.5 Hong Kong International Arbitration Centre (HKIAC)[107]

The HKIAC is popular for the resolution of complex commercial disputes, especially those involving a China component. The HKIAC offers two types of arbitration: institutional arbitration proceedings administered by the HKIAC under the HKIAC

---

104   www.adr.org/aaa/ShowPDF?doc=ADRSTG_002579 (accessed March 31 2013).
105   www.adr.org/aaa/ShowProperty?nodeId=/UCM/ADRSTG_002037&revision=latestreleased (accessed March 31 2013).
106   www.lcia.org/LCIA/Introduction.aspx (accessed March 31 2013).
107   www.hkiac.org/ (accessed March 31 2013).

Administered Arbitration Rules and *ad hoc* arbitrations that are arranged solely between the arbitrators and the parties. Under these *ad hoc* arbitrations, the parties may adopt a ready-made set of arbitration rules (such as the UNCITRAL Rules of Arbitration) or may conduct the arbitration under rules that they have drawn up. Parties to arbitrations heard at or administered by the HKIAC are free to choose the procedural rules for their arbitrations. The HKIAC has formulated several sets of rules for domestic arbitrations, short form proceedings, small claims, documents only proceedings and electronic transaction disputes, which the parties are free to adopt. In September 2008, the HKIAC issued the HKIAC Administered Arbitration Rules, which provide for a 'light touch' administered arbitration modelled on the Swiss Rules of International Arbitration[108] and may be used in either domestic or international arbitrations.

20.6 Singapore International Arbitration Centre (SIAC)[109]

Singapore is a popular arbitration centre as it provides an independent neutral third-country venue currently rated at number five in world for neutrality in the Corruption Perceptions Index. In addition to a strong multicultural environment, it is a place in which businesses from China feel comfortable due to language and cultural similarities. Moreover, the UNCITRAL Model Law is the cornerstone of Singapore's legislation on international commercial arbitration, which is regularly updated to incorporate internationally accepted codes and rules for arbitration. Parties have a freedom of choice of counsel in arbitration proceedings regardless of nationality, and there is no restriction on foreign law firms engaging in and advising on arbitration in Singapore. Non-residents do not require work permits to carry out arbitration services in Singapore.

The SIAC has just introduced new rules (2013 SIAC Rules (5th edition)), which take effect from April 1 2013 and are the primary rules of arbitration at the SIAC. Parties may also adopt the UNCITRAL Arbitration Rules (as revised in 2010) for arbitrations at the SIAC. While these rules are essentially designed for the *ad hoc* form of arbitration, parties can, with special provision, enjoy the benefit of institutional administration of the arbitration from the SIAC. The Guide to UNCITRAL Rules Arbitration provides a fuller explanation of how this can be achieved. The SIAC SGX-DT Arbitration Rules (1st edition, July 1 2005) and the SIAC SGX-DC Arbitration Rules (1st edition, March 27 2006) are designed for the conduct of expedited arbitration for disputes arising from derivative trading and derivative clearing respectively.

20.7 Swiss Chambers' Arbitration Institution[110]

The Chambers of Commerce and Industry of Basel, Bern, Geneva, Lausanne, Lugano, Neuchâtel and Zurich established the Swiss Chambers' Arbitration Institution, which offers a means of dispute resolution based on the Swiss Rules of International

108 www.swissarbitration.org/sa/download/SRIA_english_2012.pdf (accessed March 31 2013).
109 www.siac.org.sg/index.php?option=com_content&view=article&id=46&Itemid=66 (accessed March 31 2013).
110 www.swissarbitration.org/sa/en/news.php (accessed March 30 2013).

Arbitration.[111] The current revised Swiss Rules of International Arbitration took effect on June 1 2012. In 2012, the Swiss Chambers' Arbitration Institution administered 92 new cases (a 6% increase on 2011), of which 75% of the parties involved had their registered office or domicile outside Switzerland.

20.8 Arbitration Institute of the Stockholm Chamber of Commerce (SCC)[112]

The SCC is part of, but independent from, the Stockholm Chamber of Commerce and was established in 1917. It has its own board and secretariat, and provides efficient dispute resolution services. The SCC was recognised in the 1970s by the United States and the Soviet Union as a neutral centre for the resolution of East-West trade disputes, and it has since expanded its services in international commercial arbitration. In recent years, the number of cases filed with the SCC has increased as it emerges as a popular Northern arbitration destination. The SCC caseload includes both domestic and international arbitration cases. About 50% of the cases are international in that they involve at least one non-Swedish party.

20.9 World Intellectual Property Organisation (WIPO)[113]

The WIPO Arbitration and Mediation Centre is an independent branch of the World Intellectual Property Organisation (WIPO), an intergovernmental organisation with a mandate to promote the protection of intellectual property (IP). WIPO is based in Geneva, Switzerland, and has 184 member states and is largely self-financed. The WIPO Arbitration and Mediation Centre was established in 1994 to promote the resolution of IP and related disputes through ADR. To achieve this objective, it developed – with the active involvement of ADR and IP practitioners and scholars – the WIPO Mediation, Arbitration, Expedited Arbitration and Expert Determination Rules and Clauses. The centre is the only international provider that specialises in technology, entertainment and IP disputes, although its services are not limited to such disputes – it has administered arbitrations involving general contractual issues, financing transactions and employment contracts. Under the WIPO Arbitration Rules, the parties may together select a sole arbitrator. If they choose to have a three-member arbitral tribunal, each party appoints one of the arbitrators; those two persons then agree on the presiding arbitrator. Alternatively, the centre can suggest potential arbitrators with relevant expertise or may directly appoint members of the arbitral tribunal. The WIPO Rules specifically protect the confidentiality of the existence of the arbitration, any disclosures made during that procedure and the award. In certain circumstances, the WIPO Rules allow a party to restrict access to trade secrets or other confidential information that is submitted to the arbitral tribunal or to a confidentiality adviser to the tribunal.

20.10 International Centre for Settlement of Investment Disputes (ICSID)[114]

The ICSID is an autonomous international institution established under the

---

111   www.swissarbitration.org/sa/download/SRIA_english_2012.pdf (accessed March 31 2013).
112   www.sccinstitute.com/hem-3/om-oss-3.aspx (accessed April 1 2013).
113   www.wipo.int/amc/en/arbitration/ (accessed March 31 2013).
114   https://icsid.worldbank.org/ICSID/FrontServlet?requestType=CasesRH&actionVal=ShowHome&
       pageName=AboutICSID_Home (accessed March 31 2013).

Convention on the Settlement of Investment Disputes between States and Nationals of Other States (the ICSID or the Washington Convention). It has over 140 member states. The convention sets out the ICSID's mandate, organisation and core functions. The ICSID's primary purpose is to provide facilities for the conciliation and arbitration of international investment disputes.

The ICSID Convention is a multilateral treaty formulated by the executive directors of the International Bank for Reconstruction and Development (the World Bank). It was opened for signature on March 18 1965 and entered into force on October 14 1966. The convention sought to remove major impediments to the free international flows of private investment posed by non-commercial risks and the absence of specialised international methods for the settlement of investment disputes. The ICSID was created by the convention as an impartial international forum providing facilities for the resolution of legal disputes between eligible parties, through conciliation or arbitration procedures. Recourse to the ICSID facilities is always subject to the parties' consent.

As evidenced by its large membership, considerable caseload and the numerous references to its arbitration facilities in investment treaties and laws, the ICSID plays an important role in international investment and economic development. Today, the ICSID is considered the leading international arbitration institution devoted to investor-state dispute settlement.

21.   Careful drafting of clauses is critical

Example G above (see 1.1(g)) provides a good example of why it is important to draft arbitration clauses carefully and to consider the problem of two different language version contracts being equally enforceable. One of the co-authors of this chapter has seen this problem arise in a number of jurisdictions other than China, and can report that in all circumstances the courts and the government in the country worked with and only recognised the local language version of the contract as the authoritative version. Under the circumstances described in Example G, it is not clear which arbitration centre has jurisdiction thus giving rise to a claim that the agreement to arbitrate was invalid. In this situation, the jurisdiction would lie with the courts of China, since it is likely to be the country with the most significant connecting factors.

One of the advantages of in-house counsel being involved in the negotiation and drafting of a company's commercial agreements is that they can provide input to the drafting of the arbitration clause and bring the company's institutional memory (preferences, processes and prejudices) to bear on this process. It is never appropriate to leave drafting of the dispute resolution clause to an outside law firm without input from experienced internal ADR counsel or external litigation counsel with whom the company has worked in the past on such matters. Precedent files, suggested clauses from arbitration institutions and even the UNCITRAL Model Clause only go so far.

Thirty years ago, it was fairly common for lawyers who drafted commercial contracts for clients also to be involved with and represent these commercial clients in arbitrations and mediations that arose from such contracts. This was especially true in jurisdictions other than the United States and the United Kingdom, where a multinational company would often rely on a lead local legal counsel to function as the company's 'jack of all trades' in the local country they operated in. Nowadays, with the increasing emphasis of specialisation, especially early on, law firm lawyers with substantive experience in both litigation advice and transactional work are rare. Consequently, it is likely that the individual who drafted your proposed arbitration clause has little or no experience of ADR and how it works in practice.

As a result of this ADR experience deficit, it is common to find arbitration clauses that cause counsel "to miss opportunities to take a strong hand in making good process choices".[115] Some drafters, fearful that the absence of appeal on the merits will leave their arbitrating client open to an irrational award, insert provisions for judicial review for errors of law or fact. According to Professor Stipanowich, this "costly and potentially perilous 'cure' may end up being worse than the perceived malady, which is doubly unfortunate since less costly and risky alternatives exist".[116] Another reason that dispute resolution provisions are usually accorded low priority in negotiations is that the parties are more focused on closing a deal and are not inclined to examine what will happen if disputes arise. In this case, the simple alternative is to rely on the published commercial arbitration templates and procedures offered by the various major arbitration provider institutions.

The commercial provider templates make good sense unless a client is entering into a significant commercial relationship that is exceptionally complicated, when it would be worthwhile to draft a specialised ADR clause (eg, Example G). Another situation in which it might be useful to prepare a contract template is where the clause will be used many times in multiple agreements. In these circumstances, it is worthwhile for the company to invest the time to produce a sound clause. The most common compromise is that the draftsperson will use a commercial provider's suggested clause and adjust it to fit the circumstances of the particular transaction.

While this approach offers the would-be draftsperson ample sources to choose from in that at least six websites of international commercial arbitration centres offer such clauses, "few readily available and reliable guideposts exist that dependably link specific process alternatives to the varying goals and expectations parties may bring to arbitration".[117] This problem is compounded because the various international commercial arbitration centres tend to focus on providing rule-based procedures for resolving situations that may arise in the course of arbitration at the expense of providing multiple process templates under which commercial arbitration may be pursued. With the notable exception of the American Arbitration Association, which offers multiple process pathways to resolve different types of disputes based on industry-specific lines, most international commercial arbitration centres offer a 'one size fits all' set of commercial arbitration rules that will not be appropriate in all circumstances, given the size of the disputants, the scope of issues to cover and the industry sector involved.

While binding arbitration is preferred by most corporate counsel to adjudication in the international commercial sector, it is increasingly being relegated to a

---

115   Thomas J Stipanowich, Arbitration and choice: Taking charge of the 'new litigation', symposium keynote presentation, 7 *DePaul Business & Commercial Law Journal* 401, 407 (2009). Available at: SSRN: http://ssrn.com/abstract=1372291.
116   *Ibid.*
117   *Ibid.*

secondary place in a multistep dispute resolution agreement which has mediation as the first stage of the process and arbitration as the second stage in the process. In a step clause, the parties agree to use one or more dispute resolution processes to resolve disputes that may arise out of, or in connection with, the transaction. However, as the word 'step' implies, one process must be completed before the next one begins. Earlier steps call for one or more non-binding processes (eg, mediation or escalation to negotiation by top-level executives), with the final step being a binding process (eg, arbitration). The binding process of arbitration is reached if, and only if, earlier steps fail to produce a voluntary settlement. Some practitioners prefer a two-step clause, with mediation as the first step and arbitration as the second; others prefer three steps, with negotiation by the parties' corporate executives as the first step, followed by mediation and then arbitration if necessary.

Such a multi-step dispute resolution clause must be drafted with clarity in order to be enforceable. In *Sulamerica CIA Nacional de Seguros SA v Enesa Enenharia SA*,[118] the Court of Appeal ruled that a two-step clause with a mediation provision first followed by binding arbitration was not binding.

Moore-Bick LJ concluded that an agreement to mediate would be binding if:

- the mediation process was sufficiently certain and did not require further agreement to allow matters to proceed;
- the administrative processes for choosing and paying the mediator were defined; and
- the mediation process (or a sufficient model thereof) was set out so that the details of the process were sufficiently certain.

Moore-Bick LJ was of the view that the clause before him did not provide sufficient certainty and was therefore not binding. The parties had not bound themselves to mediation in clear terms; rather, they would only "seek to have the Dispute resolved amicably by mediation". Moreover, no process was set out and no provision was made for the selection of a mediator.

The ICDR has a concurrent mediation/arbitration clause[119] that makes it possible for parties to agree to mediate disputes at the same time that they agree to arbitrate. The clause provides for mediation to start automatically after the demand for arbitration is filed, which means that the parties need not reach a separate mediation agreement. Moreover, the simultaneous effect of the concurrent arbitration/ mediation clause removes the need to decide when to mediate. The concurrent clause is unique in that it allows the parties to agree to mediate before a dispute arises, eliminating the need to negotiate a separate mediation agreement at a later time or to address the timing of the mediation *vis-à-vis* the arbitration. Consequently, the mediation process does not slow down the arbitration process but proceeds on a parallel track.[120]

---

118   [2012] EWCA Civ 648.
119   Steven K Andersen, Arbitration Act: A Handbook on International Arbitration & ADR, Chapter 24 – ICDR Offers Concurrent Mediation/Arbitration Clause. Available at: www.adr.org/aaa/ShowPDF; jsessionid=n1QQPv0bYl1jBdNQQ0m08VQ9h92rQ3CZlpZ3GPhLpZypjz0hnDqn!1082660915?doc=ADR STG_012609 (accessed March 31 2013).
120   The model concurrent mediation/arbitration clause used by Northrop Grumman in its international contracts is attached as Appendix A.

22. Conclusion

In this chapter, we have considered how legal departments are using conciliation, mediation and arbitration as tools to contain legal risk. The use of these ADR techniques have evolved over the past few years and the level of complexity that is involved with using one or more of these techniques to resolve a dispute has also changed. The sophistication with which companies approach these ADR techniques and the expectations that companies have from these processes mitigate towards more thoughtful drafting of dispute resolution clauses, to incorporate not only which arbitral rules apply but also the processes to be used in such a binding arbitration. Finally, the importance of the New York Convention and the international enforceability of arbitral awards make binding arbitration preferable to adjudication at the international level.

Appendix A: Annex A to the Northrop Grumman International Dispute Clause Guidelines, November 2012

INTERNATIONAL MODEL DISPUTES CLAUSE

Disputes

1. **Amicable Negotiation:** All disputes, differences, controversies, claims or questions arising in connection with, arising out of, occurring under, or related to, the present Agreement and any subsequent amendments of this Agreement, including, without limitation, its formation, validity, binding effect, interpretation, performance, breach or termination, as well as non-contractual claims (a "Dispute") shall be reduced to writing in a document to be sent to the other Party, requesting amicable negotiation under this Article (a "Negotiation Request"). A Negotiation Request may be sent by e-mail. The negotiation process hereunder shall be submitted to mutually compatible levels of management of the respective Parties to try and resolve the Dispute amicably and the executives selected shall use their reasonable best efforts to meet and to find a mutually acceptable resolution to the Dispute.

2. **(a) Mediation:** In the event that the Dispute is not satisfactorily resolved by negotiation within forty-five (45) days after the Negotiation Request was sent, the Parties will attempt to settle the Dispute through mediation administered by the American Arbitration Association's International Centre for Dispute Resolution (ICDR) under its International Mediation Rules then in effect. Any Party may file a request for mediation (the "Mediation Request") with ICDR and the other Party(s) concerned in accordance with those Rules. The mediation will be deemed to have started as of the date the Mediation Request was received by ICDR. The Parties will use their reasonable best efforts to jointly appoint a mediator using the list of mediators provided by the International Mediation Institute (www.imimediation.org) or from ICDR's Panel of Mediators. Should the Parties fail to agree on a mediator within fifteen (15) days from the date of receipt of the Mediation Request by ICDR, ICDR shall appoint a mediator. The Parties will meet together with the mediator no later than thirty (30) days after the date of appointment of the

mediator (or such other time as the Parties shall have agreed in writing). The mediation will take place in London, England (unless otherwise agreed by the Parties in writing) and the language of the mediation proceedings shall be English. The costs of the mediation shall be shared equally by the Parties, and each Party shall bear its own expenses, including its own lawyers' fees.

(b) Arbitration: In the event that the Dispute or any part thereof is not satisfactorily settled by mediation within sixty (60) days of the appointment of the mediator (or within such further period of time as the Parties may have agreed in writing), any Party may file a request for arbitration (a "Notice of Arbitration") with ICDR, in which case the Dispute shall be referred to and finally determined by binding arbitration pursuant to ICDR's International Arbitration Rules then in effect ("the Rules"), subject to the following provisions:

(i) The Parties shall agree to the selection of one (1) or three (3) arbitrators, depending on the complexity of the case. Where a tribunal of three (3) arbitrators is to be selected, each Party shall appoint a person to serve as an arbitrator. The two Party appointed arbitrators shall then appoint the Chairperson.

(ii) If the Parties cannot jointly agree on the composition of the arbitral tribunal within thirty (30) days from the date of the Notice of Arbitration, ICDR shall appoint the arbitral tribunal in accordance with the Rules, appointing as many arbitrators and using such mechanisms to appoint them as it deems appropriate in accordance with the Rules, at its sole discretion.

(iii) The Parties and ICDR shall ensure that the arbitral tribunal shall have been appointed at the very latest forty-five (45) days from the date of the Notice of Arbitration.

(iv) All arbitrators shall be fluent in English. The arbitrator (or the chairperson of the arbitral tribunal, in the event of a three person tribunal) shall not be of the nationality of anyone of the Parties and shall be a qualified lawyer.

(v) Subject to Article 9, each party shall bear its own expenses, including lawyers' fees, in connection with the proceedings hereunder. If the Arbitration should involve multiple claimants and/or multiple respondents who cannot agree to a joint nomination of a single arbitrator for claimants and/or respondents within the time limit set out in (ii) above, the ICDR shall appoint all members of the Tribunal without regard to any Party's nomination, but considering the criteria set out in this Sub Article (b).

(vi) Where the Dispute is settled at any time after commencement of the Arbitration, but before final award, whether by way of mediation or otherwise, any settlement agreement reached may be submitted to the arbitral tribunal by any party and issued as a consent award by the Tribunal.

3. Location: The seat or legal place of any mediation or arbitration proceedings shall be London, England.[121]

---

121   Should another seat be desired, it is not to be used without Law Department approval.

4. English Language: The language of all mediation or arbitration proceedings shall be English. All documents in any other language shall be translated into English at the expense of the Party(ies) producing them.

5. Governing Law: This Agreement and all matters related to or arising therefrom including without limitation, the arbitration clause and arbitrability of the Dispute, shall be governed and construed according to the laws of England without regard to its conflict of laws rule.[122] The Tribunal shall not decide the Dispute based on *amiable compositeur* (composition) or *ex aequo et bono* (from equity and conscience).[123]

6. Confidentiality: Any settlement discussions, Mediation or Arbitration hereunder shall be conducted in strict confidence. Except as necessary to enforce an award or required by law, no information or documents produced, generated or exchanged in connection with settlement discussions, Mediation or Arbitration (including the award) shall be disclosed to any person without the prior written consent of all Parties to the settlement, Mediation or Arbitration. This restriction shall not apply to public records or other documents obtained by the Parties in the normal course of business independent of any settlement discussions, Mediation or Arbitration.

7. Scope of Tribunal's Jurisdiction: The scope of the Tribunal's jurisdiction shall not be limited because the subject matter of the Dispute implicates public policy questions or national statutory rights.

8. Discovery: Document production shall be guided by the IBA's 2010 Rules on the "Taking of Evidence in International Commercial Arbitration." The Tribunal shall ensure that document production is conducted on a timely basis and the Tribunal may impose sanctions through the allocation of the costs of the Arbitration for abuse or undue delay of the document production procedure.

9. Written Reasoning, Finality and Enforcement of Award: The Award rendered by the Tribunal shall be reasoned and in writing. The Tribunal shall have the discretion to award reasonable costs to the prevailing Party. Such costs may include the costs of the arbitrators, the Tribunal administrator, and assistance required by the Tribunal, as well as reasonable costs for legal representation. The Award rendered by the Tribunal shall be binding on the Parties and may be entered in any court having jurisdiction over the Party or Parties to the Dispute against which enforcement is sought, or a court in any other competent jurisdiction where the assets of said disputing Party or Parties are located. The Parties hereby exclude and expressly waive any right of review or appeal to any court.

---

122   English Law is preferred for the NG foreign subsidiaries – any other governing law [except where US jurisdiction is used] is not to be used without Law Department approval.

123   This means that the Tribunal must base its award on the applicable law and not general concepts of natural justice.

OPTIONAL CLAUSES TO ANNEX A

1.   When dealing with a State, Agency of a State or State controlled company add:
Sovereign Immunity. The Government of [ ] and all its agencies hereby irrevocably waive all immunity from any legal action, suit or jurisdiction, including immunity in connection with recognition and enforcement of the award and attachment in aid of enforcement of the award with respect to the Government, its agencies or any of their property. The Tribunal shall not refuse to grant relief on the basis of the Act of State Doctrine or analogous principles of law that would otherwise restrict the calling into question of a governmental act. The government of [ ] warrants that it has obtained all necessary internal approvals to make this Disputes Clause and the waiver of sovereign immunity therein enforceable, and is herewith prevented from claiming otherwise.

2.   When dealing with a subcontractor or supplier add:
Continuing Performance. The Parties shall proceed diligently with performance of the Agreement not withstanding any Dispute.

3.   When seeking to limit the scope or nature of the damages that can be awarded by the tribunal add:
Damage Limitations. The Tribunal may award compensatory damages against any Party to the Dispute or provide injunctive relief; however, under no circumstances, will the Tribunal be authorised to award, nor shall it award, indirect, consequential, incidental or special damages, multiple or punitive damages against any Party. [This provision should be drafted in conjunction with and in light of the limitation of damages provision agreed to by the parties as set forth in the Damages / Limitation of Liability section of the contract.]

Legal risk management and governance in the financial world

Boris Georg Hallik
DekaBank

1. Top keyword: risk

Every business has its top keywords. 'Legal risk management', or even 'risk', are not normally among the top keywords in financial services or other industries,[1] but phrases containing either 'financial' or 'services' are found. This does not mean that legal risk management or risk management is not important for the financial world: in practice, the more these words are used, the more efficient the legal risk management process will be.

Following the financial crisis in 2008, the word risk has become more and more important for management in banks and financial services. Projects on risk minimisation, information technology (IT) risk minimisation or information systems, risk and governance are becoming the focus of attention in the financial world. Why is this?

2. Departments dealing with risk

A financial service organisation will have a number of departments that deal with risks and publish procedures and directives on successful risk management – for example, executive management, legal and compliance, IT and services (ie, business continuity management and IT security), and sourcing, as well as most of its business segments, such as asset management and corporate management. The definitions of risk management and its overlap between departmental activities will increase with the number of departments that deal with it. Although the corporate centre has published a definition of risk, the word risk and the awareness of risk are often used in different ways.

3. Using the word risk to obtain budget approval

Today, applications for a project, for money or for board resolutions may be more successful if they include a reference to risk. Since the 2008 financial crisis, banks are more focussed on any kind of risk and are very risk averse – proposals on risk prevention in board resolutions may be more successful than proposals concerned with increasing sales of banking products. The financial services sector has been investing in the management and minimisation of risk, although often this is fragmented between different departments with no common strategy or interface.

---

1   www.wordstream.com/popular-keywords/financial-services-keywords.

Along with investments in IT and services, the number of staff dealing with risk is increasing. In Frankfurt, banking personnel resources (ie, IT security, compliance and risk management) have more than doubled in the past 10 years.

4.   Significance of legal risk management

This chapter will examine the significance and sensitivity of legal risk management for financial services, and who is responsible for its implementation. In Germany, legal risk management is not a widely used term in the financial services sector as the definition can cover a wide range of risk management. A short, representative survey of my colleagues found that the majority of them understand legal risk management to be the standard service of each legal department.

Who is aware of legal risks? What does legal risk management mean? What is the process of legal risk management? Who is in charge? What is the legal department's role?

5.   Legal risk management as a standard service of the legal department

In the financial sector, the legal department is an adviser and representative in all legal matters. It has to protect its clients from a loss of rights. It must support clients with a view to shaping the law, avoiding conflicts and settling disputes. Effective legal risk management involves the development of suitable, proactive strategies to control legal risks and opportunities. The key objective of legal risk management is to help businesses to stop operational risks becoming legal liabilities. Legal risk management is best used when its purpose is to identify, analyse and manage legal risks affecting a specific business in an organised and consistent way. An example of legal risk is the potential for problems when entering into supply contracts, whereby the business engages services or products through an external third party.[2]

5.1   Definition of legal risk management

A search of the Web for definitions of legal risk management will produce more results for UK websites than for German ones. In 2004, McCormick defined legal risk as the risk of loss to a company that is primarily caused by:

- a defective transaction;
- a claim (including a defence to a claim or a counterclaim) being made or some other event occurring which results in liability for the company or other loss;
- a failure adequately to protect assets owned by the company; or
- change in the law.[3]

This is a broad definition, but it does state what he means by the much-used term.

---

2   www.klaw.com.au/news/business-owners-managers/legal-risk-management.
3   http://lawdepartmentmanagement.typepad.com/law_department_management/2006/06/a_definition_ of.html.

6. Process involving the legal department in daily business

So how does everything start? Before signing any contract or other agreement, it is a requirement to involve the legal department, which will analyse the contract and offer a legal opinion. However, in practice the client has the choice of whether to follow that legal advice or to carry the legal risk (ie, 'business decision'). In-house lawyers may not prioritise legal risks, and legal statements may cover only liability, penalties and warranties. The information a business department needs before making a decision may not be easy to identify; further advice should be requested from the data protection officer. From the business perspective, a high-quality legal opinion should contain clear recommendations and examples of formulations. Increasingly, in my experience as a customer of a legal department, I have needed to question the difference between a legal term and a business-related term. Some legal departments only accept competence and responsibility on issues related to legal risk, such as liability and penalty clauses. However, for example, the drafting of clauses on acceptance and project management are also legal matters and need the in-house lawyers' attention. Of course, project management is business-related and businesses do know how to structure project management effectively, but they will not have the expertise to draw up the correct and specific wording for a contract.

7. Legal department and legal risk management

Although in-house lawyers will understand their client's needs, they may not be aware of the overall impact of a service (eg, framework for payment or the impact of market data for a trading and information system) or software. When setting up an IT-related project, it is essential to involve the legal department as early as possible. The larger the budget and the project, the longer the contract negotiations will be. With early involvement, the in-house lawyer will have a much better understanding of the impact of the product or services and will appreciate which clauses of the contract may contain legal risk or provide an opportunity to claim money back. In contract negotiations, management and lawyers must discuss risk and legal risk, and also decide who is in charge of legal risk management. At this stage it is preferable for the lawyer, who understands the client's needs (impact of the product/service and history of the contract negotiations and clauses), to be responsible for the legal risk management for the duration of the contractual period. However, legal departments often do not have the competence for legal risk management or they refer to a contract management tool used across the group. In practice, even businesses as a whole do not take the responsibility for the decision "who is in charge of legal risk management", so the question remains unanswered.

8. Legal risk management – business function

According to the majority of legal departments in the financial world – at least for Frankfurt banks – legal risk management is the responsibility of business departments (ie, IT control and governance). When asked for any further help – despite the legal advice and contract negotiations – in-house lawyers often tell me that risk management is purely a business function; however, they are always very happy to help in case of any further legal questions. Even when I point out that the phrase 'legal risk management' contains the word legal and ongoing support would be greatly appreciated, I get the answer that the legal department does not have enough resources to deal with ongoing support.

So how does everything start? Before discussing legal risk management further, a good basis for successful legal risk management is the structure of the contract/legal agreement and the structure of the legal opinion.

9.   Basis of legal risk management: contract structure

As a lawyer in his forties with years of legal experience and IT/sourcing management, I believe that contracts have become increasingly complex. Among the reasons for this is the increased legal demands and the complexity of legal governance and the requirements of several circulars of the Federal Financial Supervisory Authority in Germany and the Financial Services Authority in the United Kingdom. In addition, longer and more complex contracts are based on the lessons learned from first or second-generation IT outsourcing and the involvement of external law firms, which tend to use their standard contracts. At present, it is not clear whether these standard contracts will provide adequate legal risk management.

In the financial services sector and others, a standard IT outsourcing contract may be structured as one master agreement with up to 20 individual agreements, which may have to 10 to 15 attachments, and each individual agreement may have different service level agreements. Over two years, up to three new individual agreements with a number of new attachments and a renewal or exchange of a number of attachments may be added to the original contract. Clearly, not all bank contracts are as complex as this example; however, up 10% of all contracts have a similar structure. In this example the contract negotiations lasted for six months and the parties had to read up to 700 pages.

In 2012, these contract structures seem to be standard and my approach is not to change the structure or to advise the management or lawyers that using a different structure would lead to more successful legal risk management. However, it is crucial to have a good overview of the structure of the contract and the legal rights or contractual claims. Normally, these overviews are published by external consulting companies (eg, management and IT consulting companies or external law firms), just before the contract is signed, or the legal department will write a legal opinion management summary. But are these overviews helpful for legal risk management? I suggest that the answer to this question must be no.

Such an overview is a management summary intended to help management to understand the main elements of the contract before signing it. The overview would answer the usual management questions on issues such as costs, maintenance costs, service levels, liability clause, contractual penalty, duration, alteration and notice of termination of contract. Generally, the questions do not focus on IT service provider management or legal risk management. Why? My initial response is that legal risk management is not crucial for the business case of a project. In addition, there have not been many critical contractual claim cases which have generated headlines in the financial sector.

10. Process of provider management is subject of contract negotiation

It would be incorrect to say that the process of provider management is not the subject of the contract or contract negotiations for my 'contract structure 2012'. Normally, the process of provider management is specified in some detail in one of the individual agreements and its attachments, and the department provider management is usually consulted early in the contract negotiation process. Unfortunately, it is usual to find only detailed processes about service level and provider management in relation to service levels, but no real process description about legal risk management.

One example of a standard legal structure to claim contractual penalties is a very complex formula with up to five individual agreements combined with up to 10 different attachments (example 1). In summary, on the one hand, while negotiating the contract the bank concerned was very successful because the parties agreed on a contractual penalty clause; on the other hand, legal contractual penalties formulas are so complex that implementation is very difficult. In my experience, while negotiating the contract these and similar clauses are only understood by the in-house and external lawyers on both sides and the provider management. However, as explained above, neither the in-house nor the external lawyer will support the legal risk management. Their involvement ends once the contract has been concluded. What does it mean for the successful example 1? The next internal audit of provider management with reference to the contract will depend on how crucial the internal auditor considers this clause to be.

11. Legal risk management implemented by provider management?

The main issue is the implementation. Normally, the process of provider management does not provide any interface between traditional IT/service level provider management and legal claim control. The provider management analyses the results of different service levels and will contact the legal department to make contractual claims for breach of service levels when only one service level is affected. However, as clauses and contractual penalties for breach of service levels become more complex, the question arises whether provider management is able to establish that the connection between 'breach of service level 1' plus 'breach of service level 2' constitutes a contractual claim (example 1).

I believe that there are two options for establishing a successful connection between provider management (IT department responsibility) and legal risk control (legal department responsibility):

- the structure of the contract and the structure of contractual penalties, warranties and top claims; and
- ongoing legal support (active legal risk management) and the interface between provider management and legal risk management.

12. Visual representation of contractual claims

As outlined above, changing to a less complex structure will not solve this problem. However, in addition to the traditional management summary, a diagrammatic representation of the structure of the contract and diagrammatic representations of, for example, the top 20 legal contractual penalties/claims should be included. A diagrammatic representation is needed when contractual claims concern more than one contract (ie, master agreement and one or more individual agreements) and a number of attachments. Examples are contractual penalty clauses and the exceptional notice of termination clause. The latter clause in particular is a favourite of management and although these clauses are not of great practical relevance, it takes even an experienced lawyer a long time to understand the impact of an exceptional notice of termination clause. So a visual representation can be very useful, even for a lawyer.

In addition to a good structure, visual representations of top contractual claims and ongoing legal support provides another step towards implementing successful legal risk management. The process is simple. The in-house lawyer who was involved in the contract negotiations should, together with the provider management, be responsible for the ongoing legal support. At the very least, the in-house lawyer should be included in all service level reporting, should attend the internal and external meetings between the bank and the IT provider, should support management summaries and should attend the management board meetings. The drawback with this process is internal legal costs and the resources of the legal department. Legal costs can be decreased by using ongoing support from the legal department only for the bank's crucial and important contracts/agreements and the legal department's resource requirements can be reduced by using cost-efficient and cheaper contract lawyers. Is a fully qualified lawyer needed for legal risk management? Closer cooperation between service level control and legal risk control may be achieved by using a contract lawyer for the organisation's provider management.

13. Process legal risk management: ongoing support by legal department for provider management

Even with visual representations of the top contractual claims, ongoing support from either the legal department or a contract lawyer will require a process and a system to track the service level reports and the contractual claims. In my experience, even very experienced and senior business managers struggle to understand the wording of a contract, or even a very complex formula of a contract penalty clause. As lawyers are trained to write, read and understand this specific wording, they are needed for ongoing support.

One could try to re-write contracts or terms and conditions in less formal or legal English or German language, but I believe this is unlikely to be achieved as language development is a very slow process and any change of culture and the culture of the lawyer is difficult to accomplish. For example, the German government (and I am sure other European governments too) has a department at the ministry of justice tasked with checking any new law, constitution or directive for "consumer-friendly wording" and having a straightforward and logical structure. Large banks and insurance companies have departments re-writing the legal bank/insurance terms and conditions in a more consumer-friendly way. As a lawyer, it is my personal belief that the wording of any European directive incorporated into German or English law has not become more consumer-friendly or easy to understand.

14.   Contract management supporting legal risk management?

A contract management system could provide a good way of dealing with this issue. Even coming back to the definition of legal risk management, contract management systems are often considered necessary for successful legal risk management. In contrast to a legal risk management process, processes for contract management are widely used in the financial service sector. There are many IT contract management systems and solutions which support this process.

So how do contract management and legal risk management work together? There are enough standard arguments to justify implementation of a contract management solution in a bank: overview of all the contracts, financial benefits (ie, keeping deadlines and notice periods), overviews of intellectual property (IP) of the used service or data and full cost transparency and risk management. Another standard point is that a contract management system/process meets the legal requirements of Section 25 of the German Banking Act and the German Federal Financial Supervisory Authority's circular, and the UK Financial Services Authority's requirements. However, Section 25 does not prescribe a legal obligation to implement a contract management system; it cites a legal obligation of any bank or financial service for a "due and proper organisation of business".

15.   Process of contract management

The findings of the contract management work group for German private and investment banks (BME German Association Materials Management Purchasing and Logistics, Financial Services Group, Contract Management Working Group 2012) indicate that the standard process is as follows. The sourcing department has to record only the data of contracts which involve an annual payment of more than £4,500, or €5,000; master agreements must always be recorded. Recording the data of a contract means: credit-side or debit-side contract, type of contract (ie, service contract, renting contract, service level agreement, insurance contract, IT project contract, IT licence contract), status of the contract (active or not active), parties to the contract (ie, which subsidiary of the bank), entry into force of the contract, contract duration, minimum term of the contract, term of the contract, various termination options and person in charge. All these records are mandatory; other records are optional, such as contractual penalty clause, terms of payment, applicable law and technical person in charge.

The process seems to be straightforward. One advantage of an e-contract management system is that emails are generated automatically four weeks before the end of the contract, or even early enough to send the notice in time. But what is the advantage for legal risk management?

16.   Impact of contract management on legal risk management

In my opinion, there are only a few positive aspects for legal risk management supported by the e-contract management tool. First, it uses a single system where all contract data is stored centrally. Secondly, provider management can use the contract management system data to identify the beginning/end of the contract, whether the contract has a contractual penalty clause and the reason for termination.

But how can this process of contract management efficiently and successfully support legal risk management?

Using example 1 from section 11 ('breach of service level 1' plus 'breach of service level 2' constitutes a contractual claim) and the optional data, one useful piece of information that provider management receives is that there is a contractual penalty clause. The provider management must read and analyse the contract to find any further information. This again raises the issues of the legal knowledge of the provider management department and the required ongoing support of the legal department. Other issues to be considered include the quality of data in the contract management tool, a lobby for mandatory and optional data fields and an improved technical contract management tool.

Therefore, contract management tools used by banks and financial services are not sufficiently customised fully to support provider management. The ideal solution would be for the provider management to gather data for all service levels and for the system automatically to notify of any possible contractual or legal claims. However, as there is no interest group lobbying for this type of solution, either the provider management gathers data for contractual claims in a separate list or the contractual claim is not pursued.

17.   Issues of contract management

In my professional experience, the majority of possible contractual claims are not pursued or are not pursued after management discussion of unmet service levels.

Even if a contract management tool supported legal risk management as discussed above, some basic issues would still need to be resolved, such as data quality, interest groups for mandatory and optional data fields, and improved technical function.

The contract management work group also found that the quality of data provided by contract management tools in the financial sector is often poor – attributable to the process of 'procure to pay'. A comparison of the processes of 15 national and international banks found that the sourcing department, not the legal department, was responsible for data entry. An example of poor data quality is the mandatory data field 'beginning and end of the contract'. It is straightforward to establish the beginning of the contract, but defining the end of the contract is more open to error. Employees in sourcing departments may find it difficult to transpose 'legal' German or English in the correct data fields. It may even start with the date the agreement is signed. It is common to find four signatures (two from the bank, two from the provider) with at least two different dates, and non-lawyers may find it difficult to determine when the agreement will become legally effective. The practical results are either two dates (when it is technically possible) or a new date (sometimes the date between the first and the second signature). The duration of a contract may be difficult to define, and '31.12.9999' is often entered. '31.12.9999' is a technical possibility for contracts with indefinite periods, or it is often used as an easy and fast way to fill the data fields. Even employees cross-checking the data fields may be reluctant to question its use.

Contract management can support legal risk management if more data fields are reported. Comparing the mandatory and optional data records, legal risk management particularly requires completion of the optional records. In the contract management process, the legal department will be concerned with the optional data fields, but it is not responsible for the data records or data maintenance. As a result, only 5% of optional data fields are maintained, as employees in sourcing departments do not have the right skills to analyse and understand the clauses. Since the process of reporting optional data is not enforced, often very little information is provided.

In summary, the process of contract management can only support legal risk management if the data is of high quality and all optional data fields are treated as mandatory. Ideally, the software used should be customised to track the top 20 contractual claims of the contract, but this is unlikely as the business case may not be strong enough for management to justify the extra expense.

18. Business case of legal risk management

Is there a business case for legal risk management for financial services? The answer appears to be no, and that one must differentiate between contractual legal risk management and IP legal risk management. First, contractual claims – even the top 20 contractual claims – are not money-makers for banks or other financial services or individual financial services projects. A bank will be even more concerned to maintain a good relationship with its supplier than it will be to save €2 billion from a contractual penalty claim. However, it is in the management's interest to receive reports on service levels and, if possible, potential contractual claims in preparation for its meetings.

19. Contractual legal risk management

Another reason for the general reluctance of management to accept contractual legal risk management may be demonstrated by comparing the business case and the contractual claim. On the one hand are the costs of the project, the IT software implementation, the licence and the maintenance, and the criticality of a system (eg, a payment system for a bank which transfers up to €20 million daily). On the other is a contract with duration of around five years and the risks of losing the good reputation of the chief information officer/operating officer if the system fails and of legal risk management demanding, for example, €200,000 as a contractual penalty claim.

Management is more likely to be concerned with the success of the business case than with the contractual legal risk management. But, as said above, information about any possible contractual claims provided to the management will improve the provider managements' or legal departments' reputation. Management needs detailed reports about contract performance and, for example, a threatened contractual claim for thousands of euros to support its negotiating strategies.

20. IP legal risk management

It is also to be expected that management will support IP legal risk management. What does this mean?

The process of IP legal risk management is already implemented in the banking and financial services sector as licence management. In recent years, a substantial amount has been invested in licence management to minimise the risk of infringement of software licences and use of market data. One reason is that these contracts are normally subject to the laws of California or New York and contain clauses about punitive damages. For management, the risk of punitive damages is much higher than obtaining, for example, €200,000 from a contractual claim. Additionally, the loss of reputation resulting from an IP infringement claim could seriously harm a bank.

21. Licence management supporting IP legal risk management

A successful licence management procedure requires high-quality data. This is one of the biggest issues of licence management, since different systems and processes have to work together. An investment bank using market data will need a responsible market data licence manager in each department that uses the data. Market data licence managers will need information from the human resources department on employees entering and leaving the bank, the application of user authorisation, and the use of data (ie, derived data). On-site courses on using the data should be provided. Each market data licence manager must communicate with the sourcing licence manager and report the data. The sourcing licence market data manager is the source of information for the use of all data in the investment bank.

Although the process description appears to be straightforward, in practice there will be difficulties and the process should be reviewed and adapted frequently, perhaps every year, since other interface processes will change.

22. Data quality of licence management tools

Another issue is the responsibility for the process. A standard licence agreement for the use of market data may include two or three pages of IP clauses. The legal department will emphasise the legal risk of any IP infringement and will advise that either the responsible sourcing department or the IT department should provide instruction about the correct use of data. But how do you inform non-lawyers about two to three pages of legal German or English on IP use of market data in an intelligible manner? I suggest that this is extremely difficult. Even visual representations will not succeed, due to the number and complexity of IP rights. One suggestion is that the department intending to use the market data should provide a detailed description of how the data is to be used, and this should be confirmed in writing by the market data company.

Who is competent to record the data (in my example, the two to three pages of market data use/restrictions) in the licence management tool? The legal department is only competent to analyse the contract and write the legal opinion. Even for the in-house lawyer, the legal requirements for using data are complex, but it is the sourcing department or IT department that is responsible for processing data for the licensed use. Usually, these people do not have sufficient legal training and do not have enough time to consult the legal department, so there is a risk of bad data quality. Generally, however, this has not proved a problem as banks have many years' practical experience, and the sourcing department or IT department can provide sufficient support for the auditing of market data companies.

23. Legal risk management and future sourcing tools

Another good example of legal risk management is the control of risks of provider insolvency or merger and acquisition. How does it work, and who is in charge of the process and the tool?

Through my years of experience as an IT lawyer, I believe that banks and financial services are directly dependent on IT, and that their profitability is dependant on IT systems. Some banks rely on small IT companies that specialise not only in IT but also in banking processes (this practice is common in Germany). Some asset management departments work with external advisers from IT or consulting companies. However, in the majority of cases there is no exchange of expertise and knowledge with the internal bank employees. The main risks for a bank in this situation are either that the IT company goes into administration or that any of its employees who work with the bank leave the company.

One approach to managing provider risk is to implement a specific provider management sourcing tool which contains all the relevant information about the provider and its credit reports. There are several credit reports companies on the market, and all offer summaries of a provider's credit report. Many of these companies offer an early warning system that generates automatic emails if the provider's management, payment history or credit rating changes. Early warning emails can be evaluated by the strategic sourcing department, which will request more detailed information from the company and/or inform the appropriate internal department about the alerted risk.

In addition to these credit reports, annual development meetings between the provider (eg, the providers for all commodity groups: IT/management-consulting, legal consulting, HR consulting, IT, market data, miscellaneous goods and services, marketing and facility management), the department and the sourcing department shall take place with the bank's top 40 providers. These meetings may provide useful information about on change of management or creditworthiness of the provider. Again, this information should be recorded in the provider management sourcing tool.

The process of provider risk management includes the pre-monitoring of financial provider risk before entering into a contract. At DekaBank in Frankfurt, it is obligatory to write a management report for purchase orders above €500,0000 or £450,000, providing a short summary of the aims of the agreement, a cross-check of all obligatory processes (legal opinion), a price benchmarking and a detailed risk analysis of the provider.

24. Legal risk management and the legal department

In the banking/financial sector, legal departments are not essential for successful legal risk management. They certainly help to generate a legal opinion, but they do not provide sufficient support to ensure better and more professional legal risk management. The main reason for this is that in the financial sector, customarily, legal departments do not take responsibility for legal risk management.

Therefore, legal risk management provides an opportunity for legal departments to extend the in-house services they offer. I suggest the following could be added:

- improved legal opinions with more practical relevance ("the in-house lawyer shall understand the clients' needs and products");
- ongoing legal support (legal account management of the bank's major contracts) and a stronger interface between existing provider management and legal ongoing support;
- visual representation of the major contracts;
- responsibility and resources for the data records of existing contract and licence management; and
- in-house training for in-house lawyers regarding a better understanding of the client's products.

25.   Legal risk management and business

According to the definition of legal risk management provided in this chapter, banks and financial services have only partly implemented successful legal risk management. In my experience, the best available methods of implementation are the licence management tool and the provider risk management tool. However, more investment is needed in the contractual management tool and interface processes need to be adapted.

For businesses, any investment needs a good business case. Investments appear to be sufficient for a bank's top 100 contracts/agreements. The rating of 'top 100 contract' is derived not only from the money spent, but also from the importance of the provider to the business and the service of the contract. It is recommended that banks replace small, essential IT service companies with larger, more resilient suppliers to minimise the risk of their insolvency.

26.   Future of legal risk management – legal risk management 2020

In essence, legal risk management is not one of banks' and financial services' top priorities. However, I am sure it will become more important as the complexity of laws and financial regulations increases. The next top financial key words will be, and are already becoming, 'governance' and 'compliance'. Although it is not yet comprehensively defined, the governance of a bank requires strong and efficient legal risk management.

Bank departments are not always aware of, and may be unsure of how to implement, some of the German Federal Financial Supervisory Authority and the UK Financial Services Authority's regulations, and their legal and compliance departments are unable to provide adequate support.

Increasingly, the regulation of governance and compliance will force banks and financial services to manage their contracts and agreements. Efficient and successful processes of legal risk management – supported by provider management, the legal department and compliance/governance departments – will be essential to meeting the requirements.

27.   The Web and five steps of legal risk management

The recommendations given in an in-house lawyer blog by Melanie Hatton provide a useful approach to legal risk management:[4]

Conduct a legal audit: To be effective, legal risk management must be based on a thorough understanding of the business's key activities, stakeholders and objectives and this can only be achieved by conducting regular legal audits and working with the business's management team to analyse the risks, prioritise their management and anticipate the legal requirements of the business.

The audit will also facilitate the management of the 'corporate memory', essential for future due diligence exercises and the storage of key corporate data and documents, and it can lay the foundations for an ongoing compliance and risk management strategy.

Communicate, educate, cooperate: In-house counsel cannot manage legal risk single-handedly. It's imperative that the legal risks are communicated to the wider business to ensure they are supported and, vice versa, that the wider business objectives and demands are facilitated in the legal risk management strategy.

One way to achieve that communication is through legal risk awareness training sessions tailored to the audience within the business which is either most exposed to or best placed to handle the risk being communicated. Training sessions are a perfect opportunity for in-house counsel to demonstrate that they are working with the business (not against it), and are also a good precursor to introducing new business guidelines to assist colleagues with the practical day-to-day management of the legal risks which have been identified.

Although some legal risks are stand-alone, don't forget that many legal risks dovetail with financial, reputational, operational, political, regulatory and tax risks; so, legal risk management is just one part of a more broad risk management strategy within a business. It's a challenge for those new to the role of in-house counsel to balance their risk-averse nature against both these other risks and the essential quality of risk-acceptance in any successful entrepreneurial business; but, once mastered, this skill will make the commercially aware in-house lawyer stand out in the crowd from those lawyers sitting in their ivory towers.

Compliance and Governance Policies: Underpinning any legal risk management strategy is the requirement for a comprehensive set of compliance and governance policies. Policy making is a key tool which in-house counsel have within their remit to positively influence the way in which business is conducted and to set the standard for expected behaviour. It is essential that all such policies have the buy-in and support of the management team, and that the legal department has a defined role in implementing and ensuring compliance with the policies.

---

4   http://in-house-lawyer.blogspot.co.uk; http://in-house-lawyer.blogspot.de/2010/02/5-steps-to-legal-risk-management.html.

Operations: The daily operations of a business always prove to be the most fertile ground for legal input. An abundance of legal consequences can be found in supply, manufacturing and distribution chains, protection of intellectual property rights, brand protection (online and offline), pending and threatened litigation, product liability, sales and marketing practice, insurance, property matters, employment and HR practice, industry regulation as well as company secretarial, board and shareholder matters.

Good working relationships with colleagues operating in each of these areas are essential for in-house counsel to play an effective and valued role within the business; the challenge is for the lawyer to be seen as part of the team, and not as an obstacle, to achieving operational outputs and objectives.

Legal resource: The individual character of each business will determine its exposure to legal risk and the management tools required to best handle that risk. Inherent to that is the balance of matching and managing internal and external legal resource, and indeed other professional suppliers to the business. The tough economic conditions are resulting in more businesses expecting their legal teams to reduce head-count and manage costs more tightly, but arguably against a back-drop of increased legal risk. A core skill of the in-house lawyer in today's world is their ability to manage the risks in this more intense climate by better clarifying the role of the legal function within the business, demonstrating value-add and selecting, managing and getting the most out of their internal and external legal resource.

These five steps can also be used as checklist to implement successful legal risk management.

28. Legal risk management in banks and financial services

All bank and financial service businesses in Europe have already implemented parts of legal risk management. However, the meaning and importance of legal risk management differs across the sector and there is no clear definition. Efficient and successful risk management can only work if matching, high-quality processes are used by all the departments discussed in this chapter, and by highly skilled and motivated personnel.

An international overview of board structures

Jan M Eickelberg
Peter Ries
Berlin School of Economics and Law

1. Two and one-tier systems, liability and corporate governance rules

The approach towards management structure and control differs between countries with a common law legal system and those that have a civil law jurisdiction. Corporations in civil law jurisdictions (eg, the German public corporation, AG) are often structured as a mandatory two-tier system or, more correctly, a three-tier system, consisting of a board of managers, a supervisory board and the shareholders' meeting. Common law countries follow a one-tier system in which corporations have a single board of directors rather than a separate board of managers and a supervisory board.

Directors' liability is governed by national laws. In addition to their mandatory provisions, most countries have established corporate governance rules as soft law, and these rules are often similar. Globalisation has led to the introduction of international corporate governance rules such as those of the Global Corporate Governance Forum[1] and the Organisation for Economic Cooperation and Development (OECD).[2] Compliance has also become an important issue, although the level of regulation with respect to compliance varies from country to country.

2. Background

The earliest recorded board[3] was developed in the 17th century by the East India Corporation, an association of companies trading between India and Europe. Initially, the corporation had a one-tier board system, drawing directors from the individual companies to manage its affairs. This meant that members of the corporation's board managed their own companies, so in 1623 a supervisory board was introduced to control the management by attending its meetings and inspecting enterprises and business documents within the corporation. A supervisory board should also give advice to the management.

3. Germany

3.1 Two-tier board

In the German system of public corporation, a board of managers consists of one or

---

1   For further details see http://ec.europa.eu/internal_market/company/ecgforum/index_en.htm.
2   www.oecd.org/dataoecd/32/18/31557724.pdf.
3   See *Hopt/Leyens*, Board Models in Europe – Recent Developments of International Corporate Governance Structures in Germany, the United Kingdom and Italy, European Company and Financial Law Review (ECFR) 2004, 137.

more persons, who are appointed by the corporation's supervisory board for a maximum of five years. The supervisory board may remove members of the management board only for good cause. In comparison with the US-system, a German board of managers has far more independence and power than a typical US senior executive since in the United States senior executives must act on the instruction of the board of directors.

In Germany, a board of managers must consist of natural persons with full legal capacity. They must not have any convictions for fraud or similar crimes or be subject to a professional or occupational ban. The board is subject to strict competition and conflict of interests rules. Board members are appointed and removed by resolution of the supervisory board and must be registered with the commercial register. The board is responsible for running the day-to-day business of the corporation and developing its strategy. Members of the board of managers have unlimited power to represent the corporation.

Viewed in terms more familiar to the Anglo-American reader, the supervisory board plays a supervising role similar to that played by outside directors on a US board of directors. German law explicitly prohibits any person from serving on the board of managers and the supervisory board simultaneously. The members of the supervisory board must be natural persons and must have full legal capacity. Members of the supervisory board are appointed by the shareholders, sometimes on proposal by the board of managers. If the corporation has more than 500 employees, the supervisory board must consist of representatives of the shareholders and of the employees. One-third of the members of the supervisory board, or half of them if the corporation has more than 2,000 employees, must be employees' representatives (the so-called system of 'codetermination').

These rules illustrate that German corporate law protects not only the shareholders but also the employees of a corporation. They indirectly participate in strategic business decisions and control the board of managers, enabling employees to safeguard their interests at an early stage. The German system aims to harmonise the interests of the corporation, its shareholders and its employees. The supervisory board can profit from the detailed inside knowledge of the employee-representatives. The participation of employees in supervisory boards has been shown to benefit all parties, preventing strikes, mass layoffs and unfair business decisions. Since the casting vote rests with the shareholders' representative, the interests of the owners of the corporation are also represented.

The supervisory board consists of a minimum of three and a maximum of 21 members. It appoints, removes and controls the members of the board of managers; it does not manage or represent the corporation. The supervisory board provides a network with shareholders and business partners, who often are granted a seat on the supervisory board.

The supervisory board represents the corporation with respect to the board of managers. The directors must report to the supervisory board, which can control their decisions.

In practice, in the past, some directors did not fully meet their obligation to report to the supervisory board, so that the latter could not effectively control the board of managers' decisions. This disadvantage of the German two-tier system is unknown in the common law one-tier system, where managers and supervisors work together and are jointly involved in all business decisions. All board members have the same access to the same information. In contrast, members of a supervisory board have no direct access to information, so their function may be limited if information is missing or filtered.

In addition, supervisory board control was ineffective because its members had to meet only two or four times a year, and each meeting lasted less than four hours on average.[4]

Historically, the supervisory board was reactive rather than proactive. It supervised only actions already taken by the board of directors. However, under new regulations the supervisory board in German public corporations must approve certain actions, as required by law or by the corporation's articles, before they are carried out. The courts have interpreted the regulations to mean that supervisory boards must increase their involvement in strategic decisions and become advisers to the board of managers rather than functioning solely as a control body. Thus, the supervisory board must also control the future business policy of the corporation.

A supervisory board is responsible for contracts between the corporation and its managers and auditors, and it will bring actions on behalf of the corporation against members of the board of managers who do not fulfil their legal obligations.

In general, the supervisory board has enjoyed a major role in German economic development. Generally, its members included representatives of the corporation's major business partners and financing banks, both of which were often also shareholders of the corporation. In this way, supervisory boards became instruments for the expansion of large corporations and were a reason for the growth of the banking system.

In the past, it was common practice for the chief executive officer (CEO) of one corporation to sit on the supervisory boards of other corporations, thus creating a closed shop known as 'Deutschland AG'. This led to problems. Effective control requires independent controllers. Globalisation and recent scandals (eg, the so-called 'Mannesmann-scandal', where a four-member subcommittee of the supervisory board, in a 2:1 decision with one abstention, granted a $40 million 'golden handshake' to the CEOs, who sold the corporation to Vodafone) have prompted discussion on whether the independence of the members of the supervisory board should be strengthened.

3.2 Criticism regarding two-tier board system

Some scholars, in particular from the United States, have questioned the efficiency of the German two-tier board system and the influence of codetermination; from their point of view, a 'good' board requires a small size, frequent meetings, intensive flow of information, adequately qualified members and few conflicts of interest.[5] One can argue that these features do not apply to German supervisory boards.

---

4   *Jungmann*, The Effectiveness of Corporate Governance in One-tier and Two-tier Board Systems – Evidence from the UK and Germany, ECFR 2006, 454.

5   *Roe*, German Codetermination and German Securities Markets, originally published at 1998 Columbia Business Law Review 167, later included as modified in Political Determinants of Corporate Governance, Oxford 2003 (http://ssrn.com/abstract=10578), 72.

Depending on the capital of the corporation, German supervisory boards consist of up to 21 members. US boards are smaller. In addition, employee representatives sit on German boards.

Under the German Public Corporation Act, German supervisory boards may only meet two to four times a year, whereas US boards usually meet at least eight times a year.[6] Thus the decision-making process in one-tier systems is quicker than in two-tier systems. In addition, the information flow from management to the supervisory board is relatively poor in Germany. Under the two-tier system, information may be provided to the supervisory board only a short time before a board meeting.[7] This cannot happen in US corporations since in a one-tier board system both managing and supervising directors sit on the same board.

The size of German supervisory boards impedes the flow of information and the efficiency of control. Higher numbers may result in some members of the supervisory board not having the opportunity, or not seeing the necessity to speak at board meetings.[8] Some members may not prepare for board meetings, relying on other members to carry out the preparation.

Another obstacle to the efficient flow of information and control is that employee representatives sit on the board. The management may not want to provide certain confidential information to employee representatives if potentially it could lead to conflicts with the workforce. In these circumstances, the management may inform only the shareholders' representatives on the board by informal contacts. Thus, certain issues will not be discussed with the whole supervisory board.[9]

Codetermination requirements complicate the introduction of mandatory qualification standards for all members of the supervisory board.[10] Since employee representatives are elected by the employees, the introduction of qualification standards would limit free choice. Unlike US boards, until recently German supervisory boards did not require minimum qualification standards for their members, as this would have been difficult to impose. However, this may change if employees' representatives on the supervisory board are held by the courts to the same standard of liability as the shareholders' representatives, as appears likely after the Mannesmann trial mentioned above, where the employees' representative faced the same charges as the shareholders' representative for granting excessive remuneration to the managers of Mannesmann.[11]

The growing influence of foreign investors should not be underestimated when assessing the value of employee codetermination. Often, German corporations with employee codetermination find it difficult to raise capital on international capital markets as some foreign investors are reluctant to invest if global markets offer alternative instruments that are not subject to codetermination.[12]

---

6   *Ibid*, 73.
7   *Ibid*, 73 *et seq.*
8   *Ibid*, 75.
9   *Ibid*, 74 *et seq.*
10   *Jungmann*, ECFR 2006, 454, 456.
11   *Hopt/Leyens*, ECFR 2004, 137, 145.
12   *Ibid*, 146.

Some think that members of German supervisory boards are not as independent as US board members (eg, US investors who are used to independent supervising members).

Since it is common practice for members of a supervisory board to be proposed by the management board, they may be thought to lack independence. Only persons that are 'adequate' in the opinion of the management board will be elected as new members of the supervisory board by the shareholders, and only those who in the opinion of the management board 'adequately' control will remain in office.[13] In addition, for many years positions on supervisory boards were considered to be merely honorary roles.

In the past, it was standard practice in Germany that the CEO of a corporation became chairman of the supervisory board after retiring as CEO, and that a substantial proportion of the members would be former members of the management board. In addition, it is common practice for only a few individuals to hold board positions in several corporations.

Often, representatives of shareholders or financing banks are elected to the board. Banks have a significant influence on supervisory boards – about 12% of the seats in supervisory boards are taken by members of private banks.[14] Frequently, banks will have proxies to represent individual shareholders at shareholders' meetings, so they will have a threefold influence on the supervisory board: by financing the corporation; by holding shares in the corporation; and by representing other shareholders. This regularly leads to conflicts of interest, in particular since often German corporations are (partly) owned by other corporations. Consequently, managers of one corporation may sit on one or even many boards of other corporations where this corporation holds shares.

An example of a conflict of interest situation occurred at Siemens. The former CEO became chairman of the supervisory board, which had to decide whether bribery of the corporation in the years when he had been CEO had harmed the corporation. Such a conflict can also arise with regard to the employee representative, for example in the German air carrier Lufthansa. The head of the United Services Union had a seat on the supervisory board of Lufthansa. Nonetheless, he organised a strike of his union against Lufthansa in 2002.

The problem of non-independence of members of the supervisory board has been addressed by Deutsche Bank AG following pressure of international investors. The bank's corporate governance principles now state that managers of Deutsche Bank AG will not assume the chairmanship of a supervisory board outside Deutsche Bank group.

3.3 Suggested improvements for two-tier board systems

In recent years in Germany, it has become more common for individuals to be shareholders. As a result, there has been a demand for improved supervisory board independence. The 2008 financial crisis led to calls for improved corporate

---

13   *Jungmann*, ECFR 2006, 450 *et seq.*
14   *Ibid*, 458.

governance. As a result, the following proposals have been made and introduced in part.

Since September 2009:

- it is generally prohibited to become chairman of a (listed) corporation's supervisory board within two years of retiring as its CEO;
- higher qualification standards for board members of listed corporations have been introduced in part – at least one member must now have knowledge of accounting; and
- decisions regarding remuneration of directors must be taken by the entire board, not by a subcommittee.

It has been proposed to strengthen the role of the chairman. Under the proposal, the role would be a full-time position, with adequate compensation, filled by an independent person who should not have had a business relationship with the corporation for several years before his appointment. The term of the chairman would be limited. The chairman would have unlimited access to all necessary information. It has been suggested that any person who has a potential conflict of interest, such as in-house lawyer, an officer of a financing bank or a customer of the corporation, should not serve on the supervisory board.

It has been proposed to reduce the number of board positions any person may hold and to bar politicians from serving on supervisory boards. The requirements to improve the flow of information, to provide for more meetings, to introduce direct liability of board members, not only with respect to the corporation but also of shareholders, and to bring in more women[15] and foreign experts have been considered.

In addition, the German legislator has introduced rules to improve corporate governance at the management level. In particular, the rules governing remuneration of the members of the management board were amended as follows.

Remuneration packages must be based on long-term objectives rather than short-term ones. However, in Germany long-term objectives ('strategy') are usually determined by the management board, not by the supervisory board. So, management can influence its remuneration. New criteria for performance-based remunerations have been introduced. Where previously only 'shareholder value' was considered in determining compensation, now other parameters such as corporate social responsibility, employee job satisfaction and salary development, and energy efficiency must be taken into account in order to promote sustainable development of the company. If management fails to comply with these standards or if the development of the company deteriorates, remuneration may be reduced. Although the supervisory board retains responsibility for determining management remuneration, shareholders who own at least 5% of the total share capital, or at least €500,000 in par value, may now propose compensation packages. However, these proposals ('say on pay') are limited to listed companies, and only apply to past

---

15   Introduced in France, planned in The Netherlands and accomplished in Norway – 40% of the board members must be women.

compensation, are not binding on the supervisory board and cannot be challenged by a voiding action. Scholars have proposed that the quorum should be lowered and that action against shareholder votes should be permitted.[16] In practice, 27 of 30 DAX-companies opted for voluntary shareholder votes and 93% of the compensation packages were approved.[17] If the remuneration granted by the supervisory board is found to be inadequate, members of the supervisory board can be held liable. The amount of remuneration must be published in the yearly balance sheet. In Germany, the say on pay rules are voluntary; in the UK they are mandatory; in the United States, the Dodd-Frank Act provides for two separate say on pay rules, one as a non-binding vote to approve compensation and one as a non-binding vote for non-binding votes in the future.

In Germany, bonus payments to managers in the banking and insurance sector may be reduced if the corporation is in financial trouble. At the EU level, a limit on bonus payments to managers in the banking sector has been established.

The criticism regarding the German two-tier board system and in particular regarding codetermination (which is an obstacle for foreign investors) may be partly justified. In particular, German codetermination is no guarantee against excessive remuneration of managers or against strikes. Employee representatives are not independent since they have to represent the interests of trade unions and employees.

3.4 Criticism of one-tier board systems

Sometimes, Anglo-American one-tier boards do not work as they should. One-tier systems face two main problems. First, board members make decisions but then also control them. Secondly, non-executive members of the board may not be fully independent. The Enron scandal highlighted deficiencies in the US corporate governance system. Enron had no structure for control of management. Following the scandal, new proposals to improve one-tier governance systems have been put forward, and have been implemented in the United Kingdom.

It is recommended that at least half of the board of directors should be independent, non-executive members and that the positions of independent board chairman and CEO should be separated. The independent board chairmen will ensure that meetings are held in an environment in which there is a clear understanding of the different tasks of the board members and in which problems and questions can be discussed frankly and openly.[18] In the United States, the separation of the two positions has not been implemented. It has been recommended that the same objective duties and standards of care and skill should be imposed on all directors, whether executive or non-executive. Employee interests are not specifically addressed. However, the UK Corporation Act states that management must consider and disclose employee interests in what has been interpreted as "interest of the corporation". Auditors in the United Kingdom are now

---

16   *Lieder/Fischer*, The Say-on-Pay Movement – Evidence from a Comparative Perspective, ECFR 2011, 414 *et seq.*
17   *Lieder/Fischer*, ECFR 2011, 403, 411.
18   *Jungmann*, ECFR 2006, 454, 461.

elected by the shareholders rather than by the board, which adds a level of supervision of the board.

3.5 Interim conclusion

One-tier systems have similarities with two-tier systems. The separation of the positions of CEO and chairman of the board and the growing tendency to prescribe a certain number of independent non-executives on the board is similar to the two-tier system. Triggered by listing requirements of powerful stock exchanges, today audit committees contribute to the assessment of good corporate governance – which only can be guaranteed by independent supervisors asking questions and acting on the knowledge they have obtained.[19] A further improvement would be to introduce mandatory meetings between the auditors and supervisors, without any executives present.[20]

Recent studies have shown that neither of the board systems has been shown to be superior. The last study by Jungmann[21] compared the relationship between corporations' poor financial performance and the subsequent dismissal of their managers in the United Kingdom and Germany. No significant differences were found: about the same number of managers in each country was dismissed following a corporation's poor financial performance. We suggest this is evidence that both the one-tier system and the two-tier system are effective methods of control.

3.6 Liability and corporate governance rules

Under Section 93 of the German Stock Corporation Act, directors may be held liable by the company if they violate their duties. In particular, directors are liable if dividends or contributions are paid back to the shareholders in violation of the law, if shares are issued without full payment or if payments are made after insolvency. However, the law grants directors a broad discretion on the management of their company. Under the business judgment rule, directors may take entrepreneurial risks provided they carefully assess these risks.

Following several corruption cases, compliance issues have become more important in Germany. Under Section 91 of the Stock Corporation Act, directors must establish a structure to identify developments which could jeopardise the corporation. German scholars take the view that this provision only specifies the general obligation of the directors to protect the corporation from future harms. For this purpose, the directors should establish and document risk management structures. The details of such risk management systems are not stipulated by law – they depend on the size and nature of the corporation activities. In summary, risk management systems should specify who is in charge of the system, how they are supervised and which risks are relevant. The system must address how the risks will be assessed and how they can be avoided and targeted. It should make clear how information regarding the risks is disclosed to the board members.

---

19   *Hopt/Leyens*, ECFR 2004, 137, 161.
20   *Ibid.*
21   *Jungmann*, ECFR 2006, 427 *et seq.*

Within the business judgment rule, directors may be obliged to introduce compliance programmes and to appoint compliance officers. This obligation exceeds the aforementioned duty to establish risk management systems. Compliance programmes and officers are mandatory in the banking and insurance sector. German scholars are reluctant to suggest mandatory regulation of compliance in other industries, instead proposing mandatory compliance programmes and officers for large corporations.[22] In this respect, German law is not as strict as US law. The US Sarbanes-Oxley Act contains detailed and binding provisions on compliance. The introduction of compliance programmes and officers in Germany may serve to provide evidence in court proceedings that a director has fulfilled his duties and is also a convincing marketing tool. Corporations that do not introduce compliance programmes, or whose compliance programmes are inadequate, could face significantly higher premiums.

Directors cannot be held liable if their actions are based on valid shareholders' decisions.

Creditors of a company may sue its directors directly if they cannot obtain damages from the company and if the damage is caused by a failure of the directors.

The liability of members of the supervisory board is governed by Section 116 of the Stock Corporation Act and follows basically the same rules as for directors.

In a case of director's liability, members of the supervisory board must bring action against the director. Shareholders can force a company to claim damages against the directors (Section 147 of the Stock Corporation Act). Shareholders owning at least 1% of all shares or €100,000 in par value may ask the court to grant permission for actions against a director in order to pay damages to the corporation (Section 148 of the act).

The discharge of directors and of members of the supervisory board is a regular item on the agenda at the shareholders' annual meeting. However, such discharge, if granted, is not considered as a discharge of liability.

As in many other countries, Germany has introduced a Corporate Governance Codex, which contains 'soft law' rather than hard rules and applies only to listed corporations (with the recommendation that corporations that are not listed should also accept the codex). Most codex provisions are recommendations only. Corporations may deviate from the recommendations if they explain the reason for deviation ('comply or explain'). Some provisions contain suggestions. Corporations may deviate from the suggestions without explanation.

The codex provides that the management board is responsible for managing the enterprise independently, that is, only in the interest of the enterprise, thus taking into account the interests of the shareholders, the employees and other stakeholders, with the objective of sustainable creation of value. Thus, shareholder primacy is not the only value to be pursued. The stakeholders mentioned in the codex include employees as well as the public. This approach is also found in the United Kingdom: the Company Act 2006 introduced "enlightened shareholder value". This includes

---

22   *Spindler*, in: Münchener Kommentar zum Aktiengesetz, 3. ed., no. 39 zu sec. 91; *Schäfer/Baumann*, Compliance Organisationen und Sanktionen bei Verstößen, NJW 2011, 3601.

the interests of a corporation's employees. Both concepts require directors to guarantee that the corporation acts as a "good corporate citizen"[23] and pursues not only the maximisation of profits but also stable growth in order to promote the success of the corporation, which will prove useful to both shareholders and stakeholders.[24]

The provisions of the codex address issues such as:

- the composition of the management board;
- the remuneration of directors (which will also be based on the long-term performance of the corporation);
- filling management positions with respect to diversity and gender;
- the tasks of the directors (in particular, in relation to risk management and compliance with regulations);
- the composition of the supervisory board and its committees (in particular, in relation to the independence of its members and to further training and education);
- the tasks of members of the supervisory board (in particular, in relation to setting compensation packages for directors);
- the remuneration of members of the supervisory board (which will also be based on the long-term performance of the corporation);
- cooperation between the directors and members of the supervisory board;
- avoiding conflicts of interest;
- disclosure of information; and
- reporting and audit of financial statements (in particular, in relation to auditors' independence).[25]

Although the codex is only soft law, any violation of it may lead to liability of the directors or members of the supervisory board. Under Section 161 of the Stock Corporation Act, directors and members of the supervisory board must declare on a yearly basis whether they have complied with the codex and explain the reasons for any deviations. False or incomplete statements may result in liability and any discharge vote of the shareholders will be void. The codex reflects best practice and a violation of it may trigger liability under Sections 93 and 116 of the Stock Corporation Act.[26] Failure to comply with the codex may damage a corporation's reputation and discourage investors from acquiring shares, and may create an obstacle to being listed.[27]

The potential liability risk for directors and members of the supervisory board can be protected through insurance. Corporations can take out directors' and officers' liability insurance policies for their directors. Under Section 93 of the Stock Corporation Act, a deductible of at least 10% of the loss, up to at least one-and-a-half

---

23   See *Schall*, Corporate Governance after the Death of the King, the Origins of the Separation of Powers in Companies, ECFR 2011, 488. He stresses that no stakeholder will enforce its interests.

24   *Kort*, Standardization of Company Law in Germany, Other EU Member States and Turkey by Corporate Governance Rules, ECFR 2008, 391 *et seq.*

25   Source: www.ecgi.org/codes/all_codes.php.

26   *Kort*, ECFR 2008, 416.

27   As it is the case in the UK: see Kort, ECFR 2008, 410.

times the fixed annual compensation of the members of the management board, must be agreed. A similar insurance can be provided for members of the supervisory board. The Corporate Governance Codex recommends that a similar deductible is agreed in any directors' and officers' liability policy too. The introduction of deductibles to be paid by the directors may act as a deterrent to directors and members of the supervisory board violating their duties. However, in many jurisdictions this threat has only limited effect since the risk to pay deductibles can also be insured.

One major issue is corporate social responsibility – that is, whether corporations should be obliged to protect not only the interests of their shareholders but also the interests of their stakeholders (addressed in the codex, see above) and whether corporations may sponsor and pursue social activities such as sports, culture and healthcare. Many scholars approve such activities if they are not in conflict with the corporate profile, if they do not excessively burden the financial capabilities of the corporation and if no conflicts of interest are created.

Corruption cases have shown that reporting irregularities (whistle-blowing) can be relevant for improving good corporate governance. Neither the law nor the codex regulates the protection of whistle-blowers. However, German courts and the Court of Justice of the European Union have decided that whistle-blowers must not be dismissed or face other negative measures.

4. France

In France, two management systems are available to a public corporation (SA): a board of directors, headed by a chairman who is both the chairman of the board and the CEO; or a management board, which is controlled by a supervisory board.

The system commonly used is a board of directors, headed by a chairman who is both the chairman of the board and the CEO. The chairman may ask the board to appoint a general manager to assist him. The position of the chairman in this traditional system is very strong and the removal of a chairman is rare.[28]

New regulations were introduced by a law of May 15 2001 in response to scandals such as the Elf-Aquitaine case, where executives received excessive remuneration, and the Credit Lyonnais case, where the management committed obvious errors. The new regulations are similar to the UK regulations. Under the new regime:

- it is possible to separate the duties of the chairman of the board of directors and the managing director, thus weakening the power of the chairman;
- the total number of directors in a corporation is limited to 18 and one single person must not hold more than five board positions;
- specific qualification standards are imposed for directors;
- at least one-third of directors must be independent non-executives. Members coming from financing banks are not considered to be independent;
- new forms of meetings (by video conference) are introduced and committees are established (previously in France, board meetings were not held frequently enough or of sufficient duration); and
- remuneration of board members must be disclosed.

---

28 *Storck*, Corporate Governance à la Francais – Current Trends, ECFR 2004, 43.

The alternative management structure, a management board controlled by a supervisory board, is similar in concept to the German two-tier structure. Few major French corporations use this two-tier system.

France has introduced a mandatory percentage of board positions to be filled by women. From 2014, 20% of board members in listed corporations must be women, and the figure increases to 40% in 2017. Corporations that do not comply risk the resolutions electing board members being declared void.

In France, employee participation is secured since two members of the workers' council attend meetings of the board, or the supervisory board in the two-tier system, in an advisery capacity. The workers' council has the right to participate in shareholders' meetings.

French law also protects social and environmental interests. Information regarding the social and environmental consequences of a listed corporation's activities must be disclosed in its annual management report. The report must specify the measures the corporation has taken with respect to sustainable development.

Members of the management are liable towards the corporation with regard to diligent performance of their duties. Liability with respect to creditors may arise if the directors act outside their powers or if incorrect managerial decisions result in insolvency. There are approximately 3,000 cases against directors each year.[29] In particular, managers are liable for continuing to run a business when it does not have adequate legal capital. Directors are held personally liable if they do not ensure that the corporation's taxes or social security payments are made. Directors may be held personally liable in bankruptcy proceedings if they had used the corporation as a shield against personal liability.

In a two-tier structure, members of the supervisory board are liable for any negligent or tortuous acts committed by the corporation. They are not liable for the acts of the directors.

Liability actions against directors may be brought by the CEO in his capacity as the legal representative of the corporation. Any shareholder may commence actions against the director in order to pay damages to the corporation; a quorum is not required. The discharge of directors and of members of the supervisory board is a regular item on the agenda of the annual shareholders' meeting. However, if such discharge is granted, it is not a discharge of liability. Liability risks may be covered by directors' and officers' liability insurance.

France has introduced a Corporate Governance Codex. It contains soft law rather than hard rules, and applies only to listed corporations. The codex[30] explicitly states that the board should act in the interest and on behalf of all the shareholders. Members of the board must be motivated by common aims. It is recommended that the board's strategy and actions are consistent with the sustainable development of the corporation. From this perspective, the codex encourages the management to pay specific attention to social and environmental factors and to give these the same

---

29   *Lutter/Drygala*, Legal Capital in Europe, ECFR Special Volume No. 1, de Gruyter, Berlin, 2006, 242 *et seq.*
30   Source: www.ecgi.org/codes/all_codes.php.

level of consideration as it does to consolidated accounts. The provisions of the codex address issues such as:

- the independence of board members (in particular, of the CEO);
- the independence of supervising members and the separation of the function of the board's chairman from that of the CEO in one-tier boards:
- the remuneration of directors, which must not be excessive, must be linked to medium and long-term trends in the company's intrinsic worth and the relative performance of its share price, and must be consistent with the corporation's average employee compensation, dividend and earnings. Executive directors should personally hold (at risk) a significant amount of company shares and that information on their shareholdings must be provided to shareholders;
- filling management positions with respect to diversity and gender;
- the composition of the board and its committees (in particular, with respect to the independence of its members and to further training and education);
- the board of directors' internal rules and procedures (in particular, the frequency of meetings);
- avoiding conflicts of interest;
- disclosure of information; and
- reporting and audit of financial statements (in particular, with respect to the independence of the auditor).

The French Data Protection Agency[31] provides guidelines for whistle-blowers. Employees who report irregularities regarding accounts and corruption are protected against penalties, dismissals or other negative measures. Anonymous reporting is not encouraged. Persons affected by the whistle-blowing must be informed.

5.   Italy

In Italy, a public corporation (SPA) may be managed either under the traditional system (already in force before the reform of corporation law in January 2004) or under the new alternatives that are now available: the 'dualistic system' and the 'monistic system'.

Under the traditional system, corporations are managed by a sole director or by a board of directors. These directors are elected by the shareholders and may be removed by the shareholders at any time (although they are entitled to damages, to be paid by the corporation, if they are removed without good cause). The corporation's management is controlled by a board of statutory auditors, consisting of three or five members who are chartered accountants and who have been appointed by the shareholders. Auditors must be independent, and employees cannot become members of the board of auditors. The term for statutory auditors must not exceed three financial years.

Under the new dualistic system, the corporation is managed by a management board. A supervisory board, appointed by the shareholders, appoints and removes

---

31   See www.cnil.fr/.

members of the management board, approves the balance sheet and may bring actions for responsibility against the members of the management board. Unlike the traditional system,[32] members of the supervisory board are not required to be accountants. Their duties are less strict than those for auditors under the traditional system. Members of the supervisory board are not permitted individually to investigate the corporation's records.

Under the new monistic system, the corporation is managed by a board of directors, elected by the shareholders. An internal committee appointed by members controls the management, in particular by supervising the suitability of the organisational structure of the corporation and its system for internal control. At least one-third of its members must be independent, non-executive members. The supervising members of the board are directly involved in management decisions.

Italian law does not provide for codetermination of employees on the boards.

One disadvantage of the new two and one-tier models of governance is that there is no body of consolidated judicial decisions on them. This makes adopting one of the new governance models more risky for corporations.[33] Another disadvantage is that the new models require more persons than the traditional model, which adds cost. With these disadvantages, it is not surprising that very few Italian corporations (less than 1%[34]) have opted for one of the new governance models to date. In the future, the two-tier system may prove useful for corporations with external investors, as the investors may be attracted by the power to place a representative on the supervising board.

Directors may be held liable in relation to the corporation if they breach their duties. Shareholders owning 20% of the total shares may bring an action on behalf of the corporation. Even if the action against the director(s) is brought by minority shareholders, any damages awarded must be paid to the corporation.[35] It is hard for shareholders to obtain information in relation to these actions, as Italian law does not grant inspection rights to shareholders.[36] Many shareholders are deterred from starting an action due to the risk of bearing the legal expenses if they lose and no possibility of being reimbursed for individually agreed attorney fees if they win.[37]

It is possible to waive liability claims against directors by shareholders' resolution, provided the resolution is not opposed by shareholders representing at least 20% of the corporation's share capital. Liability risks can be covered by directors' and officers' liability insurance.

Italy has also introduced a Corporate Governance Codex. The codex contains soft law rather than hard rules, and applies only to listed corporations. The provisions of the codex address issues such as:

---

32   See *Ghezzi/Malberti*, The Two-tier-model and the One-tier-model of Corporate Governance in the Italian Reform of Corporate Law, ECFR 2008, 20 *et seq.*
33   *Ibid*, 25.
34   *Ibid*, 40.
35   *Giudici*, Representative Litigation in Italian Capital Markets: Italian Derivative Suits and (if ever) Securities Class Actions, ECFR 2009, 249; Latella, Shareholder Derivative Suits: A Comparative Analysis and the Implications of the European Shareholders' Rights Directive, ECFR 2009, 317 *et seq.*
36   *Giudici*, ECFR 2009, 249, 253; Latella, ECFR 2009, 317, 321.
37   *Giudici*, ECFR 2009, 249, 253.

- the independence of board members (in particular, of the supervising members in one-tier boards);
- the remuneration of directors, which will be defined in a way that aligns their interests with pursuing the priority objective of the creation of value for the shareholders in a medium to long-term timeframe. A significant part of the remuneration should be linked to achieving specific performance objectives, possibly including non-economic objectives. The remuneration of non-executive directors will be proportionate to the commitment required from each of them;
- the internal control and risk management system;
- the composition of the supervisory board, and its committees in the case of two-tier boards;
- disclosure of information; and
- reporting and audit of financial statements (in particular, with respect to the election and independence of statutory auditors).[38]

Corporate social responsibility issues are discussed within the legal community, but are not yet governed by statutory law or the provisions of the Codex.

There are no special provisions in Italian law to protect whistle-blowers. However, whistle-blowers who report irregularities and suffer dismissal or other negative measures as a result may sue for damages.

6. Spain

In Spain, a public corporation (SA) may be managed by a sole director, by two directors acting jointly, by several directors acting jointly and severally, or by a board of directors, which must consist of a minimum of three members. The board of directors system is commonly used in Spain.

Directors, who may be natural persons or legal entities, are appointed by the shareholders for a maximum of six years and may be re-appointed for subsequent maximum six-year terms. Directors may be removed by the shareholders even without good cause. The board of directors must have a chairman and a secretary. It may appoint one of its members to act as managing director. It may transfer power to an executive committee.

Under the Spanish legal regime, codetermination of employees on the board of directors is required only for large public sector corporations and charitable saving banks. Spanish law also provides that listed corporations must take measures to increase the percentage of women on boards of directors.

Directors may be held liable by the company if they violate their duties. Shareholders representing at least 5% of the share capital have the right to commence actions against directors on behalf of the corporation for breach of duties. Damages are paid to the company. It is not possible to discharge directors by shareholders' resolution. Liability risks can be covered by directors' and officers' liability insurance.

---

38   Source: www.ecgi.org/codes/all_codes.php.

Spain has introduced a Corporate Governance Codex, which contains soft law rather than hard rules and applies only to listed corporations. The codex[39] explicitly states that shareholders' interests should not be pursued at any price, that is, without regard to other groups involved in the company or the community in which it operates. The interests of stakeholders, such as employees, suppliers, creditors and customers, should also be taken into account, as well as social responsibility principles.

The provisions of the codex address such matters as:

* the independence of board members (in particular, of the CEO);
* the independence of supervising members and the control of the board's chairman, if that person is also the CEO;
* the remuneration of directors. Remuneration in the form of shares should be linked to the company's performance. Membership of pension schemes should be confined to executive directors. External directors' remuneration should be sufficient to compensate them for their work but should not be so high that it compromises their independence. In the case of variable awards, remuneration policies should include safeguards to ensure they reflect the professional performance of the beneficiaries and not simply the general progress of the markets or the company's sector, atypical or exceptional transactions or similar circumstances;
* filling management positions with respect to gender;
* the composition of the board and its committees (in particular, with respect to size, independence of its members, and further training and education);
* the board of directors' internal rules and procedures (in particular, the frequency of meetings);
* risk control and management;
* avoiding conflicts of interest;
* disclosure of information; and
* reporting and audit of financial statements (in particular, with respect to the independence of the auditor). In order to improve internal audits the audit committee may establish special channels for employees to report irregularities.

7.   The Netherlands

Two forms of Dutch corporation are available – the close corporation (BV) and the public corporation (NV). Both are managed by a board of managing directors, who are appointed and removed by the shareholders.

Supervisory directors are optional under Dutch law. These directors are appointed and removed by the shareholders and advise and supervise the managing directors. A supervisory director must not simultaneously serve as a managing director.

Corporations that are governed by the large corporations regime must have a supervisory board. A corporation will be subject to the large corporations regime if:

* its issued capital of the corporation is at least €16 million;

---

39   *Ibid.*

- it and/or an affiliated corporation has set up a works council; and
- it and its affiliates have at least 100 employees in the Netherlands.

Members of the supervisory board are nominated by the existing supervisory board and appointed by the shareholders. The shareholders and the works council may propose new members. The works council may submit nominations for one-third of the supervisory board members. Codetermination of employees in Dutch supervisory boards is not as strong as in Germany, where at least one-third (and under certain circumstances, one-half) of the supervisory board is elected directly by the corporation's employees. The shareholders may reject nominations by the existing supervisory board, and may remove all (but not single) members of the supervisory board. The supervisory board appoints and removes the managing directors and must approve important management decisions in advance.

It is planned to introduce a mandatory percentage (30%, starting 2016) of women board members in the Netherlands.

Corporation directors have a broad discretion in their business decisions (business judgment rule). They must act in the best interest of the corporation. Best interest includes the interests of all connected parties, including shareholders, employees and, in some circumstances, creditors of the corporation. Directors may be held liable in relation to the corporation if they breach their duties ('improper management'). Lawsuits against directors of close corporations are not common in the Netherlands. In order to establish improper management, shareholders owning at least 10% of the shares, public prosecutors or trade unions may request court proceedings to commence an inquiry. The open standard of the term 'improper management' means that these proceedings can be (mis)used for abusive purposes.[40] Directors may be discharged by shareholders' resolution. However, this discharge may be annulled by a court if it finds that the discharge violates good faith. Liability risks can be covered by directors' and officers' liability insurance.

The Netherlands has introduced a Corporate Governance Codex. The codex[41] explicitly states that a corporation is a long-term alliance between the various parties involved in the company. The stakeholders are the groups and individuals who, directly or indirectly, influence – or are influenced by – how the company's objects are met – that is, employees, shareholders and other lenders, suppliers, customers, the public sector, and civil society. The board members have the overall responsibility to balance these interests, generally with a view to ensuring the continuity of the enterprise, while the company endeavours to create long-term shareholder value. Board members should take into account the interests of the various stakeholders, including corporate social responsibility issues that are relevant to the corporation. The codex contains soft law rather than hard rules. It is based on a two-tier board system and applies only to listed corporations. The provisions of the codex issues such as:

- the composition of the management board;
- the remuneration of directors. The remuneration policy must serve the

---

40   *Vermeulen/Zetzsche*, The Use and Abuse of Investor Suits, ECFR 2010, 13 *et seq.*
41   Source: www.ecgi.org/codes/all_codes.php.

interests of the company and its affiliated enterprises, in other words, must be aimed at creating long-term value;

- filling management positions with respect to gender, diversity and age;
- the tasks of the directors, in particular concerning risk management and control;
- the composition of the supervisory board and its committees (in particular, with respect to the independence of its members and to further training and education);
- the tasks of the supervisory board members (in particular, with respect to determining compensation packages for the directors);
- the remuneration of the supervisory board members, which should not be based on the success of the corporation and should not include shares of the corporation or loans;
- cooperation between the directors and the members of the supervisory board;
- avoiding conflicts of interest;
- disclosure of information;
- protecting whistle-blowers;
- reporting and audit of financial statements (in particular, with respect to the independence of the auditor); and
- in case of one-tier boards, the majority of the board should be non-executive, independent members and the chairman should not be an executive officer.

Dutch law and the provisions of the codex do not require reporting on corporate social responsibility issues.

8.   Austria

The Austrian governance system is similar to the German system. An Austrian public corporation (AG) is represented by a board of managers, which is appointed by the supervisory board for a maximum term of five years and can be removed only for good cause.

The supervisory board is appointed by the shareholders and consists of a minimum of three members. The total number of members depends on the amount of share capital. Austrian law recognises codetermination. One-third of the supervisory board members are appointed by the works council if certain conditions (size, number of employees) are met.

The Austrian liability rules are similar to those in Germany. Directors may be held liable by the company if they violate their duties. Shareholders who own at least 10% of all shares may ask the court to grant permission for an action against a director in order to pay damages to the corporation. The discharge of directors and members of the supervisory board is a regular item on the agenda at the shareholders' annual meeting. However, if granted, this discharge is not a discharge of liability. Liability risks can be covered by a directors' and officers' liability insurance.

Austria has introduced a Corporate Governance Codex. The codex contains soft law rather than hard rules, and applies only to listed corporations (with the recommendation that non-listed corporations should also apply the provisions of the codex). The Codex[42] explicitly states that it aims to establish a system of management and control of companies and groups that is accountable and is geared to creating sustainable, long-term value. This objective best serves the needs of all parties whose well-being depends on the success of the corporation. The provisions of the Codex address such matters as:

- the composition of the management board ;
- the remuneration of directors, which should also contain components based on the sustainable, long-term and multi-year performance of the corporation. Measurable performance criteria for variable remuneration components should be established, as well as a limit on severance payments. Remuneration should not entice directors to take unreasonable risks;
- the tasks of the directors (in particular, concerning risk management and compliance with regulations);
- the composition and size of the supervisory board and its committees (eg, nomination and compensation committee), in particular with respect to the independence of its members, to diversity, age and gender issues, and to the remuneration of the supervisory board members, which should be proportionate to the responsibilities and scope of their work, and with the economic circumstances of the enterprise;
- the tasks of the supervisory board members (in particular, with respect to determining compensation packages for the directors);
- cooperation between the directors and the members of the supervisory board;
- avoiding conflicts of interest;
- disclosure of information (including information on directors' remuneration); and
- reporting and audit of financial statements (in particular, with respect to the independence of the auditor).

Expenditure on social, environmental and ethical issues must be included in the annual accounts.

Whistle-blowers must not be dismissed for reporting irregularities.

9. Conclusion

The European nations are working to improve corporate governance. As the questions that arise in company law are similar in every country, despite the details of the different governance systems, national legislators often find similar solutions. However, it is doubtful whether future corporate governance standards will be exactly the same throughout the European Union – national corporate laws vary in some respects due to different historical, cultural and social-economic backgrounds.[43]

One focus of current discussion is compliance. In general, compliance is less strictly regulated in European states than it is in the United States. It remains to be seen whether legal rules similar to the US Sarbanes-Oxley Act will be introduced in (all) European states.

---

42   *Ibid.*
43   *Kort*, ECFR 2008, 419.

Sarbanes-Oxley requirements and the implementation of US corporate governance controls: an overview for non-US corporates

Zabihollah Rezaee
University of Memphis

1.   Introduction

The wave of financial scandals at the turn of the 21st century and their persistence in recent years, coupled with the perceived inadequacy of market correction mechanisms, significantly eroded investor confidence. The Sarbanes-Oxley Act of 2002[1] and the Dodd-Frank Act of 2010[2] were enacted in efforts to rebuild investor confidence and improve corporate governance, and the safety, integrity and efficiency of the capital markets. More than 10 years after the passage of the Sarbanes-Oxley Act and two years after the enactment of the Dodd-Frank Act, the efficacy and sustainability of both acts have been challenged. This chapter discusses the regulatory reforms enacted in the United States in the past decade; examines provisions of the regulatory reforms and related implementation rules; addresses the global reach of the regulatory reforms and related rules; and discusses the efficacy of the regulatory reforms in terms of their expected benefits, compliance costs and sustainability.

2.   Regulatory reforms

The regulatory reforms (Sarbanes-Oxley Act and Dodd-Frank Act) passed by Congress and the related federal securities laws established by regulators to implement their provisions are intended to protect investors of public companies from receiving misleading financial reports and to improve investor confidence in the integrity and efficiency of the capital markets. The federal securities laws are primary, disclosure-based statutes that require public companies to file a periodic report with the Securities and Exchange Commission (SEC) and to disclose certain information to shareholders to inform their investment and voting decisions. Congress responded to the financial scandals of the late 1990s and early 2000s by passing the Sarbanes-

---

1   Sarbanes-Oxley Act of 2002, The Public Company Accounting Reform and Investor Protection Act (HR 3763). Available at: www.whitehouse.gov.
2   Dodd-Frank Wall Street Reform and Consumer Protection Act of 2010, Pub L 111-203 (2010).

Oxley Act, which expanded the role of federal statutes in corporate governance by providing measures to improve corporate governance, financial reporting and audit activities. The aftermath of the global 2007 to 2009 financial crisis prompted Congress to pass the Dodd-Frank Act to minimise the risk of future financial crises and systemic distress, by empowering regulators to require higher capital requirements and establish new regulatory regimes and corporate governance measures for large financial services firms. These regulatory reforms and their impacts on corporate governance, financial reporting and audit activities are discussed in the next section.

3.   Sarbanes-Oxley Act

The Sarbanes-Oxley Act was signed into law on July 30 2002, to reinforce corporate accountability and rebuild investor confidence in public financial reports. The act was intended to shift the power balance between a company's shareholders, directors and management. In the post-Sarbanes-Oxley Act era, shareholders have been more proactive in monitoring and scrutinising their corporations and thus have heightened their expectations of directors' performance on their behalf. Directors have strengthened their commitment and accountability in fulfilling their fiduciary duties by overseeing management's strategic plans, decisions and performance and spending more time on their duties, particularly in overseeing the financial reporting process. Management has stepped up its efforts in achieving sustainable shareholder value creation and enhancement, and improving the reliability of financial reports through executive certification of internal controls and financial statements. Executive certifications, vigilant oversight of the audit committee and improved audit quality together have significantly enhanced the quality of public financial information and investor confidence in the capital markets.

Early evidence indicates that the effects of Sarbanes-Oxley Act legislation are positive and should remain positive over the long term for the US economy.[3] The provisions of the act that were not previously practised by public companies and that are intended to benefit all companies include:

- creating the Public Company Accounting Oversight Board to oversee the audit of public companies and to improve the ineffective self-regulatory environment of the auditing profession;
- improving corporate governance through more independent and vigilant boards of directors and responsible executives;
- enhancing the quality, reliability, transparency and timeliness of financial disclosures through executive certifications of both financial statements and internal controls;
- prohibiting nine types of non-audit services considered to have an adverse effect on auditor independence and objectivity;
- regulating the conduct of auditors, legal counsel and financial analysts, and their potential conflicts of interest;

---

3   Jain, PK and Z Rezaee. 2006. The Sarbanes-Oxley Act of 2002 and Security Market Behavior: Early Evidence. *Contemporary Accounting Research* 23 (3). 629–654.

- increasing civil and criminal penalties for violations of security laws; and
- rebuilding public trust and investor confidence in public financial reports and financial markets.

4. Dodd-Frank Act

Congress responded to the 2007 to 2009 financial crisis by passing the Dodd-Frank Act, which is over 2,300 pages long. The act's provisions mainly govern financial services firms such as banks, hedge funds, credit rating agencies and the derivatives market. The act directs regulators to establish about 240 rules to implement its provisions and authorises the establishment of an oversight council to monitor the systemic risk of financial institutions and the creation of a consumer protection bureau within the Federal Reserve. The act is intended to minimise the risk of future financial crises and systemic distress by empowering regulators to set more effective corporate governance and higher capital requirements for financial services firms. It also establishes new regulatory regimes for large financial services firms and requires regulatory and market structures for financial derivatives, demanding the systemic risk assessment and monitoring of financial markets. The act created a Financial Services Oversight Council to identify and monitor systematic risk in the financial system. The provisions of the Dodd-Frank Act that address the corporate governance practices of financial services firms, which will be discussed in detail in the next section, introduce the following:

- shareholders are empowered with a non-binding vote ('say on pay' and 'say on golden parachutes') on executive compensation, at least every three years, with the right to vote on the frequency of say on pay every one, two or three years;
- institutional investment managers are required to disclose at least annually how they voted on say on pay and its frequency and say on golden parachute votes;
- all US public companies must incorporate so-called 'claw-back' provisions into incentive compensation arrangements for executive officers. Public companies implement and report on their policies and practices for recouping payments to current and former executives when published financial statements are subsequently restated (restatements of financial statements) following material non-compliance with financial reporting standards;
- members of the compensation committee must be independent and the committee must assess the independence of its advisers;
- incentive-based arrangements that may encourage inappropriate risk taking by management must be disclosed;
- brokers may not vote without customer instruction on some governance issues such as say on pay, say on golden parachute and board elections;
- revisions concerning the ability of brokers to vote on proxies without instruction from beneficial holders thus prohibiting brokers from voting on compensation matters; and
- provisions on shareholders' ability to nominate director candidates.

The Dodd-Frank Act was passed to minimise the likelihood of future financial crises and systemic distress of financial institutions by empowering regulators to set higher capital requirements, establishing systemic risk assessment and monitoring, developing new regulatory regimes for large financial firms and mandating regulatory and market structures for financial derivatives. Ineffective corporate governance and inadequate regulation for financial institutions can be detrimental to the global economy and economic growth and stability. Proper and timely implementation of the Dodd-Frank Act provisions may prove to be instrumental in strengthening sound and efficient operation of financial institutions worldwide.

Figure 1 provides a comparison of the purposes, provisions and implementation rules of the Sarbanes-Oxley Act and the Dodd-Frank Act.

Figure 1: Comparison of the Sarbanes-Oxley Act with the Dodd-Frank Act

Act/provisions	Dodd-Frank Act	Sarbanes-Oxley Act
Number of pages	2,300	65
Reason for enactment	The 2007 to 2009 financial crisis.	A wave of financial scandals at the turn of the 21st century.
Purpose	Rebuild public trust in the financial system, which had been eroded by a wave of subprime mortgage and other bank irregularities.	Rebuild investor confidence in public financial information and capital markets, which had been eroded by a rash of financial scandals.
Proposed implementation rules	240 rules to be established.	11 titles that describe specific mandates for financial reporting.

continued on next page

5. Key provisions of the regulatory reforms

The primary purposes of both the Sarbanes-Oxley Act and the Dodd-Frank Act are to:

- enhance reliability of public financial information;
- restore investor confidence and public trust in public financial information and the financial markets; and
- protect investors and consumers.

Both acts were passed by the US Congress in response to the wave of financial scandals, irregularities, fraud, bad practices and crises. Provisions of both acts address

Act/provisions	Dodd-Frank Act	Sarbanes-Oxley Act
Provisions	Say on pay and say on golden parachutes. Incorporate so-called 'claw-back' provisions into incentive compensation arrangements for executive officers. Members of the compensation committee must be independent. Prohibit brokers to vote on compensation matters.	Guiding principles for corporate governance. Improve the quality, reliability and transparency of financial reporting. CEOs and CFOs to certify financial reports. Ban on personal loans by companies.
Affected organisations and individuals	Private investor groups that oversee $150 million or more in assets. Financial institutions. Non-financial companies.	All investors and organisations.
Timeframe for implementation	Currently establishing regulations; full implementation by end 2012.	Implemented.
New entities	Financial Services Oversight Council. Consumer Protection Bureau.	Public Company Accounting Oversight Board.

different aspects of public companies, their governance, financial reports and related financial markets, from consumer credit to investor protection and from mandatory corporate governance practices to corporate governance education. This section examines some key provisions of both the Sarbanes-Oxley Act and the Dodd-Frank Act.[4]

5.1 Corporate governance

Corporate governance has been and will continue to be an important issue for policymakers, regulators and businesses. In the aftermath of the 2007 to 2009 global

---

4   Much of the discussion in this section comes from Z Rezaee. 2011. *Financial Services Firms: Governance. Regulations: Valuations, Mergers, and Acquisitions*. John Wiley & Sons, Inc., Hoboken, New Jersey.

financial crisis, countries worldwide have taken initiatives to improve their corporate governance. Robust corporate governance measures have been established to strengthen regulatory frameworks in order to promote economic stability, public trust and investor confidence in financial reports. The regulatory reforms in the United States (Sarbanes-Oxley Act and Dodd-Frank Act) are intended to strengthen board oversight of management, to link executive compensation schemes and practices with long-term sustainable performance and to encourage shareholders to take a more active role in the governance of their companies. Convergence in a set of globally accepted corporate governance measures can significantly improve the effectiveness of corporate governance worldwide.

The corporate governance provisions of the Sarbanes-Oxley Act introduce:

- enhanced audit committee responsibility for hiring, firing, compensating and overseeing auditors and preapproval of non-audit services;
- disclosure, in the periodic reports, of whether the audit committee has at least one member who is a financial expert and if not, why;
- chief executive officers (CEOs) and chief financial officers (CFOs) to certify the accuracy and completeness of quarterly and annual reports;
- management assessment and reporting of the effectiveness of disclosure controls and procedures;
- ban on personal loans by companies to their directors or executives other than certain regular consumer loans;
- establishment of procedures by each audit committee for receiving, retaining and handling complaints received by the company concerning accounting, internal controls or auditing matters;
- review of quarterly and annual reports (Forms 10-Q and 10-K) by officers;
- forfeiture by CEO or CFO of certain bonuses and profits when the company restates its financial statements due to its material non-compliance with any financial reporting requirements;
- ban on improper influence on the conduct of audits;
- prohibition on insider trades during pension fund blackout periods; and
- officers and directors' penalties for violations of securities laws or corporate misconduct.

The Dodd-Frank Act is expected to affect the corporate governance measures and practices of public companies in many ways, including:

- the link between pay and performance;
- the rationale for choosing a combined or separate role of CEO and the chair of the board of directors (CEO duality);
- policies and practices on the hedging of company securities;
- disclosure of the internal executive compensation ratio (the ratio of the annual total compensation of the CEO and the median annual total compensation of all employees excluding the CEO); and
- the establishment and maintenance of more effective, rewarding and protective whistle-blowing policies and procedures.

In 2011, the International Federation of Accountants made the following suggestions for improvements in global corporate governance in the post-regulatory era:

- the key driver and determinant of effective governance is the appropriate tone at the top set by directors and officers as well as organisation's leaders;
- principles-based, stakeholder-driven and lead governance measures offer a stronger likelihood of success than regulatory-led measures;
- global convergence in corporate governance measures is desirable;
- effective organisation governance mandates more board independence;
- directors should effectively and competently fulfil their fiduciary duties;
- professional risk and liability for directors need to be addressed;
- the primary responsibility of directors is performance rather than compliance;
- the overriding goal of governance is to protect the interests of all stakeholders rather than just shareholders by expanding from a shareholder to a wider stakeholder perspective;
- organisations should focus on business sustainability by improving all dimensions of an organisation's performance from social and environmental to economic performance;
- executive compensation should be aligned with the organisation's competitive sustainable performance;
- effective board oversight requires ongoing risk management and control;
- collaborative effort is required to address systemic risk;
- a set of globally accepted and coordinated systems of governance, regulation and oversight is needed to prevent future crises; and
- investors and other stakeholders should be attentive and more actively pursue their responsibilities.[5]

The proper and effective implementation of these suggestions could significantly strengthen the corporate governance of organisations of all types and sizes worldwide.

Taken together, the role of corporate governance, as addressed in the regulatory reforms, is to ensure that managers act in the best interests of the company and its shareholders and not themselves or the majority shareholders. Good corporate governance is committed to transparency, which should lead to an increase in capital inflows from domestic and foreign investors. Good corporate governance also implies the need for a network of monitoring and incentives set up by a company to ensure accountability of the board and management to shareholders and other stakeholders. The strongest form of defence against governance failure comes from an organisation's culture and behaviour. Effectiveness depends on employees' integrity and begins with the tone management sets at the top. In addition, boards should routinely oversee their own actions against the acceptable governance principles. Organisations should ensure their boards have the qualifications and

---

5   International Federation of Accountants. 2011. Integrating the Business Reporting Supply Chain (March 2011). Available at www.ifac.org.

experience to approve an organisation's strategy and to evaluate how it is executed and reported on.

The corporate governance structure is shaped by internal and external governance mechanisms, as well as by policy interventions through regulations. Corporate governance mechanisms are viewed as a series of contracts that is designed to align the interests of management with those of the shareholders. The effectiveness of both internal and external corporate governance mechanisms depends on the trade-offs among these mechanisms and is related to their availability, the extent to which they are being used, whether their marginal benefits exceed their marginal costs and the company's corporate governance structure. Countries worldwide have their own corporate governance measures and best practices, which are typically economic, political, cultural and legal. The global regulatory responses to corporate scandals and financial crises demand convergence in corporate governance across borders. The convergence is particularly important in the areas of investor rights and protections, board independence and responsibilities, and uniform financial disclosures. While complete convergence in corporate governance reforms may not be possible, uniform global corporate governance measures and cross-border standards enforcements should be promoted to improve efficiency and liquidity in the global capital markets. An unaddressed issue is whether cross-countries differences in corporate governance can be reconciled and whether full convergence in corporate governance is feasible.

5.2 Financial reporting provisions

The quality and reliability of financial reports, the effectiveness of internal control over financial reporting, and the credibility of audits of both financial statements are important in gaining public trust and investor confidence in public financial information and the capital markets. The board of directors, particularly the audit committee, is now more closely overseeing the financial reporting process. Management has stepped up its efforts in improving the reliability of financial reports through executive certification of internal controls and financial statements. Executive certifications of both financial statements under Sections 302 and 906 of the Sarbanes-Oxley Act, vigilant oversight of the audit committee under Section 301 of the Sarbanes-Oxley Act, management reporting on internal control in compliance with Section 404 (a) of the Sarbanes-Oxley Act, and audit opinion on both financial statements and internal controls together were designed to enhance the quality of public financial information and investor confidence in the capital markets.

Several provisions of the regulatory reforms (Sarbanes-Oxley Act and Dodd-Frank Act) address the quality, reliability, transparency and timeliness of public companies' financial reports:

- more vigilant oversight of the financial reporting process by the board of directors of public companies;
- the audit committee is required to oversee financial reports, internal controls and related audits;
- management (CEO, CFO) must certify the completeness and accuracy of financial reports;

- *pro forma* financial information must be presented in a manner that is not misleading and that is reconciled with published financial statements;
- the independent auditor must discuss accounting policies and practices as well as management-significant adjustments and estimates in the financial reporting process with the audit committee;
- disclosures of off-balance sheet arrangements (derivatives);
- disclosures of contractual obligations; and
- disclosure of incentive-based arrangements that may encourage inappropriate risk taking by management.

5.3 Internal control provisions

Policymakers, regulators, standard setters, the business community and the accounting profession have been debating the issue of mandatory internal control reporting for public companies for the past three decades. Traditionally, legislators, regulators and the accounting profession have advocated the establishment and maintenance of internal control systems by public companies and reporting on internal control systems by managers and auditors. Under the Sarbanes-Oxley Act and the Dodd-Frank Act, the adequacy and effectiveness of internal controls must be assessed and certified by management.

Section 302 of the Sarbanes-Oxley Act requires executives to certify the disclosure controls and procedures. Disclosure controls and procedures are accepted by the global business community and implemented without significant compliance burden or costs. Compliance with Section 302 is regarded as a cost-effective and sensible procedure that can be applied to organisations of all types, sizes and complexity to improve the quality of external disclosure. Under Section 301, the audit committee must oversee the management and independent auditor's work on internal control of financial reporting. Under Section 404(a), the management must state its responsibility for designing and maintaining effective internal control over financial reporting and its assessment of the effectiveness of those controls at the end of the company's most recent fiscal year. Management must document the effectiveness of internal control through testing related control activities and specify any limitations. When internal control is effective, material misstatements should be prevented, detected or corrected on a timely basis. Any material weaknesses identified in the internal control (or deficiencies that, taken together, result in a material weakness) must be disclosed in the management's report along with the actions taken to correct them.

Under Section 404(b) of the Sarbanes-Oxley Act, the independent auditor must verify and report on management's assessment of the company's internal control over financial reporting. The auditor's report may either be issued separately or be combined with an opinion on the financial statements, and should include an opinion on the effectiveness of the internal control. The three possible types of audit opinion on internal control are:

- an unqualified opinion if there is no material weakness in internal control;
- an adverse opinion if there is at least one material weakness or if there are deficiencies in the internal control system that together may result in a material weakness; and

- a disclaimer of opinion if the auditor cannot express an opinion due to scope limitation. Section 404 also directs the Public Company Accounting Oversight Board to issue guidance on the auditor report on internal control.

In its first report in 1987, the Committee of Sponsoring Organisations of the Treadway Commission stressed the importance of internal control in preventing and detecting fraudulent financial activities.[6] In its second report in 1992, *Internal Control – Integrated Framework*, the committee recommended that both the management and the independent auditors of public companies produce voluntary internal control reports.[7] It provided detailed guidance on the content of internal control reports, including the nature, objectives and components of internal control; the role of management, the audit committee and the independent auditor; and the limitation of internal control.

Taken together, the regulatory reforms in the United States require large public companies to prepare and publish integrated financial and internal control reports, which should include:

- the management report and certification of financial statements;
- the management report and certification of internal control over financial reporting;
- the independent auditor's opinion on fair and true presentation of financial statements;
- the independent auditor's opinion on the effectiveness of internal control over financial reporting; and
- the audit committee's review of the audited financial statements and both management and auditor reports on internal control over financial reporting.

The effectiveness of integrated financial and internal control reports depends on vigilant supervision by the board of directors, particularly the audit committee, a responsible and accountable managerial function by senior executives and a credible external audit function by the independent auditor.

(a) **Auditing provisions**

Current auditing standards require that independent auditors provide reasonable assurance that the financial statements are free from material misstatements, whether caused by error or fraud, to render an unqualified opinion on the financial statements. This level of reasonable assurance is regarded as a high level of assurance, but not absolute assurance. Reasonable assurance may mean different levels of assurance to different groups, such as investors, auditors and regulators. In the post-Enron era, investors expect independent auditors to discover and report on all

---

6   Committee of Sponsoring Organisations of the Treadway Commission (COSO). 1987. Report of the National Commission on Fraudulent Financial Reporting (October). Available at: www.coso.org/Publications/NCFFR.pdf.

7   Committee of Sponsoring Organisations of the Treadway Commission (COSO). 1992. *Internal Control – Integrated Framework*. COSO. Executive summary available at: www.coso.org/publications/executive_summary_integrated_framework.htm.

material misstatements, including errors, irregularities and fraud. On the other hand, independent auditors, in complying with their professional standards, provide reasonable assurance that financial statements are free from material misstatements. The central issue vital to the audit quality is the nature and extent of auditors' responsibility to detect financial statement fraud. Nevertheless, the gap between what auditors should be doing and what auditors are willing to accept and are capable of doing to discover fraud is widening.

The audit provisions of the Sarbanes-Oxley Act address the following functions and activities of independent auditors in the United States:

- establishment and operation of the Public Company Accounting Oversight Board, an independent, non-governmental agency;
- registration with the Public Company Accounting Oversight Board of public accounting firms that audit public companies;
- auditors must be appointed, compensated and overseen by the audit committee;
- many non-audit services are prohibited from being performed at the same time as an audit;
- rotation of the lead (or coordinating) audit partner and the lead review partner every five years;
- auditors report to the audit committee;
- prohibiting where the CEO or CFO was previously employed by the auditor;
- auditors' attestation to and reporting on management assessment of internal controls;
- limitations on partner compensation;
- disclosure of fees paid to the auditor in categories of audit, audit-related, tax and permissible non-audit services;
- requirements for preapproval of audit and permitted non-audit services by the audit committee;
- retention of audit work papers and documents for five years; and
- increased penalties for destruction of corporate audit records.

5.4 Corporate fraud and anti-fraud policies

High-quality financial information is the lifeblood of the capital markets and that quality can be adversely affected by the existence and persistence of financial reporting fraud. Financial reporting fraud is a severe threat to investor confidence in financial information and thus capital markets. The persistence of this fraud is still a significant concern for the business community and the accounting profession, and has eroded investor confidence in corporate reports. From Enron and WorldCom in 2001, to Madoff and Satyam in 2009, and Olympus in 2011, over the past decade financial reporting fraud has been a dominant news item. There has been ample evidence that financial reporting fraud has undermined the integrity and quality of financial reports and has contributed to substantial economic losses. Since the passage of the Sarbanes-Oxley Act, which was primarily intended to combat financial

---

8   Rezaee, Z and R Riley. 2009. *Financial Statement Fraud: Prevention and Detection.* 2nd edition. John Wiley & Sons, Inc., Hoboken, New Jersey.

reporting fraud, the Department of Justice has obtained nearly 1,300 fraud convictions.[8] Several of the act's provisions aim at reducing financial reporting fraud and thus improving reliability of financial reports. These provisions are:

- executives must certify the completeness and accuracy of financial statements in compliance with Sections 302 and 906 of the act;
- executives must certify and report on the effectiveness of internal control over financial reporting according to Section 404 of the act;
- under Section 301 of the act, the board of directors, particularly the audit committee, should set an appropriate 'tone at the top', promoting ethical and competent behaviour throughout the company;
- under Section 704 of the act, the SEC must analyse all enforcement actions involving violations of reporting requirements and restatements of financial statements over the previous five years to identify areas of reporting that are most susceptible to fraud;
- Section 804 of the act extends the Statute of Limitations to recover for a private action for securities fraud to the earlier of two years after the date of discovery or five years after the fraudulent activities;
- under Section 906 of the act, the maximum penalties for wilful and knowing violations of its provisions are a fine of not more than $500,000 and/or imprisonment for up to five years; and
- Sections 804, 905 and 1104 of the act authorise the US Sentencing Commission to review the sentencing guidelines for fraud, obstruction of justice and other white-collar crimes and propose changes to existing guidelines.

High-profile financial reporting fraud cases have raised serious concerns about:

- the role of corporate gatekeepers, including the board of directors and audit committees, in preventing, detecting and correcting financial reporting fraud;
- the integrity, competency and ethical reporting practices of management;
- the ineffectiveness of audit functions in detecting and reporting financial reporting fraud; and
- the important role that corporate legal counsel plays in ensuring compliance with all applicable laws, rules and regulations.

Corporate anti-fraud policies and practices should establish anti-fraud deterrence, prevention, detection and corrections mechanisms driven from the following three anti-fraud themes:

- corporate culture – corporate culture should create an environment that sets an appropriate tone at the top, promoting competent and ethical behaviour and reinforcing anti-fraud conduct, demanding to do the right thing always;
- control structure – an effective control structure should eliminate opportunities for individuals to engage in fraudulent activities; and
- anti-fraud policies and procedures – sufficient and effective anti-fraud policies and procedures should be developed and implemented to ensure the prevention and detection of potential fraud.

5.5 Say on pay and executives' performance

Typically, executive compensation consists of salary, short-term cash bonus and long-term incentive pay in terms of value of stock options, and restricted stock. Executive compensation schemes are linked to a firm's sustainable performance and are approved by shareholders – which has received considerable attention after the recent financial scandals. The provisions of the Sarbanes-Oxley Act that address executive compensation packages are:

- prohibition of personal loans to directors and executives (Section 404);
- reporting insider trading (Section 403);
- insider trading during pension fund blackout periods; and
- forfeiture of certain bonuses and profits.[9]

The Dodd-Frank Act requires say on pay as a non-binding vote by shareholders of a publicly traded company for approval or disapproval of the executive compensation programme at that company. Under the Dodd-Frank Act, public companies must disclose:

- the relationship between senior executives' compensation and the company's financial performance in the form of graphs and charts;
- the ratio of the CEO compensation and the median total to employee compensation excluding the CEO compensation; and
- whether employees or directors are allowed to hedge against a decrease in value of options included in their compensation scheme.[10]

Several suggestions are provided for improving the effectiveness of executive compensation, including the following:

- provisions of both the Sarbanes-Oxley Act and the Dodd-Frank Act should be integrated into public companies' compensation policies and procedures to ensure executive compensation is linked to sustainable performance, properly disclosed and appropriately approved by shareholders;
- the proxy statement should continue to provide adequate information on the risk profile of compensation strategies, adopting claw-back policies discussed in the next section and the trends toward shareholder say on pay votes and the use of independent compensation consultants; and
- an independent compensation committee should be established to create appropriate incentives for executives to work for the best interests of all stakeholders, including shareholders, creditors, employees, suppliers, customers, the environment and society.

5.6 Claw-back and executive compensation

Excessive and questionable executive compensation, whether caused by misconduct or lack of performance, can impose costs on shareholders if they are not

9   Sarbanes-Oxley Act of 2002.
10   Dodd-Frank Act of 2010. Dodd-Frank Wall Street Reform and Consumer Protection Act. HR 4173 Subtitle Section 951, July 21 2010.

subsequently recovered through claw-backs. Excessive executive pay has negative impacts on shareholder value and correction through claw-backs will reverse these. The Dodd-Frank Act requires that all US public companies incorporate so-called 'claw-back' provisions into incentive compensation arrangements for executive officers. It expanded the provisions of the Sarbanes-Oxley Act on claw-back practices by requiring companies to implement and report on their policies and practices for recouping payments from current and former executives when published financial statements are subsequently restated because of a material non-compliance with financial reporting standards. The recouped pay is the amount paid based on misstated financial statements and is recoverable for the three years preceding the restatement date. The Dodd-Frank Act requires national securities exchanges and associations to revise their listing standards to prohibit listings for any company that does not implement a claw-back policy.

The implementation of the claw-back provisions requires public companies to recover any excess compensation resulting from the misstated financial statements during the three years before the restatements. In addition to these mandatory claw-back policies, companies often voluntarily implement best practices of claw-back procedures. These voluntary claw-back policies of non-achievement of earnings targets or any activities deemed harmful to the company (disclosing confidential information, accepting a job with competitors) are expected to receive widespread acceptance and enforcement in the future.

5.7   Whistle-blowing

Whistle-blowing is defined as, "the disclosure by organisation members (former or current) of illegal, immoral, or illegitimate practices under the control of their employers, to persons or organisations that may be able to effect action".[11] Whistle-blowing programmes should be established and monitored because the consequences of whistle-blowing are significant and can range from personal retaliation such as termination to substantial losses to a company. Under the Sarbanes-Oxley Act and the Dodd-Frank Act, public companies must establish and enforce a whistle-blowing programme. Typically, the audit committee is responsible for ensuring it meets the requirements of the Sarbanes-Oxley Act, the Dodd-Frank Act and other related rules and regulations.

The Sarbanes-Oxley Act initially created the opportunity for confidential and anonymous submissions of complaints by requiring that a company's audit committee establish procedures for the collection and treatment of such complaints. The Dodd-Frank Act is also intended to improve the effectiveness of corporate whistle-blowing programmes by providing protection for whistle-blowers and offering rewards for the risk whistle-blowers take in reporting wrongdoers to the regulatory authorities. It provides new incentives for employees and others to blow the whistle when they become aware of law violations and fraud within a company. Under Section 922 of the Dodd-Frank Act, a person who provides "original

---

11   Miceli, MP and JP Near. 1985. Organizational Dissidence: The Case of Whistle-blowing. *Journal of Business Ethics* (February).

information" about a securities law violation to the SEC, which then leads to a successful enforcement action with penalties of $1 million or more, is now entitled to collect between 10% and 30% of the total penalties imposed by the agency.

5.8 Risk assessment and risk management

Risk management is a process of identifying, assessing and managing exposure to risks that affect a company's strategies, operations, reputation and financial reporting. Both the Sarbanes-Oxley Act and the Dodd-Frank Act address risk assessment and management as part of internal control reporting under Section 404 of the Sarbanes-Oxley Act and the executive compensation provisions of the Dodd-Frank Act. The International Organisation for Standardisation (ISO) has developed international standards (ISO 31000) aimed at helping organisations of all sizes and types to manage risk.[12] The ISO 31000 provides the framework, principles and process for assessing and managing risk in a systematic and transparent approach. Under the ISO 31000, the overriding principles of effective risk management include:

- risk management is an integral component of corporate governance;
- risk management should add value to an organisation by improving sustainable performance;
- risk management should be integrated into an organisation's objectives, strategy, operating practices and internal culture;
- risk management is a catalyst for change in the organisation's culture;
- risk management is a proactive, transparent and inclusive process; and
- responsibility for risk management should be linked to strategic vision and tone at the top in an organisation.

5.9 Legal counsel, financial advisers and analysts

Professional advisers, the legal counsel, financial analysts and investment bankers play an important role in governance and the operation of public companies. Legal counsel provides and assists the company in complying with applicable laws, regulations, rules and other legal requirements. The Sarbanes-Oxley Act makes legal counsel an integral component of the internal processes of the corporate governance structure to monitor corporate misconduct. Financial advisers provide financial advice to the company, financial analysts and investment bankers, by providing financial advice to corporations, their directors, officers and other key personnel; they make coverage and stock recommendations; and they can influence corporate governance. Institutional investors play an important role by monitoring the corporation's governance and financial reporting. Institutional investors are distinct from individual investors and consist of pension funds, hedge funds, mutual funds, insurance companies and endowments of not-for-profit entities such as foundations and universities. Several provisions of the Dodd-Frank Act concern banks, hedge funds, credit rating agencies and the derivatives market and their potential conflicts of interest. Institutional

---

12   International Organisation for Standardisation (ISO). 2009. *ISO 31000: Risk Management – Principles and Guidelines*. Available at: www.iso.org/iso/iso_catalogue/management_and_leadership_standards/risk_management.htm.

investment managers are required to disclose at least annually how they voted on say on pay and its frequency and say on golden parachute votes.

6. Efficacy of the regulatory reforms

Two conflicting theories are being used to address the efficacy of the regulatory reforms (Sarbanes-Oxley Act and Dodd-Frank Act) and their impact on shareholder wealth.[13] First, the 'loss competitiveness theory' suggests that regulatory compliance is costly because US capital markets are falling behind their foreign counterparts as public firms go private or delist from US markets. Second, the 'bonding theory' advocates that compliance with the regulatory reforms improves corporate governance and thus provides a better protection for investors worldwide. Basically, the regulatory reforms have two possible contentious effects. First, an overall positive effect of the regulatory reforms by improving investor confidence and generating a net benefit (positive externalities) for all public companies as reflected in an increase in shareholder wealth and thus firm value. Second, a compliance effect, which is a combination of the cost of establishing, implementing and enforcing compliance with the provisions of the regulatory reforms. All public companies can benefit from regulations that enhance transparency and governance, but regulatory compliance is costly. The net benefits or costs vary across firms, depending on investor's perception of the quality of a firm's governance before the regulatory reforms and the imposed compliance costs. Some believe that regulatory reforms are needed to boost customer and investor confidence in capital markets and the economy. Others believe that more regulatory reforms can be cumbersome and may tighten the spirit of free enterprise system and thus the flow of credits and capital. The following sections discuss the benefits, costs and sustainability of the regulatory reforms.

7. Benefits of the regulatory reforms

Regulatory reforms (Sarbanes-Oxley Act and Dodd-Frank Act) apply to and are intended to benefit investors and consumers of all public companies and financial institutions. Multinational and private companies and even not-for-profit organisations have also benefited from some best practices of the Sarbanes-Oxley Act and the Dodd-Frank Act in areas such as the majority of independent directors, mandatory audit committee, internal control reporting, whistle-blowing programmes, code of business conduct and ethics. Some of the provisions of the Sarbanes-Oxley Act that were not previously practised by public companies and that are intended to benefit all companies are:

- creating the Public Company Accounting Oversight Board to oversee the audit of public companies and to improve the self-regulatory environment of the auditing profession, which had been perceived as ineffective;
- improving corporate governance through more independent and vigilant boards of directors and responsible executives;

---

13   Doidge, C, GA Karolyi and RM Stulz. 2008. Has New York become Less Competitive in Global Markets? Evaluating Foreign Listing Choices over Time. The Ohio State University, Fisher College of Business Working Paper Series (WP 2007-9). Available at: www.ssrn.com/abstract=982193.

- enhancing the quality, reliability, transparency and timeliness of financial disclosures through executive certifications of both financial statements and internal controls;
- prohibiting nine types of non-audit services;
- regulating the conduct of auditors, legal counsel and analysts and their potential conflicts of interest; and
- increasing civil and criminal penalties for violations of security laws.

Many provisions of the Dodd-Frank Act can be positive and useful in protecting consumers and investors through the identification of systemically significant financial institutions and requirements of derivatives to be put on clearinghouses/exchanges. Other governance provisions of the Dodd-Frank Act are:

- establishing a new Financial Services Oversight Council to identify and address existing and emerging systematic risks that threaten the wellbeing of financial services firms;
- creation of the Consumer Financial Protection Bureau to oversee consumer and investor financial regulations and their enforcement;
- empowering shareholders with a say on pay of non-binding votes by shareholders approving executive compensation;
- directing the SEC to issue rules requiring companies to disclose in their proxy statement why they have separated, or combined, the positions of chairman and CEO;
- requirements for practices for recouping payments to current and former executives when published financial statements are subsequently restated (restatements of financial statements) due to material non-compliance with financial reporting standards;
- whistle-blowing policies and procedures; and
- disclosures of executive compensation (the ratio of the annual total compensation of the CEO and the median annual total compensation of all employees excluding the CEO).

8. Compliance cost of the regulatory reforms

The regulatory reforms can impose significant new compliance costs on public companies depending on their level of compliance with the reform provisions before their passage. The cost of compliance with Section 404 of the Sarbanes-Oxley Act is estimated to be between 0.12% and 0.62% of a company's reported revenues, and the average is a lower percentage for larger companies.[14] Nonetheless, the compliance cost of the regulatory reforms should be weighed against their possible benefits of positive impacts on investor confidence, improved reliability of financial reports, and improved effectiveness of internal controls in preventing, detecting and correcting financial statement fraud. The post-Sarbanes-Oxley Act era can be characterised by less opportunity for earnings manipulation, more effective internal

---

14   Zhang, IX. 2007. Economic Consequences of the Sarbanes-Oxley Act of 2002. *Journal of Accounting and Economics* 44. 74-115.

controls, higher audit quality, stiffer and more enforceable penalties for aggressive accounting practices, and more timely disclosure of executive compensation.

Effective compliance with Section 404 has proved to be a challenge for public companies. Two types of costs are associated with Section 404 compliance. First, the cost of compliance with the requirements of Section 404, the SEC implementation rules and the Public Company Accounting Oversight Board auditing standards to bring internal control effectiveness in line with the requirements. These costs are viewed as one-off, start-up compliance costs. The costs have been significant for companies that had an inadequate and ineffective internal control structure, requiring them to spend substantial financial and human resources in designing, implementing and operating the required internal controls. The second category of costs relate to the initial assessment, documentation, attestation and reporting on compliance with both Sections 302 and 404, and consists of costs related to ongoing, year-on-year, continuous monitoring of both the design and operation of internal controls and continuous documentation, assessment, testing and reporting requirements. Currently, it is difficult to estimate the compliance costs of the Dodd-Frank Act because many of its 240 rules have not yet been established and implemented.

The debate over the possible impacts of the regulatory reforms and their compliance costs on US capital market global competitiveness is based on two key issues. The first is that the Sarbanes-Oxley Act and its implementation rules have:

- increased compliance costs of regulation and the potential for liability;
- contributed significantly to the loss of US capital markets' global competitiveness as the majority of initial public offerings (IPOs) have recently been listed on capital markets abroad;
- encouraged US companies to go private in order to reduce their regulatory compliance costs; and
- reduced the corporate risk-taking that produces economic growth.

This view is supported by those who believe some provisions of the Sarbanes-Oxley Act should be revised and their implementation rules should be relaxed, particularly for smaller companies.[15] The second view is that the Sarbanes-Oxley Act and its implementation rules have significantly improved the accountability of corporate America, the quality and reliability of its financial reporting, and the integrity and efficiency of its capital markets, and some of its best practices have reached global adoption. This view is supported by those who believe that the Sarbanes-Oxley Act rebuilt investor confidence in the US capital markets and investors are willing to pay a premium for more protection provided by tougher regulations.[16]

It is expected that companies that already had good compliance infrastructures and were closer to compliance with the Sarbanes-Oxley Act provisions experience higher net benefits than companies that were further away from compliance, which had the substantial costs of bringing their governance practices and financial

15   The Committee on Capital Markets Regulation. 2006. Interim report of the Committee on Capital Markets Regulation (November 30). Available at: www.capmktsreg.org/research.html.
16   Norris, F. 2006. An Assault on Regulation. *The New York Times* (September 12). Available at: www.nytimes.com.

reporting process to the level required by the act. If the act has contributed to improving investor confidence in cost-effective compliance, then we expect it to have positive effects on shareholder wealth. The extent of positive effects depends on the induced net benefit, which is the difference between the realised benefit of providing investor protection and the imposed compliance costs. If the net benefit is positive and meaningful, we expect to observe positive and significant impacts of the Sarbanes-Oxley Act on shareholder value. Anecdotal evidence and empirical research on the cost-benefit analysis of the Sarbanes-Oxley Act has proved inconclusive, producing conflicting claims.[17]

9. Sustainability of the regulatory reforms

The Sarbanes-Oxley Act was once considered as the "most sweeping reform". However, it is minute in comparison with the Dodd-Frank Act. The Dodd-Frank Act requires at least 10 times more implementation rules and studies than its counterpart the Sarbanes-Oxley Act as evidenced in Figure 1 (in section 4). Like any regulations, implementation of the provisions of the two acts induced benefits and imposed costs. Induced benefits include a strengthening of the accountability of corporate America, a strengthening of its financial reporting and a strengthening of capital markets, leading to improvements in investor confidence as well as global corporate governance. Imposed costs are high initial compliance costs, possible negative effects on US capital markets' global competitiveness and potential conflicts with corporate governance reforms in other countries (eg, whistle-blowing provisions of the acts). A survey conducted by KPMG in 2012 indicates that companies worldwide are now considering the impacts of the regulatory reforms on their businesses and adapting to regulatory outlooks and the potential effects on their growth, innovation, strategies and practices.[18]

Public companies are operating to primarily enhance shareholder value by adopting the most effective and efficient corporate governance mechanisms to maximise their value. Financial scandals prove that market-correction mechanisms alone cannot prevent aggressive corporate reporting practices, and regulations such as the Sarbanes-Oxley Act and the Dodd-Frank Act are needed to protect investors from receiving misleading financial information. In its infancy, the Sarbanes-Oxley Act was viewed as a compliance document that often caused complications and substantial compliance costs for many companies, regardless of the effectiveness of their corporate governance and internal controls and despite its perceived benefits of improving investor confidence in corporate America and its capital markets. Regulations should be cost-effective, efficient and scalable to generate sustainable shareholder wealth effects. Public companies – regardless of size, earnings, type or organisational structure – can benefit from the regulatory reforms. The regulatory reforms provide positive effects for all public companies in the form of lower equity risk premiums and higher price multiples based on improved investor perception

---

17   Jain, PK and Z Rezaee. 2006. The Sarbanes-Oxley Act of 2002 and Security Market Behavior: Early Evidence. *Contemporary Accounting Research* 23 (3). 629–654.

18   KPMG. 2012. Adapting Business Strategy to the Regulatory Outlook. Available at: www.kpmg.com.

about corporate governance and financial reporting. However, firms that enjoyed positive investor perception about governance before the passage of the regulatory reforms benefit less than firms that had negative investor perception because the latter firms have a greater scope of improvement. In contrast, companies that had better compliance infrastructures before the regulatory reforms incur less incremental costs, and thus earn more net benefits from the reforms than companies that had poor compliance infrastructures.

10.   Conclusions

In conclusion, both the Sarbanes-Oxley Act and the Dodd-Frank Act regulatory reforms appear to be a step in the right direction for protecting investors and rebuilding their confidence in corporate America, its capital markets, its public financial information and its best practices. The effective regulations and best practices of the Sarbanes-Oxley Act and the Dodd-Frank Act can prevent recurrences of financial crises in the US. Cost-effective, efficient and scalable regulations such as the Sarbanes-Oxley Act and the Dodd-Frank Act can create a sound and safe environment for public companies to achieve their sustainable performance, reduce earnings management opportunities, improve accuracy and reliability of financial reports, and restore investor confidence.

Risk management and the board of directors: lessons to be learned from UBS

Roger Barker
Institute of Directors
Stuart Weinstein
Charles Wild
University of Hertfordshire

Recent risk management failures show one clear pattern: if risk is not properly understood and managed appropriately by the board of directors, any problems that arise may escalate and result in legal sanctions and reputational damage sufficient to cripple an organisation. In this chapter we examine the case of UBS AG (UBS), Switzerland's biggest bank, an example of an organisation where risk controls were lax and bank executives "failed to reform the corporate culture".[1] We then look at the risk controls that UBS has since put in place, and make a number of general recommendations on best practice in risk management at the board of directors' level.

1.   Corporate structure of UBS

Before examining the problems of UBS, it is worth looking at UBS's corporate structure. UBS has headquarters in Zurich and Basel, Switzerland, with offices in more than 50 countries, and employs approximately 63,520 people. Under Swiss company law, UBS is organised as an Aktiengesellschaft, a corporation that has issued shares of common stock to investors.[2]

UBS is the parent company of the UBS Group, which has an operational structure comprising of the corporate centre and five business divisions: wealth management, wealth management Americas, investment bank, global asset management and retail & corporate.[3]

The UBS board of directors has ultimate responsibility for the success of the UBS Group and for delivering sustainable shareholder value within a framework of prudent and effective controls.[4]

The board of directors decides UBS's strategic aims and the necessary financial

---

1   Brooke Masters, Caroline Binham, Kara Scannell and James Shotter, "Failure to reform costs UBS dearly", *Financial Times*, December 20 2012, available at: www.ft.com/cms/s/0/ef1ca832-4a95-11e2-9650-00144feab49a.html#axzz2GDDPjeRI (accessed December 27 2012).

2   UBS website, available at: www.ubs.com/global/en/about_ubs/about_us/ourprofile.html (accessed December 27 2012).

3   *Ibid.*

4   UBS website, www.ubs.com/global/en/about_ubs/corporate_governance/board-of-directors.html (accessed December 27 2012).

and human resources, upon recommendation of the Group chief executive officer (Group CEO), and sets the Group's values and standards to ensure that its obligations to its shareholders and others are met.[5]

Shareholders elect each member of the board of directors, which in turn appoints its chairman, the vice chairman/vice chairmen, the senior independent director and the chairmen and members of its various committees.[6]

Under the leadership of the Group CEO, the Group executive board has executive management responsibility for the UBS Group and its business.[7] It assumes overall responsibility for the development of the Group, and business division strategies and the implementation of the approved strategies.[8]

All Group executive board members (with the exception of the Group CEO) are proposed by the Group CEO. The appointments are approved by the UBS board of directors.[9]

2.   A spectacular series of legal governance and compliance problems at UBS

UBS had a series of spectacular legal and compliance failings across the entire spectrum of the bank's operations, from its investment banking to its wealth management division:

- in December 2012, UBS paid US $1.5 billion to global regulators – including the UK Financial Services Authority, the US Commodities Futures Trading Commission and the Swiss Federal Banking Commission – to settle claims that for six years, UBS's traders and managers, specifically at its Japanese securities subsidiary, manipulated the London interbank offered rate (LIBOR) and other borrowing standards;[10]

- in December 2012, Judge Oscar Magi ordered the confiscation of €88 million after UBS was one of four banks found guilty of fraud in a Milan court case involving the sale of derivatives to the city of Milan;[11]

- in November 2012, the UK Financial Services Authority fined UBS £29.7 million (discounted from £42.4 million for early settlement) for systems and controls failings that allowed an employee (Kweku Adoboli) to cause substantial losses totalling $2.3 billion as a result of unauthorised trading;[12]

- in July 2011, the US Federal Housing Finance Agency, the regulator for Fannie Mae (Federal National Mortgage Association) and Freddie Mac (Federal Home

5   *Ibid.*
6   *Ibid.*
7   UBS Website, www.ubs.com/global/en/about_ubs/corporate_covernance/group-executive-board.html (accessed December 27 2012).
8   *Ibid.*
9   *Ibid.*
10   Bloomberg, "Swiss banking major UBS must be shut down on LIBOR charge", December 27 2012, available at: http://economictimes.indiatimes.com/news/international-business/swiss-banking-major-ubs-must-be-shut-down-on-libor-charge/articleshow/17775826.cms (accessed December 27 2012).
11   Associated Press, "Four Banks Found Guilty of Fraud", *New York Times*, December 19 2012, available at: www.nytimes.com/2012/12/20/business/global/four-banks-found-guilty-of-fraud.html?ref=ubsag&_r=0 (accessed December 26 2012).
12   UK Financial Services Authority, Release FSN/PN/105/2012, November 26 2012, available at: www.fsa.gov.uk/library/communication/pr/2012/105.shtml (accessed December 26 2012).

Loan Mortgage Corporation), sued UBS to recover more than $900 million of losses after UBS allegedly misled the two housing agencies into buying $4.5 billion of risky mortgage debt;[13]

- in May 2011, UBS admitted that its employees had repeatedly conspired to rig bids in the municipal bond derivatives market over a five-year period, defrauding more than 100 municipalities and non-profit organisations, and agreed to pay the US Department of Justice $160 million in fines and restitution;[14]

- in February 2009, the UK Financial Services Authority fined UBS £8 million for systems and controls failures at its London-based wealth management business that enabled employees to carry out unauthorised transactions involving customer money on at least 39 accounts;[15]

- in February 2009, UBS paid $780 million in fines to US authorities after admitting helping US citizens evade paying taxes in a deferred prosecution agreement on charges of conspiring to defraud the United States by impeding the Internal Revenue Service; as part of the agreement, UBS provided the US government with the identities of, and account information for, certain US customers of UBS's cross-border business and agreed to exit the business of providing banking services to US clients with undeclared accounts;[16] and

- in December 2008, the Securities and Exchange Commission finalised a settlement with UBS that required UBS to provide almost $23 billion to tens of thousands of customers who invested in auction rate securities, resolving SEC's charges that UBS misled investors regarding the liquidity risks associated with ARS; each customer was reimbursed his or her full investment with UBS.[17]

The systems and controls failings at UBS were so flawed that Bloomberg editorialised:

There is no point in mincing words: UBS, the Swiss global bank, has been disgracing the banking profession for years and needs to be shut down. The regulators that allow it to do business in the US – the Federal Reserve, the SEC, the CFTC and the Office of Comptroller of the Currency – should see that the line in the sand was crossed last week.[18]

The same editorial pointed out that after the global financial crisis, UBS took

13   Jonathan Stempel, "Fannie/Freddie Regulator Sue UBS on $900 million Loss", Reuters, available at: www.reuters.com/article/2011/07/27/ubs-gse-lawsuit-idUSN1E76Q0Z720110727 (accessed December 26 2012).

14   US Department of Justice, "UBS AG Admits to Anticompetitive Conduct by Former Employees in the Municipal Bond Investments Market and Agrees to Pay $160 Million to Federal and State Agencies", Press Release, May 4 2011, available at: www.justice.gov/atr/public/press_releases/2011/270720.htm (accessed December 26 2012).

15   UK Financial Services Authority, Release FSN/PN/150/2009, November 5 2009, available at: www.fsa.gov.uk/library/communication/pr/2009/150.shtml (accessed December 26 2012).

16   US Department of Justice, "UBS Enters into Deferred Prosecution Agreement", Press Release, February 18 2009, available at: www.justice.gov/opa/pr/2009/February/09-tax-136.html (accessed December 26 2012).

17   US Securities and Exchange Commission, "SEC Finalizes ARS Settlements with Citigroup and UBS, Providing Nearly $30 Billion in Liquidity to Investors", Release 2008-290, available at: www.sec.gov/news/press/2008/2008-290.htm (accessed December 26 2012).

18   Bloomberg, note 10 above.

write-downs totalling some $50 billion. In an extraordinary Transparency Report to Shareholders[19] explaining the extraordinary write-downs, UBS stated: "In the aftermath of the financial market crisis it was revealed that UBS had taken a serious turn in the wrong direction under the leadership of the senior management then in charge of the bank. The result was an enormous loss of trust."[20]

3. Risk management failures at UBS in respect of the US subprime mortgage crisis

The Transparency Report identified the management failures of the UBS board of directors which led to the bank taking this extraordinary write-down. The board of directors failed to appreciate the risk that they were taking in respect of the US subprime mortgage market due to a number of factors:

- an aggressive growth strategy that was not diversified, in that UBS acquired too large an interest in investment products, which resulted in UBS being overexposed to them as a whole when the entire market for investment products collapsed;
- over-reliance on the work of ratings agencies and the false quality assurance of investment instruments rated AAA or AA by ratings agencies;
- the UBS board of directors had no clear picture of overall risk assumed by UBS in US mortgage products until it was too late;
- reliance on information from business units: the UBS board of directors relied too much on the statements of the responsible heads of the business units, leading to risk management and risk control without independent enquiry or confirmation;
- over-reliance on statistical models structured on the work of ratings agencies and not on the realities of the US housing market;
- remuneration: the remuneration models used before the financial market crisis did not distinguish sufficiently between real added value created by above-average performance and income generated by exploiting market advantages such as low funding costs. Additionally, the incentive structure encouraged the generation of revenues without adequately considering the associated risks.[21]

The then Swiss Federal Banking Commission undertook its own investigation and concluded that, in addition to inadequately identifying, limiting and monitoring its subprime exposure, UBS's governance, operational and control processes as a whole were inadequate (although to differing degrees).[22] The end result of this supervisory failure was that UBS, its Group executive board and its board of

---

19   UBS, Transparency Report to the Shareholders of UBS AG, October 2010, available at: www.static-ubs.com/global/en/about_ubs/transparencyreport/_jcr_content/rightpar/teaser/linklist/link.2141085760 .file/bGluay9wYXRoPS9jb250ZW50L2RhbS91YnNfZGVsdGEyMC9nbG9iYWwvYWJvdXRfdWJzL3RyY W5zcGFyZW5jeXJlcG9ydC8xODQ2MTRfVHJhbnNwYXJlbmN5cmVwb3J0X2VuLnBkZg==/184614_Tra nsparencyreport_en.pdf (accessed December 27 2012).
20   Bloomberg, note 10 above.
21   UBS Transparency Report, note 19 above, pp 6-7.
22   Ibid.

directors were caught unawares as to the truly dire circumstances of the US subprime mortgage market, resulting in catastrophic losses to UBS.

4.   UBS's improved risk management measures

4.1   Corporate governance
UBS has recruited new members of both the Group executive board and the board of directors from outside to bring in experience from other financial service companies and academia. At December 2012, the majority of the board of directors came from outside UBS.[23] There is now a clear separation of responsibilities between the board of directors and the Group executive board, as explained in section 1. Additionally, the chairman's office was abolished and replaced by board of directors' committees; at the same time, a new risk committee was set up, consisting exclusively of independent directors.[24]

4.2   Risk management
The recording of positions, their valuation, and the assessment of their risks and effects on the profit and loss account are now regulated on a UBS-wide basis.[25] Complex products and transactions are monitored continuously so that concentrations of risk can be identified at an early stage.[26] Business units must be able to explain their balance sheets (including risk positions) and profit and loss accounts based on standardised measurements.[27] Business plans are now assessed based on uniform criteria, both at the group level and the level of the individual business units, and are regularly examined.[28]

4.3   Risk control and finance
Before the financial market crisis, specialists, such as those in the area of risk control, reported to the head of their respective business unit only; however, structures have now been simplified and harmonised.[29] Each chief risk officer of a business unit reports directly to the group chief risk officer, and the risk control function of the group is now independent of the business divisions.[30] The quality and frequency of reporting for UBS's profit and loss statement have also been increased, requiring a monthly performance update to all members of the UBS board of directors and the Group executive board.[31] All new business is now subject to more stringent controls and has to be submitted to the risk committee of the UBS board of directors for approval.[32]

4.4   Fund-raising and balance sheet management
The Group executive board now also constitutes the asset and liability committee at

---

23   UBS website, note 4 above.
24   UBS Transparency Report, note 19 above, pp 6-7.
25   *Ibid.*
26   *Ibid.*
27   *Ibid.*
28   *Ibid.*
29   *Ibid.*
30   *Ibid.*
31   *Ibid.*
32   *Ibid.*

UBS. The committee members are accountable to the UBS board of directors for the assigning of balance sheet limits, risk-weighted assets and capital to the individual business units. The asset and liability committee also approves internal group financing. Limits for total balance sheet growth and risk-weighted assets have been introduced both on the group level and in particular at the investment bank. Financing costs are now handled on the basis of risk.

4.5 Remuneration

When making decisions regarding remuneration, greater emphasis is now placed on sustainable increases in corporate value than was the case before the crisis.[33] Variable compensation no longer contains only a bonus component, but in some cases also a malus component, which may be recorded if a loss results at the group or division level, if drastic adjustments to the consolidated balance sheet are required or if gross violations of compliance regulations or of risk guidelines are identified.[34]

5. Corporate governance and risk management – the *Roads to Ruin* study

A leading 2011 Cass Business School for AIRMIC[35] study, *Roads to Ruin, A Study of Major Risk Events: their Origin, Impact and Implications*[36] (R2R Report), examined 20 major corporate failures since 2000, including Enron, AIG, Northern Rock and Independent Insurance, in order to analyse both where things went wrong and the base causes. The R2R Report identifies competence, attitude and the behaviour of board members and non-executive directors as key factors involved in major risk events:

> *We found that the firms most badly affected had underlying weaknesses that made them especially prone both to crises and to the escalation of a crisis into a disaster. These weaknesses were found to arise from seven key risk areas that are potentially inherent in all organisations and that can pose an existential threat to any firm, however substantial, that fails to recognise and manage them.*
>
> *These risk areas are beyond the scope of insurance and mainly beyond the reach of traditional risk analysis and management techniques as they have evolved so far. In our view, they should be drawn into the risk management process.*[37]

The R2R Report goes on to identify the seven risks as follows:

> A. *Board skill and Non-Executive Directors (NEDs) control risks – limitations on board competence and the ability of the NEDs effectively to monitor and, if necessary, control the executives.*
>
> B. *Board risk blindness – the failure of boards to engage with important risks, including risks to reputation and 'licence to operate', to the same degree that they engage with reward and opportunity.*

---

33   *Ibid.*

34   *Ibid.*

35   Airmic is the UK association for risk managers. It is a members' association (1,100 individual members from over 450 companies) supporting those responsible for risk management and insurance within their own companies. See www.airmic.com/ for more information.

36   Cass Business School, "Roads to Ruin: the Analysis – A Study of Major Risk Events: Their Origins, Impact and Implications" (A Report by Cass Business School on behalf of Airmic sponsored by Crawford and Lockton), July 21 2011, available at: www.airmic.com/jresearch/roads-ruin-analysis (accessed December 29 2012).

37   *Ibid.*

C. *Poor leadership on ethos and culture – risks from a failure of board leadership and implementation on ethos and culture.*

D. *Defective communication – risks arising from the defective flow of important information within the organisation, including to board-equivalent levels.*

E. *Risks arising from excessive complexity – this includes risks following acquisitions.*

F. *Risks arising from inappropriate incentives – whether explicit or implicit.*

G. *Risk 'Glass Ceilings' – arising from the inability of risk management and internal audit teams to report on risks originating from higher levels of their organisation's hierarchy, e.g., those arising from the inability of risk management and internal audit teams to report to and discuss, with both the 'C-Suite' (leaders such as the Chief Executive, Chief Operating Officer and Chief Financial Officer) and NEDs and those emanating from higher levels of their organisation's hierarchy, including risks from ethos, behaviour, strategy and perceptions.*[38]

In the risk management failures studied by the R2R Report, it becomes clear that there were common deep-seated risks that transcended business sectors. These underlying risks were dangerous in four identified ways:

- many posed a potentially lethal threat to the organisation's business and business model;
- when they materialised, they often caused serious, sometimes devastating and almost always uninsurable losses to the business, its reputation and its owners, often putting the position of the CEO and chairman into question;
- many were also instrumental in transforming serious but potentially manageable crises into catastrophes that destroyed reputations and licences to operate; and
- most of these risks were beyond the reach of current risk analysis techniques and beyond the remit and expertise of typical risk managers.[39]

Finally, the R2R Report makes several recommendations on dealing with the risks identified:

- the scope, purpose and practicalities of risk management will need to be rethought from board level downwards in order to capture these and other risks that are not identified by current techniques;
- the education of risk professionals will need to be extended so that they feel competent to identify and analyse risks emerging from their organisation's ethos, culture and strategy, and from their leaders' activities and behaviour;
- the role and status of risk professionals will need to change so that they can confidently report all that they find on these subjects to board level; and
- chairmen and non-executive directors need to recognise the need to deal with the risks identified and work more closely with risk professionals with enhanced vision and enhanced competencies to help them do so.[40]

---

38   *Ibid.*
39   *Ibid.*
40   *Ibid.*

The R2R Report makes a number of very solid points in the debate over the competence of a board of directors to be aware of all potential future issues. One of the many problems faced by a board of directors is that its information is often provided by senior management. Since the board sets the compensation of senior management, there is a risk that their presentation and interpretation of information to the board may be skewed.

One such example is AIG. In a *Wall Street Journal* article on March 27 2009, Liam Pleven noted that the board of directors not having the right sort of information contributed to the problems at AIG before its unprecedented bailout by the US Government:

> *AIG's outside auditor and a regulator raised concerns months before the bailout about the ability of AIG's risk management to monitor what was going on in some units.*
>
> *At an AIG board-committee meeting in January 2008, AIG's auditor, PricewaterhouseCoopers LLP, "expressed concern that the access" that AIG Chief Risk Officer, Robert Lewis, and his risk management department and other top AIG executives had into the financial products unit, AIG Investments and other subsidiaries. Access "may require strengthening," according to minutes of the meeting released by Congress last fall.*
>
> *Two months later, the federal Office of Thrift Supervision, which regulated AIG's financial-products unit, sent a letter to the company, also released by Congress. OTS said the unit "was allowed to limit access of key risk control groups while material questions relating to the valuation of the [swap portfolio] were mounting." The OTS said those "control groups" included Mr. Lewis's department.*
>
> *At a congressional hearing last week, Rep. Gary Peters (D., Mich.) asked AIG Chief Executive Edward Liddy, "Where was the risk management of your company? Where was the failure of your own internal risk management procedures?"*
>
> *Mr. Liddy responded, "We had risk management practices in place. They generally were not allowed to go up into the financial-products business."*[41]

6.   The North Carolina AICPA-CIMA Study

This view is confirmed by a 2010 survey sponsored by the American Institute of Chartered Public Accountants and the Chartered Institute of Management Accountants entitled "Enterprise Risk Oversight: A Global Analysis".[42] The survey pointed out that only 39% of US companies indicated that top risk exposures facing the organisation are formally discussed when the board of directors discusses the organisation's strategic plan, in comparison with over 60% of global competitors who are discussing the top risk exposures.[43]

Noting the trend for increased discussion of enterprise risk management at board

41   Liam Pleven, "Top Risk Officers Remain at Insurer's Helm", *Wall Street Journal*, March 27 2009, available at: http://online.wsj.com/article/SB123812287215554481.html?mod=googlenews_wsj (accessed January 1 2012).

42   Mark S Beasley, Bruce C Branson and Bonnie V Hancock (North Carolina State College of Management), "Enterprise Risk Oversight: A global analysis", September 2010, available at: www.aicpa.org/InterestAreas/BusinessIndustryAndGovernment/Resources/ERM/DownloadableDocuments/Enterprise%20Risk%20v3.pdf (accessed January 2 2012).

43   *Ibid*, p 3.

level, the survey found a difference in the level of discussion about top risk exposures that may be attributable to how respondents perceive the relative completeness and robustness of their existing enterprise-wide risk management processes: for the global firms, 46% of respondents believe their organisation has a formal enterprise risk management process that regularly provides a robust, systematic report of aggregate top risk exposures to the board and senior management. In contrast, only 11% of US respondents believe they have a complete enterprise-wide risk management process in place.[44]

The study notes a differing trend between global firms and US firms with respect to assigning formal responsibility for overseeing management's risk assessment and risk management processes to one or more of the board's committees at higher rates than US organisations. Not only do global firms appear to be making these formal assignments more often than US firms, when they do they usually assign such a formal role to more than one committee:

> But, when making these assignments, a higher percentage (65%) of U.S. organisations formally assigns risk oversight responsibility to the audit committee. In comparison, global respondents noted a somewhat lower percentage (57%) of audit committees being assigned risk oversight responsibilities. Often boards are delegating aspects of risk oversight to more than one board level committee, with global firms notably more likely to make those assignments to multiple committees as compared to US firms. For global firms, there was a much higher rate of assignment of risk oversight to separate risk committees and the executive committee of the board relative to US firms. And, global firms are explicitly noting in the board committee's charter their formal risk responsibility at higher rates than US organisations. 61% of global firm boards, that delegate risk oversight responsibilities, are explicitly noting that responsibility in the committees' charters in contrast to 52% of US firms.[45]

It must be noted that the assignment of risk management to the audit committee is not surprising – the provisions of the Sarbanes Oxley Act of 2002[46] require a top-down risk assessment.[47] For more on this point, see Dr Zabihollah Rezaee's chapter.

7.   Removing the chief executive officer

In his contribution to an Institute of Directors' publication,[48] co-author Roger Barker suggests that the most important contribution to effective risk management a board of directors can make is likely to be its choice of chief executive: "If the wrong person is appointed to lead the company, then all of the board's subsequent efforts to contribute to effective risk management will be severely compromised."[49] He goes on to suggest that where the chief executive's approach to risk is not serving the

---

44   *Ibid*, p 3.
45   *Ibid*.
46   The Sarbanes Oxley Act of 2002 (Pub L 107-204, 116 Stat 745, enacted July 30 2002).
47   Sarbanes Oxley Act, Section 404 et seq. See also Zabihollah Rezaee, Kingsley O Olibe and George Minmier, "Improving corporate governance: the role of audit committee disclosures", (2003) *Managerial Auditing Journal*, Vol. 18 Issue 6/7, pp 530-7.
48   Directors Publications Ltd, Institute of Directors *et al*, "Business Risk: A practical guide for board members", June 2012, available at: www.iod.com/mainwebsite/resources/document/iod-directors-guide-business-risk-june12.pdf (accessed January 21 2013).
49   *Ibid*, p 15.

interests of the company, it is the responsibility of the board of directors to replace him or her with a more appropriate candidate.[50] Richard Moran, Chief Executive of Accretive Solutions and a board director himself, observes that this idea is easier said than done: "Boards are typically pretty poor at getting rid of CEOs ... they usually wait too long, and there's often a mentality that says, he's our guy, and we'll stick with him until the company goes down the drain."[51]

Barker's view is reinforced by Ben Heinemann, former general counsel of GE and now senior fellow at the Belfer Centre for Science and International Affairs, who suggests that the financial crisis requires a new type of CEO:

> Boards of directors must redefine the role of the CEO – and then choose a leader who meets the new spec. Under this recast role, the CEO's first foundational task is to achieve a core balance between taking economic risk (promoting creativity and innovation) and managing economic risk (within a systemic framework of financial discipline) over a sustained period of time. The second recast, foundational CEO task is to fuse this high performance with high integrity. That means tenacious adherence to the spirit and letter of formal rules, voluntary adoption of ethical standards that bind the company and its employees, and employee commitment to core values of honesty, candor, fairness, reliability and trustworthiness – which together are in the enlightened self-interest of the company, are embedded in business operations and address legal, ethical, reputational and public policy risk.[52]

8.   The role of the board: balancing risk oversight with strategy

A second basic issue for the board involves defining the nature and extent of the risks that the company is willing to take. This is not a simple exercise of listing activities, 'green-lighting' those that the company can undertake and 'red-lighting' those that the company must avoid due to its risk appetite. An Enterprise Risk Management Initiative (North Carolina State University, Poole School of Management) study suggests that "a comprehensive discussion of risk appetite should become linked to defining the overall strategy of a company, involving both top management and the board of directors".[53] A risk-educated board will take into consideration the expectations of shareholders, regulators and other stakeholders as well as the overall risk capacity of the company. Identifying those risks that the company can manage better than its competitors, clients or suppliers can be the ultimate link between risks and opportunities.[54]

The board of directors need not be involved in actual day-to-day risk management.[55] Instead, the role of the directors is to use their supervisory

---

50   *Ibid.*
51   Nicholas Rummell, "Replacing the CEO in a Crisis", January 23 2012, available at: www. corporatesecretary.com/articles/succession-planning/12124/replacing-ceo-crisis/ (accessed January 21 2013).
52   Ben Heinemann, "The Governance Crisis: First, Let's Redefine the Role of the CEO", Belfer Centre, Harvard University, available at: http://belfercenter.hks.harvard.edu/publication/19183/governance _crisis.html (accessed January 22 2013).
53   Enterprise Risk Management Initiative Faculty and Renata Heineman, "Balancing Risk Appetite and Execution", North Carolina State University, Poole College of Management, available at: www.poole.ncsu.edu/erm/index.php/articles/entry/balance-risk-strategy/ (accessed January 25 2013).
54   *Ibid.*

responsibilities to ensure proper risk management structures are in place. As US lawyer Martin Lipton writes:

> *Directors should instead, through their risk oversight role, satisfy themselves that the risk management processes designed and implemented by the company's risk managers are consistent with the company's corporate strategy and are functioning as directed, and that necessary steps are taken to foster a culture of risk-aware and risk-adjusted decision-making throughout the organisation.*[56]

This is often referred to as setting the 'tone at the top', namely, first, does the board function properly and secondly, with respect to its risk oversight function, is this function performed in a robust manner?

In addition to setting up systems and procedures to ensure proper supervision of risk management, the board of directors is involved in messaging. However, messaging of risk oversight and putting in place compliance and risk management structures alone is never enough for a board of directors. After all, a business will not make money from risk management – it makes money from prudent business strategy. As Lipton notes:

> *Through its oversight role, the board can send a message to the company's management and employees that comprehensive corporate risk management is neither an impediment to the conduct of business nor a mere supplement to a firm's overall compliance program, but is instead an integral component of the firm's corporate strategy, culture and value-generation process. Much has been said on the need for boards to find the right balance between monitoring compliance and advising on strategy. In the arena of risk oversight, these dual roles of monitor and strategic adviser converge.*[57]

The first priority for a risk management system is to ensure that the board of directors has the right information, in that it gets the appropriate material risks brought to its attention. This is far harder to determine than one would think. For instance, a $2 billion loss might be material to many companies but an argument can be made that it is not for some companies, such as JP Morgan: "All things considered, this hedging mistake is an isolated loss at JP Morgan, and the size of the loss barely breaks the threshold of materiality."[58] Each company will have a different concept of what is material for its operations, for instance, certain types of risk will be automatically material regardless of their financial value, such as an incident of insider dealing or a poor manufacturing design uncovered in a product or a safety incident. Therefore, it is important to have an appropriate risk management structure that will flag the most material risks for the board of directors, and explain them clearly so that the board can understand and act on the information.

Making sure that the board of directors recruits the right directors and that these

---

55   Martin Lipton, "Risk Management and the Board of Directors", December 17 2009, The Harvard Law School Forum on Corporate Governance and Financial Regulation, available at: https://blogs. law.harvard.edu/corpgov/2009/12/17/risk-management-and-the-board-of-directors-2/ (accessed January 25 2013).

56   *Ibid.*

57   *Ibid.*

58   RJ Towner, "The Materiality of JP Morgan's Trading Loss is Overblown", *The Motley Fool*, available at: http://beta.fool.com/valuentum/2012/05/15/materiality-jp-morgans-trading-loss-overblown/4561/ (accessed January 28 2013).

directors have the right expertise is essential to manage risk. For instance, in the US, Section 406 of the Sarbanes Oxley Act requires public companies to disclose whether their audit committee includes at least one member who is a financial expert. Accounting expertise and an understanding of financial markets is now seen as an essential qualification for the selection of directors. Ben Stein wrote in 2007 at the height of the financial crisis:

Much has been made of the failure of officers and directors to notice that something was amiss at these big banks [Merill Lynch, Citigroup and Bear Stearns]. Why didn't the directors ask the chiefs, "Gee, how can you continue to earn a far higher rate of return on debt than the market rate? How are you defying gravity this way? Can it last?"

Why were the questions not asked?

Possibly because the directors might have been chosen with an eye toward political correctness instead of an eye toward what they knew about finance and accounting. I was staggered when I read about the backgrounds of the Merrill directors. It is nice to have leaders of colleges and universities on boards (as Merrill does) but wouldn't it have been better to look for accounting expertise? Was the idea to conform to P.C. principles and not have anyone asking tough questions? What about fiduciary duty?[59]

In addition to financial expertise, companies should focus on retaining industry-appropriate expertise on their boards as well. For instance, appointing directors from related industries who are involved with companies in the upstream or downstream supply chain can provide valuable access to contacts, overcome information challenges and narrow the information gap between the board and the firm's management.[60] The research of Dass et al. suggests that appointing directors from related industries has an economically significant impact on firm value and performance. Whether this translates into better risk management is not proven, but is a logical conclusion from such research.

While appointing directors with the right expertise may ensure that the directors are capable of properly evaluating managers' decisions, the problem remains that the functional tasks performed by board members are not forward-looking mechanisms designed adequately to monitor strategic and business success – let alone risk management.[61] Nonetheless, under the corporate governance rules of the New York Stock Exchange, audit committees of its listed companies must discuss the risk

59   Ben Stein, "It's Time to Act like Grown Ups", *New York Times*, 11 November 2007, available at: www.nytimes.com/2007/11/11/business/11every.html?_r=0 (accessed January 28 2013).

60   Nishant Dass, Omesh Kini, Vikram Nanda, Bunyamin Onal and Jun Wang, "Board Expertise: Do Directors From Related Industries Help Bridge the Information Gap?", August 2011, available at: http://scheller.gatech.edu/directory/faculty/nanda/pubs/DKNOW4i.pdf (accessed January 8 2013).

61   Nicola Faith Sharpe, "Rethinking Board Function in the Wake of the Financial Crisis", *Journal of Business & Technology Law*, Vol. 5, Issue 1, 2010, Article 7, 99-111,108 available at: http://digitalcommons.law.umaryland.edu/cgi/viewcontent.cgi?article=1138&context=jbtl&sei-redir=1&referer=http%3A%2F%2Fwww.google.co.uk%2Furl%3Fsa%3Dt%26rct%3Dj%26q%3Dlack%2520of%2520expertise%2520on%2520aig%2520board%26source%3Dweb%26cd%3D3%26ved%3D0CD8QFjAC%26url%3Dhttp%253A%252F%252Fdigitalcommons.law.umaryland.edu%252Fcgi%252Fviewcontent.cgi%253Farticle%253D1138%2526context%253Djbtl%26ei%3DDjEHUZvKA4Wq0QWRsoCIBA%26usg%3DAFQjCNGr52R1Es7wQDC2wfbSPnggSnuKMw%26bvm%253Dbv.41524429%2Cd.d2k (accessed January 28 2013).

62   New York Stock Exchange, NYSE Listed Company Manual Section 303A.07 Audit Committee Additional Requirement, 2013 available at: http://nysemanual.nyse.com/LCMTools/PlatformViewer.asp?selectednode=chp%5F1%5F4%5F3%5F8&manual=%2Flcm%2Fsections%2Flcm%2Dsections%2F (accessed January 30 2013).

assessment and risk management policies of their organisations.[62] The US Securities and Exchange Commission (SEC) has expanded proxy disclosures relating to the extent of the board's role in risk supervision.[63] On July 22 2009, the rating agency Standard and Poor's (S&P) introduced reporting requirements for non-financial companies on their enterprise risk management procedures in place.[64] This information is now used as part of S&P's credit rating assessment processes.

Is there one particular structure for this risk supervision? The term 'top level' support is often used in this context. Yet, as one observer noted, top level support implies 'icing on the cake' (surface covering that is wide but thin), while in reality what is needed something that is more analogous to rock candy – in that wherever you slice it, the letters appear and the message can be seen throughout. One possible solution adapted by some companies is the creation of a separate board of directors' risk management committee. This is seen as a bit of a mixed blessing by some practitioners:

> *The benefits of a successful risk committee are obvious: improved board oversight of management and of company operations; an ability to anticipate and react to events and trends that might otherwise be inscrutable; and, not least, the projection of a sober and responsible corporate culture that will impress employees and regulators alike. But before rushing to establish a risk committee, it is worth noting that the creation of such a committee can itself create risk. The board, in delegating responsibility of monitoring risk to the new committee, will need to stay focused on the fact that managing risks, especially systemic and existential risks, is one of the core functions of the board itself. Furthermore, to the extent that other committees, especially the audit committee, maintain some role in risk management, a new risk committee could lead to uncertainty about where one committee's responsibility ends and another's begins. The result of such confusion could be overlapping efforts or in the worst case scenario, a failure to manage a certain category of risk entirely.[65]*

Where a board of directors' risk management committee is not set up, many companies assign review of risk management to the audit committee with full, periodic reviews at board level. Other companies spread the risk management functions among different committees, but this can be problematic if not coordinated properly.

9. Risk management oversight by the board: defining the nature and extent of risks that the company will take

While it is clear that it is not the board of directors' function to run the day-to-day risk management operations of the company, the board must define the nature and

---

63 Securities Exchange Commission, Final Rule: Proxy Disclosure Enhancements, December 16 2009, available at: www.sec.gov/rules/final/2009/33-9089.pdf (accessed January 30 2013).

64 Aon Global Risk Consulting, S&P Enhancement White Paper, August 2009, available at: www.aon.com/about-aon/intellectual-capital/attachments/risk-services/enterprise_risk_management _enhancement_white_paper.pdf (accessed January 30 2013).

65 W Neil Egglestone and David C Ware, "Does Your Board Need a Risk Committee?", Directors and Boards, Second Quarter 2009, 54–55, 55, available at: www.debevoise.com/files/Publication/af20c245-9373-43d5-8cd7-ab41d3b9763b/Presentation/PublicationAttachment/370af707-ef7e-4f7d-ba9b-b1c825117567/RiskCommitteeArticle.pdf (accessed January 30 2013).

extent of risks that the company will take. However, directors must support the risk management process and supervise what the company's managers have designed and implemented to manage top risk exposures. More than just setting the 'top down' message, the board of directors must ensure that the risk management programme is implemented across the enterprise and in a clear and consistent method.

COSO,[66] in its publication *Effective Enterprise Risk Management Oversight: The Role of the Board of Directors*,[67] suggests that enterprise risk management can be used better to connect the risk oversight function with the creation and protection of shareholder value. Enterprise risk management is a process effected by an entity's board of directors, management and other personnel, applied in strategy setting and across the enterprise, designed to identify potential events that may affect the entity and manage risk to be within the risk appetite, to provide reasonable assurance regarding the achievement of objectives (COSO's ERM – Integrated Framework 2004). According to the COSO publication, four areas contribute to the board of directors' enterprise risk management supervision:

- understanding the entity's risk philosophy and concurring with the entity's risk appetite;
- knowing the extent to which management has established effective enterprise risk management of the organisation;
- reviewing the entity's portfolio of risk and considering it against the entity's risk appetite; and
- being informed of the most significant risks and whether management is responding appropriately.[68]

As the board of directors is seen as being, in part, representative of the stakeholders' interest in the company, the discussions with management will go a long way to ensure that stakeholders have input into the risk management framework. Stress testing of existing risk management processes to ensure that they are robust, self-correcting and fit for purpose is also an important part of the risk oversight board's function. This must be coupled with an intimate knowledge of the particular industry within which the company operates and the issues that it faces. In addition to the general risk management procedures and policies that are in place, it is also right to assume that each company will have a specific set of risk management procedures and policies in place to deal with the specifics of the industry within which it is operating. For instance, the supermarket store Tesco obviously had a risk management failure in its food manufacturing and processing supply chain when it did not discover on its own that one of its suppliers was incorporating horse meat into Tesco beefburgers.[69] This sort of supply chain risk is obviously different from the risk issues other industries might face.

---

66   Committee of Sponsoring Organisations of the Treadway Commission (www.coso.org). The Treadway Commission consists of the American Accounting Association, American Institute of Certified Public Accountants, Financial Executives International, Institute of Management Accountants and The Institute of Internal Auditors.
67   Available at: www.coso.org/documents/COSOBoardsERM4pager-FINALRELEASEVERSION82409_001.pdf (accessed January 30 2013).
68   *Ibid.*

The board of directors must understand and appreciate the organisation's risk exposure strategies so that it can properly balance the risk portfolio against the organisation's appetite for risk. Of course, this is easier said than done. It is much more than merely adding 'Risk issues' to the board agenda and including reports in the board information packs. This is an active and evolving process so, for instance, in the case of Tesco, it may want to revisit and update its risk portfolio with respect to supply chain due diligence. Similarly, risk supervision by boards is work that involves constant monitoring and cannot be limited to reviewing static information quarterly in preparation for board meetings. Thus there is a premium on the board of directors receiving information in real time.

This reality of being able to respond quickly is reflected in the large number of products on the market that offer real time risk management solutions tailored to different risks. For instance, one product is 'pitched' for companies operating in earthquake-prone regions of the world:

A magnitude 9.0 undersea megathrust earthquake struck off the coast of Japan, 154 kilometers from the Fukushima Daiichi Nuclear Power Plant. The plant was automatically shut down following the earthquake and backup generators started the cooling process. 41 minutes later, powerful tsunami waves reached the plant at heights of up to 14 meters. A seawall was designed to protect the plant from a worst-case tsunami of 6 meters. The waves inundated the Fukushima facility, disabling the backup generators. What is your view of the risk within a resilient risk management framework?[70]

This type of scenario emphasises that some boards will need to develop catastrophic risk modelling adequately to protect their companies from risks as diverse as earthquakes and hurricanes, terrorism and infectious diseases. Of course, there is much demand by financial institutions for such sophisticated risk management modelling technology. Another vendor makes an enterprise-readiness hub available which balances crisis avoidance with crisis containment, suggesting that the balance between the two lies in the hands of management working with partners and influencers.[71] Bearing in mind the advice attributed to Warren Buffett that "it takes 20 years to build a reputation and five minutes to ruin it", boards must also consider reputation management and the high cost of failing to protect the company's reputation: BP, Shell, AIG, Arthur Andersen, Pan Am and many other companies have failed due to reputational issues.

As befits a lawyer, Lipton identifies a more specific task list for the board of directors in pursuance of their risk oversight function. These include:

- review with management the company's risk appetite and risk tolerance, the ways in which risk is measured on an aggregate, company-wide basis, the setting of aggregate and individual risk limits (quantitative and qualitative, as

---

69   Rosa Silverman and Alice Philipson, "Tesco Beef Burgers Found to Contain 29pc Horse Meat", *The Telegraph*, January 19 2013, available at: www.telegraph.co.uk/news/uknews/9804632/Tesco-beef-burgers-found-to-contain-29-horse-meat.html (accessed January 30 2013).

70   Risk Management Solutions website, available at: www.rms.com/www.rms.com/ (accessed January 31 2013).

71   Risk Readiness Corporate website, available at: http://riskreadinesscorp.com/solution/ (accessed January 31 2013).

appropriate), the policies and procedures in place to hedge against or mitigate risks, and the actions to be taken if risk limits are exceeded;

- review with management the categories of risk the company faces, including any risk concentrations and risk interrelationships, as well as the likelihood of occurrence, the potential impact of those risks and mitigating measures;
- review with management the assumptions and analysis underpinning the determination of the company's principal risks and whether adequate procedures are in place to ensure that new or materially changed risks are properly and promptly identified, understood and accounted for in the actions of the company;
- review with committees and management the board's expectations of each group's respective responsibilities for risk oversight and management of specific risks to ensure a shared understanding of accountabilities and roles;
- review the company's executive compensation structure to ensure it is appropriate in light of the company's articulated risk appetite and to ensure it is creating proper incentives in the light of the risks the company faces;
- review the risk policies and procedures adopted by management, including procedures for reporting matters to the board and appropriate committees and providing updates, in order to assess whether they are appropriate and comprehensive;
- review management's implementation of its risk policies and procedures, to assess whether they are being followed and are effective;
- review with management the quality, type and format of risk-related information provided to directors;
- review the steps taken by management to ensure adequate independence of the risk management function and the processes for resolution and escalation of differences that might arise between risk management and business functions;
- review with management the design of the company's risk management functions, as well as the qualifications and backgrounds of senior risk officers and the personnel policies applicable to risk management, to assess whether they are appropriate given the company's size and scope of operations;
- review with management the means by which the company's risk management strategy is communicated to all appropriate groups within the company so that it is properly integrated into the company's enterprise-wide business strategy;
- review internal systems of formal and informal communication across divisions and control functions to encourage the prompt and coherent flow of risk-related information within and across business units and, as needed, the prompt escalation of information to management (and to the board or board committees as appropriate); and
- review reports from management, independent auditors, internal auditors, legal counsel, regulators, stock analysts and outside experts as considered appropriate regarding risks the company faces and the company's risk management function.[72]

In sum, the risk appetite of an organisation must be clearly defined by its board of directors working alongside senior management. Once this is done, it then becomes the responsibility of the board of directors and senior management to communicate the company's risk tolerance/aversion fulcrum. This is needed to ensure that all activity of the company falls within the limits set out between those risk activities the company will tolerate and those that are against the company's policy. In proscribing risk tolerance, it is useful for the company to state clearly and precisely the maximum risk levels the organisation will tolerate. It is also useful for the company to divide specific categories of risk into appropriate subgroups – strategic, operational, financial and legal/compliance. All of these risks will be measured and managed in their own ways and by their own experts, almost as wholly separate sectors. Nonetheless, the 'silo mentality' as so often seen in profound corporate risk management failures, for example, AIG or UBS, must be avoided. Someone at the top should be aware of all the risk activities of the company and must be able to control all personnel: in other words, the chief executive must be the number one risk manager at his or her company – the term popularised by US President Harry S Truman comes to mind: "the buck stops here".

10. Balancing risk and reward

Since the financial crisis, there has been a reshaping of the way in which boards handle the balance between risk and reward. In particular, a 2011 Ernst & Young/Institute of International Finance survey found that 83% of institutions had increased their board's supervision of risk.[73] Board-level risk committees and chief risk officers with direct reporting lines to the non-executive directors are now much more common. More non-executive directors with expertise in risk assessment are being appointed so that management is engaged in the process of rigorous defence of their risk appetite.

According to the Ernst & Young/Institute of International Finance report, 96% of the financial institutions they surveyed have increased their focus on risk appetite.[74] This raises the question of what we mean by the term risk appetite. Risk appetite can be defined as the quantity and types of risk that an organisation is willing to assume in pursuit of its strategic objectives.[75] The SAS White Paper, "The Art of Balancing Risk and Reward: The role of the board in setting, implementing and monitoring risk", sets out the parameters by which boards should determine risk:

> Boards must determine an appropriate risk appetite, unambiguously document it and sufficiently quantify it so it can be acted upon. Further, boards must also make management accountable for ensuring that everyone in the institution is in compliance

---

72   Lipton, note 55 above.

73   Ernst & Young/Institute of International Finance, "Making Strides in Financial Services Risk Management", 2011, available at: www.ey.com/Publication/vwLUAssets/Making_strides_in_financial_services_risk_management/$FILE/Making%20strides%20in%20financial%20services%20risk%20management.pdf (accessed February 1 2013).

74   Ibid.

75   SAS Institute Inc., "The Art of Balancing Risk and Reward: The role of the board in setting, implementing and monitoring risk appetite", 2011, available at: www.sas.com/offices/europe/uk/industries/capital_markets/pdf/balancing-risk.pdf (accessed February 1 2013).

with the risk appetite. A framework will evolve to address gaps in current practices relative to risk appetite. This framework will include data, a variety of metrics, collaboration structures, analytical processes, and contextual translations and reconciliations that bridge the areas of capital management, risk management and corporate strategy.

The SAS White Paper stresses that it is not enough for the board of directors to "talk the talk" (the authors' term) of defining risk appetite for the company. The board must also ensure that the company also "walks the walk" (again, the authors' term) – in other words, operationalises the risk appetite of the company as expressed by the board of directors. This task is far more subtle than merely developing a risk appetite statement or defining broad areas of coverage along with measuring tools. 'Walking the walk' involves cascading "more granular risk-taking limits down to the most fundamental operating unit level".[76] Monitoring alone is not enough if it is done on a rigid and static basis, as both risk appetite and the environment in which the company operates will change: just as strategy needs to evolve in response to changing internal and external conditions, so too must the risk appetite "live and breathe".[77]

The views set out in the SAS White Paper echo those contained in the Report of the National Association of Corporate Directors Blue Ribbon Commission, "Risk Governance: Balancing Risk and Reward".[78] The report defines the role of the board of directors as not being involved in risk management, which is only part of the picture, but rather emphasises that the role of the board of directors is to engage in risk governance – the key to this being improving the processes by which the company oversees risk management. The report set out 10 principles to guide directors in their risk oversight function:

1. *Understand the company's key drivers of success.*
2. *Assess the risk in the company's strategy.*
3. *Define the role of the full board and its standing committees with regard to risk oversight.*
4. *Consider whether the company's risk management system – including people and processes – is appropriate and has sufficient resources.*
5. *Work with management to understand and agree on the types (and format) of risk information the board requires.*
6. *Encourage a dynamic and constructive risk dialogue between management and the board, including a willingness to challenge assumptions.*
7. *Closely monitor the potential risks in the company's culture and its incentive structure.*
8. *Monitor critical alignments – of strategy, risk, controls, compliance, incentives, and people.*
9. *Consider emerging and interrelated risks: What's around the next corner?*
10. *Periodically assess the board's risk oversight processes: Do they enable the board to achieve its risk oversight objectives?*

---

76   *Ibid.*
77   *Ibid.*
78   Report of the National Association of Corporate Directors Blue Ribbon Commission, "Risk Governance: Balancing Risk and Reward" (2009) available at: www.oliverwyman.com/media/riskbrc-execsummary(2).pdf (accessed February 1 2013).

11. The role of the non-executive director

In the risk oversight process set out by the Blue Ribbon Commission report, a question should be asked: does the non-executive director have a particular role to play in this process? Barker[79] points out that, generally, non-executive directors will have less information than management on the risk facing the company. In addition, non-executive directors will receive information about risk management and containment filtered through senior management. The perspective of senior management may be marred with self-serving information as well as self-delusional thinking. One need only think of the last weekend before Lehman Brothers filed for bankruptcy and the testimony of its last chief executive, Dick Fuld, before the Financial Inquiry Crisis Commission to understand the possibility that self-delusional thinking on the part of senior management may cloud risk management judgment:

> By early September 2008, Lehman's situation was deteriorating quickly. The stock was falling, clients were clamoring to get money out, and the bank was forced to turn over billions of dollars in additional collateral to its prime broker, depleting its cash on hand.
>
> But in his testimony to the commission, Mr. Fuld said that even in Lehman's final days he believed that the 158-year-old Wall Street firm, which started as an Alabama cotton brokerage firm, would survive.
>
> "I didn't go into that weekend with anything that resembled failure on my brain," Mr. Fuld said. "I must tell you that."[80]

So how does the non-executive director go beyond senior management and obtain information from the lower levels of personnel, who will often have a different view of risk governance issues than senior management?

Richard Anderson, in his research for the Organisation for Economic Cooperation and Development,[81] points out that the corporate governance standards promulgated by the New York Stock Exchange, Financial Reporting Council and their French counterparts provide for a board of directors consisting of a majority of independent directors or non-executive directors and for the possibility that the independent directors or non-executive directors may want to meet alone, without the presence of executive directors, with such managers in the organisation as they require. As such, the non-executive directors cannot claim that they were unaware of or prevented from finding the right risk management information they needed to perform their oversight function. Moreover, Anderson calls for the risk management function of the independent directors or non-executive directors to be closely linked to the remit of the remuneration committee in that there must be clear alignment between risk management and oversight and remuneration, especially if there is a high level of conditional remuneration (bonuses), which, of course, significantly influences the nature of risk taking in the organisation.[82]

---

79   See note 84 below.
80   Susanne Craig, "In former C.E.O.'s Words, the Last Days of Lehman Brothers", *New York Times*, February 14 2011, available at: http://dealbook.nytimes.com/2011/02/14/a-different-side-to-dick-fuld/ (accessed February 1 2013).
81   Richard Anderson & Associates, "Risk Management & Corporate Governance", undated, available at: www.oecd.org/daf/corporateaffairs/corporategovernanceprinciples/42670210.pdf (accessed February 1 2013).
82   *Ibid.*

12.   Changing world of risk management

In drawing conclusions to our review of UBS and its governance reforms in the wake of an unprecedented series of legal, compliance and risk management challenges, it becomes apparent that now is not the time for self-congratulations or complacence on the part of UBS or others. In a Spring 2012 survey of 192 US executives from companies in the consumer and industrial products, life sciences, health care and technology/media/telecommunications industries, Deloitte and Forbes Insights found that many are still working hard to make sense of the environment as they deal with the current effects of the world economic crisis that began with the collapse of the US subprime mortgage market. In fact, 91% of these executives plan to reorganise and reprioritise their approaches to risk management in some form in the coming three years.[83] Not only are these executives fearful of further financial challenges to the world economy (eg, the continuing euro crisis), but they are also fearful of geopolitical changes, technological developments and their impact on society (eg, social media), and the impact of new regulation and compliance regimes.

As such, it is now more important than ever for the board of directors to 'step up to the plate' and take on the critical role of supervising risk to provide the right balance between risk and reward. Non-executive directors have an important function to play in the process as well, as they have the independence to ensure that the board's risk appetite is balanced, appropriate and followed throughout the company, not just at the C-level. To achieve this, companies are implementing programmes such as enterprise risk management to bridge the gap between C-suite executives and general personnel, as well as trying to ensure the right level of risk supervision is available. Computer automation and complex risk modelling have a role to play in ensuring the right risk management structures are in place. However, nothing can substitute for the indispensable ingredient for successful risk management on the part of today's board of directors – having independent directors on the board who are engaged and asking the right questions at all levels of the company and who can make tough decisions without fear of strong managerial personalities so as to ensure the appropriate risk management structure is in place, operational and effective.

13.   Final note of caution[84]

In trying to draw lessons to be learned from the problems faced by UBS or other companies in respect of risk management, one must consider the difficulty – and perhaps impossibility – for a small group of individuals such as the board of directors (especially the non-executive directors among them) truly to understand and anticipate all the risks facing large organisations. Perhaps it is unrealistic (to turn a famous phrase of Sir Winston Churchill) for so many to expect so much from so few!

Sir David Walker, in his review of the corporate governance of the UK banking industry, wrote of this problem:

---

83   Deloitte and Forbes Insights, "Aftershock: Adjusting to the New World of Risk Management", June 2012, available at: http://images.forbes.com/forbesinsights/StudyPDFs/deloitte_risk_management_2012.pdf (accessed February 1 2013).

84   The genesis for this section is co-author Roger Barker's Institute of Directors' January 2013 working paper entitled "The Challenge of Board Governance in the 21st Century" [2].

Doubts have been aired in some quarters whether it is, in practice, realistic to rely on a significant contribution from NEDs in future in the governance of BOFIs [banks and other financial institutions] which, already heavily regulated and becoming more so, will continue to engage in risk business of substantial complexity. A sceptical answer might acknowledge the important potential contribution of non-executives to board deliberation and decisions on other matters including audit, remuneration and nomination, but would leave core decisions on risk and strategy to be taken largely by the executive on the basis that the NED cannot be expected to get under the skin of complex risk issues in a way that is likely to be useful.[85]

Nonetheless, the Walker Review 2009 concludes that the role of the non-executive director and his or her input into the risk management oversight function is important, especially insofar as it can sometimes prevent internal executive decisions from "going off the rails":

The reasonable and legitimate expectation of the shareholder in a company governed by a unitary board has, at any rate until now, been that there will be a material input from the non-executive directors to decisions on strategy and in oversight of its implementation; and that such shared decision-taking between executive and non-executive directors is likely, at any rate in general and over time, to yield better performance for their company than if strategy were determined exclusively by the executive without external input independently of the executive. And certainly in the light of recent experience on both sides of the Atlantic, several banks whose strategies appear to have been determined by long-entrenched executives with little external input to their decision-taking appear to have fared materially worse than those where there was opportunity for effective challenge in the boardroom.

While in some recent situations NEDs may have made little effective input, it seems clear that the NED contribution was materially helpful in financial institutions that have weathered the storm better than others. This, and similar experience in many non-financial companies, suggests that the most relevant question is how to identify and draw lessons from recent experience so that best practice is more widely and dependably attained.

Of course, none of this removes the need for the board of directors to meet its responsibilities. It is important to note that although the institution of the board of directors faces major challenges, no one has yet suggested an alternative mechanism of governance that could viably take its place. Nonetheless, it is worth stressing that we expect a great deal from boards of directors; in fact, perhaps too much. As a result, the board of directors' functioning in the context of risk management is still a work in progress and, sad to conclude, it is unlikely that we have experienced the last ever corporate disaster.

---

85   Sir David Walker, "A review of Corporate Governance in UK Banks and Other Financial Industry Entities – Final Recommendation", November 26 2009, p 37, available at: http://webarchive. nationalarchives.gov.uk/+/www.hm-treasury.gov.uk/d/walker_review_261109.pdf (accessed February 18 2013).

Understanding the role of the independent director in family-controlled listed enterprises

Richard L Narva
Narva & Company LLC

All happy families resemble each other.
Each unhappy family is unhappy in its own way.
L Tolstoy[1]

I don't know if a company can have a soul, but I
like to think it can. And if it can, I'd like our soul
to be an old soul – and everything that implies.
I'd like to talk about things like values and soul.
These things aren't transient. These are things
You build forever.
William Clay Ford III, Chairman, Ford Motor Company[2]

1. Introduction

This chapter is about large-scale business enterprises, listed on stock exchanges across the world, that are controlled by families. It focuses on the impact the 'familiness' of a family shareholder control group has on the listed enterprise generally, and in particular on how controlling shareholders of family-controlled listed enterprises and the managers of their enterprises interact with the independent directors. Particular attention will be paid to how the independent directors perform their duties in this singular setting. Reference will also be made to how the role of the independent director of a family-controlled listed enterprise is different from the role and duties of independent directors of other enterprises controlled by single or small groups of shareholders, such as venture capital and private equity funds, governments, cooperatives, or other controlling parties not connected by the family ties that bind members to each other and to the enterprise. Finally, the chapter addresses the paradoxical and unexpected impact that effective performance of corporate governance responsibilities by independent directors may have on both family-controlled listed enterprises and the family shareholder groups that control them.

---

1   L Tolstoy, *Anna Karenina* (1877).
2   M Sherrill, "The Buddha of Detroit", *NY Times Magazine*, November 26 2000.

Readers should distinguish between business-owning families, that is, businesses where stockholders share a common name, but not necessarily any cohesive family behaviour or values,[3] and enduring, values-driven family-controlled enterprises, whether publicly traded or privately held, which succeed because they are built to last.[4] This chapter addresses only family-controlled (listed) enterprises because, in the author's experience,[5] such enterprises present corporate governance 'balance sheets' with recurring thematic assets and liabilities, so that corporate counsel, other corporate executives and members of the boards of directors may reasonably anticipate the consequences of decisions that they make. Such decisions and their predictable consequences are primarily a function of one's understanding and acceptance of the foundational values that underlie both family and corporate culture, and the foreseeable behaviours that flow from these family-sourced, cultural norms. On the other hand, business-owning families offer a variety, range and randomness of behaviour and, therefore, lie outside the scope of this chapter.

The chapter is based on two central principles. First, truly effective corporate governance in a family-controlled listed enterprise is rare. It is a difficult role and few individuals have all the required knowledge and skills to serve as an independent director of such an enterprise. Second, even if there were many independent director candidates, there is little demand for their services from family shareholder control groups (for reasons described below). It is perhaps for these reasons that articles focusing on the power of the family system and how it buttresses not only a family shareholder control group but also the enterprise itself are uncommon.[6] But I suggest another reason, and that is simply a bias that many (particularly American) observers of, or participants in, corporate governance believe, with or without evidence – that all family-controlled enterprises are misfits in the global economy. Holders of this view are entitled to their opinions, but obviously should not stand for election to the boards of family-controlled enterprises, whether listed or unlisted.

The opportunity to serve as an independent director of a family-controlled listed enterprise is rarely available to non-executive directors. The role is the most challenging of any corporate governance assignment. Effective corporate governance of such an enterprise requires:

- outstanding performance by directors who are independent of management, the controlling shareholder(s) and the family itself'
- utilising all of the sources of information discussed in this chapter to support their judgment on complex issues, and their judgment; and
- must be exercised consistently with full understanding of the numerous roles such directors play that are unique to the family-controlled listed enterprise setting.

3   D Dreux IV and J Goodman, *Business Succession Planning and Beyond: A Multidisciplinary Approach to Representing the Family-Owned Business*, American Bar Association (1997).
4   J Collins and J Porras, *Built to Last: Successful Habits of Visionary Companies*, New York (1997).
5   See generally, R Narva, "Heritage and Tradition in Family Business: How Family-Controlled Enterprises Connect the Experience of their Past to the Promise of their Future", in *Family Business Gathering 2001 The Holistic Model: "Destroying Myths and Creating Value in Family Business"*, Stetson University (2001), also available at: www.narvaandcompany.com/pdfs/Heritage-and-Tradition-in-Family%20-Business.pdf.
6   See RC Andersen and DM Reeb, "Founding-Family Ownership and Firm Performance: Evidence from the S & P 500", 58 *J of Finance* 3 (2003).

As well as being able to communicate effectively in corporate governance terms in the boardroom, the independent director must also be able to communicate effectively with the controlling family and understand its ethnicity, culture and values. Perhaps the most important necessary skill is for the independent director to bring to the assignment an emotional intelligence that is rarely found, appreciated or addressed in the curricula of the world's business schools or other training grounds where one goes to prepare to become a director of a listed company.

If independent directors are allowed to serve effectively in a family shareholder control group, they will contribute to good governance and better corporate performance.[7] An independent director may modify the controlling family's culture, supporting harmony within the family and helping it to stay in control. Although this is not a formally defined aspect of their role, the introduction of new ideas and ways of behaving that independent directors of family-controlled listed enterprises may contribute can lead to continued corporate growth and competitive strength.

2.   The difficulty of defining a family-controlled listed enterprise

For more than thirty years the literature on family business has struggled with the basic issue: "What is a family business?"[8] This chapter will not contribute further to that academic debate; instead it will discuss a group of businesses that are readily identifiable: enterprises with widely held shares and listed on a stock exchange, but controlled by a family shareholder control group. The first two characteristics are easily identifiable, but the definition of 'controlled by a family shareholder group' may vary, even individually by family (see Tolstoy's observation about families at the beginning of the chapter). Primarily, it is a function of the culture, nation, origin and/or ethnicity of the family shareholder control group. Consider the power of an observation such as that of US Supreme Court Justice Potter Stewart as he tried to explain hard core pornography or what is obscene:

> I shall not today attempt further to define the kinds of material I understand to be embraced ... but I know it when I see it ...[9]

I believe that anyone who is employed by or serves on the board of a family-controlled enterprise knows the reality of being in such an enterprise. For example, both Giovanni Agnelli and Edmund Safra held title of Honorary Chairman, but they exercised complete control. These two honorary chairmen were born on different continents, spoke different languages and were active in different industries. What they shared was a deep commitment to their multi-generational families and their lifelong commitment to global corporate endeavour. Virtually everyone within the senior management or governance of a family-controlled listed enterprise can define family control without recourse to an academic definition to verify the experience. They know family control when they see it.

---

7   *Ibid.*
8   See, eg, W Handler, "Methodological Issues and Consideration in Studying Family Business", 2(3) *Fam Bus Rev* 257 (1992).
9   *Jacobellis v Ohio*, 378 US 184, 197 (1964).

3. Governance in family-controlled listed enterprise

Many entrepreneurs and/or patriarchs and matriarchs of family-controlled listed enterprises rarely think about governance issues. A business adviser may think it illogical or even imprudent that a business founder, or a member of a succeeding generation of the family shareholder control group who leads a listed company, seldom contemplates whether effective governance will serve their enterprise well in the long term; the issue appears too remote to be seen as a pressing, current problem. Dynastic succession may override good business judgment, on the part of both the family chairman and chief executive officer (CEO) and the board of directors. Many observers of family shareholder control groups – whether sympathetic or hostile – would confirm that families have this sense of priorities. Focus on the family leads many to believe that "... the antiseptic ethos of the industrial era, stigma surrounds family business, as if the involvement of family was somehow unbusinesslike".[10]

Analysis of many family-controlled listed enterprises may show that the enterprise's governance policy is a token used to improve image rather than to focus on effective supervision of management. (In this respect, family-controlled enterprises may be neither better nor worse than non-family listed companies. Consider the poor governance issues that contributed to recent scandals such as Enron in the USA and Ahold in the Netherlands.) The developmental nature of change within the family that controls such an enterprise, whether listed or unlisted, is the first premise one must understand in order to design and execute effective governance. As one leading commentator has observed:

Family companies with public shareholders are interesting simply because they may exhibit many of the characteristics of family businesses more generally. Individuals' roles – as family member, equity owner, or participant in business management or operations – may overlap, and, at times, collide. Tensions within the family may be reflected in decisions that formally concern the business or its ownership structure.[11]

In family-controlled listed enterprises, there is a risk that personal family issues will intrude into the business and interfere with its management. This makes good governance more difficult.

4. Distinguishing the family-control listed enterprise from the private equity, venture capital or government led controlled company

An independent director in the family-controlled listed enterprise setting must be more than independent of management as that term is commonly understood in American securities law. In addition, he must be independent of both the founder/patriarch/CEO and of the family shareholder control group as a whole. In this setting, 'independent' does not mean that there should be no personal relationship with the family owners or family members who serve on the board of directors. Paradoxically, a real relationship may be seen as a condition precedent to true independence.

---

10   T Petzinger Jr, *The New Pioneers*, New York (1999) at 217.

11   D DeMott, "Guests and the Table?: Independent Directors in Family-Influenced Public Companies", 33 *J Corporation Law* 819-863 (2009), available at: http://scholarship.law.duke.edu/faculty_scholarship/1918.

Directors who are independent of both management and the founding family serve distinct functions within the complex environment of a family-influenced public company. Independent directors are the sole actors at the highest level of firm governance who have the capacity to bring appropriate detachment to bear in resolving difficult questions that implicate family ties as well as business necessity, including management succession and external threats to the firm's position and separate existence.[12]

5. Linking corporate governance to performance of family-controlled listed enterprises

Ronald Andersen and David Reeb's pioneering study of Standard & Poor's 500 largest firms (S & P 500) between 1992 and 1999[13] provides a good basis for understanding the performance of family-controlled listed enterprises. In what was the first analysis of how family-controlled listed enterprises in the index performed relative to other index enterprises (the larger proportion) of the S & P 500:

Andersen and Reeb's 2003 study found that family-associated firms in the Standard and Poor's Index performed better than non-family firms, controlling for industry and other firm characteristics and measuring firm performance by Tobin's q and return on assets.[14]

What is most striking is not that founder and family-controlled enterprises modestly outperformed the non-family S & P index companies based on a particular metric, but that they performed materially better than the commonly held belief that family-controlled companies perform less well than non family-controlled listed enterprises. Andersen and Reeb provided the first serious indication that anecdotal evidence of family business collapses reported by the financial media should not define how family-controlled listed enterprises perform generally. For purposes of this chapter, the occasional family-controlled listed enterprise collapse will be treated as an outlier with respect to the impact of governance on corporate performance, just as neither Enron nor Ahold will be deemed representative of how corporate governance in non family-controlled listed enterprises impacts performance.[15]

This chapter assumes simply that the commonplace, clichéd understanding of family-controlled listed enterprises is myth, not fact. Clearly, family firm collapses do occur, often because the management is focused on family prerogatives or needs instead of the business enterprise. Again, the literature does not support the myth that this is the norm. Thus, the following sections will focus on how the independent director can gather information, apply skills and add value to the family-controlled listed enterprise (that, like all other listed companies, can benefit from best practices in corporate governance), and on how the special knowledge and skills an independent director can bring to the family-controlled listed enterprise to help meet the particular demands of governing an enterprise controlled by a specific family.

---

12   *Ibid*, at 824.
13   Andersen and Reeb, note 6 above.
14   DeMott, note 11 above, at 17.
15   There is an enormous bibliography on Rupert Murdoch's dynastic ambitions, but see specifically, D Carr, "The Cozy Compliance of the News Corp. Board", *NY Times*, May 7 2012.

6. Family as the primary source of corporate culture

A primary objective of this chapter is to highlight the sources of information for the corporate officer charged with compliance with securities and other legal obligations of a family-controlled listed enterprise. Some sources of information are identical to those of any other listed company; others are particular to family-controlled enterprises generally, whether listed or unlisted; and yet others are particular to individual family-controlled listed enterprises. Although not usually included within the ambit of securities regulation, the culture or ethnicity of the founding family/family shareholder control group is important for any corporate compliance officer of a family-controlled listed enterprise. In practice, it may be considered to be material non-public information. Monica McGoldrick, a leading scholar on culture and ethnicity and family therapy,[16] and a co-author have concluded that, given two business enterprises similar in all respects except for the culture and ethnicity of the family shareholder control group, any effective consulting intervention must be designed primarily with the cultural practices of the controlling family in mind.[17] My own firm's consulting experience with over 400 family-controlled enterprises, both listed and unlisted, validates this approach to family business advising.

Consider the following example from my consulting experience. My firm had been retained by a manufacturing firm, based in the United States but producing goods for export to global markets. The founder and his wife were both of South Asian origin, one having been born in India, the other in the expatriate Indian community of East Africa. They married and moved to the United States. In the course of the initial interview with the wife, he told me that they had an arranged marriage and did that matter in the context of their family business issues. My response was swift: "Perhaps so, but how is an American born-and-bred adviser with absolutely no experience of arranged marriages to answer that question based upon his own knowledge?" He then inquired whether the fact that her husband was born into a high caste had any impact on his inability to relate well to his senior management team. I suggested that her inference was probably correct, but that my first-hand experience of the implications of a caste system for corporate team-building was more limited than my familiarity with arranged marriages, since at least two of my grandparents had had a marriage broker arrange their marriage.

Service on the board of directors of a family-controlled listed enterprise requires more than respect for and understanding of cultural differences. Interest in learning about and knowledge of the primary cultural motivations of the family shareholder control group are as essential as the ability to read a balance sheet is to any director of a listed company. What one finds when discussing these topics with members of the family shareholder control group can be illuminating. Two decades ago, I taught a course, 'Managing the Family Business', to a class of seniors at a major American university, one of whom was a Arab woman from a very traditional family that controlled a substantial business in her nation of origin. During a private conversation

---

16   See generally, M McGoldrick *et al*, *Culture and Ethnicity in Family Therapy*, 3rd edn, New York City (2005).
17   M McGoldrick and J Troast Jr, "Ethnicity, Families, and Family Business: Implications for Practitioners", VI Fam *Bus Rev* 3 (2004).

he told me that her younger brother had been provided with funding to attend an American university to study business. In contrast, she had to win a scholarship in order to attend college in the United States. She had done this in order to return home and run the family business. When I inquired whether her gender might constrain her leadership, she replied that this would not be a problem. Before her marriage, she invoked the power of her father as the author of her management directives. Now that she was married, she would (with her more modern-thinking husband's full and knowing consent) invoke his authority in the same way. It may be true that such indirection may no longer be necessary in this woman's family-controlled enterprise. I certainly hope so. But what is compelling to me about this memory is not the culturally specific burden under which this woman had to manage her company, but rather how imaginatively she had intuited how to convert the norms of her culture of origin from constraint to a compelling source of leadership.

7. Protecting the directors' independence in a family-controlled listed enterprise setting

For purposes of this chapter, it is presumed that in order for a director to assume the full independence required to offer objective advice and accountability, and even to resign on a matter of principle if necessary, an independent director must be a non-executive director (ie, a director not employed on a full-time basis by the family-controlled listed enterprise) and must not depend on income from service to the family-controlled listed enterprise for a material portion of his or her income. Financial dependency and independence are antonyms, not concurrent relationships in this setting. Thus, by definition, a trustee of a trust for the benefit of a material shareholder, legal or financial counsel, or the proprietor of or a partner in a firm that advises the shareholder control group or a member of it, cannot be independent. This definition of independence applies to any listed company. However, another criterion must be added for the family-controlled listed enterprise – avoiding over-involvement with the family of the controlling shareholder group.

> Directors who are independent of both management and the founding family serve distinct functions within the complex environment of a family-influenced company. Independent directors are the sole actors at the highest level of firm governance who have the capacity to bring appropriate detachment to bear in resolving difficult questions that implicate family ties as well as business necessity, including management succession and external threats to the firm's position and separate existence.[18]

An independent director of a family-controlled listed enterprise may derive personal satisfaction from roles which indicate that a relationship of trust has developed (eg, godparent, legal counsel, or trustee to a member of the family), and any such role may support effective service as an independent director. However, it will also be a warning sign that the director lacks independence from the family. Roles that create too much intimacy with the controlling shareholder/family may introduce problems, sometimes undetectable, for a director who is not trained to understand their full impact.

---

18   *Ibid.*

In this context, training in family systems, which is rarely taught in law or business schools, may be compared to the military training of a bomb disposal expert, skilled at finding and defusing land mines. While understanding that the power of the family is the "oxygen that feeds the fires of entrepreneurship"[19] and usually the original source of the culture of strategically powerful family-controlled listed enterprises, knowledge of the power of a particular family's culture, ethnicity and interpersonal dynamics is not the same as the expertise to intervene in family conflicts within the enterprise. Family systems are at least as complex as the enterprises they may control, and require some directors with the same familiarity and understanding of the family dynamics that other directors have of the balance sheet of the enterprise. There is a reason why chartered or certified public accountants are required by law to serve as auditors of listed companies. Similarly, experts licensed to charge fees to provide services regarding understanding and counselling families are an absolute requirement for a fully functional group of advisers to the board of a family-controlled listed enterprise.

Conflict is a normal process in family life. Some families develop the tools and skills to resolve interpersonal conflict; others seek recourse to outside professionals; many go it alone. Some succeed; some fail. But it is only in the family firm context that the failure to resolve interpersonal conflict can affect the livelihoods of the many individuals who have placed their confidence and economic well-being in the hands of a family shareholder control group. A failure to resolve existing and foreseeable family relationship issues often presents the greatest potential to destroy family control of a business enterprise, and even the enterprise itself. Independent directors of family-controlled listed enterprises must recognise that communication patterns and relationship dynamics within families play a crucial role in determining both business success and family harmony. Normal family dynamics such as sibling rivalry and intergenerational conflict can sabotage the family enterprise if not addressed and resolved. Recourse to experts in this area should be as normal a pattern of director conduct as seeking fairness opinions in the unsolicited takeover offer setting. But it is almost never so.

8. Roles played by a director independent of the family shareholder control group

The remainder of this chapter examines the multiple, concurrent roles that constitute the job description of an independent director of a family-controlled listed enterprise and how successful execution of these responsibilities can enhance corporate performance while strengthening family systems of the controlling shareholder group. When I first addressed the issue of independent directors of a family-controlled listed enterprise 33 years ago, it was in the context of evaluating the board of directors of the listed shoe company founded by my grandfather and his brother in 1921. It was 1979 and the company had been listed for about a dozen years. I was recruited from a leading corporate law firm in Boston by my brother to

---

19   See RZ Heck, "Evolving Research in Entrepreneurship and Family Business: Recognizing Family as the Oxygen that Feeds the Fire of Entrepreneurship", 18 J *Business Venturing* 559 (2003).

assist the family in addressing several concurrent leadership crises. The company had four apparently independent directors, all of whom, I learned eventually, had essentially a two-word vocabulary at board meetings, "Yes, Mort" – Mort being my father and the CEO of the company. I learned first hand the cost of the so-called 'independent director' who was really a sycophant, and persuaded my father to purge the board of its directors and start again. Since the recruitment of a crew of talented, truly independent directors for our family-controlled listed enterprise's board, I have advised on the creation or overhaul of more than six dozen boards, and have served on numerous listed and unlisted companies' boards of directors. From all of these experiences, I have learned that there are many different important roles – many of which are specific to the family-controlled listed enterprise – that independent directors can, and often must, assume. The roles discussed in the following sections are not intended to be a comprehensive list, but only to highlight some of the most important roles the independent director of a family-controlled listed enterprise may play that his counterpart in a non family-controlled listed enterprise may be free to ignore.

8.1 Prometheus, the bearer of fire

In her seminal article, "Guests at the Table?: Independent Directors in Family Influenced Companies", Professor Deborah DeMott emphasizes that: "unlike a reliably affable guest at the family dinner table, an effective director in a public company brings a capacity for skeptical assessment to the boardroom table."[20] While clearly a correct statement of the best case theory of corporate governance, DeMott does not explain fully why an independent director of a family-controlled listed enterprise is a guest at the table. In my view, one should look at the 'table' not as the Formica-covered kitchen table around which the prototypical small business family gathered in the climactic scene of the movie comedy. Moonstruck, but rather as one of the many salon tables in Vienna in the early 20th century. In these salons, where intellectual ferment was the main course, being a guest at the table created the inference that one had been invited to the table less for affability than as an exemplar of intellectual energy and provocative ideas.

It is in this sense that being a guest at the table invites favourable comparison with governance at companies chaired by executives who are simultaneously CEO and chairman. The impact of CEO as emperor on the quality of governance has been eloquently described and analysed in the career of Michael Eisner at Disney[21] in a book that illustrates how an imperial chairman, who stocks his board with luminaries the way a pond is stocked with trout, and who is more concerned with the optics of governance than the challenges and accountability knowledgeable, independent directors bring to the process of corporate governance, brings about his own downfall when he does battle with the last remaining scion of a founding family of a major listed company.

---

20   DeMott, note 11 above, at 863.
21   James B Stewart, *Disney Wars*, (2005).

8.2 Guardians of protocols, formality and process

Family systems issues are like magma moving beneath the earth's crust. Magma erupts, becoming a volcano, when and where tectonic forces command – there is little humankind can do about it. Similarly, when long-term, unresolved, emotionally powerful family issues erupt in a family-controlled listed company, there is nothing directors can do to stop it. A corporate governance regime is unlikely to address such issues. What directors independent of the family can do is:

- anticipate foreseeable eruptions;
- identify independent resources such as consultants specialised in family-controlled enterprises – especially advisory firms expert in family systems issues as well as in corporate and business affairs – to assist in management of the aftermath; and
- educate themselves about the impact of family issues on family-controlled listed enterprises.

This is not to say that directors should become family therapists any more than they should become chief financial officers or chief information officers. Rather, directors learn about the thematic family issues that arise in family-controlled listed enterprises, whether listed or unlisted. As a board, they can retain expert advisers who can warn of an impending eruption in the same way that they retain investment bankers to advise the board on other major events, such as an unsolicited takeover offer. Finally, they can:

- insist that standard corporate governance procedures are followed, for example management succession planning.

For an example of the benefit of such planning, compare the consequences of the management succession planning process of Warren Buffett with that of Rupert Murdoch on the stock prices of their respective enterprises.

8.3 Ombudsman for the disempowered

If one person enjoys the total control exercised by the family, many stakeholders will be powerless – family members, especially women and in-laws engaged in both management and corporate governance, senior non-family executives, minority shareholders, professional advisers and many members of the board of directors. In this setting, the independent director may be the sole voice for the stakeholders and other shareholders if their concerns are dismissed by the controlling shareholder, either through fiat or a failure to understand. This is not a role without substantial power.

The main power of the independent director in a family-controlled listed enterprise is the power to resign, either quietly and privately, or publicly and proclaiming a message. While most fiduciary directors in such enterprises are ultimately advisery (ie, they serve at the will of the controlling shareholders, and can be replaced at will by the family shareholder control group as a whole or, in some cases, by the paterfamilias), they nonetheless have one deterrent power: their power to resign, either privately or publicly. Speaking from the personal experience of having resigned on a matter of principle – albeit quietly – from a billion dollar family-controlled private company with a CEO who had held the post for 42 years, and watching it get sold within six months of the resignation of two of the three independent directors, I see this power as real deterrent to management malfeasance or nonfeasance by a long-term CEO who has dominated his or her company.

One of America's greatest Supreme Court justices, Louis Brandeis, once observed that "Sunlight is the best disinfectant." One need look no further than the assignment undertaken by the independent directors of News Corporation's Management Standards and Practices Committee, who have been empowered by the corporation's board of directors to manage the telephone tapping and police bribery scandal of its English newspaper subsidiary, to witness the power of Brandeis' dictum. At the other end of the continuum is South Africa's Pick n Pay Stores Ltd, frequently awarded the status of most admired company in South Africa and best governed company in that nation, whose second generation chairman, Gareth Ackerman, has written about how the duties of the family shareholder control group include a duty of loyalty to all stakeholders imposed on shareholder control groups by virtue of ownership control.[22] Most family-controlled listed enterprises fall in between these two poles of the continuum, often moving along the continuum as both family system and corporate enterprise encounter and respond to the realities of the marketplace. How far and how fast a family-controlled listed enterprise moves along this continuum may often be determined by the efficacy of its independent directors' performance of their numerous, concurrent roles.

8.4 Window on the world

Decades ago I heard a Portuguese family business adviser speak on the subject of privacy in family business consulting. He noted that, in his client base, family shareholder control groups spanned the entire spectrum of attitudes on privacy – from completely private to hermetically sealed, and everything in between. Thirty years in the same field have taught me that this European adviser was speaking accurately for family shareholder control groups across the globe. In private companies, it is relatively easy to maintain a culture of silence and non-cooperation with authorities. For a family-controlled listed enterprise with statutory and regulatory disclosure requirements, it is a more difficult task, albeit one that is usually assumed willingly.

However great the advantage of maintaining privacy, the disadvantages for members of a family shareholder control group are:

- in addition to governmental mandates to disclose material inside information, normal business practice requires discretion from all senior managers and directors of a listed company;
- any violation of this legal constraint by a family member may lead to ostracism for violating a family mandate of silence that meets the legal

---

22   G Ackerman, Business Day, Rosebank, RSA, March 1 2012, also available at http://article.wn.com/view/2012/03/01/GARETH_ACKERMAN_SA_needs_more_businesses_run_by_families_not/. See also www.howwemadeitinafrica.com/the-case-for-family-businesses/15469/.

standard and to reduction of the family's wealth and reputation if non-public information is disclosed;

- commitment to both immediate and extended family and long work hours within the family-controlled listed enterprise can leave the family shareholder control group without the energy or inclination to explore ideas and people outside their relatively closed world; and
- the power of some cultural norms move the standards of corporate conduct from intensely private to hermetically sealed.

The independent director of a family-controlled listed enterprise can open up a closed system. Ultimately, it is the values shared by the shareholder control group and the independent director that introduce ideas and ways of doing business. Directors may speak different languages, come from a different continent or express these values from a completely different religious tradition, but it is the shared values that provide the enterprising independent director with an opportunity to widen the approach of the family-controlled listed enterprise's controlling shareholders.

8.5 Counsellor/mentor to individual family members

Over the years, the new independent director will move from being an alien visitor to guest at the table, to respected independent voice, to a wise adviser and trusted confidante. Speaking from substantial personal experience, this journey may take at least five to 10 years. Serving too long in the role of director may compromise independence, especially if the director respects the controlling family of shareholders for their community commitment and fundamental decency as well as their business acumen. Notwithstanding this risk, remaining a guest at the table is a plausible and sustainable stance – when it can be maintained, such an independent director has the access, the trust and the independent insight to offer information, advice and guidance that may not otherwise be available to the patriarch/matriarch and/or other members of the family shareholder control group. When an independent director has earned this status, and the need arises, he, based solely on trust and competence, can have profound impact on the affairs of the enterprise, relationships within the family and, ultimately, on the durability of family control of the enterprise.

8.6 Architects of continuity

Much of the academic literature on family business emphasises the issue of management succession in family firms. Yet this emphasis is misplaced. It assumes that all family firms are small or medium-sized, owner/managed companies where the ownership control and management succession occurs between two generations. As a result, much of the literature is of little use to the family shareholder groups who control listed companies, who often transfer control over more than two generations. Management succession plans are an important part of the planning process that families who control capital invested in operating companies need to undertake, and are a primary responsibility of all boards of all listed enterprises. However, succession plans are only a small part of the overall process of meeting the strategic objectives of controlling family shareholder groups. Independent directors of these enterprises should make themselves aware of continuity planning and of professional firms qualified by their expertise in both family systems and corporate life. Continuity planning is a holistic planning and implementation process that requires several independent, concurrent planning activities led by several different primary professional advisers. In addition to the development of both family and corporate governance, it will include a range of schemes that enable the family shareholder control group to achieve three concurrent objectives:

- continued strengthening of corporate strategy, growth and financial performance;
- continued family control of the enterprise; and
- continued enhancement of family harmony.

In order to achieve these objectives, families who control listed enterprises must undertake the same kind of sustained, comprehensive planning that the management teams and boards of directors of the companies they control assume. Failure to plan for future ownership control generally, and failure to address underlying family systems issues within the family shareholder control group, will have a negative impact on achieving the goals of continuity planning.

At a minimum, family shareholder control groups should regularly undertake:

- resolution of existing and foreseeable family relationship issues;
- personal financial, tax and estate planning;
- corporate strategic planning;
- development of family and corporate governance; and
- design of financial architecture appropriate and capable of funding both corporate strategic plans and controlling family/shareholder needs.

8.7   Mediator of intra-family disputes

On some occasions, the guest at the table is asked to mediate disputes between members of the family or between family members and management. Such assignments should not be accepted by independent directors acting individually, if at all. Governance is a collective enterprise. If mediation is required, the independent directors as a group should retain a skilled mediator experienced in dealing with family-controlled listed enterprises, or at least with family-controlled business enterprises generally. Families may ask for mediation, but directors should stay within their remit – corporate governance – and refer such requests to professionals specialised in mediation. Without advanced professional education in family systems and counselling, no director, however empathic and sympathetic, should undertake a service which he is unlicensed to perform.

9.   Eleven rules for recruiting and retaining outstanding independent directors for a family-controlled listed enterprise

Finding an independent director for a family-controlled listed enterprise is a time-consuming, expensive and difficult task. Based on my experience of assembling nearly 70 boards for substantial family-controlled enterprises, both listed and unlisted, certain thematic issues arise over and over again. Set out below are eleven thoughts for family shareholder control groups and the individuals who wish to serve on their boards to consider.

- if complete control is important to you, do not consider recruiting independent directors. Truly independent directors can contribute significantly to family-controlled listed enterprises, but their independence, however subtle, does not suit the culture of every family shareholder control group. Closed systems do not become open systems simply because some new directors are elected;

- you must be able to define your vision for your family-controlled listed enterprise, your family's values and your company's core competencies and strategy before you ask anyone to serve as a member of your board of directors, because it is primarily the lure of being a guest at your particular table that will attract the best talent;

- if you want only advice, form a council of advisers. Do not recruit independent directors who will challenge the controlling family on issues and will have the legal authority to enforce their views;

- independent directors of family-controlled listed enterprises earn a premium to market rates for non family-controlled listed enterprises directors. Be prepared to pay for what you need. Fully qualified directors for family-controlled listed enterprises are rare. Even qualifiable ones are hard to find. Money should not be an object when the future of the family, its control of the enterprise and the enterprise itself are on the line;

- choose directors who have experience, judgment, passion, emotional intelligence and character. Everything else is a non-essential bonus;

- remember that a director's primary duties are to the corporation, not to the CEO or to the family that owns a controlling interest in the company. If this idea is not inspiring, try a different initiative. As noted above, if the family shareholder control group needs mediation of a family dispute, look to a qualified, experienced professional firm, not to the board of directors;

- do not recruit any directors who need the money. Directors who depend on their fees are never truly independent, and you want and need independent directors;

- subject every potential director to a thorough set of screening interviews. A formal vetting process shows both your managers and your potential directors just how serious you are about having an effective board. Candidates who are otherwise excellent candidates but who cannot demonstrate listening and communications skills with many different, and even difficult, people are not fully qualified for this role;

- avoid famous people. Governance is a collegial task easily subverted by prima donnas and narcissists;

- your board should be willing and able to evaluate all senior family and non-family executives and, therefore, be willing to have their performance as directors evaluated as well; and

- governance is an investment, not an expense. It will take at least three years for a new board of directors to start to become effective. But some contributions begin immediately, such as pointing out where not to step in a minefield.

Corporate social responsibility

Richard Smerdon

Editor, *CCH Corporate Governance Handbook*

---

1.   Corporate social responsibility in the context of corporate governance

Corporate governance may be defined in several ways. The 1992 Cadbury review[1] adopted a 'narrow' definition of the financial aspects of corporate governance – "the system by which companies are directed and controlled". The Organisation for Economic Cooperation and Development (OECD) uses a broader definition:

> *Corporate governance involves a set of relationships between a company's management, its board, its shareholders and other stakeholders. Corporate governance also provides the structure through which the objectives of the company are set, and the means of attaining those objectives and monitoring performance are determined.*[2]

The narrow definition, which emphasises structure and process, does not include corporate social responsibility, although many companies which use this definition do practise corporate social responsibility. The broader definition emphasises that relationships with a broad range of stakeholders are essential to good governance, and this approach is the one adopted in the chapter.

2.   The background to corporate social responsibility

In recent years, several factors have emerged to explain why many public companies explicitly adopt corporate social responsibility.

2.1   Sustainability and public pressure

In 2012, Professor David Grayson, Director of the Doughty Centre for Corporate Responsibility, was quoted in the Financial Times in the context of the excesses in the financial markets as saying that:

> *... the world has been equally profligate in its use of natural resources. We've been living way beyond our means in relation to credit, but in the way in which we've been growing, you could say exactly the same thing about the models for how we pay social and environmental costs.*[3]

In the same year, a group of protesters calling themselves the Occupy movement occupied an area round St Paul's Cathedral in London to protest against the excesses

---

1   The Committee on the Financial Aspects of Corporate Governance, available at: www.jbs.cam.ac.uk/cadbury/report/index.html (accessed November 5 2012).

2   www.oecd.org/daf/corporateaffairs/corporategovernanceprinciples/31557724.pdf (accessed November 20 2012).

3   Responsible Business: Special Report, *Financial Times*, May 30 2012, available at: http://media.ft.com/cms/f52cfc76-a866-11e1-8fbb-00144feabdc0.pdf (accessed November 30 2012).

of the banking community in the City of London. Professor Grayson commented that the Occupy movement served as an important reminder to corporations about their responsibility to society.

In 1980, business leaders and others formed Business in the Community, which aimed to drive responsible corporate practice. The organisation developed a corporate responsibility index (BITC CR Index[4]) and now makes annual awards to companies achieving outstanding progress – in everything from environmental leadership to sustainable innovation and design. In 2012, companies such as BT Group, EDF Energy, Unilever and the Wates group were listed in the index's 'Platinum Plus' category.

In 2010, Unilever (which produces some of the UK's leading brands) unveiled a new business model,[5] putting sustainability at the heart of its global operations. It pledged to halve the environmental impact of its products while doubling sales over the following 10 years, and to produce an annual report on its progress towards achieving these goals. It made three overarching commitments to achieve by 2020:

- to reduce the environmental impact of its products in terms of water, waste and greenhouse gases by 50%;
- to source 100% of its agricultural supplies from sustainable sources; and
- to improve the health and well-being of one billion people across the world.

Unilever outlined a number of ways in which it would meet these commitments, including doubling its use of renewable energy to 40% of total energy use; reducing its water consumption by 65% on 1995 levels; reducing waste sent for disposal by 70% on 1995 levels; and reducing levels of salt, fat and sugar in its food products.

In its 2011 annual report, the Royal Bank of Scotland (RBS) put the issue thus:

We want to be a bank that is socially useful. Lending responsibly is absolutely what we need to do. We took significant steps in 2011 to promote sustainable business practices internally. As part of the wider responsibility we all have to our communities, our people should be out there getting involved to give something back. And that's what we encourage at RBS.

It is unlikely that this approach would have been included in annual reports a few years ago, let alone become a driver for change in business models, but the concern for developing sustainable business models has become so common as not to be worth remarking upon – rather, what is remarked upon is the extent to which models are effective and measurable.

2.2 A change in the attitude of senior executives towards corporate social responsibility

A 2006 survey of business executives by McKinsey found that the majority of respondents acknowledged a wider role for corporations than just maximising

---

4   Available at: www.bitc.org.uk/cr_index/about_the_cr_index/cr_index_framework.html (accessed November 30 2012).

5   www.unilever.com/investorrelations/annual_reports/AnnualReportandAccounts2011/Ourbusiness modelforsustainablegrowth.aspx (accessed November 30 2012).

investor returns, "though this finding is remarkable in itself".[6] In addition, respondents saw environmental concerns, the offshoring debate and other sensitive matters as potential threats to the creation of value and conceded that their companies handled these issues poorly.

2.3 The Companies Act 2006

Section 172 of the UK Companies Act 2006 imposes a primary duty on directors to promote the success of a company for the benefit of its members as a whole ('enlightened shareholder value'), but provides that, in arriving at decisions for the benefit of members as a whole, directors must "have regard to" a number of pluralist factors which encompass corporate social responsibility, such as "the impact of the company's operations on the community and the environment", "the interests of the company's employees" and "the need to foster the company's business relationships with suppliers, customers and others".

2.4 The ABI Disclosure Guidelines on socially responsible investment, reissued in 2007

In 2007, the Association of British Insurers, which represents 440 members that own approximately 20% of the FTSE All-Share Index and have over £1.5 trillion assets, reissued its 2001 Socially Responsible Investment Guidelines. It stated:

Public debate on corporate responsibility and new legislation in both the EU and UK has furthered understanding of corporate responsibility to the point where it seems helpful for institutional shareholders to set out fresh disclosure principles, which will guide them in assessing narrative reporting and seeking to engage with companies in which they invest.[7]

The amended 2007 guidelines incorporate provisions of the EU Accounts Modernisation Directive and the Companies Act 2006, as well as experience of narrative reporting and the UK government's clarification of directors' liability for narrative statements. They have not changed substantially, but they now highlight those aspects of responsibility reporting on which shareholders place particular value. This is narrative reporting which:

- sets environmental, social and governance risks in the context of the whole range of risks and opportunities facing a company;
- contains a forward-looking perspective; and
- describes the actions of the company's board in mitigating these risks.[8]

Institutional shareholders are concerned to avoid unnecessary prescription and the imposition of expensive burdens, which can restrict the ability of companies to generate returns. The 2007 guidelines are not intended to add to the reporting

6 McKinsey Quarterly, 2006 Number 2, *When Social Issues Become Strategic*, available at: https://bspace. berkeley.edu/access/content/group/fe2bfb5b-adc6-40b2-813e-381775070de0/01.%20_Business,%20 Social%20Responsibility,%20and%20Human%20Rights_:%20What%20and%20Why/When%20Social% 20Issues%20Become%20Strategic,%20McKinsey%20Q.pdf (accessed November 30 2012).
7 www.ivis.co.uk/ResponsibleInvestmentDisclosure.aspx (accessed December 10 2012).
8 *Ibid.*

burden facing companies, but rather they aim to help companies to understand and respond to the needs of investors when complying with new reporting requirements under UK and European company law.

For investors, by focusing on the need to identify and manage environmental, social and corporate governance risks to the long and short-term value of the business, the guidelines highlight an opportunity to enhance value. The positive response of companies to the original guidelines has been built on, setting the reporting of these risks in the context of the full range of strategic, financial and operational risks facing businesses. Investors value forward-looking assessment of risks in the annual reports of companies in which they invest.

2.5   The business review/operating and financial review

Section 417 of the Companies Act 2006 implemented the Accounts Modernisation Directive's requirement for a business review in the annual report, and also requires quoted companies, "to the extent necessary for an understanding of the development, performance or position of the company's business",[9] to include not only narrative reporting on the main trends and factors likely to affect development, but also information on environmental matters, the company's employees and social and community issues (covering the company's policies on these matters and their effectiveness) and contracts or arrangements essential to the business. The benchmark guidance on accounting treatment best practice in relation to the operating and financial review is *Reporting Standard 1 Operating and Financial Review*,[10] published in May 2005 by the Accounting Standards Board division of the Financial Reporting Council.

3.   What does corporate social responsibility mean in practice?

In its 2001 report, Investing in Social Responsibility: Risks and opportunities, the Association of British Insurers stated that corporate social responsibility is about "how profits are made rather than how much profit there is or how much is given away".[11]

It pointed out that the subject embraces a diverse range of issues, which may change rapidly and will differ from company to company. However, the key areas are:

- *employment:* ensuring diversity in the workforce, and providing suitable conditions, including subcontractors' and suppliers' labour;
- *environment:* minimising the impact of products and processes on the quality of land, air, water and ecosystems that make up the environment;
- *human rights:* working to uphold basic human rights wherever the company operates, including issues such as child labour, sexual harassment,

---

9   Companies Act 2006, Section 417(5), available at: www.legislation.gov.uk/ukpga/2006/46/section/417 (accessed November 30 2012).

10   www.dti.gov.uk/files/file31529.doc (accessed November 30 2012).

11   Association of British Insurers, "Investing in Social Responsibility – Risks and Opportunities" (2001), available at: www.abi.org.uk/Publications/Investing_in_Social_Responsibility__Risks_and_Opportunities 1.aspx (accessed December 17 2012).

discrimination and abuse, genetic testing, and monitoring emails;

- *communities:* maximising the positive impact of the company's operations through support for and involvement in the communities where it operates; and

- *business relationships:* operating fairly as regards suppliers and customers.[12]

The Association of British Insurers urges it members to use their influence on investee companies to see corporate social responsibility as essentially a risk management tool, and to measure the management of that risk by reporting annually. The annual report should contain information reflecting the ABI Disclosure Guidelines.

3.1 The ABI Disclosure Guidelines

The guidelines take the form of disclosures which institutions would expect to see included in the annual report of listed companies. Specifically, they refer to disclosures relating to board responsibilities and to policies, procedures and verification.

With regard to the board, a company should state in its annual report whether:

- as part of its regular risk assessment procedures, the board takes account of the significance of environmental, social and governance matters to the business of the company;

- the board has identified and assessed the significant environmental, social and governance risks to the company's short and long-term value, as well as the opportunities to enhance value that may arise from an appropriate response;

- the board has received adequate information to make this assessment and whether account is taken of environmental, social and governance matters in the training of directors; and

- the board has ensured that the company has in place effective systems for managing and mitigating significant risks which, where relevant, incorporate performance management systems and appropriate remuneration incentives.

With regard to policies, procedures and verification, the annual report should:

- include information on environmental, social and governance-related risks and opportunities that may significantly affect the company's short and long-term value, and how they might impact on the future of the business;

- include in the description of the company's policies and procedures for managing risks the possible impact on short and long-term value arising from environmental, social and governance matters. If the annual report and accounts state that the company has no such policies and procedures, the board should provide reasons for their absence;

- include information, where appropriate using key performance indicators, on the extent to which the company has complied with its policies and

---

12   *Ibid.*

procedures for managing material risks arising from environmental, social and governance matters and about the role of the board in providing supervision;

- where performance falls short of the objectives, describe the remedial measures that the board has taken to; and
- describe the procedures for verification of environmental, social and governance disclosures. The verification procedure should be adequate to achieve a reasonable level of credibility.

With regard to the board, the company should state in its remuneration report:

- whether the remuneration committee is able to consider corporate performance on environmental, social and governance issues when setting the remuneration of executive directors. If the report states that the committee has no such discretion, then a reason should be provided for its absence; and
- whether the remuneration committee has ensured that the incentive structure for senior management does not raise environmental, social and governance risks by inadvertently motivating irresponsible behaviour.[13]

4. The business case for corporate social responsibility

4.1 Management of reputational risk

Risks to reputation can arise from a variety of sources, such as:

- product quality concerns;
- pressure group action; and
- failure to comply with laws, regulations or reasonable expectations of integrity and professionalism (eg, BP's oil spill in the Gulf of Mexico in 2011).

Sometimes, mere association with a market sector can contribute to reputational damage, for example, the banking industry following the 2007 financial sector collapse.

Thus the successful management of reputational risk through responsible practices such as scrupulous environmental behaviour can be a significant hedge against disaster.

4.2 Share price performance

A study conducted by UBS investment bank in 2001 concluded that:

> ... we find no evidence that socially responsible investing confers any sustainable performance advantage in the long run ... Having said that, however, we do not believe that investing responsibly necessarily entails financial sacrifices.[14]

---

13 Association of British Insurers, "Guidelines on Responsible Investment Disclosure", February 2007, available at: www.ivis.co.uk/ResponsibleInvestmentDisclosure.aspx (accessed December 10 2012).

14 UBS Warburg, "Sustainability Investment: The Merits of Socially Responsible Inventing", unpublished manuscript, August 2001; Roger Cowe, Risk, Returns and Responsibility, Association of British Insurers (2004).

Similar findings arose from research conducted by the investment bank West LB Panmure in 2002 and by the Swiss private bank Pictet in 2002.[15]

4.3 Reduced operating costs

Many initiatives aimed at improving environmental performance – such as reducing emissions of gases that contribute to global climate change or reducing the use of agrochemicals – are said also to lower costs. Many recycling initiatives reduce waste-disposal costs and generate income from the sale of recycled materials. In the human resources sector, flexible scheduling and other work-life programmes that result in reduced absenteeism and increased retention of employees are thought to save companies money through increased productivity and reduction of hiring and training costs.

4.4 Enhanced brand image and reputation

It is claimed that customers are often drawn to brands and companies with good reputations in corporate social responsibility-related areas – for example, Bodyshop. A company that is considered to be socially responsible can benefit both from its enhanced reputation with the public and from its reputation within the business community, increasing its ability to attract capital and trading partners.

In the Millennium Poll on Corporate Social Responsibility, 56% of the respondents cited social responsibility as the factor most influencing public impressions of individual companies.[16]

4.5 Increased sales and customer loyalty

Anecdotal evidence suggests a large and growing market for the products and services of companies perceived to be socially responsible. While businesses must first satisfy customers' key buying criteria (such as price, quality, availability, safety and convenience), some studies have also shown a growing desire to buy (or not to buy) because of other values-based criteria, such as 'sweatshop-free' and 'child-labour-free' clothing, lower environmental impact, and the absence of genetically modified materials or ingredients.[17]

4.6 Increased productivity and quality

Company efforts to improve working conditions, lessen environmental impact or increase employee involvement in decision-making are thought to increase productivity and reduce error rate.

---

15   Dr Henrich Garz, Claudia Volk and Martin Gilles, "More Gain than Pain: SRI: Sustainability pays off", WestLB Panmure, November 2002, available at: http://s3.amazonaws.com/zanran_storage/www.djindexes.com/ContentPages/10244444.pdf (accessed December 10 2012); Pictet, "Decomposing SRI Performance", September 30 2003, available at: www.pictet.com/en/home/about/sustainability/sri_reports/decomposing_sri_performance.html (accessed December 10 2012).

16   Environics International Ltd, "The Millennium Poll on Corporate Social Responsibility", Executive Briefing, 2000, available at: www.globescan.com/news_archives/MPExecBrief.pdf (accessed December 10 2012).

17   See , for example, http://ethicalconsumer.org

4.7 Increased ability to attract and retain employees

Companies perceived to have strong corporate social responsibility commitments are thought to recruit and retain employees more easily, resulting in a reduced staff turnover and associated recruitment and training costs.

4.8 Reduced regulatory oversight

Companies that satisfy or go beyond regulatory compliance requirements may be given more freedom by both national and local government entities. For example, in the United States, the federal and state agencies that supervise environmental and workplace regulations have formal programmes which recognise and reward companies that have taken proactive measures to reduce adverse environmental, health and safety impacts. In many cases, such companies are subject to fewer inspections and paperwork, and may be given preference or fast-track treatment when applying for operating permits, zoning variances or other forms of governmental permission. The US Federal Sentencing Guidelines[18] allow penalties and fines against corporations to be reduced or even eliminated if the company can show that it has taken "good corporate citizenship" actions and has an effective ethics programme in place.

4.9 Access to capital

It is claimed that following the growth of socially responsible investment, companies with strong corporate social responsibility performance have increased access to capital that might not otherwise have been available.

5. The argument against corporate social responsibility

The main argument against corporate social responsibility is that it diverts a company's attention and resources from its primary obligation to maximise profit for the benefit of the company and its shareholders. It is also said that corporate social responsibility has become a 'greenwash' exercise in public relations that does not achieve much lasting social good.

In an article in the Wall Street Journal in 2010, Professor Aneel Karnani of the University of Michigan's School of Business argued that the idea that companies have a responsibility to act in the public interest and will profit from doing so is fundamentally flawed.[19]

This approach is an extreme view, but variations of it are held by a significant number of business entities and managers, and may be one of the reasons why movements such as the Occupy movement gain traction. However, the mainstream view in the UK business sector is that corporate social responsibility is established and will grow in influence. Insurance institutions encourage companies into

---

18   United States Sentencing Commission, 2011 Federal Sentencing Guidelines Manual (effective November 1 2011), available at: www.ussc.gov/Guidelines/2011_Guidelines/Manual.../index.cfm (accessed December 11 2012).

19   See Aneel Karnani, "The Case Against Corporate Social Responsibility", *Wall Street Journal*, June 14 2012, available at: http://online.wsj.com/article/SB10001424052748703338004575230112664504890.html (accessed November 20 2012).

corporate social responsibility practices because they have a vested interest in ensuring sustainability, especially in relation to the environment and carbon reduction.

6. Governance structures for corporate social responsibility

Governance structures will differ from company to company, and individual companies may change their structures from time to time. However, an example of a possible model might be:

- the corporate social responsibility committee of the board supervises the group's corporate social responsibility and sustainability policies and advises the board, committees of the board and executive management;
- the committee meets at least four times a year;
- the committee comprises four non-executive directors and three external members; and
- there may also be a corporate social responsibility executive steering group.[20]

The executive steering group would supervise the implementation of corporate social responsibility policies, performance evaluation and communications. The steering group would comprise executives from business functions that influence the overall corporate social responsibility performance, and it would also act as a conduit for keeping the corporate social responsibility committee of the board informed.

7. The views of institutional investors

7.1 The Association of British Insurers

In 2001, the Association of British Insurers published disclosure guidelines on social responsibility.[21] The guidelines take the form of disclosures which institutions should expect to see included in the annual report of listed companies. Specifically, they refer to disclosures relating to board responsibilities and to policies, procedures and verification.

In summary, a company should state in its annual report:

- the board:
  - the extent to which the board takes regular account of the significance of social, environment and ethical matters to the company;
  - whether the board has identified and assessed the significant risks to the company's short and long-term value arising from social, environment and ethical matters, as well as the opportunity to enhance value that may arise from an appropriate response;
  - whether the board has received adequate information to make this assessment, and that account is taken of social, environment and ethical matters in the training of directors;

---

20   President and Fellows of Harvard University, The Initiative Defining Corporate Social Responsibility, available at: www.hks.harvard.edu/m-rcbg/CSRI/init_define.html (accessed December 11 2012).
21   See note 13 above.

- whether the board has been assured that the company has effective systems in place for managing significant risks. Where relevant, these should incorporate performance management systems and appropriate remuneration incentives;
- policies, procedures and verification:
  - information on social, environment and ethical-related risks and opportunities and how this might impact on the business;
  - a description of the policies and procedures for managing and verifying such risks, the extent to which compliance has occurred and, in the absence of policies or compliance, an explanation;
  - information on the extent to which the company has complied with its policies and procedures for managing social, environment and ethical risks; and
  - a description of the procedures for verification of social, environment and ethical disclosures. They should be sufficient to achieve a reasonable level of credibility.[22]

The association argues that there are two business cases for corporate social responsibility:

- the control and elimination of business risks associated with the environmental impact, poor labour relations, human rights abuses and bad management of stakeholders; and
- competitive advantage – or rather features which in the minds of investors distinguish in a positive fashion the socially responsible organisation.[23]

To these, one might add the argument of share price advantage as investors gradually take positions in socially acceptable companies under increasing public pressure to do so.

7.2 The UK Stewardship Code[24]

The UK Stewardship Code was published by the Financial Reporting Council in July 2010 with the intention of enhancing the quality of engagement between institutional investors and companies – its objective is to help improve long-term returns to shareholders and the efficient exercise of governance responsibilities, by setting out good practice on engagement with investee companies to which the council believes institutional investors should aspire.

The code is based on the Institutional Shareholders Committee publication "The Responsibilities of Institutional Shareholders and Agents: Statement of Principles" (2005 and converted to a code by the committee in 2009, the same year that the Walker review of the corporate governance of UK banks invited the committee to

---

22   *Ibid.*
23   *Ibid.*
24   Financial Reporting Council, The Stewardship Code, available at: www.frc.org.uk/Our-Work/Codes-Standards/Corporate-governance/UK-Stewardship-Code.aspx (accessed December 17 2012), UK Stewardship Code 2012 edition, frc.org.uk.

take responsibility). The Stewardship Code is still developing in terms of usage by institutions, and in particular by non-UK institutions and sovereign funds.

It will take time for the code's full impact to be felt. In April 2002, the Financial Reporting Council published a feedback paper in which it stated that it was appropriate at that stage in the code's life to build on a "promising start" – only to reinforce it where necessary, but not fundamentally to change it.

The consultation had received 51 responses: 12 from asset managers, seven from asset owners and two from listed companies. In addition, nine respondents were from service providers, 17 were from representative bodies, three were from membership organisations and one was from an academic institute.

Most respondents felt that the proposed wording on stewardship[25] was useful and appropriate, and the majority of respondents welcomed the proposed clarification of the role of asset owners in exercising their stewardship responsibilities. There was strong support for improved disclosure on conflicts of interest, with some respondents wanting the revisions to the guidance to Principle 2 (see below) to be stronger. Some asset owners wished to see their managers describe more fully their organisational context – for example, whether they were part of a wider financial services group, and the reporting lines between the manager and the wider group. In response, the Financial Reporting Council stated that it will assess the quality of disclosure under the revised code before considering whether further changes are needed in future editions.

There was strong support for the council's proposals to improve disclosure of investors' use of proxy voting agencies, with several respondents commenting that the code needs to be strengthened even further in this area.

Investors are to be encouraged to disclose their policy on voting and the use made of any proxy voting or other voting advisory service. The guidance for Principle 6 reflects this, and has been extended to encourage investors also to describe what types of services are provided and to disclose the extent to which they follow or rely upon recommendations made by such services. In addition, under the revised code, signatories will be asked to identify the providers of proxy voting or other voting advisery services, in the same way as changes being made to the UK Corporate Governance Code will require companies to identify external advisers to the board and committees.

In considering the responses, the Financial Reporting Council concluded that it was not necessary to change or add to the code's seven principles. Instead, it proposed introductory sections intended to replace the preface. In the words of the Financial Reporting Council, "this replacement is because there appears no common understanding of what is meant by 'stewardship', or of the respective roles and responsibilities of asset owners and managers: the revised Code will attempt to clarify these issues".

The principles of the Code

Institutional investors should:

> *1. publicly disclose their policy on how they will discharge their stewardship responsibilities.*

---

25   *Ibid.*

2. have a robust policy on managing conflicts of interest in relation to stewardship and this policy should be publicly disclosed.

3. monitor their investee companies.

4. establish clear guidelines on when and how they will escalate their activities as a method of protecting and enhancing shareholder value.

5 be willing to act collectively with other investors where appropriate.

have a clear policy on voting and disclosure of voting activity.

6. report periodically on their stewardship and voting activities.[26]

8. Policies of the UK government, the United Nations and the OECD

8.1 The UK government

The UK government's approach includes:

- the role of facilitator in the context of general sustainability policy initiatives;
- imposing specific reporting requirements, for example, the reporting by trustees of their corporate social responsibility policy in investment decisions under the Pensions Act 2001, and the enhanced business review in the annual directors' report which Section 417 of the Companies Act 2006 requires; and
- the use of public procurement policies which are claimed to favour environmentally sensitive companies.

(a) Reporting requirements

Under the business review provisions of Section 417 of the Companies Act 2006, every quoted company must produce an annual business review which must, to the extent necessary for an understanding of the development, performance and operation of the business of the company, include analysis using key performance indicators of information relating, amongst other things,[27] to environmental matters.

In order to provide assistance in relation to this analysis, the Department of Environment Food and Rural Affairs has produced a set of "Environmental Reporting Guidelines – Key Performance Indicators" (KPIs).

The guidelines outline how environmental impacts may be measured through key performance indicators (eg, KPI 1 concerns greenhouse gases). The intention is to enable companies to make use of existing standard business data, as well as provide guidance on how data should be reported.

8.2 The United Nations

On April 27 2006, the secretary general of the United Nations, Mr Kofi Annan, launched the UN Principles for Responsible Investment. These were sponsored by investment banks and institutional funds managing funds worth over $6 trillion. They comprise six principles which require institutional investors to "engage in and report on investment policies which encourage the development of sound practices

---

26   *Ibid.*
27   See note 9 above.

on environmental, social and corporate governance matters (ESG) by investee companies".[28]

> *There is a growing view among investment professionals that environmental, social and corporate governance issues can affect the performance of investment portfolios. Investors fulfilling their fiduciary (or equivalent) duty therefore need to give appropriate consideration to these issues, but to date have lacked a framework for doing so. The 'Principles for Responsible Investment' provide this framework.*

The principles are voluntary and provide goals. They are not prescriptive, but instead provide a menu of possible actions for incorporating environmental, social and governance issues into mainstream investment decision-making and ownership practices.

The UN Global Compact[29] is an initiative to encourage businesses worldwide to adopt sustainable and socially responsible policies, and to report on them. Under the compact, companies are brought together with UN agencies, labour groups and civil society.

The Global Compact was officially launched in New York on July 26 2000. By 2006, it included more than 1,800 companies from all regions of the world.

(a)   *The Ruggie Guiding Principles on Business and Human Rights*[30]

Published by the UN in March 2011, the Guiding Principles are the product of six years of research and extensive consultations, led by the secretary general's special representative for business and human rights, Harvard Professor John Ruggie, involving governments, companies, business associations, civil society, affected individuals and groups, investors, and others around the world.

The guiding principles seek to provide for the first time an authoritative global standard for preventing and addressing the risk of adverse human rights impacts linked to business activity. The UN Human Rights Council gave formal endorsement of the text at its June 2011 session.

The guiding principles outline how states and businesses should implement the UN 'Protect, Respect and Remedy' framework in order better to manage business and human rights challenges. The framework, proposed by Professor Ruggie in 2008, was unanimously welcomed by the Human Rights Council at the time, and has since enjoyed extensive uptake by international and national governmental organisations, businesses, non-governmental organisations and other stakeholders.

The guiding principles set out what steps states should take to foster business respect for human rights; they provide a blueprint for companies to know and show that they respect human rights, and reduce the risk of causing or contributing to human rights harm; and they constitute a set of benchmarks for stakeholders to assess business respect for human rights. The principles are organised under the UN

---

28   PRI Association, "Principles for Responsible Investment", available at: http://unpri.org (accessed December 17 2012).
29   United Nations Global Compact, available at: www.unglobalcompact.org/ (accessed December 17 2012).
30   UN Human Rights Council, "Guiding Principles on Business and Human Rights: Implementing the United Nations 'Protect, Respect and Remedy' Framework", available at: www.business-humanrights.org/ SpecialRepPortal/Home/Protect-Respect-Remedy-Framework/GuidingPrinciples (accessed December 17 2012).

framework's three pillars:

- the duty of the state to protect human rights;
- the corporate responsibility to respect human rights; and
- the need for greater access to remedy for victims of business-related abuse.

Professor Ruggie stated:

The Human Rights Council has been extremely supportive of the consultative approach I've taken throughout my mandate, and I look forward to formally presenting the Guiding Principles at the Council's June session. Endorsement by the Council would enable the global community to move beyond the confusion and polarization of the past by establishing an authoritative point of reference that recognizes the central role that States need to play, gives businesses predictability in what is expected of them, and provides other stakeholders, including civil society and investors, the tools to measure progress where it matters most – in the daily lives of people.[31]

8.3 The OECD

The OECD Guidelines for Multinational Enterprises[32] are an international benchmark for corporate responsibility. They contain voluntary principles and standards for responsible business conduct in such areas as human rights, supply chain management, disclosure of information, anti-corruption, taxation, labour relations, environment, competition, and consumer welfare. They aim to promote the positive contributions multinational enterprises can make to economic, environmental and social progress.

The Guidelines are stated to express the shared values of the 39 countries that have adhered to them (the 30 OECD member states and nine non-member countries). The adhering countries are said to be the source of almost 90% of the world's foreign direct investment and most major multinational enterprises are based within them. Although many business codes of conduct are now publicly available, the OECD guidelines are the only multilaterally endorsed and comprehensive code that governments are committed to promoting. The guidelines are part of a broader package of instruments, most of which address government responsibility – they promote open and transparent policy frameworks for international investment.

9. Independent verification

Some companies choose to have their reports on corporate social responsibility policy implementation audited or verified by external third parties to assess the quality of information presented by the corporation and the integrity of management reporting systems.

The following are among the more widely recognised organisations for measurement of corporate social responsibility.

---

31   *Ibid.*
32   Organisation for Economic Cooperation and Development, Guidelines for Multinational Enterprises, available at: www.oecd.org/daf/internationalinvestment/guidelinesformultinationalenterprises/ (accessed December 17 2012).

9.1 AccountAbility 1000 Series (AA1000)[33]

AA1000 is a framework developed by the Institute of Social and Ethical Accountability which companies can use to understand and improve their ethical performance. It focuses on providing a framework through which quality social and ethical accounting, auditing and reporting may be achieved. It comprises principles and a set of process standards. The standard has been revised with five specialised modules: calibration and communication of quality of stakeholder engagement; integration with existing management and metrics systems; quality assurance and external verification; governance and risk management; and application to small- and medium-sized enterprises.

9.2 Global Reporting Initiative (GRI)[34]

The GRI issues guidelines covering three areas: economic (eg, wages and benefits); environmental (eg, impacts on bio-diversity); and social (eg, labour rights). It has also developed sustainability reporting guidelines.

9.3 Social Accountability 8000 (SA8000)[35]

SA8000 was developed in conjunction with representatives from trade unions, businesses and non-governmental organisations and is now operated by Social Accountability International. The standard is based on a number of existing international human rights and labour standards, including International Labour Organisation conventions relating to employment, the Universal Declaration of Human Rights and the United Nations Convention on the Rights of the Child. The standard aims to provide "transparent, measurable, verifiable" standards for certifying the performance of organisations in nine areas: child labour; forced labour; health and safety compensation; working hours; discrimination; discipline; free association; collective bargaining systems; and management systems.

9.4 The Association of British Insurers[36]

As described above, the Association of British Insurers scrutinises the reports and accounts of selected listed companies to monitor the extent to which its Disclosure Guidelines on socially responsible investment are being observed. There is no public access to the criteria used by the association in making its assessments.

9.5 Ceres Principles[37]

The Ceres Principles were created by a coalition of environmental groups, socially responsible investors and public pension administrators. The coalition uses shareholder resolutions to initiate discussions on environmental responsibility with companies, with the goal of getting companies to endorse the Ceres Principles.

---

33   www.accountability.org/standards/index.html (accessed December 17 2012).
34   www.globalreporting.org (accessed December 17 2012).
35   www.sa-intl.org/sa8000 (accessed December 17 2012).
36   www.abi.org.uk/ (accessed December 17 2012)
37   The Ceres Principles, www.ceres.org/about-us/our-history/ceres-principles (accessed December 17 2012).

9.6   The Goodcorporation[38]

The Goodcorporation is a global standard of corporate social responsibility which has been designed to address the needs of all types and sizes of organisation. It covers an organisation's fairness to its employees, suppliers, customers, providers of finance, community and environment. Verification tests the charter principles of the organisation on four levels, from the existence of policies to evidence of these being implemented effectively.

9.7   FTSE4Good[39]

FTSE4Good is an index for socially responsible investment. It consists of a series of benchmarks and tradable indices facilitating investment in companies with good records of corporate social responsibility. The selection criteria cover three areas: working towards environmental sustainability; developing positive relationships with stakeholders; and upholding and supporting universal human rights. An independent advisery committee is responsible for the design of the selection criteria, deletions from the index, the management of the index and the ongoing review process to strengthen the selection criteria. At present, a number of sectors are excluded, including tobacco producers and nuclear weapons manufacturers.

9.8   Business in the Community Corporate Responsibility Index[40]

This index is based on a framework that Business in the Community developed with businesses through a series of consultations and workshops with over 80 companies and engagement with a number of other stakeholders during 2002. Following the launch of the first year's results in March 2003, Business in the Community has continued this process – it has engaged with representatives from over 110 companies and made a number of modifications to the survey.

9.9   The Institute of Business Ethics[41]

The Institute of Business Ethics is a non-profit organisation established to emphasise the essentially ethical nature of wealth creation, to encourage higher standards of behaviour by companies and to help to develop and publicise the best ethical practices. The institute holds consultations and conferences, publishes research, and identifies effective actions for business organisations, offering practical advice to companies wishing to establish and implement effective ethics policies. It has produced many publications, including "Demonstrating Corporate Values", which compares the relative merits of some the standards-testing organisations referred to above.

10.   Conclusion

There are still many sceptics as to the value or even propriety of companies using resources on corporate social responsibility activity. In the Financial Times of May 30

---

38   The Goodcorporation, www.goodcorporation.com/ (accessed December 17 2012).
39   FTSE4GOOD Index Series, www.ftse.co.uk/Indices/FTSE4Good_Index_Series/index.jsp (accessed December 17 2012).
40   See note 4 above.
41   www.ibe.org.uk/ (accessed November 20 2012).

2006, the correspondent Stefan Stern expressed the view that "true believers in free markets and rigorous competition find the warm words of public relations driven CSR. ridiculous ... The emergence and growth of CSR betrays the deep crisis of confidence that afflicts too many business leaders",[42]

At the opposite end of the spectrum are pressure groups and others who believe that, so far, the response of the corporate sector to issues of sustainability has been inadequate. They point to the apparent disconnect between the words of the corporate social responsibility reports and the actions in recent years of companies such as Tesco, BP and Shell as evidence that, in reality, the corporate sector regards corporate social responsibility with indifference

However, both are wrong. Anyone who studies the corporate social responsibility reports of many public companies (and the key features of some of them appear earlier in this chapter) would surely find it impossible to characterise the numerous outstanding initiatives by many of the FTSE 350 companies as indicating a 'deep crisis of confidence' or an inadequate response.

11.   Appendix: terminology

11.1   Corporate social responsibility (CSR)
Defined by the Institute of Business Ethics[43] as:

> How an organisation approaches the social and environmental impacts of its business operations and its voluntary contribution to the wellbeing of the global and local communities in which it operates.

The Harvard Kennedy School of Government develops this definition as follows:
> It goes beyond philanthropy and compliance and addresses how companies manage their economic, social, and environmental impacts, as well as their relationships in all key spheres of influence: the workplace, the marketplace, the supply chain, the community, and the public policy realm.[44]

11.2   Corporate responsibility (CR)
The Institute of Business Ethics believes that an organisation cannot be genuinely responsible without an embedded and inherent culture that is based on ethical values such as trust, openness, respect and integrity. "This is why the IBE prefers to talk about Corporate Responsibility (CR) as a wider concern, rather than using the more limiting 'social' tag'."

11.3   Environmental, social, and corporate governance (ESG)
Used by the Association of British Insurers (ABI) in the ABI Disclosure Guidelines on Socially Responsible Investment and described as:

> ... narrative reporting which:

---

42   Stefan Stern, "Business Life – Corporate Responsibility and the Curse of the three-letter acronym", *Financial Times*, May 30 2006.
43   www.ibe.org.uk/ (accessed November 20 2012).
44   Corporate Social Responsibility Initiative, Harvard Kennedy School of Government, available at: www.hks.harvard.edu/m-rcbg/CSRI/init_define.html (accessed November 30 2012).

- *sets environmental, social and governance (ESG) risks in the context of the whole range of risks and opportunities facing the company*
- *contains a forward looking perspective, and*
- *describes the actions of the board in mitigating these risks.*[45]

11.4 Social, environmental and ethical (SEE)

Social, environmental and ethical matters.

11.5 Sustainable and responsible investing (SRI)

Defined by the US Social Investment Forum[46] as

> *... a broad-based approach to investing ... that corporate responsibility and societal concerns are valid parts of investment decisions. SRI considers both the investor's financial needs and an investment's impact on society. SRI investors encourage corporations to improve their practices on environmental, social and governance issues.*

---

45   IVIS institutional voting guidelines, available at: www.ivis.co.uk/ResponsibleInvestmentDisclosure.aspx (accessed December 10 2012).

46   US SIF, The Forum for Sustainable and Responsible Investment, available at: http://ussif.org/resources/sriguide/ (accessed November 5 2012).

'Tone at the top' and corporate governance

Peter Giblin
Cass Business School

1. Introduction

Proper corporate governance is about the standards set by those who are in a position to establish and enforce those standards. It is about leaders who know what appropriate attitudes and systems are required and how to deliver the message from positions of power.

Much is written and spoken about crisis management and risk management, but too little attention is paid to risk awareness and risk readiness. This whole area is a continuum, a reflection of problematic evolution, so let us start at the beginning. Everyone faces risks every day; everyone makes a decision explicitly/implicitly to accept risks, addressing and accepting cost/benefit or risk/reward. Driving a car to work is a risk – the car might break down, run out of petrol or an accident could incur. There is no realistic travel alternative, so the risk is accepted by millions, because it is minimal, and more than counterbalanced by financial gain, job satisfaction or prestige. The same can be said for thousands of other decisions made by billions every day, affecting health, safety and a myriad of other concerns.

In this chapter we will focus on this phenomenon as it affects senior level decision-makers in a wide range of institutions, private and public, and consider how these leaders address the simple challenge outlined above in much more complex circumstances. The issue at its core can be reduced to the question: what is the probability of something happening and, if it does, what is the impact? The goal is to calculate exactly what it costs to be 'ahead' at all times.

On a personal level, taking out a 20-year life insurance policy seems to have been a significant waste of money after 21 years, but death in year two seems to be an excellent financial return for the estate. The policies are sold, because the insured/beneficiaries believe the comfort level benefits outweigh the cost.

In a corporate environment the issues are more complex, nuanced and ambiguous, and may involve huge numbers from a financial perspective, and a potentially catastrophic impact on reputations – individual and entity – if things go wrong.

Every day the media has coverage of someone, or group of people, who 'got it wrong' by failing to get the risk/reward ratio properly balanced – accidentally or deliberately – and may or will pay the price, corporately or personally, or both.

What happened to Enron, WorldCom, Arthur Andersen, Siemens, aspects of the British banking sector and certain members of their respective senior management? What will happen to Wal-Mart, and how long will the Libor scandal continue?

In all cases, risks were taken, and for certain individuals the rewards were high, at least temporarily, but the probability of something going wrong was underestimated, and the impact in every case was very large.

This chapter is about the positive aspects of corporate governance, assessment of values and attitudes, and behaviour that drives people and institutions towards an atmosphere that recognises the omnipresence of risks, boundaries that will not be crossed, and focuses on those who lead in this constantly evolving world of complexity.

We will look at corporate cultures – where do they come from, what drives them; is there a difference between old and new, public and private? Are 'old values' less relevant as the speed and access to information changes? Who decides? Who holds the keys to the kingdom?

Even if there is a 'message' from the top, how does it get disseminated? How do we know that all our people will do the right thing?

As this focus turns to specific individuals, how do we determine that this person is the right one at the right time? Many institutions get it wrong because they underestimate the risks of making ill-informed decisions, and they underestimate the potential damage that an ill-informed decision may cause.

This is about having a culture, a view, values, foresight as well as hindsight, and a base line that puts shareholders as well as other stakeholders in the forefront.

Assuming that we can get to this stage with a sense of comfort, how does a senior leader function in the boardroom with conflicting objectives (and perhaps conflicting personal values)? For example, what if the chairman and the chief executive officer (CEO) do not like each other, do not trust each other, do not share information and have different personal objectives. How does this impact on the drive for proper corporate governance?

2. Tone at the top

When people speak of 'tone at the top' they are normally referring to a perception of appearance or behaviour that delivers a message of some sort, directly or indirectly. It is sometimes thought of as an impression that others have, such as "she makes a good first impression". We are concerned with the depth that actually supports that impression, and the impact it makes on the supporting cast, and the stakeholder community.

It is quite clear that 'tone' reflects a 'talk the talk' and 'walk the walk' approach, and that any disconnect is evident to those affected. The relevance is particularly important when distinguishing between corporate governance and compliance. The latter may form a piece of the former in certain circumstances, particularly in highly legalistic environments, but proper corporate governance, or the lack thereof, is much more pervasive. It exists in any circumstance where an individual or small group has an impact on a larger body.

If the CEO of a large multinational organisation, public, private or not-for-profit, makes a statement or initiates a practice, he will or will not be taken seriously depending on the attendant behaviour. For example, suppose a message from the top is issued that, "The Anti-Bribery Act has just been passed, and what follows is what you can and cannot do, and we always act responsibly toward our staff, customers, etc, and obey the law", and a copy or version of this message is sent to all staff, and that is it! This feels like compliance – "I told everyone, that's what I was required to do, my job is done". There is no sense of serious concern or commitment, and others will know that, and, perhaps, act accordingly. On the other hand, if the message is more comprehensive and includes a series of steps that will be implemented over an extended period of time, the impact will be much more significant. Such a message might announce an information dissemination, training and tracking programme, and the establishment of a whistle-blowing hotline, as well as clear guidelines for reporting and protection. The purpose of this programme is to ensure that anyone potentially affected by such legislation knows what it is about, how it impacts on them, and the penalties to personal and employer reputation, as well as possible job loss, fines and jail. Imagine the power a message has internally and externally if it is:

We take this very seriously, and we are instituting a series of explanatory sessions with all relevant staff, and have arranged for an online training programme, linked to a short quiz to ensure that we are all comfortable knowing what to do when. We will be able to track when you received the case studies pack and quiz, when you opened it, when you took the quiz, how long it took, and what your answers were. We will periodically update the entire process, and encourage you to ask questions of your manager on any points at any time to ensure full understanding and compliance [that word again!].

Suppose you are a regulator with full powers to investigate and penalise, and you have suspicions and information indicating that an entity has breached the provisions of the Bribery Act 2010 in a very serious manner. You are presented with the two written messages, as outlined above. Both may claim to be doing what is required, but how will the regulator react? Will he see or feel the difference in the tone at the top? Probably. Assuming that an infringement did take place, it is entirely possible that the penalty in the first case will be imposed in full, and lead to a search for further breaches. In the second case, the reaction could well be, "they have taken this seriously, done what they could reasonably be expected to, and put procedures in place to deliver and track the message". Result? Perhaps a lesser penalty, and an earlier closure to the investigation.

The author recently engaged with the CEO and director of human resources of a 200-year-old Swiss company to consider initiating a programme along the lines of the second alternative above. The company, although not a household name, is the world leader in the manufacture of certain types of components, and has 40,000 employees in many countries. For the first 90 minutes of the two-hour meeting, the CEO spoke of the history of the company, the brand, the reputation, the absolute necessity of delivering clear behavioural messages to all staff and his strong concern not to breach any transnational laws and guidelines. Only then did he actually ask for details of our firm's services. The tone at the top was very clear.

It was also clear that he believed what he said, and that he expected others to believe and act accordingly. He would do his very best to deliver his values and message to all of his staff and use the latest methods to ensure this was effected.

This leads to a result which may be underused by even the most effective leaders – the effective use of the internal audit function.

Historically, the internal audit function has been used to ensure the cohesion, honesty and financial integrity of an entity, by collecting a 'picture' of what is happening throughout the organisation on a selective 'snapshot' basis. At its most basic, it periodically visits all departments/divisions of the entity, probes to check for veracity of the facts, as well as compliance with standards systems and procedures, and makes suggestions for improvements based on, for example, what other parts of the organisation may be doing or contemplating. It will then issue a management letter to the auditee in draft form, highlighting findings, and asking for a response and a plan of action; but it does not make management decisions. Once completed, the report goes to the CEO and the chairperson of the board audit committee for review, comments and action if required. (An entity's audit charter must provide for independence of thought as well as of action, and as such it exists in an ambiguous environment. The head of the audit department must report functionally to the chair of the board audit committee, as well as administratively to someone within the organisation – the CEO or a delegate therefrom.)

Regretfully, while it is clear that the audit function has a unique brief to visit any part of the entity at any time, and a broad knowledge of the daily functioning of the entity, it is generally underused as a communicator of risk challenges and concerns. This is not to suggest that such function should have line management authority for making risk-related decisions, but rather as it perpetually moves around performing its audit function, it should keep its risk register up to date, and make suggestions that may be of value to the auditee, and perhaps to the entity as a whole.

The effective master of the tone at the top understands the value of the audit function, and supports its independence implicitly and explicitly, and uses its structure, brief and power to help address the key challenge of risk awareness and risk readiness, so as to minimise the need for risk management and crisis management.

3.   Why will all of our people do the right thing?

So who are these people, and who pays attention to them?

They are effective leaders who set the right tone at the top. They are credible, respected and appear to do what say they will do. That leads us to an examination of what these people are. They are resourceful, astute, compatible and knowledgeable.

Resourcefulness indicates action-oriented drive, with a will to accomplish and eagerness to be involved, with an ability to innovate, to seek new and better ways, to champion original ideas. It reflects intellectual curiosity, a willingness to improve, and a propensity for mobility and challenges, and a fear of the 'comfort zone'. It also reflects speed of thought, although not always speed of response, stamina, willpower, and tenacity, and an ability to act, while rejecting gratuitous perfectionism.

Astuteness indicates an innate knowledge of when and how to act, a sense of timing and limits, good judgement, as well as a commercial, technical or financial understanding. This often shows as a 'feeling', and ability to be 'to the point', to channel time and energy on key issues; in essence a focus on quality not quantity. It also indicates a long-term vision, and ability to keep sight of goals, a clear view of future objectives. This is balanced by flexibility in execution, and a balance between acting directly and delegating responsibilities. An ability to adapt to circumstances is prevalent, a practical and political common sense, with an innate recognition of the need to plan for contingencies. It also demonstrates an ease with ambiguity, an instinct for addressing real problems, and understanding covert messages and paradoxical information.

Compatibility indicates skills in dealing with others, and the ability to use people effectively; empathy, and open-mindedness – hearing what is said and, most importantly, what is not said. It means effectiveness as a communicator, convincing, adept salesmanship, coupled with a sense of when to accept disagreement and rejection. This is often demonstrated as diplomatic skills, tact and a respect for others – an ability to see others' possibilities and to develop their potential, and a sense of team spirit and how to develop the interpersonal skills of others. This is closely related to negotiating skills, as well as psychological and emotional intelligence. In essence, an ability to inspire others, to motivate and to communicate a 'can do' attitude.

Knowledge is intellectual prowess, demonstrated reliability, a presence of know-how, a projection of being 'on top of' any specific problem of relevance. This is often accompanied by excellent analytical skills, the ability to dissect a problem and to detect relationships and consequences. It also reflects an ability to be abstract, to be comfortable tackling complex problems with a clear mind, which demonstrates logical thinking and the skill to rehearse the sequence of future events. This is about the ability to integrate all facets of a problem, to sort out relevant details, to summarise and synthesise, and requires an excellent memory, as well as accumulated experience or competence. Organisational skills are essential; being effective, practical and capable of finding concrete solutions. In summary, always having or finding the time, at ease under pressure, and in complete self-control.

An individual who is seen by others as being particularly resourceful, generally astute in his or her decision-making, compatible with most of those with whom he comes into contact and knowledgeable in the area of focus is likely to be regarded as a leader. If such an individual expects to be considered a true leader, he will have been resourceful in defining his or her objectives (while separating the means from the end), will have been astute in recognising various priorities, will have made an effort to be compatible with the target group, and will know what is required.

The leader with the right tone at the top, and with the most effective combination of attributes outlined above, now has an obligation to ensure that the people in their organisation know what is expected of them, understand what this means to them personally, and to the organisation as a whole, and believe in the message and course of action, and will be capable of doing what is expected of them.

4.   So who is this person?

We now have a sense of what a proper tone at the top is, who can set this tone and what leadership looks like. That is fine up to a point, but now we have to find out who that person is, and how to assist him or her in being effective to a maximum extent. Whether the individual is new to the position, internally or externally, or is involved in a periodic performance review, it is essential to focus on what is expected from the 'decision-makers'. For sake of this discussion, let us assume that the board of directors of a corporate entity has decided to change the international strategy of the organisation, and needs to be confident that the chief executive, who has been in place for a relatively short time, not only knows what is expected of him or her, but also genuinely understands, and believes, and has the capability to do what is necessary.

The exercise should include not only the formulation of a clear goal, together with rationale, strategy and tactics, but also a realistic, cogent job description for the incumbent, and a professional approach to review and assessment, particularly given the change of direction. The proper management of this process is extremely important so that the perceived need is clear, and the appropriateness and interest of the incumbent is assessed, That can be addressed by a series of interviews, which may be sufficient, but the inclusion of a properly presented, explained and executed psychometric questionnaire may be very valuable, particularly one that focuses on real needs and interests.

Psychometric testing continues to evolve, in part influenced by the proliferation of the internet and online assessment tools. Some are very good, some are out-of-date and some are irrelevant. The very best can be a major contributor to assessing and minimising risk when selecting or assessing senior executives; and the standard-bearer for this purpose will focus on personal preferences rather than abilities. This is because those who work in areas and on matters that are of interest tend to spend more time on them and become more knowledgeable; the task becomes the vocation.

By definition, one cannot be interested in everything, and most effective in all areas. So let us examine the possibilities, and draw some conclusions. First, how does a key person deal with challenges and problems? Can he properly evaluate them, using credible methods and tools of analysis? Can he then investigate emergent issues with purpose and intent to ensure that available resources are brought to bear on what matters. Can he then foster an environment which encourages open debate, and possible innovation in dealing with these problems – that is, find the solutions and implement them?

Second, how effective is he at influencing people? Can he build effective relationships with the necessary team or followers, or other stakeholders? Generally, it is not too difficult to work with someone who shares the same ideas, philosophy and objectives; it is not so easy to work with someone who does not. How does he work with the latter? How does leadership emerge in these circumstances, and how does one accept that it exists? Pearson CEO Marjorie Scardino, the late Steve Jobs of Apple or Virgin's founder, Richard Branson, clearly are people of influence but their vision, styles and focus were all different. Third, how effective is the leader when faced with serious roadblocks? Can he adapt new circumstances? Is there resilience when faced with technical, regulatory or competitive issues? Who takes the next step? Having demonstrated resilience, does he have the ability to change direction, without losing the followers, who expect decisiveness from their leader? How about giving support to those in need? This requires an ability to explain and motivate at the same time as saying: 'We value your efforts and commitment, but we are obliged to go in a different direction for the following reasons …'

Fourth, it is all about delivering results. Does he know enough about the essence, the details of the challenge, to be confident of making the right decision and bringing the stakeholders behind her? Has he ensured that the tasks required to reach the agreed goals are clear, and that the attendant authority and resources are available?

The Wave questionnaire, created and developed by Saville Consulting,[1] is the leading provider of answers to these crucial questions. It is able to link ipsative and normative evaluations within a single instrument in a unique manner and accordingly its conclusions are valid and highly credible.

Certain other observations emerge from an examination of the results from this questionnaire across a wide variety of organisations. Those who succeed or excel at the top clearly demonstrate leadership for the entity in question, show resilience and can adjust to change. They are also effective in communicating information, building relations and encouraging innovation (not necessarily new products, but new ways to approach issues), and are driven by achieving 'success', however that may be defined. Nevertheless, perhaps surprisingly, such people tend not to evaluate difficult situations or investigate issues personally – how often have we heard the expression 'don't bring me problems, bring me solutions'? They are less likely to be involved in processing details or structuring specific tasks.

A clear explanation of the purpose for taking the questionnaire, coupled with proper administration and professionally provided feedback, should reduce the risk of hiring or promoting inappropriate individuals into positions to which they aspire but which require skills, interests or attitudes which they do not have. No person is omni-skilled or interested in everything. It is not possible to spend all day thinking of the next product, and reading documents, and speaking to key colleagues, and visiting essential customers, and meeting with regulators to discuss or influence impending legislation. What we are seeking to do to is clarify what the position requires, to determine who this person in front of us is, and thus minimise the risk of permitting or encouraging enterprise damage.

5. Into the boardroom

The chapter began with some comments on risk, highlighting the crucial need to be aware of enterprise risk in all stages of life, and at all levels; to maximise risk awareness and risk readiness, so there should be less reliance on risk management and crisis management. We are well aware that organisations are run by people, and that the more effective leaders must be identified – internally or externally – attracted or retained, and certainly developed, properly managed and promoted, in the broadest sense of the word. We have considered the need to have a proper corporate culture with a clear and well-understood tone at the top, which should have the effect of a strong magnet – attracting and holding the best talent. We have considered what attributes successful leaders should possess and demonstrate, and outlined a way to determine what is necessary about specific individuals.

Now we are going to incorporate this into an individual who has recently joined the board of a large enterprise. For the purposes of the argument, we will not

---

1   http://www.savilleconsulting.com/products/wave.aspx.

categorise the individual as chairman, CEO, an internal director or non-executive director, but rather call them an 'integrated individual'. We will not address the issue of whether this person is an internal promotion or external hire, because we want to place the person, as the 'right' type (for whatever position) based on what we are hoping for, in an environment with personal and professional conflict to observe, think, reflect and possibly act on.

Bearing in mind that the chairman runs the board and the CEO runs the company, we are looking at the interaction of these two individuals: is there clarity regarding their roles, are there expressions of honesty, mutual trust and self-confidence? This translates into open, effective communication, which should minimise risk by encouraging discussion of emerging problems – being risk-aware and risk-ready, rather than reactive and in crisis mode (think BP and the Deepwater Horizon disaster – billions of dollars paid or set aside for fines and payments). Does vigorous debate exist; is there respect for the abilities of others? Are the other members of the board fully informed of the current issues, briefed for discussion, and certainly briefed on the implications arising from a major change of corporate direction? (Imagine our 'integrated individual' being told that the FT 100 company is moving out of telecoms equipment manufacturing and into software development, or moving from oil exploration to commodity trading without any prior information, and told 'you are new – you don't really need to concern yourself with this' – it has happened!) Proper preparation and distribution of management information encourages the best people to join, stay, participate professionally and absorb the ethos of good governance. This reduces the risk attendant with a weak atmosphere which reflects weak values, or values which are not conceived with the best interests of all stakeholders in mind. Think Enron – a disappearing entity, fines and jail-time for some at the top. Where was the trust, the serious debate? Was it fear and greed that governed?

Implicit in our discussion is that tone at the top, and a very professional approach to recruitment and promotion, should enhance the objective of some transitions. Think GE under Jack Welch, one of the great preparers. Possible successors were subject to vigorous operational, staff, and geographical challenges for years before a successor was appointed. This did not mean a 'cookie cutter' procedure, nor did it envision the production of a 'plain vanilla' cast of characters, but rather a very explicit goal of risk awareness and risk readiness, including preparation for the unthinkable. Those who were not successful moved on, did very well elsewhere and brought with them the rigorous attitudes to proper corporate governance, having participated in a very demanding succession planning exercise – not the knee-jerk reaction seen in media converge when a lack of risk-awareness has led to a state of crisis management, attendant departures and the elevation of compromise and surprise.

Where do we see this?

A strong-minded chairman with a weaker chief executive can lead to an assumption that the chairman will make all the important decisions, and that the CEO is just a rubber stamp, and thus is less important; when or if the chairman leaves, the team left behind could be weak, with low credibility down and an increased risk of damage to the entity.

A strong CEO and a weak chairman could mean that the board simply does not function adequately; it becomes the fiefdom of the CEO and his inner team, and possible problems will be buried because there is not practical mechanism for visibility. If something goes wrong, it may be a surprise because dissenting views may not be visible, or, if they are, disfunctionality joins the party.

Of course, a weak chairman combined with a weak CEO is likely to be disastrous. Risk, apparent or otherwise, will be rampant. The potential star will not show up, or will disappear and the risk of endemic weak management will be high. This is often manifested in an 'it will be all right on the night' attitude, an unknown, unexpected accident waiting to happen.

The other possibility is a strong chairman and a strong CEO who are able, confident, and knowledgeable, and communicate with trust 'ahead of the curve'. One would like to think that such a team would reflect the best values, by implicitly, and hopefully explicitly, setting the proper tone at the top, and disseminating proper corporate beliefs and values. By following the path outlined above, it should be possible to create an environment of pride and respect together with professionalism and effectiveness, which does become the magnet for the best people available.

Reflecting on what we have addressed in this chapter, let us hope for the best result as we consider a final scenario which may occur more often than we would like.

6.   Mr Pandora and his briefcase

Mr Pandora parked his modest car at the far end of the spaces allotted for the State Licensing Authority. He had worked for many years for a large multinational energy company in various somewhat menial positions, and had agreed the day before to drop off the comprehensive, bulky drilling application for permission to extend the company's search for additional gas reserves on its leased property. Tucked inside this jacket pocket was a bank draft made out to the SLA for £500,000 to cover the filing fees, research, investigation and review, and hopefully approval, of the application.

As he approached the door to the SLA offices, he remembered that his driver's licence had just expired, and decided to try to get that renewed at the same time.

After waiting a few minutes, he was shown into a small conference room where he was soon joined by Mr Smiley, a representative of the SLA, who closed the door, seated himself and noted that he was briefed on the reason for Mr Pandora's visit. The latter placed the application file on the table, together with the bank draft, confirmed that everything should be in order and that he had been told by his manager that, assuming all was well, approval to proceed would be forthcoming very soon.

Mr Smiley pulled the file and bank draft towards himself and said in a pleasant manner that while processing normally took two to three months, they were very busy at the SLA and somewhat under-staffed, and so the company might have to wait for eight to ten months for a response, unless an additional payment of £250,000 was made to Mr Smiley – in cash. Mr Pandora had never been faced with a situation like this before, and was completely at a loss as to how he should respond.

Stalling for time, he mentioned that, by the way, his driver's licence had expired, and could the SLA issue him with a renewal? Mr Smiley responded that this was certainly the case; the fee was £25 and it would normally take six weeks to process. However, if Mr Pandora provided an addition £20 to Mr Smiley with his renewal application, in cash, the licence would be issued while he waited.

Mr Pandora asked for some time to consider what had transpired, and said he would return after some reflection.

Mr Smiley reminded him that the SLA would be closing early that day in preparation for the long weekend holiday, so Mr Pandora should not delay for long. He also told him not to use his car without his new driver's licence as there would be increased police presence in the next few days due to the expected arrival of an increased number of visitors from out of state.

Mr Pandora picked up the drilling application and banker's draft, put them in his briefcase, politely excused himself and left the office. He returned to his car, rolled down the window and began to think about what had just happened, his career and how to get home.

He remembered, vaguely, something about corporate governance. There had been some presentations on the subject, he had taken a sort of online course and a test which he guessed everyone eventually passed, and occasionally an email would show up. It was all about how to react to situations like those he was facing – or perhaps there was more to it. Seems to have been the result of widespread panic in the energy world, and elsewhere following the collapse of a big company – couldn't remember the name – lots of people lost their jobs, and some went to jail.

In his company, there was talk of 'tone at the top', leadership talking about everyone behaving properly and being a representative of the company, together with a message that doing what the CEO and the board said was the answer. But he wondered – after a while messages seemed to arrive less frequently and stories still floated around about extravagant entertainment and doing business in other countries 'in a different way'. Did anyone really care? Was he in a lose-lose situation?

He could pay 'extra' to get his driver's licence renewed, but was it right to do so? Was it any different from the 'other' payment? Was one a 'facility payment' and the other a bribe?

Who should he speak to for advice? His boss? Not sure about that; he would say sort your driver's licence out yourself, that is a private matter – "you could always take a bus" – although that was not really true. Was his job was on the line if the drilling license just didn't come in on schedule and various costs went up? What if his bonus was cut because targets were not reached? Maybe there is extra money around to deal with things like this – call it consulting fees; maybe there was a way.

He could always speak to the company's whistle-blower, although he did not know much about this. Would his identity be protected? Would he be in trouble with the government if he did not say anything to anyone, and they later found out? Maybe he was already in trouble because he did not say no to Mr Smiley!

Maybe someone in the family, a friend … Would just mentioning the situation possibly get them into trouble?

What should he feel? What should he think? Who cares?

What happens next?

The Foreign Corrupt Practices Act: compliance to protect business clients globally

Aaron Schildhaus
Law Offices of Aaron Schildhaus

1.   Introduction

The US Foreign Corrupt Practices Act (15 USC Section 78dd-1ff) and the anti-corruption laws of other countries, including notably the UK Bribery Act 2010, have a major impact on business throughout the world.

Although this chapter focuses on the Foreign Corrupt Practices Act, the concepts and the compliance methodology discussed here are applicable to the laws of other countries, as well. Generally, businesses that comply with the Foreign Corrupt Practices Act will be able to adapt their policies and programmes relatively easily to conform with the requirements of the Bribery Act 2010 and other countries' anti-bribery legislation.

The Foreign Corrupt Practices Act makes it a crime for a US person to make a corrupt payment to a foreign official for the purpose of obtaining or retaining business for or with, or directing business to, any person. The law also applies to foreign firms and persons engaging in any act involving a corrupt payment while in the United States.

The act is taken very seriously by US businesses and their lawyers. Its extension abroad and application to companies around the world has increased significantly in the past few years. No one doing international business with any link to the United States can ignore it. Those who do, do so at their peril.

Two key US government agencies take the lead in enforcement. The Department of Justice is responsible for all criminal enforcement and for civil enforcement of the anti-bribery provisions with respect to domestic concerns and foreign companies and nationals.

The Securities and Exchange Commission (SEC) is responsible for civil enforcement of the anti-bribery provisions with respect to issuers – the Foreign Corrupt Practices Act requires companies with US-listed securities to meet its accounting provisions (15 USC Section 78m). These provisions operate together with the anti-bribery provisions of the Foreign Corrupt Practices Act. Corporations covered by its provisions must keep books and records that fairly and accurately reflect their transactions and are required to maintain proper internal accounting controls.

Other statutes, such as the mail and wire fraud statutes (18 USC Sections 1341, 1343) and the Travel Act (18 USC Section 1952), which provide for federal prosecution of violations of state commercial bribery statutes, may also apply.

In addition, the general conspiracy statute (18 USC Section 371) enables the

Department of Justice to charge companies with conspiracy to violate the anti-bribery provisions of the Foreign Corrupt Practices Act. It is easier for a prosecutor to prove conspiracy to commit an anti-bribery violation than it is to prove the underlying anti-bribery violation itself. To prove conspiracy, the prosecutor only has to prove an agreement by two or more persons to commit a Foreign Corrupt Practices Act violation with knowledge of, and participation in, the conspiracy. One overt act in furtherance of the conspiracy will suffice.

Because US companies must comply with the Foreign Corrupt Practices Act and, when applicable, the UK Bribery Act 2010 and the anti-bribery laws of other countries in which they operate, in their dealings outside their home countries, they must be able to show that their officers, employees, subsidiaries, affiliates, agents and partners around the world do not and will not transgress the these laws in their own operations. The best way for a company to do this is to have in force a fully effective anti-corruption compliance programme, adapted to its own business and structure, as further discussed below.

2. Relevance and background of the Foreign Corrupt Practices Act

The increasing number of investigations, prosecutions, settlements and convictions in the United States has created a sense of urgency in corporate boardrooms and officers' suites, not only in the United States, but also in countries where business relationships exist with US entities or are contemplated. Officers' and directors' concerns include:

- lost opportunities/revenues for their companies that may not pass the anti-corruption tests; and
- possible imprisonment and fines for officers and directors, as well as extremely large financial fines and penalties for the companies themselves.

It is helpful to review the background of the Foreign Corrupt Practices Act, which was enacted in the United States in 1977. At that time, foreign companies (except for those which were qualified as 'issuers') and foreign nationals were not covered. However, in 1998 the law was amended to provide territorial jurisdiction over foreign companies and nationals. Presently, a non-US company or person is also subject to the act if it causes, directly or through agents, any act taking place in US territory in furtherance of a corrupt payment.

Although, initially, many US businesses trying to compete in international markets did not welcome the Foreign Corrupt Practices Act, its criminalisation of corrupt behaviour and increasing enforcement has forced corporations and their management to take the matter very seriously – to the point where today any company that is not taking active steps to comply with the act is at risk.

In the years since passage of the act, the US government has worked successfully to assist in the drafting and ratification of international anti-corruption conventions by the Organisation of American States, the Organisation for Economic Cooperation and Development, the Council of Europe and the United Nations.

Aimed at modifying the behaviour of US businesses outside the United States, the Foreign Corrupt Practices Act has forced governments, business and the public to recognise that corruption is a major impediment to economic growth. This applies particularly to developing countries, where bribery and 'kickbacks' often are part everyday life. In those countries, which critically need economic development, corruption diverts scarce financial resources into the pockets of corrupt government officials and their associates. Eventually, investment flows into those countries are seriously reduced – foreign investors find more secure environments in which to invest, and the corrupt countries suffer even more. When corruption is contained and curtailed, investment flows more readily, and the standard of living in the country can increase.

Since 1977, criminal actions have been taken by the Securities and Exchange Commission (SEC) and by the US Department of Justice against companies and individuals violating various provisions of the act. In particular, in the past decade, investigations and prosecutions have increased sharply. Various factors underlie this acceleration, including the growing use of electronic communications and the availability, easy transfer and duplication of data across the Internet, providing more opportunities to secure evidence (and jurisdiction). Scandals such as Enron and WorldCom and the passage of new, tougher and expansive legislation, such as the Sarbanes-Oxley Act and the Dodd-Frank Act, have forced additional transparency and accountability on the acts of corporate officials and helped to change how corporations meet their ethical responsibilities.

More internal due diligence has become the rule, and more cooperation – not only among US government agencies, but also with foreign prosecutors – has led to a large increase in the number of Foreign Corrupt Practices Act investigations taking place. One effect is that regulators outside the United States are more confident and better able to cooperate with one another to fight corruption and to prosecute violators worldwide.

The past few years give a graphic example of the increase in prosecutions. In 2005, there were five Foreign Corrupt Practices Act assessments of fines and penalties, totalling approximately $15 million; in 2009, 52 companies were found liable and were fined over $1 billion. In December 2008, Siemens of Germany was fined a total of $450 million by the United States and more than twice that amount by Germany, receiving a total penalty of over $1.5 billion.

Non-US companies have been among the Department of Justice and SEC targets. On March 1 2010, the UK's BAE pleaded guilty to violating the Foreign Corrupt Practices Act and was fined $400 million; in actions by the SEC and Department of Justice in March and April 2010, German and Russian divisions of Daimler AG were fined and penalised a total of $185 million; and in the November 2010 Panalpina case, seven corporate entities were prosecuted – only one was a US entity – and assessed at $81.9 million in fines.[1] It should be noted that the investigation into Panalpina started in 2006, which proves that the investigations are lengthy, detailed and comprehensive, as well as very costly!

The trend is continuing, and many companies are under investigation, agreeing to

---

1   See www.sec.gov/spotlight/fcpa/fcpa-cases.shtml and www.forbes.com/sites/nathanvardi/2011/12/13/feds-charge-former-siemens-executives-with-bribery/

deferred prosecution and otherwise settling cases with the government, paying fines, implementing robust compliance programmes (imposed upon them by the government as a part of the penalties). Fines, disgorgements of profits and more are at hand. Moreover, the suspension and debarment of companies from federal procurement contracting and the imprisonment of their employees and officers is increasing.

3. Other countries' anti-corruption enforcement increasing

For years following the enactment of the Foreign Corrupt Practices Act, many US companies had complained that they were at a disadvantage compared with foreign companies which routinely paid bribes and, in some countries, were even permitted to deduct the cost of these bribes as business expenses on their taxes. The United States started negotiations in the Organisation of Economic Cooperation and Development (OECD) to obtain the agreement of its major trading partners to enact legislation similar to the Foreign Corrupt Practices Act. In 1997, the United States and 33 other countries signed the OECD Convention on Combating Bribery of Foreign Public Officials in International Business Transactions. (The United States ratified this convention and enacted implementing legislation in 1998.)

The passage of the OECD Convention, and its gradual implementation in the member countries, has been enhanced by ratification in 2005 of the United Nations Convention Against Corruption, by the passage of more explicit anti-corruption laws by various countries and by increasing public scrutiny of OECD implementation on a country-by-country basis.

In addition to this increased governmental anti-corruption activity, the multilateral lending institutions, led by the World Bank, have established special internal units with trained investigative staff to review the actions of their employees and contractors for any improprieties. They are now rigorously examining and debarring individual companies from working on bank-funded projects if they are found to have engaged in corrupt practices during any bank projects. In 2011, the World Bank's anti-graft unit investigated allegations in 97 countries and in connection with 367 projects, and suspended 32 individuals, firms and non-governmental organisations from bidding on bank projects. On May 30 2012, the World Bank published its Sanctions Board Decisions for the first time,[2] and clearly and publicly indicated the importance it attaches to the implementation of effective anti-corruption compliance programmes (similar to the Foreign Corrupt Practices Act) in determining the extent to which, or whether, sanctions would be imposed against a company found to have engaged in corruption.

Today, corporate compliance is the rule. In order to avoid the negative consequences of allegations of corruption, many corporations have been implementing detailed compliance programmes, aimed at identifying and preventing any improper payments by their employees and agents.

In order to appreciate the compliance climate, and before examining the process, it is helpful to review the elements of a Foreign Corrupt Practices Act violation.

---

2   see http://web.worldbank.org/WBSITE/EXTERNAL/EXTABOUTUS/ORGANIZATION/ORGUNITS/EXT OFFEVASUS/0,,contentMDK:23059612~pagePK:64168445~piPK:64168309~theSitePK:3601046,00.html

4. To whom does the Foreign Corrupt Practices Act apply?

The Foreign Corrupt Practices Act applies to any individual, firm, officer, director, employee or agent of a firm and any stockholder acting on behalf of a firm. Individuals and firms may also be penalised if they order, authorise or assist someone else to violate the anti-bribery provisions or if they conspire to violate those provisions.

Under the Foreign Corrupt Practices Act, US jurisdiction over corrupt payments to foreign officials depends upon whether the violator is an "issuer", a "domestic concern", or a foreign national or business.

An issuer is a corporation that has issued securities that have been registered in the United States or which is required to file periodic reports with the SEC. A domestic concern is any individual who is a citizen, national or resident of the United States, or any corporation, partnership, association, joint-stock company, business trust, unincorporated organisation or sole proprietorship which has its principal place of business in the United States, or which is organised under the laws of a state of the United States, or a territory, possession or commonwealth of the United States.

Issuers and domestic concerns may be held liable under the Foreign Corrupt Practices Act under either territorial or nationality jurisdiction principles. For acts taken within the territory of the United States, issuers and domestic concerns are liable if they take an act in furtherance of a corrupt payment to a foreign official using the US mails or other means of interstate commerce, including telephone calls, facsimile transmissions, wire transfers and interstate or international travel. In addition, issuers and domestic concerns may be held liable for any act in furtherance of a corrupt payment taken outside the United States. Thus, a US company or national may be held liable for a corrupt payment authorised by its employees or agents operating entirely outside the United States, using money from foreign bank accounts, and without any involvement by personnel located within the United States.

A foreign company or person is subject to the Foreign Corrupt Practices Act if it causes, directly or through agents, an act in furtherance of the corrupt payment to take place within the territory of the United States. There is no requirement for the act to use the US mails or other means of interstate commerce.

Finally, a US parent corporation may be held liable for the acts of foreign subsidiaries if it authorised, directed or controlled the activity in question. In the same way, US citizens or residents are considered to be domestic concerns (and thus liable under the act) if they were employed by or acting on behalf of such foreign-incorporated subsidiaries.

4.1 Corrupt intent

The person making or authorising the payment must have a corrupt intent, and the payment must be intended to induce the recipient to misuse his or her official position to direct business wrongfully to the payer or to any other person. It is important to note that the Foreign Corrupt Practices Act does not require that a corrupt act succeeds in its purpose. The offer or promise of a corrupt payment can constitute a violation of the statute. The Foreign Corrupt Practices Act prohibits any corrupt payment intended to influence any act or decision of a foreign official to do or fail to do any act in violation of his or her lawful duty, to obtain any improper advantage, or to induce a foreign official to use his or her influence improperly to affect or influence any act or decision.

4.2 Payment

The Foreign Corrupt Practices Act prohibits the paying, offering, promising to pay (or authorising to pay or offer) of money or anything of value. For example, offering or promising (even if never carried out) to pay for the education of a relative of a government official, or for the travel expenses of an official or official's family member, would satisfy this element.

4.3 Recipient

The prohibition extends only to corrupt payments to a foreign official, a foreign political party or party official, or any candidate for foreign political office. A 'foreign official' means any officer or employee of a foreign government, a public international organisation, or any department or agency of it, or any person acting in an official capacity. What constitutes a foreign official is often an important question. For example, is a member of a royal family, a member of a legislative body or an official of a state-owned business enterprise considered to be a foreign official?

The Foreign Corrupt Practices Act applies to payments to any public official, regardless of their rank or position. The act focuses on the purpose of the payment, not the particular duties of the official receiving the payment, offer or promise of payment, and there are exceptions to the anti-bribery provision for "facilitating payments for routine governmental action" (see below).

4.4 Business purpose test

The Foreign Corrupt Practices Act prohibits payments made in order to assist the firm in obtaining or retaining business for or with, or directing business to, any person. "Obtaining or retaining business" is interpreted very broadly by the Department of Justice; it encompasses more than the mere award or renewal of a contract. The business to be obtained or retained need not be just with a foreign government or foreign government entity.

5. Third party payments

The Foreign Corrupt Practices Act prohibits corrupt payments through intermediaries. It is unlawful to make a payment to a third party knowing that all or a portion of the payment will go, directly or indirectly, to a foreign official. The term 'knowing' includes conscious disregard and deliberate ignorance. The elements of an offence are essentially the same as described above, except that here the recipient is the intermediary who is making the payment to the foreign official.

Intermediaries may include joint venture partners or agents. To avoid being held liable for corrupt third party payments, US companies are encouraged to exercise due diligence and to take all necessary precautions to ensure that their business relationships are with reputable and qualified partners and representatives.

Proper due diligence includes investigating the potential foreign representatives and joint venture partners to determine:

- their qualifications for the position;
- the extent to which they have personal or professional links to government entities or officials;
- the numbers, types and reputations of their clients;
- their reputation with the US and the UK's and other enforcing countries' embassies or consulates, and with local bankers, clients and other business associates; and
- in addition, in negotiating a business relationship, the US firm should be aware of so-called 'red flags' (see section 13.4(g) for a detailed discussion of red flags).

6. Permissible payments: affirmative defences

The Foreign Corrupt Practices Act contains an explicit exception to the bribery prohibition for "facilitating payments" for "routine governmental action", and also provides for affirmative defences against alleged violations of the act.

6.1 Facilitating payments for routine governmental actions

There is an exception to the anti-bribery prohibition for payments to facilitate or expedite performance of a "routine governmental action". The Foreign Corrupt Practices Act lists the following examples: obtaining permits, licences or other official documents; processing governmental papers, such as visas and work orders; providing police protection, mail pick-up and delivery; providing phone service, power and water supply; loading and unloading cargo, or protecting perishable products; and scheduling inspections associated with contract performance or transit of goods across country. Actions "similar" to these would also be covered by this exception.

The exception for facilitating payments under the act sets it apart from other anti-bribery laws, such as the UK Bribery Act 2010, which do not provide for any exceptions. The predominant view is that corruption is corruption, and that making exceptions is confusing and unfair. Therefore, in structuring compliance programmes that need to conform to the legislative norms of other countries as well as the United States, it is advisable to practise zero tolerance of any payments, regardless of whether they may be definable as facilitating. Obviously, under the Foreign Corrupt Practices Act or otherwise, routine governmental action does not include any decision by a foreign official to award new business to or continue business with a particular party.

6.2 Affirmative defences

A person charged with a violation of the Foreign Corrupt Practices Act's anti-bribery provisions may assert as a defence that the payment was lawful under the written laws of the foreign country or that the money was spent as part of demonstrating a product or performing a contractual obligation.

It may be difficult to determine whether a payment was lawful under the written laws of the foreign country. Moreover, because these defences are affirmative defences, the defendant is required to show in the first instance that the payment met these requirements. The prosecution does not bear the burden of demonstrating in the first instance that the payments did not constitute this type of payment.

7.   Criminal sanctions against bribery

The following criminal penalties may be imposed for violations of the Foreign Corrupt Practices Act's anti-bribery provisions:

- corporations and other business entities are subject to a fine of up to $2 million; and
- officers, directors, stockholders, employees and agents (including non-US nationals) are subject to a fine of up to $100,000 and imprisonment for up to five years.

See 15 USC Sections 78dd-2(g), 78dd-3(e), 78ff(c).

Under the Alternative Fines Act, these fines may be higher – the actual fine may be up to twice the benefit that the defendant sought to obtain by making the corrupt payment (see 18 USC Section 3571(d)). Fines imposed on individuals may not be paid by their employer or principal (see 15 USC Sections 78dd-2(g)(3), 78dd-3(e)(3), 78ff(c)(3)).

A violation of the Foreign Corrupt Practices Act may also result in the civil and criminal forfeiture of assets. The Civil Asset Forfeiture Reform Act of 2000 expanded the list of civil forfeiture predicates to include each offence listed as a specified unlawful activity in the Money Laundering Control Act (18 USC Section 1956(c)(7)). The 2000 act further provides for criminal forfeiture for all offences for which civil forfeiture was authorised (see 28 USC Section 2461(c)). Any property, real or personal, which constitutes or is derived from proceeds traceable to a violation of, or a conspiracy to violate, the Foreign Corrupt Practices Act may be forfeited (see 18 USC Section 981).

8.   Civil sanctions

In addition to the criminal sanctions, the attorney general or the SEC, as appropriate, may bring a civil action to enjoin any act or practice of a firm if it appears that the firm (or an officer, director, employee, agent or stockholder acting on behalf of the firm) is in violation (or about to be) of the Foreign Corrupt Practices Act anti-bribery provisions (see 15 USC Sections 78u, 78dd-2(d), 78dd-3(d)). In such a civil action, a fine of $10,000 may be assessed for each act committed in furtherance of the offence, potentially bringing the total fine to more than $10,000 (see 15 USC Sections 78dd-2(g), 78dd-3(e), 78ff(c)).

A person or firm found to be in violation of the Foreign Corrupt Practices Act may be barred from doing business with the federal government. Indictment alone can lead to suspension of the right to do business with the government. A person or firm found guilty of violating the act may be ruled ineligible to receive export licences; the SEC may suspend or bar persons from the securities business and impose civil penalties on persons in the securities business for violations of the act; the

Commodity Futures Trading Commission and the Overseas Private Investment Corporation both provide for possible suspension or debarment from agency programmes for violation of the act; and an unlawful payment under the act cannot be deducted under the tax laws as a business expense.

As mentioned above, fines imposed on individuals may not be paid by their employer or principal. Therefore, corporations should be aware that the traditional corporate officers' and directors' liability insurance policies are likely to be of limited use in protecting their officers and directors from the expenses of defending themselves from the costs of investigations and prosecutions.

9. Private cause of action

Conduct that violates the anti-bribery provisions of the Foreign Corrupt Practices Act may also give rise to a private cause of action for triple damages under the Racketeer Influenced and Corrupt Organisations Act, or to actions under other federal or state laws. For example, an action may be brought under the act by a competitor who alleges that the bribery led to the defendant winning a foreign contract.

10. Foreign Corrupt Practices Act investigations: whistle-blowing

Foreign Corrupt Practices Act investigations may be initiated by the US government whenever it feels there is likelihood of corruption. It relies on a variety of sources to justify an investigation, including complaints from competitors and news reports, and whistle-blowing is now a major source, stemming from the new rules under the provisions of the Dodd-Frank Act. Whistle-blowing is encouraged under Section 21F of the act, which provides bounties to whistle-blowers of 10% to 30% of monetary sanctions for SEC violations.

US prosecutors are pursuing violators rigorously and successfully, but have demonstrated a willingness towards leniency if a US violator self-reports, particularly if it offers complete cooperation, not hiding anything. However, there is concern that the whistle-blower provisions noted above are making it more difficult for companies to investigate internally and self-report. Given the high value of the whistle-blower sanctions, individuals familiar with violations may be more likely to seek the very high rewards provided by the legislation.

11. Guidance from the government

The Department of Justice has established a Foreign Corrupt Practices Act Opinion Procedure by which any US company or national may request a statement of the department's present enforcement intentions under the anti-bribery provisions of the Foreign Corrupt Practices Act regarding any proposed business conduct. The details of the opinion procedure may be found at 28 CFR Part 80. Under the procedure, the attorney general will issue an opinion in response to a specific inquiry from a person or firm within 30 days of the receipt by Department of Justice of all the information it requires to issue the opinion. Conduct for which the department has issued an opinion stating that the conduct conforms with current enforcement policy will be entitled to a presumption of conformity with the Foreign Corrupt Practices Act in any subsequent enforcement action.

A major concern on the part of non-US law firms is how to counsel their clients in light of the exponential increase in US prosecutions and the fact that today, in the boardrooms of most US companies, there is a real fear that any Foreign Corrupt Practices Act transgression will result in substantial and possibly crippling fines for their companies, coupled with fines and imprisonment for the officers and employees who actively or tacitly may have participated in making prohibited payments. Another factor to consider is the extent to which adverse publicity in the United States, or inquiries by US regulators to their foreign counterparts, may put local companies at risk.

The reality today is that US businesses overwhelmingly are unlikely to go forward on any deal with a foreign partner that cannot or will not certify that it is now or will be Foreign Corrupt Practices Act-compliant. The situation is worse if the US party uncovers hard evidence that corrupt acts have occurred and might represent a pattern of corruption, actionable under the statute. In addition to the Foreign Corrupt Practices Act, other federal laws relating to conspiracy, record-keeping, money-laundering, and so on, may be applicable, and all are used by federal prosecutors to pursue violators of the act. Clearly, prosecutors have many resources, all of which they are using to pursue all leads, and they benefit from their close relationships with prosecutors in other countries, with whom they share much information and close cooperation.

12.   Privileged attorney-client communications

One of the concerns expressed outside the United States is the extent to which non-US law firms need to be concerned about the erosion or waiver of privileged communications between themselves and their clients. A US party's fear of punishment may lead it to decide to provide everything – all documentation, data, results of internal investigations and communications – to US prosecutors in order to minimise their own criminal consequences, including the reduction of fines, deferred prosecutions, and other attempts at plea-bargaining. Cooperation by US parties tends to be extensive, with compromising results sometimes on their industry and on their partners and related parties.

Because US and UK companies must comply with the Foreign Corrupt Practices Act or the Anti-Bribery Act 2010 in their dealings outside their home countries, they are insisting that their subsidiaries, affiliates, agents and partners around the world provide them with assurances that they do not and will not transgress these laws in their own operations. The best way for a company to do this is to have its own anti-corruption (or Foreign Corrupt Practices Act) compliance programme, adapted to its particular business and structure.

The internal costs of self-investigation before the fact are always significantly less than the costs of investigation and due diligence once the Department of Justice or SEC launch an investigation. Companies that have been able to prove that they have a robust compliance programme in place are able to shield themselves from indictment and much of the associated direct and indirect costs.

13. Elements of a Foreign Corrupt Practices Act compliance programme

There is no one-size-fits-all compliance programme, since no two companies are alike and no two companies face the same issues internally and externally. It is essential that each company designs its own compliance programme. However, most deferred prosecution agreements and settlements and decisions contain references and details of compliance programmes, as do the US Sentencing Guidelines published by the Department of Justice,[3] and all are worth examining.

Although not all guidelines may be applicable in every case, when designing a corporate compliance programme, there are a number of elements that are universal and must be included in one form or another. A non-exhaustive list of the necessary elements is discussed in the following sections.

13.1 Corporate policy

To be effective (and compliant), anti-corruption compliance must be integrated into a corporation's written policies and be very clear. I recommend that the corporation adopts as official, written corporate policy that it has zero tolerance for corruption. It should cite the law in its own country, and refer to laws in other countries, stating that it will adopt the highest standard of conduct prescribed by the laws in the countries of actual or prospective operation. A clearly articulated corporate policy against violations of the Foreign Corrupt Practices Act, including its anti-bribery, books and records, and internal controls provisions, and other applicable counterparts (collectively, the 'anti-corruption laws') must be in place.

The existence of a written programme alone will not satisfy the Department of Justice. Prosecutors always inquire whether a company's compliance programme is being adequately enforced – that is, whether it is a 'paper programme'. Primarily, companies should focus on the actual implementation of their compliance programme, but they should also ensure that its communication and enforcement is transparent and obvious. The existence of various identifiable channels for communication, implementation and enforcement of a company's Foreign Corrupt Practices Act policies through the legal and/or compliance department and the requirements for documenting the compliance are all important indicators of an effective and robust compliance programme.

In addition to having a documented procedure in place, it is essential that all issues and situations that arise that have any bearing on the policy are thoroughly documented, so there is a clear record available to show that the policy not only exists, but that it is properly and completely implemented.[4]

13.2 Top-down approach

The anti-corruption compliance message must be conveyed with authority and must be consistent and applicable to every officer, director and employee, as well as to all contractors, agents, representatives, joint venture partners, and all who work with

---

3   see www.ussc.gov/Guidelines/2011_Guidelines/Manual_HTML/2c1_1.htm
4   See *US v Depuy, Inc* (DDC, filed April 8 2011); *SEC v Johnson & Johnson*, Civil Action 1:11-cv-00686 (DDC, filed April 8 2011).

them. Communications to the employees in newsletters and other media should include periodic memoranda, regular restatement of the policy and articles on compliance.

No one is exempt or above the policy. The chief executive officer must make it clear to all that he endorses the policy completely and that any violation discovered will result in the dismissal of employees involved or the termination of business relationships if the business partner has engaged in corruption. A corporate culture of compliance must exist. To the extent that this can be shown, it will benefit the company and all contractors, representatives, joint venture or teaming partners, and all who work with as well as for them.

The Department of Justice has emphasised the importance of having at least one member of a company's senior management responsible for the enforcement of policies, standards and procedures. In its settlement made with the department, Johnson & Johnson and its subsidiaries and operating companies (collectively Johnson & Johnson), agreed to "appoint a … Chief Compliance Officer … [with] reporting obligations directly to the Audit Committee of the Board of Directors". Johnson & Johnson also agreed to "appoint heads of compliance within each business sector and corporate function … [with] … reporting obligations to the Chief Compliance Officer and the Audit Committee". It further agreed to: "Maintain a global compliance leadership team, including regional compliance leaders and business segment compliance leaders, with responsibility for overseeing its company-wide compliance programme. That leadership team will have reporting obligations directly to the Chief Compliance Officer." See *US v Depuy, Inc*, cited above.

13.3 Due diligence

A programme of ongoing due diligence for past, present and proposed corporate activities is one of the pillars upon which an effective compliance programme is built. If a potential business deal comes under suspicion, or if a due diligence investigation discloses suspicious circumstances, the US party must resolve it, or face possibly serious consequences. See section 13.4(g) for a discussion of red flags and their importance in meeting the due diligence requirements of the Foreign Corrupt Practices Act.

If a company has a history of corrupt payments and the employees and/or managers or others are asked to disclose them, they may decide upon non-disclosure in order to protect their jobs or contracts. Whistle-blowing protections and actual corporate history must be openly discussed with special counsel in order to deal with such compromising situations. Anonymous channels of disclosure, such as telephone hotlines and suggestion boxes, will enable whistle-blowers to inform top management of violations without fear of losing their positions.

The implementation of a regular compliance audit is one of the elements necessary to ensure the due diligence is undertaken properly. Detailed guidelines are contained in the Johnson & Johnson case cited above, and in a great many other cases, although they are always tailored to the company in question. However, they are all instructive in helping a company to establish its own audit procedures, which must include a detailed review of all accounts, books, records, documents and correspondence on a regular basis. The audit must address the company and its partners, its activities and its potential and proposed activities, contracts, and partners and affiliates with whom it does, or plans to do, business.

13.4   Relevance and risk assessment

The programme must be relevant to the company and its operations. Because risks differ in type and size from country to country, and because no two companies are the same, a compliance programme requires the following.

(a)   Advance analysis of the risks of the industry sectors

This is necessary as each business sector has different levels of risk.

(b)   Analysis of the country and the region

This is necessary because geography often influences behaviour. It is suggested that reference is made to indicators such as Transparency International's Corruption Perception Index (see http://cpi.transparency.org/cpi2011/).

(c)   Size of the business and size of the company

The size of the business and the size of the company are relevant to the likelihood of corruption.

(d)   Types of company's products and activities

The types of the company's products and activities may affect the likelihood of corruption.

(e)   Level of interface with government officials

The more regulatory contact and the more discretionary authority exerted by government officials, the higher are the corruption risk factors. The specific contact points between the company and foreign officials must be identified.

(f)   Quality of contractors, agents, distributors and partners

Due diligence must be carried out on those with whom the company is working, or intends to work.

(g)   Red flags

'Red flags' relate to persons with whom the company may be working or planning to work, who may be potential partners, representatives, agents or others. It is necessary to obtain information about them before going forward, as a part of the required due diligence. If there are any red flags, counsel must increase its due diligence and obtain as many facts as possible. Red flags include any of the following:
- request for payment in cash;
- request for payments to be made in a third country, or to a third party;
- history of having requested any payment to be made to a third, unrelated party;
- direct/indirect family relationship with a government official;

- history of asking for false invoices or other false documentation;
- refusal of a person to agree in writing to comply with the Foreign Corrupt Practices Act or other laws;
- prospective activities in a country with a reputation for corruption and bribery;
- previous convictions or charges against a payee for violation of local or foreign laws or regulations relating to the award of government contracts;
- inadequately explained break-up of an association with one or more foreign companies;
- relationship problems with other foreign companies;
- heavy reliance on political/government contacts, as opposed to time and effort to be expended;
- expressed preference for keeping representation secret; and
- other suspicious conduct on the part of the representative that would raise questions in the eyes of a prudent person.

Whenever there is a red flag, a deep and detailed investigation, and complete resolution of all concerns/questions, is required; otherwise, the company should refuse to enter into any agreement with the representative. Detailed investigation may include retention of an outside investigative firm or counsel, interviewing the principals of the foreign representative, and other independent research and discussions within the other country.

(h) Number of contractors, agents and partners

The more third parties involved, the higher the risk. The risk is reduced proportionally to the extent that corporate management has effective internal contacts and controls in place and relies upon itself, rather than outside entities, which are inherently more difficult to supervise.

(i) Corporate code of conduct

Management's adherence to a comprehensive written programme, and its promulgation of an effective code of conduct incorporating all the elements of the programme, must be effectively communicated and updated on a regular basis to all employees and business partners. The code should be specific, identifying corporate policy regarding the following, and approvals by whom and how, in writing:

- bribes or solicitations for bribes or other irregular payments – prohibited;
- gifts, hospitality and travel policies must be designed appropriately. The following restrictions on such policies were agreed by Johnson & Johnson with Department of Justice:
  - Gifts must be modest in value, appropriate under the circumstances, and given in accordance with anti-corruption laws and regulations, including those of the government official's home country;
  - Hospitality shall be limited to reasonably priced meals, accommodations, and incidental expenses that are part of product education and training programs, professional training, and conferences or business meetings ...

> Travel shall be limited to product education and training programs, professional training, and conferences or business meetings; and
> - Gifts, hospitality, and travel shall not include expenses for anyone other than the official.

- charitable contributions need very careful scrutiny and approval;
- contributions to political parties – prohibited;
- entertainment – generally prohibited;
- facilitating payments – recommendation is not to permit these;
- actions of employees through third parties – a major danger point, requiring due diligence as described above;
- third-party transaction partner – due diligence is essential here, too;
- accounting for agency/license fees – need itemised accounts and receipts;
- petty cash must be accounted for; and
- loans and advances must be accounted for.

13.5   Training and certification

One of the key elements of an effective compliance programme is education, and updated materials must be generated and presented to employees in a live and effective manner on a regular basis. The educational process must require all persons to attend presentations/seminars and to provide adequate proof that they understand what is being taught to them.

The presentation should provide relevant documents, including a copy of the Foreign Corrupt Practices Act and recent decisions/opinions that may have particular resonance for the industry or the structure of the corporate client. It should consist of lectures and workshops, documentation, videos, online materials, and live, interactive discussions (Q&As). Potential scenarios should be explored and discussed and questions and active discussion should be encouraged. The provisions of the applicable laws and fact patterns of recent cases should be covered.

Red flags should be described, and all participants should be encouraged to consult a corporate checklist of questions and concerns that apply to their own company and its operations. In the event of any questions, employees should be taught to discuss with their supervisors and/or with specially designated anti-corruption management personnel, as well as with specialised counsel, where appropriate. The in-house procedures for investigations and for dealing with possible violations of policy should be thoroughly discussed, and the types of detailed reports that will be required must also be reviewed.

13.6   Contractual provisions for Foreign Corrupt Practices Act compliance

Business partners and existing and prospective employees at all levels must be willing to certify that they will not engage in any corrupt conduct and that they accept the consequences if they break this commitment. They must renew their commitment on a regular, at least annual, basis.

From the perspective of compliant US companies, all agreements with international distributors or representatives must highlight the importance of Foreign Corrupt Practices Act compliance. Every potential representative should be advised that there can be no agreement, and that no payments or advances can be made or given for any services rendered, until an agreement containing sufficient contractual provisions is completed and executed by both sides. Ideally, the client company should discuss the Foreign Corrupt Practices Act (and other laws and company policies) as early as possible in the evaluation and negotiation process. In any event, no payment should be made to the representative until preliminary due diligence has been satisfactory, no red flags exist and the representative has warranted its compliance and commitment to continue compliance.

Each representative/distributor/joint venture party must agree to abide by the provisions of the Foreign Corrupt Practices Act. Compliance provisions should be explicitly set forth in the agency, representative, joint venture or other relevant agreement. Because company agents have implicit authority to bind the company legally, the contractual provisions for agents and representatives must be more comprehensive and stringent than in agreements with distributors.

The following contractual requirements are recommended:

- agreement that the company will be given access to books and records;
- periodic full audit rights;
- provision that any information relating to a suspected violation may be disclosed to government agencies, for example, the Department of Justice, or to other entities that may have a legitimate need to know;
- rights to immediate termination of the agreement upon a good-faith belief that the agent, representative or partner has violated the Foreign Corrupt Practices Act or caused client risk of a Foreign Corrupt Practices Act violation;
- agent, representative or partner warranty that it/they have obtained an opinion letter from local counsel acknowledging that the terms of the agreement do not violate any local laws;
- payment of travel, entertainment and other expenses, including charitable contributions or payments to third persons of any type, require advance written approval by management or in-house counsel;
- certification by agents/distributors/partners that they are not official representatives of the government of the country in which the transaction is to take place, and that no payments to them will be transferred to a foreign official, political party or official thereof, or to a political candidate;
- obligation to notify as soon as possible if there is any material change in their ownership structure;
- certification that they understand and agree to comply with the terms of the Foreign Corrupt Practices Act and other applicable laws as specified in the client's written compliance procedures;
- undertaking fully to observe and abide by the client's written compliance procedures;
- obligation to report immediately any information received that may indicate that a Foreign Corrupt Practices Act violation or an improper payment has been made;
- requirement to certify on an annual basis that the party has no knowledge of any Foreign Corrupt Practices Act violations;

- no assignment or subcontracting of rights or obligations to third parties; and
- right to terminate immediately upon any breach of such provisions.

14. How a well-designed and robustly enforced compliance programme matters

In the preceding paragraphs, we have described the necessary elements of an effective compliance programme. A recent and graphic example of how such a programme is effective is that of Morgan Stanley, whose effective and well-implemented programme saved it from prosecution. Morgan Stanley found itself under investigation for Foreign Corrupt Practices Act violations; yet, the SEC's description of Morgan Stanley's compliance programme and its active and diligent implementation of it saved the company from prosecution (see citation www.sec.gov/news/press/2012/2012-78.htm).

Following an extensive investigation, on April 25 2012, the SEC charged Garth Peterson, a former executive at Morgan Stanley, with violating the Foreign Corrupt Practices Act as well as securities laws for investment advisers by secretly acquiring millions of dollars-worth of real estate investments for himself and an influential Chinese official with a state-owned enterprise, steering business to Morgan Stanley's funds. Yet, because of its robust Foreign Corrupt Practices Act compliance programme, Morgan Stanley was able to shield itself from prosecution, and its rogue employee was pursued instead. The SEC commended Morgan Stanley, citing its compliance system relative to the violations. Morgan Stanley's compliance as officially described by the SEC is most instructive and should give practitioners a valuable perspective and confirmation of the need for a compliance programme to include all the elements described above and for it to be vigorously enforced:

- *training:* it "trained Peterson on anti-corruption policies and the Foreign Corrupt Practices Act at least seven times" in both live and web-based sessions. Between 2000 and 2008, it held "at least 54 training programs for various groups of Asia-based employees on anti-corruption policies, including the Foreign Corrupt Practices Act";
- *compliance personnel:* it employed "over 500 dedicated compliance officers, and its compliance department had direct lines to MS's Board of Directors and regularly reported through the Chief Legal Officer to the Chief Executive Officer and senior management committees";
- *regional compliance personnel:* it employed "regional compliance officers who specialised in particular regions, including China, in order to evaluate region-specific risks";
- *audit:* it "randomly audited selected personnel in high-risk areas" and "regularly audited and tested MS's business units";
- *hotline:* it provided a toll-free compliance hotline 24/7, "staffed to field calls in every major language, including Chinese";
- *written compliance materials:* it "distributed written training materials specifically addressing the Foreign Corrupt Practices Act, which Peterson kept in his office";
- *frequent compliance reminders:* "Peterson personally received more than 35

Foreign Corrupt Practices Act compliance reminders during the time he was working for MS in China. These included a distribution of the MS Code of Conduct, reminders concerning policies on gift giving and entertainment and guidance on the engagement of consultants";

- *written certifications:* it "required Peterson on multiple occasions to certify his compliance with the Foreign Corrupt Practices Act. These written certifications were maintained in Peterson's permanent employment record";
- *disclosure of outside business interests:* "it required Peterson, along with other employees, to annually disclose his outside business interests"; and
- *review and update policies:* it "conducted, 'in conjunction with outside counsel,' a formal review annually of each of its anti-corruption policies."

Morgan Stanley also had specific policies to conduct due diligence on its foreign business partners.

- it conducted due diligence on the "Chinese Official" and Yongye (the state-owned enterprise) before initially doing business with them;
- it imposed an approval process for payments made in the course of its real estate investments to prevent improper payments;
- an in-house compliance officer specifically informed Peterson in 2004 that employees of Yongye, a Chinese state-owned entity, were government officials for purposes of the Foreign Corrupt Practices Act;
- it maintained a substantial system of controls to detect and prevent improper payments, including required multiple employees to be involved in the approval of payments; and
- it "continually evaluated and improved its compliance programme and internal controls", including "risk-based Foreign Corrupt Practices Act auditing intended to detect transactions, payments and partnerships that suggested increased risks".

See www.sec.gov/news/press/2012/2012-78.htm.

15. Conclusion: compliance programmes are essential

Non-US counsel have an interest in understanding the Foreign Corrupt Practices Act and in counselling their clients about the act's enforcement, which includes the design and implementation of dynamic (and individually tailored) compliance programmes in third countries for foreign clients, and about introducing programmes that will meet compliance requirements in the host country as well as in the United States.

Anti-corruption is here to stay, and lawyers should initiate discussions with their business clients about the dangers sooner rather than later, because later may well be too late. Lawyers and compliance professionals should urge corporate leadership to examine their local and global operations in the light of the Foreign Corrupt Practices Act, and should urge them to design and implement proper compliance programmes.

The rising tide of a new international phenomenon: carbon-copy prosecutions

Andrew S Boutros*
United States Attorney's Office for the Northern District of Illinois
T Markus Funk
Perkins Coie LLP

1.   Introduction

A lot has been written about the Foreign Corrupt Practices Act[1] over the past few years. However, this chapter concentrates instead on a critical, yet very under-recognised anti-corruption trend that is gaining worldwide recognition in enforcement circles: carbon-copy prosecutions.[2]

The phrase 'carbon-copy prosecutions'[3] refers to successive, duplicate prosecutions by different states for conduct that is illegal under each of their national laws but arises out of the same common facts. Put another way, prosecutors in different countries each punish transnational conduct that violates their own domestic laws, but elect to do so after an offender has admitted to the wrongful conduct in an earlier foreign proceeding. The number of carbon-copy prosecutions in the transnational anti-corruption sector is increasing, and this type of prosecution has altered the equation for conducting and resolving international anti-corruption investigations. It appears that these proceedings will be more widely used in international anti-corruption enforcement in the future. Carbon-copy prosecutions appear to be here to stay and they should be a part of any desktop reference tool about legal risk management, governance and compliance.

This chapter is divided into five sections. Section 1 provides an overview of the Foreign Corrupt Practices Act and its constituent parts. It also examines recent Foreign Corrupt Practices Act enforcement statistics and trends, and places that data in the context of the historical enforcement development of the statute. Section 2 examines the concept of carbon-copy prosecutions. It defines the phenomenon,

---

*In his personal capacity.

1   15 USC §§ 78dd-1, *et seq.*

2   Andrew Boutros coined the term 'carbon copy prosecutions' during a panel presentation at the 2011 ABA Annual Meeting Presidential Showcase Panel in Toronto, Canada. See Juliet Sorensen, *The Globalization of Anti-Corruption Law*, Foreign Corrupt Practices Act Professor Blog (August 16 2011), at www.fcpaprofessor.com/the-globalization-of-anti-corruption-law (summarising a panel presentation on the globalisation of anti-corruption law and noting that: "Boutros also pointed out an increased trend in what he termed 'carbon copy' prosecutions, a phenomenon where foreign authorities rely on the factual findings emerging out of US enforcement actions to vindicate the local laws of their own jurisdiction - often the site of the bribe payment or bribe receipt").

3   For another comprehensive examination of carbon copy prosecutions and their collateral effects and attendant considerations, *see* Andrew S Boutros and T Markus Funk, *'Carbon Copy' Prosecutions: A Growing Anti-Corruption Phenomenon in a Shrinking World*, 2012 U Chi Legal F 259.

explains its analytical base and examines certain key lessons that emerge from the carbon copy trend. Section 3 identifies several key cases in which states have brought successive, duplicate enforcement actions arising out of the admissions and factual findings of earlier (and often US-led) government investigations and negotiated resolutions. Section 4 analyses the cost-benefit considerations of a company's decision to make a joint voluntary front-end disclosure to foreign authorities along with its decision to disclose potential Foreign Corrupt Practices Act violations to US authorities. The main consideration is the double jeopardy implication of successive, multiple transnational prosecutions arising from common facts. Finally, Section 5 concludes with some observations on the current state of international anti-corruption enforcement, including the future of carbon-copy prosecutions.

2. The Foreign Corrupt Practices Act

In the mid-1970s, more than 400 US companies admitted to making improper payments of more than $300 million to foreign government officials, politicians and political parties.[4] In 1977, Congress responded by enacting the Foreign Corrupt Practices Act, which was intended to reduce the bribing of foreign officials, criminally to punish those who undermine the core values of the US business system in international transactions and to re-establish worldwide confidence in the legitimacy of US business practices.

2.1 Foreign Corrupt Practices Act fundamentals

Under the Foreign Corrupt Practices Act, it is a federal crime for an "issuer",[5] "domestic concern"[6] and others[7] corruptly to offer, promise or provide anything of value to a foreign government official for the purpose of improperly obtaining or retaining business. The classic scenario is the bribery of a foreign official on foreign soil by a non-US third party agent to win a valuable contract or licence on behalf of a multinational company – this is an international crime which has not originated in the United States, but the Foreign Corrupt Practices Act's extraterritorial provision governs and prohibits precisely this sort of conduct, so long as it is committed by persons, issuers, companies or others[8] that have a legally defined connection to the United States. Violations of the Foreign Corrupt Practices Act are prosecuted by the Department of Justice and the Securities and Exchange Commission (SEC).

The decision tree[9] shown in Figure 1 outlines the logic, decision processes and liability attachment in a standard Foreign Corrupt Practices Act anti-bribery case.

---

4   See US Department of Justice and US Department of Commerce, *Lay-Person's Guide to Foreign Corrupt Practices Act*, www.usdoj.gov/criminal/fraud/docs/dojdocb.html (visited June 16 2012).
5   15 USC § 78dd-1 (making the Foreign Corrupt Practices Act applicable to 'issuers', that is, any company that has securities registered in the United States or is otherwise required to file periodic reports with the SEC).
6   15 USC § 78dd-2 (making the Foreign Corrupt Practices Act applicable to "domestic concerns", that is, (i) any individual who is a citizen, national or resident of the United States, or (ii) any corporation, partnership, association, joint-stock company, business trust, unincorporated organisation or sole proprietorship with its principal place of business in the United States or organised under the laws of a state of the United States).
7   15 USC § 78dd-3 (making the Foreign Corrupt Practices Act applicable to "persons" other than "issuers" or "domestic concerns" who undertake an act "while in the territory of the United States").
8   See *ibid*.

Figure 1. Walking through the Foreign Corrupt Practices Act and Travel Act's anti-bribery provisions

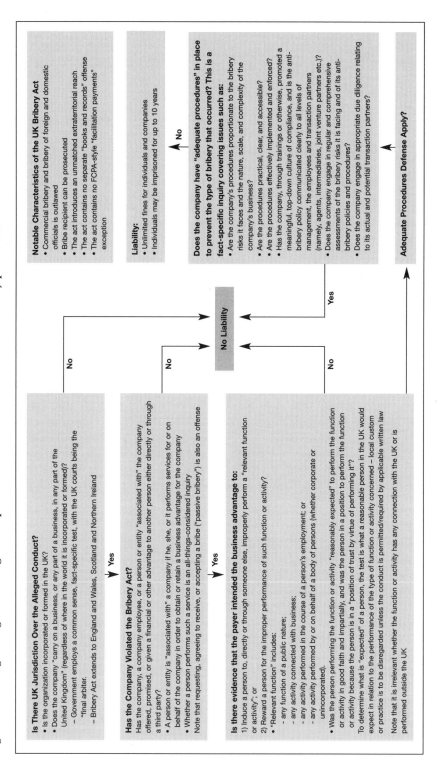

Is There UK Jurisdiction Over the Alleged Conduct?
- Is the organization incorporated or formed in the UK?
- Does the company "carry on a business, or any part of the United Kingdom" (regardless of where in the world it is incorporated or formed)?
  - Government employs a common sense, fact-specific test, with the UK courts being the "final arbiter."
  - Bribery Act extends to England and Wales, Scotland and Northern Ireland

Has the Company Violated the Bribery Act?
Has the company, a company employee, or a person or entity "associated with" the company offered, promised, or given a financial or other advantage to another person either directly or through a third party?
- A person or entity is "associated with" a company if he, she, or it performs services for or on behalf of the company in order to obtain or retain a business advantage for the company
- Whether a person performs such a service is an all-things-considered inquiry
Note that requesting, agreeing to receive, or accepting a bribe ("passive bribery") is also an offense

Is there evidence that the payer intended the business advantage to:
1) Induce a person to, directly or through someone else, improperly perform a "relevant function or activity"; or
2) Reward a person for the improper performance of such function or activity?
- "Relevant function" includes:
  - any function of a public nature;
  - any activity connected with business;
  - any activity performed in the course of a person's employment; or
  - any activity performed by or on behalf of a body of persons (whether corporate or unincorporated).
- Was the person performing the function or activity "reasonably expected" to perform the function or activity in good faith and impartially, and was the person in a position to perform the function or activity because the person is in a "position of trust by virtue of performing it"?
To determine what is "expected" of a person, the test is what a reasonable person in the UK would expect in relation to the performance of the type of function or activity concerned – local custom or practice is to be disregarded unless the conduct is permitted/required by applicable written law
Note that it is irrelevant whether the function or activity has any connection with the UK or is performed outside the UK

Notable Characteristics of the UK Bribery Act
- Commercial bribery and bribery of foreign and domestic officials is outlawed
- Bribe recipient can be prosecuted
- The act introduces an unmatched extraterritorial reach
- The act contains no separate "books and records" offense
- The act contains no FCPA-style "facilitation payments" exception

Liability:
- Unlimited fines for individuals and companies
- Individuals may be imprisoned for up to 10 years

Does the company have "adequate procedures" in place to prevent the type of bribery that occurred? This is a fact-specific inquiry covering issues such as:
- Are the company's procedures proportionate to the bribery risks it faces and the nature, scale, and complexity of the company's business?
- Are the procedures practical, clear, and accessible?
- Are the procedures effectively implemented and enforced?
- Has the company, through trainings or otherwise, promoted a meaningful, top-down culture of compliance, and is the anti-bribery policy communicated clearly to all levels of management, the employees and transaction partners (namely, agents, intermediaries, joint venture partners etc.)?
- Does the company engage in regular and comprehensive assessments of the bribery risks it is facing and of its anti-bribery policies and procedures?
- Does the company engage in appropriate due diligence relating to its actual and potential transaction partners?

Adequate Procedures Defense Apply?

No Liability

Yes

No

Yes

No

No

Yes

No

In addition to the anti-bribery provisions, the Foreign Corrupt Practices Act contains two accounting-related mandates:

- the books-and-records provision; and
- the internal controls provision.

The books-and-records provision requires issuers to "make and keep books, records, and accounts, which, in reasonable detail, accurately and fairly reflect the transactions and dispositions of the assets of the issuer".[10] The internal controls provision requires issuers to "devise and maintain a system of internal accounting controls sufficient to provide reasonable assurances", among other requirements, that:

- "transactions are executed in accordance with management's general or specific authorization";
- "access to assets is permitted only in accordance with management's general or specific authorization"; and
- "transactions are recorded as necessary to permit a preparation of financial statements in conformity with generally accepted accounting principles … and to maintain accountability for assets".[11]

2.2 Foreign Corrupt Practices Act enforcement: past, present and future

Over the years, the Foreign Corrupt Practices Act has become more effective. For example, in November 2011, the US Assistant Attorney General, Lanny Breuer, addressing the 26th National Conference on the Foreign Corrupt Practices Act, noted that while in 2010 US authorities achieved a record number of enforcement successes, in 2011 there were more Foreign Corrupt Practices Act trials than ever and one violator received the longest prison sentence – 15 years – ever imposed under the act[12]

As Breuer observed, 2011 was another strong year for the Foreign Corrupt Practices Act enforcers.[13] Within just a few years, the Foreign Corrupt Practices Act had developed from a weakly enforced anti-corruption instrument to a major enforcement tool that is whispered about in corporate boardrooms across the globe.[14] As Breuer put it:

---

9   Mr Funk's decision tree has been selected as an effective reference tool for those interested in the anti-corruption subject matter. See Perkins Coie Press Release, *Funk Publishes First-Of-Its-Kind Foreign Corrupt Practices Act/Travel Act Decision Tree*, at www.perkinscoie.com/a-hrefhttpwwwperkinscoiec omfilesuploadiwcd_11_12fcpatravelactflowchartpdffunk-publishes-first-of-its-kind-fcpatravel-act-decision-tree-12-14-2011/ (visited August 24 2012); *The Editors Back-To-School Resources*, The Foreign Corrupt Practices Act Blog (August 15 2012), at www.fcpablog.com/blog/2012/8/15/the-editors-back-to-school-resources.html (visited August 24 2012).

10   15 USC § 78m(b)(2)(A).

11   15 USC § 78m(b)(2).

12   See Lanny A Breuer, *Assistant Attorney General Lanny A. Breuer Speaks at the 26th National Conference on the Foreign Corrupt Practices Act* (DOJ 2011), at www.justice.gov/criminal/pr/speeches/2011/crm-speech-111108.html (visited August 24 2012).

13   See T Markus Funk and M Bridget Minder, *The Foreign Corrupt Practices Act in 2011 and Beyond: Is Targeted Foreign Corrupt Practices Act Reform Really the 'Wrong Thing at the Wrong Time'?*, 6 Bloomberg Finance LP 1 (2011). But see Mike Koehler, *Writer's Cramp At The DOJ?*, Foreign Corrupt Practices Act Professor Blog (February 3 2012), at www.fcpaprofessor.com/writers-cramp-at-the-doj (visited August 24 2012) (summarising the Department of Justice's string of Foreign Corrupt Practices Act trial losses).

14   See generally T Markus Funk, *Another Landmark Year: 2010 Foreign Corrupt Practices Act Year-In-Review and Trends for 2011* (Bloomberg Law Reports 2011), at www.perkinscoie.com/files/upload/11_01_03_FunkArticle.pdf (visited August 24 2012).

In the Criminal Division, we have dramatically increased our enforcement of the Foreign Corrupt Practices Act in recent years. That statute, which was once seen as slumbering, is now very much alive and well ... We recently promoted a new head of the Section's [Foreign Corrupt Practices Act] Unit and two assistant chiefs, and we have also increased the number of line prosecutors in the Unit, attracting high caliber attorneys with extensive experience – including Assistant US Attorneys with significant trial and prosecutorial experience and attorneys from private practice with defense-side knowledge and experience. These changes have significantly increased our [Foreign Corrupt Practices Act] enforcement capabilities.[15]

SEC Director of Enforcement Robert Khuzami echoed AAG Breuer's warnings: "Word is getting out that bribery is bad business, and we will continue to work closely with the business community and our colleagues in law enforcement in the fight against global corruption."[16] Today, the Foreign Corrupt Practices Act is undoubtedly both feared and respected; it affects how companies conduct business and it has emerged as one of the hottest corporate compliance issues facing multinational businesses – period.

(a) *Corporate Foreign Corrupt Practices Act enforcement actions*

The number of corporate enforcement actions between 2004 and 2011 shows the increasing effectiveness of the Foreign Corrupt Practices Act (see Figure 2).[17]

Figure 2: Summary of Department of Justice and SEC enforcement actions brought between 2004 and 2011[18]

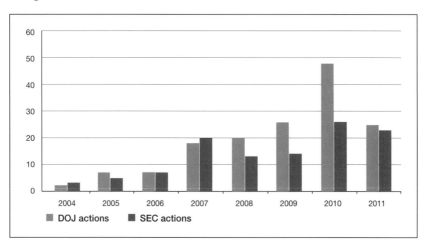

■ DOJ actions   ■ SEC actions

---

15 Lanny A Breuer, *Remarks at the Annual Meeting of the Washington Metropolitan Area Corporate Counsel Association* (2011), at www.justice.gov/criminal/pr/speeches/2011/crm-speech-110126.html (visited August 24 2012).

16 US Securities and Exchange Commission, *OECD Commends US Regulators for Efforts to Fight Transnational Bribery* (SEC 2010), at www.sec.gov/news/press/2010/2010-200.htm (visited August 24 2012).

17 See generally Funk, *Another Landmark Year* (cited in note 14).

18 See *2011 Year-End FCPA Update* (Gibson Dunn 2012), at www.gibsondunn.com/publications/Pages/2011YearEndFCPAUpdate.aspx (visited August 24 2012).

The United States is a global leader in anti-corruption enforcement.[19] For instance, in 2010, three out of every four worldwide anti-corruption enforcement actions were brought by the United States, and it continues to file more than 70% of the world's foreign anti-bribery charges, with the United Kingdom in second place at 4.3%.[20] According to TRACE International, Inc between 2000 and 2010, the US government brought more than 3.5 times more bribery-based enforcement actions than the combined charges filed by all other countries in the rest of the world.[21] As TRACE International put it:

> Foreign bribery enforcement by countries other than the United States actually fell in 2010, while the United States surged ahead with a more than a doubling of its formal enforcement figures between 2009 and 2010 ... The United States has accumulated over 14 times as many anti-bribery enforcement actions as the country with the next highest total, the United Kingdom. Many countries worldwide have not pursued a single enforcement action in the 34-year period.

(b)   *Top 10 list of Foreign Corrupt Practices Act corporate enforcement actions*
The US government's current list of top 10 resolved Foreign Corrupt Practices Act enforcement actions shows that not only have US authorities been bringing more anti-bribery related enforcement actions, but also they have been bringing bigger enforcement actions, with each of the 10 largest enforcement actions occurring between 2009 and 2011 and nine of them being brought against foreign companies (see Table 1).[22]

Table 1: Top 10 Foreign Corrupt Practices Act corporate enforcement actions

Position	Company	Enforcement action
1	Siemens (Germany)	Judgment entered January 6 2009: $448.5 million criminal fine; SEC disgorged $350 million in profits.
2	KBR/Halliburton (United States)	Judgment entered February 12 2009: $402 million criminal fine; SEC disgorged $177 million in profits.
3	BAE (United Kingdom)	Pleaded guilty March 1 2010: $400 million criminal fine.
4	Snamprogetti Netherlands BV/ENI SpA (Holland/Italy)	Deferred prosecution agreement filed July 7 2010: $240 million criminal fine; SEC disgorged $125 million in profits.

continued on next page

Position	Company	Enforcement action
5	Technip SA (France)	Deferred prosecution agreement filed in June 2010: $240 million criminal fine; SEC disgorged $98 million in profits.
6	JGC Corporation (Japan)	Deferred prosecution filed April 6 2011: $218.8 million criminal fine.
7	Daimler AG (Germany)	Deferred prosecution agreement placed in the record April 1 2010: $29.1 million criminal fine (in total, Daimler AG and its subsidiaries liable for $93.6 million in criminal fines); SEC disgorged $91.4 million in profits.
8	Alcatel-Lucent (France)	Deferred prosecution agreement and guilty plea placed in the record December 27 2010: $92 million criminal fine; SEC disgorged $45.3 in profits.
9	Magyar Telekom/Deutsche Telekom (Hungary/Germany)	Deferred prosecution agreement filed December 29 2011: $63.9 million criminal fine; SEC disgorged $31.2 million in profits.
10	Panalpina (Switzerland)	Deferred prosecution agreement filed November 4 2010: $70.5 criminal fine; SEC disgorged $11.3 million in profits.

19   See generally Funk, *Another Landmark Year* (cited in note 14).
20   See Funk and Minder, *The Foreign Corrupt Practices Act in 2011 and Beyond* (cited in note 13).
21   See TRACE International, Inc, *Global Enforcement Report 2011* (TRACE 2011), at https://secure.traceinternational.org/data/public/documents/Global_Enforcement_Report_2011-67720-1.pdf (visited August 24 2012).
22   For the most recent top ten Foreign Corrupt Practices Act actions, see *Who Will Crack the Top Ten*, The Foreign Corrupt Practices Act Blog (August 3 2012), at www.fcpablog.com/blog/2012/8/3/who-will-crack-the-top-ten.html (visited August 24 2012); see also *With Magyar In New Top Ten, It's 90% Non-US*, The Foreign Corrupt Practices Act Blog (December 29 2011), at www.fcpablog.com/blog/2011/12/29/with-magyar-in-new-top-ten-its-90-non-us.html (visited August 24 2012). As the Foreign Corrupt Practices Act Blog points out, four of the top six largest Foreign Corrupt Practices Act resolutions of all time involve the TSKJ consortium partners. See *Marubeni Pays $54.6 Million To Settle TSKJ Nigeria Case*, The Foreign Corrupt Practices Act Blog (January 17 2012), at www.fcpablog.com/blog/2012/1/17/marubeni-pays-546-million-to-settle-tskj-nigeria-case.html (visited August 24 2012); see also *Pfizer Joins Our Top Ten Disgorgement List*, The Foreign Corrupt Practices Act Blog (August 8 202), at www.fcpablog.com/blog/2012/8/8/pfizer-joins-our-top-ten-disgorgement-list.html (visited August 24 2012).

(c)   *Foreign Corrupt Practices Act actions against individuals*

Under US law, the enforcement of the Foreign Corrupt Practices Act is not limited to domestic, foreign and multinational corporations – individuals who violate the act will be prosecuted. In 2011, a federal judge handed down the longest prison sentence ever (15 years) under the Foreign Corrupt Practices Act,[23] while another judge imposed a $149 million forfeiture judgment against an individual – the largest of its kind in the act's history.[24] The increased enforcement activity against individuals continues. During 2004 and 2005, the Department of Justice and SEC brought Foreign Corrupt Practices Act charges against 10 individuals;[25] the number for 2009 and 2010 was 60, representing a 600% increase in enforcement activity over five years. There have been some setbacks (eg, on March 27 2012, 22 defendants once charged by the Department of Justice in its famous undercover sting operation, known as 'Shot Show', were dismissed with prejudice[26]), but the overall trend shows an increase in individual Foreign Corrupt Practices Act prosecutions (see Figure 3).

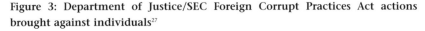

Figure 3: Department of Justice/SEC Foreign Corrupt Practices Act actions brought against individuals[27]

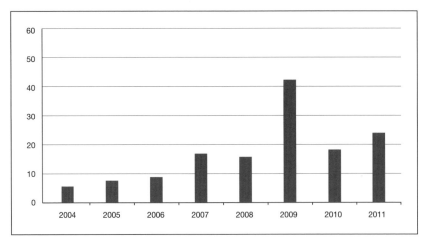

---

23   See US Department of Justice, *Executive Sentenced to 15 Years in Prison for Scheme to Bribe Officials at State-Owned Telecommunications Company in Haiti (Longest Prison Term Ever Imposed in a Foreign Corrupt Practices Act Case)* (DOJ 2011), at www.justice.gov/opa/pr/2011/October/11-crm-1407.html (visited August 24 2012).

24   See US Department of Justice, *UK Solicitor Pleads Guilty for Role in Bribing Nigerian Government Officials as Part of KBR Joint Venture Scheme* (DOJ 2011), at www.justice.gov/opa/pr/2011/March/11-crm-313.html (visited August 24 2012).

25   *Ibid.*

26   *All charges dismissed in the Department of Justice's Foreign Corrupt Practices Act Africa Sting case*, TRACE Blog (March 28 2012), at http://traceblog.org/2012/03/28/all-charges-dismissed-in-the-department-of-justices-fcpa-africa-sting-case/ (visited August 24 2012visited [2]).

27   *FCPA Digest: Recent Trends and Patterns in the Enforcement of the Foreign Corrupt Practices Act* (Shearman & Sterling 2012), at www.shearman.com/files/Publication/bb1a7bff-ad52-4cf9-88b9-9d99e001dd5f/ Presentation/PublicationAttachment/6ec0766a-25aa-41ec-8731-041a672267a6/FCPA-Digest-Trends-and-Patterns-Jan2012.pdf (visited August 24 2012).

(d) Increasing enforcement trends and developments

In addition to the 2010 and 2011 enforcement figures, emerging enforcement trends indicate a continued hard-hitting expansion of the fight against global anti-corruption, such as:

- specialised law enforcement agents have promoted more effective industry-specific enforcement;
- with reportedly more than 150 open/pending investigations, investigative approaches and techniques are becoming increasingly proactive and aggressive – Foreign Corrupt Practices Act violations are now investigated in the same way as sophisticated 'street' crimes, using techniques such as undercover agents and informants, court-authorised electronic surveillance, and searches and seizures;
- the prosecution of individual defendants continues to be a top enforcement priority;
- the Dodd-Frank Act's whistleblower bounty provisions are encouraging more informants;[28]
- increased compliance and promises of leniency encourage self-disclosure;
- multi-jurisdictional cooperation and parallel investigations and prosecutions are becoming more common;
- the 'demand side' of the enforcement net is being widened to catch bribe recipients and the middlemen who assist them; and
- Congress is considering mandatory debarment of any government contractors that are found to violate the Foreign Corrupt Practices Act.[29]

Perhaps most important on this list is the developing trend that is the subject of this chapter – transnational carbon-copy prosecutions, that is, serial prosecutions and/or investigations in more than one jurisdiction for the same (or similar) underlying conduct. Although reasonable minds can agree to disagree on whether this spreading enforcement phenomenon should be characterised as a 'race to the top' or a 'race to the bottom',[30] the United States is likely to be the global anti-corruption leader in the foreseeable future.

3. Anatomy of a carbon copy prosecution

Carbon Copy Prosecution: When foreign or domestic Jurisdiction A files an enforcement action based on a charging document or guilty plea from Jurisdiction B.

---

28 On May 25 2011, the SEC issued its final rules to establish a new whistleblower program, as required by Section 922 of the Dodd-Frank Act, paying awards to whistleblowers who voluntarily provide the SEC with original information about a violation of the securities laws, including the Foreign Corrupt Practices Act. The amount of the award is required to equal between 10% and 30% of the monetary sanction. See generally T Markus Funk, *Meeting (and Exceeding) Our Obligations: Will OECD's Anti-Bribery Convention Cause the Dodd-Frank Act's 'Whistleblower Bounty' Incentives to Go Global?*, 5 BNA White Collar Crime Report (Bureau of National Affairs 2010).

29 See Overseas Contractor Reform Act, H 3588, 112th Cong, 1st Sess (December 7 2011).

30 Compare David Kennedy and Dan Danielsen, *Busting Bribery: Sustaining the Global Momentum of the Foreign Corrupt Practices Act* (Open Society Foundations 2011) (defending the soundness of the statutory Foreign Corrupt Practices Act scheme, as currently drafted), with Funk and Minder, *The Foreign Corrupt Practices Act in 2011 and Beyond* (cited in note 13) (calling for Foreign Corrupt Practices Act reforms and setting out the foundations of such reforms).

3.1 Definition and explanation

In general, the type of bribery that the Foreign Corrupt Practices Act criminalises will also be prohibited under the domestic laws of the foreign nation where the bribe was offered, paid or received. As such, a person or company found to violate the Foreign Corrupt Practices Act (particularly, eg, by admitting to such violations in the public record via a guilty plea, a deferred prosecution agreement or a non-prosecution agreement) risks successive prosecutions by the United States and the other foreign nation for similar, if not identical, conduct. Thus, carbon-copy prosecutions refer to multiple sovereigns bringing successive, duplicate prosecutions (or, at least, investigations) for the same (or similar) underlying transnational criminal conduct, which by its nature violates the laws of several nations. As this definition sets out, the two fundamental features of these prosecutions are (1) the timing in which foreign sovereigns bring their follow-on actions and (2) the subject matter of those actions.

The movement in carbon-copy prosecutions teaches two critical lessons:

- *resolutions with authorities must be carefully tailored:* a business entity that enters into a negotiated resolution with a sovereign on transnational bribery-related charges, whether through a guilty plea, deferred prosecution agreement or non-prosecution agreement, must understand that other nations may initiate prosecutions based on the same common facts and admissions that form the basis of the original resolution; and
- *even non-parties to agreements have a strong interest in how agreements are worded:* individual corporate executives who are implicated or involved in a negotiated resolution (even marginally, and even if not identified in the resolution) must be aware of the increased likelihood that other nations will bring enforcement proceedings based on the resolved conduct, and should ensure that the resolution either does not cite their involvement or portrays their conduct positively, or at least neutrally.

3.2 Understanding carbon-copy prosecutions' analytical force and effectiveness

Recent transnational enforcement actions show a trend of foreign nations bringing largely similar – if not nearly identical – proceedings with increased frequency after a company has already resolved its Foreign Corrupt Practices Act liability with US authorities. The reason for this is that when a company enters into a negotiated criminal resolution with the Department of Justice, it must allocute – that is, it must admit, acknowledge and accept responsibility for the underlying conduct which gives rise to the criminal liability. In the case of guilty pleas, a federal court may not accept a guilty plea unless it "determine[s] that there is a factual basis for the plea".[31] A district court's acceptance of a guilty plea is a "factual finding" that the charged defendant is, indeed, guilty of the allegations set out in the charge.[32]

By comparison, and until January 2012, the SEC had a long-standing policy to resolve cases without requiring the charged party to admit to the allegations; a party could neither admit nor deny the agency's allegations in the civil injunctive complaint or administrative order.[33] On January 6 2012, the SEC announced a shift in its

---

31   Fed R Crim P 11(b)(3).

"settlement language for cases involving criminal convictions where a defendant has admitted violations of the criminal law".[34] The "new policy does not require admissions or adjudications of fact beyond those already made in criminal cases, but eliminates language that may be construed as inconsistent with admissions or findings that have already been made in the criminal cases", whether the criminal resolution it through a conviction, deferred prosecution agreement or non-prosecution agreement.[35]

Thus, negotiating a criminal plea agreement's factual statement (especially now in those cases with companion SEC enforcement exposure) may be the most negotiated (and contested) portion of any such resolution. Similarly, when a company admits to the underlying facts in a Department of Justice-based non-prosecution agreement or deferred prosecution agreement,[36] usually the terms of the agreement will bar a company from making any public statements contradicting the factual basis.[37] Typically, these agreements will empower the Department of Justice to

---

32   See, for example, *United States v Hildenbrand*, 527 F3d 466, 475 (5th Cir 2008) ("[The Fifth Circuit] regards the district court's acceptance of a guilty plea as a factual finding to be reviewed for clear error."). See also *Gray v Commissioner of Internal Revenue*, 708 F2d 243, 246 (6th Cir 1983) (holding that a "guilty plea is as much a conviction as a conviction following jury trial" and explaining further in the tax context that "numerous federal courts have held that a conviction for federal income tax evasion, either upon a plea of guilty, or upon a jury verdict of guilt, conclusively establishes fraud in a subsequent civil tax fraud proceeding through application of the doctrine of collateral estoppel") (collecting cases).

33   See Consent Decrees in Judicial or Administrative Proceedings, Securities Act Release No 33-337 (November 28 1972) (formally permitting respondent to avoid admitting or denying the allegations). See also *SEC v Citigroup Global Markets, Inc*, 2011 WL 5903733 *4 (SDNY 2011) (describing as "long-standing" the SEC's policy "of allowing defendants to enter into Consent Judgments without admitting or denying the underlying allegations"); *SEC v Vitesse Semiconductor Corp*, 771 F Supp 2d 304, 308-10 (SDNY 2010) (examining the history of the SEC's policy). In recent years, this policy has led to increasing criticism and scrutiny by the federal courts. See *SEC v Citigroup Global Markets, Inc*, 2011 WL 5903733 *2 (SDNY 2011) ("[T]he Court concludes that it cannot approve [the consent judgment], because the Court has not been provided with any proven or admitted facts upon which to exercise even a modest degree of independent judgment."), 673 F3d 158, 169 (2d Cir 2012) (granting a stay of the district court's proceedings on the ground that the SEC and Citigroup had made a "strong showing of likelihood of success in setting aside the district court's rejection of their settlement"). See also Letter to Pl's Counsel, *SEC v Koss Corp*, No 11-cv-00991, at 2 (ED Wis December 20 2011) (relying on the district court's decision in *SEC v Citigroup Global Markets, Inc*, to reject an SEC settlement with Koss Corporation and requesting "a written factual predicate" for the settlement); *SEC v Bank of America Corp*, 653 F Supp 2d 507, 508 (SDNY 2009) (denying an SEC-proposed $33 million settlement with Bank of America because, in part, the bank neither admitted nor denied the allegations in the consent judgment and took the position in its court submission that "the proxy statement in issue was totally in accordance with the law").

34   *SEC Changes 'Neither Admit Nor Deny' Settlement Policy (When There is a Parallel Criminal Case)*, TheCorporateCounsel.net (January 9 2012), at www.thecorporatecounsel.net/Blog/2012/01/cf-disclosure-guidance-topics-topic.html (visited May 6 2012).

35   *Ibid*. As the SEC noted, the new policy change "does not affect [the SEC's] traditional 'neither admit nor deny' approach in settlements that do not involve criminal convictions or admissions of criminal law violations". *Ibid*.

36   The SEC has recently expanded its settlement vehicles to include deferred prosecution and non-prosecution agreements. See SEC Enforcement Manual, Sections 6.2.3 to 6.2.4, pp 129-33, (March 9 2012), at www.sec.gov/divisions/enforce/enforcementmanual.pdf (visited May 6 2012). See also US Securities and Exchange Commission, *Tenaris to Pay $5.4 Million in SEC's First-Ever Deferred Prosecution Agreement* (SEC 2011), at www.sec.gov/news/press/2011/2011-112.htm (visited May 6 2012).

37   See *2009 Year-End Update on Corporate Deferred Prosecution and Non-Prosecution Agreements* (Gibson Dunn 2010), at www.gibsondunn.com/publications/pages/2009YearEndUpdateCorpDeferredProsecution Agreements.aspx (visited August 24 2012) (observing that "the terms and conditions of DPAs and NPAs have become more homogenous over the past few years" and that "the vast majority of DPAs and NPAs contained provisions ... prohibiting the company for making any statement that contradicts the facts as laid out in the agreement"). See also *SEC Changes "Neither Admit Nor Deny" Settlement Policy (When There is a Parallel Criminal Case)* (TheCorporateCounsel.net 2012) (cited in note 34) ("Under the new approach, for those settlements we will ... retain the current prohibition on denying the allegations of the Complaint/[order instituting proceedings] or making statements suggesting the Commission's allegations are without factual basis.")

determine in its sole discretion whether a company has breached its agreement and taken a position inconsistent with the factual basis.[38]

The combined effect is that when a company enters into a negotiated criminal resolution with the Department of Justice (in particular, in those cases with parallel SEC enforcement actions that are no longer subject to the SEC's 'neither admit nor deny' policy), for all practical purposes, the company is effectively powerless to defend against, much less deny, the underlying facts that form the basis of the resolution.[39] These features (which are based on US criminal resolutions) help explain why carbon-copy prosecutions are especially effective when US authorities bring the original enforcement action. They also virtually ensure that a company which settles with the Department of Justice (or both the Department of Justice and SEC in companion proceedings) will have no choice but to settle with any successive foreign sovereign that elects to enforce its own anti-bribery (or other similar) laws against the violating transnational conduct.

These new cross-border considerations mark a shift in negotiated settlement strategy. Historically, the principal motivation for companies to negotiate short and simple factual statements was to reduce the possibility of any follow-on civil or securities actions, or class actions.[40] However, in the current transnational anti-corruption environment, the concern over follow-on private causes of action is only one of several important factors: businesses and their employees and agents faced with allegations of transnational misconduct must consider the additional possibility that foreign authorities will seek to punish the same conduct that formed the basis of the original resolution, regardless of the resolution's original source.[41]

3.3   Exposure to carbon-copy prosecutions

As discussed, serious consideration must be given to the increasing possibility of successive prosecutions by multiple sovereigns for the same core conduct that gives rise to original liability.[42] This is especially true given the increasing number of countries that are enacting, or at least contemplating, new and enhanced anti-

---

38   See Gibson, Dunn and Crutcher, *2009 Year-End Update* (cited in note 37) (observing that pre-trial diversion agreements routinely "give DOJ sole discretion to determine whether the agreement has been breached by the company").

39   See F Joseph Warin and Andrew S Boutros, *Response, Deferred Prosecution Agreements: A View from the Trenches and a Proposal for Reform*, 93 Va L Rev In Brief 121, 128-29 (2007) (describing FirstEnergy's predicament of potentially violating its DPA because of a "highly nuanced, legalistic argument" it made in submitting a claim for insurance coverage).

40   See generally Warin and Boutros, *Response, Deferred Prosecution Agreements*, at 129 (cited in note 39). ("As should be obvious, the whole point of a DPA is that companies may not be able to weather the storm of an indictment without it; upon indictment, companies are likely to face fundamental instability, downgrading of creditworthiness, loss of market share, diminution of stock value, market and reputational damage, debarment from certain industries, regulatory proceedings, and class actions.")

41   For a discussion of the interplay and potential implications of the United Nations Convention Against Corruption (UNCAC) on successive multi-sovereign enforcement actions, see *The United Nations Convention Against Corruption: A New Focus?* (KYC360 2011), at www.kyc360.com/hot_topic/show/238?set=1 (visited August 24 2012) ("An enforcement action based upon Article 53 could allow a country such as Nigeria to come into a US court and seek compensation from a US company which has committed bribery in Nigeria or require the DOJ/SEC to recognize a foreign country which has ratified the UNCAC as the 'legitimate owner' of profits disgorged or fines and penalties paid to the US government as a result of a Foreign Corrupt Practices Act violation.").

42   See, for example, *Significant China Law Development*, Foreign Corrupt Practices Act Professor Blog (March 3 2011), at www.fcpaprofessor.com/significant-china-law-development (visited August 24 2012).

corruption laws. For example, China, Russia and the United Kingdom have passed new, stricter anti-corruption legislation, while Brazil and India are in the process of doing so.[43] Indonesia, Jordan, Morocco, Taiwan and the Ukraine are among the countries that have recently proposed or adopted new anti-corruption measures.[44] More importantly for purposes of this chapter, and as demonstrated by recent foreign enforcement actions, an increased number of nations are not only 'talking the talk', but they are actively enforcing their own local anti-corruption laws.[45]

With the increase of extraterritorial provisions in the criminal laws of nations prohibiting international bribery, including, for example, countries such as the United Kingdom and China, a single illegal payment can set off liability not only under the Foreign Corrupt Practices Act and the local laws where the bribe was made or offered, but in all jurisdictions that prohibit international bribery by citizens and others who seek access to their capital markets or otherwise undertake business, or part of a business, within their territories.[46] This risk is not hypothetical.

The Socio-Economic Rights and Accountability Project (SERAP) recently called on the Nigerian government to "urgently take steps to seek adequate damages and compensation against multinational corporations who have been found guilty in the US of committing foreign bribery in Nigeria".[47] Indeed, SERAP took the extra step of providing detailed, case-specific information to the Nigerian authorities to support its request – it identified by name those companies that publicly admitted

---

43 See PRC Anti-Unfair Competition Law, Article 8 (People's Republic of China); PRC Criminal Law, Article 164 (2011) (Amendment 8 criminalises the payment of bribes to non-PRC government officials and international public organisations). See also *Federal Law On Amendments to the Criminal Code and the Code of Administrative Offences of the Russian Federation to Improve State Anti-Corruption Management*, at http://eng.kremlin.ru/news/2164 (visited August 24 2012) (raising fines to up to 100 times the amount of the bribe given or received with a cap of Rb 500 million (approximately $18.3 million)); and UK Bribery Act 2010, c 23.

44 See *2011 Mid-Year Foreign Corrupt Practices Act Update* (Gibson Dunn 2011), at www.gibsondunn. com/publications/pages/2011Mid-YearForeign Corrupt Practices ActUpdate.aspx (visited August 24 2012).

45 See F Joseph Warin, *2008 Year-End Foreign Corrupt Practices Act Update*, 1737 PLI/Corp 503, 506-07 (2009) (quoting the Department of Justice's then acting assistant attorney general as stating the "United States is not the only player at the table" when it comes to "fighting global corruption").
But the statistics also show that foreign enforcements continue to lag behind US enforcement activities. See Funk and Minder, *The Foreign Corrupt Practices Act in 2011 and Beyond* (cited in note 13) ("Although the world may, indeed, be ... passing more local anti-corruption legislation ... its collective zeal to actually enforce anti-corruption laws continues to significantly lag.").

46 One such example is the UK Bribery Act 2010, which includes a jurisdictional provision that captures within its reach all entities and partnerships that "carry on a business, or part of a business, in any part of the United Kingdom" c 23, Section 7, Schedule 5, even if the prohibited payment itself, has no territorial nexus to the United Kingdom. Another example is the People's Republic of China Criminal Law, Article 164 (2011), where Amendment 8 criminalises the payment of bribes to non-PRC government officials and international public organisations.

47 See Marcus Cohen, David Elesinmogun and Obumneme Egwuatu, *Will Nigeria Take Another Bite?*, The Foreign Corrupt Practices Act Blog (August 4 2011), at www.fcpablog.com/blog/2011/8/4/will-nigeria-take-another-bite.html (visited August 24 2012) (quoting SERAP's August 2 2011 petition to Nigeria's Economic and Financial Crimes Commission). See also Chinyere Amalu, *Bribery: SERAP Asks EFFC to Seek Damages Against Halliburton, Others* (Leadership 2011), at www.leadership.ng/nga/articles/3165/2011/08/03/bribery_serap_asks_efcc_seek_damages_against_halliburton_others.html (visited August 24 2012) (summarising SERAP's petition).
But as some have observed, "many Nigerians, both those serving in public office as well as those on the street, may not want to pursue multinational corporations already dinged for Foreign Corrupt Practices Act violations" because to do so "may scare off foreign companies willing to invest in Nigeria" and lead to "loss of jobs ultimately, if unintentionally, punishing the Nigerian people". See Cohen, Elesinmogun, and Egwuatu, *Will Nigeria Take Another Bite?* (cited *ibid*).

to paying Foreign Corrupt Practices Act-prohibited bribes in Nigeria, yet remained unpunished or in SERAP's view, modestly punished by the Nigerian authorities. In SERAP's words:

> While settlement by Halliburton Co and Kellogg Brown & Root LLC (KBR) in Nigeria has amounted only to US $35 million, the corporation has paid over $727 million in settlement and damages in the US. Similarly, Technip SA has paid $338 million in settlement in the US, but has not paid any damages in Nigeria. Snamprogetti Netherlands BV and ENI SpA paid only $32.5 million in Nigeria, but has paid $365 million in the US.

> JGC Corp paid $28.5 million in Nigeria but paid $218.8 million in the US; MW Kellogg paid no damages in Nigeria, but has paid £7 million in the UK. Also, Julius Berger Nigeria Plc has paid only $29.5 million in Nigeria, while Willbros International has paid over $41 million in the US but has made no payment in Nigeria. Panalpina paid $82 million in US, but no payment has been made in Nigeria. The Royal Dutch Shell Plc has paid only $10 million in Nigeria whereas it has paid $48.2 million in the US.

> ... Pride International paid $56.1 million in the US but made no payment in Nigeria; Noble Corp has paid $8.1 million in the US but no payment made in Nigeria; Tidewater Inc has paid $15.7 million in the US but no payment in Nigeria; Transocean Inc made payment of $20.6 million in the US but no payment made in Nigeria; Shell Nigerian Exploration and Production Co. Ltd paid $18 million in the US but no payment in Nigeria; and Siemens AG paid only $46 million in Nigeria, whereas it paid $800 million in the US ...[48]

Similarly, the Department of Justice has received a request to initiate a carbon copy prosecution: the international anti-corruption watchdog organisation, Transparency International, has petitioned the department to "examine" Oklahoma-based Walters Power International's $20 million fraud conviction in Pakistan and to "take action against" it and others under the Foreign Corrupt Practices Act based on a finding of guilt from the Pakistan Supreme Court.[49] As these calls for carbon copy enforcement actions demonstrate, the carbon copy trend is not theoretical. Indeed, taking the carbon copy concept to its logical limit, a multinational US company with operations in the United Kingdom and China that resolves a Foreign Corrupt Practices Act case with US authorities for foreign bribes paid in Russia, Costa Rica and Nigeria, faces serial prosecution in the United States, the United Kingdom, China, Russia, Costa Rica, Nigeria and every other country that has applicable

---

48   See Amalu, *Bribery: SERAP Asks EFFC to Seek Damages Against Halliburton, Others* (cited in note 47). For another helpful list identifying companies that have entered into foreign resolutions for bribe-related conduct also resolved through US-based Foreign Corrupt Practices Act enforcement actions, see *Who Paid Foreign Corrupt Practices Act-Related Fines Overseas?*, The Foreign Corrupt Practices Act Blog (August 8 2011), at www.fcpablog.com/blog/2011/8/8/who-paid-fcpa-related-fines-overseas.html (visited May 6 2012).

49   See Usman Manzoor, *US Urged to Take Action Against RPP Firm for $20m Fraud*, The News International (April 10 2012), at www.thenews.com.pk/Todays-News-2-102194-US-urged-to-take-action-against-RPP-firm-for-$20m-fraud (visited May 6 2012) (stating that "Transparency International Pakistan requests Chief, Fraud Section US Department of Justice Criminal Division to kindly examine this case and take action against the US firms under the anti-bribery provisions of the Foreign Corrupt Practices Act 1977 ...").

extraterritorial jurisdictional provisions, absent, of course, some relevant limiting principle or other canon, such as a country's double jeopardy doctrine.

4.   Carbon copy prosecutions in action

4.1   KBR/Halliburton: a carbon copy prosecution case study

In February 2009, Halliburton's former subsidiary, Kellogg Brown & Root LLC (KBR), pleaded guilty to five counts of Foreign Corrupt Practices Act violations and agreed to pay a $402 million criminal fine.[50] As part of the resolution, KBR admitted to being part of the TSKJ consortium[51] that paid at least $182 million in 'consulting fees' that were partly used to bribe Nigerian government officials between 1995 and 2004 to obtain engineering, procurement and construction contracts to build liquefied natural gas facilities on Bonny Island, Nigeria.[52] The contracts were valued at approximately $6 billion, which in turn led to KBR profits of approximately $235.5 million.

In a companion action to its guilty plea, KBR's current and former parent companies KBR, Inc and Halliburton, respectively, settled a civil action with the SEC based on their internal control failures and falsified corporate books and records. Both parent companies agreed jointly to disgorge $177 million in profits derived from the Foreign Corrupt Practices Act violations.[53] In total, Halliburton, KBR, Inc and KBR collectively agreed to pay $579 million to resolve their various Foreign Corrupt Practices Act matters. But it turned out that these substantial US-based resolutions were not the end of KBR's (or its executives') criminal troubles.

In early December 2010, less than two years after its resolution with US authorities, headline news broke that Nigeria's anti-corruption agency, the Economic and Financial Crimes Commission, had lodged a 16-count criminal complaint against KBR, Halliburton, and their current and former executives, among others – including former United States Vice President Richard Cheney[54] – arising out of the same Bonny Island, TSKJ consortium bribe payments.[55] The commission filed charges against KBR's current CEO even though KBR publicly announced that its new CEO joined KBR after the conclusion of the Bonny Island misconduct. As KBR's press

---

50   See generally US Department of Justice, *Kellogg Brown & Root LLC Pleads Guilty to Foreign Bribery Charges and Agrees to Pay $402 Million Criminal Fine* (DOJ 2009), at www.justice.gov/opa/pr/2009/February/09-crm-112.html (visited August 24 2012). See also *Halliburton Announces Settlement of Department of Justice and Securities and Exchange Commission Foreign Corrupt Practices Act Investigations* (Halliburton 2009), at www.halliburton.com/public/news/pubsdata/press_release/2009/corpnws_021109.html (visited August 24 2012).

51   The joint venture, known as the TSKJ consortium, consisted of four companies from four different countries: (1) Technip, SA (France); (2) Snamprogetti (Netherlands); (3) KBR, acquired by Halliburton (United States); and (4) JGC Corporation (Japan). See US Department of Justice, *JGC Corporation Resolves Foreign Corrupt Practices Act Investigation and Agrees to Pay a $218.8 Million Criminal Penalty* (DOJ 2011), at www.justice.gov/opa/pr/2011/April/11-crm-431.html (visited August 24 2012).

52   See Plea Agreement, *United States v Kellogg, Brown & Root LLC*, Case No 4:09-cr-00071, Exhibit 3 Statement of Facts, ¶¶ 11-12 (SD Tex 2010), at www.justice.gov/criminal/fraud/fcpa/cases/kelloggb/02-11-09kbr-plea-agree.pdf (visited August 24 2012).

53   See US Securities and Exchange Commission, *SEC Charges KBR, Inc. with Foreign Bribery; Charges Halliburton Co. and KBR, Inc with Related Accounting Violations - Companies to Pay Disgorgement of $177 Million; KBR Subsidiary to Pay Criminal Fines of $402 Million; Total Payments to be $579 Million* (SEC 2009), at www.sec.gov/litigation/litreleases/2009/lr20897.htm (visited August 24 2012).

release announced: "No one on KBR's current executive team was involved in the Foreign Corrupt Practices Act violations."[56]

Similarly, the Nigerian government filed charges against Vice President Cheney even though, according to Cheney's lawyer, "the ... Department of Justice and the Securities and Exchange Commission investigated that joint venture extensively and found no suggestion of any impropriety by Dick Cheney in his role of CEO of Halliburton".[57] According to some, "[i]t is believed the Nigerian authorities want to probe the case further from their perspective", notwithstanding "the US investigation".[58] Yet others opined that the Nigerian probe was politically motivated: "There could be political calculations at play in the new charges. Nigerian President Goodluck Jonathan faces a coming primary election in the nation's ruling party against former Vice President Atiku Abubakar", and "the charges come as the election looms".[59] Whatever the motivation, news outlets reported that the Nigerian authorities would seek the arrest and extradition of former Vice President Cheney[60] and several other executives, invoking Nigeria's 75-year-old extradition treaty with the United States.[61]

When news broke, KBR's initial response was to defend its position. It stated that it would "continue to vigorously defend itself and its executives if necessary, in this matter", and it characterised the actions of the Nigerian government as "wildly and wrongly asserting blame".[62] But within two weeks, KBR announced it would fight no more as news emerged that Halliburton would pay $35 million to the Nigerian authorities to resolve charges of "distribution of gratification to public officials".[63] Halliburton's press statement announced that:

---

54   According to news stories, those charged included US Vice President Dick Cheney (Halliburton's onetime CEO), Halliburton CEO David Lesar, Halliburton, Halliburton Nigeria Limited, KBR, former KBR CEO Albert 'Jack' Stanley, KBR CEO William P Utt, TSKJ Nigeria Limited, and TSKJ Consortium. See *Nigeria Files Bribery Charges against Dick Cheney* (domain-b.com 2010), at www.domainb.com/economy/worldeconomy/20101209_bribery_charges.html (visited August 24 2012). See also Jon Gambrell, *Nigeria Charges Dick Cheney in Halliburton Bribery Case* (MSNBC.com 2010), at www.msnbc.msn.com/id/40555171/ns/world_news-africa (visited August 24 2012).

55   See American Bar Association Global Anti-Corruption Task Force, *Nigeria Charges Former US Vice President Dick Cheney and Others with Public Corruption* (ABA 2010), at www2.americanbar.org/sections/criminaljustice/CR121212/Pages/news.aspx (visited August 24 2012). See also Elisha Bala-Gbogbo, *Nigeria to Charge Dick Cheney in Pipeline Bribery Case* (Bloomberg 2010), at www.bloomberg.com/news/2010-12-01/nigeria-to-file-charges-against-former-u-s-vice-president-over-bribery.html (visited August 24 2012).

56   See *KBR Statement Regarding Latest Nigeria Foreign Corrupt Practices Act Charges* (KBR 2010), at www.kbr.com/Newsroom/Press-Releases/2010/12/07/KBR-Statement-Regarding-Latest-Nigerian-Foreign Corrupt Practices Act-Charges/ (visited August 24 2012).

57   See Gambrell, *Nigeria Charges Dick Cheney in Halliburton Bribery Case* (MSNBC.com 2010) (cited in note 54) (further stating that "any suggestion of misconduct on his [Cheney's] part, made now, years later, is entirely baseless").

58   See *ibid* (emphasis added).

59   *Ibid.* See also *Halliburton Settles Nigeria Bribery Claims for $35 Million* (CNN 2010), at http://articles.cnn.com/2010-12-21/world/nigeria.halliburton_1_tskj-nigerian-officials-financial-crimes-commission?_s=PM:WORLD (visited August 24 2012) ("Many observers in Nigeria regarded the charges as a publicity stunt by the Financial Crimes Commission ahead of national elections in April and as a symbolic effort to display resolve against government corruption.").

60   Bala-Gbogbo, *Nigeria to Charge Dick Cheney in Pipeline Bribery Case* (Bloomberg 2010) (cited in note 5). See also Gambrell, *Nigeria Charges Dick Cheney in Halliburton Bribery Case* (MSNBC.com 2010) (cited in note 54) (quoting a Nigerian spokesperson as stating that: "we are following the laws of the land. We want to follow the laws and see where it will go ... we're very convinced by the time the trial commences, we'd make application for appropriate court orders to be issued.").

61   The United States and Nigeria entered into an extradition treaty on December 22 1931, which went into effect on June 24 1935. See 47 Stat 2122 (1931), codified at 18 USC §§ 3181-3196.

pursuant to [the settlement] agreement, all lawsuits and charges against KBR and Halliburton corporate entities and associated persons have been withdrawn, [the Federal Government of Nigeria (FGN)] agreed not to bring any further criminal charges or civil claims against those entities or persons, and Halliburton agreed to pay US$32.5 million to the FGN and to pay an additional US$2.5 million for FGN's attorneys' fees and other expenses.[64]

Halliburton further "agreed to provide reasonable assistance in the FGN's effort to recover amounts frozen in a Swiss bank account of a former ... agent [associated with underlying conduct] and affirmed a continuing commitment with regard to corporate governance".[65]

4.2 More examples of carbon-copy prosecutions

Although the threatened arrest and extradition of Vice President Cheney makes the KBR/Halliburton carbon copy prosecution fairly unique, it is not an isolated incident. In just the last two years, at least five other companies have faced carbon-copy prosecutions,[66] with three of those actions brought by the Nigerian authorities and two initiated by US enforcers.[67] Specifically:

- in December 2008, Siemens AG paid $800 million to the US authorities to resolve the largest ever Foreign Corrupt Practices Act matter in US history while simultaneously paying an additional $569 million to the Public Prosecutor's Office in Munich, Germany, for a total combined payment of nearly $1.4 billion,[68] followed by an additional $100 million to the World Bank Group (among a variety of other concessions),[69] $46.5 million to the

---

62   See *KBR Statement* (cited in note 56).

63   See *Halliburton Confirms Agreement to Settle with Federal Government of Nigeria* (Halliburton 2010), at www.halliburton.com/public/news/pubsdata/press_release/2010/corpnws_12212010.html?SRC=Nigeria (visited August 24 2012). See also *Halliburton Settles Nigeria Bribery Claims for $35 Million* (CNN 2010) (cited in note 59).

64   See *ibid*.

65   *Ibid*.

66   Carbon copy prosecutions are also to be distinguished from global resolutions across countries, such as the global settlements (or proposed global settlements) involving (1) Siemens (resolution with United States and Germany), (2) BAE Systems plc (resolution with the United States and United Kingdom), and (3) Innospec Inc (resolution with the United States and United Kingdom).

67   In addition to actual enforcement actions brought by Nigerian authorities, there are also open carbon copy Nigerian-led investigations. See Claudius O Sokenu, *2010 Foreign Corrupt Practices Act Enforcement Year-End Review*, 1883 PLI/Corp 395, 410 (Practicing Law Institute 2011) ("Panalpina itself is under investigation in Nigeria for bribery, after paying $82 million in civil and criminal penalties to settle bribery allegations in the US") (citing Joe Palazzolo, *2011: The Year of the Foreign Corrupt Practices Act Piggyback?*, Wall St J (December 29 2010)).

68   See US Department of Justice, *Siemens AG and Three Subsidiaries Plead Guilty to Foreign Corrupt Practices Act Violations and Agree to Pay $450 Million in Combined Criminal Fines* (DOJ 2008), at www.justice.gov/opa/pr/2008/December/08-crm-1105.html (visited August 24 2012). Specifically, Siemens agreed to pay a criminal fine of $450 million to the Department of Justice and $350 million in disgorgement of profits to the SEC. In the German prosecution, Siemens agreed to pay €395 million (approximately $569 million), in addition to the €201 million (approximately $287 million) it paid in October 2007 to settle another related enforcement action brought by the Munich public prosecutor.

69   See The World Bank, *Siemens to Pay $100m to Fight Corruption as Part of World Bank Group Settlement* (World Bank 2009), at http://web.worldbank.org/WBSITE/EXTERNAL/NEWS/0,,contentMDK:22234573 ~pagePK:34370~piPK:34424~theSitePK:4607,00.html (visited August 24 2012).

70   See *Recent Domestic Bribery Enforcement Developments in Nigeria* (Traceblog.com 2010), at http://traceblog.org/2010/12/23/recent-domestic-bribery-enforcement-developments-in-nigeria/ (visited August 24 2012).

> Nigerian authorities,[70] another €270 million (approximately $336 million) to Greece,[71] while still remaining "subject to corruption-related investigations in several jurisdictions around the world";[72]

- in a reversal of the typical order of transnational enforcement proceedings, in January 2010, the French-based telecommunications equipment and services provider, Alcatel-Lucent SA, paid $10 million to the Costa Rican government,[73] followed by an additional combined $137.4 million in criminal fines and disgorgement to the US authorities in December 2010 covering bribe payments that included those resolved previously by Alcatel-Lucent in Costa Rica.[74] Two days after its US resolution, the Honduran authorities announced that they would reopen their investigation against Alcatel-Lucent and, more specifically, into the now-admitted conduct that gave rise to Alcatel-Lucent's US-based liability for bribe payments in Honduras;[75]

- in July 2010, the Italian energy company ENI SpA and its Dutch subsidiary Snamprogetti paid $365 million in criminal fines and disgorgement to the US authorities,[76] followed by an additional $32.5 million to the Nigerian authorities in December 2010;[77]

- in November 2010, Royal Dutch Shell Plc paid $48.15 million in criminal fines, disgorgement of profits and interest to the US authorities,[78] followed by an additional $10 million to the Nigerian authorities in December 2010;[79] and

- in another reversal of order in the sequence of carbon-copy prosecutions, in January 2011, JGC Corporation paid $28.5 million to the Nigerian authorities,[80] followed by an additional $218.8 million in criminal fines to the Department of Justice.[81]

---

71   *Siemens in Greek Settlement*, The Foreign Corrupt Practices Act Blog (March 12 2012), at www.fcpablog.com/blog/2012/3/12/siemens-in-greek-settlement.html (August 24 2012).

72   Statement of Legal Proceedings, Siemens AG (May 4 2011), at www.siemens.com/press/pool/de/events/2011/corporate/2011-q2/2011-q2-legal-proceedings-e.pdf (visited August 24 2012).

73   See Leslie Josephs, *1-Alcatel-Lucent to Pay $10 mill in Costa Rica Case* (Reuters 2010), at www.reuters.com/article/2010/01/21/alcatellucent-costarica-idUSN2121041320100121 (visited August 24 2012).

74   See *Alcatel-Lucent S.A. and Three Subsidiaries Agree to Pay $92 Million to Resolve Foreign Corrupt Practices Act Investigation* (US Attorney's Office, SD Fla 2010), at www.justice.gov/usao/fls/PressReleases/101227-01.html (visited August 24 2012).

75   See *Honduras Reopens Alcatel Bribe Case on SEC Ruling*, Bloomberg Businessweek (Bloomberg 2010), at www.businessweek.com/ap/financialnews/D9KDN1F00.htm (visited August 24 2012).

76   See *Snamprogetti Netherlands BV Enters Agreement with Federal Government of Nigeria* (saipem 2010), at www.saipem.com/site/Home/Press/Corporate/articolo6034.html (visited August 24 2012).

77   See US Department of Justice, *Snamprogetti Netherlands B.V. Resolves Foreign Corrupt Practices Act Investigation and Agrees to Pay $240 Million Criminal Penalty* (DOJ 2010), at www.justice.gov/opa/pr/2010/July/10-crm-780.html (visited August 24 2012).

78   See US Department of Justice, *Oil Services Companies and a Freight Forwarding Company Agree to Resolve Foreign Bribery Investigations and to Pay More Than $156 Million in Criminal Penalties* (DOJ 2010), at www.justice.gov/opa/pr/2010/November/10-crm-1251.html (visited August 24 2012).

79   See Elisha Bala-Gbogbo, *Shell Pays $10 Million Fine to Nigerian Government* (Bloomberg 2010), at www.bloomberg.com/news/2010-12-22/shell-pays-10-million-fine-to-nigerian-government-update1-.html (visited August 24 2012).

80   See Consolidated Financial Statements – Summary (JGC 2010), at www.jgc.co.jp/en/06ir/pdf/financial_statements_summary/FY10/fy10_yem.pdf (visited August 24 2012).

81   See US Department of Justice, *JGC Corporation Resolves Foreign Corrupt Practices Act Investigation and Agrees to Pay a $218.8 Million Criminal Penalty* (DOJ 2011), at www.justice.gov/opa/pr/2011/April/11-crm-431.html (visited August 24 2012).

4.3 A carbon copy offshoot

The precedent-setting actions discussed above suggest that current enforcement practice is moving towards increased successive international enforcement activity. But it also suggests that offshoots of the carbon copy concept will be an area of considered focus, deliberation and activity in the future. For example, following SERAP's petitioning of the Nigerian government to initiate Nigerian-based carbon-copy prosecutions (discussed in section 3.3), it later petitioned the SEC on a supplemental request for serial, duplicate prosecutions. In a letter filed in March 2012, SERAP requested the SEC to "establish an efficient case-by-case process for the payment of some or all of [the Foreign Corrupt Practices Act] civil penalty and disgorgement proceeds to or for the benefit of the victimised foreign government agency or the citizens of the affected foreign country like Nigeria".[82]

In SERAP's view, although "local law can, in theory, provide for a remedy":

... litigation in the local courts is often fraught with political risk, and can be time-consuming and expensive in the best of circumstances; even if such cases are eventually successful, enforcement of judgments, locally and internationally, present formidable challenges as well.[83]

SERAP proposed a variant of the carbon copy prosecution concept:

After, and only after, publication of a Foreign Corrupt Practices Act settlement agreement, the victim foreign government entity [should be allowed to] file a request that the Enforcement Division pay some or all of the agreed payment proceeds to or for the benefit of the victim government entity or to a US-based NGO ...[84]

In SERAP's own words, its "proposal would only come into play after a Foreign Corrupt Practices Act matter has been resolved, typically as a result of a settlement with the company".[85] In May 2012, the SEC responded to SERAP's proposal by pointing out that the "framework of [US] securities laws requires a proximate connection to the harm caused by a particular violation".[86] Whether the SEC's response ends the matter remains to be seen.

5. The cost-benefit considerations of carbon-copy prosecutions

The emerging trend of transnational carbon-copy prosecutions has complicated the manner in which companies conduct internal investigations and interact with US and foreign authorities. For example, at the disclosure stage, companies now must

---

82   Letter from Alexander W Sierck to Robert Khuzami (March 15 2012), at Foreign Corrupt Practices Act Blog (March 16 2012), www.fcpablog.com/blog/2012/3/16/african-ngo-asks-for-distribution-of-fcpa-recoveries.html (visited August 24 2012).
83   *Ibid.*
84   *Ibid* (emphasis added).
85   *Ibid* (emphasis added).
86   *Giving Back to the Victims*, The Foreign Corrupt Practices Act Blog (May 2 2012), at www.fcpablog.com/blog/2012/5/2/giving-back-to-the-victims.html (visited August 24 2012).
87   See US Department of Justice, *Principles of Federal Prosecutions of Business Organizations* 4 (DOJ 2008), at www.justice.gov/opa/documents/corp-charging-guidelines.pdf (visited August 24 2012) (instructing prosecutors to consider, among other things, "the corporation's timely and voluntary disclosure of wrongdoing and its willingness to cooperate in the investigation of its agents", and "to replace responsible management, to discipline or terminate wrongdoers, to pay restitution, and to cooperate with the relevant government agencies").
For a detailed discussion of the effect of the Dodd-Frank Whistleblower Protection Act on that calculus, see Funk, *Another Landmark Year* (cited in note 14).

assess not only whether voluntarily to disclose potential Foreign Corrupt Practices Act violations to US authorities,[87] but also decide whether (and to what extent) to make concurrent (or near concurrent) front-end self-disclosures to foreign sovereigns. Like so many of these decisions, real costs and benefits are at issue.

5.1 Early multi-sovereign disclosures to us and foreign authorities: potential benefits

(a) *Economies of scale achieved on the front end of early, multi-sovereign disclosures*
Concurrent multi-national disclosures to US and foreign authorities ensure that all potentially interested government authorities are informed at the same time – and, just as importantly, are informed by the entity responsible for, or at least that benefitted from, the bribe payments. In this regard, multi-national disclosures have the effect of treating all implicated sovereigns equally. Early multi-sovereign disclosures are an acknowledgement that the foreign jurisdictions that are the sites of the crimes, and whose government officials may have been corrupted, have a stake at least equal to, if not greater than, the United States in vindicating their own domestic laws.

The US authorities are likely to view such voluntary multi-sovereign disclosures favourably. They demonstrate a company's commitment to accepting responsibility for the wrongs it committed in a foreign jurisdiction in violation of local law, and it reflects a basic respect for the laws of the local jurisdiction. Early and direct multi-sovereign disclosures also avoid the unfortunate scenario of foreign governments learning of corruption and scandals from news outlets or outside governments.

There can be little doubt that in transnational criminal investigations, the "United States informally cooperates and shares information with other jurisdictions".[88] Indeed, a variety of US-based negotiated resolutions have explicitly required corporations to cooperate with foreign authorities as a condition to resolving charges with the US authorities. For example, as part of their deferred prosecution agreements, Alcatel-Lucent, BizJet and Shell (just to name three) each agreed to "cooperate fully with such other domestic or foreign law enforcement authorities and agencies", at the request of Department of Justice.[89] Thus, regardless of whether a company elects voluntarily to disclose potential bribery violations to foreign authorities, those authorities might well be notified of the possibility of a transnational crime sooner than once expected.

---

88   Gary R Spratling and D Jarrett Arp, *International Cartel Investigations: Evaluating Options and Managing Risk in Multi-Jurisdictional Criminal Antitrust Investigations*, 1788 Practising L Inst Corp 229, 258-59 (2010) (explaining that through international cooperation among sovereigns, "a firm can make simultaneous amnesty applications to authorities in the United States and other countries"); see also Lanny A Breuer, *Assistant Attorney General Lanny A. Breuer Speaks at the 26th National Conference on the Foreign Corrupt Practices Act* (DOJ 2011), at www.justice.gov/criminal/pr/speeches/2011/crm-speech-111108.html (visited August 24 2012) ("In partnership with the US Department of State, we have for years placed legal advisers and law enforcement professionals in countries around the world, including throughout North and Sub-Saharan Africa and the Middle East, to work with foreign prosecutors, judges and police to develop and sustain effective criminal justice and law enforcement institutions.").

89   Deferred Prosecution Agreement, ¶ 5, *United States v Alcatel-Lucent*, SA, Case No 10-20907 CR-Moore (SD Fla 2010), at http://lib.law.virginia.edu/Garrett/prosecution_agreements/pdf/alcatel_lucent.pdf (visited August 24 2012); Deferred Prosecution Agreement ¶ 6, *United States v Shell Nigeria Exploration & Prod Co*, No 10-00767 (SD Tex 2010), at www.justice.gov/opa/documents/shell-dpa.pdf (visited August 24 2012); Deferred Prosecution Agreement ¶ 5, *United States v BizJet Int'l Sales and Support, Inc*, No 12-61 (ND Okla 2012), at http://lib.law.virginia.edu/Garrett/prosecution_agreements/pdf/bizjet.pdf (visited May 6 2012).

By disclosing wrongdoing to foreign authorities, these governments are in a better position to get ahead of a potential media crisis.[90] Such information empowers local authorities to gain control of a situation; to remove (or at least contain) corrupt government officials early in the process; and proactively to respond to allegations of public corruption. Thus, a company's early voluntary multi-sovereign disclosures are likely to place the company in good (or at least, better) stead with local jurisdictions than might otherwise be the case.

Multi-jurisdiction disclosures also have the potential to lead to economies of scale by reducing duplication of investigatory work for both private counsel and law enforcement authorities. Early disclosures help to ensure that interested foreign and domestic governments are consulted on an investigation from the start, including, for example, on important matters such as how the investigation should be conducted; what, if any, additional follow-up items should be pursued; and what local legal or factual concerns ought be addressed, or at least not overlooked, during the otherwise US-targeted investigation. Such cross-border sharing of information also makes it more likely that foreign authorities will be more willing to cooperate and coordinate with US authorities – and company counsel – in their collective efforts to interview witnesses, obtain visas, remove travel restrictions and otherwise collect and export relevant material from the local jurisdictions to the United States, while at the same time remaining compliant with local laws.[91]

(b) Economies of scale achieved on the back end of early, multi-sovereign disclosures

Early multi-sovereign disclosures are also more likely to lead to global settlements, with all the advantages of coordinated resolutions and across-the-board finality.[92] For instance, coordinated global disclosures and ensuing investigations increase the prospect that a corporation will be able successfully to petition the US authorities for one-for-one credit for any compensatory payment or penal fine made to local authorities as part of a worldwide resolution.[93] The converse is also true: by cooperating and complying with local authorities from the beginning of an

---

90   See F Joseph Warin and Andrew S Boutros, *Foreign Corrupt Practices Act Investigations: Working Through A Media Crisis* (Andrews Litigation Reporter 2007), at www.gibsondunn.com/publications/ Documents/Warin-Foreign Corrupt Practices Act_InvestigationsMediaCrisis.pdf (visited March 26 2012).

91   One such example is China's *Law on the Protection of State Secrets*. See Congressional-Executive Commission on China, *Law of the People's Republic of China on Guarding State Secrets*, at http:// www.cecc.gov/pages/newLaws/protectSecretsENG.php (visited May 6 2012) (providing a translation into English); see also Congressional-Executive Commission on China, *National People's Congress Standing Committee Issues Revises State Secrets Law* (May 20 2010), at www.cecc.gov/pages/virtualAcad/ index.phpd?showsingle=140456 (visited May 6 2012). The law covers "matters that relate to state security and national interests", see *ibid*, which could extend to information collected as part of an internal investigation. See also 3rd Quarter 2011 Anti-Corruption Quarterly (Sidley Austin 2011), at www.sidley.com/files/upload/Anti-Corruption.pdf (August 24 2012) ("Foreign companies, therefore, should take a very cautious approach to conducting internal investigations in China, even where the documents at issue would not commonly be considered to implicate a state secret.").

92   See Sokenu, 1883 PLI/Corp at 412 (cited in note 67) ("While such settlements offer closure, they can be incredibly tricky to negotiate and even trickier to get approved through courts that are not familiar with US-style settlement.").

93   See Warin, 1737 PLI/Corp at 513 (cited in note 45) (summarising comments made by the Department of Justice's then Foreign Corrupt Practices Act Chief Mark Mendelsohn and citing "the 2006 Statoil and 2007 Akzo Nobel prosecutions as examples in which DOJ has credited penalties paid in foreign jurisdiction against those to be paid in the United States").

investigation, a company might achieve more success in convincing a foreign government – or even the United States – not to bring a follow-on enforcement action, that is, a carbon copy prosecution, with its corresponding fines, penalties and unwanted publicity.[94] Even beyond matters of prosecutorial discretion, the substantive laws of other nations and other related treaty obligations might well create advantages that favour – or disadvantages that cut against – early front-end multi-sovereign disclosure. Chief among these considerations is the double jeopardy doctrine.

(c)   *International double jeopardy as a consideration*

Under US law, "the ... Constitution of the United States has not adopted the doctrine of international double jeopardy".[95] That is, a "prosecution by a foreign sovereign does not preclude the United States from bringing criminal charges",[96] nor does the double jeopardy clause "prevent extradition from the United States for the purpose of a foreign prosecution following prosecution in the United States for the same offense".[97] However, not all other nations subscribe to this interpretation of double jeopardy: in some countries, "there are ... limitations on multiple prosecutions by different sovereign jurisdictions established by treaty or [foreign] domestic laws".[98]

For example, while director of the UK's Serious Fraud Office,[99] Richard Alderman discussed critical differences between the US and UK approach to the double jeopardy doctrine, as well as the doctrine's effects on the UK's ability to bring carbon-copy prosecutions. Using the BAE enforcement action[100] as the case study example to

---

94   See *ibid* (quoting former Foreign Corrupt Practices Act Chief Mendelsohn as stating, "there are other cases that are not public where we have elected to do nothing in deference to ongoing foreign investigations - or to sit back and wait to see what the outcome of that foreign investigation will be."). See also *ibid* ("If that foreign investigation results in some enforcement action, we may elect to do nothing. On the other hand, if ... that foreign prosecution never gets off the ground, we may step in and proceed with our investigation.").

95   *United States v Martin*, 574 F2d 1359, 1360 (5th Cir 1978). See also *Chua Han Mow v United States*, 730 F2d 1308 (9th Cir 1984) (describing a contrary argument as "frivolous").

96   *United States v Richardson*, 580 F2d 946, 947 (9th Cir 1978). Similarly, as the Supreme Court stated in the context of successive state-state prosecutions, "when a defendant in a single act violates the peace and dignity of two sovereigns by breaking the laws of each, he has committed two distinct offences", and as such, "it cannot be truly averred that the offender has been twice punished for the same offence; but only that by one act he has committed two offences, for each of which he is justly punishable". See *Heath v Alabama*, 474 US 82, 93 (1985).

97   *Elcock v United States*, 80 F Supp 2d 70, 75 (EDNY 2000) ("The Double Jeopardy Clause of the Constitution does not prevent extradition from the United States for the purpose of a foreign prosecution following prosecution in the United States for the same offense."). See also *In re Ryan*, 360 F Supp 270, 274 (EDNY 1973), affd 478 F2d 1397 (2d Cir 1973) ("There is no constitutional right to be free from double jeopardy resulting from extradition to the demanding country.").

98   See generally Linda E Carter, *The Principle of Complementarity and the International Criminal Court: The Role of Ne Bis in Idem*, 8 Santa Clara J Intl L 165, 172-73 (2010). See, for example, *Treacy v Director of Public Prosecutions* [1971] 1 All ER 110 (HL 1970) (UK) (Lord Diplock); see also Lissa Griffin, *Two Sides of a 'Sargasso Sea': Successive Prosecution for the 'Same Offence' in the United States and the United Kingdom*, Pace Law Faculty Publications, Paper 471 (2003) ("Protection against successive prosecution under United Kingdom law is afforded in two different ways: first, there is a core 'same-elements' protection that is based on the pleas of autrefois acquit and autrefois convict; second, this narrow protection is supplemented by a broad judicial discretion to stay successive prosecutions under the doctrine of 'abuse of process'.").

99   Richard Alderman stepped down as the Serious Fraud Office's director on April 20 2012. See Lindsay Fortado, *U.K. Serious Fraud Chief Walks Away From Agency in Flux* (Bloomberg 2012), at www.bloomberg.com/news/2012-04-20/u-k-serious-fraud-office-chief-walks-away-from-agency-in-flux.html (visited May 6 2012).

discuss the UK double jeopardy doctrine, Alderman explained that when BAE "agreed to plead guilty to offences brought by the US Department of Justice", that "plea of guilty had consequences so far as the SFO's investigation was concerned".[101]

According to Alderman, because BAE "pleaded guilty in the US to offences relating to Central and Eastern Europe", under "the UK law of double jeopardy, it was no longer possible for the SFO investigation relating to Central and Eastern Europe to continue …".[102] Since the "law on double jeopardy differs as between the US and the UK",[103] according to Alderman, "the SFO needed to terminate the investigations relating to Central and Eastern Europe once [BAE's] plea of guilty was entered in the US".[104]

Alderman also explained that the basis of the UK double jeopardy analysis depends not on the charged offence brought by the original charging jurisdiction, but on the underlying facts used to support the offence, irrespective of the charging offence itself. In this regard, Alderman responded to the question on the SFO's prosecution of BAE after BAE entered into its negotiated resolution with US authorities as follows:

> *[Question]: As to the double jeopardy issue, the offense BAE pleaded guilty to in the US was not a corruption offense, but rather a charge of conspiracy to make false statements to the US government including as to its compliance with the provisions of the Foreign Corrupt Practices Act. You are correct that certain of the factual allegations supporting this non-corruption offense related to Central and Eastern Europe. Are you suggesting that simply because facts are alleged in a US prosecution to support a non-corruption charge, that the U.K. is thereby prohibited from bringing a corruption charge as to those facts?*
>
> *[Alderman's Answer]: Yes. [The UK] double jeopardy law looks at the facts in issue in the other jurisdiction and not the precise offence. Our law does not allow someone to be prosecuted here in relation to a set of facts if that person has been in jeopardy of a conviction in relation to those facts in another jurisdiction. As a result I could not continue to consider whether to prosecute BAE for an offence relating to Central and Eastern Europe once BAE had pleaded guilty in the US.*[105]

Thus, in deciding whether to make front-end or back-end multi-sovereign disclosures, if at all, one significant factor to be considered is the double jeopardy doctrine as interpreted by local jurisdictions – as well as by other interested nations with extraterritorial anti-corruption jurisdiction.

5.2   Potential costs of early multi-sovereign disclosures to US and foreign authorities

Early multi-sovereign disclosures – and the roll-on effects that they trigger – do have

---

100   The BAE enforcement action with US authorities ranks as the third all-time largest Foreign Corrupt Practices Act resolution. See note 22.

101   Mike Koehler, *A Conversation with Richard Alderman Regarding BAE*, Foreign Corrupt Practices Act Professor Blog (March 15 2011), at www.fcpaprofessor.com/a-conversation-with-richard-alderman-regarding-bae (visited August 24 2012), with the full questions and answers available at www.scribd.com/doc/50759481/A-Conversation-With-Richard-Alderman-Regarding-BAE (August 24 2012); see *ibid* at Q&A 1.

102   *Ibid*.

103   *Ibid*.

104   *Ibid*.

105   *Ibid* at Q&A 3.

distinct potential disadvantages. Such disclosures may increase the complexities of already-complicated investigations. They can lead to the division of resources across different nations, with teams of professionals interfacing with different – and conflicting – government officials, constituents, cultures and priorities. They can require companies to staff and coordinate global investigations that are progressing at different rates, with different focuses and scopes, responding to varying levels of enforcement sophistication.

Parallel multi-sovereign investigations can also involve conflicting, intersecting substantive laws, procedural rules, modes of evidence gathering and data privacy rights. They can expose both persons and companies to serial prosecutions in several jurisdictions, absent a treaty or local law to the contrary.[106] They may prompt foreign sovereigns to charge – and seek the extradition of – US executives or other non-US personnel before the US investigation is complete. They have the potential to cause local persons implicated in misconduct – or even material witnesses with relevant information – not to cooperate with the joint US-local investigations out of fear of local reprisal and prosecution. Eearly multi-sovereign disclosures to – and coordinated efforts among – foreign jurisdictions could lead foreign governments to exercise their discretion to bring their own follow-on enforcement actions. In doing so, the foreign government may well utilize its enforcement action to show that it is committed to fighting corruption. In addition, such a carbon copy action would benefit the foreign jurisdiction's treasury, in exchange for its assistance and effort in the transnational investigation. Furthermore, in global investigations involving multiple jurisdictions, one foreign jurisdiction might decide to become a 'first actor', insisting on settling its matter first, even when the global investigation as a whole is not complete and not fully understood.[107]

As one practitioner summed it up:

interest from law enforcement agencies from other countries significantly increases the complexities surrounding when, and to whom, to self-report, how and when to conduct internal investigations, what to do with the results of the internal investigation, and how to structure global settlements with multiple countries with conflicting legal jurisprudence.[108]

6.   Conclusion

Increasingly, the global law enforcement community is working together. Although transnational cooperation was once a cumbersome and time-consuming rarity, today it has become routine. Formal cooperation and collaboration mechanisms such as

---

106   See *United States v Jeong*, 624 F3d 706, 711-12 (5th Cir 2010) (upholding a defendant's sequential US-based conviction following his South Korean conviction for the same conduct and holding that Article 4.3 of the OECD's Anti-Bribery Convention "does not prohibit two signatory countries [such as the United States and South Korea] from prosecuting the same offense"; rather, the OECD only requires countries with concurrent jurisdiction to consult with one another upon request).

107   One such example could be Alcatel-Lucent's resolution with Honduran authorities, which occurred nearly a year before Alcatel-Lucent settled its Foreign Corrupt Practices Act case with US authorities. See *Honduras Reopens Alcatel Bribe Case on SEC Ruling* (Bloomberg 2010) (cited in note 75). See also *Honduran Court of Auditors Investigated Alcatel-Lucent* (Honduras News 2010), at www.hondurasnews.com/auditors-investigate-alcatele/ (visited March 24 2012).

108   Sokenu, 1883 PLI/Corp at 409 (cited in note 67).

mutual legal assistance treaties and letters rogatory are regularly supplemented by informal methods of sharing information and providing off-the-record assistance, particularly between countries with friendly diplomatic relations.

Therefore, it is not surprising that, in the global law enforcement arena, bribery and transnational public corruption have become a focus for what Boutros first termed carbon-copy prosecutions. Whether this is due to lengthy and ongoing transnational investigations and collaboration, or simply because a prosecutor in Country A read about, say, a company's plea agreement in Country B, serial prosecutions that allege the same or similar conduct appear to be the next step in the internationalisation of the criminal law. In short, law enforcement officials and private counsel working in this area must monitor the trend and be prepared to plan a few steps ahead.

The Bribery Act 2010

Paul Feldberg
Willkie Farr & Gallagher LLP
Ian Leist QC
Fulcrum Chambers LLP

1. Introduction

The UK Bribery Act 2010 received royal assent on April 8 2010. The act aimed to modernise and consolidate the UK's anti-corruption laws, to regulate the UK's international businesses and to demonstrate the UK's continued commitment to the international fight against corruption.

Lord Templeman described bribery clearly and concisely in the leading case of *Attorney General for Hong Kong v Reid* [1994] [1994] AC 324, 330:

A bribe is a gift accepted by a fiduciary as an inducement to him to betray his trust ... a person who provides the bribe and the fiduciary who accepts the bribe may each be guilty of a criminal offence ... Bribery is an evil practice which threatens the foundations of any civilised society. In particular bribery of policemen and prosecutors brings the administration of justice into disrepute.

In his foreword to the 2004 UN Convention against Corruption (UNCAC), the then UN Secretary General, Kofi Annan, described the serious effects of corruption:

Corruption is an insidious plague that has a wide range of corrosive effects on societies. It undermines democracy and the rule of law, leads to violations of human rights, distorts markets, erodes the quality of life and allows organised crime, terrorism and other threats to human security to flourish ... Corruption is a key element in economic under-performance and a major obstacle to poverty alleviation and development.

The United Kingdom is a signatory to a number of international anti-corruption instruments, including the UN Convention against Corruption (2004), the Organisation for Economic Cooperation and Development (OECD) Convention on Combating Bribery of Foreign Public Officials (1997), and the Council of Europe Criminal Law Convention on Corruption (1998) and additional Protocol (2005).

In 2009, the World Bank estimated that around a trillion dollars of bribes were paid each year, adding 10% to the cost of doing business globally and as much as 25% to the cost of procurement contracts in developing countries. This distortion of free markets and the diversion of resources damaged society and increased, directly and indirectly, poverty and human suffering.

In the United Kingdom in February 2007, the Association of Chief Police Officers estimated that the cost of corruption to the domestic economy was £13.9 billion a year.[1]

---

1   Association of Chief Police Officers, *The nature, extent and economic impact of fraud in the UK*, February 2007, available at http://www.acpo.police.uk/asp/policies/Data/Fraud%20in%20the%20UK.pdf

Between 2003 and 2007 the OECD had been critical of "deficiencies" in the UK's bribery laws and in 2008 stated that it was "disappointed and seriously concerned with the unsatisfactory implementation of the [OECD] Convention by the UK".

It called on the UK government to enact modern bribery legislation and establish effective corporate liability for bribery as a matter of "high priority" and warned that:

... failing to enact effective and comprehensive legislation undermines the credibility of the UK legal framework and potentially triggers the need for increased due diligence over UK companies by their commercial partners or Multilateral Development Banks.[2]

The government did not accept that the United Kingdom was non-compliant with any of its international obligations, but was concerned that the UK's commitment to the OECD Convention could be questioned if it did not implement law reform. Thus, the introduction of the Bribery Act 2010 confirmed the UK's policy objective as a member of the OECD, the Council of Europe, the European Union and the United Nations, by aiming to raise standards and to provide equal opportunities for businesses competing solely on the basis of merit.

The act reflects the UK's continued commitment to combat bribery and provides a modern, comprehensive scheme of bribery offences. It covers all forms of bribery but there is a clear focus on commercial bribery – two of its four offences are business-related. The government declared its intention that over time the act will contribute to international and national efforts towards ensuring a shift away from a culture of bribery that may persist in certain sectors or markets and help ensure high ethical standards in international business transactions.

The introduction of Bribery Act 2010, supported by guidance given in March 2011, deals with bribery both domestically and abroad and provides for a strict and far-reaching anti-corruption legislative scheme which is intended to foster a culture of zero tolerance towards corruption in business, driven from the top down by officers and managers to all levels of each organisation.

1.1 The guidance

The guidance to the Bribery Act 2010 is a pragmatic explanation of the Bribery Act 2010. It is a statutory document issued under Section 9 of the act. The act and the guidance need to be read together.

The guidance sets out policy objectives and is designed to reassure the UK business community, which saw the introduction of the act at a time of a global economic downturn as unduly burdensome. It describes the balance the government intends to strike between compliance and zero tolerance on the one hand, and business practicalities and the public interest on the other.

Therefore, on March 30 2011, Secretary for State for Justice Kenneth Clarke published the official Ministry of Justice guidance on the meaning of "adequate procedures" as they relate to Section 7 of the Bribery Act 2010, which came into force on July 1 2011. Section 7 creates an offence by which corporates can be prosecuted for failing to prevent bribery.

In his foreword to the guidance, he stated that the rules are directed at making

---

2   OECD working Group Report 2008

life difficult for those responsible for corruption and are not intended to burden "the vast majority of decent law abiding individuals". Seeking to reassure business further, he added: "We don't have to decide between tackling corruption and supporting growth. Addressing bribery is good for business because it creates the conditions for free markets to flourish." The act is meant to be workable in a common sense way by all sizes of business, even those with limited resources.

Commenting on the guidance at the time in The Telegraph (2011), Richard Alderman, then director of the Serious Fraud Office, signalled his organisation's approach to deploying the act. "I want to see companies police themselves and develop an anti-corruption culture," he said. "I want to get on and investigate those companies that are putting our ethical UK businesses at disadvantage by offering bribes."

Kenneth Clarke offered clarity on how the law should operate by referring immediately to the question of hospitality. "Rest assured no one wants to stop firms getting to know their clients by taking them to Wimbledon or the Grand Prix."

The guidance explains that to prosecute an allegation that hospitality was intended as a bribe would require proof that the hospitality "was intended to induce conduct that amounts to a breach of an expectation that a person will act in good faith, impartially or in accordance with a position of trust".

The guidance is stricter on the discrete offence of bribing a public foreign official under Section 6 of the Act. It says:

Bona fide hospitality and promotional or other business expenditure which seeks to improve the image of a commercial organisation, better to present products and services or establish cordial relations is recognised as an established and important part of doing business and it is not the intention of the Act to criminalise such behaviour. It is, however clear that hospitality and promotional or other similar business expenditure can be employed as bribes.

It continues: "The more lavish the hospitality or other similar business expenditure provided to a foreign public official, then generally, the greater the inference that it is intended to influence the official."

The guidance states that "very careful consideration" on public interest grounds must be given before a decision is taken to prosecute an allegation where hospitality, promotional expenditure or facilitation payments do trigger the provisions of the act.

Elsewhere, it is made plain that the objective of the act is not to bring the "full force of the criminal law to bear upon well run commercial organisations that experience an isolated incident of bribery" and "in order to achieve an appropriate balance, Section 7 provides a full defence".

The guidance recognises that this area of new law is extremely fact sensitive. "The onus will remain on the organisation to demonstrate that it is well run and has adequate procedures in place, or risk prosecution."

A departure from the suggested procedures set out in the guidance does not create a presumption that an organisation does not have adequate procedures.

However, the guidance is issued under Section 9 of the act and so all organisations must be familiar with the principles which underpin the legislation and take appropriate action. These six key principles are referred to at pages 20 to 31 of the guidance and are dealt with in more detail below.

1.2   Key considerations

The bribery of foreign public officials is a significant target of the Bribery Act 2010 and different levels of risk are more likely to face companies operating in high-risk foreign markets. The government accepts that changes in dealings with existing associated persons may take time and may depend on the level of control and practicability in achieving change, but steps to influence change must be taken.

Prosecutorial discretion and public interest criteria must be appreciated in order to understand how the act is to operate. It is clear that self-policing and corporate self-reporting with the prospect of civil settlements and deferred prosecution agreements are designed to encourage the corporate community to overhaul its own culture.

2.   The Bribery Act 2010

The Bribery Act 2010 abolishes the offences of bribery at common law and the statutory offences in the Public Bodies Corrupt Practices Act 1889 and the Prevention of Corruption Act 1906 (Section 17 and Schedule 2).

2.1   Active bribery

Section 1 creates a single offence that can be committed in two main ways. A person is guilty of bribery if he offers, promises, or gives a financial or other advantage to another, either directly or through a third party, and:

- in doing so. intends to reward a person for, or to induce a person to undertake, the improper performance of a relevant function or activity (Case 1); or
- knows or believes that the acceptance of such advantage would itself constitute the improper performance of a relevant function or activity (Case 2).

A person may be an individual or a body corporate. In Cases 1 and 2 the advantage may be offered, promised or given through a third party (Section 1(5)).

In each case the act criminalises offering, promising or giving to another an advantage, financial or otherwise. The first method of committing the offence requires that a person intends that the financial or other advantage will either induce the improper performance of a relevant function or activity, or reward a person for such improper performance (Case 1).

The second form of the offence requires proof that the briber knows or believes that the acceptance by the recipient of the financial or other advantage would amount to improper performance of a relevant function or activity (Case 2).

There is no definition of 'financial or other advantage'. The Explanatory Notes accompanying the Bribery Bill indicate that the words are to be determined as a "'matter of common sense" by the tribunal of fact.

Both cases require proof that the briber intends or knows that the financial advantage offered produces the "improper performance" of a "relevant function".

(a)   'Relevant function'

For the purposes of the general offences under Sections 1 and 2, a 'relevant function' to which the alleged bribery relates must fall into one of four categories:

- any function of a public nature (Section 3(2)(a));

- any activity connected with a business (Section 3(2)(b));
- any activity performed in the course of a person's employment (Section 3(2)(c)); or
- any activity performed by or on behalf of a body of persons (whether corporate or unincorporated) (Section 3(2)(d)).

(b)   Improper performance

'Improper performance' of a relevant function for the purposes of the general offences is defined by Section 4 of the act.

> *(1) A relevant function will be performed improperly if it—*
>> *(a) is performed in breach of a 'relevant expectation', and*
>> *(b) is to be treated as being performed improperly if there is a failure to perform the function or activity and that failure is itself a breach of a 'relevant expectation'*
> *(2) In subsection (1) "relevant expectation"—*
>> *(a) in relation to a function or activity which meets condition A or B, means the expectation mentioned in the condition concerned, and*
>> *(b) in relation to a function or activity which meets condition C, means any expectation as to the manner in which, or the reasons for which, the function or activity will be performed that arises from the position of trust mentioned in that condition.*
> *(3) Anything that a person does (or omits to do) arising from or in connection with that person's past performance of a relevant function or activity is to be treated for the purposes of this Act as being done (or omitted) by that person in the performance of that function or activity.*

It is important to note that in deciding what such a person would expect in relation to the performance of a function or activity where the performance is not subject to the law of any part of the United Kingdom, any local custom or practice is to be disregarded unless it is permitted or required by the written law applicable to the country or territory concerned. 'Written law' is defined in Section 5:

> *(3) In subsection (2) "written law" means law contained in—*
>> *(a) any written constitution, or provision made by or under legislation, applicable to the country or territory concerned, or*
>> *(b) any judicial decision which is so applicable and is evidenced in published written sources.*

Therefore, the standard to be applied is what a reasonable person in the United Kingdom would expect of a person performing the relevant function or activity. All local customs and traditions should be disregarded.

2.2   Passive bribery (offences relating to being bribed)

The second general offence is created by Section 2 of the act. It is intended to deal with those who solicit or accept bribes. There are four cases (Cases 3 to 6) of passive bribery. The recipient in each case must request, agree to receive or accept a financial or other advantage for himself or for another.

Section 2 provides as follows.

In Cases 3 to 5, a person is guilty of being bribed if he requests, agrees to receive or accepts a financial or other advantage:

- intending that, in consequence, a relevant function or activity should be performed improperly (whether by himself or another) (Case 3);
    - the person must intend that he or someone else will improperly perform a relevant function or activity as a consequence of the advantage he has received, requested or agreed to receive;
    - this version of the offence applies even if the person from whom the money was requested had no intention of paying;
    - it applies where he intends to perform his function improperly but fails to do so;
- where the request, agreement or acceptance itself constitutes the improper performance by the person of a relevant function or activity (Case 4);
    - all that is required to make out the offence is the request, agreement or acceptance of the advantage;
    - it is irrelevant that he knows or believes that the performance of the function or activity is improper, provided it is in the act;
    - There is no *mens rea* requirement;
    - he must be the person who performs or is due to perform the relevant function or activity;
- as a reward for the improper performance (whether by himself or another person) of a relevant function or activity (Case 5);
    - it does not matter that the person believed the performance of the function was improper;
    - the act necessary for the commission of the offence is that he requests or agrees to receive a reward for improper performance.

In Case 6, where a relevant function or activity is performed improperly by a person, or by another at his request or with his assent or acquiescence (whether or not that other knows or believes that the performance of the function or activity is improper), in anticipation or in consequence of a requesting, agreeing to receive or accepting a financial or other advantage, that person commits an offence.

This section deals with the situation where there is improper performance of a relevant function or activity in anticipation of a request, agreement to receive or acceptance of a financial or other advantage.

In Cases 3, 4 and 5 there is a requirement that the recipient or potential recipient of a bribe "requests, agrees to receive or accepts" an advantage, but no requirement to prove that he actually receives it. What must be shown is that the request, agreement or acceptance is linked with the "improper performance" of a "relevant function or activity" as defined in Sections 3 to 5.

In Cases 3 and 5 the improper performance may be by the recipient of the advantage or another, whereas in Case 4 it is the request, agreement to receive or actual acceptance of the advantage which constitutes improper performance.

3. Bribing a foreign public official (Section 6)

Questions are often asked as to why the Bribery Act 2010 has a specific section dealing with bribing a foreign public official when Section 1 of the act could be used to prosecute the same action.

The answer is that the Section 6 offence of bribing a foreign public official has been inserted to ensure the United Kingdom meets its obligations under the OECD Convention. Unlike the Section 1 offence, the Section 6 offence does not require a prosecutor to prove that the person offering the bribe intended the recipient improperly to perform a relevant function. All that is required is that the person, through his offer of financial advantage, is attempting to influence the foreign public official in his capacity as an official. Consequently, this will be a much easier offence for a prosecutor to prove.

Section 6 reads as follows:

(1) A person who bribes a foreign public official is guilty of an offence if—

> *(a) his intention is to influence that official in his capacity as a foreign public official, and*

> *(b) he intends to obtain or retain business, trade or profession, or an advantage in the conduct of business, trade or profession.*

(2) A person bribes a foreign official if, and only if—

> *(a) directly or through a third party, he offers, promises or gives any financial or other advantage to that official or to another person at that official's request or with that official's assent or acquiescence, and*

> *(b) that official is neither permitted nor required by the written law applicable to him to be influenced in his capacity as a foreign public official by the offer, promise or gift.*

The reference to influencing a foreign official in his capacity as a foreign public official includes any omission to exercise those functions, and any use of his position as such an official, even if not within his authority.

3.1 What is a foreign public official?

The definition of foreign public official (Section 6(5)) is widely drafted and includes all those who hold legislative, administrative or judicial positions of any kind, those who exercise a public function or an official or agent of a public international organisation whose members comprise countries, governments or other international organisations.

3.2 Wide jurisdictional reach

The general bribery offences are committed within the jurisdiction if any part of the conduct element of the offence takes place in any part of the United Kingdom.[3] It is made clear that even where all relevant actions take place outside the United Kingdom, those actions will still constitute an offence if the person performing them is a British national or a person ordinarily resident in the United Kingdom, a body incorporated in the United Kingdom, or a Scottish partnership. As such, the Bribery Act 2010 has, and is intended to have, a wide jurisdictional reach.

---

3   Bribery Act 2010, Section 12(2)-(4).

4. Corporate bribery

The Bribery Act 2010 creates a new offence of failure of a commercial organisation to prevent bribery by persons associated with it (Section 7).

This new corporate offence of failing to prevent bribery has been the subject of much comment and has caused many companies to review their global compliance programmes. The offence can be triggered by the commission of an offence under Section 1 or 6, as discussed above. It is worth highlighting that there is no requirement for there to have to been a prosecution of a Section 1 or 6 offence for the corporate offence to be triggered. To trigger the corporate offence, the prosecution only needs to prove that a person 'associated' with the corporate would be guilty of one or other of the Section 1 or 6 offences. A Section 2 offence (accepting a bribe) cannot trigger the Section 7 offence.

Section 7 provides as follows:

> (1) A relevant commercial organisation ("C") is guilty of an offence under this section if a person ("A") associated with C bribes another person intending—
>> (a) to obtain or retain business for C, or
>> (b) to obtain or retain an advantage in the conduct of business for C.
>
> (2) But it is a defence for C to prove that C had in place adequate procedures designed to prevent persons associated with C from undertaking such conduct.
>
> (3) For the purposes of this section, A bribes another person if, and only if, A—
>> (a) is, or would be, guilty of an offence under section 1 or 6 (whether or not A has been prosecuted for such an offence), or
>> (b) would be guilty of such an offence if section 12(2)(c) and (4) were omitted.

Therefore, the corporate offence can be committed by a company or a partnership if a person associated with that organisation bribes another person to obtain or retain either business or a business advantage for the company. The organisation will have a defence if it can prove that it had adequate procedures in place designed to prevent that associated person committing bribery. Once the prosecution has proved that a bribe was paid for the benefit of the company, the burden will shift to the company to prove to the civil standard of proof (balance of probabilities) that it had adequate procedures in place.

4.1 Who is 'associated'?

A person will be associated with a corporate enterprise if he performs services on behalf of that company. The Bribery Act 2010 is clear that the capacity in which the associated person acts for the company does not matter and that whether a person performs services for a company will be determined by reference to all relevant circumstances and not merely to the nature of the relationship between the parties. Corporates will need to examine all their associated parties, agents and intermediates to ascertain whether or not they 'provide a service' for the company and then establish appropriate procedure to prevent those individuals committing bribery. The meaning of 'associated' is yet to be tested by the courts. In the meantime, regulators will be seeking to interpret this section as widely as possible.

In this respect, Section 14 provides that the corporate offence will apply to corporate bodies and partnerships incorporated or formed outside the United

Kingdom which carry on business in the United Kingdom.

Section 9 of the act required the Secretary of State to issue guidance on the procedures that relevant commercial organisations could put in place to prevent associated persons committing bribery on a company's behalf for the purposes of Section 7. In March 2010, the Ministry of Justice published the guidance. The government considered that the procedures to be put in place by commercial organisations wishing to prevent bribery being committed on their behalf should be informed by six principles:

- **Proportionate procedures** – *the procedures should be proportionate to the size and type of organisation and the risks that the organisation may face;*

- **Top-level commitment** – *there should be a clear and demonstrable top level commitment and involvement in the prevention of bribery by persons associated with the organisation.*

    The purpose of advocating top-level commitment is to encourage the involvement of senior management in the engagement of bribery prevention procedures. It also aims to achieve top-level involvement in key decision-making in relation to bribery risk where it is appropriate for the organisation's management structure. The result of this should be to foster a culture of zero tolerance and effective bribery prevention controls within the company. The guidance states that there should be a formal statement, brought to the attention of employees on a regular basis. The Ministry of Justice has advised that effective formal statements would be likely to include:[4]

    - *a commitment to carry out business openly and fairly;*
    - *a commitment to zero tolerance towards bribery;*
    - *the consequences of breaching policy for employees and managers;*
    - *with regard to 'associated persons', a statement of the consequences of breaching contractual provisions relating to bribery prevention;*
    - *articulation of the business benefits of rejecting bribery;*
    - *reference to the range of bribery prevention procedures the commercial organisation has or is putting in place, including any protection and procedures for confidential reporting of bribery (whistle-blowing);*
    - *key individuals and departments involved in the development and implementation of the organisation's bribery prevention procedure; and*
    - *reference to the organisation's involvement in any collective action against bribery in, for example, the same business sector.*

    The Ministry of Justice has recognised that in large multinational organisations the top of the organisation cannot be involved in the daily implementation and monitoring of bribery prevention. However, the guidance does place a clear burden on the board to be responsible for setting bribery prevention policies, tasking management to design, operate and monitor bribery prevention procedures, and keeping these policies and procedures under regular review. The guidance also suggests that the regulators would be looking for evidence of the following:[5]

---

4   Ministry of Justice Guidance: The Bribery Act 2010, March 2011, page 23

- *selection and training of senior managers to lead anti-bribery work where appropriate;*
- *leadership on key measures such as a code of conduct;*
- *endorsement of all bribery prevention-related publications;*
- *leadership in awareness raising and encouraging transparent dialogue throughout the organisation so as to seek to ensure effective dissemination of anti-bribery policies and procedures to employees, subsidiaries and associated persons;*
- *engagement with relevant associated persons and external bodies, such as sectoral organisations and the media, to help articulate the organisation's policies;*
- *specific involvement in high-profile and critical decision-making where appropriate;*
- *assurance of risk assessment; and*
- *general oversight of breaches of procedures and the provision of feedback to the board or equivalent, where appropriate, on levels of compliance;*

- **Risk assessments** – *the guidance states that companies should implement a risk-based approach to managing bribery risks. Bribery prevention procedures that are both adequate and proportionate require "an initial risk assessment as a necessary first step". The guidance explains that commonly encountered risks are likely to fall into five broad risk groups:*
  - *country risks, such as those countries scoring badly on the Transparency International Corruption Perception Index;*
  - *sectoral risk, such as the large-scale infrastructure sector;*
  - *transaction risks, such as those involving charitable or political contributions;*
  - *business opportunity risks, such as high-value projects with many contractors or intermediaries; and*
  - *business partnership risks, such as those with politically exposed persons linked to a prominent public official.*

  Risk analysis procedures need to be embedded across the business in order develop a continuing anti-corruption culture within the company. For example, there is no specific mention of the internal audit function within the guidance, but the head of internal audit, like any other manager, has a duty to ensure that people involved in the work of internal audit are aware of the act, their own responsibilities, and the company's relevant policies, procedures and documentation.

  It will be prudent to review the controls over the processing of international transactions and assess the organisation's ability to address the UK's anti-corruption legislation since obtaining the necessary information from appropriately informed people is an essential part of the background work. Hence, checking suppliers, particularly those with agency or consultancy roles, and methods of payment should always be part of due diligence. Data analysis in order to identify suspect transactions, accounts and persons should be considered essential good practice.

  However, a well-run company will be able to demonstrate that risk assessment

---

5   Ministry of Justice Guidance: The Bribery Act 2010, March 2011, page 24

procedures enable it to "identify and prioritise the risks" and adapt to changes in its exposure to risk. As a company grows, its internal and external bribery prevention procedures should seek to ensure there is a practical and realistic means of achieving the organisation's stated policy objectives across the company;

- *Due diligence – Principle 4 reinforces this integrated approach to risk analysis. Due diligence is required in respect of persons who will perform services on behalf of organisations in order to mitigate bribery risks. The guidance is clear that "organisations will need to take considerable care in entering into certain business relationships".*

   Thus, compliance and internal audit departments are key to bribery and corruption prevention and are capable of providing forensic evidence of corruption for management to act upon. The level of the risk will vary with the type and nature of the persons associated with it, the type of business it transacts, the nature of the business relationships involved and the country where it is being done.

   Where departments merely check that existing procedures have been properly complied with rather than assessing the adequacy of the underlying due diligence or the rationale for third party payments, they will be falling below the standards expected under the guidance;

- *Communication and training – the government also expects that training, which is proportionate to the risk, should form part of this commitment to establish an anti-bribery culture and could be mandatory for new employees or for agents on a weighted risk basis. Consequently, compliance and internal audit staff found to have inadequate knowledge of bribery and corruption issues due to inadequate training are likely to have fallen short of the guidance. The Financial Services Authority identified in 2010 that it is good practice that audit and compliance staff receive specialist training and review, not only compliance with process but also the adequacy of the process itself;*

- *Monitor and review – once the culture is established, it should be demonstrated that its procedures are monitored, reviewed and where necessary improved. The guidance encourages organisations to consider seeking some form of external verification or assurance of the effectiveness of its anti-bribery procedures, but such certification may not necessarily mean that the company has established its adequate procedures defence to a charge under Section 7 of the Bribery Act 2010.*

By describing the act as "common-sense" the guidance seeks to encourage businesses to find practical solutions to actual, not theoretical, risks.

The guidance specifically states it is not "prescriptive" and "not a one size fits all document". This is an important observation because, in May 2010, a report into the insurance industry by the Financial Services Authority found that most firms were still adopting flawed thinking in their corruption risk management.[6] In doing so,

---

6   FSA Anti Bribery & Corruption in commercial insurance Broking May 2010

companies frequently failed to take into account the different risk profiles of jurisdictions and industries, and, even where they did, they did not document their findings or take remedial action by changing their procedures.

The guidance recognises no company policy or procedure can guarantee the detection and prevention of all bribery, but a risk-based approach will focus the effort where it is most needed and will have most impact, bearing in mind that the threat to organisations varies according to the nature of their business. In the context of a prosecution, the question of whether an organisation had adequate procedures in place to prevent bribery can ultimately only be decided by the courts, bearing in mind all the particular facts and circumstances of the case. However, it is clear that affirmative, proportionate action by all organisations in response to the risk of bribery is expected and, accordingly, the language in the guidance reflects its non-prescriptive nature.

4.2 Prosecution of senior officers in a company (Section 14)

Section 14 of the Bribery Act 2010 is aimed at senior individuals within organisations who consent or connive to bribery committed by a body corporate (contrary to Section 1, 2 or 6). It does not apply to the offence in Section 7 (failure of a commercial organisation to prevent bribery). Therefore, senior officials cannot be individually prosecuted for consenting or conniving to their commercial organisation failing to prevent bribery.

It must first be established that the body corporate partnership has been found guilty of an offence under Section 1, 2 or 6. The section then provides that a director, partner or similar senior manager of the body is guilty of the same offence if he has "consented to or connived" in the commission of the offence.

In this scenario, the senior manager would be charged with the same main bribery offence as the body corporate and, if convicted, both the corporate and senior manager would be guilty of the same main bribery offence. This section does not create a separate offence of 'consent or connivance'.

Section 14(3) makes clear that for a "senior officer" or similar person to be guilty he must have a close connection to the United Kingdom as defined in Section 12(4).

The offences under the Sections 1, 2 and 6 of the act carry a maximum penalty of 10 years' imprisonment and/or a fine following conviction on indictment. Summary conviction carries a maximum of 12 months' imprisonment and/or a fine limited to a statutory maximum. The Section 7 offence carries an unlimited fine.

4.3 Summary

The Bribery Act 2010 uses everyday language of offering, promising or giving (active bribery) request in agreeing to receive or accepting an advantage (passive bribery). It is also clear that, except where the allegation is that the advantage was given or received, there is no need for the transaction to have been completed. It is enough to show that a financial advantage was offered or promised. The concept of improper performance (Section 4) of a relevant function is central to the general offences, and also indirectly to the offence of failure of commercial organisations to prevent bribery, since an offence under Section 7 requires a general bribery and for it to have been committed but not proved.

A good rule of thumb when assessing whether or not a gift, reward, incentive or other financial advantage could fall foul of the act is to ask whether that gift, reward or incentive could be considered large enough, covert enough, and so on to have induced the recipient to perform his function improperly. If the answer is yes, whoever offers the gift may be in breach of one of the sections of the act.

A commercial organisation may be liable for bribes by an associated person. The offences of giving a bribe (Section 1), receiving a bribe (Section 2) and bribing a foreign public official (Section 6) may also be committed directly by a corporate body.

5. Prosecution decisions

Bribery is a serious offence, and it is in the public interest for bribery to be prosecuted. However, the Bribery Act 2010 not only sets the law governing bribery – it also aims to change the commercial culture of business in the United Kingdom over time. To understand the act, it is essential to appreciate how Bribery Act offences are to be prosecuted.

Under the old law (Public Bodies Corrupt Practices Act 1889 and Prevention of Corruption Act 1906), the attorney general's consent was required for a prosecution to proceed. In 1972, a Home Office memorandum to the Franks Committee gave its reasons for this, including the need for consistency in prosecution as this area of law deals with important considerations of public policy and international law.

Section 10 of the act removes this requirement and provides that a prosecution under the Bribery Act 2010 requires the consent of the Director of Public Prosecutions and the Director of the Serious Fraud Office. Under Section 10(4) this consent must be given personally by the appropriate director, except in certain defined circumstances.

This change does not affect the Attorney General's supervision of the of the prosecution authority. The relationship with the two directors is formalised in a 2009 protocol (to be updated following the 2010 act), which seeks to harmonise the prosecutorial decisions of independent directors.

On March 30 2011, the two directors published the Joint Prosecution guidance of the Director of the Serious Fraud Office and the Director of Public Prosecutions.

The guidance sets out the directors' approach to prosecutorial decision-making in respect of offences under the act. It is not intended to be exhaustive and prosecutors are advised to consider the wide range of circumstances in which culpability may arise in any particular case.

This guidance is subject to the Code for Crown Prosecutors. When considering corporate prosecutions, it should be read in conjunction with the guidance on Corporate Prosecutions, which sets out the approach to the prosecution in England and Wales of corporate offenders. Prosecution of a company should not be seen as a substitute for the prosecution of criminally culpable individuals such as directors, officers, employees or shareholders. Prosecuting such individuals provides a strong deterrent against future corporate wrongdoing. Equally, when considering prosecuting individuals, it is important to consider the possible liability of the company where the criminal conduct is for corporate gain.

5.1 General approach to bribery prosecutions

However, as with other criminal offences, prosecutors will make their decisions in accordance with the Full Code Test as set out in the Code for Crown Prosecutors. It has two stages: (i) the evidential stage; and (ii) the public interest stage. The evidential stage must be considered before the public interest stage.

A case which does not pass the evidential stage must not proceed, no matter how serious or sensitive it may be. Where there is sufficient evidence to justify a prosecution, prosecutors must always go on to consider whether a prosecution is required in the public interest. Assessing the public interest is not simply an arithmetical exercise, adding up the number of factors on each side and seeing which side has the greater number. The absence of a factor does not necessarily mean that it should be taken as a factor tending in the opposite direction. Each case will have to be rigorously considered on its own facts and merits in accordance with the code.

Acknowledging the important policy objective in combating bribery of foreign officials, prosecutors are reminded of the UK's commitment to abide by Article 5 of the OECD Convention on Combating Bribery of Foreign Public Officials in International Business Transactions:

> *Investigation and prosecution of the bribery of a foreign public official … shall not be influenced by considerations of national economic interest, the potential effect upon relations with another State or the identity of the natural or legal persons involved.*

6. Public interest considerations

In general, unless the prosecutor is sure that there are public interest factors tending against prosecution which outweigh those tending in favour, a prosecution will take place.

6.1 Factors tending in favour of prosecution

The code sets out a number of general factors tending in favour of prosecution. When applied in the context of bribery offences, the following may be particularly relevant:

- a conviction for bribery is likely to attract a significant sentence (Code 4.16a);
- offences will often be premeditated and may include an element of corruption of the person bribed (Code 4.16e and k);
- offences may be committed in order to facilitate more serious offending (4.16i); and
- those involved in bribery may be in positions of authority or trust and take advantage of their positions (Code 4.16n).

The more serious the offence, the more likely it is that a prosecution will be needed in the public interest. Indicators of seriousness include not just the value of any gain or loss, but also the risk of harm to the public, to unidentified victims, shareholders, employees and creditors, and to the stability and integrity of financial markets and international trade.

The impact of the offending in other countries should be taken into account, not just the consequences in the United Kingdom. See Annex A for additional factors in favour of and against a prosecution.

7. Self-reporting

The guidance to the Bribery Act 2010 states that the government is not targeting companies that show a commitment to zero tolerance to bribery. The guidance advises that the government does not intend to bring the full force of the criminal law to bear against "well run" commercial organisations that experience an "isolated incident" of bribery, but rather against the "mavericks" who undermine the majority of ethical UK business.

In order to achieve its policy objectives, the government is encouraging companies to self-report and to take positive, robust action from the top down to prevent bribery and corruption. In its guidance to Overseas Corruption, the Serious Fraud Office explains its policies and the benefits of self-reporting. The benefit to the corporate will be the prospect – in "appropriate cases" – of a civil rather than a criminal outcome, as well as the opportunity to manage, with the Serious Fraud Office, the issues and any publicity. The corporate will be seen to have acted responsibly by the wider community in taking action to remedy what has happened in the past and to have moved on to a new and better corporate culture. Furthermore, a negotiated civil settlement rather than a criminal prosecution means that the mandatory debarment provisions under Article 45 of the 2004 EU Public Sector Procurement Directive will not apply.

The Serious Fraud Office believes that the system creates effective and proportionate sanctions for this type of case and that they will help to produce a new corporate culture in which no corruption is tolerated. Under this guidance, self-referral leading to a civil outcome in appropriate cases is one tool. However, criminal prosecution and confiscation in other cases is described as "another vital tool".

Hence, the guidance strikes a cautionary note for those who may assume that they will be treated leniently:

> Without knowing the facts, no prosecutor can ever give an unconditional guarantee that there will not be a prosecution of the corporate. The aim is to settle self-referral cases ... civilly wherever possible. An exception to this would be if board members of the corporate had engaged personally in the corrupt activities.

Before deciding to self-report, a chief executive officer or chief financial officer is likely to ask his legal representative: is anyone going to prison? Is this the best way to protect the company? Is there no alternative to self-reporting and precipitating an investigation?

Those who decide to self-report may be disappointed unless they can answer yes to the following questions:

- Is the board of the corporate genuinely committed to resolving the issue and moving to a better corporate culture?
- Is the corporate prepared to work with the prosecution authority on the scope and handling of any additional investigation considered necessary?
- At the end of the investigation (and assuming acknowledgement of a problem), will the corporate be prepared to discuss resolution of the issue on the basis, for example, of restitution through civil recovery, a programme of training and culture change, appropriate action where necessary against individuals, and, at least in some cases, external monitoring in a proportionate manner?

- Does the corporate understand that any resolution must satisfy the public interest and must be transparent? This will almost invariably involve a public statement, although the terms of this will be discussed and agreed by the parties; and
- Will the corporate want, where possible, to work with regulators and criminal enforcement authorities, both in the United Kingdom and abroad, in order to reach a global settlement?

Cases in which the director of a prosecution authority decides cannot be dealt with through a civil action must be dealt with through criminal proceedings. Criminal proceedings may lead to long and expensive trials if they cannot be compromised or settled by the parties on satisfactory terms, often called 'plea bargains'.

Following the enactment of Bribery Act 2010, the government and prosecution authorities predict that all prosecutions will be dealt with through pleas of guilty. However, unlike in the United States, plea bargains and negotiated non-criminal settlements have had a difficult history in the criminal justice system in the United Kingdom. It is against this difficult background that the government proposes to introduce a statutory system of deferred prosecution agreements.

In 2006, the UK Government Fraud Review recommended the introduction of a plea bargaining framework because it would save an estimated £50 million in trial costs.

However, plea bargaining remains problematic. On the one hand, it is seen as a mechanism by which a guilty person is treated more lightly than he should be; on the other, it is seen as a pressure on innocent people to admit to crimes they have not committed. Even the word itself – 'bargain' – may suggest a cheap deal struck in private between lawyers, whereas justice should be public and transparent and involve the judges.

A short expression of the principle is set out in *R v Dougall* [2010] EWCA Crim 1048, when the Lord Chief Justice stated "agreements between the prosecution and defence about the sentence to be imposed on a defendant are not to be countenanced".

In *R v Innospec Ltd* [2010] Crim LR 665, Lord Justice Thomas noted that:

It will therefore rarely be appropriate for criminal conduct by a company to be dealt with by means of a civil recovery order … It is of the greatest public interest that the serious criminality of any, including companies, who engage in the corruption of foreign governments, is made patent for all to see by the imposition of criminal and not civil sanctions.

The case involved sales to Indonesia of a lead-based petrol additive (tetraethyl lead), which has been banned in Europe and the United States for a long time because it damages children's brains. Innospec pleaded guilty to paying $12 million to agents, who then bribed Indonesian officials. This was no ordinary commercial bribery case. The money was paid not only to secure sales of the chemical but also to persuade the Indonesian legislature to delay the introduction of lead-free petrol by six years.

In comparison, the result in *R v Mabey & Johnson Ltd* (2009), where a pre-trial settlement was endorsed by the court, was publicised on the Serious Fraud Office website in a mixed message to its corporate readers:

> *We are working together with companies to manage plea negotiations and achieve settlements which satisfy all parties. But this is just the start; we shall be using all of the tools at our disposal in identifying and prosecuting cases.*[7]

In the case of *R v Dougall*[8] in April 2010 the defendant also cooperated and a plea agreement was reached in which both sides submitted to the court that his sentence of imprisonment should be suspended. However, Mr Justice Bean sentenced Dougall to 12 months' imprisonment – not suspended – and said:

> *In this jurisdiction a plea agreement between the prosecution and the defence in which they agree what the sentence should be or present what is an agreed package for the courts acquiescence is contrary to principle.*

The defendant later successfully appealed his sentence (*R v Dougall* [2010] EWCA Crim 1048), which was suspended for different stated reasons. While some argue the outcome reflected the pre-trial settlement for leniency on sentence, the Court of Appeal criticised the prosecution's approach to plea bargains in white collar fraud cases.

> *… although the prosecution should be involved in the process by which the sentencing court is fully informed about any matters arising from the evidence which may reflect on the defendant's criminality and culpability … this process does not involve an agreement about the level of sentence.*

The court rejected the suggestion that the only practicable way of prosecuting white collar crime is by a guarantee of a non-custodial sentences to whistle-blowers. It also addressed a second important point on self-referral cases and subsequent pre-trial settlements:

> *… in our jurisdiction there is no principle of any legitimate expectation to be enjoyed by the first person to co-operate with an investigating authority, that he (or she) will be the beneficiary of the most favourable sentencing outcome … The answer to the question, "who first co-operated?" does not answer the separate question of the appropriate level of sentence discount for that defendant.*

On February 5 2010, the long-running BAE Systems case[9] was finally settled after BAE Systems reached a settlement with the Serious Fraud Office. It was no part of the Serious Fraud Office's case that the company was involved in making payments which were improperly used or that the company was party to any agreement to corrupt in Tanzania.

On December 21 2010, and by way of contrast, this settlement was commented on by the court. In his opening remarks on sentence, Mr Justice Bean stated:

> *The laying of the information on 5th November 2010 came after a Settlement Agreement between the company and the Serious Fraud Office … (but) the fine for the offence admitted shall be imposed by the court.*

Bean J went on to say that he had "no power to vary or set aside the settlement agreement … I also cannot sentence for an offence which the prosecution has chosen not to charge".

---

7   www.sfo.gov.uk/
8   *R v Dougall* [2010] EWCA Crim 1048).
9   *R v BAE Systems*, Southwark Crown Court, 21st December 2010. Case No: S2010565

There is no indication that the judiciary intends to endorse the type of pre-trial negotiated settlements that regularly feature in other jurisdictions. Responsibility for the sentencing decision in cases of fraud or corruption lies exclusively in the sentencing court and there are no circumstances in which it may be displaced.

In complex commercial fraud cases, prosecutors and defendants seek certainty when settlements are sought. However, cases are fact sensitive, and trials are unpredictable, expensive, time-consuming and commercially distracting. Unless the Serious Fraud Office decides that cases will be dealt with in civil actions, or through agreed criminal charges, the United Kingdom is some way off US-style settlements in cases of this kind. In the United States, such agreements are a long-standing prosecutorial tool. By 2007, there were 39 deferred prosecution agreements and non-prosecution agreements a year and agreements have been averaging at approximately 30 per year.

Consequently, there has been growth in the total amount of fines in the United States. The combined total for 2010 and 2011 was $7.6 billion. The growth is consistent with the Department of Justice's priorities in relation to the Foreign Corrupt Practices Act, healthcare fraud and anti-trust. According to a report by the US law firm Gibson, Dunn & Crutcher,[10] Foreign Corrupt Practices Act violations account for 45% of all economic crime prosecuted by the Department of Justice.

7.1 Deferred prosecution agreements

In March 2012, the UK's Solicitor General, Edward Garnier QC, admitted that the government had learnt the lessons of *Innospec* and BAE Systems – "we don't want to get kicked around by the court again". He acknowledged that the UK courts had already made it very clear that prosecutors are not permitted to make so-called 'private deals' with the defence and that sentencing was purely within the jurisdiction of the court. In Innospec (2010), Lord Justice Thomas explained that sentence must remain a matter for the judiciary so that the basis of any plea can be rigorously scrutinised by the judiciary in open court, "in the interests of transparency and good governance".

Mr Garnier confirmed to Parliament that so-called deferred prosecution agreements will be available to prosecutors in the United Kingdom through legislation to be introduced no later than Spring 2013. This type of agreement is an important step forward in the search for effective, multinational and cross-jurisdiction settlements, which are the final stage of the process beginning with self-reporting and non-criminal civil settlements envisaged by the Bribery Act 2010 and the guidance.

Mr Garnier acknowledged that in order for deferred prosecution agreements to work, English judges will need to be involved at a much earlier stage of the criminal proceedings so that they can oversee the parties' negotiations and indicate their opinion: "I am going to need judicial buy-in to deferred prosecution agreements and to ensure that judicial control is preserved for the judiciary."

However, the Solicitor General confirmed that:

- there would be no non-prosecution agreements, but only deferred

---

10   FCPA Update, Gibson, Dunn & Crutcher LLP, January 5, 2009

prosecution agreements conditional on compliance with measures designed to avoid any repetition of misconduct; and

- the new regime would apply only to corporate defendants, and not to individuals.

The details of the proposed deferred prosecution agreements are to be found in Schedule 17 of the Crime and Courts Bill. A full analysis of the proposed legislation is beyond the scope of this chapter. However, it is immediately clear from the Crime and Courts Bill that the government has taken care to put the judiciary at the heart of the deferred prosecution agreement process in an effort to ensure that these agreements are seen as "fair and transparent". It will be interesting to see what approach the judiciary takes to its new role.

8.   Conclusion

The government reacted decisively to criticism that it was failing to set high standards in commercial public life and to fulfil its international obligations, by enacting a new Bribery Act 2010 which consolidated a body of anti-corruption legislation. The United Kingdom now has an anti-corruption regime which, arguably, is stricter than the US Foreign and Corrupt Practices Act from which it took its cue.

The act is supported by an integrated, prosecutorial policy overseen by the directors of the two main prosecution authorities, which is designed to encourage compliance, particularly in overseas markets. By encouraging self-policing and self-reporting, it has been made clear to corporates that they will be given a reasonable opportunity to bring their practices in line with the requirements and that they will be monitored and given assistance where necessary.

The offer to deal with corruption through civil settlements and deferred prosecution agreements in appropriate cases sends a message that while bribery is a serious offence there are alternatives to criminal prosecution, and that companies who are prepared to isolate and report the criminal behaviour of culpable individuals may avoid the consequences of a damaging investigation and expensive prosecution. It remains to be seen how deferred prosecution agreements will work in practice after 2013. The judiciary has made it clear that it will not countenance pre-trial, non-criminal settlements which appear to exculpate or show undue leniency to white collar criminals, who should be punished like any other criminal. The judiciary's approach to overseeing deferred prosecution agreements is likely to prove the key to success in establishing a workable system of resolving cases where corporates and individuals find themselves in the dock together.

Annex A: Factors influencing the decision to prosecute

Factors tending in favour of prosecution

Additional factors tending in favour of prosecution include:

- a history of similar conduct (including prior criminal, civil and regulatory enforcement actions against the company). Failing to prosecute in circumstances where there have been repeated and flagrant breaches of the law may not be a proportionate response and may not provide adequate deterrent effects;
- the conduct alleged is part of the established business practices of the company;
- the offence was committed at a time when the company had an ineffective corporate compliance programme;
- the company had been previously subject to warning, sanctions or criminal charges but had failed to take adequate action to prevent future unlawful conduct, or had continued to engage in the conduct;
- failure to report wrongdoing within reasonable time after becoming aware of the offence (the prosecutor will also need to consider whether it is appropriate to charge the company officers responsible for the failures/breaches); and
- failure properly and fully to report the true extent of the wrongdoing.

Factors tending against prosecution

The factors tending against prosecution may include cases where:

- the court is likely to impose only a nominal penalty (Code 4.17a); and
- the harm can be described as minor and was the result of a single incident (Code 4.17e).

Additional factors will include:

- the corporate management team has adopted a genuinely proactive approach involving self-reporting and remedial action when the offending is brought to their notice, including the compensation of victims. In applying this factor the prosecutor needs to establish whether sufficient information about the operation of the company in its entirety has been supplied in order to assess whether the company has been proactively compliant. This will include making witnesses available and the disclosure of the details of any internal investigation;
- no history of similar conduct involving prior criminal, civil and regulatory enforcement actions against the company. The relevant regulatory departments should be asked whether investigations are being conducted in relation to the due diligence of the company;
- the existence of a genuinely proactive and effective corporate compliance programme;
- the availability of civil or regulatory remedies that are likely to be effective and more proportionate. Appropriate alternatives to prosecution may include civil recovery orders combined with a range of agreed regulatory measures.

However, the totality of the offending needs to have been identified. A fine after conviction may not be the most effective and just outcome if the company cannot pay;

- the offending represents isolated actions by individuals, for example, by a rogue director;

- the offending is not recent, and the company in its current form is effectively a different body to that which committed the offences – for example, it has been taken over by another company, it no longer operates in the relevant industry or market, all of the culpable individuals have left or been dismissed, or corporate structures or processes have been changed in such a way that repetition of the offending is impossible.

- a conviction is likely to have adverse consequences for the company under European law. Any candidate or tenderer (including company directors and any person having powers of representation, decision or control) who has been convicted of fraud relating to the protection of the financial interests of the European Communities, corruption or a money laundering offence is excluded from participation in public contracts within the European Union (Article 45 of Directive 2004/18/EC of the European Parliament and of the Council on the coordination of procedures for the award of public works contracts, public supply contracts and public service contracts).The directive is intended to be severe in its effect, and companies can be assumed to have been aware of the potential consequences at the time when they embarked on the offending. Prosecutors should bear in mind that a decision not to prosecute because the directive is engaged will tend to undermine its deterrent effect; and

- the company is in the process of being wound up.

Issues relating to health, safety and environment practice

Jon Cooper
Bond Pearce LLP

1.   Introduction

In the recent past, there has been a significant change in the approach of companies and managers to the administration of health, safety and environmental issues. Most public limited companies now include in their annual reports a stated commitment to attaining and maintaining the highest standards of health, safety and environmental management. This is in marked contrast to the past, when these issues were less important in the corporate agenda. In the higher regulated industries, the management of health and safety and environmental issues was of operational importance, but it did not often feature prominently in the public-facing documentation and approach of those organisations. This has now changed – high standards of health and safety and environmental management are the stated objectives of most reputable organisations, including those which operate in what would normally be regarded as low risk sectors.

A number of factors have driven this change, some of which will be explored in greater detail in this chapter. However, the change in attitude in boardrooms to a large extent reflects the attitude of society as a whole. Health and safety and environmental failings are no longer acceptable to the public. Whenever there is a major incident involving safety or environmental issues, there is significant, and in some cases intense, media interest and a call for those who are perceived to have been responsible for any shortcomings to be punished for their failings. There is an increasing expectation not only that those who suffer harm or loss as a result of such incidents will be compensated, but also that prosecution of the perceived wrongdoers will follow. This change in public attitude was driven by major incidents involving risks to public safety. However, failings in workplace safety and environmental management now also attract media and public attention and, crucially, significantly damage the reputation of a company or brand. It is that risk of reputational damage which has become one of the most significant driving forces behind efforts on the part of organisations to manage their businesses in a safe, sustainable and environmentally compliant manner. It was the failure of prosecutions of corporate manslaughter against large corporates that led to the calls for a change in the law, culminating in the UK Corporate Manslaughter and Corporate Homicide Act 2007. The old common law was unable to meet the challenges of modern, large corporate structures and the problem of identifying and establishing gross negligence at the strategic or 'controlling mind' level of an organisation. The Herald of Free Enterprise[1] prosecution and the prosecution arising from the Paddington rail crash[2] are clear examples.

The Corporate Manslaughter and Homicide Act 2007 took a long time to bring into law, reflecting not only the challenges of legislating for criminal breaches by corporate bodies, but also the opposition in some sectors of industry. The Law Commission report Legislating the Criminal Code: Involuntary Manslaughter[3] was the starting point of the new legislation and in 2000 the then Labour government published its proposals "Reforming the Law on Involuntary Manslaughter". A draft bill was not presented to Parliament until March 2005 and the legislation was enacted in July 2007, finally coming into force on April 6 2008. To date, there have been two successful prosecutions in England and Wales.[4] Neither of those cases offers any guidance to this area of law on the scope and extent of who might be termed 'senior management' and what might be considered a 'gross breach of duty'. In the Cotswold Geotechnical case, although it was contested, the company was too small for any useful inferences to be drawn. Lion Steel Equipment Limited pleaded guilty. A prosecution under similar legislation in Northern Ireland also went by way of a plea of guilty.[5] Finally, on November 7 2012 the Crown Prosecution Service announced that it had charged a Norfolk-based company, PS and JE Ward Limited, with an offence of corporate manslaughter. Again, the defendant company is modest in size and it is unlikely that the key parts of the legislation, such as what constitutes 'senior management', will be explored in any great detail. The real test of the legislation will come when a substantial corporate defendant is charged with and contests an allegation of corporate manslaughter.

Throughout the period of failed prosecutions under common law for corporate manslaughter and the lengthy gestation of the 2007 act, the Health and Safety at Work etc Act 1974 and regulations made under it have been in force and have remained the principal enforcement tool, in terms of criminal sanction, for breaches of health and safety legislation. There have been significant changes in the courts' approach to sentencing for breaches of the 1974 act, and a greater willingness to impose significant penalties. That too, it is submitted, has been an influence in the changing attitude within companies to compliance. However, the statistics published by the Health and Safety Executive for the year ending March 2012 indicate that executive prosecuted 551, cases with convictions secured in 517 (a conviction rate of 94%), but the average penalty was only £24,005 per offence. Those figures have to be treated with some caution and against the backdrop of the Definitive Guideline issued by the Sentencing Guidelines Council, *Corporate Manslaughter and Health and Safety Offences Causing Death*, but even so the average penalties do not appear to be a significant driver towards ensuring high standards of health, safety and environmental management. It is submitted that penalties are secondary to the risk of brand and reputational damage.

---

1   *R v P&O European Ferries (Dover) Limited* [1990] 93 Cr App Rep 72.

2   *R v Great Western Trains Co* (June 30 1999, unreported), Scott Baker J.

3   Law Com 237, March 1996.

4   R v Cotswold Geotechnical Holdings Limited [2011] EWCA Crim 1337 and *R v Lion Steel Equipment Limited* (July 3 2012, unreported), Manchester Crown Court.

5   *R v JMW Farm Limited* (May 8 2012, unreported), Belfast Crown Court.

Furthermore, tarnished or bad health, safety and environmental records are a disadvantage to companies in their everyday operations. Tender documentation, particularly in the public sector, usually requires details of prosecutions and other enforcement actions relating to health, safety and environmental issues to be disclosed. A bad record will stand against a company in a tender application.

Of course, communication in the modern world is both instant and widespread through the Internet and social media. The failing of an organisation is likely to receive far greater scrutiny and comment, much of it uncontrolled, and that too has repercussions for brand and reputation.

Non-executive directors now take a more active role in policing the managerial attitude of companies to health, safety and environmental obligations. This is not, as sometimes stated, through risk of personal prosecution. It is driven more by non-executive directors' desire not to be associated with organisations which cannot demonstrate commitment to health, safety and environmental management at the highest level. Again, reputation is paramount.

This chapter will inevitably deal with the practicalities of investigations into health, safety and environmental failings and the potential liabilities that might result from such incidents for corporate bodies and individuals. However, a common thread will be the need to ensure proper systems of governance and management to prevent or limit such liabilities. This is an increasingly active and important area of the law. However, the principles of risk management and governance that should be followed to avoid such incidents are those which can be applied broadly to the entire corporate risk portfolio.

2. Enforcing health, safety and environmental legislation

In general, the Health and Safety Executive and local authorities are responsible for enforcing health and safety legislation, which is governed by the Health and Safety (Enforcing Authority) Regulations 1998 as amended. The executive is the primary enforcing authority, but local authorities are responsible for enforcement in some work activities, including office work, catering services, the provision of childcare or nursery facilities and, most significantly, the retail sector.

The Environment Agency is the principal enforcement body for environmental legislation although local authorities also have some responsibilities. The legislation covers a wide range of activities and statutory responsibilities, including the carriage, keeping and disposal of waste, packing responsibilities, compliance with environmental permits, and obligations imposed by the Water Resources Act 1991.

Sometimes, the bodies responsible for health and safety enforcement and the Environment Agency will undertake joint investigations. For example, if a health and safety breach has potential environmental consequences, such as an explosion in industrial premises leading to loss of containment of potentially polluting substances, or where, as in the case of the Control of Major Accident Hazards Regulations 1999, the Health and Safety Executive and the Environment Agency are jointly responsible for enforcement as the 'competent authority' as defined by the regulations.

The investigation into and prosecutions arising from the explosions at the

Buncefield Oil Terminal in Hertfordshire in December 2005 were conducted jointly by the Health and Safety Executive and the Environment Agency as the competent authority under the 1999 regulations.

The Office of Rail Regulation is responsible for enforcing work-related health and safety legislation in the railway sector.

In England and Wales, the fire and rescue authorities are responsible for enforcing the Regulatory Reform (Fire Safety) Order 2005 in all types of premises, with the exception of premises in a house which is occupied as a single private dwelling.

Other authorities and agencies have responsibility for the investigation and enforcement of health and safety legislation in specific circumstances, such as the Maritime and Coastguard Agency, the Civil Aviation Authority and the Care Quality Commission.

However, the role of the police is worthy of mention.

In work-related deaths, the police will be involved in the initial investigation. The interaction between the police and other enforcement authorities is governed by the Work-Related Death Protocol. The Protocol sets out principles governing such investigations and applies not only to incidents resulting in immediate fatality, but also where "the victim suffers injuries in such an incident that is so serious that there is a clear indication, according to medical opinion, of a strong likelihood of death".[6]

Where prosecutions are brought against companies under the Corporate Manslaughter and Corporate Homicide Act 2007, the principle investigating body will be the police and the prosecution will be undertaken by the Director of Public Prosecutions/Crown Prosecution Service. The same applies to prosecutions of individuals for gross negligence manslaughter. In contrast, prosecutions brought for breaches of health and safety and environmental legislation are, except in limited circumstances, brought by the Health and Safety Executive/local authorities and the Environment Agency.

3.   Investigations into health, safety and environmental incidents

Health, safety and environmental incidents are regarded as major criminal investigations, particularly if they involve death, serious injury or serious environmental damage, and appropriate resourcing to the investigations is given by the enforcement authorities.

As these are investigations into potential breaches of criminal law, they are governed by the Criminal Procedure and Investigations Act 1996, which, among other obligations, requires investigators to follow all reasonable lines of enquiry.

The act also sets out detailed provisions and obligations for the investigating and prosecuting authorities in relation to disclosure. Accordingly, and particularly in relation to major incidents, investigations of this nature are technical, formal and, on many occasions, lengthy. A company or organisation that is subject to such an investigation should be under no illusion as to the cost, need for resource and strain that will be put on the organisation during the course of the investigation.

---

6   Work-related Deaths: A Protocol for Liaison.

If the Work-Related Death Protocol applies to the investigation, primacy for the investigation will in the initial stages rest with the police. It is only at the stage where the police, usually on advice from the Crown Prosecution Service, reach the conclusion that there is or is likely to be no evidence to warrant prosecution for offences for which the police/Crown Prosecution Service have jurisdiction (in this context, primarily corporate manslaughter or gross negligence manslaughter) that the investigation will pass to the Health and Safety Executive/local authority. In such cases, if new evidence emerges or it is thought that further reasonable lines of enquiry need to be pursued, the normal procedure is for there to be a review of the decision on which organisations should lead the investigation.

The powers available to the police are limited in comparison with those granted to the Health and Safety Executive. It is submitted that the limited, and in many respects considerable, powers of the police to investigate work-related deaths may be one reason why there have been so few prosecutions under the Corporate Manslaughter and Corporate Homicide Act 2007 and why ongoing investigations into breaches of the act are often protracted and lose momentum.

The police powers are mainly governed by the Police and Criminal Evidence Act 1984 and the associated codes of practice. For example, they may arrest and interview under caution a person reasonably suspected of having committed a criminal offence. As many of these investigations relate to a potential breach of duty by a corporate entity, the power of arrest does not arise. Individuals cannot be arrested in connection with a corporate manslaughter investigation as no personal liability arises under the act. The police may arrest and interview under caution individuals who they have reasonable suspicion may have committed the offence of gross negligence manslaughter, but evidence so obtained will not be admissible against any party other than the person interviewed.

The police have no power to force persons to answer questions or to give witness statements. Unless access to premises is granted on a voluntary basis, the police must obtain from court a search warrant to enter premises and seize documents. This will only be granted if the court is satisfied that there are reasonable grounds for believing that an offence has been committed and that there is likely to be material on the premises that is relevant evidence.

These limited powers should be contrasted with those granted to authorised inspectors (Health and Safety Executive and local authority) under Section 20(2) of the Health and Safety at Work etc Act 1974, under which inspectors are empowered to:

- enter premises (taking with them a police officer if there is reasonable cause to apprehend any serious obstruction in the execution of the inspector's duty) and to take with him any other person duly authorised by the enforcing authority and any equipment and materials required for any purpose for which the power of entry is being exercised;
- make such examination and investigation as may in the circumstances be necessary;
- direct that premises or part of them must be left undisturbed as long as is reasonably necessary for any examination or investigation (often known as a 'do not disturb' notice);

- take measurements, photographs and records;
- take samples of any articles or substances;
- dismantle or subject articles to dismantling and/or testing;
- take possession of and detain articles or substances for examination and ensure that they are available for use as evidence in subsequent proceedings;
- require any person whom the inspector has reasonable cause to believe to be able to give information relevant to any examination or investigation to answer questions and sign a declaration on the truth of the answers;
- require the production of, inspection and copies of any books or documents kept by virtue of statutory provisions or any other books or documents considered necessary to see for the purposes of the investigation or examination;
- require any person to afford such facilities and assistance as are necessary to enable the inspector to exercise any powers under Section 20; and
- exercise any other power which is necessary for the purpose of the investigation.

Under Section 108 of the Environment Act 1995, in environmental investigations, almost identical powers are granted to the Environment Agency as those contained in Section 20 of the 1974 act.

Section 20 and Section 108 powers are extremely wide-ranging. Failure to comply with a request or requirement under the sections is itself an offence. It is submitted that the powers should be exercised by inspectors proportionately, consistently and in accordance with the published procedures of the investigating organisation. A failure to exercise Section 20/Section 108 powers this way could lead to an application to exclude evidence so obtained in any subsequent trial.

In practice, enforcement authorities will often ask for documents, reports, inspection facilities and the like, that can be requested under Section 20 powers, to be provided on a voluntary basis. It is important, particularly in terms of health and safety investigations arising from fatalities, that companies are prepared to deal with such investigations and have in place at an early stage a strategy for dealing with the regulatory authorities. This is particularly so in the light of the contents of the Sentencing Guidelines Council Definitive Guideline referred to above, which sets out what will be regarded as both aggravating and mitigating features in the event of sentencing. One mitigating feature is: "A high level of cooperation with the investigation, beyond that which will always be expected."[7] Increasingly, at sentencing hearings, the prosecuting authorities do not accept that the level of cooperation required for it to be a mitigating feature (and this can impact significantly on a sentence) is present if the prosecuting authority has had to use statutory powers to gather evidence rather than it being provided on a voluntary basis. This is an issue which needs to be addressed by an organisation subject to investigation at an early stage, and a clear strategy agreed. It may also require the involvement and consent of the company's insurers, as some insurance policies

---

7   Paragraph 8 (a) of the SGC Definitive Guideline, February 2010.

prohibit the passing of documentation to investigatory authorities unless there is a legal obligation to do so. Therefore, providing such documentation on a voluntary basis may amount to a breach of policy and potential arguments on indemnity.

In addition to taking in possession of relevant documentation, the investigating authorities, whether police, Health and Safety Executive/local authority or Environment Agency, will want to interview potential witnesses. As stated above, the police cannot compel individuals to answer questions or make witness statements. On the other hand, the Health and Safety Executive/local authorities and the Environment Agency have the statutory power to require persons to answer questions under Section 20 of the Health and Safety at Work etc Act 1974 and Section 108 of the Environment Act 1995.

Inevitably, in a workplace-related incident, many of the individuals able to give evidence on the incident and the background will be employees of the company that is subject to investigation and potential prosecution. This is not a feature of other criminal investigations and raises a number of issues which need to be considered by the company.

First, it is the individuals who are asked to provide witness statements that decide whether they wish to do so on a voluntary basis (under Section 9 of the Criminal Justice Act 1967) or under statutory powers, not their employers. On occasions, companies will encourage their employees fully to cooperate with the investigation authorities, and it is submitted that such an action by the company would amount to cooperation of the sort necessary to make it a mitigating feature. On the other hand, particularly in non-unionised workplaces, employees are sometimes reluctant to be seen to be giving witness statements on a voluntary basis and so prefer the protection of answering questions under statutory powers, where they can explain to their employer that they would be at risk of prosecution if they did not cooperate.

The inherent conflict for an employee providing a witness statement, either voluntarily or under statutory powers, to the investigating authorities also gives rise to potential legal conflict issues. In many investigations, companies will seek legal advice at a very early stage and the company's solicitors will take an active part in the investigation process and communicate with the investigating authorities. The solicitors will also seek to sit in on interviews of the employer's employees. This has caused some friction between legal representatives of employers and the Health and Safety Executive, and led to the Rules and Ethics Committee of the Law Society issuing in March 2006 (revised in November 2008) guidance to solicitors on whether it is ethically appropriate for solicitors acting for an employer to be present at interviews of employees following work-related incidents. The guidance is not mandatory. It covers a number of topics, in particular the following:

- whether there is a conflict or potential conflict between the employer and the employee;
- the duty to tell the employer (as client) about information provided by the employee during the course of the interview and whether that may conflict with the duty of confidentiality owed to the employee;
- conflicts between employees where attending interviews of more than one employee;

- where acting solely for the employer, the need to explain to the employee that the solicitor owes them no duty but only a duty to the employer, that advice cannot be provided to the solicitor for the employee and that anything said by the employee will not be treated as confidential;
- public interest considerations – for example, whether the presence of the employer's solicitor would inhibit the employee from making full and proper disclosure of facts relevant to the enquiry; and
- the role of the employer's solicitor.

It is fair to say that the enforcement authorities were not happy with the failure of the Law Society to prohibit solicitors instructed by employers representing employees at interviews as well. This remains an area of conflict in investigations and needs to be approached sensitively on a case-by-case basis. Again, the need, if asserting it as a mitigating feature, to show that cooperation is "beyond that which will always be expected" may be an important factor in an employer's decision whether to insist, or try to insist, that its solicitor sits in on interviews of potential prosecution witnesses.

Once the investigating authorities have completed their investigation and gathered evidence which gives rise to a reasonable suspicion that an offence may have been committed, they are likely to move to the interview under caution stage. This is always a critical stage of the investigation, and the company must carefully consider its response.

As already stated, the police cannot, as is the usual process, arrest a potential defendant if the defendant is a company suspected of a breach of the Corporate Manslaughter and Corporate Homicide Act 2007. Similarly, there is no obligation on a company facing investigation for potential health and safety and/or environmental offences to attend an interview under caution. It is for the company, usually with the benefit of legal advice, to decide on whether it will attend an interview. There are generally three options open to a company in these circumstances:

- to decline to attend an interview;
- to decline to attend to but submit a written statement acknowledged to be in response to the request to attend an interview under caution and acknowledging its admissibility in evidence against the company; or
- to nominate an individual to attend an interview under caution.

Increasingly, particularly in large organisations, the practice is for a written statement to be submitted in response to a request to attend an interview under caution. The reasoning behind this approach is that in a large organisation it is difficult to identify one individual who will be able to deal with all questions that are likely to arise during the interview under caution and who has sufficient seniority to speak on behalf of the company.

Generally, investigating authorities prefer to interview in person a representative of a company rather than receive a written response. However, there is often little to be gained evidentially or tactically (from the company's perspective) from a company nominating a representative to attend an interview under caution. One consideration is that it may be thought that attending an interview under caution will perhaps 'tip the balance' in the enforcement authority taking a decision not to prosecute. In incidents involving fatalities, it is unlikely to be a significant consideration, since the Health and Safety Executive's Enforcement Policy Statement provides an expectation that prosecution will follow where breach of duty has led to death.

An interview under caution requires careful preparation, whether the response is through a written submission or attending a tape-recorded interview. In particular, consideration should be given to the question of pre-interview disclosure. This is governed by the Police and Criminal Evidence Act 1984 and the codes of practice. There is no obligation on an investigator to disclose all the evidence against a suspect before an interview.[8] The obligation on the investigating authority is to disclose sufficient information to enable a suspect to take legal advice. In practice, at the very least, it is advisable to seek copies of any documents or technical reports which will be referred to specifically during the course of interview via pre-interview disclosure.

In subsequent prosecutions, failure to attend an interview under caution is sometimes claimed to be a lack of cooperation. It is submitted that that is not correct; it is difficult to see how exercising a legal right (and there is a right not to attend an interview under caution) amounts to a lack of cooperation. Whether the failure to attend will be cited as a failure to meet the degree of cooperation required to make it a mitigating feature is likely to be determined by judges on a case-by-case basis.

Interviews under caution are admissible in evidence only against the person or legal entity being interviewed and not against any other person.

4. Enforcement options

If, following an investigation involving the police, the Director of Public Prosecutions/Crown Prosecution Service is satisfied that the evidential test is made out in relation to an offence and it is in the public interest to prosecute, prosecution will follow. However, these cases are relatively rare and, generally, the task of enforcement falls to the Health and Safety Executive/local authorities, in relation to health and safety matters, and the Environment Agency, in relation to breaches of environmental obligations. The Health and Safety Executive and Environment Agency have a number of enforcement options open to them.

5. Environmental breaches

The Environment Agency's approach to enforcement is outcome-based. Its policy is to use the enforcement options available to it to achieve environmental outcomes, and specifically to:
- stop offending;
- restore and/or remediate;
- bring under regulatory control; and
- punish and/or deter.

---

8   *R v Imran and Hussain* [1997] Crim LR 754.

The enforcement powers available to the agency include:

- enforcement notices and works notices (where contravention can be prevented or needs to be remedied);
- prohibition notices (where there is an imminent risk of serious environmental damage);
- suspension or revocation of environmental permits and licences;
- variation of permit conditions;
- injunctions;
- carrying out remedial work (where the agency carries out remedial works it will seek to recover the full costs incurred from those responsible);
- criminal sanctions, including prosecution; and
- civil sanctions, including financial penalties.

The enforcement powers for health and safety obligations include:

- improvement notices (where an inspector is of the opinion that a person is contravening a relevant statutory provision or has contravened such a provision in circumstances that make it likely that the contravention will continue or be repeated);
- prohibition notices (where an inspector is of the opinion that, as carried on or is likely to be carried on, the activities involve, or will involve, a risk of serious personal injury); and
- prosecution.

There is a significant difference between the approach to enforcement by the Environment Agency and by the Health and Safety Executive as the principal enforcing agency for health and safety legislation in relation to civil sanctions. Since January 2011, the Environment Agency has adopted the concept of civil sanctions and they form a part of the agency's enforcement regime. However, to date, the Health and Safety Executive has not used civil sanctions, stating that it is satisfied that its existing enforcement powers and provisions are sufficient.

There are six types of civil sanctions, namely:

- compliance notice – a regulator's written notice requiring actions to comply with the law or to return to compliance within a specified period;
- restoration notice – a regulator's written notice requiring steps to be taken within stated period to restore harm caused by non-compliance, so far as is possible;
- fixed monetary penalty – a low level fine fixed by legislation that the regulator may impose for specified minor offences;
- enforcement undertaking – an offer, formally accepted by the regulator, to take steps that will make amends for non-compliance and its effects;
- variable monetary policy – a proportionate monetary penalty, which the regulator may impose for a more serious offence; and
- stop notice – a written notice which requires an immediate stop to an activity that is causing serious harm or presents a significant risk of causing serious harm.

Another material difference in the enforcement strategies of the agency and the executive relates to the use of simple cautions as an alternative to prosecution. According to the Health and Safety Executive's Enforcement Guide, "it would be very unusual for HSE to offer a simple caution. In order for a simple caution to be offered there would need to be exceptional circumstances specifically relating to the proposed Defendant that outweighed the public interest factors". This is in contrast to the Environment Agency, where the use of simple cautions is not uncommon. It is further complicated because many local authorities, which also have responsibilities for enforcing health and safety legislation, do utilise simple cautions.

6. Prosecution

The ultimate sanction available for breaches of health and safety legislation and environmental legislation is prosecution.

The Crown Prosecution Service (in relation to corporate manslaughter and gross negligence manslaughter offences), the Health and Safety Executive/local authorities (in relation to health and safety prosecutions) and the Environment Agency (in relation to environmental prosecutions) must all follow the Code for Crown Prosecutors.

Before any enforcement authority can start a prosecution, it must be satisfied that the evidential test is made out. This means that the prosecutor must be satisfied that there is sufficient evidence to provide a realistic prospect of conviction.

Thereafter, but only if satisfied that the evidential test is made out, the prosecuting authority must consider whether prosecution is in the public interest.

Both the Health and Safety Executive and the Environment Agency have published what they consider to be relevant public interest criteria.

The Health and Safety Executive considers that the common public interest factors which, if present, would normally lead to prosecution are:[9]

- death was a result of the breach of legislation;
- the gravity of an alleged offence, taken together with the seriousness of any actual or potential harm, or the general record and approach of the offender warrants it;
- there has been a reckless disregard of health and safety requirements;
- there have been repeated breaches which give rise to significant risk, or persistent and significant poor compliance;
- work has been carried out without or in serious non-compliance with an appropriate licence or safety case;
- a dutyholder's standard of managing health and safety is found to be far below that required by health and safety law and is giving rise to significant risk;
- there has been a failure to comply with an improvement or prohibition notice, or there has been a repetition of a breach that was subject to a formal caution;
- false information has been supplied wilfully, or there has been an intent to deceive, in relation to a matter which gives rise to significant risk;

---

9   Health and Safety Executive Enforcement Policy Statement.

- inspectors have been intentionally obstructed in the lawful course of their duties; and
- it is appropriate through prosecution to draw attention to the need for compliance with the law and to deter others, or if a breach that gave rise to significant risk continued despite relevant warnings.

The Environment Agency's public interest criteria are set out in their Enforcement and Sanctions – Guidance Document issued on January 4 2011. The document acknowledges that the importance of each public interest factor may vary on a case-by-case basis. In summary, the relevant factors are:

- intent – offences that are committed deliberately, recklessly or with gross negligence are more likely to result in prosecution;
- foreseeability – if the circumstances leading to the offence could reasonably be foreseen and no avoiding and/or preventative measures were taken;
- environmental effect – the potential and actual harm to people and the environment;
- nature of the offence – impact on the agency's ability to be an efficient and effective regulator;
- financial implications – where a legitimate business is undercut or where profits are made or costs are avoided as a result of the breach;
- deterrent effect – prosecutions, because of their greater stigma, may be appropriate even for minor non-compliances where they might contribute to a greater level of overall deterrents;
- previous history – the degree of offending and/or non-compliance by the offender;
- attitude of the offender – a poor attitude towards the offence and/or lack of cooperation may be more likely to lead to prosecution;
- personal circumstances;
- repeat offending – where offending has been continued or repeated despite enforcement action previously, prosecution is more likely;
- failure to comply with a notice – likely to result in prosecution; and
- operating without a permit, licence or other authority – where necessary authorisation has not been obtained, prosecution is more likely.

The public interest factors set out above in relation to both the Health and Safety Executive and the Environment Agency are not exhaustive. However, it is unusual for either organisation to depart from its published enforcement criteria, as failure to do so may lead to a challenge, either to the prosecution as an abuse of process or, by way of judicial review, to the actual decision to prosecute.

7.   Corporate and personal liability

Health and safety legislation imposes obligations on employers, the self-employed and employees.

The Corporate Manslaughter and Corporate Homicide Act 2007 imposes a duty on "organisations" but does not impose personal liability.

Environmental legislation is more wide-ranging, and the dutyholder tends to vary between specific statutes and regulations.

Where an individual has personal responsibility under the legislation and is in breach of that legislation, they may be subject to enforcement action, including prosecution.

However, of greater concern to those involved in the management of companies, in particular directors, will be the statutory provisions which enable those individuals to be prosecuted personally as well as, or instead of, the corporate body.

Section 37 of the Health and Safety at Work etc Act 1974 provides as follows:

(1) *Where an offence under any of the relevant statutory provisions committed by a body corporate is proved to have been committed with the consent or connivance of, or to have been attributable to any neglect on the part of, any director, manager secretary or other similar officer of the body corporate or a person who is purporting to act in any such capacity, he as well as the body corporate shall be guilty of that offence and shall be liable to be proceeded against and punished accordingly.*

(2) *Where the affairs of a body corporate are managed by its members the preceding section shall apply in relation to the acts and defaults of a member in connection with its functions or management as if he were a director of the body corporate.*

The mere fact that an individual has a title of 'director' or 'manager' may not be sufficient to attract personal liability. The issue was examined in a case brought under virtually identical wording contained in the Fire Precautions Act 1971.[10] In that case, it was held that only those responsible for deciding corporate policy and strategy fell within the scope of the Section 37 equivalent. However, in those circumstances liability may be imposed on the individual under Section 7 of the Health and Safety at Work etc Act 1974, which imposes a duty on every employee while at work:

(a) *to take reasonable care for the health and safety of himself and of other persons who may be affected by his acts or omissions at work; and*

(b) *as regards any duty or requirement imposed on his employer, or any other person by or under any of the relevant statutory provisions, to cooperate with him so far as is necessary to enable that duty or requirement to be performed or complied with.*

The potential liability on directors and managers under Section 37 of the Health and Safety at Work etc Act 1974 is repeated in much of the environmental legislation. In particular, there is an identical provision imposed by Section 157 of the Environmental Protection Act 1990. Similar provisions are also found in Section 217(1) of the Water Resources Act 1991.

The wording of the sections refers to an offence that is "proved to have been committed ...". It is submitted that it is not a prerequisite that the company is prosecuted and convicted, provided that sufficient evidence is called to prove the offence on the part of the company. This is what happens in practice when it is not in the public interest to prosecute the company, for example, because it is in administration or liquidation, but it is felt that the evidential and public interest test is made out in prosecuting individual directors personally.

---

10   *R v Boal* [1992] QB 591, CA.

8. The consequences of non-compliance for companies and those concerned with their management

As stated in the introduction to this chapter, the potential brand/reputational damage arising from a health and safety or environmental incident may well be the primary concern of those charged with the management of an organisation and hence the guardianship of its reputation. Those concerns will be fuelled by the financial and legal consequences of a serious incident.

In addition to the criminal consequences, which are set out more fully below, it is likely that a serious health and safety/environmental incident will lead to claims for compensation by individuals and organisations who allege that they have suffered harm or loss as a result of the incident. The Buncefield explosion is again a good example. In addition to prosecution under health and safety and environmental legislation, those responsible were faced with civil proceedings running to hundreds of millions of pounds based on causes of action that included negligence, nuisance, *Rylands v Fletcher*[11] and breach of contract. While insurance may be in place in relation to such liabilities, the management time and resources in dealing with these claims, in addition to and often simultaneously with an investigation by the regulatory authorities, should not be underestimated. It is also likely to lead to increased insurance premiums, payments under deductibles and potentially provisioning for losses in accounts. In the most serious of cases this may have an impact on a company's share price, as can the adverse reputational consequences, as evidenced by the impact on BP following the Deepwater Horizon incident in the Gulf of Mexico in April 2010.

However, the criminal sanctions imposed following a prosecution and the adverse publicity following a conviction may be the greatest concern to the board of a company. As has been stated above, the financial penalty in some respects is secondary to the reputational damage attendant upon it. Since the coming into force of the Health and Safety (Offences) Act 2008, the maximum penalty that can be imposed in the magistrates' court for a breach of the act or regulations made under it is £20,000. In addition, if an offence is committed by an individual, that individual may be imprisoned for a term not exceeding 12 months.

If a case is dealt with on indictment, and the majority of incidents involving fatalities and severe injuries are dealt with in the Crown Court, there is no limit on the fine that can be imposed and the maximum period of imprisonment is increased to two years.

Whereas some years ago it was relatively rare for a health and safety case to go to the Crown Court, that is not the case now. The Sentencing Guidelines Council has issued clear guidelines on sentencing and the approach to be taken by the courts. Under Section 142 of the Criminal Justice Act 2003, courts must have regard to the guidelines when passing sentence.

The Definitive Guideline applies only to corporate manslaughter offences and health and safety offences resulting in death. However, the aggravating and mitigating features largely reflect those contained in the seminal sentencing case of

---

11   (1878) LR 3 HL 330.

Howe,[12] and these features will be of relevance to non-fatal prosecutions and in prosecutions of individuals (the guideline applies only and specifically to the sentencing of corporate defendants).

The Definitive Guideline recognises the broad range of potential fines and the need for them to be punitive and sufficient to have an impact on the defendant, but makes the point that they cannot and do not attempt to value human life in monetary terms.

In determining the appropriate penalty, the guideline requires the court to consider a number of factors, namely:

- the effect on the employment of the innocent may be relevant;
- any effect on shareholders will not normally be relevant – those who invest in and finance a company take a risk that its management will result in financial loss;
- likewise, the effect on directors will not normally be relevant;
- it would not ordinarily be relevant that prices charged by a defendant might in consequence be raised unless the defendant is a monopoly supplier of public services;
- the effect on the provision of services to the public will be relevant;
- the liability to pay civil compensation will not ordinarily be relevant;
- the cost of meeting any remedial order will not ordinarily be relevant – such an order requires no more than should already have been done; and
- whether the fine will have the effect of putting the defendant out of business will be relevant – in some cases this may be an acceptable consequence.

In relation to the final point, the Court of Appeal in the Cotswold Geotechnical case, the first and only conviction for corporate manslaughter in England and Wales, acknowledged that the penalty imposed would put the company into liquidation. This was stated to be "unfortunate" but was "unavoidable and inevitable".

The Definitive Guideline states at paragraph 24 that, "In relation to corporate manslaughter, the appropriate fine will seldom be less than £500,000.00 and may be measured in millions of pounds", and, in relation to breaches of health and safety legislation short of corporate manslaughter resulting in death, "The appropriate fine will seldom be less than £100,000.00 and may be measured in hundreds of thousands of pounds or more".

The guideline was considered by the Court of Appeal in the case of *R v Marble City Limited*,[13] an appeal against sentence on a health and safety rather than a corporate manslaughter case. The judgment itself was unremarkable. However, the transcript of the exchanges between counsel for the appellant company and the bench is illuminating. It included the following comment by the court:

In this particular case, the Sentencing Guidelines Council looked at matters such as percentages, starting points and they have abandoned all of that. This guideline is quite unlike any other; there are no starting points in it. The indications "will be seldom less

---

12   *R v F Howe & Sons (Engineers)* [1999] 2 All ER 249.
13   [2010] EWCA Crim 1872.

than" and "something more" were just a general steer.

The Definitive Guideline also sets out what will be regarded as aggravating features and mitigating features in an offence and hence reflected in the penalty imposed.

Aggravating features identified were:

- more than one death, or very grave personal injury in addition to death;
- failure to heed warnings or advice, whether from officials such as the inspectorate, or from employees (especially health and safety representatives or other persons) or to respond appropriately to 'near misses' arising in similar circumstances;
- cost-cutting at the expense of safety;
- deliberate failure to obtain or comply with relevant licences, at least where the process of licensing involves some degree of control, assessment or observation by independent authorities with the health and safety responsibility; and
- injury to vulnerable persons.

Mitigating features recognised in the guideline are:

- a prompt acceptance of responsibility;
- a high level of cooperation with the investigation, beyond that which will always be expected;
- genuine efforts to remedy the defect;
- a good health and safety record; and
- a responsible attitude to health and safety, such as the commissioning of expert advice or the consultation of employees or others affected by the organisation's activities.

The guideline also sets out factors likely to affect the seriousness of the offence namely:

- how foreseeable was serious injury – usually, the more foreseeable it was the graver will be the effects;
- how far short of the applicable standard did the defendant fall;
- how common is this kind of breach in this organisation; and
- how far up the organisation does the breach go.

When sentencing for corporate manslaughter, the court also has the power to make publicity orders specifying:

- the fact of conviction;
- specified particulars of the offence;
- the amount of any fine; and
- the terms of any remedial order.

According to paragraph 31 of the Definitive Guideline: "Such an Order should ordinarily be imposed in the case of corporate manslaughter. The object is deterrence and punishment." This may also be recognition that the real damage to an organisation being convicted of corporate manslaughter is reputational.

Similarly, for offences of corporate manslaughter, the court may impose a remedial order requiring a convicted defendant to remedy any identified defects. This provision in the Corporate Manslaughter and Corporate Homicide Act 2007 has attracted a lot of publicity, but there is a similar provision in Section 42 of the Health and Safety at Work etc Act 1974, which, to my knowledge, has been used only on one occasion.[14]

The Definitive Guideline at paragraph 29 provides that: "The Defendant ought ordinarily (subject to means) to be ordered to pay the properly incurred costs of the prosecution."

The prosecution costs may, and usually do, include the prosecuting authority's investigative costs, which can be substantial. For example, in the Buncefield prosecution, costs ordered to be paid by the defendants exceeded £4 million and, were it not for the impecuniosity of two defendants, would have exceeded £5 million.

When imposing financial penalties on companies, the courts are entitled to allow more time for the fine to be paid than that for an individual, thus allowing higher penalties to be imposed.[15]

The Court of Appeal has recognised that in environmental cases, there is "clearly an overlap with the sentencing principles to health and safety cases".[16] The relevant sentencing authorities and other documents, such as the Sentencing Advisery Panel Advice to the Court of Appeal (March 2000) and the Sentencing Guidelines Council Definitive Guideline on Overarching Principles: Seriousness (December 2004), indicate an acceptance of the following aggravating and mitigating features.

Aggravating features identified in environmental offences are:

- the actual or potential extent of the damage caused to the environment, human and animal health, and lawful activities;
- the extent to which the defendant fell short of its duty;
- the deliberate breaching of a duty in order to maximise profit;
- the skimping of proper precautions to make or save money, or to gain a competitive advantage;
- evidence of repletion or failure to heed advice, caution, concerns or warnings from the regulatory authorities, employees or others;
- a poor attitude and/or response after the event; and
- any previous conviction.

Mitigating features include:

- a good record of compliance with the law;
- a good attitude and/or response after the event – including prompt reporting of the offence, cooperation with the enforcement authorities, taking prompt

---

14   *HSE v Neil Vesma* (May 25 2004, unreported), Gloucester Magistrates' Court – court made an order that the defendant, an architect, should not accept any further appointments to act as planning supervisor under the Construction (Design and Management) Regulations 1994 until he had undergone appropriate training.

15   *R v Rollco Screw and Rivet Co Ltd* CA No 98/6278/W4, March 26 1999.

16   *R v Thames Water Utilities Limited* [2010] EWCA Crim 202.

and effective measures to rectify any failures, and paying compensation; and
• a timely admission of guilt and a plea of guilty at an early opportunity.

While there are similar principles in relation to sentencing for health and safety and environmental offences, companies and those who manage them should take particular note of two features of environmental prosecutions.

First, in pollution-based prosecutions, the importance of taking effective and prompt remedial measures cannot be overstated. It was a feature of the Thames Water case,[17] that great weight was given by the Court of Appeal to the remedial measures taken by the defendant after the incident. The court said that the steps taken by Thames Water were sufficient to reduce the deterrent element of the fine imposed to nil, resulting in the fine being decreased from that imposed in the Crown Court by 60%.

The second point is the need to be aware of the willingness of the Environment Agency to use wider criminal sanctions against those convicted of environmental offences, in particular, applications for confiscation of the proceeds of crime under the Proceeds of Crime Act 2002. This is particularly relevant if a defendant has carried out an activity over time, for example, in relation to the disposal of waste without a waste management licence or in contravention of such a licence, and is a significant sanction for regulators. It is anticipated that enforcement authorities will increasingly give consideration to using the 2002 act as a means of recovering assets from defendants.

Generally, the principles of sentencing set out above are applicable to individuals.

In terms of financial penalties, the court must have regard to the ability of a defendant to pay and, particularly if the defendant is a director of a company which has also been prosecuted, to make sure that there is no 'double jeopardy'. That is particularly relevant in relation to smaller companies where the directors are also the only, or major, shareholders. In those circumstances any impact on the profitability of the company or its ability to pay dividends would impact directly on the directors as shareholders.

However, there are two additional potential criminal sanctions that the court may impose on individuals.

First, sentences of imprisonment may be imposed. Since the Health and Safety (Offences) Act 2008 came into force, the use of custodial sentences has been rare. Generally, they are imposed only for the breach of an improvement/prohibition notice with immediate and gross risk to health and safety.

Imprisonment of individuals has been a sentencing option in relation to a range of environmental offences for considerably longer. Under the Environmental Protection Act 1990, the maximum term of imprisonment that may be imposed after conviction on indictment is five years for offences relating to the deposit of controlled special waste, and two years for offences relating to the carrying on of prescribed processes in breach of authorisation under the act. Offences under the

---

17   *Ibid.*

Water Resources Act 1991 also carry a maximum custodial sentence on indictment of two years.

Again, the courts use their powers of imprisonment sparingly – they tend to be reserved for deliberate and wilful breaches which have caused or potentially caused significant environmental damage and led to significant financial advantage.

It is submitted that, with current public attitudes to environmental and health and safety offences hardening, the courts may be more willing to impose custodial sentences in the future.

Finally, the criminal courts, when sentencing directors for breaches of health and safety and/or environmental legislation, may use the powers granted by the Company Directors Disqualification Act 1986. Under the act, a court may make a disqualification order against a person convicted of an indictable offence (whether on indictment or summarily) "in connection with the promotion, formation, management or liquidation of a company ...".

The maximum period of disqualification that a magistrates' court may impose is five years or, on indictment, 15 years.

Increasingly, in prosecutions involving prosecutions of directors as individuals under health and safety or environmental legislation, prosecuting authorities are drawing the attention of the courts to their powers under the 1986 Act.

9.   Managing the risk

As will be apparent from the foregoing, the failure to manage, to the highest possible standard, health, safety and environmental issues may lead to severe consequences for companies and those individuals concerned with their management.

It is essential that health, safety and environmental issues are given appropriate priority and resourcing.

A company's internal governance systems and procedures should reflect best practice and should be enforced internally through human resources systems and procedures and externally by appropriate contractual provision.

Health and safety and environmental management systems should be based on an appropriate and dynamic system of risk assessment and risk review.

While the objective of companies and their directors will be to manage their organisation so as to avoid becoming involved in an extensive investigation, it is also sensible for directors to plan for such an eventuality. This should include ensuring that:

- a critical incident policy for dealing with such incidents is in place;
- the company has access to specialist legal advice on a 24/7 basis;
- there is appropriate insurance cover in place for both the company and its directors/senior managers as individuals; and
- a strategy is developed at a very early stage following an incident to deal with regulatory investigations.

Finally, companies and their directors should consider Section 8(3) of the Corporate Manslaughter and Homicide Act 2007, which provides that:

The jury may also –

> *(a)* *consider the extent to which the evidence shows that there were attitudes, policies, systems or accepted practices within the organisation that were likely to encourage any such failure as is mentioned in sub-section (2) or to have produced a tolerance of it;*
>
> *(b)* *have regard to any health and safety guidance that relates to the alleged* breach.

Section 8(2) governs evidence showing whether the defendant company failed to comply with any health and safety legislation relating to the alleged breach and, if so, how serious the failure was and how great a risk of death it posed.

Section 8(3) is in effect an invitation to a jury to consider the health and safety culture within an organisation. Companies must be prepared to deal with such probing and this section is a good benchmark against which a company can judge its own governance and risk management procedures.

Human resources issues for managers

Marjorie Hurwitz Bremner
Berg Kaprow Lewis LLP
Thushara Polpitiye
Astute HR Ltd

People are at the heart of every business, determining its success and profitability, and they are a manager's most important resource.

However, being a manager can be a minefield with a myriad of legal responsibilities and obligations.

Managers must ensure that fairness, respect and best non-discriminatory HR practice is applied in all aspects of their work, to get the most from their people and pre-empt problems before they arise.

1. Recruitment and selection

One of the most important tasks of any manager is the recruitment and selection of staff. The recruitment process is time-consuming and can be costly. Poor recruitment policies and procedures may result in high labour turnover, poor performance and disruption for other staff.

A rigorous and systematic approach to recruitment, from job analysis through to appointment and induction, is essential (see Appendix 1.1, Human resources planning programme).

1.1 Legislation and recommended codes of practice

The legislation governing discrimination in all aspects of employment, including recruitment, is extensive. Everyone involved in the recruitment process must be fully conversant with the equal opportunities legislation.

The recruitment process involves many steps, which can be grouped into three stages:

- job analysis – defining the job role and profiling the applicant;
- the 'attraction strategy' – that is, consideration of alternative sources of applicants; and
- the selection process – evaluating applications, selection, interviewing and testing of applicants, the use of assessment centres, and references.

1.2 The job description

A job description sets out the overall objective of the position and the basic details, including reporting relationships, main activities, training and development opportunities, and key standards of performance (see Appendix 1.2, Outline job description pro forma).

1.3 The person specification

The person specification defines the education, training, qualifications, experience and competencies required (see Appendix 1.3, Person specification pro forma).

There are two well-known person specification schemes: the Rodger seven-point plan and the Munro Fraser fivefold grading system (see Appendix 1.4, Person-specific plans).

However, increasingly, interviewers are using a competency-based approach, which focuses on areas where a candidate may demonstrate competence in their working or academic life (see Appendix 1.5, Example competency-based interview questions).

1.4 Attraction strategy – sources and methods of recruitment

The type of vacancy will determine the recruitment source – the press or Internet, employment agencies, or networking and personal recommendations. For graduate or trainee appointments, it may be useful to contact universities, schools and colleges. Social networking websites such as LinkedIn are being used more frequently.

An organisation should keep the vacancy section of its website up to date. It can be useful to keep a waiting list of speculative CVs.

There are many websites for general recruitment agencies available, as well as specialist websites for specific professions.

1.5 Advertising and agencies

Many firms run a referral system and offer a 'bounty' to team members who introduce a new team member.

Job advertisements must be designed to attract the reader's attention and to create a desire to apply within a matter of seconds.

The standard of service provided by agencies varies, and it is essential that any agency used to design a job advertisement is briefed thoroughly on what is essential for the job and the organisation.

Jobs should also be advertised internally to ensure that all employees are aware of the current vacancies.

1.6 Methods of selection

As much objective evidence as possible should be obtained – that is, from the information provided on the application form or CV, from interviews and from references. This can be supplemented by psychometric tests, appropriate work-based tests or evaluation at an assessment centre. Psychometric tests include ability, personality, attainment and aptitude tests. Group exercises assess a number of skills, including analytical skills, team working, leadership and motivation.

However, is essential that the tests are evaluated and validated to ensure a consistent and ethical approach.

An interview on its own is a notoriously unreliable predictor of performance, but it is considered very important by employers.

1.7 The selection interview

The purpose of the interview is to identify the most suitable candidate, to give the candidate a complete picture of the job and the firm and to demonstrate fairness and respect for all candidates.

Remember the public relations aspect of the selection process. I recall hearing the chairman of Cadbury speak, and he said: "We turn down thousands of applicants but we still want them to eat Cadbury's chocolate"!

The principle 'be ruthless with time but gracious with people' applies to recruitment as to all other human resources processes.

Each applicant should have at least two interviews and, ideally, should see more than one interviewer to avoid allegations of bias.

The skills required in the selection process are effective questioning, active listening and interpretation of non-verbal communication and body language.

Beware of the barriers to communication – stereotypes, 'halo and horns effect', 'projection and perceptual defence'.

The halo effect occurs when an interviewer's judgement of a candidate is affected by an overall positive impression or by one or two good points which results in more negative factors being ignored or 'screened out'. The horns effect is the opposite phenomenon.

Projection and perceptual defence are similar mechanisms whereby the interviewer disregards some attributes or information and does not obtain a full picture of the interviewee.

1.8 The offer

Employers are responsible for checking that applicants have the right to work in the United Kingdom. Under the Equality Act 2010 it is unlawful to ask candidates to complete a medical questionnaire. However, it is advisable in the letter or telephone call inviting a candidate to interview to ask whether any adjustments need to be made for them for the interview or tests.

A verbal offer is legally binding.

Most offers are conditional or subject to the receipt of references satisfactory to the organisation and to the completion of a probationary period.

1.9 Costs of recruitment

The cost of recruitment should be monitored to ensure that the processes are cost-effective and that the correct media have been used.

The entire selection process should be evaluated and validated.

1.10 Documentation

Ensure that your interview notes and all other documentation will pass scrutiny and keep all relevant recruitment documentation for 12 months. It is good practice to monitor all applications to ensure that the equalities legislation is being followed.

Appendix 1.1: Human resources planning programme

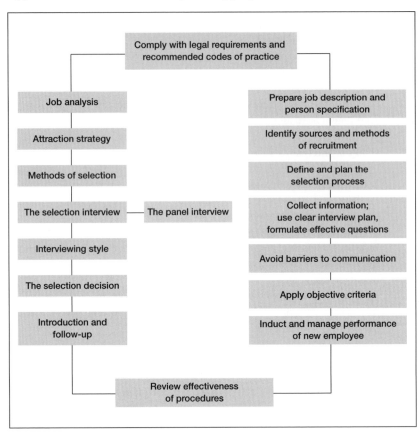

Appendix 1.2: Outline job description pro forma

JOB DESCRIPTION
Job title:
Responsible to:
Responsible for (team members and resources)
Main purpose of job/primary role

Continued on next page

Key responsibilities
1
2
3
4
5
Standards of performance/measures of effectiveness
1
2
3
4
5
Development expectations

The company reserves the right to require you to perform other duties outside your normal work duties as the company may reasonably require.

Appendix 1.3: Person specification pro forma

Person specification			
Job title:			
	Essential	Desirable	Method of assessment
Impression Overall impact			Interview
Qualifications/training			CV Interview Certificate check
Attainments/experience			CV Interview Tests References
Knowledge/skills/ability Intelligence			CV Interview Tests References

Continued on the next page

Personal qualities/disposition			CV Interview Tests References
Special aptitudes			CV Interview
General (motivation/ expectations)			CV Interview References

Appendix 1.4: Person-specific plans

Rodger's seven-point plan[1]
1   Physical make up – physique, bearing.
2   Attainments – education qualifications and experience.
3   General intelligence.
4   Special attitudes – numeracy, verbal reasoning, typing, etc.
5   Interests – intellectual, social physical, etc.
6   Disposition – dependability, influencing skills, etc.
7   Circumstances.

Munro Fraser's fivefold grading system[2]
1   Impact on others – physical make-up speech and manner.
2   Acquired qualifications – education, work experience.
3   Innate abilities – aptitude for learning, etc.
4   Motivation.
5   Adjustment – ability to withstand stress, ability to get on with people.

1   Michael Armstrong, A Handbook of Human Resource Management Practice, 8th edn, Kogan Page, London and Philadelphia, 2001
2   Michael Armstrong, A Handbook of Human Resource Management Practice, 8th edn, Kogan Page, London and Philadelphia, 2001

Appendix 1.5: Example competency-based interview questions

INTERVIEW PLAN	
A Exceeds the standard required B Meets the standard required C Nearly meets the standard required D Does not meet the standard required	
Name:	Date:
Interviewed by:	
How was the journey?	
Brief information about the organisation.	
Why did you apply for this position?	
Would you talk me through your CV?	
Intelligence	**A B C D**
Describe your learning ability.	
Describe a complex situation in which you had to learn a lot quickly. How did you go about learning and how successful were the outcomes?	
Judgement/decision-making	**A B C D**
Describe your decision-making approach when faced with difficult situations (decisive and quick, thorough, intuitive, etc).	
Describe one or two of the best and the worst decisions you have made in the past year.	
Risk-taking	**A B C D**
What are the biggest risks you have taken in recent years (include ones that worked well and ones that did not work so well)?	

Continued on the next page

Best practice	A	B	C	D
How have you copied, created or applied best practice?				
How will references rate and describe your technical expertise?				
Describe your professional network.				
Track record	**A**	**B**	**C**	**D**
Looking back on your career, what were your most and least successful jobs?				
Experience	**A**	**B**	**C**	**D**
The questions in this section relate to your current/most recent position.				
What were your expectations for the job?				
What were your responsibilities and accountabilities?				
What were the most rewarding/enjoyable aspects of the job?				
What circumstances contributed to you leaving/wanting to leave?				
What are the most important lessons you have learned in your career (when, where, what, etc)?				
What do you consider to be your strengths?				
What are your weaknesses?				
Initiative/problem solving	**A**	**B**	**C**	**D**
Tell me about any achievements that you are particularly proud of.				
What sort of obstacles have you faced in your present/most recent job and what did you do?				

Continued on the next page

Organisation/planning	A	B	C	D
How well organised are you? What do you do to be more organised and what, if anything, do you feel you ought to do to become better organised?				
When was the last time you missed a significant deadline?				
Are you better at juggling a number of priorities or projects simultaneously or at attacking a few projects, one at a time?				
Describe a situation that did not go as well as planned. What would you have done differently?				
Relationships/team player	**A**	**B**	**C**	**D**
What sort of impression do you think you make at different levels in an organisation?				
Can you describe a situation in which you have had to deal with a difficult person? How was this situation resolved?				
What sort of obstacles have you faced in your present/most recent job and what did you do?				
What will reference checks disclose to be the common perception among others of how much of a team player you are?				
Self-awareness	**A**	**B**	**C**	**D**
Have you received any sort of systematic or regular feedback from supervisors, peers, etc and, if so, what did you learn?				
What have been the most difficult criticisms for you to accept?				
Assertiveness	**A**	**B**	**C**	**D**

Continued on the next page

How would you describe your level of assertiveness?				
Stress	**A**	**B**	**C**	**D**
Describe yourself in terms of emotional control. What sort of things irritate you the most or get you down?				
How do you handle yourself under stress and pressure?				
What do you do to alleviate stress?				
Motivation	**A**	**B**	**C**	**D**
What motivates you?				
How many hours per week do you work on average?				
How would you rate yourself in enthusiasm and energy?				
Technical	**A**	**B**	**C**	**D**
What IT packages are you familiar with, and do you find it easy to pick up new systems?				
General circumstances	**A**	**B**	**C**	**D**
What are your interests outside work?				
Do you have any commitments which may affect you working the hours required?				
What is your current remuneration package?				
What are you looking for?				
How much notice would you have to give your current employer?				
Further information about the company.				
Information about future action.				

Continued on the next page

Tests – where applicable.				
Observations	**A**	**B**	**C**	**D**
Physical presence:				
Listening and understanding of questions:				
Poise and confidence:				
Sense of humour:				

2. Legal responsibility

There are three pillars or components that together govern employment law in the United Kingdom:

- common law, which provides a concept of duties and ethical principles of fairness;
- statutory law, which is approved by Parliament in the form of a statute, either an act of Parliament or a statutory instrument, and which gives protection and rights to employees and places obligations on employers; and
- case law, which is derived from decisions made by judges and provides guidance on the interpretation of statutory law.

European community (EC) legislation also has a major impact on English employment law.[3]

2.1 Health and safety

Employers have a duty to ensure the health, safety and welfare of their employees and others. Health and safety is governed by the Health and Safety at Work etc Act 1974 and the Management of Health and Safety at Work Regulations 1999 and enforced by the Health and Safety Executive.

2.2 Data Protection Act 1998

The Data Protection Act 1998 was introduced to regulate personal data held either on computer or within a manual filing system. Employers must ensure that the information held is relevant, accurate and, where necessary, kept up to date.[4]

Under the act, any data held must be processed fairly and lawfully, and in accordance with the rights of data subjects prescribed by the act.

Upon written request, employees have the right to be told what personal data about them is being processed, the source of the data and to whom it may be disclosed.

---

3   CIPD Employment Law Workbook 1 – The Origins of UK Employment Law, Valerie Francis and Sandra Madigan,2011
4   Employment Law: The Essentials, Lewis, Sargeant and Schwab, Chartered Institute of Personnel and Development; 11 edition (2011)

2.3 Equality Act 2010

In 2010, following a review of the UK discrimination legislation in response to an EC directive, the Equality Act 2010 replaced eight major UK acts of Parliament and many statutory regulations (see Appendix 2.1, Statutes replaced by the Equality Act 2010).

The main purpose of the Equality Act is to harmonise and strengthen the previous law on discrimination, to promote equality and to provide a simpler, more consistent framework for the effective prevention of discrimination.

In addition, the act addresses the perceived lack of progress in achieving equal pay between men and women.

The act promotes equality by extending the definitions of direct and indirect discrimination, harassment and victimisation, and introducing new concepts, including discrimination arising from a disability. Under the act, employment tribunals' powers to make recommendations to reduce the effect of discrimination in an organisation are extended, for example by specifying that equal opportunities training should be undertaken.

2.4 The protected characteristics

There are nine "protected characteristics" and people are protected from unlawful discrimination on the basis of one or more of these characteristics.

The protected characteristics are age, disability, gender reassignment, marriage and civil partnership, pregnancy and maternity, race, religion or belief, and sex and sexual orientation.

2.5 Conscious motivation or intent?

In any act of discrimination or perceived discrimination, it is not necessary to show that the perpetrator intended to cause less favourable treatment.

2.6 Liability

An employer is automatically liable for the discriminatory acts of its employees unless it has taken all reasonable steps to prevent the discrimination from occurring. The employer can argue this defence if it can show that it provides anti-discrimination training, has an anti-discrimination policy in place and monitors that policy, so that only an offending employee can be held responsible.

2.7 Direct and indirect discrimination

Direct discrimination occurs when an employee is treated less favourably because of a protected characteristic.

Indirect discrimination occurs where a provision, criterion or practice applies to everyone but has a disproportionate adverse effect on people with a protected characteristic. To justify indirect discrimination, an employer must show it was a proportionate means of achieving a legitimate aim.

Associative discrimination occurs where someone is less favourably treated because of an association with someone who has a protected characteristic.

Perceptive discrimination is discrimination against a person because the discriminator mistakenly thinks that person possesses a protected characteristic.

2.8   Disability discrimination

(See Appendix 2.2, Definition of disability.)

The main changes in terms of disability discrimination include indirect discrimination, associative and perceptive discrimination. Discrimination "arising" from a disability will be forbidden. Employers must consider possible reasonable adjustments to assist the disabled person.

It is now unlawful to require a pre-employment health questionnaire and questions about a prospective employee's health can only be asked in limited circumstances, as follows:

- establishing whether reasonable adjustments are necessary to the assessment process;
- establishing whether the applicant can carry out a function intrinsic to the work;
- taking positive action in relation to disabled people;
- establishing whether the applicant has a particular disability that is a requirement for the job; and
- in pursuing the employer's diversity monitoring.

2.9   Genuine occupational requirements

A genuine occupational requirement enables employers to treat those with a protected characteristic differently, if it can be shown that this is a proportionate means of achieving a legitimate end.

2.10   Positive action

The provision on positive action became law on April 6 2011 and can be justified by showing that people with a particular characteristic are underrepresented in the workforce. A person in an underrepresented group could be offered a job instead of other candidates if they are "as qualified".

However, this may be a risky strategy, and will generally require a high level of justification.

2.11   Pay secrecy and gender pay reporting

Any clause in a contract of employment which requires pay secrecy is unenforceable and any organisation which employs 250 or more staff must produce public reports on differences between male and female pay.

2.12   Inappropriate behaviour/prohibited conduct

The Equality Act 2010 defines prohibited conduct under a number of headings, including direct and indirect discrimination, discrimination arising from disability, gender reassignment discrimination, pregnancy and maternity discrimination and failure to comply with the duty to make reasonable adjustments.

It also identifies harassment and victimisation.

2.13   Harassment

Harassment is defined as unwanted conduct related to relevant protected characteristic, which has a purpose or effect of violating an individual's dignity or creating an intimidating, hostile, degrading, humiliating or offensive environment.

The act materially widens the scope of harassment:

- employees may complain of harassment even if they do not have a protected characteristic or the harassment is not directed at them; and
- employers may be liable for harassment of their staff by non-employees (eg, customers or clients).

An employer will only be liable to such harassment if it knows that an employee has been harassed on at least two other occasions by a third party.

2.14 Bullying

There is no legal definition of bullying. However, it usually refers to offensive or insulting behaviour which makes an individual feel threatened, humiliated or demoralised.

2.15 Victimisation

Victimisation is treating someone less favourably for carrying out a protected act or believing they have done so.

2.16 Jokes and banter

Jokes and banter frequently get employers into trouble, as what is perceived as funny or humorous by some employees may be perceived as offensive by others.

2.17 Best non-discriminatory practice

Employers must ensure best non-discriminatory practice and fairness is applied to all aspects of their human resources practices and processes. They should attempt to foster a culture where diversity is valued and celebrated.

All human resources policies and practices, from recruitment (including the wording of job advertisements), training and promotion, and managing performance in the appraisal interview to redundancy and other termination of employment, should be reviewed to ensure non-discriminatory best practice.

(see Appendix 2.3, Good equality practice.)

Appendix 2.1: Statutes replaced by the Equality Act 2010

- Equal Pay Act 1970;
- Sex Discrimination Act 1975;
- Race Relations Act 1976;
- Disability Discrimination Act 1995;
- Employment Equality (Religion or Belief) Regulations 2003;
- Employment Equality (Sexual Orientation) Regulations 2003;
- Employed Equality (Age) Regulations 2006;
- Equality Act 2006; and
- Equality Act (Sexual Orientation) Regulations 2007.

Appendix 2.2: Definition of disability

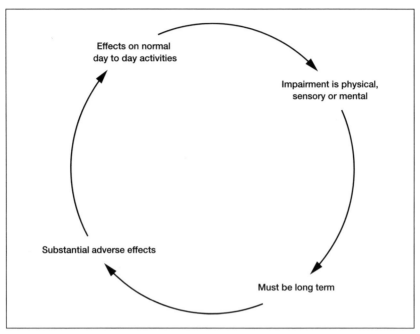

Tracey Proudlock, MCIPD, Proudlock Associates, www.proudlockassociates.com

Appendix 2.3: Good equality practice
- review equal opportunities, bullying and harassment policies to ensure that they are consistent with the new provisions;
- review recruitment processes and procedures to remove inappropriate pre-employment medical questions;
- communicate with and involve staff in writing and monitoring the policies;
- consider in what circumstances employees might encounter harassment from third parties and what steps may reasonably be taken to avoid it;
- review all policies and procedures to avoid discrimination claims;
- ensure that line managers and managers responsible for recruitment are trained;
- train managers in managing performance and give positive feedback;
- train all managers not to punish or treat someone unfairly if they have raised a grievance – unlawful victimisation;
- decisions on recruitment, promotion, granting training, appraisal, flexible working etc should be made on objective fair grounds;
- discount any decisions on absences relating to a woman's pregnancy, maternity leave or childbirth from any absence management or capability process which could result in a detriment, loss of pay, promotion or selection for redundancy;
- establish a zero tolerance policy to avoid potential incidents of harassment or bullying;
- act on any evidence that a person may be disabled and make enquiries to see

whether you can make reasonable adjustments for them – reassure them about the reason for doing this;

- handle disputes quickly and sensitively;
- consider mediation;
- include equality statements in job advertisements;
- build education and awareness of gender reassignment and transexuality into your equal opportunities policy;
- take account of different religions when planning events and functions;
- check for unjustifiable differences between the pay of male and female employees;
- make all reasonable adjustments that are required to remove or limit any substantial disadvantage caused to a disabled person; and
- document everything – a clear paper trail will help to defend any claims.

3. Effective attendance and absence management

Employee absence can be costly and disruptive to a business and can result in poor customer service, loss of productivity and profitability.

It is essential that an employer has a rigorous attendance management policy which is fairly and consistently applied. This can be especially important at times such as the Olympic games and other sporting events, when absenteeism may increase.

The key aim of an attendance procedure is to encourage reliable attendance. The policy must be communicated to staff and managers trained in how to apply it.

Employers must attempt to rehabilitate and support those staff with genuine health problems, but also must deal with those with unacceptable or unauthorised absence levels.

Good attendance initiatives such as flexible working, provision of health care, gym facilities, improving working conditions and employee assistance programmes can be introduced if they are within the organisation's budget.

There are the numbers of reasons why employees take time off work:

- short-term sickness absence;
- long-term sickness absence;
- unauthorised absence and lateness; and
- other authorised absence, for example, annual leave, maternity and paternity adoption or parental leave, time off to care for dependents, compassionate or study leave, trade union duties, and jury service.

Employers must have strategies for dealing with authorised and unauthorised absence.[5]

3.1 Measuring absence

Employers must accurately assess and measure absence levels and identify any patterns.

A number of methods are available to measure absence such as 'lost time' rate, frequency rate and the Bradford factor, which measures persistent short-term absences (see Appendix 3.1, Measuring absence).

---

5   Absence measurement and management CIPD Factsheet (www.cipd.co.uk/hr-resources/factsheets/)

3.2 Absence policy

An absence policy should contain absence notification procedures and certification requirements. If possible, employees should not be allowed to leave messages about their absence with reception or on voicemail. Details of any contractual sick pay and the right to require employees to attend a medical examination should be provided (see Appendix 3.2, Developing a successful attendance management policy).]

3.3 Management of short-term absence

One of the most effective methods for controlling short-term absence is the return to work interview. However, this needs to be handled sensitively and managers who conduct such interviews should be trained. In many cases, the reason initially given for an absence may not be correct and the underlying issues can be discussed.

The return to work interview should be WARM.

Welcome the employee back to work

Ask the reason

Responsibility – it may not be their fault, but their job is their responsibility

Move the employee sensitively back to work.

Other interventions include the use of trigger points, involving occupational health professionals and allowing family leave and flexible working.

Absence should be managed proactively, and early intervention can prevent issues escalating.

Some organisations withhold paid sick leave if an employee has less than six months' or one year's service.

Other reason for non-attendance may include low motivation, poor employee relations, poor management or leadership, and uncomfortable working conditions. The return to work interview and informal meetings with the employee might identify any underlying concerns.

3.4 Self-certification and doctor's certificates

Most employers operate a system of self-certification for sickness absences of one calendar week or less.

3.5 Fit notes

From April 6 2010, the traditional doctor's sick note was replaced by a statement of fitness for work, or a 'fit note'.

The fit note allows doctors to state either that the employee is "not fit for work" or that he "may be fit for work" taking account of specified advice from the doctor.

The doctor can highlight a number of options, including a phased return, amended job duties, altered hours and workplace adaptations.

3.6 Management of long-term absence

Employers should maintain contact with employees on long-term sick leave to avoid them feeling isolated and keep them up-to-date with changes in the workplace.

However, some employers feel that contact can be intrusive, particularly if the employee is off work due to stress.

The manager should write to the employee to ask how the employee would like to be contacted – via email, a personal visit or telephone.

The rehabilitation process should be managed proactively, and a structured return to work plan should be devised and agreed with the employee.

3.7 Disability discrimination

The Equality Act 2010 stipulates that reasonable adjustments may have to be made for employees who have become disabled. The types of adjustment include physical adjustments, altering the working hours, including the time for travel, providing special equipment and finding an alternative job.

3.8 Unauthorised absence and lateness

The reason for any absence or lateness should be investigated and discussed with the employee. If their behaviour does not improve, a formal attendance review meeting may be held, which may result in disciplinary action.

3.9 Other authorised absence

Other authorised leave includes annual leave, maternity, paternity adoption or parental leave, time off to care for dependents, compassionate leave, study leave, and time off for trade union activities or jury service.

Appendix 3.1 Measuring absence

Different measures of absence focus on different aspects of measuring time lost.

'Lost time' rate

This measure expresses the percentage of total time available which has been lost due to absence, and can be calculated separately for different departments to identify areas of concern.

$$\frac{\text{Total absence (hours or days) in the period} \times 100}{\text{Possible total (hours or days) in the period}}$$

Frequency rate

This measure shows the average number of absences per employee expressed as a percentage. It gives no indication of the length of each absence, or any indication of employees who take more than one spell of absence.

$$\frac{\text{No of spells of absence in the period} \times 100}{\text{No of employees}}$$

Source CIPD

By counting the number of employees who take at least one spell of absence in the period rather than the total number of spells of absence, this calculation gives an individual frequency rate.

Bradford factor

By measuring the number of spells of absence, the Bradford factor identifies persistent short-term absence for individuals and so is a useful measure of the disruption caused by this type of absence. It is calculated using the formula:

$S \times S \times D$

Where

S = number of spells of absence in 52 weeks taken by an individual.

D = number of days of absence in 52 weeks taken by that individual.

Source CIPD

Appendix 3.2 Developing a successful attendance management policy

- monitor absence of new starters during their probationary period;
- ensure all staff are aware of absence notification procedures and certification requirements;
- interview all staff on return to work after sickness absence;
- initially counsel employees whose absence is unsatisfactory;
- invoke disciplinary procedure if counselling does not improve the situation; and
- ensure consistency of approach.

4. Handling disciplinary and grievance issues

Employers and employees should try to resolve workplace disputes informally, promptly and respectfully before the issues escalate and attitudes become fixed. However, this is not always possible and formalised discipline and grievance procedures may become necessary.

Disciplinary procedures set the standards of behaviour that are necessary to maintain good employee relations, provide the level of service required and make clear what conduct is acceptable in the workplace.

Grievance procedures allow employees to raise their concerns or complaints and enable grievances to be dealt with fairly and without fear of recrimination or victimisation.

In both cases, it is essential that the procedures are clearly communicated to employees and that line managers are trained in their interpretation and application.

There are many categories of disciplinary situations, including work conduct, job performance, absence, poor timekeeping, health and safety (endangering the safety of others), and personal behaviour, including theft, assault or fraud.[6]

Grievances are concerns or complaints that employees raise with their employers. They may concern working relationships, pay or other conditions in the work environment.

4.1 ACAS Code of Practice on Disciplinary and Grievance Procedures

The Employment Act 2008 regulates various aspects of employment law, including dealing with discipline and grievance issues. The act came into force in 2009.

---

6   Employment Law: The Essentials, Lewis, Sargeant and Schwab, Chartered Institute of Personnel and Development; 11 edition (2011)

The act paved the way for the revision of the UK's Advisery, Conciliation and Arbitration Service (ACAS) Code of Practice to reflect the abolition of the statutory three-step dismissal and grievance procedures.[7]

The aim was to provide a simpler and more flexible framework for employers and employees. However, many people feel that the code is still too complicated and that further simplification is needed. A 'call for evidence' was opened in June 2012 to obtain employers' views on the code.

The code provides basic practical guidelines on handling discipline and grievances. The concept of fairness is central to the code, which specifies that:

- issues should be dealt with promptly;
- issues should be dealt with consistently;
- investigations should be conducted to establish the facts;
- employees should be informed that there is a problem and be allowed to put their case;
- employees should be allowed to be accompanied at formal meetings; and
- employees should be allowed to appeal against any disciplinary sanction.

However, if an employer followed the ACAS code but did not follow its own procedures, any dismissal may be found to be unfair by an employment tribunal.

4.2 Effective performance management

The management of an employee's performance should start at the recruitment and selection stage and continue throughout their employment. It should not be restricted to an annual performance review (see Appendix 4.1, Performance management).

An employee should be made aware of the standards of performance that are expected of them. The standards should be SMART:

Specific;
Measurable;
Achievable;
Realistic; and
Time bound.

Ideally, although this is not always possible, the standards should also be Stretching, Motivating, Agreed, Relevant and Timely. However, if an employee's performance is unsatisfactory and informal counselling has not worked, their employer may need to invoke the organisation's capability procedures.

4.3 Capability procedures

In many cases, organisations deal with poor performance and ill-health under their disciplinary procedures. Others have a separate capability procedure to deal with an employee's poor performance or sick leave record. However, even if performance issues are dealt with under a separate procedure, they are still subject to the ACAS Code.

It is essential to identify the causes of an unsatisfactory performance and explore

---

7   ACAS Code of Practice 1 – Disciplinary and Grievance Procedures, www.acas.org.uk/dgcode2009

all avenues with the employee, such as retraining, support, etc. The employer should agree review periods with the employee, with a view to achieving satisfactory performance. Following this, and if there is insufficient improvement, it may be necessary to instigate the disciplinary procedures.

4.4 Investigation

The importance of a fair, transparent and a rigorous investigation cannot be overestimated in handling disciplinary and grievance issues. Where possible, the employee should be informed of how long the investigation will take, whether witnesses will be interviewed and what the next stage in the process will be. All the usual rules of confidentiality should apply to the investigation process.

4.5 Employment tribunal changes

Employment tribunals are relatively informal, but can be extremely stressful, time-consuming and expensive for both employers and employees.

A number of proposals aimed at simplifying the employment tribunal process and reducing the number of claims that are made and a significant reform in the way in which employment tribunals are operated will be introduced in 2012.

The principal amendments are as follows:

- an increase in the qualifying period from one to two years' continuous employment before an employee may pursue a claim for unfair dismissal;
- employment judges will be permitted to sit alone in deciding unfair dismissal cases. Witness statements will be taken as read at tribunal hearings;
- it will be a requirement to pay a fee to issue a claim, with the possibility of a further fee should the matter progress to a full hearing;
- there will be an increased role for ACAS;
- employment judges will have an increased power to strike out cases which have no reasonable prospect of success;
- in some instances, certain court officials will be able to make minor decisions on applications; and
- junior judge positions may be created to sit on the more straightforward cases.

Proposals currently under consideration include early ACAS conciliation – pre-claim conciliation, financial penalties for employers and the introduction of fees for those seeking to pursue employment tribunal claims.

While the increased qualifying service requirement will reduce some claims, it may result in more discrimination claims, which required no service, being raised.

4.6 Mediation

Mediation may be used at any stage in an employment dispute, but usually the earlier it is introduced the better.

Mediation is an informal, flexible process conducted confidentially by a neutral person.

Unlike other forms of intervention, the parties are in control of the decision to settle and the terms of the resolution.

Mediation can be used effectively for relationship breakdown, allegations of bullying, harassment and discrimination, personality clashes, and communication problems.

It is useful to introduce a mediation clause, either into the contract of employment or into the organisation's disputes procedures, so that both parties realise there is a useful alternative approach that is far less adversarial.

Appendix 4.1: Performance management

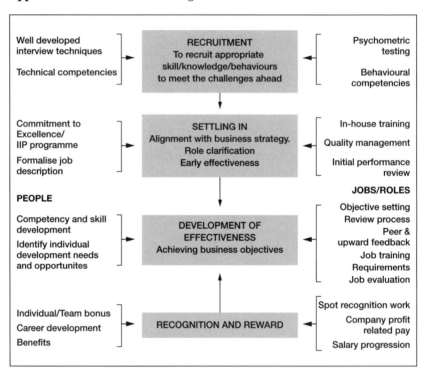

5. **Transfer of Undertakings (Protection of Employment) Regulations 2006**
The Transfer of Undertakings (Protection of Employment) Regulations 2006 (TUPE) apply to what are known as 'relevant transfers', which may occur in a wide range of situations.

TUPE can be a legal minefield. The question of when TUPE does and does not apply is complex. Each case is fact-sensitive, and two very similar situations could result in one scenario where TUPE applies and another where it does not. The aim of TUPE is to protect employees if a business changes ownership. TUPE can apply regardless of the size of the business or the number of employees.

The legal effect is that employees who are employed in the business which is being transferred have their employment transferred to the new employer. Employees have a choice of refusing to transfer if they wish, but can lose valuable legal rights if they do so. The law states that, apart from criminal liabilities, "all the transferor's rights, powers, duties and liabilities under or in connection with the transferring employees' contracts of employment are transferred to the transferee".[8] This covers rights under the contract of employment, statutory rights and continuity of employment, and includes employees' rights to sue their employer, such as for unfair dismissal, redundancy, discrimination, unpaid wages, bonuses or holidays or personal injury claims.[9]

Therefore, employees have a legal right to transfer to the new employer under their existing terms and conditions of employment and with all of their existing employment rights and liabilities intact (although there are special provisions that deal with pensions). Essentially, the new employer replaces the previous employer as if the employee's contract of employment had always been with the new employer. The previous employer is legally obligated to provide the new employer with written details of all the employee rights and liabilities that will transfer.

Any dismissal will be automatically unfair if the sole or principal reason for the dismissal is the transfer, or is connected with the transfer. The only defence is where such dismissals are for an economic, technical or organisational (ETO) reason requiring a change in the workforce. This ETO reason can be difficult to rely on, but even if the employer can rely on an ETO defence and the dismissal is not automatically unfair, it may still be unfair for other reasons, such as a failure properly to consult in a redundancy situation.

Since the new employer must take on the employees under their same terms and conditions of employment as before the transfer, it is not permitted to make any changes to the terms and conditions of employment of the transferred employees if the sole or principal reason for the variation is the transfer. The same applies if the sole or principal reason is connected to the transfer, unless there is an ETO reason for the change, usually requiring a change in number of the workforce. This often makes it difficult, if not impossible, for incoming employers to harmonise terms and conditions of employment of employees after a TUPE transfer.

The two broad categories where TUPE applies are business transfers and service provisions changes.

In order for TUPE to apply, there must be a "relevant transfer" of an "undertaking or of business" situated immediately before the transfer. This includes the following elements:

- There must be a relevant transfer – this means the transfer of an economic entity which retains its identity. This will be either where there is a service provision change or where a business is transferred. A business is transferred or there is a service provision change or outsourcing in the following situations:
  - the sale or purchase of part or all of a business as a going concern;
  - an initial outsourcing of a service, such as a services transfer from a business to an external contractor;
  - a subsequent transfer, such as a services transfer from the first external contractor to a different external contractor;

---

8   Butterworths Employment Law Handbook 20th edition.
9   See Pinsent Masons guide: http://www.out-law.com/page-448

- the transfer of a service back in-house, such as from an external contractor back to the business; and
- the grant or takeover of a lease or licence of premises if the same business is operating from those premises; and
- There must a relevant transfer of an undertaking. This means activities that the business carries out or which to some extent are separate and self-contained from the remainder of the business – for example, an operating division which is autonomous, such as an accounts department. The key is that there is an economic entity that retains its identity.[10]

5.1 Business transfers

The key issue in the regulations is whether there is a "transfer of an economic entity that retains its identity". The factors to consider in deciding whether there is a stable economic entity that is capable of being transferred include:[11]

- the type of undertaking that is being transferred;
- whether any tangible assets (eg, buildings or moveable property) are transferred;
- whether any intangible assets are transferred and the extent of their value;
- whether the majority of the employees are taken on by the new employer;
- whether any customers are transferred;
- the degree of similarity between activities carried on before and after the transfer; and
- the period for which the activities were suspended.

The question of whether there is a 'stable economic entity' is essentially one of fact for an employment tribunal to determine. There is no single factor that will necessarily determine whether TUPE applies – all the above must be considered and an overall view made on whether TUPE applies or not.

5.2 Service provision changes

A service provision change is more common in work contracts for cleaning, workplace catering and security businesses. It normally happens in one of three situations, as follows:[12]

- A service previously undertaken by the employer is awarded to a contractor – that is, contracting out or outsourcing;
- The contract is assigned to a new contractor during a re-tendering process; or
- The contract ends with the service being performed in-house – that is, contracting in or insourcing.

There are two exceptions to when a service provision change will be protected by TUPE:

- The contract is for the supply of goods for the company's use (eg, a restaurant changing food suppliers); or

---

10   See CIPD website: www.cipd.co.uk/hr-resources/factsheets/transfer-of-undertakings-tupe.aspx.
11   *Ibid.*
12   Tolley's Employment Handbook 26th edition.

- The contract is carried out in connection with a single specific event or short-term task (eg, a catering company being used to cater for a large corporate event).

Some transfers will be both a business transfer and a service provision change. The transfer need not be a sale and the undertaking may be involved in any form of activity. Courts and tribunals will seek to ascertain whether there was a continuing economic entity before and after the transfer to help to decide whether the TUPE regulations apply in any particular situation.

Employers must inform appropriate representatives of the affected employees and any measures or changes which may affect employees resulting from the transfer. Certain specified information must be provided to the representatives sufficiently far in advance of the transfer to enable the outgoing employer to consult with them about it.

If there are any changes or proposals for changes following the transfer, these measures must be discussed with the representatives of the affected employees. The incoming employer must provide the outgoing employer with information on the proposed measures to allow the outgoing employer to comply with its duty to inform and consult. While there is no set timetable for consultation, the more complex the transaction and the more employees affected, the longer the timetable must be.

The consequences of a failure to inform and consult is that a complaint can be made to an employment tribunal. If successful, the tribunal will award whatever compensation it considers fair and reasonable, taking into account the seriousness of the employer's failure. This can mean up to 13 weeks' pay for each affected employee. Information and consultation failures can result in joint and severable liability between the outgoing and incoming employer, although the contract governing the transfer may determine the apportionment of liability.

The outgoing employer has a duty to provide the incoming employer with written details of the transferring employees (including identity, age, particulars of employment, disciplinary and grievance records, employee claims and collective agreements), together with the associated rights and liabilities that will transfer. This information must be given not less than 14 days before the transfer.

If the outgoing employer fails to comply with this duty, the incoming employer can apply to the tribunal for compensation – which will be assessed with regard to the losses suffered, with a minimum award of £500 per employee. Therefore, a failure to comply with TUPE could expose employers to claims large enough to undermine the entire transaction if not carried out properly.[13]

TUPE protects employers only if the exiting employer is insolvent, in which case iability for redundancy, notice and some other payments to employees will not transfer to the incoming employer. The terms and conditions of employment may be changed (without an ETO) if the change is designed to save a failing business, where this is agreed with a trade union or employee representatives. In these circumstances companies will be more inclined to rescue insolvent businesses, thereby safeguarding employment, where the inherited liabilities are not so onerous.

---

13 See Pinsent Masons guide: http://www.out-law.com/page-448

However, TUPE will not apply in the following circumstances:[14]

- transfer by share takeover, because when a company's shares are sold to new shareholders, there is no transfer of business – the same company continues to be the employer;
- transfer of assets only – for instance, the sale of equipment alone would not be covered, but the sale of a going concern including equipment would be covered;
- transfer of a contract to provide goods or services, where this does not involve the transfer of a business or part of a business; and
- transfers of undertakings situated outside the United Kingdom.

Although there is nothing that anyone can do to prevent TUPE applying (it is not possible to contract out of TUPE), there are steps which both the outgoing and the incoming employers can take contractually to divide the TUPE liabilities between them. Although, under TUPE, employment liabilities connected with the transferring employees will always transfer to the incoming employer (so employee claims should always be made against the new employer), the parties may still contractually agree to divide the liabilities between them in a different way. This should be done through contractual indemnities, and it is recommended that specialist legal advice is sought.

6. Redundancy

Redundancy is a very stressful process for both employers and employees and needs to be handled legally, promptly and sensitively.

Before embarking on a programme of compulsory redundancies, employers should consider all feasible alternatives. According to ACAS, these may include reduction of overtime, natural wastage, introduction of short-time working or temporary layoff, if provided in the contract of employment, restrictions on recruitment and seeking applicants for voluntary redundancy.

While it is good practice to ask if any employee wishes to volunteer for redundancy, an employer is not obliged to accept an employee's application.

6.1 A fair reason for dismissal

Potentially, redundancy is a fair reason for dismissal. An employee will be taken to be dismissed by reason of redundancy, if the dismissal is wholly or mainly attributable to:

- the fact that his or her employer has ceased or intends to cease:
  - to carry on the business for the purposes of which the employee was employed; or
  - to carry on the business in a place where the employee was employed; or
- the requirements of the business have ceased or diminished or are expected to cease or diminish:
  - for employees to carry out work of a particular kind; or
  - for employees to carry out work of a particular kind, in the place where

---

14   Tolley's Employment Handbook 26th edition.

the employees were employed by the employer.
(Section139(1)(a) and (b) of the Employment Rights Act 1996.)

6.2 A fair redundancy

The tests which apply at an employment tribunal to ascertain the fairness or otherwise of a redundancy are:

- there was a genuine business reason for the redundancy;
- there was a fair and objective selection process which was applied reasonably; and
- there was genuine meaningful consultation.

It is also essential that an employer considers all alternatives to redundancy, including alternative ways of working and alternative positions, which may require retraining.

Potentially redundant employees should be informed of all current and possible future vacancies, even if the position seems to be a demotion or the duties appear quite different.

If the alternative employment offered is different from their previous position, an employee may have a four-week trial period, unless a longer period has been agreed in advance, as further training is necessary.

If either side then terminates or gives notice to terminate, the employee will be treated for redundancy payment purposes as having been dismissed on the date the previous contract ended.

6.3 The selection process

There must be a fair and objective selection process for redundancy which is applied reasonably.

The process may be more straightforward if the potentially redundant position or role is unique; however, the size and appropriateness of the selection pool may lead to a claim in an employment tribunal.

The selection criteria chosen must be objective and fair (see Appendix 6.1, Example redundancy selection).

It is good practice to inform employees of the criteria on which selection will be made at the outset of any potential redundancy programme, so that they can make suggestions or raise objections at an early stage.

It is essential to guard against potentially discriminatory selection criteria or reasons which are automatically unfair. When including attendance in the scoring, absences due to maternity or a disability should be discounted.

More than one person should be involved in the selection process to avoid allegations of bias.

6.4 Redundancy and maternity leave or adoption leave

The selection of an employee for redundancy for any reason related to maternity or adoption leave will automatically be unfair. It may also be direct sex discrimination.

If there is a suitable and appropriate alternative vacancy for an employee on maternity or adoption leave, they will be entitled to be offered that position.

6.5 Consultation

The consultation must be genuine and meaningful. Consultation is a process of considering proposals, not a process of implementing a decision, and should take place when proposals are still at a formative stage. The employer should consult about ways of avoiding redundancies or of reducing the number of employees to be dismissed, and mitigating the consequences in the event that no alternative to redundancy is found.

Collective consultation is essential if it is proposed to dismiss 20 or more employees at one establishment during a period of 90 days or less. However, individual consultation is still essential.

If the employer recognises an independent trade union representative, he should be consulted. If not, employee representatives should be elected and consulted.

The timetable for consultation depends on the number of employees potentially involved.

The penalties for failure to consult or notify the secretary of state, where the number of employees concerned requires it, are severe.

(See Appendix 6.2, Timetable for consultation and notification of the secretary of state.)

6.6 Statutory redundancy pay

Employees must have a minimum of two years' continuous service to be entitled to statutory redundancy pay. Redundancy pay is based on an employee's age, length of service and gross weekly pay, subject to a statutory maximum (see Appendix 6.3, Statutory redundancy pay).

Statutory redundancy payments are expressly exempt from income tax and there is a £30,000 tax-free limit.

6.7 Preparation and due diligence

Before embarking on a redundancy programme, employers should prepare thoroughly by ensuring they have up-to-date job descriptions and specifications, updated contracts of employment and documented annual or regular appraisals or reviews. It is also essential to train any managers who will be involved in the process to use appropriate language, such as 'proposed' 'potential' and 'possible' until the final consultation is completed and a decision is made.

6.8 Practicalities

Employers should do everything possible to minimise the effects of redundancy. Outplacement services can be invaluable, but they are expensive for a small employer. Consider what benefits, if any, can be given (such as tax benefits) or maintained (such as healthcare and mobile phones).

Following a redundancy programme, staff morale may be low and the remaining employees may be anxious and unsettled. Managers should be as supportive as possible at this time and give the employees as much time to talk as possible.

As in all human resources procedures, the entire process should be documented, and records must be checked to ensure they will stand up to scrutiny.

---

15   XpertHR (http://www.xperthr.co.uk/)

Appendix 6.1: Example redundancy selection[15]

Redundancy selection matrix			
Name of employee:		Job title:	
Department:		Length of service:	
Name(s) of manager(s) making assessment:			
Criteria	**Score (1-10)**	**Weighting (1-5)**	**Total score**
Knowledge (eg, of job, customers, the company)			
Skills			
Breadth and depth of relevant experience			
Versatility (in terms of ability/willingness to perform different functions/duties)			
Relevant qualifications/training			
Job performance			
Attendance			
Time-keeping			
Disciplinary record			
Total score			
Manager's signature:		Date:	
Approval of senior manager:		Date:	

Notes:

The range of 1 to10 for employees' point scores should be applied as follows:

10 = highest (eg, the employee's skills are exceptionally relevant and useful to the organisation)

1 = lowest (eg, the employee does not have suitable or adequate skills to do the job)

Appendix 6.2: Timetable for consultation and notification of the secretary of state

Timetable for consultation

Consultation on the proposed redundancies should take place:

- if 100 or more redundancies are proposed, at least 90 days before the first of the dismissals takes effect; and
- if between 20 and 99 redundancies are proposed, at least 30 days before the first of the dismissals takes effect.

Penalties for failure to consult collectively

Penalties may be imposed for a failure to consult collectively:

- can be up to 90 days' actual pay for each employee.

Notifying the secretary of state

The secretary of state must be notified of redundancy proposals under the following circumstances:

- an employer proposing to dismiss as redundant 100 or more employees at one establishment within a period of 90 days or less must notify the secretary of state in writing of its proposal at least 90 days before the first of the dismissals take effect; and
- if the proposals concern between 20 and 99 employees, the notice period is 30 days.

Failure to comply with this requirement is a criminal offence punishable by a fine.

7.   Dismissals

Dismissing an employee is a serious undertaking for any employer.

Certain legal procedures and codes of practice concerning dismissals must be followed in addition to the terms of the contract of employment. However, as in most areas of human resources, often it is the way the procedure is handled that makes a difference, not only to the employee affected but also to the remaining employees and on how the employer is viewed externally.

An employee will be treated as dismissed if his or her contract of employment is terminated with or without notice, if a limited or fixed-term contract expires without renewal, or if the employee terminates the contract as a result of the employer's conduct (constructive dismissal).

7.1   The legislation

Principally, unfair dismissal is governed by the Employment Rights Act 1996, as amended by various statutes, including the Employment Act 2008, which repealed the statutory disciplinary and dismissal procedures, the Employment Equality (Repeal of Retirement Age Provisions) Regulations 2011 and the Unfair Dismissal and Statement of Reasons for Dismissal (Variation of Qualifying Period) Order 2012 (Employment Rights Act 1996).[16]

---

16   CIPD Factsheet – Dismissal (http://www.cipd.co.uk/hr-resources/factsheets/)

Appendix 6.3: Statutory redundancy pay

	COMPLETE YEARS' SERVICE																		
Age	2	3	4	5	6	7	8	9	10	11	12	13	14	15	16	17	18	19	20
16	1.0	–	–	–	–	–	–	–	–	–	–	–	–	–	–	–	–	–	–
17	1.0	1.5	–	–	–	–	–	–	–	–	–	–	–	–	–	–	–	–	–
18	1.0	1.5	2.0	–	–	–	–	–	–	–	–	–	–	–	–	–	–	–	–
19	1.0	1.5	2.0	2.5	–	–	–	–	–	–	–	–	–	–	–	–	–	–	–
20	1.0	1.5	2.0	2.5	3.0	–	–	–	–	–	–	–	–	–	–	–	–	–	–
21	1.0	1.5	2.0	2.5	3.0	3.5	–	–	–	–	–	–	–	–	–	–	–	–	–
22	1.0	1.5	2.0	2.5	3.0	3.5	4.0	–	–	–	–	–	–	–	–	–	–	–	–
23	1.5	2.0	2.5	3.0	3.5	4.0	4.5	5.0	–	–	–	–	–	–	–	–	–	–	–
24	2.0	2.5	3.0	3.5	4.0	4.5	5.0	5.5	6.0	–	–	–	–	–	–	–	–	–	–
25	2.0	3.0	3.5	4.0	4.5	5.0	5.5	6.0	6.5	7.0	–	–	–	–	–	–	–	–	–
26	2.0	3.0	4.0	4.5	5.0	5.5	6.0	6.5	7.0	7.5	8.0	–	–	–	–	–	–	–	–
27	2.0	3.0	4.0	5.0	5.5	6.0	6.5	7.0	7.5	8.0	8.5	9.0	–	–	–	–	–	–	–
28	2.0	3.0	4.0	5.0	6.0	6.5	7.0	7.5	8.0	8.5	9.0	9.5	10.0	–	–	–	–	–	–
29	2.0	3.0	4.0	5.0	6.0	7.0	7.5	8.0	8.5	9.0	9.5	10.0	10.5	11.0	–	–	–	–	–
30	2.0	3.0	4.0	5.0	6.0	7.0	8.0	8.5	9.0	9.5	10.0	10.5	11.0	11.5	12.0	–	–	–	–
31	2.0	3.0	4.0	5.0	6.0	7.0	8.0	9.0	9.5	10.0	10.5	11.0	11.5	12.0	12.5	13.0	–	–	–
32	2.0	3.0	4.0	5.0	6.0	7.0	8.0	9.0	10.0	10.5	11.0	11.5	12.0	12.5	13.0	13.5	14.0	–	–
33	2.0	3.0	4.0	5.0	6.0	7.0	8.0	9.0	10.0	11.0	11.5	12.0	12.5	13.0	13.5	14.0	14.5	15.0	–
34	2.0	3.0	4.0	5.0	6.0	7.0	8.0	9.0	10.0	11.0	12.0	12.5	13.0	13.5	14.0	14.5	15.0	15.5	16.0
35	2.0	3.0	4.0	5.0	6.0	7.0	8.0	9.0	10.0	11.0	12.0	13.0	13.5	14.0	14.5	15.0	15.5	16.0	16.5
36	2.0	3.0	4.0	5.0	6.0	7.0	8.0	9.0	10.0	11.0	12.0	13.0	14.0	14.5	15.0	15.5	16.0	16.5	17.0
37	2.0	3.0	4.0	5.0	6.0	7.0	8.0	9.0	10.0	11.0	12.0	13.0	14.0	15.0	15.5	16.0	16.5	17.0	17.5
38	2.0	3.0	4.0	5.0	6.0	7.0	8.0	9.0	10.0	11.0	12.0	13.0	14.0	15.0	16.0	16.5	17.0	17.5	18.0
39	2.0	3.0	4.0	5.0	6.0	7.0	8.0	9.0	10.0	11.0	12.0	13.0	14.0	15.0	16.0	17.0	17.5	18.0	18.5
40	2.0	3.0	4.0	5.0	6.0	7.0	8.0	9.0	10.0	11.0	12.0	13.0	14.0	15.0	16.0	17.0	18.0	18.5	19.0
41	2.0	3.0	4.0	5.0	6.0	7.0	8.0	9.0	10.0	11.0	12.0	13.0	14.0	15.0	16.0	17.0	18.0	19.0	19.5
42	2.5	3.5	4.5	5.5	6.5	7.5	8.5	9.5	10.5	11.5	12.5	13.5	14.5	15.5	16.5	17.5	18.5	19.5	20.5
43	3.0	4.0	5.0	6.0	7.0	8.0	9.0	10.0	11.0	12.0	13.0	14.0	15.0	16.0	17.0	18.0	19.0	20.0	21.0
44	3.0	4.5	5.5	6.5	7.5	8.5	9.5	10.5	11.5	12.5	13.5	14.5	15.5	16.5	17.5	18.5	19.5	20.5	21.5
45	3.0	4.5	6.0	7.0	8.0	9.0	10.0	11.0	12.0	13.0	14.0	15.0	16.0	17.0	18.0	19.0	20.0	21.0	22.0
46	3.0	4.5	6.0	7.5	8.5	9.5	10.5	11.5	12.5	13.5	14.5	15.5	16.5	17.5	18.5	19.5	20.5	21.5	22.5
47	3.0	4.5	6.0	7.5	9.0	10.0	11.0	12.0	13.0	14.0	15.0	16.0	17.0	18.0	19.0	20.0	21.0	22.0	23.0
48	3.0	4.5	6.0	7.5	9.0	10.5	11.5	12.5	13.5	14.5	15.5	16.5	17.5	18.5	19.5	20.5	21.5	22.5	23.5
49	3.0	4.5	6.0	7.5	9.0	10.5	12.0	13.0	14.0	15.0	16.0	17.0	18.0	19.0	20.0	21.0	22.0	23.0	24.0
50	3.0	4.5	6.0	7.5	9.0	10.5	12.0	13.5	14.5	15.5	16.5	17.5	18.5	19.5	20.5	21.5	22.5	23.5	24.5
51	3.0	4.5	6.0	7.5	9.0	10.5	12.0	13.5	15.0	16.0	17.0	18.0	19.0	20.0	21.0	22.0	23.0	24.0	25.0
52	3.0	4.5	6.0	7.5	9.0	10.5	12.0	13.5	15.0	16.5	17.5	18.5	19.5	20.5	21.5	22.5	23.5	24.5	25.5
53	3.0	4.5	6.0	7.5	9.0	10.5	12.0	13.5	15.0	16.5	18.0	19.0	20.0	21.0	22.0	23.0	24.0	25.0	26.0
54	3.0	4.5	6.0	7.5	9.0	10.5	12.0	13.5	15.0	16.5	18.0	19.5	20.5	21.5	22.5	23.5	24.5	25.5	26.5

Continued on the next page

								COMPLETE YEARS' SERVICE										
Age	2	3	4	5	6	7	8	9	10	11	12	13	14	15	16	17	18	19	20
55	3.0	4.5	6.0	7.5	9.0	10.5	12.0	13.5	15.0	16.5	18.0	19.5	21.0	22.0	23.0	24.0	25.0	26.0	27.0
56	3.0	4.5	6.0	7.5	9.0	10.5	12.0	13.5	15.0	16.5	18.0	19.5	21.0	22.5	23.5	24.5	25.5	26.5	27.5
57	3.0	4.5	6.0	7.5	9.0	10.5	12.0	13.5	15.0	16.5	18.0	19.5	21.0	22.5	24.0	25.0	26.0	27.0	28.0
58	3.0	4.5	6.0	7.5	9.0	10.5	12.0	13.5	15.0	16.5	18.0	19.5	21.0	22.5	24.0	25.5	26.5	27.5	28.5
59	3.0	4.5	6.0	7.5	9.0	10.5	12.0	13.5	15.0	16.5	18.0	19.5	21.0	22.5	24.0	25.5	27.0	28.0	29.0
60	3.0	4.5	6.0	7.5	9.0	10.5	12.0	13.5	15.0	16.5	18.0	19.5	21.0	22.5	24.0	25.5	27.0	28.5	29.5
61	3.0	4.5	6.0	7.5	9.0	10.5	12.0	13.5	15.0	16.5	18.0	19.5	21.0	22.5	24.0	25.5	27.0	28.5	30.0
62	3.0	4.5	6.0	7.5	9.0	10.5	12.0	13.5	15.0	16.5	18.0	19.5	21.0	22.5	24.0	25.5	27.0	28.5	30.0
63	3.0	4.5	6.0	7.5	9.0	10.5	12.0	13.5	15.0	16.5	18.0	19.5	21.0	22.5	24.0	25.5	27.0	28.5	30.0
64	3.0	4.5	6.0	7.5	9.0	10.5	12.0	13.5	15.0	16.5	18.0	19.5	21.0	22.5	24.0	25.5	27.0	28.5	30.0
65	3.0	4.5	6.0	7.5	9.0	10.5	12.0	13.5	15.0	16.5	18.0	19.5	21.0	22.5	24.0	25.5	27.0	28.5	30.0
66	3.0	4.5	6.0	7.5	9.0	10.5	12.0	13.5	15.0	16.5	18.0	19.5	21.0	22.5	24.0	25.5	27.0	28.5	30.0
67	3.0	4.5	6.0	7.5	9.0	10.5	12.0	13.5	15.0	16.5	18.0	19.5	21.0	22.5	24.0	25.5	27.0	28.5	30.0
68	3.0	4.5	6.0	7.5	9.0	10.5	12.0	13.5	15.0	16.5	18.0	19.5	21.0	22.5	24.0	25.5	27.0	28.5	30.0
69	3.0	4.5	6.0	7.5	9.0	10.5	12.0	13.5	15.0	16.5	18.0	19.5	21.0	22.5	24.0	25.5	27.0	28.5	30.0
70	3.0	4.5	6.0	7.5	9.0	10.5	12.0	13.5	15.0	16.5	18.0	19.5	21.0	22.5	24.0	25.5	27.0	28.5	30.0
71	3.0	4.5	6.0	7.5	9.0	10.5	12.0	13.5	15.0	16.5	18.0	19.5	21.0	22.5	24.0	25.5	27.0	28.5	30.0
72	3.0	4.5	6.0	7.5	9.0	10.5	12.0	13.5	15.0	16.5	18.0	19.5	21.0	22.5	24.0	25.5	27.0	28.5	30.0
73	3.0	4.5	6.0	7.5	9.0	10.5	12.0	13.5	15.0	16.5	18.0	19.5	21.0	22.5	24.0	25.5	27.0	28.5	30.0
74	3.0	4.5	6.0	7.5	9.0	10.5	12.0	13.5	15.0	16.5	18.0	19.5	21.0	22.5	24.0	25.5	27.0	28.5	30.0
75	3.0	4.5	6.0	7.5	9.0	10.5	12.0	13.5	15.0	16.5	18.0	19.5	21.0	22.5	24.0	25.5	27.0	28.5	30.0

There are potentially five fair reasons for dismissal:

- capability or qualifications;
- conduct;
- illegality or contravention of a statutory duty;
- some other substantial reason; and
- redundancy

An employer must be able to prove that it acted fairly and reasonably when dismissing an employee. However, an employment tribunal will take into account the employer's size and administrative resources in determining the fairness or otherwise of the dismissal.

The concept of reasonableness includes the employee being informed of the nature of the complaint, being given the opportunity to explain and give any mitigating circumstances, and being given the right to appeal.

7.2 Terms

(a) Wrongful dismissal

Wrongful dismissal is dismissal without giving the contractual notice period or a dismissal which is in breach of agreed procedures.

(b) *Automatic termination of employment – frustration of contract*

A contract is frustrated where events make it impossible or unlawful for the contract to be performed, for example a prison sentence may be a frustrating event.

(c) *Termination without notice – summary dismissal*

A summary dismissal occurs when an employer terminates a contract of employment without notice. No notice period is given or payment in lieu of notice made. However, payment will be made for any accrued and untaken holiday.

To justify summary dismissal, the employee must be in breach of an express or implied term of their contract.

'Instant dismissal' has no legal meaning. It usually refers to dismissal without a fair investigation and is likely to be procedurally flawed.

(d) *Constructive dismissal*

Constructive dismissal occurs when an employee resigns as a result of the actions of their employer which amount to a fundamental breach of the contract. The most common breach is a breach of the implied term of mutual trust and confidence.

7.3 Automatically unfair dismissals

There are many dismissals which are automatically unfair (see Appendix 7.1, Automatically Unfair Dismissal). In addition, it is automatically unfair to dismiss an employee for asserting a statutory right (see Appendix 7.2, Asserting a statutory right).

7.4 Qualification to make a claim of unfair dismissal

Historically, employees were not protected from unfair dismissal if they had less than one year's continuous service. From April 6 2012, the qualifying period has doubled to two years. This only applies to new recruits and not to those who are already employed.

However, there may now be an increased risk of other types of employment claims, such as automatic unfair dismissals on the grounds of a protected characteristic such as age, sex, a disability, or race and ethnic origin. These claims do not require a minimum length of service and there is no cap on the award which can be granted.

If an employee has not accrued unfair dismissal rights, some lawyers feel that a modified disciplinary, capability or redundancy procedure could be adopted.

However, if there is any risk of an automatically unfair dismissal claim, a more detailed procedure should be followed. It is always advisable to follow a fair procedure to mitigate any risk.

7.5 Compensated 'no fault' dismissal for micro-businesses

The government launched a 'call for evidence' to introduce a system of no-fault compensated dismissals for employers with less than 10 employees. However, it has now formally confirmed that it will not be pursuing this proposal.

7.6 Compromise agreement

A compromise agreement allows an employer to manage an employee out of the business while protecting themselves against the risk of a tribunal claim.

The employee must receive independent legal advice and it is usual for the employer to pay for this advice.

The government plans to launch a consultation on compromise agreements later in the year. It has been suggested that the rules are too onerous for employers and that they should be simplified. They may also be renamed as 'settlement agreements'.

7.7 Following a fair procedure

It is essential that a fair procedure is followed, but there can be a wide interpretation of what the word 'fair' means.

A fundamental aspect of a fair procedure is a thorough and impartial investigation. It is essential to establish the facts and there may be strong mitigating factors or other matters that are outside the employee's control which must be taken into consideration.

It is good practice to inform an employee who is under investigation that an investigation will be taking place, what procedure will be followed and how long the whole process will take.

Although an investigation in itself can be stressful, it allows the employee to speak with someone on an informal basis prior to any hearing. In some cases, following an investigation no disciplinary action takes place and other action such as coaching or counselling can achieve the required standards. In addition, a properly conducted investigation means that the employer will have all the evidence or at least much of the evidence before the hearing to help him or her come to a decision.

The burden of proof that an employee committed an offence is not as high as in a criminal court. However, an employer must be able to show that it had a reasonable belief that the employee had committed the offence.

Although the ACAS Code of Practice does not have the force of law, employers should follow it. Any compensation awarded may be increased or decreased by up to 25% if the employer or employee, respectively, failed to comply with the code.

Currently, the ACAS Code is under review – in March 2012, the government issued a 'call for evidence' to survey employers' views.

According to ACAS, as a minimum, three stages should be followed:

- inform the employee of the alleged offence and give him or her all the evidence that will be relied on;
- arrange a meeting with the employee to discuss the alleged offence and allow the employee to be represented by a colleague or trade union representative; and
- allow the employee the right to appeal.

Appendix 7.1: Automatically unfair dismissal

A dismissal for any of the following reasons will be automatically unfair:

- taking time off for dependant's leave;
- pregnancy, childbirth or family leave (eg, maternity or adoption leave);
- health and safety;
- the entitlement to paid annual leave and other rights under the Working Time Regulations 1998;
- carrying out the duties of an employee representative;
- the national minimum wage;
- entitlement to working tax records;
- the right to request flexible working;
- trade union membership and activities or use of union services;
- an application or campaign for trade union recognition or securing collective bargaining rights;
- the right to be accompanied at a disciplinary or grievance hearing;
- carrying out any official function or activity as a member/representative of a European works council;
- the rights of fixed-term employees;
- information and consultation rights under the Information and Consultation of Employees Regulations 2004;
- based on a spent conviction (under the Rehabilitation of Offenders Act 1974);
- a refusal to work on Sundays as a shop or betting worker;
- the employee applied for or took jury service;
- making a protected disclosure – that is, whistle-blowing;
- the principal reason is a transfer of undertakings;
- taking official industrial action; or
- the employee was made redundant for a reason connected with any of the above.

Source: News and Action Plans Employment May 2012 indicator/FLM Meme

Appendix 7.2: Asserting a statutory right

Reasons include a right to:

- receive a written statement of employment particulars;
- receive wages;
- receive a guarantee payment;
- not suffer any detriment, for example, for paid time off to study or train;
- time off to carry out public duties;
- time off for ante-natal care;
- remuneration on suspension on medical grounds;
- alternative work and remuneration for maternity suspension;
- minimum statutory notice;
- receive a written statement of reasons for dismissal;
- receive a redundancy payment;
- not to have unauthorised deduction from wages in respect of a union political fund;

- not to be offered an inducement to give up trade union membership or activities; and
- paid time off for union officials to carry out union duties or learning and training activities.

Source: News and Action Plans Employment May 2012 indicator/FLM Meme

Data privacy: data transfers, offshoring and the cloud

Hazel Grant
Mark Watts
Bristows

1.   Overview

Over the past 10 years or so, data privacy (or data protection, as it is usually referred to in Europe) has become one of the most important compliance issues for multinational companies. This can be seen in a number of ways, but the dramatic increase in membership of the International Association of Privacy Professionals (essentially, a global organisation that represents privacy professionals such as chief privacy officers) is perhaps as good a measure as any. In 2000, it had 300 members; by 2012, its membership had exceeded 8,000 (source: IAPP) – a rise of over 2,500%!

There are several possible reasons why data privacy compliance has become such a key issue for organisations in terms of corporate governance:

- *reputation:* perhaps the most compelling reason for a company to make sure that it protects and handles personal data appropriately is to avoid the negative publicity that a significant data breach inevitably attracts, whether the incident was intentional, negligent or merely an accident. Over the years, there have been many high-profile incidents involving the mishandling of personal data in different ways, from data losses on portal media (such as USB drives and laptops), to illegal data collection, to unlawful interception of electronic communications. What they all have in common is that in each case it has been the adverse publicity and tarnishing of the company's brand that has been most damaging, usually more so than any regulatory enforcement taken, although the latter can always make already bad publicity even worse;
- *regulatory compliance:* for many companies, it is enough that protecting personal data and handling it appropriately is a legal requirement in the countries where they do business – companies often have an ethics policy requiring compliance with applicable laws. This is particularly the case where a failure to comply with data privacy laws may lead to criminal sanctions, either on the company itself or on its corporate officers (although the latter is rare). While many breaches of data privacy laws around the world attract comparatively minor sanctions, there have been numerous situations where enforcement action by regulators and prosecutors in Europe and elsewhere has led to sizeable fines, long-lasting undertakings to comply in the future and even criminal liability. As the authorities around the world charged with enforcing privacy laws have become more active, so too have companies realised that prevention (in the form of compliance) is generally better than cure;
- *business advantage:* there can be many different aspects to this. For example,

when implementing a major business project, such as (say) rolling out a new human resources system internationally, a company will usually find that the project proceeds more smoothly, and their business is less disrupted, if data privacy compliance is taken seriously at the outset rather than treated as an afterthought (or not even considered at all). To the extent that compliance must be achieved by designing and configuring the new system in a particular way (eg, limiting particular data fields and setting access controls), this is much easier to accomplish if the privacy compliance features are identified during the requirements definition phase when the system is being designed than if attempts are made to retrofit them to the system afterwards. There have been many examples of system roll-outs costing millions of pounds being significantly delayed or of particularly problematic countries (ie, those with the strictest laws) being omitted from 'go live' or even being scrapped altogether, as a result of data privacy being considered too late in the process, so as to have become an insurmountable obstacle. Another example of data privacy compliance offering companies a business advantage is where, as companies become increasingly global in their outlook and operations, their business processes (eg, human resources, sales and marketing, internal investigations) become more global too. Any such globalisation will require increased data sharing between group companies, potentially all over the world. As data privacy laws may act as a bar to such data sharing, companies have been strongly incentivised to implement compliance programmes internally, such as binding corporate rules, which enable data sharing in a compliant way. It would be inadvisable for a multinational company to change its internal processes globally without giving sufficient thought to data privacy requirements; and

- *competitive edge:* as data privacy considerations have been rising up the corporate governance agenda, so too have they been rising up the list of concerns expressed by online consumers. Concerns over how their information is handled and protected online have topped survey after survey in recent years. Companies which have been perceived by the public to have acted in a privacy-unfriendly way have been the subject of significant public outcry. As a result, many companies, particularly those who direct their goods and services at consumers, have come to appreciate that being seen as a responsible organisation when handling personal data can be a decisive factor for individuals when choosing companies to do business with. This is often summed up by the word trust – if consumers do not trust a company with their data then why would they give it to them?

2.   Principles and rights

Most developed economies around the world either have, soon will have or are seriously considering introducing some form of data privacy law. Over the last 10 to 15 years, data privacy has ceased to be the EU-only issue that it once was, although the privacy laws in the European Union still tend to have the greatest impact on the operations of multinational companies.

In very broad terms, data privacy regimes around the world divide into those that are 'comprehensive' (sometimes referred to as omnibus or horizontal) and those that are vertical or 'sectoral'. Comprehensive regimes apply to the processing of personal data generally, such as the laws in the European Union, while sectoral regimes apply to privacy issues arising within particular sectors, such as the healthcare and financial services sectors, or to certain categories of data, such as information about children, or particular types of high-risk processing, such as direct marketing by email. (The United States has adopted this approach, having passed the Health Insurance Portability and Accountability Act of 1996, the Gramm-Leach-Bliley Act of 1999, the Children's Online Privacy Protection Act of 1998 and the CAN-SPAM Act 2003 in each of these areas.) In countries adopting a sectoral approach to data-privacy laws, such as the US, self-regulatory programmes – that is, voluntary industry initiatives – also play a significant role. This has particularly been the case, for example, with the privacy issues arising from online behavioural advertising (ie, serving a consumer with adverts on the basis of his or her online browsing history).

It is not possible in a single chapter to provide a comparative analysis of all of the individual privacy laws around the world. However, whether comprehensive or sectoral, most privacy laws have more in common than not. The most significant variations in countries' laws arise from different cultural approaches to regulation and its enforcement, rather than any fundamental differences in how personal data should be handled.

In order to describe the key data compliance steps that multinational companies should consider taking, the most common features found in those regimes which apply a comprehensive approach to data privacy are described below. Although the sectoral approach continues to be popular in the United States, the majority of countries that have recently introduced a specific privacy law have done so in a comprehensive manner. Even those countries that have spurned the overly broad, expansive and bureaucratic approach to data protection taken in the European Union have nevertheless taken an approach that applies to the processing of personal data generally, rather than restricting it to particular sectors. The best example of this is the Privacy Framework adopted by the members of the Asia-Pacific Economic Cooperation (APEC) in 2004.

Comprehensive privacy laws tend to work by setting out 'principles' which must be followed by organisations processing personal data (ie, obligations to process personal data in a particular way) and providing 'rights' to the individuals to whom that personal data relates (ie, legal rights and remedies to ensure processing in accordance with the principles). The most common and significant of these principles and rights are described below.

2.1 The principles
The following principles apply (at least to some extent) under most comprehensive data privacy laws.

(a) Fair processing
In some countries, this is also referred to as the transparency principle or

occasionally the notice principle. It refers (in part) to the principle that individuals should be informed about various aspects of how their personal data will be processed. Typically, this fair processing information (or 'notice') should be provided either before or at the time that the data is collected. The idea is that the individual should be provided with sufficient information about how their personal data will be processed, and any potential consequences, to enable them to (if possible) decline to provide his personal data, to limit the personal data they provide (eg, by providing the minimum required) or to restrict the other purposes for which it is processed (eg, in the case of an online purchase, to opt out of subsequent direct marketing). Even where the circumstances are such that the individual cannot exercise any control over what they provide, for example, where the personal data must be provided by law, the provision of 'fair processing' information should at least inform the individual about the identity of the organisation processing their data and how they may exercise thier legal rights.

At a minimum, individuals should be informed of which organisation is collecting their personal data, and of the purpose for which it is being collected, details of any third parties with whom the personal data may be shared (unless this is obvious) and, in many countries, any further information that is required in order to ensure that the data processing is fair. It is this requirement to provide fair processing information that gives rise to companies developing privacy policies, particularly with regard to online data collection.

Although the fairness principle is most often considered at the time of collecting personal data and summarised as providing notice to the individual, the principle is usually far broader and imposes an obligation to ensure that the personal data is processed fairly (from the point of view of the individual) for as long as it continues to be held by the organisation.

(b) **Purpose limitation**

This refers to the principle that personal data must be collected for a specific purpose (the purpose communicated to the individual in the fair processing information above) and not subsequently used or processed in a way that is incompatible with that purpose. For example, generally it is not possible for a company to collect personal data from an individual as part of a recruitment process and then subsequently use it to send them direct marketing materials (whether the individual was successfully recruited or not). It is the purpose communicated by a company at the time that it collected the data that determines the scope of what the company can do with that data for as long as it continues to hold it – a company cannot recycle personal data if doing so would involve a change of purpose, irrespective of whether the company owns the data concerned (in an intellectual property sense). However, it is usually permissible for a company to collect personal data for more than one purpose, as long as each of the purposes is clearly communicated in the fair processing notice when the data is collected.

(c) **Proportionality**

This refers to the principle that the amount of personal data processed should be the minimum necessary for the purpose for which it is being processed (again, this purpose having been communicated in the fair processing information described above). In practice, this means that personal data should not be collected from an individual if it is not necessary for the particular purpose concerned. For example, it is not necessary for a company to collect bank account details from job applicants as part of its recruitment process, even though it will undoubtedly need the information in due course to pay the successful applicant. By collecting bank account details from all candidates, it would have collected a disproportionate amount of personal data about the other, unsuccessful candidates. It is the proportionality principle that prevents companies from collecting personal data 'just in case'.

(d) Data quality

Personal data should be accurate and kept as up-to-date as necessary for the purpose for which it is being processed. This is particularly important when a company is making decisions affecting an individual based on personal data that they hold about him, such as a salary review based on his performance at work. Obviously, it is important that such decisions are made on the basis of the best possible information.

(e) Data retention

Companies processing personal data (and this includes companies continuing to store personal data) should only do so for as long as it is necessary for the purpose for which that data was originally collected. Once this purpose has been satisfied, the personal data associated with it should be deleted or rendered anonymous (ie, so that it longer qualifies as personal data). For example, if during a recruitment process a company receives 100 job applications and eventually selects one successful applicant, the resumes of the other 99 applicants should be deleted once the period within which the hiring decision can be challenged on legal grounds has expired (eg, in some countries, a period of six months), unless the company wishes to keep some of the applicants' details on file for future opportunities and has their permission to do so.

(f) Data security

All data privacy laws impose an obligation to safeguard personal data that is being processed – without sufficient data security there can be no data privacy. Under the laws of some countries, this security principle is expressed as a relatively high-level requirement to implement appropriate organisational and technical measures to protect personal data from unlawful or unauthorised processing and accidental loss or destruction. In other countries, a general obligation may be coupled with a more prescriptive list of specific security measures that must be applied, for example, dealing with issues such as the encryption of data and the length of user passwords that must be used in IT systems that process personal data.

In many countries additional requirements are imposed in circumstances where a third party, such as an information technology (IT) supplier, is being engaged by a company to process personal data on its behalf. A description of these additional requirements, their potential impact and how to deal with them in practice is included in section 7.

(g) Data transfers

The principle that has probably attracted the most publicity and certainly driven a lot of the compliance activity by multinational companies is the principle that personal data may not be transferred across country borders – that is, from one country to another. While privacy laws in the European Union are best known for such restrictions, similar restrictions exist in many other countries, such as Switzerland, Argentina, Russia, Canada and Japan. It is these restrictions that can present companies with some of the greatest legal challenges when considering moving the processing of personal data 'offshore' to a service provider based in another country. The restrictions on transferring personal data out of the European Union are described in more detail in section 6.

2.2 Individual rights

As mentioned above, as well as requiring companies to process personal data in accordance with certain principles, data privacy laws also provide the individuals whose personal data is processed with certain legal rights and remedies in respect of its processing. The most significant of these rights are set out below.

(a) Access

Most data privacy laws provide an individual with a right of access to the personal data that an organisation is processing about him, usually by providing a copy of this information in tangible form, such as a printout. Usually, but not always, the right must be exercised in writing. Generally, the right is coupled with a right to have inaccurate personal data corrected. Companies may charge a fee to individuals seeking to exercise this right, but it is usually extremely low compared with the actual cost associated with providing an individual with such 'subject access' (as it is often referred to). Since the right of access can and often does extend to all personal data that a company holds about a particular individual (including emails to and from the individual), locating the personal data required to respond can be an enormous task. However, there are often exceptions to this right of access, for example, where the personal data is legally privileged or where providing access would require an organisation to expend a disproportionate amount of effort. However, these exceptions are relatively narrow so the access right itself remains fairly broad.

(b) Right of objection

Data privacy laws often give individuals a right to object to the processing of their own personal data in certain circumstances – essentially, the right to prevent certain processing of their personal data. For example, a right to object to the processing of personal data for direct marketing purposes is relatively common (often referred to as an 'opt-out'). An individual may also have the right to object to processing on certain compelling grounds, such as where the processing is unwarranted and may have a significant effect on the individual concerned, or where the processing complained of is unlawful or does not comply with the principles described above.

(c) *Compensation*

Some countries' data privacy laws give individuals the right to claim compensation if they have suffered loss as a result of a company misprocessing their personal data (ie, processing it other than in compliance with the principles). This would usually be for any financial losses but may, more exceptionally, include damages for emotional distress suffered. However, while enforcement action by a data protection authority is fairly common, often prompted by an individual complaining to the authority, private causes of action remain rare, at least for the time being. This is perhaps because of the expense of commencing litigation compared with the loss suffered, which in many cases may be modest, difficult to ascertain or even non-existent. However annoying it may be, does any real harm arise from the receipt of unwanted marketing materials?

3. **Data privacy laws in the European Union: old and new**

Data privacy laws in the European Union originate from the Data Protection Directive (Directive 46/95/EC) and largely follow the description of principles and rights set out above. However, there are certain additional requirements and differences that are worth mentioning, particularly as they can significantly impact on efforts to move data processing offshore or to make use of cloud computing providers.

Each of the EU member states that is subject to the directive has implemented its own local law giving effect to the directive. In some countries, this is simply a copying out of the directive word for word, while in other countries, implementation may have involved rewriting certain aspects of the directive in different words, amending existing data privacy legislation, or a combined approach of all three. Coupled with different cultural approaches to enforcement from country to country, the result is something of a legal patchwork. In practice, this means while a multinational company that adopts a 'one size fits all' approach to compliance can often achieve a good, or even very good, level of compliance, there may be situations or particular forms of data processing, such as communications monitoring and biometrics, where the country variations simply cannot be ignored.

One other aspect of EU data privacy laws that is rare outside the European Union but likely soon to be abolished is the process of 'notification' and 'authorisation'. This refers to the heavily bureaucratic administrative requirement that companies processing personal data must file notifications with the various data protection authorities in the countries where they are established. The notification must describe in minute detail the processing that takes place. In some situations, where the processing is of a particular type that is considered to present a higher level of risk, the data protection authority must issue an authorisation (ie, give its approval) before the processing may proceed. Overall, the notification and authorisation requirements are relatively poorly complied with by companies and are often neglected or deliberately ignored, despite the possibility of sanctions being imposed by a data protection authority in the event of non-compliance. The situation is not helped by a general lack of resources on the part of many data protection authorities, so that obtaining their response to a request for an authorisation may take many months or even, on occasion, years.

The directive (and the various member state laws that implement it) applies to the processing of 'personal data'. This is a much broader concept than many of the equivalent definitions used in other countries, such as 'personal information' and 'personally identifiable information', which can in some cases be defined by a closed list of specific categories of information (eg, name, address, social security number). The wider definition may and often does have the effect of expanding the jurisdiction of privacy laws in the European Union compared with those of other countries, simply because the category of information to which the directive applies is so broad.

Essentially, 'personal data' refers to data that 'relates to' (ie, is about) an individual who is either 'identified' or 'identifiable'. The breadth of the definition comes from data being considered as 'about' someone not only in the everyday meaning of it, but also when the processing of the data is in order to treat an individual in a particular way or might impact on them in a particular way. Equally, the circumstances when an individual may be considered as identifiable are also broadly interpreted, with some highly theoretical and unlikely circumstances being considered sufficient to raise the possibility of an individual being identified. Obvious examples of personal data include names and addresses, résumés and credit card information. Less obvious examples (where there is also less consistency between countries) include IP addresses and other online identifiers, such as cookies and mobile device identifiers.

Within the definition of personal data is a subset of data referred to as 'sensitive personal data', on which the directive imposes additional restrictions. Sensitive personal data refers to personal data about an individual's:

- racial or ethnic origin;
- political opinions;
- religious or similar beliefs;
- trade union membership;
- physical or mental health;
- sexual life; and
- criminal activity and criminal proceedings.

In order to process sensitive personal data lawfully, a company must identify at least one of a closed and relatively short list of processing criteria set out in the directive (examples include that the individual has consented to the processing or the processing is required by employment law). It is often not appreciated that in order even to process 'ordinary' (ie, non-sensitive) personal data, a company must identify a 'processing criterion'. However, for personal data this is a relatively straightforward task because the list of available criteria under the directive is much broader. When it comes to sensitive personal data, it may be difficult to find a processing criterion, and this is one of the reasons why many companies try to minimise their processing of sensitive personal data.

With definitions of personal data and sensitive personal data, as well as other legal terms such as confidential information, there is often confusion with respect to the relationship between these categories. For example, personal data and confidential information are sometimes used interchangeably as if they are either synonymous (which they are not) or as if personal data is invariably a subset of confidential information (which it is not). Sensitive personal data is sometimes talked of as if it is not also personal data (which it is). Figure 1 shows the relationship between information generally, confidential information, personal data and sensitive personal data.

Figure 1: The relationship between general and confidential information and personal and sensitive personal data

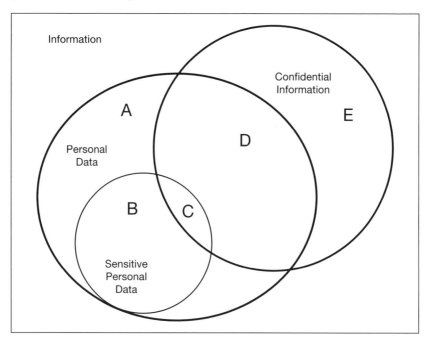

In Figure 1, 'Information' encapsulates everything, whether it is recorded in some way (eg, processed on a computer or in writing) or not (eg, communicated verbally). Some data privacy laws, including those of many EU member states, differentiate between 'information' and 'data', the main distinction being that data is recorded whereas information is not. Figure 1 does not make this distinction because it seldom matters in terms of the practicalities of compliance.

The circle labelled 'Personal Data' represents that information which is subject to the principles and rights described in section 2. Information outside this circle may be subject to other legal restrictions, such as those of confidentiality and/or intellectual property, but it is not subject to EU data privacy laws.

From the smaller circle labelled 'Sensitive Personal Data', it can be seen that sensitive personal data is a subset of personal data.

Intersecting both the personal data and sensitive personal data circles is a circle labelled 'Confidential Information'. This represents a separate category of information to which an obligation of confidence applies, which can arise contractually (eg, under a non-disclosure agreement), because of the existence of a particular relationship (eg, doctor and patient), or by some other means where the information is not already publicly known. A consequence of information qualifying as confidential information is that the organisation handling it is usually subject to an obligation of secrecy (ie, non-disclosure) and restricted in terms of what the confidential information may be used for.

The different categories of personal data and confidential information are summarised in Table 1.

Table 1: Categories of personal data and confidential information

Category	Description	Example	Obligation to comply with data privacy laws	Obligation to comply with confidentiality obligations
A	Personal data that is not confidential information.	An individual's name and contact details on an organisation's website.	Yes	No
B	Sensitive personal data that is not confidential information.	Information about a medical condition (eg, a skiing accident) made widely known by the individual concerned on a social network.	Yes	No

continued on next page

Category	Description	Example	Obligation to comply with data privacy laws	Obligation to comply with confidentiality obligations
C	Sensitive personal data that is also confidential information.	A hospital's patient records.	Yes	Yes
D	Personal data that is also confidential information.	Employee salary records stored within a human resources department.	Yes	Yes
E	Confidential information that is not personal data.	An organisation's confidential manufacturing processes.	No	Yes

3.1   The proposal for a new regulation

On January 25 2012, the European Commission published its proposal for a new EU Data Protection Regulation. One significant consequence of the regulation is that it would replace the Data Protection Directive and all the implementing laws of the EU member states in their entirety and, as a regulation, it would take effect without the need for EU member states to pass any local laws. It would also be the most comprehensive update of EU data privacy laws since the directive was introduced in 1995. At present it is merely a proposal, so it is likely to be around three years before the impact of any new regulation is felt in practice. Moreover, it is likely that many of the proposed amendments set out in the regulation will be modified through extensive lobbying during the legislative process. However, we have highlighted in the appropriate places in this chapter the provisions of the regulation which we consider are likely to remain in some form and to have an impact on compliance in practice.

One amendment that offers the prospect of significantly reducing some of the compliance cost and burden for multinational companies under the current regime is that the regulation proposes to abolish almost all the notification and authorisation requirements currently in place (as described in section 3). While it is likely that the existing external bureaucracy will be replaced, in part, by an internal bureaucracy (as described in section 5.1), the removal of the costly and time-consuming external notification and authorisation requirements is potentially a big advantage for businesses.

4.   Data breach notification

One significant requirement found under some countries' data privacy laws is the area of 'data breach notification' – that is, the requirement that the existence of a data breach (eg, a loss of personal data due to a stolen laptop, or an unauthorised disclosure of personal data due to hacking by a third party) should be brought to the attention of either the relevant regulator or, potentially, each of the individuals whose data may have been comprised by the breach. Although the United States is often (incorrectly) described as a country with laws that offer only a minimal degree of privacy protection, there can be little doubt that in the area of data breach notification, it has led the way. Starting in California in 2002, almost all US states now have some form of legal requirement to notify data breaches, and there have been many attempts to introduce federal data breach notification legislation.

In the European Union, the Data Protection Directive does not contain a requirement to notify data breaches, although some countries, such as Germany, have introduced this requirement. However, a stringent and wide-ranging data breach notification regime is likely to be introduced under the proposed regulation, requiring both data protection authorities and individuals to be notified within very short timeframes and with significant sanctions in place for those companies that fail to do so.

5.   Governance framework

Having set out numerous reasons why a company should want to comply with data privacy laws and described the common elements of the laws of most countries, it is helpful to consider a possible 'information governance' structure that would enable a company to comply with data privacy laws in a consistent and proportionate way. 'Proportionate' is the key word here, referring to the need to implement an effective and achievable compliance programme that is appropriate for the level of risk arising from the company's processing of personal data. It also refers, albeit implicitly, to the fact that it is probably impossible for any organisation to achieve 100% compliance, no matter what level of money and resources it dedicates to its compliance programme.

The level of compliance risk will vary from company to company and will generally be greater for companies that are data-rich (eg, companies processing medical information, companies offering social network platforms, credit card companies) than for companies for which processing personal data is something relatively minor and incidental to their business operations (eg, a UK-based manufacturing organisation with a fairly small workforce). In addition, the level of risk that an organisation faces will also depend on several other factors, such as the size of its work force, the complexity of its internal IT systems, the laws to which it is subject around the world and the extent of its international transfers. Described below is an information governance programme that is proportionate (ie, not too much) for most companies above a certain size, while being scalable for much larger companies, including those that may be contemplating implementing binding corporate rules internationally (these are discussed further in section 6).

Essentially, the structure set out below can be summed up as the 'Three Ps' – practices, people and paper. While there is some overlap between the 'P's, they provide a simple framework for describing the key ingredients of an information governance structure (as it relates to data privacy).

(a)   *Practices*

Some countries' data privacy laws mandate that an organisation must have a documented data privacy policy. Even in those countries where there is no such requirement, having a comprehensive and effective policy is a good idea. 'Practices' in the present structure refers to the process of documenting the various Dos and Don'ts for handling personal data internally, so that the company's handling of personal data complies in practice with applicable data privacy laws. The precise terminology used to describe the documents forming part of the governance structure may vary from company to company – in some it may be a policy, in others an instruction, procedure or guidelines. What these documents have in common, and what the 'practices' part seeks to achieve, is that they set out a comprehensive and detailed set of rules for the handling of personal data in the context of that particular company's business operations. The policy (or whatever it is called) is specific to the privacy risks faced by that company in its business operations (rather than theoretical risks faced by some hypothetical organisation processing personal data).

Such a policy may be (and often may be better) divided across several different documents, but this depends on the existing governance structure within the company. The most important consideration should be to find the best way to communicate the rules for handling personal data, so that they are readily understood and most likely to become part of the company's culture. There is little point in writing an all-encompassing, very detailed policy if in practice it will remain on the company's intranet site and be read by no one except the person who wrote it.

It is better to incorporate the data privacy policy within the company's existing hierarchy of documents, perhaps having at the top a fairly short and high-level statement of the principles that the company (and its staff) will abide by when processing personal data. Beneath this top level there may be one, two or even three further levels (depending on the company), each going into greater levels of detail about precisely how personal data should be processed in particular situations. Typically, the level of detail increases as the documents move from general statements of principle (eg, "Personal data must be collected fairly") to specific requirements that must be followed (eg, "The following call-centre script must be read out before collecting personal data on all in-bound calls"). It is also usual for the size of the intended audience for particular documents to get smaller as the level of specificity increases, with some being directed at particular groups internally, such as procurement, human resources, marketing.

(b)   *People*

No matter how good a company's data privacy policy is, and no matter how clearly communicated it may be, a company's governance programme will be less effective if it is not supported by a network of people who are knowledgeable about data privacy compliance within the company. It is hard to overstate the importance of an effective compliance network. At a senior level, the company will need to evolve its compliance programme over time for a variety of reasons – as the company's business operations develop, as laws change, as it opens offices in new countries or as it decides to roll out new systems internally. An effective privacy programme should never be fixed; it should be designed to respond to new privacy challenges faced by the company. At an operational level, someone needs to run training programmes to bring the policy to life and to respond to queries from various business units or from data protection authorities, to handle data breaches, or whatever else might be required. The policy should be thought of as just the beginning – the document that sets out what the company will do in various situations, but a successful privacy programme based on it will also require significant day-to-day direction.

How a company organises itself internally to manage data privacy compliance varies from company to company, and decision-making can often be quite fraught. Arguments over which internal function should be responsible – legal? human resources? chief information officer? marketing? compliance? – are fairly common, as is haggling over headcount and budget. Putting such internal politics to one side, the following are likely to be present in a company that takes data privacy compliance seriously:

- a dedicated privacy function;
- senior leadership of the privacy function (eg, a chief privacy officer);
- support for the privacy function at a senior management level;
- knowledgeable and experienced individuals within the privacy function;
- a network of trained data privacy 'champions' representing key parts of the company such as human resources, legal or marketing, with responsibility for privacy issues arising from day-to-day operations and a 'dotted' reporting line to, and support from, the privacy function; and
- clearly delineated responsibilities for auditing compliance.

The number of people involved, particularly in forming part of the privacy function, will depend on the size of the company and how international its operations are.

(c)   *Paper*
Although closely related to both the practices and people parts of this example information governance structure, 'paper' refers to ensuring that the paperwork aspects of compliance are not overlooked. Of particular importance for a multinational corporation is ensuring that, for as long as notifying and/or requesting authorisations from data protection authorities continues to be a legal requirement in certain countries, it has at least its key processing systems and operations notified in the countries where it has the greatest headcount or does a significant amount of business.

Various other compliance requirements fall within the paper part of the compliance programme. Depending on the solution to the data transfers issue that a multinational company has adopted, there may be more or less additional paperwork.

For example, if a multinational corporation is implementing a network of EU model clauses (described below), there will be an internal requirement to manage the signature process (particularly as companies leave or join the group) and to obtain any necessary approvals from EU data protection authorities. If a multinational company decides to implement binding corporate rules (described below), there are various formalities to be complied with, such as maintaining a list of the companies within the group which are subject to the rules. Even if a company has relatively simple operations so that it does not need to concern itself greatly with transfers of data internationally, it may still need to document certain decisions it takes, such as risk assessments made with respect to particular high-risk data processing.

5.1   Governance under the new regulation

Although the information governance structure described above is merely voluntary and best practice at present, it is likely that companies will be required to implement some or all of it once the Data Protection Regulation comes into effect, as part of the European Commission's efforts to introduce the so-called 'accountability' principle. Under this principle, companies will be required not only to comply with the regulation, but also to be able to demonstrate that they do so.

As mentioned above, the proposed regulation is likely to be modified as it is examined by the various European institutions involved. However, it seems likely that the following requirements relating to information governance will remain in one form or another.

- *policies:* companies will be required to have clear, understandable and easily available data protection policies covering their processing of personal data, together with documented procedures to ensure and to demonstrate compliance with data privacy laws;
- *detailed data protection notices:* companies will be required to provide more detailed, more helpful information to individuals regarding the processing of their personal data;
- *internal system documentation:* although companies will no longer be required to file notifications and requests for authorisations externally with data protection authorities, it is likely that they will be required to maintain internally detailed descriptions of their main data processing operations;
- *impact assessments:* companies will need to carry out and document an impact assessment in respect of processing that may present particular risks to individuals, such as certain processing of sensitive personal data or processing that could be said to be profiling individuals in a significant way; and
- *data protection officers:* companies above a certain size (in terms of headcount) are likely to be required to appoint a suitably qualified data protection officer.

6.   Data transfers

Under the Data Protection Directive, personal data may not be transferred to a country outside the European Economic Area (EEA) unless the protection in place for the data is "adequate". Although the word 'transfer' is sometimes used to refer to the sharing of personal data between two organisations, strictly speaking, under the directive, a 'transfer' refers to the movement of personal data across country or other geographical borders, which is how it is used in this section.

In order to appreciate the breath and significance of a restriction on transferring personal data out of the EEA, it is necessary to consider some examples of what amounts to a 'data transfer'.

- *example 1:* if a server storing a company's human resources information is located in an EU member state but access to it is provided to (say) senior human resources management at that company's parent company in the United States, there is a data transfer of the personal data that they access on the EU-based server;
- *example 2:* if an employee in the marketing department of a multinational company read the details of a marketing list over the phone to a colleague in the United States for him to include those details in the US marketing system, this would be a data transfer, despite the fact that the personal data has been transmitted verbally;
- *example 3:* an employee in a multinational company has an international role that causes him to travel extensively. When travelling, the employee carries a laptop containing personal data about each of his team members. This would be considered a data transfer of the personal data stored on that laptop.

Having demonstrated how broadly the concept of 'transfer' is interpreted, one can see how the restriction on transferring personal data out of the EEA could potentially disrupt the operations of many multinational companies. Fortunately, the directive also provides for certain exceptions for when personal data may lawfully be transferred out of the EEA.

- *adequacy findings:* although not exceptions as such, the European Commission has determined that the laws of certain non-EEA countries do ensure adequate protection for personal data. These countries include Switzerland, Canada (depending on the circumstances) and Argentina, as well a few other smaller countries. However, the list is very short, and not something that a multinational company will be able to rely on for its international operations generally. In particular, many of the most popular destinations for offshore outsourcing, such as India, have not been found to be adequate;
- *US Safe Harbour:* rather than being an exception, the US Safe Harbour is actually a specific form of adequacy finding in favour of the United States. Essentially, personal data may be transferred to US companies that have signed up to the US Department of Commerce's Safe Harbour scheme. The scheme creates a voluntary mechanism enabling US companies to qualify as offering adequate protection for personal data transferred to them from the European Union. In order to sign up for the US Safe Harbour, a US company must implement a privacy policy that incorporates the Safe Harbour principles, which are substantially the same as the principles and rights set

out in section 2. This is often a helpful solution to data transfer issues for companies that transfer personal data mostly to the United States, such as to their US parent company;

- *EU model clauses:* among the exceptions allowed under the directive, the European Commission has approved various sets of model contractual clauses which can be entered into between a company based in the European Union and a recipient based outside the EEA. Essentially, the EU model clauses have the effect of contractually requiring the non-EEA recipient of the personal data to handle it in accordance with the directive. Although this is a popular solution with some multinational companies, it can lead to significant complexity when implemented within a large group of companies, often requiring thousands of contracts to be put in place;

- *binding corporate rules:* in order to overcome many of the administrative difficulties associated with EU model clauses, several multinational companies, particularly larger ones, have sought to rely on binding corporate rules. Under these rules, companies implement detailed 'rules' (ie, policies and procedures that in many respects are similar to those set out in section 2) with a view to achieving a level of adequacy internally that will enable personal data to be transferred more freely from company to company. The rules must be approved by all of the relevant EU data protection authorities, although the process of doing so is made easier by a mutual recognition procedure (whereby certain data protection authorities have agreed to accept the approval of other data protection authorities without conducting a review themselves);

- *consent and other exceptions:* personal data may be transferred with an individual's consent or in certain other, rather narrow, circumstances, such as where it is necessary for the performance of a contract with the individual concerned. However, many of the EU's data protection authorities have expressed significant reservations about a company's ability to rely on consent or several of the other exceptions. Moreover, relying on individual consent will often not be the best solution because it may be withdrawn by the individual at any time and, in addition, in the context of employee data, there may be difficulties with obtaining valid consent due to the perception of unequal bargaining power between the employer and employee.

Finally, it should be mentioned that in addition to the solutions described above, for transfers of personal data out of the United Kingdom (only), a company may make its own assessment of whether there is adequate protection for the personal data, based on the particular circumstances. This often provides companies in the United Kingdom with considerably greater flexibility than in respect of transfers of personal data from other EEA countries.

The new regulation largely preserves the existing position in relation to data transfers from the EEA. Therefore, finding ways to transfer personal data out of the EEA lawfully (even within the same group of companies) will continue to be an issue that companies operating in the European Union struggle with for the foreseeable future.

7.   Outsourcing

Most companies outsource some aspects of their non-core operations to third party suppliers, whether just for a relatively small and specialised part of their operations (eg, payroll processing) or a more comprehensive, 'full scope' outsourcing of their business processes (eg, IT, human resources, procurement, and finance and accounting). In these circumstances, it is almost inevitable that the company will share personal data with the supplier concerned. This may create a very significant compliance issue for the company involved. Even if its own handling of personal data is secure and compliant with the applicable data privacy law, when a company shares personal data with a third party supplier, its compliance (in legal terms) is only as good as that of the supplier it chooses to use. In other words, although a company may outsource its personal data processing, it is not able to contract out of its legal responsibility for the personal data processed on its behalf by the supplier.

The compliance challenges presented in an outsourcing situation may increase when the third party supplier is located in a different country (at least in theory), or in other words, when the data processing is moving offshore. Offshoring presents two significant compliance requirements, the first relating to data security (including the process of selecting and contracting with the supplier), and the second relating to data transfers across country borders (as already discussed). A company contemplating offshoring its data processing should consider these two issues separately.

7.1   Controllers and processors

The data privacy laws of many countries, particularly those in the EEA, recognise a distinction between the company that 'owns' or controls the personal data (typically, the customer in an outsourcing situation) and the company that merely processes personal data on behalf of the customer (typically, the outsourcing supplier). Using the terminology of the directive, the company that controls the personal data processing – that is, the company that determines what data is collected, what it is used for, how it is processed – is referred to as the 'controller', and the company that is performing data processing under the direction of the controller is referred to as the 'processor'.

The distinction between a controller and a processor is fundamentally important for both companies. Controllers are subject to an obligation to comply with applicable data privacy laws; usually, processors are not, or at least have far fewer obligations, typically limited to implementing security measures to protect the personal data that they are processing. In other words, an outsourcing supplier is unlikely to be subject to statutory obligations with respect to the personal data that it processes on behalf of its customer, although it may have significant contractual obligations under its services agreement with that customer.

Wherever such a controller-processor relationship arises, the controller is under obligation and would be well-advised to:

- select an appropriate processor;
- contract with that processor in a manner that protects the personal data; and
- take steps to ensure compliance by the processor with its obligations with respect to the data.

7.2   Selecting a 'safe pair of hands'

Since the controller remains responsible for breaches and misprocessing by its processor, it is important that the controller selects a processor that is a 'safe pair of hands' with respect to personal data. There are many different factors that a controller should take into account when selecting a processor and, ideally, these factors should be included on the controller's selection checklist alongside other important commercial matters, such as price and quality of service. However, out of the various factors that should be considered, the following are the most significant.

(a)   *Standing, reputation and reliability*

The controller should assess its proposed processor in terms of its reputation with respect to data security and data privacy. For example, it should ascertain whether the processor has been involved in any significant data breaches and understand what the causes of these were. It should take steps to satisfy itself that culturally the processor (including its senior management) understands data privacy and security compliance and takes them seriously. Since the controller will be imposing its data security and privacy requirements on the processor contractually, it should also satisfy itself that the processor has sufficient financial resources to enable the processor's data privacy obligations to be enforceable. A contract that cannot be enforced may be no better than no contract at all.

(b)   *Data security*

The controller should ask the processor specific questions regarding the data security measures that will be used to protect the controller's personal data. A documented security policy should be put in place, which may either be the controller's own (typically incorporated into the services agreement) or that of the processor. The latter option is more likely where the processor offers a standard service, such as in cloud computing. The controller should also consider the level of security risk created by making use of the processor and take proportionate and effective steps to protect its data. In some cases, these steps will include only choosing a processor with appropriate industry security certifications (such as SSAE 16 and/or ISO 27701).

(c)   *Country-specific risks*

Particularly when considering moving data processing offshore, the controller should consider whether the location of the proposed processor (and/or its data centre) creates any specific risks that may not be obvious. Such risks may be geographical, such as a risk of the processor's data centre flooding in certain countries, or legal, such as the possibility of government access to data located in, or accessible from, a country where the processor has its operations.

(d)   *Staff training, vetting and attrition*

If the processor's staff will need to have access to the controller's personal data, it is important that they have a good understanding of their data security and privacy obligations. In practice, this makes it important that the processor can demonstrate to the controller that it has an effective staff training programme in place. This becomes even more important if the processor is located in a country that does not have a domestic data protection law because there is unlikely to be a strong data protection culture. If a processor is known to have high staff attrition rates, further enquiries should be made about the processor's training programme. High attrition levels make it essential that staff training is an ongoing process and not just a one-off event.

(e)   *Data transfers*

Although the data transfer considerations involved in offshoring are considered separately below and most data transfer restrictions can be overcome using one or more of the approaches described in section 6, if faced with a choice between a processor offering to host the controller's data in Europe and a processor using data centres distributed all around the world, the controller may decide that it prefers to choose a processor that involves the least, or least complex, transfers of data out of Europe.

7.3   Contracting with a data processor

The controller should ensure that its services agreement with its processor (ie, the outsourcing supplier) contains appropriate language to ensure that the personal data it processes is appropriately protected – a mere confidentiality agreement is not sufficient. Indeed, if the data processing is subject to the EU laws that implement the Data Protection Directive, there are certain mandatory clauses which, if they are not included in the services agreement with the outsourcing supplier, will put the controller in breach of its obligations at the outset of the engagement.

If personal data that is subject to the directive is being processed by a processor, the services agreement must, at a minimum, include:

- a requirement that the processor will only process personal data on behalf of the controller in accordance with the controller's instructions (ie, a requirement that the processor will not process the personal data for its own purposes);
- a requirement that the processor will apply appropriate organisational and technical measures to protect the personal data against unauthorised or unlawful processing and against accidental loss or destruction of, or damage to, personal data. It is common to see agreements with processors where this obligation is set out almost word for word, but the controller may express the obligation in other ways, for example, by reference to a detailed data security schedule or policy, provided the effect of the clause is that the processor is subject to a contractual obligation that is equivalent to the controller's obligation under the directive; and
- a requirement that the processor must take reasonable steps to ensure the reliability of any of its staff who may have access to the personal data.

The clauses above are the bare minimum. However, a controller that is entrusting significant data processing to a processor would be well-advised to include other protections in its services agreement, such as:

- a requirement to comply with applicable data privacy laws, at least as they apply to the processor when providing the services;
- a requirement to inform the controller of, and to assist with, any requests for access from individuals and to provide a copy of their data in tangible form. This is particularly important where the processor is processing personal data on behalf of the controller and the controller no longer holds a copy of the data itself;
- a requirement to notify the controller promptly of any unauthorised or unlawful use, disclosure or processing of any personal data of which the processor becomes aware. This is essential where the controller is subject to a data privacy laws that require it to notify data protection authorities and/or individuals of any data breaches;
- a restriction on subcontracting without the controller's prior written consent. The steps that controller has taken to choose a processor that can be trusted with its personal data may be defeated if the processor is able to delegate or subcontract part of its performance to a third party;
- a right for the controller (or its representatives) to inspect the processor's facilities where the controller's personal data is being processed. Since the controller remains responsible for the processor's processing of its personal data, it would be well-advised to give itself the means to check up on the processor's compliance with the services agreement. Under the directive, the controller is required to take reasonable steps to monitor the processor's performance of its obligations;
- a provision specifically dealing with data transfers. The content of the clause will vary depending on the particular circumstances, ranging from an outright ban on transfers out of a particular country or geography (with or without exceptions for particular named countries), to a requirement to implement EU model clauses, or to remain in the US Safe Harbour. It is important that the controller retains some knowledge and/or control over where its personal data is being processed, although, as explained in section 8, this can sometimes be difficult in the context of cloud computing;
- a requirement that, at the request of the controller, the processor should promptly return or destroy all of the controller's personal data in the processor's possession; and
- a clause specifying the controller's remedies in the event of the processor breaching the services agreement in respect of the personal data. Typically, this remedy will be expressed in the form of an indemnity, but it can be in the form of a damages claim either subject to an enhanced damages cap or possibly no cap at all. This is often one of the most hotly contested discussions in negotiations between controllers and processors.

7.4   Offshoring and data transfers

The second issue to consider when moving data processing offshore to a processor are data transfers. The restrictions on transferring personal data out of the EEA, as well as other countries with similar restrictions, are described in section 6. Faced with a situation where a processor (or one of its affiliates or subcontractors) may process personal data offshore, the controller must implement one of the solutions identified in section 6 to make the data transfers lawful.

Realistically, there are only three options available to a controller established in the EEA. The first option only applies where the controller is established in the United Kingdom and not in other EEA countries, so that only the UK legal requirements for transferring personal data need to be satisfied. As described in section 6, in this situation it is possible for the controller to make its own assessment of 'adequacy' and, if it is satisfied that the level of protection is sufficient, it may transfer the data to the processor without taking further steps. One very significant factor that can lead a UK controller to conclude that it may transfer personal data out of the EEA is where it has implemented a sufficiently robust data processing agreement with the processor concerned, such as, for example, one that includes the provisions set out in section 7.3.

The second option applies EEA-wide – that is, in respect of data transfers from all EEA countries – but only where the processor is located in the United States and is a member of the US Safe Harbour. However, even in this situation it is essential to have a data processing agreement in place with the processor, irrespective of where the processor is located. A second point to check is that the processor's Safe Harbour certification actually covers the controller's data, as opposed to the processor's own data; this is a common failing on the part of processors seeking to rely on the US Safe Harbour to persuade controllers to hand their personal data over to them. Under the US Safe Harbour arrangement, it is possible for the processor to subcontract some of its processing to third parties, including those in other countries, subject to meeting certain requirements. When contracting with a processor in the US Safe Harbour, the controller should enquire whether there may be such onward transfers.

Where the controller's EEA operations are not limited to the United Kingdom and the processor is not within the EEA (or any of the countries that have an 'adequacy finding') and either not in the United States or not a member of the US Safe Harbour, currently there is only one other option available to the controller to make its data transfers lawful. It must require the processor to sign with the processor the EU model clauses (described in section 6) for data transfers between controllers and processors.

7.5 Offshoring and the new regulation

The new regulation will not ease the process of moving personal data processing offshore to a processor significantly. First, the underlying restrictions on transferring personal data out of the EEA largely remain intact, as does the relative lack of solutions available for overcoming them. One additional possibility that may emerge and which is mentioned in the new regulation is the possibility of so-called 'processor binding corporate rules', under which a multinational company that acts as a processor and has multiple data centres and companies involved in processing on behalf of a controller may be designated as offering adequate safeguards, such that the controller's personal data may be more freely, and lawfully, transferred between the processor's data centres.

The new regulation is also likely to introduce additional requirements for the agreements between controllers and processors, including, for example, requirements that the processor may only subcontract with the controller's permission, and must hand over to both the controller and the data protection authority details of its compliance processes and procedures.

8.   Engaging a cloud computing provider

A full description of cloud computing is beyond the scope of this chapter, but essentially the term is used here to refer to situations where an IT supplier delivers 'computing' as a service via the Internet or some other communications link. 'Computing' in this sense may be computing infrastructure, such as additional storage capacity or functionality, such as access to a particular software application online. Rather than a company having to purchase additional hardware and license software itself, it receives as a service the benefit of the supplier's hardware and software by using them remotely. Cloud computing can offer a company great flexibility and scalability in its operations, with the ability to grow its computing resources without having to invest in expensive IT assets itself. This, together with the possibility of it being at a lower overall cost than a more traditional IT set up, has made it very popular.

On the whole, everything that has been described with respect to engaging a supplier and moving data processing offshore applies with full force when engaging a cloud computing supplier; indeed, many suppliers' methods of delivery could probably have been described as cloud computing long before the phrase became popular. Nevertheless, there are some additional considerations that may be particularly relevant when considering engaging a supplier of cloud computing.

(a)   Location of data centres

It is highly likely that the cloud provider will make use of various data centres, and these may be distributed around the world and potentially managed by various third parties. Inevitably, this increases the complexity of data transfers involved and makes it more difficult for the controller to achieve a good level of compliance with applicable data privacy laws, even where the cloud provider is willing to cooperate by executing EU model clauses or joining the US Safe Harbour. The controller's difficulties become almost insurmountable when the cloud provider is unwilling to cooperate in this way and also refuses to accept a restriction on transferring the controller's personal data out of the EEA.

(b)   Data security

One of the well-publicised concerns expressed about cloud computing is on data security – how can a company know that its data is safe if it is 'somewhere' in the cloud, particularly if it is being stored within data centres all over the world? In practice, it is likely that the controller's data is better protected in the hands of a large cloud provider with robust data security practices in place than in the hands of the (often less sophisticated) controller itself. Moreover, it is in the interests of the cloud provider, and its reputation, to make sure that all data is properly protected.

However, when it comes to contracting, it is often the case that the standard terms and conditions of the cloud provider do not enable controllers to satisfy their statutory obligations with respect to data security. In other words, there is often a significant gap between the security measures a cloud provider applies in practice (and 'sells' to the customer) and what they actually offer from a contractual point of view. From the controller's perspective, the way their data is protected in practice is more important than what is written on paper.

(c)   *Standard terms and conditions*

All too often in negotiations with cloud providers, controllers are told, "It's a standard (or commoditised) offering and so we cannot change our terms". Certainly, there is a significant reluctance on the part of most cloud providers to move away from their standard contractual positions on most issues. Nevertheless, faced with the prospect of losing a large deal or a trophy client, many will negotiate. Controllers should not be afraid to ask, particularly in respect of any significant concerns and changes required for them to meet their obligations under applicable data privacy laws, but they should be realistic too. Cloud computing providers are generally reluctant to agree changes to their terms that would require them to handle the data differently in practice (because their systems are standardised), but may be more willing to change terms that do not have any operational consequences.

(d)   *Law enforcement access*

Concerns have been raised, particularly in Europe, over foreign governments, and overseas law enforcement in particular, obtaining access to a controller's data. Often, such discussions focus on the USA Patriot Act, legislation that allows the Federal Bureau of Investigation to require a company subject to US jurisdiction to hand over certain business records if they are necessary for foreign intelligence purposes. Most of the concerns have been expressed by EEA-based companies and data protection authorities, who fear that personal data being processed by a US-owned cloud provider (whether in the United States or elsewhere) may be subject to such an order. In fact, the scope of the bureau's rights under the Patriot Act is far narrower than many assume. A discussion of the act is beyond the scope of this chapter, but in practice it is unlikely to be an issue.

9.   Conclusion

It has never been more important that companies at least make serious efforts to comply with data privacy laws, even if they do not ever achieve full compliance. Indeed, full compliance is likely to be an unachievable goal, bearing in mind the complexity of most multinational companies' systems and processes and the plethora of applicable data privacy laws around the world. It could even be argued that it is better not even to aim for full compliance, but rather just good compliance (or perhaps very good), because all too often, by attempting to do everything, companies end up achieving very little, becoming bogged down in the magnitude of the task and all the detail involved. Generally, it is far better for a company to acknowledge that realistically it will not be able to achieve full compliance for a long time (if ever) and to focus on those systems, processes and operations that present the greatest compliance risk to the company. It should identify these risks and deal with them as a priority, before moving on to the next greatest risks. By addressing compliance in this way and continually prioritising, a company can make sure that, at any point in time, it is spending its time, money and efforts on the compliance steps that from a business point of view will have the greatest positive impact.

Corporate information risk management

Rita Esen
University of Northumbria

1. Introduction

Generally, risk is viewed in a negative sense as it is often defined in terms of an event that may have an adverse effect on a defined goal. Risk management is the process of taking systematic steps to identify risks and to analyse and respond to those risks. Risk management is not a new process. What is relatively new is the management of risks associated with information assets and the use of information systems. Managing risks to information collected, stored and shared on systems/networks requires continuous assessment of the adequacy of controls that are in place to protect data and the systems on which they are stored. In today's information age, organisations have to manage many aspects of information risk, including the risk of attack from outsiders, errors and mistakes in information processing, deliberate inappropriate activities by insiders, and information technology (IT) system failures. These risks have to be managed on an ongoing basis in order to determine the security control requirements for each class of information. Although periodic assessments of information risks can identify the magnitude of harm that could result from specific incidents, they must be followed up with mitigating actions in order to ensure that appropriate controls are implemented to address identified risks.

This chapter highlights the need to manage information risk in today's global information network systems and provides a breakdown of the key areas of information risk management – establishing the context, information risk assessment, and discussion of the various elements of risk analysis and evaluation. An examination of the treatment of identified risk is used to illustrate that mitigation is not the only option for organisations – they may also avoid, transfer or accept. The final part of the chapter looks at the important aspects of communicating the result of the risk assessment process with key stakeholders and the monitoring of risks on an ongoing basis to ensure that new threats are identified.

2. Establishing the context

Before an organisation can effectively manage its information risks, it must set the context of the risk management programme by identifying its structure, capabilities, goals, strategic objectives and operational processes. This should help the organisation to determine the acceptable level of risk to its information and information systems and in turn should form the basis for the control and mitigating actions that are to be effected. Establishing the context requires identifying the boundaries of the process with a clear indication of the scope of the risk management activities. The risk management process may require prioritising the most critical information assets and processes of the organisation, in which case a phased approach would be the preferred option for carrying out an organisation-wide risk assessment.

In order to establish the context for effective information risk management, the organisation's strengths, weaknesses, threat and opportunities must be understood. Before conducting the risk assessment, the timeframe needed to complete the process and the geographical location to be covered must be considered. To establish the context, the key stakeholders must be identified and channels of communication with them must be set up. As individual stakeholder's circumstances may change over time, their information requirements and the risks to such information should be reviewed regularly to enable the effective management of such risks. During this preparatory phase, the resources required for the risk assessment process need to be identified and should include both internal and external resources.

3.   Information risk assessment

The process of information risk assessment determines the value of information assets in an organisation, identifies the potential threat and vulnerability to such information and the existing controls that are in place to protect it. The information risk assessment consists of the following processes.

3.1   Risk identification

Risk identification is the process that is used to determine what could happen to cause a potential loss of information. It answers the questions of how, where and why loss to information assets may happen in an organisation. Information risk identification should include all risks that affect the organisation, whether the source of the risk is internal or external.

3.2   Identifying the assets

For risk to be effectively identified, the assets that are at risk must be determined. An asset is anything that is of value to an organisation which needs to be protected. Without knowing what information needs protection and what happens when the protection fails, it would be impossible to identify the risks to such information. All corporate information assets should be identified with enough detail to enable an efficient assessment of risks that they could be subject to. Information assets often take the form of databases, financial information, corporate intellectual property and other vital business information. Asset identification should aim to include the IT systems, resources and information that are critical to the business operations of the organisation.[1] As each entry in the database does not need to be treated individually, the whole collection of data in the database may be treated as one information asset that is subject to certain privacy and storage risks. Irrespective of the nature and form of information assets, they normally have one or more of the following characteristics:

---

1   Scot Laliberte, Risk Assessment for IT Security, August 2004, *Bank Accounting & Finance*, 39.

- they are recognised to be of value to the organisation;
- they are not easily replaceable without cost, skill, time or resources; and/or
- they form part of the organisation's corporate identity, without which the organisation may be threatened.

Information asset owners should be identified in each service and operational area to provide responsibility and accountability for identified assets. The asset owners should provide assurance that information risk is being managed effectively for the information assets that they 'own'. The main responsibilities of an information asset owner are to understand 'owned assets', what information is associated with their asset and the nature/justification of information flows to and from the assets.

Asset identification should include identifying the storage media and systems that allow information to be grouped. The more a group of information assets contributes to the organisational objectives, the greater its value to the organisation. During identification, information assets may be ranked in an order of priority for risk assessment and treatment; this is determined by how critical they are to the organisational objectives. Asset identification should include some form of classification to identify and rank data, systems and applications in their order of importance, which will allow the organisation to ensure consistent protection of information assets in a system. This enables it to focus its efforts in a structured manner. The classification given to an information asset determines how it is protected, who has access to it and what system/network it runs on.

3.3   Identifying the threats

Apart from identifying information assets and owners, a key element of risk identification is the process of identifying the threats to these assets. A threat is an indication, circumstance or event with the potential to cause loss of or damage to an asset. Another way of defining threat is the possibility for an information asset to have its security breached. Threat identification is the process of determining threat sources that have the potential to exploit some weakness in the information system. All information threats should be identified generically and by type, with individual threats within a generic class being identified in such a way that no potential threat is overlooked. Information asset owners in different business areas are the people with the knowledge to identify potential threats to their information assets and the likelihood of the threat occurring. Past experience from information incidents and threat assessments should be taken into consideration when identifying a possible threat to information and information systems.

Information threat may be classified into four groups:

- deliberate actions by individuals, which may result from the activities of those inside an organisation or from outsiders, and may be further classified into malicious and non-malicious threats. An example of an insider malicious threat is an employee shredding an accounts document to destroy evidence of fraudulent accounting in the finance department;
- accidental actions by individuals, occurring when the activity was an

unintended action by either an insider or an outsider;[2]

- systems problems, including hardware problems, software problems and malicious code. An example of this is a server crashing with the result that files on the hard drive are unrecoverable; and

- environmental/natural factors – any weather, physical or environmental conditions that could cause threat to information assets, such as earthquakes, fire, flood and power cuts.

During this phase, it is important to identify all threat sources that could cause harm to corporate information assets.

3.4   Identifying existing controls

Existing controls and security safeguards may be classified as administrative, technical or physical security controls. Administrative security controls are primarily policies and procedures that are already in place to define and guide employee actions in dealing with an organisation's information assets – for example, the organisation's information security awareness programme, which is used to make employees aware of their information security roles and responsibilities. Technical security controls (also known as logical controls) are devices, processes and protocols used in protecting an organisation's information assets, such as firewalls, intrusion detection systems and encryption systems. Physical security controls are devices used to control physical access to information and to protect the availability of the information, including physical access barriers such as fences, physical intrusion detection systems such as motion detectors, and physical protection systems such as backup generators.

The technical and physical security controls may each be categorised into three groups – preventive, detective and corrective controls. Usually, preventive security controls are put in place to prevent intentional or unintentional disclosure, alteration or destruction of information. Examples of these include a statement in a policy document that unauthorised network connections are prohibited and the use of firewall in an organisation to block unauthorised network connections. Detective security controls identify and report any unauthorised or undesired event in an organisation's information systems. These controls are invoked after the undesired event has occurred and may be in the form of a systems audit, log monitoring or motion detection. Corrective security controls are used to respond to or fix a security incident with the aim of eliminating, limiting or reducing the damage caused by the attack, for example, removing a virus from an organisation's infected system after an attack by a malicious code.

Existing controls should be identified in order to avoid the duplication of controls and unnecessary costs. The existing controls should be checked to ensure that they are working as a non-functional control may result in vulnerabilities. The

---

2   Stefan Fenz and Andreas Ekelhart recognise that that human threats to information may exploit a vulnerability either deliberately or accidentally: Fenz, Stefan; Ekelhart, Andreas; and Neubauer, Thomas (2011) "Information Security Risk Management: In Which Security Solutions Is It Worth Investing?," *Communications of the Association for Information Systems*: Vol. 28, Article 22.

key aim of identifying existing controls is to check their ability to reduce the threat likelihood and to ease any exploitation of the vulnerability. If an existing control is identified as insufficient or ineffective, it should be replaced. The identification of existing controls may involve conducting an on-site review of the physical controls and checking implemented controls to ensure that they are effective.

3.5   Identifying vulnerabilities

The identification of risks to information assets must include the identification of vulnerabilities associated with information and information systems. Vulnerability describes the problem that allows a system to be attacked or broken into. It denotes a weakness in the system that allows an attacker to violate the system's integrity. Attackers exploit existing security vulnerabilities on systems to gain unauthorised access to the systems and the data they hold. Vulnerability may be technical, such as bugs in software, or non-technical, such as a user disclosing their personal password to an unauthorised person. The aim of identifying vulnerabilities is to develop a list of possible flaws and weaknesses that could be exploited by the potential threat sources. An example of a vulnerability is a terminated employee's system identifiers (ID) not being removed after termination, with the threat source being the terminated employee. The threat to information assets in this case is the possibility of the ex-employee dialling into the company's information systems and network to access confidential corporate data.

Vulnerabilities with no corresponding threat may not require a control to be established, but should simply be identified and monitored for future changes. Vulnerability can be grouped into two categories – general vulnerabilities and information-specific vulnerabilities. General vulnerabilities include basic weaknesses in software, hardware, information resources, processes and procedures. Information-specific vulnerabilities include the use of unsecured computers and unsecured wireless systems. System vulnerabilities are identified using vulnerability sources, system security testing and a security requirement checklist. Vulnerability sources may be identified from previous risk assessment documentation, systems audit reports and system testing/evaluation reports. System security testing and evaluation can be used to identify IT system vulnerabilities during a risk assessment process. The purpose should be to test the effectiveness of security controls as they have been applied in an operational environment. Penetration testing may be used to assess the system's ability to withstand intentional breach of security controls.

In addition to these methods of systems testing, an automated vulnerability scanning tool can be used to scan a network for known vulnerable services. Another method of identifying vulnerability sources is to use a security requirement checklist. Generally, this shows the basic security standards that are used to evaluate and identify the vulnerabilities of an information asset, and may be presented in table form. It is used to evaluate whether the identified controls are effective and, where they are not implemented, they will be regarded as a vulnerability source. A suggested list of security criteria for technical and personnel security is given in Table 1 on the following page.

Table 1: Technical and personnel security checklist

Technical security	• Access control • Authentication • Encryption • Network access • Firewalls • Remote access
Personnel security	• Background • Confidentiality • Supervision • Qualification/certification • Training • Termination processes

3.6 Identifying consequences

Identifying consequences is the process of highlighting the damage to an organisation that could be caused by an incident scenario. An incident scenario is the description of a threat exploiting a certain vulnerability or a set of vulnerabilities in an information security incident. The process of identifying consequences identifies the effect that losses of confidentiality, integrity and availability may have on information assets. During this phase, the damage to an organisation's information and systems that could result if any identified threats occur is highlighted and documented. The likelihood of a threat becoming a reality and the magnitude of the consequences of the event depends on the effectiveness of the controls that are in place.

4. Risk analysis

Risk analysis focuses on the extent of the consequences that would arise from a risk event and the likelihood of the event occurring. During risk analysis, potential threats to information assets are mapped to the risks associated with them. Risk is a function of the likelihood of a given threat exercising a particular potential vulnerability and the resulting impact of that adverse event on an organisation. In order to determine the likelihood of an adverse event occurring, the potential vulnerability must be analysed in conjunction with the security controls in place to protect the information. Consequence refers to the magnitude of impact that could be caused by a threat's exercise of potential vulnerabilities. The result of the combination enables an organisation to determine situations that would give rise to major and unacceptable risks rather than minor and acceptable ones.

4.1 Risk analysis methodology

There are two methods of risk analysis – qualitative and quantitative. The preferred methodology depends on the circumstance of the case. A qualitative risk analysis is based on applying the categories, consequence and likelihood to each of the two-dimensional risk attributes. Unlike the quantitative method, a qualitative risk analysis does not involve numerical probabilities or predictions of loss. Instead, it defines the various threats, determining the extent of vulnerabilities, and devises countermeasures to address the identified risks. Therefore, it involves using specific descriptive scales to determine the likelihood of an event occurring and the extent of the consequence. In qualitative analysis, the magnitude and likelihood of potential consequences are presented and described in detail. The scales used can be formed or adjusted to suit the circumstances, and different descriptions may be used for different risks. If the quantitative approach is used, the risk analysis team must agree on the probability estimates.[3] The benefits of the qualitative approach are that it overcomes the challenge of calculating accurate figures for asset values and the process is much less demanding on staff. The drawback of this method is that the results can be vague and may not be a very useful tool for corporate decision-makers.

The aim of a quantitative risk analysis method is to provide a numerical value for each of the components, that is, to determine a numerical value for the probabilities of various adverse events and the likely extent of the losses if a particular event took place. Numerical values are assigned to both impact and likelihood, and these values are derived from a range of sources. The quality of the entire analysis depends on the accuracy of the assigned values and the validity of the statistical models used. Determining the monetary value of an asset is an important part of risk management, and the quantitative approach is the method used to estimate the monetary value of the cost of information assets to an organisation in the event of a compromise. Estimations are usually made with regard to what it would cost the organisation in terms of lost productivity, loss of reputation, legal actions, and other direct or indirect costs. The value attached to information assets enables an organisation to determine the budget and time that should be spent in securing the information. The benefit of using this method is that information assets are prioritised by financial values and the results are expressed in management-specific terminology – monetary value. The drawbacks are that the values assigned to various risks are based on the subjective views of the analyst and the process is a complex, time-consuming one.

4.2 Threat analysis

Information threats are the agents that violate the protection of information assets and site security policy. Usually, threat analysis will assume a level of access skill that a particular attacker may possess. A key challenge in threat analysis is that the intent of the attacker cannot be determined. A threat source may be either internal or external to the organisation. An internal attack, which requires inside access to information systems, should be differentiated from external attacks. An external threat may be a structured, an unstructured or a transnational threat. Generally, a structured external threat will be quite sophisticated. An unstructured external threat

---

3   Rex Rainer, Jr, Charles Synder and Houston Carr, Risk Analysis for Information Technology, 1991, 8(1) *Journal of Management Information Systems*, 133.

is usually caused by an individual, such as a hacker or cracker, and normally lacks the sophistication of the structured threat. Generally, unstructured threats limit their attacks to information system targets and the motivation of the attacker is usually less hostile than its structured counterpart.

4.3 Vulnerability analysis

In order to determine the risk that a set of information assets are exposed to, the potential vulnerabilities that may be exploited must be analysed. Vulnerabilities are configuration errors and operation errors which allow unauthorised users to enter systems and take unauthorised actions in breach of legal or regulatory requirements. Vulnerabilities may be exploited intentionally (malicious) or unintentionally (non-malicious), with the result that the confidentiality, integrity and/or availability of the organisation's information assets may be impacted. When analysing the vulnerability of an information asset, a range of potential vulnerabilities should be taken into consideration, from obvious ones such as failure to authenticate down to subtle ones such as symmetrical key management. The aim of this phase of risk analysis is to develop a list of possible vulnerabilities that could be intentionally exploited or accidentally triggered with a resulting security breach or violation of systems security policy.

A major study, the Program Analysis study,[4] has classified vulnerability causes into four categories:

- improper protection, initialisation and enforcement, as a result of incorrect initial assignment of security privilege level at when the system is initialised or set up. It could also be a result of improper isolation of implementation details, which allows users to bypass operating system controls and manipulate a hidden data structure;
- improper validation, which is the result of failure to check critical conditions and parameters;
- improper synchronisation, such as improper sequencing, which may allow actions in an incorrect order; and
- improper choice of operation by the use of unfair scheduling algorithms that block certain processes or users.

4.4 Assessment of likelihood

Once it has been determined what potential vulnerabilities may be exploited, the next step is to estimate the likelihood of this happening. Likelihood is the probability that a potential threat may be exercised against the asset under review. It is a qualitative estimation of how probable a successful attack is, based on past experience. Identifying the likelihood of most events occurring can be subjective; it is based on the knowledge and expertise of those involved in the risk analysis. However, evidence and statistics may be available on the recurrence of certain events and this information will help in assessing the likelihood level. The following factors

---

4   R Bisbey and D Hollingsworth, Protection Analysis Project Final Report, 1978, Information Sciences Institute, University of Southern California.

are normally taken into consideration when analysing likelihood: the threat motivation and capability; the vulnerability impact; and the effectiveness of existing controls.

Threat motivation depends mainly on the knowledge of the actor or the reason behind his or her activities. For example, a dismissed employee may be more motivated to hack into a university information system than a first year student who simply hacks into the system for the fun of it. Direct vulnerabilities tend to result in a highly likely severe impact on the assets; if the vulnerability is indirect, the likelihood will be low. Existing controls and their effectiveness can determine how likely or unlikely it is that a vulnerability will be exploited. If strong, effective controls are in place, they will work to prevent, or at least significantly impede, the vulnerability from being exploited.

Table 2: Likelihood descriptions

Descriptor	Frequency of event occurring
Unlikely	Not expected to happen but definite potential exists – unlikely to occur.
Possible	May occur occasionally, has happened before on occasions – reasonable chance of occurring.
Likely	Strong possibility that this could occur – could occur several times.
Almost certain	This is expected to happen frequently/in most circumstances – more likely to occur than not.

4.5   Assessment of consequence

Once the likelihood is determined, the consequence of the risk on the organisation must be agreed. In identifying the consequence level, the worst-case scenario has priority. This phase involves determining the impact that would result from a successful threat exercise of a known vulnerability, and impact is the degree of harm to information that can be caused by risk.[5] In assessing the impact of an incident on an organisation and its information assets, account should be taken of the consequences of the breach of information security – the loss of confidentiality, integrity and availability.

(a)   Loss of confidentiality

Confidentiality is used to prevent information from being disclosed to unauthorised

---

5   George Tolbert, Residual Risk Reduction: Systematically Deciding What is Safe, November 2005, *Professional Safety*, 26.

persons and can be enforced on information by encryption in order to prevent unauthorised disclosure during transmission. By controlling access to information and preventing unauthorised disclosure, a system can achieve confidentiality. The value of confidential information is high when it involves personal information, as individuals expect that their personal information will remain confidential. An example of loss of confidentiality is an insecure email, sent to several recipients, which contain confidential information and discussions by staff outside the office about their colleague's sensitive information.

(b) Loss of integrity

Loss of integrity occurs if information is modified without authorisation, by a party that is authorised to access the information/system or by an unauthorised party. When information integrity loss is malicious, the user purposely adds, deletes or modifies the information.

(c) Loss of availability

Information availability is the assurance that information and communications systems will be ready to use when expected. Loss of availability may be caused by denial of service attack, through trojans, worms or viruses, which work to deny the user access to information or systems. As information is now the lifeline of businesses, it is extremely important that users are able to access information when they need it.

5. Risk evaluation

The level of risk to information assets is determined by the likelihood of the threat being exercised and its consequence or impact on the organisation. In assessing the likelihood and impact, existing controls must be taken into consideration. During the risk evaluation phase, decisions must be made on which risks need treatment and which do not, and on the treatment priorities. Analysts need to compare the level of risk determined during the analysis process with risk criteria established in the risk management context (ie, in the risk criteria identification stage). It is important to note that in some cases the risk evaluation may lead to a decision to undertake further analysis. Risk evaluation must also take into account the organisation's objectives, the stakeholder views and, of course, the scope and objective of the risk management process itself.

The overall risk level is normally determined on the basis of inputs from threat likelihood and threat consequence categories. The likelihood and consequence levels are then cross tabulated to give a risk exposure rating and this determines whether a risk is categorised as red, amber, yellow or green. Use of colour coding facilitates rapid communication and understanding of risks. Prioritising of risks that are assigned the same risk exposure rating is achieved by examining the strength of the control measures in place for those risks. For example, a 'high' rated risk could have effective control measures in place that cannot be improved upon, whereas a 'medium' rated risk may not have any control measures in place, and this is the risk that should be prioritised for action by the team. The matrix in Table 3 shows the rating of low, moderate, high and extreme risk that an organisation's information assets may be exposed to if a specific vulnerability is exercised. Table 4 outlines the prioritisation of actions following a risk assessment.

Table 3: Determining risk level

Impact	Likelihood				
	1	2	3	4	5
	Rare	Unlikely	Possible	Likely	Almost certain
5 Catastrophic					
4 Major					
3 Moderate					
2 Minor					
1 Negligible					

Key 1 to 3 Low risk ▨ 4 to 7 Moderate risk ■ 8 to 14 High risk ■ 15 to 25 Extreme risk

Table 4: Prioritising action following a risk assessment

Risk level	Action and time scale
Low Risk value 1 to 3	No action is required to deal with trivial risks, and no documentary records need to be kept.
Moderate Risk value 4 to 7	No further preventive action is necessary, but consideration should be given to more cost-effective solutions, or improvements that impose no additional cost burden. Monitoring is required to ensure that the controls are maintained.
High Risk value 8 to 14	Efforts should be made to reduce the risk, but the costs of prevention should be carefully measured and limited. Normally, risk reduction measures should be implemented within three to six months, depending on the number of people exposed to the hazard. Where the significant risk is associated with extremely harmful consequences, further risk assessment may be necessary to establish more precisely the likelihood of harm as a basis for determining the need for improved control measures. *Enter the risk on the risk register.*
Extreme Risk value 15 to 25	Work should not be started or continued until the risk has been reduced. Considerable resources may have to be allocated to reduce the risk. Normally, if the risk involves work in progress, the problem should be remedied within one to three months, depending on the number of people exposed to hazard. *Enter the risk on the risk register.*

7. Risk treatment

Risk treatment is the process of selecting and implementing actions that are to be taken to address identified risks to information assets. The output of the risk matrix will determine the actions to be taken by risk treatment. As the elimination of risk is impracticable, the least expensive and most effective approach should be used in treating identified risks. Risk treatment involves identifying a range of options to reduce the consequences and/or likelihood of an identified risk. Possible treatments include avoidance, transference, mitigation and acceptance.

7.1 Avoidance

Some information risks are not worth taking, and the best action is to avoid the risk completely. Avoidance is the risk control action that prevents the exploitation of the vulnerability. It may be achieved by removing vulnerabilities in information assets and limiting access to assets, using three methods – application of policy, training/awareness and application of technology. Risk avoidance through application of policy allows management to mandate that certain procedures should always be followed or that specific actions should be taken by system users. An example is a clause in a corporate security policy stating that users of personal computers should not install unauthorised software. This should work to reduce the risk of unauthorised software infecting an organisation's information system.

Whenever new technological systems are installed, all potential users should be given training to ensure that they are aware of the risks and that they use the system in a safe way and do not put corporate information assets at risk. With the fast changes in IT and its uses, training on new systems should not be a one-off process but should be refreshed regularly so that staff remain up-to-date in the use of such systems. Ongoing technical support should be built into the awareness programme so that users are continuously supported in the use of the systems. Apart from risk to information assets, failure to train staff in the use of IT systems may result in productivity falling and business operations being disrupted. The application of appropriate technology may have the effect of avoiding risks to corporate information assets, for example, the use of one-time passwords that are valid for only one log-in session or transaction. One-time passwords help to avoid the risks associated with the use of traditional passwords, such as replay attacks.

7.2 Transference

Risk transference is the process of shifting any losses incurred as a result of the risk to a third party. Although risks can be transferred in a number of ways, a typical method is the use of an insurance policy. The insurance policy does not alter the threat or likelihood of the risk occurring, but simply reduces the impact that the risk has on the organisation – the impact cannot be removed completely from the organisation but is instead shared between the organisation and the insurance company. Another method of transferring risk is to outsource the relevant activities to a third party. Usually, outsourced activities are not the core business of the outsourcing organisation and may include back-office functions such as payroll, human resources and data entry.

A key element of modern-day outsourcing is business process outsourcing, which encompasses call centre outsourcing, human resources, finance and accounting outsourcing. Although outsourcing allows an organisation to transfer the risk associated with the management of its information systems to another, it is not without its own risks. In recognition of the risk of outsourcing, Kumar warns that before organisations decide to outsource, they should give due consideration to these risks.[6] Organisations that outsource must ensure that the service level agreements with their service provider address information privacy and security. Disaster recovery plans and business continuity plans should be key features of the service agreements. A disaster recovery plan should identify the processes that have been put in place to limit losses before and during disasters and help recovery from an information incident. A business continuity plan should highlight the steps necessary to ensure the continuity of the organisation when a disaster occurs that affects outsourced information assets.

7.3 Mitigation

Mitigation is the process of taking steps to reduce the negative effect caused by the exploitation of vulnerability on the organisation. There are three possible ways of reducing risk to corporate information assets – by reducing the threat, by reducing the vulnerability or by reducing the impact. In order to reduce the threat to information assets, the threat source must first be identified. An effective method of reducing threat is by removing or preventing the threat source, for example, removing the threat of a malicious insider who accesses and changes information on systems without authorisation by denying access to such systems or termination of employment. The vulnerability of the systems may be easily reduced by disabling the employee's access log-in on termination or tightening the security setting of the system if the individual remains an employee of the organisation. The business impact may be reduced by effective mitigating actions through the implementation of appropriate controls.

There are three main categories of control that can be used to reduce the impact of identified information risks in an organisation – administrative controls, physical controls and logical control.

(a) Administrative controls

Administrative controls, often referred to as procedural controls, make up the framework used in running a business and managing the people involved. They comprise of approved policies, procedures, standards and guidelines. They inform staff how the business is to be run and how business operations are to be conducted. Administrative controls form the basis for the selection and implementation of physical and logical controls. Some sectors have specific standards and guidelines that must be followed by organisations within the sector. For example, all organisations within the health sector must adhere to the NHS Code of Confidentiality and the NHS Information Security Code of Practice.[7]

(b) Physical controls

Physical controls work to monitor and restrict the workplace by ensuring that only

---

6   Nayak Kumar, IT Risk Management Program: Managing Risk in Organisations, December 2009, 2(12) *Advances in Management*, 5.
7   Department of Health, Information Security Management: NHS Code of Practice, 2007.

authorised persons have access to workplace facilities. They address the design implementation and maintenance of countermeasures that protect the physical resources of an organisation. Physical controls work to protect the people, systems, hardware and resources associated with corporate information assets. Most physical control devices are aimed at restricting the movement of people as well as safeguarding information assets within the workplace, for example, the use of smartcards to control access to locked rooms and information system resources. Another key aspect of physical control is the prevention of physical interception of data. The three methods of data interception – direct observation, interception of data transmission and electromagnetic interception – must be effectively controlled to ensure risk mitigation.

(c) **Logical controls**

Logical controls, also referred to as technical controls, are the use of software to monitor and control access to information and computer systems. Although some logical controls are easy to circumvent, such as passwords, a number are quite robust and difficult to break, such as encryption, which is used to protect data in transit, such as data transferred via networks and mobile telephones. The process of encryption transforms data to make it unintelligible to anyone without the decryption key, and may also be used to protect data at rest, such as files in computers and storage devices. Risks such as loss of personal information through the theft of laptops or memory sticks can be controlled through the use of encryption technologies. An important aspect of logical control is the process of least privilege, which requires that an individual or program is not granted any more access privilege than is necessary to perform the required task.

7.4   Residual risk

Even after the different types of control – administrative, physical and logical – have been implemented, usually some risk remains which cannot be completely removed, and this is referred to as residual risk. Residual risk is the risk that remains after all attempts have been made to counter, mitigate or eliminate known information risks in an organisation. According to Whitman and Mattord, the goal of information risk management is not to bring residual risk to zero but to ensure that residual risk is in line with an organisation's risk appetite.[8] If residual risk is below the acceptable level, no action need be taken, but if it is above acceptable risk, additional controls must be used to mitigate those risks. If the residual risk is above the acceptable level and the cost of decreasing such risks would be higher than the impact, a prudent action would be to accept the residual risk.

7.5   Acceptance

When an organisation accepts identified risks after they have been evaluated, it simply acknowledges that the risks exist but does not take any action to mitigate

---

8   Michael Whitman and Herbert Mattord, *Principles of Information Security,* Second Edition, 2005, Thomson Course Technology, 163.

them. Therefore, risk acceptance is about making cost-effective decisions on resource investment.[9] Generally, this strategy would be used after an organisation has assessed the probability of the attack, estimated the potential impact, performed a cost/benefit analysis and decided that the assets do not justify the cost of protection. When mitigating risks to information assets, the organisation has to decide the level of risk it is willing to operate with – this is referred to as the risk appetite of the organisation. Risk appetite is the nature and level of risk that an organisation is willing to accept as a balance between achieving extreme security and enjoying accessibility. It is an indication of the extent to which an organisation is willing to take risk in order to meet its strategic goals.

Every organisation has an appetite for some types of risk and is adverse to others – this depends on the nature of the assets and their role in the organisation. An organisation should clearly identify its risk appetite in order to provide guidance to its staff on the level of risk permitted so that there is consistency of approach in the organisation. The importance of risk appetite in the risk management process has been stressed by the UK Corporate Governance Code, which states that "the board is responsible for determining the nature and extent of the significant risks it is willing to take in achieving its strategic objectives".[10]

8. Risk communication

Risk communication is two-way process between the various stakeholders on the existence, nature, form, severity and acceptability of identified risks. It is the process of providing information asset stakeholders with awareness of the risk assessment undertaken, the analysis and the treatment processes, and their outcome. The communication process should work to improve stakeholders' understanding of identified risks and the steps taken to address them. Risk communication is essential as it helps to achieve consensus among the stakeholders on the appropriate method to be used to manage identified risks and the acceptable level of risk. Effective communication should disseminate the result of the risk assessment and present the risk treatment plan to stakeholders, as they are the group that will implement the plan. Risk communication documents should aim to give stakeholders and decision-makers a sense of responsibility in agreed risk treatment methods.

9. Monitoring and reviewing risks

All identified risks and their components, such as threats, vulnerabilities, probability of occurrence and consequences, should be monitored on an ongoing basis. The monitoring is necessary to ensure that new threats that are brought about by changes in the organisation are identified. Regular reviews of risk factors are used to verify that the criteria used in measuring the risk remain consistent with the business goals. During monitoring, steps should be taken to ensure that identified risk response measures have been completely and correctly implemented. Failure to implement

---

9   Thomas Longstaff, Clyde Chittister, Rich Pethia and Yaco Haimes, Are We Forgetting the Risks of Information Technology?, December 2000, *Computer*, 44.

10   Principle C.2, UK Corporate Governance Code, June 2010.

agreed controls may result in the breach of corporate information-related policies or procedures and regulatory requirements. Where implemented risk response measures fail to achieve the desired level of effectiveness, the likelihood is that the controls have either not been correctly implemented or that they are not functioning as expected.

Monitoring and reviewing the risk factors as well as controls enables the organisation to identify changes to information processes, systems and the environment in which information assets are handled. New types of risk can arise with changes to information systems, such as software, hardware and infrastructure. Changes in information processing environments may change existing risks or introduce a new set of information risks – for example, if an organisation decides to outsource some of its services to a third party, which may require the organisation to revisit its underlying risk assumptions as there will be significant changes to its threat, vulnerabilities and likelihood identification processes. Usually, the frequency of risk monitoring and review is determined by the impact of the risk if not properly controlled and the level of change to the organisation's information, systems and infrastructure.

10. Conclusion

Every organisation, both private and public, is experiencing some form of information risk as data has become the lifeblood of organisations worldwide. The ever-growing use of information, systems and networks comes with the potential threats and risks to corporate information assets. The current globalisation of business processes has created an increasing amount of data, so effective information risk management is crucial. Today, corporate bodies must meet legal and regulatory requirements in personal information processing, with the result that the classification of information has become the key to the effective protection of person-identifiable information. In order to ensure the continued confidentiality, integrity and availability of information, organisations must identify, assess and effectively treat risks to their information assets. As the requirement to manage corporate information assets improves its profile, discussions on risks associated with IT failure are finding their way to the boardroom. Organisations have to take positive steps to protect their information assets, as the value of corporate information is directly linked to the success of business operations.

Managing legal risks in China

Fang Ma

University of Hertfordshire

1.   Introduction

With China's increasing drive towards full integration with the global economy, both Chinese and foreign investors have been presented with tremendous business opportunities. Due to the relative immaturity of the Chinese stock markets for raising capital, Chinese companies may look to foreign investors to invest in Chinese business. When foreign investors purchase shares in a Chinese company, they become shareholders and they may also sit on the board of directors. As such, legal risks may arise from ineffective corporate governance and insufficient protection of shareholders' interests under Chinese law. In light of the increasing foreign investment in China, more lawyers, even outside of China, are required directly or indirectly to manage China-related legal compliance risks. In order to manage and minimise such risks, it is essential to examine the legal framework on corporate governance and the protection of shareholders' interests in China. The distinct legal, economic, political and social background to company law should also be taken into account.

The Chinese Company Law 1993[1] played a significant part in the economic development of China and the state-owned enterprise reform of the 1990s;[2] however, it was unable to adapt to the new changes as the market economic reforms intensified. In particular, the poor protection given to minority shareholders was considered to be a major obstacle to China's economic growth.[3] As a result, there had been increasing demand for comprehensive reform of the Company Law 1993 in order to facilitate the market economic reforms.[4] The Chinese Company Law 2005[5] is regarded as being "unusually broad in scope introducing a large number of truly bold new measures" and it brings the provisions of Chinese company law more closely in line with its counterparts in more developed economies.[6] Many Western investors who are used to more sophisticated corporate governance might expect similar standards in China; nevertheless, there are key differences in relation to the

---

1   The Company Law of People's Republic of China 1993 came into force on January 1 1994.
2   Xiaosong Xu, *The Company Law and the Research of SOE Reform* (Law Press, Beijing, 2002), pp 161-170.
3   L Miles, "The Implications of the State's Majority Shareholder on Corporate Governance in China" (2005) 8 *Company Law Newsletter* 1, 3.
4   Fei Li (ed), *Annotation of the Amendments to the PRC Securities Law* (Law Press, Beijing, 2005), p 3.
5   The Company law of People's Republic of China 2005 was promulgated on October 27 2005 and came into force on January 1 2006. It replaced the Company Law 1993.
6   Baoshu Wang and Hui Huang, "China's New Company Law and Securities Law: An Overview and Assessment" (2006) 19 *Australian Journal of Corporate Law* 229, 242. C Hawes, "Interpreting the PRC Company Law Through the Lens of Chinese Political and Corporate Culture" (2007) *University of New South Wales Law Journal* 813, 813.

corporate governance structure and the protection of shareholders' interests in China and Western countries such as the United Kingdom.

Through comparison with English law, this chapter examines how foreign investors manage legal risks when investing in a Chinese company; in particular, when their shareholders' rights have been infringed or when directors or supervisors breach their duties. Part 2 considers the economic, political and legal background to the development of Chinese company law. Part 3 evaluates the problems with corporate governance structure in China in relation to the allocation of power among shareholder meetings, board of directors and board of supervisors. Part 4 analyses the current law on shareholders' rights and remedies. It is argued that an effective corporate governance structure together with a sound system for enforcing directors' duties and protecting shareholders' interests are essential to reduce legal risks for foreign investors in China.

2. Economic, political and legal background

Historically, the nature of a country's economy is the major driving force behind its corporate development, while specific economic conditions and political policies at a particular time can combine to influence the nature, structure and development of corporate governance.[7] In China, the introduction and development of companies has happened over a very short, recent time. This is in sharp contrast to the gradual emergence and centuries-old growth and development of companies in England, during which commercial considerations of a market-orientated economy have always been paramount. However, in China, corporate development has been very closely linked to political objectives and as such has not necessarily reflected the actual needs of a market-orientated economy.[8] Therefore, it does not serve the same purpose as that in England.

After 1949, a socialist or planned economy based on public ownership was established in China. Private companies were soon nationalised or collectivised[9] and state-owned enterprises established. The latter remained as the main driving force and business vehicle in China until the end of the 1970s. The government not only owned all the properties of state-owned enterprises but also enjoyed managerial powers. As such, state-owned enterprises were not independent legal entities, but simply channels through which the government organised economic resources and activities.[10] In the late 1970s, China initiated a series of economic reforms designed to transform the economy into a market economy.[11] One crucial area was improving state-owned enterprises' performance by delegating responsibility to them for their own gains and losses in the market.[12]

---

7   Yuwa Wei, *Comparative Corporate Governance – A Chinese Perspective* (Kluwer Law International, 2003), p.177.
8   Fu Jian and Yuan Jie, *PRC Company & Securities Laws – A Practical Guide* (CCH Asia Pte Limited, 2006), pp 16-17.
9   Kirby, "China Unincorporated: Company Law and Business Enterprise in Twentieth-Century China" (1995) 54 J Asian Stud 43, 58.
10 Mei Shenshi, *Research on the Structure of Modern Corporate Organs' Power: A Legal Analysis of Corporate Governance* (Publishing House of China University of Political Science and Law, 2006), p 33.
11 Yuwa Wei (2003), p 74.
12 Miles (2005), p.1.

In the early 1990s, the Chinese central government launched a new series of economic reforms[13] with the aim of incorporating state-owned enterprises into independent business enterprises such as companies. The Company Law 1993 was promulgated to facilitate this reform by providing, for example, a legal foundation for the establishment and operation of limited liability and joint stock companies. Many traditional state-owned enterprises were restructured and incorporated as joint stock companies or listed on the Shanghai and Shenzhen Stock Exchanges, which had been established in 1990 and 1991 respectively.[14] In this way, the government was able to utilise Chinese citizens' personal savings and foreign investment as useful capital to boost economic development.[15]

Currently, China is still in a transitional stage in developing its aim of a full-blown socialist market economy. After more than two decades of reform, beginning with the mid-1980s separation of state from enterprises, the government's intervention in the management of corporatised state-owned enterprises is still considered by some commentators as the fundamental reason for the failure of such reforms.[16] In reality, the government continues to interfere frequently and directly with the management of its enterprises in various ways, such as requiring its approval of board decisions, bypassing general meetings and directly appointing directors and executives.[17] Yu has correctly argued that China cannot achieve the goal of using Western law to improve the inefficiency of corporatised-state-owned enterprises unless the state withdraws or considerably reduces its exercise of ownership in these companies.[18] A crucial and fine line needs to be drawn between the government's right as a majority shareholder and its governmental power. Olaerts convincingly suggests that European investors in China have to take into account the fact that "they will not be able to operate their business as autonomously as they might be used to in their own legal system since they can be confronted with governmental interference".[19]

3. Corporate governance structure in China

Managing legal risks for investors should be considered in the broader context of corporate governance, which is concerned with "the relationship between the board of directors, management and shareholders".[20] As many management powers are delegated to boards of directors, who are regarded as agents of both the company and

---

13   For detailed discussion, see A Chen, *Introduction to the Legal System of the PRC*, 3rd edn, (Butterworths Asia, Hong Kong, 1999).

14   Liu Ban, "Private Sector Catches Listing Fever", *China Daily*, February 25 2003.

15   Fred Hu, "Beijing's Paradigm Shift", *Asian Wall Street Journal*, July 4 2000.

16   Li and Hua, "To Reform the SOEs in a Way of Seeking Truth from the Facts", in *The Analysis and Forecast of The Chinese Economic Situation of 1998 – A Blue Paper of the Economy* (Li Guo-Guang (ed), Soc Sci Literature Press, 1997), p 209.

17   Schipani and Liu, "Corporate Governance in China: Then and Now" (2002) Colum Bus L Rev 1, 29.

18   Guanghua Yu, "Using Western Law to Improve China's State-owned Enterprises: Of Takeovers and Securities Fraud" (2005) 39 Val U L Rev 339, 340.

19   M Olaerts, "Euro-Chinese Company Models: An Exploratory Journal into the Position of Directors, Shareholders and Stakeholders in Chinese and European Company Law" (2009) *Maastricht Journal of European and Comparative Law* 171, 180.

20   Department for Trade and Industry, *Modern Company Law for a Competitive Economy* (HMSO, March 1998), para 3.5.

shareholders collectively, there is a risk that agents may act dishonestly or incompetently as a result of the separation of ownership and control.[21] Effective corporate governance can provide an internal solution to redress disputes within a company and, to some extent, prevent misconduct by majority shareholders or directors. This section examines, by comparison with English law, the main types of companies in China and the allocation of power among shareholder meetings, the board of directors and the board of supervisors.

In China, only limited liability companies and joint stock companies may be set up under the Company Law 2005.[22] They share the same two identifying features as the companies limited by shares in England – the principles of limited liability and separate legal personality.[23] In a limited liability company, the number of shareholders is limited to 50 and the liability of a shareholder is limited to the capital contribution he subscribes.[24] In a joint stock company, there is no maximum limit to the number of shareholders. Its capital must be divided into shares of equal value and the liability of a shareholder is limited to the number of shares he subscribes.[25] It is well recognised that limited liability companies are broadly similar to private companies limited by shares in England, while joint stock companies are broadly similar to public companies limited by shares in England.[26]

In England, the unitary board model operates with a single board of directors composed of both executive and non-executive directors. In China, similar corporate governance requires the establishment of shareholders' general meetings, a board of directors and a board of supervisors for both limited liability companies and joint stock companies.[27] A general meeting is regarded as the supreme organ of authority of a company, with extensive powers to exercise control over the company's affairs.[28] The board of directors is responsible for managing the company,[29] while a board of supervisors has the right to supervise corporate management and the activities of directors and managers.[30]

The one-tier structure in England aims to create an internal form of supervision whereby non-executive directors oversee management by executive directors. The two-tier system in China aims to create a hierarchical system with a supervisory board above a board of directors. Although different in form, the rationale underlying corporate governance in both jurisdictions is the same: to put restraints

---

21   Berle and Means, *The Modern Corporations and Private Property* (Transaction Publishers, 1991, originally published in 1932), p 51.
22   Access to Chinese company formation is more restricted for foreign investors. The two main types of companies – limited liability company and joint stock company – are not available to foreign investors. Foreign investors may set up an equity joint venture, a contractual joint venture, a wholly foreign-owned enterprise or a foreign-invested company limited by shares. Despite the specific rules on foreign investments in China, a knowledge of Chinese company law is essential for foreign investors because the Company Law 2005 applies to foreign-invested companies with limited liability and such companies limited by shares (Article 218).
23   *Salomon v Salomon & Co* (1897) AC 22.
24   Company Law 2005, Articles 3 and 24.
25   *Ibid*, Articles 3 and 126.
26   Fu and Yuan (2006), p 13.
27   S Shim, "Corporate Governance Reform in China" (2005) 26 Comp Law 375, 376.
28   Company Law 2005, Article 100.
29   *Ibid*, Article 109.
30   *Ibid*, Article 119.

on directors' power and therefore to reduce agency costs. This is because the management of a company is delegated to directors who do not have ownership of the company and who may not act in the best interests of their company. It is argued that the corporate governance structure in China is ineffective in protecting the interests of minority shareholders, although the corporate standards in China have been brought much more in line with those of the developed market economies under the Company Law 2005.

3.1 Shareholders' general meeting

The shareholders' general meeting in a limited liability company or joint stock company, as the supreme organ of the company,[31] is granted extensive rights and absolute control.[32] It is entitled to determine the business operation policies and investment plans of the company; to elect and remove directors or supervisors who are not employee representatives; and to determine the remuneration of directors and supervisors. The general meeting can review and approve the reports of the board of directors or board of supervisors as well as the plans for annual financial budget, profit distribution and the recovery of losses. It also has the power to decide on a reduction or increase in the company's capital, the issue of debentures, and the merger or winding-up of the company. Most importantly, it may alter the articles of association and enjoy other powers conferred by the articles. A general meeting therefore has control of all the company's powers, including the management of business; by contrast, the board of directors only carries out resolutions passed at general meetings.

When shareholders exercise their extensive powers by voting, they must not abuse their rights and cause losses to the company or other shareholders; otherwise, they will be liable for compensation. Moreover, if they abuse the principles of corporate legal personality and limited liability and infringe the company creditors' interests, shareholders will be jointly and severally liable for the company's debt.[33] Thus, investors have to take into account the interests of their company and other shareholders when exercising their rights.

3.2 Board of directors

The board of directors, which is accountable to shareholders' general meetings, must consist of between three and 13 directors in a limited liability company[34] and between five and 19 directors in a joint stock company.[35] It has the power conferred by the articles of association, including the power to convene and report to shareholder meetings, to carry out resolutions passed at shareholder meetings, to decide the company's management and investment plans, to draft plans on the company's annual budget and profit-distribution, to increase or decrease the share capital, and

---

31   *Ibid*, Article 37 (for limited liability companies) and Article 99 (for joint stock companies).
32   *Ibid*, Article 38 (limited liability companies) and Article 100 (joint stock companies). Jinzhu Yang, "Shareholder Meeting and Voting Rights in China: Some Empirical Evidence" (2007) 18 ICCLR 4, 6.
33   *Ibid*, Article 20.
34   *Ibid*, Article 45. In a small limited liability company, an executive director may be appointed instead of setting up a board of directors (*Ibid*, Article 51). A small limited liability company is defined as a company with a small number of shareholders or with small business.
35   *Ibid*, Article 109.

winding-up or merger. The board is also entitled to determine the appointment and removal of the company's managers and their remuneration.[36] Although the board of directors provides information and proposals to shareholders, it is the shareholders who make business decisions and the board of directors that implements them.

As a general meeting has the power to appoint and remove directors, doubts have been cast on the independence and integrity of the board to run the company, especially if there is a majority shareholder. Without strict duties imposed on them, directors may act in their own best interest and that of the majority shareholders rather than that of the company. For the first time, the Company Law 2005 expressly imposes the duty of loyalty and the duty of care on directors, supervisors and senior managers.[37]

(a)   *The duty of loyalty*

Directors, supervisors and senior managers must comply with laws, administrative regulations and the company's articles of association; they must not misappropriate the company's property or accept bribes or other illegal gains by taking advantage of their authority.[38] Article 149 of the Company Law 2005 provides a detailed list of activities that directors, supervisors and senior managers must not engage in, such as misappropriating company's funds or depositing the company's funds in an account in their own or another's name. They are prohibited from self-dealings;[39] for example, they should not, in violation of the company's articles of association or without the consent of the shareholder meeting or the board of directors, enter into contracts or carry out transactions with the company. Similarly, they must not take advantage of their position to acquire business opportunities for themselves or any other person, or to engage in a business identical to the company's business for the benefit of themselves or any other person. They must not lend the company's funds to others or provide any guarantee to any other person by using the company's property. Moreover, they are prohibited from taking commissions on the transactions between their company and others, and from disclosing the company's secrets without permission. Above all, a catch-all provision is included in Article 149(8), where directors, supervisors and senior managers are refrained from undertaking "other acts that breach their duty of loyalty". The duty of loyalty, although similar to the concept of fiduciary duty in England, is not clearly defined in China; further judicial interpretations may help to clarify the meaning and scope of such duty.

(b)   *The duty of care*

The duty of care is of great significance for the protection of the interests of shareholders and the company. As directors have the discretion to propose business strategies and prepare reports for shareholder meetings, without such a duty, they

---

36   *Ibid*, Article 47 (limited liability company) and Article 109 (joint stock company).
37   Senior manager is defined in Article 217 of the Company Law 2005 as "a manager, deputy manager, any person in charge of a company's finance, the secretary of the board of directors of a listed company as well as any other person as stated in the articles of association".
38   Company Law 2005, Article 148.
39   *Ibid*, Article 149.

could misuse their power and infringe shareholders' interests. The Company Law 2005 clearly imposes the duty of care on directors, supervisors and senior managers[40] but, unlike the duty of loyalty, it fails to address any specific rules, such as defining the duty of diligence and which standards should be adopted. It does not specifically require directors to have any expertise or knowledge of the company's business. The lack of essential knowledge might put the interests of the company and shareholders at risk. It is suggested that the English approach, which combines both objective and subjective standards for the duty of care, skill and diligence,[41] may be of benefit to future Chinese company law reforms because they are well-established and have been tested in practice over a long period of time.

(c)   *Corporate social responsibility*
When directors make business decisions, they must also consider corporate social responsibilities. Article 5 of the Company Law 2005 states that:

> *When undertaking business operations, a company shall comply with all laws and administrative regulations, and respect social and business morality. It shall act in good faith, accept the supervision of the government and the general public, and bear social responsibilities.*

This mandatory approach is in stark contrast to the approach of enlightened shareholder value in England, where directors are required only to take into account the interests of other stakeholders when making management decisions.[42] Hawes is of the view that the mandatory requirement of social responsibility "clearly reflects the Chinese Government's wish to guide and closely monitor corporate behaviour".[43]

3.3   Board of supervisors
In a limited liability or joint stock company, the board of supervisors must consist of at least three people,[44] including representatives of shareholders and the company's employees. At least one-third must be representatives of the company's employees. In theory, a board of supervisors should be in a position to monitor the activities of the board of directors as they attend board meetings and have first-hand knowledge. However, the question arises as to what extent a supervisory board can effectively monitor the board of directors and safeguard the interests of the company. Based on the discussion below, it is argued that the board has only limited supervisory power and it lacks independence, especially in listed companies with the state as the majority shareholder.

First, the powers of the supervisory board have been enhanced under the Company Law 2005.[45] The supervisory board may now propose to dismiss directors;[46]

---

40   *Ibid*, Article 148.
41   Section 174 of the Companies Act 2006. *Re Barings plc* (No 5) [1999] 1 BCLC 433.
42   Section 172 of the Companies Act 2006.
43   C Hawes, "Interpreting the PRC Company Law Through the Lens of Chinese Political and Corporate Culture" (2007) *University of New South Wales Law Journal* 813, 821.
44   Company Law 2005, Articles 52 and 108. In a small limited liability company, there should be one or more supervisors; there is no requirement for setting up a board of supervisors.
45   *Ibid*, Articles 54 and 119.
46   *Ibid*, Article 54(2).

to convene and hold interim shareholders' meetings;[47] and to initiate litigation against directors on the request of shareholders.[48] However, it still has no power to dismiss directors because the final decision lies with the general meeting.[49] In companies with a highly concentrated share ownership, it is doubtful whether the supervisory board can challenge the misconduct of directors who are connected with the majority shareholders.

Secondly, supervisors are still not totally free from the influence of directors or the controlling shareholders because of the supervisory board's required composition. There is a lack of independence as a supervisory board must include representatives from shareholders and employees.[50] As employees rely on management superiors for promotions, remuneration and personal progression, it is difficult for them to be totally independent when conducting the company's affairs. Moreover, in most cases, shareholders on the supervisory board are appointed by the majority shareholders and tend to represent only the latter's interests, while members from relevant government authorities are usually appointed as supervisors in corporatised-state-owned enterprises.[51] By creating such boards, the government can continue to influence the operation of a company through the placement of administrative bureaucrats on them, even when it loses its controlling interest in the company. Therefore, it is easy to compromise the independence of supervisors and any supervision of the board of directors is at best perfunctory and at worst non-existent.

Thirdly, the inadequate regulations on supervisory powers and implementing procedures ultimately affect the management and the performance of a company's business.[52] Moreover, all Chinese-listed companies must use the independent director system, which is designed to supervise the board of directors and improve the corporate governance of listed companies.[53] Thus, the role and functions of the board of supervisors and independent directors overlap to a great extent and further law reforms are urgently required to clarify their functions. In conclusion, a supervisory board under the current law does not function efficiently or independently to monitor either a board of directors or a management team.

The allocation of power among shareholders' general meetings and the boards of directors and supervisors allows majority shareholders to be in total control of the company. The situation for minority shareholders in China is comparably worse than that in England because of the extensive power given to shareholders' general meetings, the lack of independence of boards of directors and the lack of real supervisory power of the boards of supervisors. Compared with the well-established directors' duties in England, the vague and undefined duties in China make it more difficult for directors and supervisors to perform their duties, for shareholders to detect breaches of such duties and for judges to enforce them. Thus, the interests of

---

47   *Ibid*, Article 54(4).
48   *Ibid*, Articles 54(6) and 152.
49   *Ibid*, Article 100.
50   *Ibid*, Article 118.
51   Fu and Yuan (2006), p 11.
52   *Ibid*.
53   *The CSRC Guideline Opinions on the Establishment of Independent Directors within Listed Companies* (2001).

a company and its minority shareholders may be infringed either by the misconduct of majority shareholders or by the management. In most cases, shareholders resort to litigation when corporate governance fails to function properly.

4. Shareholders' rights and remedies

Shareholders' remedies are important tools to prevent and address management inefficiencies and directors' breach of duties, and thereby protect the interests of companies and shareholders. In China, the interests of minority shareholders were not clearly recognised or well protected until the company law reform of 2005. The Company Law 2005 contains a number of ground-breaking mechanisms to protect minority shareholders' interests. Shareholders in China are afforded a wide variety of rights, similar to those enjoyed by their counterparts in England. For example, shareholders are entitled to participate in corporate management by proposing resolutions at shareholder meetings,[54] and they may access corporate information by examining the original corporate accounts of limited liability companies for bona fide purposes.[55] The cumulative voting system for the election of directors and supervisors in joint stock companies is used.[56] In addition, shareholders' protection has been greatly enhanced in relation to personal actions and derivative actions. It is argued here that these rules have filled some of the gaps left by the Company Law 1993; however, these new remedies are still inadequate in protecting the interests of minority shareholders.

4.1 Shareholders' personal actions

Shareholders are entitled to challenge the validity of resolutions passed at a shareholders' meeting or decisions adopted at a board of directors meeting.[57] They are also entitled to bring personal actions against directors and senior managers,[58] and against other shareholders, including majority shareholders.[59] Moreover, they may be bought out by the company when they disagree with certain management policies;[60] and they have the right to petition the court to wind up the company in certain extreme circumstances.[61] However, it is argued that these remedies are vague in their scope and inadequate for addressing any misconduct of majority shareholders or management; for example, shareholders have no remedy if the company's affairs are conducted in accordance with the law but are unfairly prejudicial to the interests of minority shareholders.[62]

(a) The right to challenge the validity of shareholder resolutions or board decisions

Article 22 grants shareholders of both limited liability companies and joint stock

---

54 Company Law 2005, Article 103.
55 *Ibid*, Articles 34 and 98.
56 *Ibid*, Article 106.
57 *Ibid*, Article 22.
58 *Ibid*, Article 153.
59 *Ibid*, Article 20(2).
60 *Ibid*, Articles 75 and 143.
61 *Ibid*, Article 183.
62 By contrast, the unfair prejudice remedy is available to shareholders in England under Section 994 of the Companies Act 2006.

companies the right to challenge the validity of resolutions passed at shareholders' meetings or decisions made at board of directors meetings. If their content violates any law or administrative regulations, the resolutions or decisions will be void; for example, if a resolution requires all the shareholders to provide a guarantee for a company's debt, the resolution will be void from the time of passing. If their content violates only the company's articles of association or if the procedure in convening or voting violates the laws or administrative regulations, such resolutions or decisions should be voidable; for example, if shareholders are not notified of a shareholders' meeting in advance or the notice does not include the proposals for the resolutions before the meeting, or the minimum requirement of the votes is not satisfied for the passing of resolution. Article 22 aims to protect the interests of third parties from violation of a company's articles of association, since they are unlikely to be familiar with the articles, which regulate the internal relationships within the company.[63]

In order to achieve the certainty of various transactions between a company and a third party, a shareholder must exercise the right to revoke the voidable resolutions or decisions within 60 days of the resolution being passed.[64] This time limit has been criticised as being too restrictive and unfair in some situations; for example, if the majority shareholders pass a resolution without notifying the minority shareholders, who then do not find out about the resolution until after the 60-day limit.[65] In order to prevent undue interference in a company's management, the court may require the claimant shareholders to provide an appropriate guarantee or security for expenses if requested by a company.[66] The criteria for such security are not specified and therefore which factors the courts take into account is unclear.

Article 22 aims to strike a proper balance between the certainty of the resolutions and the effectiveness of the protection of shareholders' interests.[67] It appears that Article 22 allows shareholders too much freedom to interfere with a company's management because they are always entitled to request the court to revoke resolutions or decisions subject to the statutory requirements, no matter whether their rights or interests are infringed, or even if they are invoking trivial procedural irregularities. It is unclear whether a court will allow shareholders to sue when a majority or all of the shareholders agree to ratify an irregularity. There is a danger of malicious actions and an increase in the amount of litigation coming before the courts, which will disrupt a company's ordinary course of management. In order to strike the right balance between minority shareholders' protection and the company's day-to-day management, it is recommended that the English "internal irregularity principle"[68] should be introduced into China to filter out vexatious shareholder actions.[69]

---

63   Liu Junhai, *Institutional Innovations of New Corporate Law: Legislative and Judicial Controversies* (China Law Press, 2006), p 239. Yulin Qian, "Voidable Resolutions of Shareholders' Meetings" (2006) *Legal Science* 11, 37.
64   Company Law 2005, Article 22(2).
65   Zonglin Chen, "The Validity of Companies' Resolutions and the Protection of Minority Shareholders' Interests – Art 22 of the Amended Company Law", www.chinacourt.org, August 29 2006.
66   Company Law 2005, Article 22(3).
67   Ping Jiang and Guoguang Li (eds), *The Interpretation of The Amended Company Law* (People's Court Publishing House, 2005), p 118.

(b)   The appraisal rights

The Company Law 2005 entitles shareholders who disagree with a number of specified transactions to demand that the company buys their shares at fair value. These appraisal rights aim to strike an appropriate balance between majority shareholders who wish to reform their company strategies and dissenting minority shareholders who want to sell their shares and leave the company. The appraisal rights, which allow dissenting shareholders to withdraw their investments from companies, not only facilitate the companies' management operation but also protect minority shareholders' interests.[70] Due to the different nature of limited liability companies and joint stock companies, they have separate and different provisions for the appraisal rights of their shareholders.

A limited liability company shareholder may request the company to purchase his shares at a reasonable price if he votes against the resolution at the shareholder meeting in one of the three situations:[71]

- if the company has been making profits and meets the conditions for distributing profits as prescribed in Article 167 but fails to distribute its profits to the shareholders for five consecutive years;
- if the company merges, divides or transfers its substantial assets; and
- if the period of business stipulated by the company's articles of association expires or if other situations as stipulated by the articles arise for the dissolution of the company but a resolution is adopted at shareholder meetings to revise the articles in order to continue the company's existence.

Article 75 also outlines the procedure for the enforcement of appraisal rights. If within 60 days from the date of a resolution, passed at a shareholders' meeting, the shareholders and the company cannot reach an agreement about the purchase of the shares, shareholders may file an action within 90 days of the date of the resolution.

A joint stock company shareholder may request the company to purchase his shares if he objects to a resolution on merger or division made at a shareholders' general meeting.[72] This scope is much narrower than that for limited liability companies. Jianzhu An has suggested that joint stock company shareholders who are dissatisfied with the company's management may sell their shares and leave the company.[73] In terms of procedure, Article 143 stipulates that shares should be purchased within six months; nevertheless, it fails to specify the date from which the six months should run. Moreover, it fails to specify the procedure for the valuation of shares. There is no guidance as to what a reasonable price is. If a fair price cannot be reached, as Qian has correctly argued, the appraisal rights might well be used as a means of disadvantaging the dissenting minority shareholders.[74]

---

68   *Foss v Harbottle* (1843) 67 ER 189.
69   F Ma, "A Challenge for China: Is it Possible to Introduce Unfair Prejudice Remedies? Part 1" (2009) ICCLR 417, 424.
70   Junhai Liu (2006), p 216.
71   Company Law 2005, Article 75.
72   *Ibid*, Article 143(1).
73   Jianzhu An (ed), *Interpretations of the Company Law of the People's Republic of China* (Law Press, 2005), p 203.
74   Weiqing Qian, *Corporate Litigations – Judicial Remedies* (People's Court Press, 2006), p 111.

Despite their shortcomings, the appraisal rights provide a win-win solution for both dissenting shareholders and their company. However, they are 'no-fault' provisions: there is no need to prove misconduct of the company or directors' breach of duties.[75] As long as minority shareholders are unsatisfied with the resolutions in certain situations, they may ask the company to purchase their shares. The permission of the unilateral withdrawal may be abused by minority shareholders who deliberately object to resolutions in order to be bought out.

(c)   The winding-up remedy

The winding-up remedy is essential for the protection of minority shareholders when disputes within a company cannot be resolved by other means.[76] Shareholders may petition for a winding-up only if all four requirements under Article 183 are met:

- shareholders hold 10% or more of the voting rights of the company;
- the company's operation or management is in serious difficulty;
- the shareholders will suffer heavy losses if it continues to exist; and
- the dispute cannot be resolved by any other means.

This remedy is justly criticised as being abstract, vague and inadequate for the following three reasons.[77] First, the lack of restrictions on the shareholding period may be used for malicious actions by shareholders – in particular, those who bought shares for short-term profit on the stock exchange market. Secondly, there is no guidance on the interpretation of "serious difficulty in a company's operation or management" or "heavy loss" suffered by shareholders. Gu has suggested that it should also apply to situations in which minority shareholders suffer oppression from the majority and will suffer great loss if the company continues to exist.[78] Thirdly, Article 183 does not explain "by any other means". Due to the drastic consequences of a winding-up order, it is likely that the Chinese courts will regard it as the weapon of last resort, as is the case in England.

4.2   Derivative actions

Derivative actions play an important part in building a better regime for corporate governance, in particular, in deterring directors from breaching their duties, in holding directors accountable to their companies, and in protecting the interests of companies and shareholders.[79] Derivative actions were introduced for the first time in China under Article 152 of the Company Law 2005. Under this article, if a director, supervisor, senior manager or "any other person" violates the laws or administrative regulations, and has caused losses to the company, shareholders who have the right to bring an action and who meet the procedural requirements may challenge the misconduct. This is an extremely broad scope of respondents compared with that in England, where it

---

75   Ma (2009), p 424.

76   See the case of *Jian v Chuangtaiwo Ltd* [2006] Foshan Court No 330 where the claimant successfully requested the court to wind up the company.

77   Ma (2009), p 425.

78   Gengyun Gu, *Interpretation of China's New Company Law* (Beijing University Press, 2006), p 175.

79   F Ma, 'The Deficiencies of Derivative Actions in China' (2010) *Company Lawyer* 150, 150.

only applies to directors.[80] Different rights requirements are laid down on the shareholding percentage and period for both joint stock companies and limited liability companies. Joint stock company shareholders must hold separately or aggregately no less than 1% of the company's shares for at least 180 days.[81] These requirements are not imposed on limited liability company shareholders; any shareholder in a limited liability company is qualified as a claimant in a derivative action. The less restrictive approach reflects the sympathies for limited liability company shareholders due to their difficulties in transferring their shares and leaving the company;[82] however, an easy access to judicial remedies is often accompanied by the risk of increased litigation and potentially a rise in the number of malicious actions.

In terms of procedure, shareholders who wish to bring derivative actions must make a written demand to either the board of directors or the board of supervisors.[83] If the directors or senior managers breach their duties under Article 150,[84] the written demand should be made to the board of supervisors. If the supervisors breach their duties under Article 150, the demand should be made to the board of directors, or to an executive director of a limited liability company which does not have a board of directors. This cross-demand aims to avoid a conflict of interests when the board makes its decision on the litigation. If the board of directors or supervisors refuses to start the litigation, or fails to bring an action within 30 days of receipt of the request, a shareholder is entitled to bring a derivative action.[85] In order to provide a timely remedy for shareholders when the demand is not met, the demand requirement may be exempted in "emergency situations" or "when the damage to the company will be irrecoverable if shareholders do not bring proceedings immediately".[86] However, the meaning of the emergency situations is unclear.

The demand rule aims to make full use of all the company's internal remedies and to save the time and expense of litigation if the board decides to ratify the misconduct or to sue the wrongdoer. However, it can be criticised for the lack of requirements on the content of the demand and of rules for shareholders to take over actions from either another claimant or the company if it has failed to do so diligently. There are also concerns about whether a board can make independent and impartial decisions on the shareholders' demand because it is not required to investigate the veracity of the content of the demand or to justify their decisions. The shareholders' lack of access to relevant information and the inflexibility of the time limit are additional concerns.[87]

---

80   Companies Act 2006, Section 263.
81   Company Law 2005, Article 152(1). In 2006, the Supreme People's Court promulgated the judicial interpretation entitled "Regulations on the Application of Company Law of the People's Republic of China". Article 4 states that claimants for derivative actions must be shareholders for at least 180 days until the day when the litigation is initiated.
82   Zhiyong Zhang, "The Rules on Derivative Actions in the Company Law Reform Proposal Draft 2005" (2005) 5 *Chinese Lawyer* 52, 52.
83   Company Law 2005, Article 152(3).
84   Article 150 of the Company Law 2005 states that: "Where a director, supervisor or senior manager violates laws, administrative regulations or the company's articles of association in performance of his duties for the company and thus cause losses to the company, he shall be liable for compensation."
85   Company Law 2005, Article 152.
86   *Ibid*, Article 152(2).
87   Ma (2010), p 154.

In the light of the ineffective corporate governance and the serious problems of the abuse of power by directors and majority shareholders, the adoption of derivative actions may be perceived to be a good opportunity to address these issues. The broad scope and relaxed procedure could appear to maximise their functions and show the courts' willingness to allow derivative claims, to redress corporate wrongs and to protect the interests of both the company and minority shareholders.[88] This is consistent with the main objective of the Company Law 2005 – to protect the interests of the company and its shareholders. It also complies with socialist ideology and is of great significance to state-owned enterprises where the state is the majority shareholder. However, if derivative actions are used inappropriately, they have the potential to disrupt the management of a company, so it is essential to strike the proper balance between the protection of minority shareholders' rights and the protection of a company's day-to-day management.[89]

The establishment of a modern framework of shareholders' remedies has been regarded as a milestone in Chinese company law reform.[90] However, the lack of detailed guidance may result in inconsistent interpretations by different courts. This problem is compounded by the complexity of shareholders' disputes, and a lack of both detailed judicial interpretations and trial experience. The effectiveness of these measures in protecting shareholders' interests depends to a large extent on the rules of procedure, the allocation of costs and, more importantly, how the courts interpret and enforce them in practice.

5. Conclusion

While the Company Law 2005 has brought the standards of corporate governance and shareholders' protection closer to those of the Anglo-American models, it is "riddled with much vague wording".[91] Under the influence of political and economic factors, the corporate governance structure appears to have been designed to maintain the government's controlling position in corporatised state-owned enterprises and to uphold socialist ideology – and not to protect the rights of individual investors. It is argued that the corporate governance structure has failed to reduce legal risks in Chinese companies, largely due to the extensive power given to shareholders' general meetings, the lack of independence of boards of directors and the lack of real supervisory power for boards of supervisors. Moreover, the ill-defined duties of directors and supervisors in China make it difficult for judges to enforce them.

The Company Law 2005 is certainly a very important and necessary move in the right direction for the improvement of shareholders' rights and remedies in China. However, these new remedies still do not adequately protect minority shareholders,

---

88   See the derivative cases such as *Guangzhou Tianhe Science & Technology Park Construction Ltd v Guangdong Zhujiang Investment Ltd* (2003 Yue Gao FaminYi No 5. Hengzhong Guo, "Minority Shareholder Recovered Corporate Losses of Nearly RMB 5Billion – The Judgement of the Largest Amount of Derivative Claims in China", *Legal Daily*, April 22 2007.

89   Ma (2010), p 157.

90   Krause and Qin, "An Overview of China's New Company Law" (2007) *Company Lawyer* 316, 316.

91   D Clarke, "Lost in Translation? Corporate Legal Transplants in China" (2006) George Washington University Law School Public Law Research Paper No 213, pp 12-13.

particularly those in corporatised state-owned enterprises. Moreover, shareholders may be discouraged from bringing personal or derivative actions by the high cost of litigation, the difficulties in getting access to information, the distrust of local courts stemming from judges' inexperience (whether actual or merely perceived), and the difficulties in enforcing judgments. In order to reduce legal risks for foreign investors, it is crucial to build up an effective corporate governance structure in Chinese companies and to establish a sound system for enforcing directors' duties and protecting shareholders' interests in China. A sound system of investor protection may also help to build up shareholders' confidence in their companies and the stock market generally, to create investment incentives and ultimately to contribute to national economic growth.

Third parties, agents and supply chain due diligence

David Curran
Risk Readiness Corporation
Wolf Juergen von Kumberg
Northrop Grumman
Peter Mancusi
Weber Shandwick

1.   Introduction

The Good Wife is a popular American TV show about a wife and mother who restarts her legal career at a prestigious Chicago law firm after her husband is convicted on corruption charges stemming from a highly public political and sex scandal. For its millions of fans, it is compelling weekly viewing, mixing the central character's struggles and the firm's internal intrigues with cut-throat legal warfare and courtroom drama.

So how did talk of supply chain problems find its way into the script of a recent episode of the show? And what does the fact that it did say about how supply-chain risks have evolved during the past decade?

First, a recap: Lockhard-Gardner, the fictional firm at the heart of *The Good Wife*, is called upon to defend a dairy company after its cheese is suspected of causing of an outbreak of listeria affecting dozens of school children, whose sickness has been captured live on video and is being played around the clock on cable TV.

While the chief executive officer (CEO), persuaded by a Lockhard-Gardner partner, declares at a press conference that the company will do all it can to find the source of the problem and fix it, the firm's investigator, Kalinda, sets off to see what she can learn. Her inquiry leads to a brief exchange with the driver of one of the company's refrigerated trucks. He tells her the trucks are always kept within one degree of accuracy, "so I don't think it's a refrigeration problem".

"So what do you think?" Kalinda asks.

"I think it used to be easy to find the source", the driver replies. "Now, you've got some of these cheeses, they're a blend of three or four lines from three or four companies. So all I can say is, 'good luck'."

Good luck, indeed. These few sentences neatly sum up the unsettling reality many companies in Europe and the United States face today: they do not have a firm grasp on their supply chains and are susceptible to many risks that may develop into crises, with the potential to inflict severe damage on their businesses, stock prices and – most worrisome in today's world of instant communications – their reputations. *The Good Wife* writers were well aware of this. Viewers never learn the ultimate fate of the dairy company with the bad cheese, but a brief scene in which the company's hapless CEO is mobbed by reporters outside his home makes it clear that the company will take a long time to recover from the bad publicity and its seeming lack of supervision of its suppliers.

In the recent past, companies often had complete control over their supply chains. As FM Global, the commercial and industrial insurer, noted in a 2006 paper,[1] companies often created and shipped products from the same place. Their supply chains were models of vertical integration, ideally suited for domestic production and sales. They allowed companies to maintain direct and constant monitoring over vital related matters, particularly workplace rules and safety conditions. As companies began selling products in foreign countries, they could simply replicate the supply chain and production processes that had served them so well for so long.

But globalisation of the marketplace changed this – companies began searching for the lowest possible production costs. As the world became "flat", to use *New York Times* columnist Thomas Friedman's term, it became easier to outsource production to faraway suppliers in China, India, the Philippines, Central America and elsewhere. In addition, companies abandoned the old way of stockpiling materials, which added to expenses, and adopted just-in-time inventory programmes that stressed speed and cost reduction.

The result is that the nature of supply chain operations has changed dramatically. They are stretched farther than ever and can be surprisingly fragile – one mishap in a distant plant can have major consequences. In a 2012 survey of risk professionals at 110 North American companies, Marsh & McLennan emphasised how much more complex supply chains have become, noting that they require "many more handoffs between parties" that increase "the risk of delays and product integrity issues".[2] This is so whether a company sources materials from overseas or, like the dairy company in *The Good Wife*, relies on multiple domestic suppliers. The survey also stressed that "supply chain shipments can also cross more hot spots that are vulnerable to natural hazards, political risks, cargo theft and diversion and raise the cost of recovering from delays".

Although supply chains are most commonly identified with the manufacture of materials used to create products, there are 'knowledge' supply chains as well – the thousands of contract workers companies often employ (Hewlett Packard has 40,000 of them) at home and around the world and depend on to provide an array of important services. The rise of the contract worker, like the inevitable movement toward basing supply chains in remote locations, is a phenomenon of the continuing move to cut costs. And, like physical supply chains, contract workers also pose potential risks that arise both from their actions in carrying out their jobs and from the extensive access they often have to company information and processes.

Undoubtedly, and no matter how one defines a supply chain, there are more ways in which things may go wrong in supply chain operations today. It is also beyond debate, as even a casual scan of the daily news will confirm, that when they do go wrong, the media, customers, investors, regulators, politicians and every other group with an interest in the matter will blame the company the supply chain serves.

---

1 "The New Supply Chain Challenge: Risk Management in a Global Economy," FM Global, 2006.
2 "Risk Business. Tackling the Rising Supply Chain Threat." Marsh & McLennan, 2012

The Marsh & McLennan survey put it succinctly: "Companies are learning that while you may be able to outsource physical supply chain activities to other organisations, you can't outsource the related supply chain risk."

Even though companies are aware of the potential problems and damage that supply chain issues can cause, they do not appear to be doing all they can to ensure the risks do not escalate into public crises. In the Marsh & McLennan survey, 73% of the companies said their overall supply chain risk had increased since 2005, while 71% reported that the financial impact of supply chain disruptions had also risen. Yet most of these organisations also said that despite their rising concerns they did not believe they were adequately assessing and addressing these risks. None of the survey participants said their supervision practices were highly effective and only 35% said they were moderately effective.

Marsh & McLennan also found that "at most companies, supply chain risk management processes are piecemeal, informal, *ad hoc* and inconsistent". The participants estimated that their companies were conducting annual risk assessments of just 25% of their end-to-end supply chains, with the survey adding that "[a] lack of staff time and resources – combined with the complexity of supply chain processes that can involve thousands of internal and external organisations – create daunting challenges".

There are likely other dynamics at play that help explain why companies have done so little. For all the risks they face from their supply chain operations, the majority of companies have never experienced a major public crisis because of one of them. Senior executives, focused on keeping costs down and maximising revenues, may view spending corporate funds to assess supply chain risks that may never harm their businesses as a waste of money. The attitude may be that as long as they're doing something – like the 25% in the Marsh & McLennan survey – they will probably be OK.

But events have a way of making converts, or at least forcing action. For years, many companies were reluctant to pay for crisis communications plans which would help them quickly and confidently to respond to a crisis. In 2005, a prominent crisis management expert estimated that less than one-fifth of U.S. corporations had such plans.[3] The same circular logic applied: "We've never faced a crisis, so we're unlikely to face a crisis. Why spend the money?" However, with the rise of social and digital media, consumers were able to organise online boycotts or post negative comments in reaction to a company decision they did not like; stories about controversies facing companies – executive pay, unexpectedly poor financial performance, employee complaints – could spread in minutes. Now, almost all major companies, and many smaller ones, have established a rapid-response process, and many have prepared to react to a few specific scenarios that represent particular threats to their businesses.

Inevitably, the same forces that prompted the rapid adoption of general crisis communications plans will pressure companies to assess their supply chains, take

---

[3]   James Surowiecki, "In Case of Emergency", *New Yorker*, June 13, 2005, http://www.newyorker.com/archive/2005/06/13/050613ta_talk_surowiecki

action to minimise the inherent risks they pose and prepare to handle the crises that might arise from them. It is clear that the new supply chain model centred on overseas sourcing has created a host of issues that may become public controversies in an instant. Apple has millions of devoted customers and its stock, both literally and figuratively, has never been higher. Nevertheless, it has faced unrelenting scrutiny from media and non-governmental organisations in 2012 over how Foxconn, its primary Chinese supplier, treats its thousands of workers. In the face of mounting criticism, Apple quickly announced that it would press for full compliance on work hour limits and for remedial action to address health and safety issues, worker representation and compensation.

A cynic might say the spotlight on Apple's supply chain operations has cost it very little – there are no signs that its business has suffered and it remains the most highly valued company in the world. But, arguably, no company has as much reputational capital as Apple. While Apple executives have said little about the controversy, it is safe to assume that, in hindsight, they believe they should have dealt with Foxconn before its harsh working conditions became a worldwide story and a major embarrassment to the company. As the leader in producing innovative consumer electronics, Apple could have been the leader in sustainable supply chain practices as well, further enhancing its reputation. Instead, it was shamed into taking action, and will be closely watched for years to come to see whether it is meeting its commitments to improving conditions at Foxconn and its other suppliers.

This kind of attention on supply chain practices is unlikely to decrease. If anything, companies are facing growing demands to raise environmental and social standards across their supply chain operations, as a recent report by the European Sustainable Investment Forum[4] (Eurosif) makes clear. In addition, it is no longer considered best practice for companies to monitor only their main suppliers. The Eurosif report states that the scope of a company's responsibilities "has expanded from direct suppliers to further up the supply chain involving sub-suppliers and raw materials suppliers". In other words, companies will be held accountable for practices of third parties whose identities and track records may not even be known to them, and thus will be even more vulnerable to supply-chain crises. As one commentator on supply chain risks has noted: "When a company's reputation is only as good as the worst-behaving supplier in its supply chain, it is exposed to guilt by association."[5]

In addition to requiring that its suppliers – and their suppliers – follow sound environmental and social practices, a company must ensure the quality of the materials they source. Failure to monitor for quality control can lead to devastating crises if there is a major product recall that damages sales or, worse, causes physical harm and injuries. Issues such as lead paint in toys, contaminated pharmaceuticals, tainted pet food and defective medical devices have made headlines and have caused business and reputational harm in recent years. Nearly every case highlighted the same problem: poor supervision of a supplier that had made a preventable mistake,

---

4   Eurosif Procurement Report, March 2010.
5   Greenconduct.com, "5 Reputational Risks to Revenue without Sustainability Strategies, by Bob Willard, October 18 2011.

or cut a corner, or done a poor job monitoring subcontractors providing it with materials. No one believes supply chains should never experience a serious problem – no business is immune from risks or their consequences. That is why commercial insurance is available. But the media, the public and the regulators will not hesitate, in the face of a crisis caused by a supply chain issue, to deride companies that have failed to pay a proper level of attention to their suppliers and their suppliers' practices.

So how does a company ensure that it is meeting its obligations, and that it is 'risk ready' – focused on the issues particular to its supply chain operations, vigilant in taking steps to mitigate them and ready to respond effectively if a crisis develops that becomes a matter of public concern?

Some steps that companies should consider to ensure adequate monitoring of their supply chains and to reduce the chance that they will be confronted with a public crisis resulting from a sourcing issue are discussed in the next section.

2.   Supply chain readiness

2.1   Develop an accurate picture of your vulnerabilities

Before a company can mitigate supply chain risks, it must know what its vulnerabilities are. An audit designed to uncover supply chain issues need not be expensive or time-consuming. The results can both highlight new problems and provide the impetus to take action.

Consider the case of a major consumer US retail company that sources thousands of items from China. The company had acquired several companies in recent years, and there were concerns about the sourcing protocols and standards of the new businesses. There were also worries about the company's operations in Europe and emerging markets, which had their own practices for sourcing, auditing factory operations and testing products.

The company hired a consultant, who developed a simple plan to interview some 20 executives – those directly responsible for supply chain operations in the US and China and those with related supervisory responsibilities, including the general counsel, the vice president for environmental affairs and the vice president for business ethics. In a meeting with the company's supply chain executives, the consultant presented the details of what he had found through a series of questions.

For example, did they know that one acquired company had set up a voluntary recall of a children's product because of high lead concentrations? Or that another had recalled a toaster oven because several had exploded? Were they aware that while their European operations monitored factories in China, they relied on third-party agents instead of company employees, raising possible conflict of interest issues? Had they heard about the whistle-blower who had called Newsweek alleging that a company factory in China was mistreating workers? The answer to all these questions was "no". Armed with the findings, the executives began coordinating with their European counterparts and the acquired companies in an effort to make sourcing practices and supervision more consistent. They instituted Web-based training for all supply-chain employees to teach them the kinds of situations they should report to headquarters. They created a 24-hour hotline to take calls from the field and a process for reporting them to senior management, along with guidelines for communicating both internally and externally if a crisis in the supply chain became a public controversy.

Simply by getting a more complete picture of its supply chain and then taking some basic steps based on that new view, the company had come a long way in being better able to protect its business and its reputation.

2.2 Develop a risk readiness attitude

It is not enough simply to know the weaknesses in a supply chain operation. Like the company in the example above, there must also be a cultural shift toward dealing with these risks. The CEO and other senior executives must make it clear throughout their organisation that avoiding preventable risks is everyone's job. The days when handling risk was mainly a matter for operations are gone, especially when it comes to supply chains, which no longer are judged merely on whether they are sourcing goods in an efficient manner but also are expected to reflect a company's values and its ability to maintain high standards of quality.

2.3 Create an enterprise-wide supply chain risk management group that convenes on a regular basis

Along with a risk readiness attitude comes the need to address the daily challenges of monitoring supply chain risks – they are not static and can change over time – and minimising the threats they pose. A group composed of operational managers and executives whose duties involve the supply chain should create a simple guide detailing goals (reflecting expectations for suppliers and the employees who oversee them); how it will go about identifying risks in the supply chain on an ongoing basis; and the processes it will use to mitigate these risks.

The group should document the actions it takes and make certain it can access any materials concerning supply chain operations, such as supplier contracts, inspection reports and violation notices. The group can convene physically or online, and an online platform should be developed to house documents so that they are easily accessible to all group members. However it convenes, the group should hold regular meetings, with an agenda that includes progress reports on pending matters and new issues the group needs to consider. The group should strive to maintain a rhythm to its work, and regular meetings will help ensure that it does.

Implementing an enterprise-wide risk management programme will pay dividends in a time of crisis. The ability to demonstrate to the media and stakeholders that you have taken supply-chain risk seriously and have a system in place to correct problems can go a long way toward preventing negative coverage from escalating. In real life, crises happen. The companies that can deal with them quickly and move on will be able to limit the damage.

2.4 Drill and then drill some more

The probability that a company will face reputational harm at some point from a risk that develops into a crisis is higher than ever. All the meetings and planning will be worthless if a company cannot respond confidently should the worst happen. Thus, risk readiness programmes should include periodic drills, the more realistic and spontaneous the better. Assume a government agency has just asked for all the records involving the operations of a Chinese supplier accused of abusing workers. Or that a reporter has called with questions about the financial condition of your main sourcing facility. How quickly can you gather the crucial documents or craft a credible answer to a media inquiry? Surprise drills are a way to find out and gather intelligence to improve response capabilities.

It is important when conducting these drills – and in all preparedness projects you undertake – to include outside lawyers, public relations firms and any other outside consultants on risk and communications. In a real situation, companies rely on all these players, and the more practice you have working with them in simulations the better you will coordinate with these advisers if there is an actual crisis event.

2.5 Bring the board of directors and CEO along

Too many companies seek to shield their boards and CEOs from the 'nitty gritty' of corporate operations like supply chains. However, supply chain failures often carry financial risks. Credit rating agencies and investors are likely to become involved if there are problems that seriously hurt revenues, and supply chains are only as good as the financial health of their suppliers. Following the worldwide recession, the failure of a main supplier can also have serious effects for a company. More than ever, company boards and CEOs need to focus on supply chain risk and include it in both drills and, at least from time to time, the work of the supply chain management group.

2.6 Measure and monitor

As part of any overall risk management programme, companies should develop systems to monitor and measure how the work is going. Has the company made substantial progress in addressing preventable risks? How has it done this? What has it learned in the process? What gaps in supply chain remain and how serious are they? Answering questions like these on a quarterly or at least annual basis will further advance the work of supply chain risk management and ensure that the company is working toward its goal of become risk-ready.

2.7 Reward performance for success in addressing risk in the supply chain

Companies routinely align compensation plans with performance in implementing various strategies and goals.

The same should be true for supply chain risk management programmes. Providing compensation and other awards to those who help a company progress toward risk readiness in the supply chain will send a clear message that assessing and mitigating supply chain risk is a main corporate priority.

Beyond these steps, one other important initiative warrants a slightly longer discussion.

2.8 Develop a comprehensive supplier policy

Today, it is common for companies to require their suppliers to follow certain general policies, which are often contained in supplier contracts. However, many companies need to set out their expectations to suppliers more clearly and to obtain their cooperation in meeting goals for sourcing in a responsible way.

Suppliers are a key component of any business that is sourcing goods and materials. A company's business reputation and credibility often rests with its overseas suppliers, who should at least be working to meet the same standards of ethics and business conduct the company follows. Ultimately, tainted suppliers will taint the company and raise questions from customers, employees, shareholders and regulators. A related, but extremely important, reason is that companies must also treat their suppliers fairly and equitably and put systems in place to provide regular, honest feedback on their performance so the suppliers can correct any problems.

Thus, creating what we call a Statement of Principles for Global Ethical Procurement should be a key priority for any company trying to improve its supply chain operations. There is no set model for such a statement; they will obviously differ somewhat from company to company and from sector to sector. But we believe that it is useful for companies to consider the following guidelines:

- the standards in the statement must be achievable, particularly where local standards are low. This is not to say that companies should let local standards dictate, but simply ordering that suppliers implement standards that far exceed those followed in a particular location is unlikely to result in much progress;
- to the extent a company is willing to consider different legal codes and cultural expectations in the home countries of its suppliers, it should address these issues with a supplier early on and determine whether these codes and expectations will support the company's goals for its statement of principles; and
- whatever the final goals and standards are, they should be achievable within a certain, agreed-upon time. There should be performance milestones and a policy for discussing conflicts and resolving them according to an established approach. The statement should emphasise a policy of openness that includes access to work sites and to information from suppliers.

The overall goal here is not to create a contract or establish regulations that make a company, in effect, a policeman (with all the liabilities that can arise if a supplier fails to adhere to the rules). The goal is to develop a statement of principles that sets out a company's expectations and makes it clear that a supplier's ongoing relationship with the company will depend in large part on its performance in meeting these expectations. In other words, the statement must convince suppliers that following policies outlined in the statement is not only an ethical requirement but also makes good business sense.

There are other, more specific elements that should be addressed in the statement of principles, including:

- a demonstration of responsible environmental performance and health and safety standards in line with ISO 14001 (an environmental management standard);

- a commitment to permit freedom of association and a right to collective bargaining for workers, where permitted by local law, and not to discriminate on any basis, including gender, race, colour or religious creed; to eliminate the use of child labour and forced and bonded labour; to pay a living wage based on local conditions and limit the amount of hours worked by each employee to acceptable maximums;
- a clear statement that the company strictly forbids the offer, promise or payment of anything by the supplier to a public official and that any gifts and gratuities are in line with company policies; and
- an expectation that suppliers will avoid conflicts of interest between their responsibilities to the company and the suppliers' other active interests.

Finally, a statement of principles should also detail how a company will audit a supplier's adherence to supply chain policies and the scope of such audits, and include expectations for how a supplier will protect important company information. The statement should make clear that:

- where relevant, time records accurately and precisely reflect how a supplier's time was spent;
- expenses must be documented accurately and adequately, submitted promptly and reflect special care when customers or suppliers are involved;
- any action by any person acting on the company's behalf to circumvent its system of internal controls or provide misleading information about company documents or records is strictly prohibited;
- property, especially electronic media, should never be used for purposes which are disruptive or which violate company procedures in some other way;
- company information must be protected as an asset as valuable as money and may not be used for personal gain. All classified information must be handled and safeguarded in strict compliance with security procedures;
- suppliers should not seek information to which they are not entitled, especially sensitive source selection procurement details;
- the company will not violate other third-party copyrights or licensing agreements; and
- the company has adopted an open-book policy with its suppliers, which includes access to conduct independent audits (there may be various books kept by foreign suppliers that show the 'true' version of accounts).

3.   The Northrop Grumman experience

One company that has successfully implemented many of the above principles is Northrop Grumman, a multinational defence and security company, which has developed a critical supply chain not only in the United States but also in many countries overseas. The company's Principles for Global Ethical Procurement encourage its suppliers to develop high standards for sourcing to help them achieve that goal.

The programme is aimed at providing guidance, rather than forcing compliance through coercive means. The incentive for suppliers is that high operating standards lead to more productive and ultimately successful businesses with which Northrop Grumman is willing to establish long-term relationships.

A copy of the Northrop Grumman Principles can be seen at this web address: http://www.es.northropgrumman.com/ourvalues/assets/Principles_for_Global_Ethic al_.pdf Every company must assess its own supply chain risks and priorities, but these principles may provide a useful starting point.

Implementing compliance management systems: an organisational learning process

Lutz-Ulrich Haack
German Graduate School of Management and Law, Heilbronn
Robert Nothhelfer
Former head of GRC Lidl International and University of Freiburg, Asperg

1.   Introduction

Newspapers have been reporting financial law violations (the Libor scandal is a recent example) and very large fines and penalties imposed on companies or their management for infringements almost every week. In response, many corporate management and supervisory boards are introducing a compliance management system, or expanding their existing one, to ensure they meet legal and internal regulations, not only in individual cases but also systematically, thus helping their boards to avoid liability. The available literature and guidance on this topic focus heavily on the legal issues, on the set up and on the subcomponents of a compliance management system. The questions of how such a system is introduced, how the implementation process should be managed, how such a project is perceived by employees and how this perception may be controlled through communication frequently play a subordinate role.

This chapter examines the learning processes necessary when introducing a compliance management system to an organisation and how it may be supported by management. It uses IDW PS 980, "Generally accepted standards for audit of Compliance Management Systems",[1] as a model compliance management system. This follows the prevalent measures for implementation cited in current literature. The chapter develops a typical project workflow for the introduction of these structures to implement the various basic elements in an organisation. Finally, the learning processes for participants and how they may be supported are examined.

2.   Basic elements of a compliance management system and typical implementation measures

In response to the current high demand for appropriate audits, the Institute of Public Auditors in Germany has adopted a new auditing standard, PS 980 "Generally accepted standards for audit of compliance management systems". This provides a formalised auditing framework. PS 980 defines a compliance management system as follows:

---

1   Institute of Public Auditors in Germany, Generally accepted standards for audit of Compliance Management Systems (PS 980), 2011.

A Compliance Management System means introduced company policies, procedures and measures which are based on the objectives ... established by the legal representatives directed toward the safeguarding of code-compliant conduct of the legal representatives and employees of the company as well as, if applicable, third parties, ... to the end of compliance with certain rules and thus the prevention of substantial violations.[2]

The standard defines seven basic elements of a compliance management system; these and a short description are contained in the first two columns of Table 1. Typical implementation measures recommended in the literature are assigned to the third column; this listing is however not exhaustive but only exemplary as it should be decided which measures are appropriate for the respective organisation and how they can be implemented within the scope of each project.

Table 1: The seven basic elements of a compliance management system

Basic element[3]	Description[4]	Typical implementation measures[5]
Compliance culture	"influences the importance which the employees ... attribute to the compliance with rules."	• formulation of corporate values • developing behaviour guidelines/codices • adapting incentives systems • integration into human resource development programme • principles for the sanctioning of misconduct • regular control through company management
Compliance objectives	"Objectives which are to be achieved with CMS ... Basics for the assessment of compliance risks."	• delineation of the scope of the respective legal spheres and the measurability of the objectives • integration into corporate objectives

continued on next page

---

2 *Ibid*, margin no. 6.
3 *Ibid*, margin no. 23.
4 *Ibid*, margin no. 23.
5 For example, Schulz/Kuhnke, BB, 2012, 143ff; Behringer, *Waldzus/Behringer*, Compliance kompakt, 2010, 337ff; Behringer, *Behringer*, Compliance kompakt, 2010, 383ff; Moosmayer, Compliance, 2012, 33ff; Hauschka, Lampert, Corporate Compliance, 2010, § 9; Hauschka, *Schlaghecke*, Corporate Compliance, 2010, § 14; Wieland/Steinmeyer/Grüninger, *Kaptein*, Handbuch Compliance Management, 2010, 291ff; Wieland/Steinmeyer/Grüninger, *Fürst*, Handbuch Compliance Management, 2010, 333ff; Wieland/Steinmeyer/Grüninger, *von Oertzen/Hoffmann/Oppitz*, Handbuch Compliance Management, 2010, 415ff; Wieland/Steinmeyer/Grüninger, *Tur*, Handbuch Compliance Management, 2010, 437ff; Wieland/Steinmeyer/Grüninger, *Knoll/Kaven*, Handbuch Compliance Management, 2010, 457ff; with regard to media design, eg, www.compcor.info/trainingsprodukte.html.

Basic element[3]	Description[4]	Typical implementation measures[5]
Compliance risks	"Systematic risk detection …, in terms of probability of occurrence and potential consequences analysed."	• systematic baseline study (risk assessment) • definition of a materiality limit/take-up threshold
Compliance programme	"Principles and measures … which are directed to the limitation of compliance risks."	• presence and online training, compliance games, media support • development/adaptation of guidelines/handbooks/ standards • redesigning workflows/business processes • documentation of processes/decisions • IT technical support
Compliance organisation	"The roles and responsibilities … as well as the setup and workflow management."	• job description/role definition of the compliance officer • setting up a compliance committee/panel • scope of resources • integration into existing structures
Compliance communication	"Employees … will … be informed so that they sufficiently understand their tasks in the CMS … [It] is established how … information … is reported."	• verbal/written communication of corporate management • media support • intranet pages/consultation hotline • Ombudsman/whistle-blower system
Compliance monitoring and improvement	"Suitability and effectiveness … are … monitored … the elimination of the defect and the improvement of the system."	• clarification of responsibility • generation of a monitoring plan • allocation of resources

3. Typical workflow of an implementation project

Under the description of the basic elements of a compliance management system and established measures for their implementation, a typical project workflow should now be described. First, what a project is and who the project participants are should be defined.

3.1 Project definition

The current literature has developed the following characteristics of a project. A project is an "intention which is characterised by the uniqueness of its conditions as a whole", meaning in particular that projects are "innovative, complex in their scope, [have] a clear objective, [have] a deadline, [have] a specific organisation".[6]

Generally, for larger organisations, the implementation of a compliance management system will meet these criteria and will be organised as a project. Frequently, at the start, a project team is set up to prepare the system's introduction, implement it and manage its operation as a fixed organisational process.

3.2 Project participants

Ultimately, the entire company will be involved in a comprehensive compliance project. The task at this point is to develop specific functions which are linked to the decision-making and coordination processes so that the interplay between the functions is defined. The essential project participants are as follows.

(a) Corporate management

The project must be introduced by corporate management. As one of its main tasks, the management must ensure compliance with legal requirements. It must also inspect and approve the project's results on an ongoing basis, and inform all employees of the significance of the project and ensure their compliance.

Regardless of the compliance requirements for individual departments in a business, the fundamental issues, in particular the objectives, culture, organisation and communication, must be decided and supported by the entire corporate management or its chairperson because these affect all areas of the company.

(b) The project team

Once the corporate management has decided to implement a compliance management system, a project team must be set up to coordinate and implement its introduction.

(c) The rest of company

The project will affect all of the company to varying degrees because information must be collected by the project team, employees must be trained by the project team and workflows must be adjusted. All areas must be made aware of the processes developed by the project team and implement them in day-to-day business practice; otherwise no real compliance will be achieved.

---

6   For example, Keßler/Winkelhofer, Projektmanagement, 2002, 9ff.

3.3 A typical project workflow

A typical project workflow is shown in Figure 1.

Figure 1

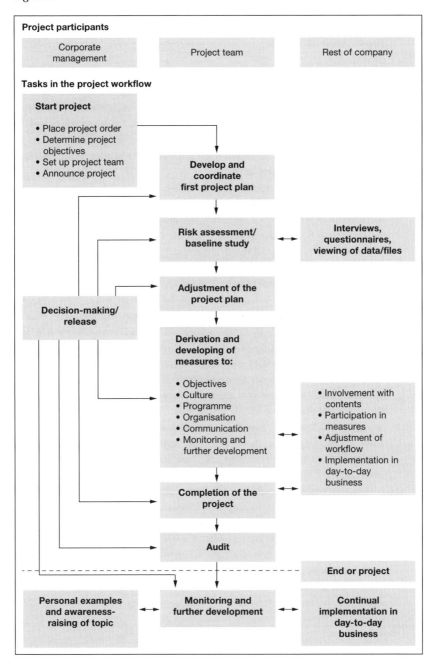

The workflow should show the tasks of the project participants, the management, the project team and the rest of company and put them in an operational time sequence. The precise arrangement of the project will depend on individual circumstances and will focus on the specific company requirements. The single arrows in Figure 1 connect tasks which are consecutively related to each other, meaning the next task only starts when the previous task is completed. The double arrows represent communication processes between the individual project participants.

The project is introduced by corporate management, which will define the project objectives and the basis upon which the project team is formed. From the outset, the project objectives should follow the compliance objectives. As the compliance objectives may develop over time, they are listed again with the basic elements in the development of measures. To give the project team its necessary authority, corporate management must announce the project to the company before the team starts work (tone at the top).

The project team's first step is to develop an initial project plan, that is, to organise the project order in defined task packages, for both content and facts, and allocate the expected costs. Typically, the project plan will be adjusted throughout the project as new information is received. The initial project plan is assessed by corporate management, adjusted if necessary and then adopted as a set approach with a defined budget.

Usually, a risk assessment or baseline study is carried out after the initial planning phase. Most companies intending to implement a compliance management system will have previously undertaken compliance activities in individual areas; it would be rare that a company had not carried out any advance compliance activities – without it, any business activity would be difficult. Thus, the project team will have to establish what activities, regulations, training and so on already exist. It is recommended that all departments are consulted during the baseline study. This step should include interviews and questionnaires and examining documents, data and files. It should provide an evaluation of which legal risks the company is exposed to, how these risks are to be assessed (gross risk) and which measures have already been taken so far (net risk). Based on this, further approaches and focuses can be developed in detail so that any areas previously overlooked and at risk may be processed.[7]

The results and conclusions of the risk assessment, along with suggestions for the next stages, are presented to corporate management for evaluation, amendment and approval.

The next stage is the central part of every implementation project. The project team develops a matrix from the basic elements of culture, programme, organisation, communication, monitoring and further development, and from any legal areas where there are compliance risks (typically, corruption guidelines, anti-trust law, data protection, product liability law, tax law, accounting fraud and, depending on the

---

7   For a more detailed presentation of a possible approach, see Wieland/Steinmeyer/Grüninger, *Knoll/Kaven*, Handbuch Compliance-Management, 457ff.

corporate activity, other legal areas). If necessary, additional systems will be set up for specific elements or legal areas. Where possible, this development should be carried out in consultation with all affected departments, to address as many practical questions as possible and so simplify implementation into the day-to-day business. The participation of the rest of the company or affected departments may vary here: cooperating in particular areas of the project; participating in actions such as training; adapting the project team's workflows and, if applicable, adapting guidelines or process descriptions up to 'simple' compliance with newly introduced regulations in the day-to-day business.

Not all parts of a company will be affected by all measures: anti-trust law and corruption guidelines may primarily affect sales and purchasing; tax law and accounting fraud may affect accounting and the tax department. The project team must design a coherent overall plan which specifies the scope of the measures so that they are effective but easily implementable.

Already, the individual buzzwords will define the extent of each compliance area for the whole company. As such, the basic measures developed must be presented to and approved by corporate management before they are implemented, then followed. It is counterproductive to rule-consistent behaviour in day-to-day business if corporate management shows inconsistency between its compliance management system and its ongoing decisions ("when things get serious"), possibly creating conflict for employees in deciding what is more important: business or compliance.

If all the measures developed have been implemented, or at least are in the process of being implemented, the project may be concluded. Typically, this is achieved through a report from the project team to corporate management, which the management will either approve or else arrange for any reworking or improvements.

If an audit of the compliance management system (eg, according to IDW PS 980) is planned by corporate management, it may be carried out at this stage. However, the audit should have already been prepared. In particular, the project team should clarify early on which documents and other information must be provided for future audits and in what form. Generating audit-suitable documentation during the development of measures and their implementation will save additional work.[8]

Upon a successful audit, the implementation is concluded and the system can be integrated into regular operations, particularly issues such as monitoring and further development, and the company will apply issues of compliance on a daily basis. In particular, corporate management should not consider the compliance management system to be concluded but must view it as a long-term commitment – first, by exemplary conduct, that is, personally meeting the compliance regulations, and, secondly, by regularly drawing attention to the importance of the system.

4. Learning process within the framework of an implementation project

4.1 Terms and systemisation of learning processes
Knowledge can be defined as the effective capacity to act, while information requires

---

8   Cf Görtz, BB 2012, 178ff.

further interpretation. If knowledge is the capacity to act, learning may be seen as the change in the capacity to act.[9] The consequence of this knowledge term is also the understanding that a company and its environment, for example its product market or society, influence each other. External influences – in this context changes in legal regulations – lead to adjustment reactions in the company which can only be considered successful when (regardless of what has been generated within the company in terms of preliminary work, guidelines or training) the behaviour of the employees of the company is in compliance with the law. In these terms, a company has learned successfully if it reacts to a change in the legal framework with an appropriate change in behaviour – that is, it can convey the intellectual understanding of the legal change to those who must comply with this standard and these persons actually do so.

Learning processes in organisations may be further distinguished by whether individuals learn or whether, beyond the individual, groups learn in a social context, especially through communication. An organisation may only learn if individual people learn. This is important because a 'supra-personnel' development of an organisation without the further development of at least one part of its membership is not possible. Because the reach of the individual is limited, particularly in larger organisations, learning in groups in social communication processes is very important for the dissemination of knowledge.[10]

In addition to the learning processes, the question of how knowledge may be stored independently of individuals must be asked. In the current context, rules in the form of guidelines, instructions, handbooks or other documentation to be used are particularly important. One characteristic of these rules is that the person who uses them uses the knowledge of the person who developed the rules without possessing or needing to possess this knowledge himself. This is the same principle as driving a car without understanding how a car is constructed. Through this so-called knowledge surrogate, documented knowledge can be disseminated quickly and efficiently in an organisation. An important component of an organisational knowledge base is the rules which are to be applied in that organisation by default. Thus every larger company has several knowledge bases in which the rules to be applied differ from department to department.[11]

4.2 Specifics in the implementation of a compliance management system

The implementation of a compliance management system has the following features:

- acquisition of the required knowledge is easy to plan in contrast to, for example, the development of new products. The knowledge which the company lacks is easily defined based on the established compliance

---

9   Nothhelfer, Lernprozesse in Organisationen, 2001, 25ff; Probst/Raub/Romhardt, Wissen managen, 2010, 15ff.

10 Nothhelfer, Lernprozesse in Organisationen, 2001, 68ff; cf Probst/Raub/Romhardt, Wissen managen, 2010, 117ff.

11 Nothhelfer, Lernprozesse in Organisationen, 2001, 50ff; Pautzke, Die Evolution der organisatorischen Wissensbasis, 1989, 76ff.

objectives and the risk assessment: which legal provisions are relevant and how they may be applied. This knowledge usually already exists – at least in part, not in the company, but with consultants, lawyers, auditors or other service providers;

- because it is primarily about the systematic and consistent implementation of legal provisions, that is, external regulations, imposed on the company, the focus of the learning processes is also regulation-oriented, with less emphasis on individual or informal learning processes, such as product innovations or creative marketing concepts; and

- the typical project workflow illustrated in Figure 1 shows that the learning processes taking place affect the entire organisation, not only every hierarchical level but also all functional areas. This presents a special challenge with regard to the scope of the learning processes.

4.3 The learning processes in the implementation of a compliance management system in detail

In the following, the aforementioned tasks in the project workflow are examined in terms of whether and how learning takes place in each phase, who learns and whether the organisational knowledge base changes.

When classifying learners, the term 'directly involved' should mean that these are the people who are involved with the project tasks in detail and develop the specific results, creating new knowledge adapted to the company – initially for themselves and, depending on the dissemination, to others. 'Indirectly involved' should mean that the directly involved people must involve other people at the end of the particular project phase, especially the corporate management. Each project result will be presented to corporate management. To obtain a sound decision, they must immerse themselves in the situation, understand the relevant questions/problems and the solutions developed for them. This, too, is a learning process with those affected because they must adopt new knowledge in the organisation.

For simplicity, the project participants are not subdivided any further at this point. Depending on the size of the project team, not every team member will work on all topics and all factual issues – here, too, there are specialisations. The same is true for corporate management and the rest of the company.

The integration of corporate management should be illustrated by way of examples of several possible measures assigned to the above basic elements as follows.

(a) Compliance culture

Behaviour guidelines/codices: Behaviour guidelines or codices set a framework on how employees should conduct themselves in certain situations. Typical regulation contents are: dealing with gifts, invitations and other presents or benefits, dealing with donations, and dealing with conflicts of interest. Due to the sensitive nature and the large sphere of influence, corporate management must not only approve of

Table 2: Learning and the knowledge base

Task in the project workflow	Learners		Changes in the knowledge base
	Directly involved	Indirectly involved	
Start project	Corporate management	None	None
Develop and coordinate initial project plan	Project team	Corporate management	None
Risk assessment	Project team and rest of company (provided they are directly involved)	Corporate management	None
Adjusting the project plan	Project team	Corporate management	None
Derivation and development of measures	Project team and rest of company (as far as they are directly involved with the project)	Rest of company (provided they are only participating) and corporate management	Yes – dependent on the results:

new guidelines and training, new workflows |
| Conclusion of project | Project team | Corporate management | Documentation of lessons learned from the project |
| Audit | If applicable, project team | None – provided there are no essential audit findings | None – provided there are no essential audit findings |

such principles or decide on them, but must also look in detail at the regulations to determine whether they are appropriate or correspond to the culture of the company. It is important for corporate management to communicate the approved principles to the company when they are initiated to give them their necessary importance and to enforce them.[12]

Adjustment of incentive systems: Incentive systems should guide the behaviour of the employees through the use of targeted rewards. The objectives may be both qualitative and quantitative. These systems are frequently a part of individual employment contracts or corresponding additional agreements. If these systems are enhanced with compliance elements, this affects all employees with such agreements in a very basic manner, usually involving an employee's income. Accordingly, changes clearly affect the motivation and behaviour of employees. Based on the consequences for the employees and the necessary decisions regarding which targets should be rewarded in which manner while considering all corporate objectives, corporate management must contemplate adapting incentive systems and explain any changes in connection with the compliance project and the pursued compliance objectives.

Principles on the sanctioning of misconduct: If it is emphasised within the framework of the compliance project that, beginning with the implementation, all misconduct will be appropriately sanctioned, it is necessary to establish principles for sanctioning to prevent arbitrary decisions. In addition to possible sanctions, this includes organisational questions, in particular, who sanctions, how is it documented and, if applicable, communicated. Corporate management should be involved because contestable cases must ultimately be decided at that level and the issue is generally subject to worker participation.

(b) Compliance organisation

The objective of a compliance management system is to avoid the possible liability of corporate management based on organisational culpability. However, this is only possible if the corresponding tasks are properly assigned. In addition to a "clear and unambiguous" assignment of responsibilities, this also includes "the necessary authority and material means to carry out ... necessary tasks ...".[13] This responsibility is incumbent on corporate management, which will also have to deal in detail with practical measures such as a job description for the compliance officer or an agenda for a compliance committee.

Despite correct delegation, corporate management also must continue to monitor the delegated tasks.[14] Generally, this is achieved through regular reporting by those responsible for compliance, either in meetings through verbal reports or, additionally, through a reporting system which records all significant compliance cases and developments in the company.

5. Conclusions

The following conditions are necessary for the successful implementation of a compliance management system.

---

12 Cf Behringer, *Waldzus/Behringer*, Compliance kompakt, 2010, 346ff; cf Moosmayer, Compliance, 2012, 49ff.
13 Hauschka, *Schmidt-Husson*, Corporate Compliance, 2010, § 7, margin nos 20 and 23.
14 *Ibid*, margin nos 10 and 27ff.

5.1 Changes in behaviour must be wanted

An organisational learning process is only successful if it leads to an actual change in the behaviour of the members of the organisation. Accordingly, a project must be set up to implement a compliance management system and modify the behaviour of the organisation. This does not mean a general change in market launches, purchasing strategies or the like; it can also mean only that more is documented or that one is more careful when dealing with invitations or gifts and, if applicable, also more reserved. In other words: A project whereby the behaviour of an organisation is not changed at all, is only a paper tiger and must be considered to be a failure.

These changes in behaviour are only partially foreseeable at the start of the project. If corporate management deals with the implementation of a compliance management system, it has to be willing to change the corporate behaviour – otherwise the project is superfluous.

5.2 Continual involvement of corporate management

Following the initiation, corporate management must be continually involved in the project due to the many questions which have to be addressed; examples were given above. In particular, the temporal availability of one or the other members of the corporate management may lead to a bottleneck. The tone at the top is the starting point and this alone is not enough.

5.3 Corporate management's willingness to learn

It is necessary that corporate management is willing to learn in order to complete each of the project steps successfully. This requires an individual willingness to learn, and especially the willingness to learn in groups which, as a rule, are not hierarchically homogeneous. An attitude that the company should go ahead and learn but corporate management does not have to change will not lead to successful learning processes.

5.4 The entire company's willingness to learn

All company areas are affected by a compliance management system. In order for the implementation to be successful, all employees must become familiar with the new procedures and guidelines and adapt their behaviour in the day-to-day business. This means that every person in the company must be willing to learn.

Creating an open environment that promotes learning is particularly useful, and this requires a corporate management which is willing to learn.

5.5 Communication is the essential motor

Essential learning results from the creation of new knowledge through mutual exchange and the quick dissemination of this knowledge in the company to all involved levels. In this way, clear and efficient communication of the contents becomes a key element for the successful implementation project. This requires particular attention to communication skills when selecting the project team. If necessary, this ability should be reinforced through specific training in moderation and public speaking.

European debt capital markets regulation in the context of retail market risks

Ferdinando Bruno
University of Lugano, Switzerland

1.   Introduction

As noted by one commentator:

> ... a quick survey of some of the financial frauds that have occurred in the past few years – Enron, WorldCom, Parmalat, Adelphia – reveals how corporate debt securities loomed large as instruments involved in the losses suffered by investors.[1]

The year before WorldCom, Inc collapsed it had raised at least $12 billion in a public debt offering. Parmalat Finanziaria SpA, which had debt securities listed on the Milan and Luxembourg securities exchanges, had approximately $9.4 billion in bonds outstanding at the time insolvency proceedings were instituted, a substantial portion of which were held by retail and non-Italian investors. As Kung points out:

> ... debt holders were left holding billions of dollars in losses as a result of these frauds, most of which involved accounting irregularities and, in many cases, questionable related-party transactions that enabled companies to hide their losses through the use of related companies and special purposes vehicles.[2]

For the purposes of this chapter, it is worth noting that, "these recent corporate debacles have highlighted the need for full and fair disclosure to investors when issuers raise capital in the markets through debt offerings and listings, particularly when retail investors are involved".[3] Following the recent scandals in the European debt capital markets, the European regulator became concerned about the lack of strong and effective rules to protect the retail domestic market, especially debt financial instruments. These securities attract large numbers of investors as they provide a fixed return (the coupon) with redemption at maturity, thus apparently offering a no or low-risk investment. Many of the potential investors are retail investors, that is, investors – usually individuals – with no (or limited) financial experience. As debt financial instruments are tailored for institutional investors (and are therefore higher risk), over the past few years the European Union has issued a number of directives and regulations aimed at creating a high-standard legal framework to reduce and avoid these risks.

This chapter focuses on a selection of the instruments for primary and secondary markets, including the relevant provisions of Directive 2003/71/EC of the European

---

1   Felicia H Kung, *The Regulation of Corporate Bond Offerings: A Comparative Analysis*, 26 U PA J INT'L ECON L 409, 427 (Fall, 2005), 410.
2   *Ibid*, 410-411.
3   *Ibid*, 411.

Parliament and the Council of November 4 2003 on the prospectus to be published when securities are offered to the public or admitted to trading and amending Directive 2001/34/EC (the Prospectus Directive, as amended by Directive 2010/73/EC,[4] the Amending Directive). Although the Prospectus Directive was recently amended, an analysis of both the previous and the current regime is relevant. In addition to the Prospectus Directive, the chapter focuses on the Directive 2004/39/EC by the European Parliament and the Council, dated April 21 2004, referring to the markets of the financial instruments (the MiFID). Compliance with the provisions contained in the European directives and regulations – as implemented by EU member states – is mandatory for issuers and financial intermediaries working in debt capital markets, and any breach will expose them to legal risk and to reputational risk, both of which can damage their business.

2.   The retail cascade

2.1   The previous regime

Under the public offers rules, following the implementation of the Prospectus Directive in EU member states, an offer of securities must be accompanied by the publication of an offering prospectus approved by the home member state's regulator or hold a European passport in another member state. A European passport is issued to a prospectus following approval by the EEA competent authority in its home state (home authority), and may be used as a passport for offers or listings in any other EEA country without further review or the imposition of further disclosure requirements by the authority of that EEA country (host authority). This reduces the delay and cost of obtaining approval in each EEA country. The issuer simply files a request with the home authority to notify the host authority in the EEA country where the offer or admission is to be made, and the home authority will provide the host authority with a statement that the prospectus has been drawn up in accordance with the Prospectus Directive (certificate of approval).[5]

One important aspect of public offers is the so-called 'retail cascade' issue – the possibility that an intermediary (qualified investor) purchasing securities with the intention of selling them on (either immediately or shortly afterwards) to retail investors may use the prospectus prepared by the issuer. This issue arises because, under Article 3(2) of the Prospectus Directive, any resale of securities which were previously subject to an offer exempt from the obligation to publish an offering prospectus (eg, an offer addressed exclusively to qualified investors) is regarded as a separate offer and the definition of "offer of securities to the public", set out in Article 2(1)(d), will apply for the purpose of deciding whether that resale is an offer of securities to the public. This issue was treated differently before July 1 2012. In this section we will analyse the previous regime in order to clarify the changes to the

---

4   Directive 2010/73/EU of the European Parliament and of the Council of 24 November 2010 amending Directive 2003/71/EC on the prospectus to be published when securities are offered to the public or admitted to trading and 2004/109/EC on the harmonisation of transparency requirements in relation to information about issuers whose securities are admitted to trading on a regulated market.

5   www.nortonrose.com/knowledge/publications/30873/european-passporting.

current regime, which is discussed in the next section.

Under this provision, the offeror (ie, the entity that will carry out the on-sale characterised as a re-offer under Article 3(2) of the Prospectus Directive) would be the intermediary and, accordingly, would be required to prepare an offering prospectus since its re-offer activity is open to the public in the relevant member state. The responsibility for the preparation/publication of the prospectus would then lie with the authorised intermediary offering/placing the securities with retail investors.

If an institutional investor buys bonds issued by the issuer without a prospectus (ie, an exempted offer) and then sells the bonds to the public, it will be considered to be making a public offer and so must draft a prospectus. Otherwise, the offer will be void.

The competent authorities of some member states took a different approach, requiring a detailed disclosure in the issuer's offering prospectus to ensure that it contained all the information necessary for the final investor to make an informed evaluation of the securities and of the terms of the offer (including the responsibilities of the issuer and intermediaries involved).

In order to avoid the risk of misunderstanding for retail investors, the offering documentation should make it clear that the entity which drafts the prospectus (ie, the issuer) is the actual offeror.

Even if the competent authorities do not raise any issues in relation to the compliance of an offer with the Prospectus Directive, investors could argue that:

- the prospectus has not been drafted by the actual offeror; and
- in case of passported offers, the prospectus could not have been properly passported in the relevant host member state, since the entity responsible for the prospectus (ie, the issuer) is not carrying out any public offer in that state.

If an entity is acting as manager and the prospectus indicates that the manager is re-offering the securities to the public, it is possible that the relevant authority will not consider the manager to be the offeror, but instead will consider the issuer to be the offeror and the manager to be the 'placer'. This may raise additional issues if the manager is not authorised to conduct placement activity with retail investors in the host state.

Several countries have investigated this practice. The United Kingdom has noted that since the introduction of the Prospectus Directive on July 1 2005, there have been practical issues in addressing the disclosure items relating to the 'Terms and Conditions of the Offer' set out in Annexes V.5 and XII.5 of the Prospectus Directive Regulation.[6] If a debt offer is through a retail cascade (which, as defined by the European Securities and Markets Authority,[7] is a distribution mechanism where securities are offered to retail investors not directly by the issuer, but by a distribution

---

6   Regulation (EC) No 809/2004 implementing Directive 2003/71/EC of the European Parliament and of the Council as regards information contained in prospectuses as well as the format, incorporation by reference and publication of such prospectuses and dissemination of advertisements, as amended by Commission Regulation (EC) No 211/2007 of 27 February 2007, Commission Delegated Regulation (EU) No 486/2012 of 30 March 2012 and Commission Delegated Regulation (EU) No 862/2012 of 4 June 2012

7   European Securities and Markets Authority (ESMA), www.esma.europa.eu. Formerly the Committee of European Securities Regulators (CESR).

network of financial intermediaries[8]), the regulation requires detailed disclosure of all offers in the distribution chain, as set out in Annexes V and XII.[9]

However, the requirement creates problems when preparing a prospectus for a retail cascade offer, since the detailed information required by Annex V.5 or Annex XII.5 to be included in the prospectus is not known at the time the prospectus is prepared, and also it may change during the course of the retail cascade.[10]

A specific area of concern is how an investor will know whether an entity offering securities is acting in association with the issuer (which will determine whether the offer is one to which the prospectus relates or whether it is a separate, unrelated offer).[11]

The ability to address this point is fundamental to any approach put forward as a solution to the retail cascade issue.[12]

The UK Listing Authority's proposed approach is for issuers to utilise Article 23.4 of the Prospectus Directive Regulation, which the authority believes is applicable to the situation. Article 23.4 allows information required by Articles 4–20 of the regulation to be omitted if the information is not relevant to the offer.

If the information required to be disclosed under Annexes V.5 and XII.5 of the Prospectus Directive Regulation is not relevant to a specific retail cascade offer, it may be omitted under Article 23.4. An issuer wishing to use Article 23.4 must make this clear in the comment box (against the V.5/XII.5 rules) when submitting the relevant checklists.[13]

If an issuer uses this derogation and does not identify all authorised distribution agents in its prospectus, the UK Listing Authority would require a prominent statement on the front page of the prospectus advising that investors should check with the securities distributor whether it is acting in association with the issuer as part of the offer to which the prospectus relates. The prospectus should also state that if the distributor is not acting in association with the issuer, investors may not have recourse against the issuer in respect of information in the prospectus.[14]

ESMA expressly addressed the matter in its Frequently Asked Questions.[15] Q&A 56 ('Retail cascade offers'), stressing that the objectives of the Prospectus Directive – investor protection and lowering the cost of capital – are the key priorities for ESMA[16] in deciding the best way forward. When the Prospectus Directive was introduced,

---

8   The ESMA definition covers both schemes in which securities are sold by the issuer to financial intermediaries (eg, on the basis of an underwriting agreement) and subsequently resold by intermediaries to retail investors and schemes where financial intermediaries are responsible for the final placement of the securities without any previous underwriting or acquisition of the securities: SMA, Final Report, ESMA's technical advice on possible delegated acts concerning the Prospectus Directive as amended by the Directive 2010/73/EU, February 29 2012, ESMA/2012/137, www.esma.europa.eu/system/files/2012-137.pdf.

9   Financial Services Authority, UKLA Publications List!, Issue 16, July 2007, page 11 www.fsa.gov.uk/pubs/ukla/list_jul07.pdf.

10   Ibid.

11   Ibid.

12   Ibid.

13   Ibid.

14   Ibid.

15   Frequently Asked Questions, Prospectuses: common positions agreed by ESMA Members, 13th updated version, June 2011, www.esma.europa.eu/system/files/11_85.pdf.

16   In this chapter ESMA is used instead of CESR, even if the original text there was the mention to CESR.

other relevant FSAP[17] legislation such as the MiFID and the Transparency Directive had not been introduced, and the full impact of other key legislation, such as the Market Abuse Directive, had not been realised. The objectives of the Prospectus Directive will not be met if a new prospectus must be drawn up each time an offer/sub-offer is made within the 12-month validity period of the prospectus in a retail cascade context, when the other directives provide sufficient regulatory protection. ESMA considers that these FSAP directives must be viewed as a whole.[18]

Article 3.2 of the Prospectus Directive must be viewed in this light. ESMA considers that the rationale for the article is to ensure that when a non-exempt public offer takes place, an offeror is not able to circumvent the publication of a prospectus by relying on an earlier exemption.[19]

A ESMA fact-finding exercise found that the current practice in most jurisdictions is that intermediaries acting in association with an issuer may use the issuer's prospectus for their offers, but intermediaries not acting in association with the issuer may not use its prospectus – they must draw up a separate one.[20]

ESMA acknowledged that the solution described in the Q&A for retail cascade is a temporary one, based on the current provisions of the directive, and a recommendation to amend the regulation based on a more robust regulatory solution may be made to the EU Commission.[21]

ESMA members consider that the key principle is the distinction between intermediaries who are acting in association with the issuer and those that are not. ESMA members encourage issuers clearly to disclose in the prospectus (or supplement) or through public announcements the identity of the intermediaries acting in association with them. In addition, ESMA members consider that it is good practice to insert a bold notice in a suitable place in the prospectus, informing investors that they should verify with the offeror whether the offeror is acting in association with the issuer.[22]

As mentioned above, ESMA provides a clear definition of retail cascade – the term used to describe the distribution mechanism of debt securities to retail investors through a distribution network of intermediaries. Offers from an issuer to intermediaries are usually exempt offers under Article 3.2 of the directive. Usually, however, the final placement of the securities to the retail investors is not exempt from the obligation to produce a prospectus.

---

17   "Specific Community legislation promoting the single market was introduced in the 1980s, and since then there have been two step changes; the first was the Financial Services Action Plan (FSAP), launched in 1999; the second, the significant legislative programme initiated in response to the financial crisis. The FSAP consists of 42 measures, including 24 EC Directives to be transposed into the law of each Member State, and Regulations, which are directly applicable in all Member States. The FSAP has three specific objectives: (i) to create a single EU wholesale market; (ii) to achieve open and secure retail markets; and (iii) to create state-of-the-art prudential rules and structures of supervision. These objectives are designed to promote Europe's wider economy by removing barriers and increasing competition among financial services firms, thereby making markets more efficient and reducing the cost of raising capital to the wider economy." www.fsa.gov.uk/about/what/international/european.

18   Frequently Asked Questions, Prospectuses: common positions agreed by ESMA Members, 13th updated version, June 2011, www.esma.europa.eu/system/files/11_85.pdf.

19   *Ibid.*

20   *Ibid.*

21   *Ibid.*

22   *Ibid.*

In response to market participants' requests for clarification of the directive, in particular how the definition of a public offer and its interaction with last paragraph of Article 3.2 applies when a retail cascade is used, ESMA has identified the three key issues.

First, who is responsible for producing the prospectus? Under the current provisions of the directive, anyone who makes a public offer is responsible for drawing up its prospectus (Article 3.1). If an offer includes sub-offers from intermediaries to the end-investor, the intermediaries should be able to rely on the issuer's prospectus without having to draw up a separate prospectus, in particular where the issuer has consented to this: if intermediaries are acting in association with the issuer, an additional prospectus should not be required. However, intermediaries that sell securities on their own account – that is, not acting in association with the issuer – must have a separate prospectus.[23]

The second issue is who is responsible for the publication of supplements to the prospectus under Article 16 of the directive. An issuer must update the prospectus while sub-offers from the intermediaries acting in association with it subsist. Intermediaries that do not act in association with the issuer must update their own prospectus.[24]

The third issue relates to the information to be included in the prospectus. As regards the completeness of the prospectus in respect of the information relating to the sub-offers, the information in the prospectus is usually sufficient except that some of the information, in particular the information required by Annex V, Item 5 (Terms and Conditions), will not be available at the time the prospectus is published. The information on allocation, distribution and pricing will be provided by the intermediaries to the end-investor at the time of any sub-offer, so may be omitted under Article 23.4 of the Prospectus Regulation. ESMA considers that it is good practice to insert a bold notice in a suitable place in the prospectus informing investors that such information will be provided at the time of any sub-offers.[25]

The EU Commission examined the issue in the Frequently Asked Questions of its Prospectus Directive,[26] explaining that the obligations attached to retail cascade offers need some clarification. A retail cascade typically occurs when securities are sold to investors (other than qualified investors) by intermediaries and not directly by the issuer. In particular, it is unclear how the requirement to produce and update a prospectus, and the provisions on responsibility and liability, should apply when securities are placed by the issuer with financial intermediaries and are subsequently, over a period that may run to many months, sold on to retail investors, possibly through one or more additional tiers of intermediaries. This may increase costs for issuers and intermediaries and in certain cases result in the duplication of disclosure requirements. A valid prospectus, drawn up by the issuer or the offeror and available to the public in the final placement of securities through financial intermediaries or

---

23 *Ibid.*
24 *Ibid.*
25 *Ibid.*
26 http://europa.eu/rapid/pressReleasesAction.do?reference=MEMO/09/412&format=HTML&aged=0&
    language=EN&guiLanguage=en.

in any subsequent resale of securities, will provide sufficient information for investors to make informed decisions. Therefore, financial intermediaries placing or subsequently reselling the securities should be entitled to rely on the initial prospectus published by the issuer or the offeror, provided that it is valid and supplemented as necessary and that the issuer or the offeror responsible for drawing it up consents to its use. In this case, no other prospectus should be required. If the issuer or the offeror responsible for drawing up the initial prospectus does not consent to its use, the financial intermediary should be required to publish a new prospectus. The financial intermediary could use the initial prospectus by incorporating the relevant parts by reference into its new prospectus.[27]

2.2 The new regime

As mentioned above, the retail cascade regime has changed recently.

On January 20 2011, the European Commission mandated the ESMA to provide technical advice on possible "delegated acts" concerning the Prospectus Directive as amended by the Amending Prospectus Directive.[28]

On October 4 2011, ESMA submitted its Technical Advice on Part I of the mandate related to, among other things, (i) the format and content of final terms to a base prospectus and (ii) the prospectus summaries required for low denomination debt and equity prospectuses to the European Commission (the 'Part I Technical Advice').[29]

On February 29 2012, ESMA submitted its Technical Advice on Part II of the mandate relating, among other things, to the consent to use a prospectus in a retail cascade (the 'Part II Technical Advice').[30]

In ESMA's 'Advice on the Consent to use a Prospectus in a Retail Cascade', it noted that the intermediaries, when subsequently reselling or placing the securities, may either act in association with the issuer, on the basis of an individual agreement between the parties involved, or act independently from the issuer, on the basis of the issuer's general consent to rely on its initial prospectus. Such offers by intermediaries to retail investors, which are often seen as a series of different offers, may take place over a period of several weeks or months.[31]

ESMA's view is that if a financial intermediary wishes to make an offer or sub-offer and none of the exemptions from the obligation to publish a prospectus stated in Article 3.2.1 of the Prospectus Directive apply, the offer or sub-offer must comply with the terms and conditions described in the prospectus, or base prospectus/final terms, in order to be able to rely on the prospectus published by the issuer under Article 3.2.3 of the Prospectus Directive. In particular, the terms and conditions of the securities must not deviate from the terms and conditions in the prospectus.

---

27   *Ibid.*
28   www.linklaters.com/pdfs/mkt/london/120501_EUPD_Amending_Directive_FAQs.pdf, Frequently asked questions on the Prospectus Amending Directive, June 1 2012.
29   *Ibid.*
30   ESMA, Final Report, ESMA's technical advice on possible delegated acts concerning the Prospectus Directive as amended by the Directive 2010/73/EU, February 29 2012, ESMA/2012/137, www.esma.europa.eu/system/files/2012-137.pdf.
31   *Ibid.*

However, due to the nature of offers or sub-offers made within a retail cascade by different financial intermediaries over time, it may not be possible for the issuer or person responsible for drawing up the prospectus to include in the prospectus or the final terms information on the terms and conditions of the offers or sub-offers subsequently made by the financial intermediaries, since these may be unknown when the prospectus is approved or its final terms are filed.

This is particularly the case for offers by intermediaries acting independently from the issuer. Therefore, such information may be omitted in the prospectus under Article 23.4 of the Prospectus Regulation and will be provided by the financial intermediaries at the time of any sub-offers and will be the responsibility of each financial intermediary. It is assumed that the information would in particular relate to the offer price, which is generally expected to fluctuate in accordance with prevailing market conditions, but could also relate to any other information on the intermediary's specific sub-offer (except for the location and offer period in which public offers or sub-offers in retail cascade can be made).[32]

Issuers granting consent to use a prospectus for sub-offers must insert in a suitable place in the prospectus a bold notice informing investors that information regarding such sub-offers will be provided at the time of the sub-offers. ESMA expects such notice to be included in the prospectus in the context of the other information items required in case of retail cascades.[33]

Therefore, from July 1 2012, an issuer's consent to the use of its prospectus by a third party must be included in the relevant prospectus or base prospectus.

The above analysis indicates that ESMA's understanding of current market practice in a retail cascade is that financial intermediaries, when subsequently reselling or placing the securities, may act either (i) in association with the issuer, on the basis of an individual agreement between the parties involved (the individual consent approach), or act independently from the issuer, on the basis of the issuer's general consent to rely on its initial prospectus (the general consent approach).

In the individual consent approach, an issuer must include in the prospectus the identities of the financial intermediaries that are granted consent to use the prospectus or base prospectus, together with any conditions attached to the consent. The underlying written agreement between the issuer and the relevant financial intermediaries does not need to be disclosed to investors as it contains provisions which are only relevant to the parties to the agreement. In the case of a base prospectus, certain information that is not known at the time it is approved may be included in the relevant final terms. ESMA acknowledges that certain information may only be known after the prospectus or base prospectus has been approved by, or final terms filed with, the competent authority (eg, information on the identity of additional financial intermediaries if the group of financial intermediaries appointed on an issue of securities will change frequently). In this case, the information may be published at a later date in the manner prescribed in Article 14.2(c) of the Prospectus Directive (ie, on the issuer's and the relevant financial intermediaries' websites).

---

32   *Ibid.*
33   *Ibid.*

In the general consent approach, an issuer must include in the prospectus a general consent to use the prospectus together with any conditions attached to the consent. This general consent constitutes an offer by the issuer to any financial intermediary (that meets any relevant conditions) to use and rely on the issuer's prospectus. Any financial intermediary wishing to accept this offer must publish on its website the fact that it is relying on the prospectus for its offer of securities with the consent of the issuer. The financial intermediary must also inform investors that the prospectus has been published and where it can be obtained. As there is no separate underlying individual written agreement between the parties involved (as would be the case for the individual consent approach), ESMA considers it essential that any information on retail cascades, including any conditions attached to the consent, must (other than information on the offer period upon which public offers or sub-offers of securities can be made by financial intermediaries) be included within the prospectus or base prospectus itself.[34]

ESMA has advised that the information which the issuer should disclose in the prospectus must include:

- a statement that the issuer consents to the use of the prospectus for public offers of its securities by financial intermediaries, together with any conditions attached to the consent;
- a statement that the issuer's responsibility for the content of the prospectus will extend to any public offers of its securities by financial intermediaries that have been granted consent to use the prospectus;
- the period for which consent to use the prospectus for public offers of its securities by financial intermediaries is granted;
- the offer period upon which public offers or sub-offers of its securities can be made by financial intermediaries or a place holder in the form of final terms for such information to be disclosed in the relevant final terms.[35]

On the terms and conditions of offers or sub-offers, ESMA acknowledges that offers or sub-offers made within a retail cascade may be made by different financial intermediaries over time. As a result, it may not be possible for an issuer to include in the prospectus, or base prospectus/final terms, information on the terms and conditions of the offers or sub-offers to be made by the financial intermediaries (eg, because the information may not be known at the time the prospectus or base prospectus is approved by, or the relevant final terms filed with, the competent authority). This is particularly relevant to public offers of securities by financial intermediaries acting independently from the issuer (ie, under the general consent approach). Therefore, ESMA has concluded that, with the exception of information on the duration and location of the offers and sub-offers, all the other information required by Item 5 of Annex V of the Prospectus Regulation (or, eg, Item 5 of Annex XII) may be omitted from the prospectus or base prospectus/final terms. The

---

34 www.linklaters.com/pdfs/mkt/london/120501_EUPD_Amending_Directive_FAQs.pdf, Frequently asked questions on the Prospectus Amending Directive, June 1 2012.
35 *Ibid.*

information may be provided by the financial intermediaries to the investors at the time of the relevant offer and each financial intermediary must accept responsibility for the information that it provides.[36]

In the individual consent approach, ESMA's view is that new information on financial intermediaries that is not known at the time the prospectus or base prospectus is approved by, or final terms filed with, the competent authority may be published at a later date. This information should have no effect on the assessment of the securities and should, therefore, not trigger the requirement for a supplement. However, if such information does constitute a new factor, material mistake or inaccuracy relating to information in the prospectus which is capable of affecting the assessment of the securities, the issuer must publish a supplement in accordance with Article 16 of the Prospectus Directive.[37]

ESMA has issued a new version of its Prospectus FAQs, in which question 56 (retail cascades) is deleted and a new question 81 (consents to retail cascades) is added.[38]

Question 81 of the new version of FAQs[39] is: "What are the information items on and conditions to the consent to use the prospectus for subsequent resale of securities or final placement through financial intermediaries ("retail cascade") as contained in Article 3 (2) subparagraph 3 of the amended Prospectus Directive?" In answering, ESMA clarifies that in order to ensure maximum consistency in the application of the Prospectus Directive, as amended pending the official publication and entry into force of the Commission Delegated Regulation amending Regulation 809/2004/EC as regards information on the consent to use of the prospectus, information on underlying indices and the requirement for a report prepared by independent accountants or auditors (COM DR 2), adopted by the Commission on June 4 2012, ESMA recommends that any prospectus which grants its use in subsequent resale of securities or final placement of securities through financial intermediaries should anticipate the requirements of COM DR 2.

Article 10 of the Amending Directive provides that

A valid prospectus, drawn up by the issuer or the person responsible for drawing up the prospectus and available to the public at the time of the final placement of securities through financial intermediaries or in any subsequent resale of securities, provides sufficient information for investors to make informed investment decisions. Therefore, financial intermediaries placing or subsequently reselling the securities should be entitled to rely upon the initial prospectus published by the issuer or the person responsible for drawing up the prospectus as long as this is valid and duly supplemented in accordance with Articles 9 and 16 of Directive 2003/71/EC and the issuer or the person responsible for drawing up the prospectus consents to its use. The issuer or the person responsible for drawing up the prospectus should be able to attach conditions to his or her consent. The consent, including any conditions attached thereto, should be given in a written agreement between the parties involved enabling assessment by

---

36   *Ibid.*
37   *Ibid.*
38   SNR Denton ESMA updates prospectus FAQs on retail cascades, July 27 2012, www.lexology.com/library/detail.aspx?g=2daa7787-922c-4564-a649-7197afddb765.
39   ESMA, Questions and Answers, Prospectuses, 16th updated version, July 2012.

relevant parties of whether the resale or final placement of securities complies with the agreement. In the event that consent to use the prospectus has been given, the issuer or person responsible for drawing up the initial prospectus should be liable for the information stated therein and in case of a base prospectus, for providing and filing final terms and no other prospectus should be required. However, in case the issuer or the person responsible for drawing up such initial prospectus does not consent to its use, the financial intermediary should be required to publish a new prospectus. In that case, the financial intermediary should be liable for the information in the prospectus, including all information incorporated by reference and, in case of a base prospectus, final terms.

Consequently, in complying with the requirements of Article 3(2), subparagraph 3 of the amended Prospectus Directive, the issuer, offeror or person seeking admission to trading on a regulated market should so far as possible apply the requirements of COM DR 2 as published on June 4 2012 on the European Commission' website when drawing up a prospectus to be used in retail cascades. In particular, these steps should be taken immediately upon communication of this Q&A in the light of the implementation of the amendments to the amended Prospectus Directive on July 1 2012.[40]

3. The supplement to the prospectus

3.1 The previous regime

Another risk related to retail debt capital markets concerns the supplement to the prospectus.

Article 16 of the Prospectus Directive (Supplements to the prospectus) provides that every significant new factor, material mistake or inaccuracy relating to the information included in the prospectus which is capable of affecting the assessment of the securities and which arises or is noted between the time that the prospectus is approved and the final closing of the offer to the public or, as the case may be, the time when trading on a regulated market begins, must be stated in a supplement to the prospectus. The supplement must be approved in the same way within seven working days and published in accordance with at least the same arrangements as were applied when the original prospectus was published. The summary, and any translations of it, must also be supplemented, if necessary, to take into account the new information included in the supplement. Investors who have already agreed to purchase or subscribe for the securities before the supplement is published will have the right to withdraw their acceptances, exercisable within a time limit of not less than two working days after the publication of the supplement.

This provision will have a significant effect on public offers and on retail investors. The decision to publish or not to publish supplement can affect the investment decisions made or to be made by retail investors. The rules also have practical consequences which must be considered by the issuers. Generally, an offer period lasts between two and four weeks, during which investment requests are received by the financial intermediaries and communicated to the issuers for the

---

40   *Ibid.*

issue of the requested amount of bonds. Settlement takes place after the close of the offer period (usually within two or three days), commonly through a delivery versus payment (DVP) system where the issuer receives the funds and the investors receive their securities. If during the offer period a supplement is published by the issuer, investors who have already agreed to purchase or subscribe for the securities will have the right to withdraw their acceptances, exercisable within a time limit of not less than two working days after the publication of the supplement.

If the issuer publishes a supplement on the last day of the offer, or even the first day after the offer closes, investors must be given the opportunity to withdraw. The settlement date may be postponed, or the issuer may undertake to buy securities already issued in the case of withdrawal after the settlement date. The planning of a public offer should consider the risk of a supplement being published, and structure the timing to account for this.

This possibility is so risky for the debt capital market that ESMA has dedicated several Q&As[41] to it.

Q&A 19 addresses the question of whether the publication of interim financial statements is considered to be a significant new factor that requires the publication of a supplement under Article 16 of the directive. In this respect, there is no systematic requirement to supplement the prospectus when interim financial statements are produced. It will depend on the specific circumstances in particular, the relevance of the information included in the interim financial statements (such as any significant deviation from previous financial information) or the type of securities to which the prospectus refers. In the case of doubt, ESMA members recommend that the issuer produces the supplement.

Q&A 20 addresses the question of whether the publication of a profit forecast before the final closing of the offer is a significant new factor that requires the publication of a supplement under Article 16. This is relevant since, under the regulation, the insertion of a profit forecast in a prospectus is optional. The answer emphasises that paragraph 44 of ESMA's "recommendations for the consistent implementation of the European Commission's Regulation on Prospectuses" (Regulation 809/2004/EC) states:

> CESR considers that there is a presumption that an outstanding forecast made other than in a previous prospectus will be material in the case of shares issues (especially in the context of an IPO). This is not necessarily the presumption in case of non-equity securities.

Although the issuer will decide when a supplement is needed, according to this statement there would be a presumption in the case described in ESMA's recommendations that the publication of a profit forecast before the final closing of the offer would constitute material information. Therefore, in such a case a supplement should be prepared including the profit forecast and complying with item 13 of Annex I of the regulation.[42]

It has been asked whether the right of withdrawal related to a publication of a

41 Frequently Asked Questions, Prospectuses: common positions agreed by ESMA Members, 13th updated version, June 2011, www.esma.europa.eu/system/files/11_85.pdf.
42 Ibid.

supplement should be the right of withdrawal and the actual period for the right mentioned in the supplement. The answer is positive, as ESMA considers that, provided investors are allowed to withdraw their subscription in accordance with Article 16 of the Prospectus Directive, this would be necessary information for investors under Article 5 of the Prospectus Directive.[43]

Under Article 16 of the directive, the issuer must file a supplement with the competent authority for approval as soon as practicable if a significant new factor arises or a material mistake or inaccuracy is discovered.

Non-relevant information in relation to a published prospectus does not trigger the obligation to publish a supplement.[44]

ESMA members considered how to deal with information that arises after the publication of the prospectus which is not significant in terms of the Prospectus Directive (ie, does not significantly affect the assessment of the securities and therefore does not require a supplement), but could be useful for investors. The directive states that the text and the format of the prospectus, and/or the supplements to the prospectus, published or made available to the public, must at all times be identical to the original version approved by the home authority (Article 14.6). Under Article 16.1, every significant new factor, material mistake or inaccuracy relating to the information included in the prospectus which is capable of affecting the assessment of the securities must be published through a supplement to the prospectus. There are cases when the information is not significant in terms of the Prospectus Directive, but could be useful for investors – for example, where the prospectus contains mistakes or inaccuracies which are not material.[45]

As prescribed by Article 14, the prospectus approved by the competent authority cannot subsequently be modified (apart from the supplement procedure). However, if the prospectus contains a mistake or inaccuracy that is not material or significant under to Article 16 of the directive, the issuer is entitled to make an announcement to the market explaining the mistake or inaccuracy.[46]

The above comments are without prejudice to the obligations imposed on issuers of securities admitted to trading on a regulated market by other directives, in particular Directive 2003/6/EC on Market Abuse.

In Poland, if new factors arise that refer only to the organisation of the subscription or admission to trading of the securities and are not material or significant under Article 16 of the directive, the competent authority permits the issuer to make an announcement to the market explaining that new factor.

There are many issues related to supplement which are beyond the scope of this chapter. However, one scenario which should be considered is where a passported public offer in which a supplement to base prospectus is published before the offer period starts, but is not provided to the distributor and so is not published on the distributor's website together with the base prospectus. In this case, the non-publication should not create legal responsibility because, under Article 14 of the

---

43   *Ibid.*
44   *Ibid.*
45   *Ibid.*
46   *Ibid.*

Prospectus Directive and as disclosed in the final terms, the base prospectus and any supplements to it are published on the relevant authority's website as well as on the issuer's website. Publication on the distributor's website is at the party's option; it is not a legal requirement. ESMA, in its Q&A 3, clarified that if the issuer complies with the publication requirements set out in Article 14.2 of the Prospectus Directive, the host authority is not entitled to intervene in the publication of the prospectus. Article 14 of the directive provides a list of methods of publication of the prospectus, all of which are valid for investors within the European Union (in the home member state and in the host member states). Normally, foreign prospectuses are published in accordance with Article 14(d) and (e), so any additional method of publication is at the party's option.

3.2 The new regime

For the sake of completeness, it must highlighted that under the amendments to the Prospectus Directive on retail disclosure discussed above, some amendments have been made to the regime for supplements:

- supplements may only be used to describe something which is a significant new factor, material mistake or inaccuracy relating to information described in the prospectus;
- withdrawal rights following publication of a supplement have been standardised at two days across Europe – so this period will be reduced from five days in Sweden and 15 days in Hungary; and
- if a supplement affects only certain securities, the withdrawal rights will only apply to the affected securities.[47]

4. MiFID – conflict of interests

We have analysed some of the relevant issues related to the primary debt capital markets. However, there are significant risks in secondary debt capital markets that cannot be left out of this discussion. This sector of the market is governed mainly by the Markets in Financial Instruments Directive (MiFID),[48] which is designed to help to integrate Europe's financial markets and to establish a common regulatory framework for Europe's securities markets. MiFID incorporates the following European legislation:

- Directive 2004/39/EC (MiFID), adopted in April 2004 – a 'framework' Level 1 Directive which has been supplemented by technical implementing measures (see the Level 2 legislation below);
- Implementing Directive 2006/73/EC and Implementing Regulation 1287/2006/EC (the Level 2 legislation);[49] and

---

47 Prospectus Directive amendments came into force on July 1 2012 – impact on debt capital markets, www.ashurst.com/doc.aspx?id_Content=7932.
48 Directive 2004/39/EC by the European Parliament and the Council, dated April 21 2004, referring to the markets of the financial instruments (MiFID).
49 Modifying Directives 85/611/EEC and 93/6/EEC of the Council and the Directive 2000/12/EC of the European Parliament and of the Council abrogating the Directive 93/22/EEC of the Council, as well as the Directive 2006/31/ EC of the European Parliament and of the Council, dated April 5 2006 which modifies the Directive 2004/39/EC.

- MiFID Implementing Regulation: Commission Regulation (EC) No 1287/2006 of 10 August 2006 implementing Directive 2004/39/EC of the European Parliament and of the Council as regards record-keeping obligations for investment firms, transaction reporting, market transparency, admission of financial instruments to trading, and defined terms for the purposes of that directive.

Clause 2 of MiFID points out that in recent years more investors have become active in the financial markets and are being offered an even more complex wide-ranging set of services and instruments. In view of these developments, the legal framework of the Community should encompass the full range of investor-oriented activities. To this end, it is necessary to provide for the degree of harmonisation needed to offer investors a high level of protection and to allow investment firms to provide services throughout the Community, being a single market, on the basis of home country supervision. In view of this, Directive 93/22/EEC has been replaced by MiFID.

Clause 5 notes that it is necessary to establish a comprehensive regulatory regime governing the execution of transactions in financial instruments, irrespective of the trading methods used to conclude those transactions, to ensure a high quality of execution of investor transactions and to uphold the integrity and overall efficiency of the financial system. In emphasising that a coherent and risk-sensitive framework for regulating the main types of order-execution arrangements currently active in the European financial marketplace should be provided for, it is noted that it is necessary to recognise the emergence of a new generation of organised trading systems alongside regulated markets. These new trading systems should also be subjected to obligations designed to preserve the efficient and orderly functioning of financial markets. With a view to establishing a proportionate regulatory framework, provision should be made for the inclusion of a new investment service which relates to the operation of a multilateral trading facility.

MiFID identifies several risks for the secondary retail market, the first and most significant of which is the problem of conflict of interest.[50]

Under Article 18 of MiFID, member states may prescribe that the investment firms[51] adopt all reasonable measures to identify the conflicts of interests which could arise. This applies to managers, employees and the other agents or the persons directly or indirectly connected with the firms and their clients (or between two clients) at the moment of the performance of the investment or accessory service, or of a combination of such services. If the organisation or administrative provisions

---

50   The following discussion is based on author's article: Ferdinando Bruno (together with Andrea Rozzi) *The Eligible Operator in the Italian Market*, 3(12) *International In-house Counsel Journal* (Summer, 2010), 11.

51   Article 4, no. 1, of the directive defines as 'investment firm' any legal person whose regular occupation or business is the provision of one or more investment services to third parties and/or the performance of one or more investment activities on a professional basis. It also provides that member states may include in the definition of investment firms undertakings which are not legal persons, provided that: a) their legal status ensures a level of protection for third parties' interests equivalent to that afforded by legal persons, and b) they are subject to equivalent prudential supervision appropriate to their legal form.

adopted by the investment firm[52] to manage the conflicts of interest are sufficient to assure, with reasonable certainty, that the risk of damage to the interests of the clients can be avoided, the investment firm must clearly inform the clients, before acting upon their behalf, about the general nature and/or about the sources of such conflicts of interest.[53]

MiFID[54] also provides that investment firms maintain and enforce organisation and administrative provisions that are effective in order to adopt all the reasonable measures to ensure that any conflicts of interest[55] do not harm the interests of their clients.

The Community legislator has placed responsibility for the management conflicts of interest on investment firms. The two stages for addressing conflicts of interest are identification and management, with the latter aimed at avoiding the negative impact that the conflicts may cause.

The definition of conflict of interest is provided by the Level 2 Directive: recital 24 provides that the circumstances which should be treated as giving rise to a conflict of interest are cases where there is a conflict between the interests of the firm or certain persons connected to the firm or the firm's group and the duty the firm owes to a client; or between the differing interests of two or more of its clients, to both of which the firm has a duty. It is not enough that the firm may gain a benefit if there is not also a possible disadvantage to a client, or that one client to whom the firm owes a duty may make a gain or avoid a loss without there being a concomitant possible loss to another client.

When an investment service or an accessory service is supplied by an investment firm, it is the management of conflicts of interest that is regulated; the status of the client to whom the service is supplied (retail client, professional client or eligible counterparty) is not important.[56] An investment firm supplying an investment service or accessory service should always regulate the conflicts of interest.

The Level 2 Directive[57] identifies the most significant causes of conflict and provides that, in fulfilling its duty to have in place a management policy for conflicts of interest that complies with the directive and identifies the circumstances giving rise to a conflict of interest, the firm should pay special attention to the activities of investment research and advice, proprietary trading, portfolio management and corporate finance business, including underwriting or selling in an offering of securities and advising on mergers and acquisitions.[58]

These provisions place a strict burden on firms in producing a conflicts of interest policy.

5.   Best execution and elimination of the concentration obligation

The significant Community provisions supporting the best execution and elimination of the concentration obligation are found mainly in Article 19 of MiFID,

---

52   Under MiFID, Article 13, paragraph 3.
53   Under *ibid*, Article 18, paragraph 2.
54   Under *ibid*, Article 13, paragraph 3.
55   As defined by *ibid*, Article 18.
56   *Ibid*, Recital 25.
57   Level 2 Directive, Recital 26.
58   In particular, such attention is appropriate when it results from a control report that the firm or a subject which is linked directly or indirectly to the firm carries out two or more of the above referred activities.

under which member states may prescribe that the investment firms, when providing investment services and/or ancillary services to clients, act honestly, fairly and professionally in accordance with the best interests of their clients.[59]

Article 21 of MiFID sets an obligation for investment firms to execute orders on the most favourable terms to their clients. Member states must require investment firms, when executing orders, to take all reasonable steps to obtain the best possible result for their clients, taking into account price, costs, speed, likelihood of execution and settlement, size, nature, or any other consideration relevant to the execution of the order. However, if a client gives a specific instruction, the investment firm must follow it.

Member states require investment firms to establish and implement effective arrangements for complying with the best execution requirement: investment firms must establish and implement an order execution policy to allow them to obtain the best possible result for their client orders. Such a strategy should include, in respect of each class of instruments, information on the different venues where the investment firm executes its client orders and the factors affecting the choice of execution venue.[60]

6. The classes of clients

MiFID establishes the general criteria of conduct to be observed by the entities eligible for supplying investment services and activities, and ancillary services, based on care of the clients' interests, taking into account the integrity of the market and the specific needs of each category of investors, such as retail clients, professional clients and the eligible counterparties.

One of the objectives of the directive is to protect investors.[61] This means that the measures designed to protect investors must be adapted to meet the needs of each category of investor, defined as (i) retail clients, (ii) professional clients and (iii) eligible counterparties.[62] The professional client is set apart from retail clients, satisfying the criteria established in Annex II of MiFID.[63] Retail clients[64] are clients who are not professional clients (ie, clients who do not satisfy the Annex II criteria);[65] eligible counterparty is a sub-category of professional clients.[66]

The interchangeability of the terms client and investor must be considered. In Community law, an investor is only defined in MiFID, which distinguishes between retail investor and wholesale investor is made, thus addressing the level of 'professional experience' of the investor rather than to its status as a consumer.[67]

---

59   "and that they comply, in particular, with the principles set out in paragraphs 2 to 8".
60   It defines at least the seats allowing the investment firm to obtain the best possible result for the execution of the client orders along the time.
61   MiFID, Recital 16.
62   *Ibid*, Recital 31.
63   bid, Article 4, no 11.
64   7.3.1. Retail clients form a residual category, defined negatively as those clients who are not professionals (Article 4(1)(10) of MiFID): CESR, Background note for the draft implementing directive, February 2006, http://ec.europa.eu/internal_market/securities/docs/isd/dir-2004-39-implement/dir-backgroundnote_en.pdf.
65   MiFID, Article 12.
66   *Ibid*, Article 24.

Annex II of the directive defines 'professional client' as a client possessing the experience, knowledge and expertise necessary to make its own investment decisions and properly to assess the risks it incurs. The annex identifies the entities who, for all services and instruments governed by the directive, should be considered as professional clients.[68]

One unfortunate consequence of the attribution of the status of professional client[69] is the misapplication of a series of important provisions that should not apply to professional clients, such as:

- information about the investment firm and its services for retail clients and potential retail clients;[70]
- information about financial instruments;[71] and
- information requirements concerning safeguarding of client financial instruments or client funds.[72]

It is then provided that these entities, although considered to be professional clients, must be allowed to request non-professional treatment, and investment firms may agree to provide a higher level of protection. This gives rise to an unconditional right for a professional client to request information which would not normally be made available to it.

If a client is an undertaking, before providing any services an investment firm must inform the client that, on the basis of the information available to the firm, it is deemed to be a professional client, and will be treated as such unless the firm and client agree otherwise. The firm must inform the client that it may request a variation of the terms of the agreement in order to secure a higher degree of protection. It is the responsibility of the client considered to be a professional client to ask for a higher level of protection if it considers that it is unable properly to assess or to manage the risks involved.[73]

---

67   Speech by Dr Enrico Cervone, Consumer's week, Settimana di dialogo tra Aziende e Consumatori, Giornata di apertura: Consumatori, Istituzioni, Legislazione, Unioncamere, Rome, November 28 2005, L'azione delle Autorita` di Garanzia, La Consob e la tutela dell'investitore, www.consob.it/ main/documenti/Pubblicazioni/Audizioni/intervento_cervone28_11_2005.html?hkeywords=mifid&doc id=8&page=0&-hits=16.

68   (1) Entities which are required to be authorised or regulated to operate in the financial markets; (2) Large undertakings meeting two of three size requirements on a company basis; (3) National and regional governments, public bodies that manage public debt, Central Banks, international and supranational institutions such as the World Bank, the IMF, the ECB, the EIB and other similar international organisations; (4) Other institutional investors whose main activity is to invest in financial instruments, including entities dedicated to the securitisation of assets or other financing transactions.

69   7.3.2. Professional clients: "Annex II of the level 1 Directive establishes which clients are considered as professionals. Undertakings listed in Section I of Annex II are automatically recognised as professional clients. These are the so called 'per se professionals'. For example, investment firms, credit institutions, insurance companies, some institutional investors as well as defined large undertakings are in this category. Additionally, clients that are not on the list of per se professionals in Section I of Annex II may be treated as professional clients on their request, provided that they fulfil the criteria and follow the procedure set out in Section II of Annex II. Furthermore, per se professionals may request the protection granted to retail clients. The procedure for this is set out in paragraphs 2 to 4 of Section I of Annex II." Background note for the draft implementing Directive, February 2006, http://ec.europa.eu/ internal_market/securities/docs/isd/dir-2004-39-implement/dir-backgroundnote_en.pdf.

70   Level 2 Directive, Article 30.

71   *Ibid*, Article 31.

72   *Ibid*, Article 32.

This option to request different treatment by the investment firm is granted also to retail clients under Annex II of MiFID, which expressly provides that clients other than those mentioned in Section I, including public sector bodies and private individual investors, may also be allowed to waive some of the protections afforded by the conduct of business rules.[74]

MiFID provides a detailed procedure for retail clients to waive the standard protections:

- the client must state in writing to the investment firm that it wishes to be treated as a professional client, either generally or in respect of a particular investment service or transaction, or a type of transaction or product;
- the investment firm must give the client a clear written warning of the protections and investor compensation rights that it may lose;
- the client must state in writing, in a separate document from the contract, that it is aware of the consequences of losing such protections.

Under the directive, investment firms must implement appropriate written internal policies and procedures to categorise clients. Professional clients must inform the firm of any change which could affect their current categorisation. However, if the investment firm becomes aware that the client no longer meets the initial criteria that made it eligible for professional status, the investment firm must take appropriate action.

Particular attention should be given to the category of eligible counterparties. For the purposes of MiFID, eligible counterparties must be considered as acting as clients.[75] For the purposes of ensuring that conduct of business rules (including rules on best execution and handling of client orders) are enforced in respect of those investors most in need of these protections, and to reflect well-established market practice throughout the Community, it is appropriate to clarify that conduct of business rules may be waived in the case of transactions entered into or brought about between eligible counterparties.[76]

In respect of transactions executed between eligible counterparties, the obligation to disclose client limit orders will only apply where a counterparty is explicitly sending a limit order to an investment firm for its execution.[77]

Article 24 of MiFID defines eligible counterparties, recognising them as investment firms, credit institutions, insurance companies, UCITS[78] and their management companies, pension funds and their management companies, other

---

73 "This higher level of protection will be provided when a client who is considered to be a professional enters into a written agreement with the investment firm to the effect that it shall not be treated as a professional for the purposes of the applicable conduct of business regime. Such agreement should specify whether this applies to one or more particular services or transactions, or to one or more types of product or transaction." MiFID, Annex II.

74 The investment firms should therefore be authorised to treat these clients as professional clients, provided that the relevant criteria and procedures are respected. However, they should not assume that these clients have a market knowledge and experience comparable to that of the categories listed in Section I.

75 MiFID, Recital 40.

76 *Ibid*, Recital 41.

77 *Ibid*, Recital 42.

financial institutions authorised or regulated under Community legislation or the national law of a member state, undertakings exempted from the application of MiFID under Article 2(1)(k) and (l), national governments and their corresponding offices, including public bodies that deal with public debt, central banks, and supranational organisations.[79]

A consequence of the status of eligible counterparties[80] is the misapplication of specific protection rules, as it is provided that:

> *Member States shall ensure that investment firms authorised to execute orders on behalf of clients and/or to deal on own account and/or to receive and transmit orders, may bring about or enter into transactions with eligible counterparties without being obliged to comply with the obligations under Articles 19, 21 and 22(1) in respect of those transactions or in respect of any ancillary service directly related to those transactions.[81]*

In this particular case, the misapplied rules concern the provision on the conduct of business obligations when providing investment services to clients,[82] the provision on the obligation to execute orders on terms most favourable to the client (best execution),[83] and the provision on the client order handling rules.[84]

Also, it is possible for eligible counterparties to renounce to the exemption system as it is provided that the classification as eligible counterparty will be without prejudice to the right of the entities to request, either on a general form or on a trade-

---

78   Undertakings for Collective Investments in Transferable Securities (UCITS). It refers to an EU directive adopted in 1985. The objective of UCITS was to allow collective investments to operate throughout the EU with a single authorisation from one member state, allowing funds authorised in one member state to be sold to the public in other member states. In practice, UCITS was not successful as many EU nations have imposed additional regulatory requirements in order to protect local asset managers. www.nasdaq.com/investing/glossary/u/undertakings-for-collective-investments-in-transferable-securities.

79   MiFID, Article 24, paragraph 2.

80   7.3.3. Eligible counterparties: "The level 1 Directive recognises that the most sophisticated classes of investors and capital market participants – the so-called "eligible counterparties" – do not need some of the protections afforded by the conduct of business rules. Thus, Articles 19, 21 and 22(1) of the level 1 Directive do not apply to investment firms when providing the following services to eligible counterparties: execution of orders, dealing on own account, reception and transmission of orders, or any directly related ancillary service. The fact that certain entities are treated as eligible counterparties only in respect of these specific services is crucial to an understanding of the overlap between the categories of professional clients and eligible counterparties. For example, investment firms are both professional clients and eligible counterparties, but their status as eligible counterparty is limited only to the services mentioned above. Entities that are explicitly mentioned in Article 24(2) of the level 1 Directive are automatically recognised as eligible counterparties. These are the "per se eligible counterparties" and include, for example, investment firms, UCITS and their management companies. Per se eligible counterparties may also request treatment as a class of client which benefits from the protection given under the conduct of business rules. Furthermore, the level 1 Directive gives Member States the option to recognise as eligible counterparties entities other than the per se eligible counterparties defined in Article 24(2) of the MiFID, provided that such entities meet certain criteria and have requested to be treated as eligible counterparties. The proposed implementing Directive sets out those criteria." Background note for the draft implementing Directive, February 2006, http://ec.europa.eu/internal_market/securities/docs/isd/dir-2004-39-implement/dir-backgroundnote_en .pdf.

81   MiFID, Article 24, paragraph 1.

82   *Ibid*, Article 19.

83   *Ibid*, Article 21.

84   "Member States shall require that investment firms authorised to execute orders on behalf of clients implement procedures and arrangements which provide for the prompt, fair and expeditious execution of client orders, relative to other client orders or the trading interests of the investment firm. These procedures or arrangements shall allow for the execution of otherwise comparable client orders in accordance with the time of their reception by the investment firm." MiFID, Article 22, paragraph 1.

by-trade basis, treatment as clients whose business with the investments firm is subject to Articles 19, 21 and 22.[85]

In the event of such a request, if the eligible counterparty does not expressly request treatment as a retail client, and the investment firm agrees to that request, the firm must treat the eligible counterparty as a professional client.[86] However, if the eligible counterparty expressly requests treatment as a retail client, the provisions in respect of requests for non-professional treatment specified in the second, third and fourth sub-paragraphs of Section I of Annex II to MiFID will apply.[87]

Under Article 24 of MiFID, member states must ensure that when an investment firm enters into transactions with such undertakings in accordance with paragraph 1, it obtains the express confirmation of the prospective counterparty that it agrees to be treated as an eligible counterparty.[88] Member states will allow the investment firm to obtain this confirmation either in the form of a general agreement or in respect of each individual transaction.

The category of eligible counterparty is not a fixed category. Member states may also recognise as eligible counterparties other undertakings meeting pre-determined proportionate requirements, including quantitative thresholds. In the event of a transaction where the prospective counterparties are located in different jurisdictions, the investment firm must defer to the status of the other undertaking as determined by the law or measures of the member state in which that undertaking is established.[89] Member states may recognise an undertaking as an eligible counterparty if it falls within a category of clients that are to be considered professional clients under paragraphs 1, 2 and 3 of Section I of Annex II to MiFID, excluding any category which is explicitly mentioned in Article 24(2) of the directive.

On request, member states may also recognise as eligible counterparties undertakings that fall within a category of clients which are categorised as professional clients under Section II of Annex II to MiFID. However, in such cases, the undertaking concerned will be recognised as an eligible counterparty only in respect of the services or transactions for which it could be treated as a professional client.[90]

The closing condition provided by the legislator, which requires an investment firm to notify new and existing clients if it changes their categorisation as a retail client, a professional client or an eligible counterparty in accordance with MiFID.[91]

Member states must ensure that investment firms inform their clients in a durable medium of any right that client has to request a different categorisation and of any limitations to the level of client protection that it would entail. Member states will permit investment firms, either on their own initiative or at the request of the

---

85   MiFID, Article 24, paragraph 2.
86   Level 2 Directive, Article 50.
87   *Ibid.*
88   "Member States shall allow the investment firm to obtain this confirmation either in the form of a general agreement or in respect of each individual transaction." MiFID, Article 24, paragraph 3.
89   MiFID, Article 24, paragraph 3.
90   Level 2 Directive, Article 50.
91   *Ibid*, Article 28.

client concerned to treat as a professional or retail client a client that might otherwise be classified as an eligible counterparty, and to treat as a retail client a client that is considered to be a professional client.[92]

7. Conclusions

At the beginning of the chapter it was stated that the recent legislative developments aim to protect retail debt capital markets, and to avoid a recurrence of past financial frauds. Have these goals been achieved? We can answer yes. Today, the new rules discussed in this chapter provide protection for both sides of the debt arena. From the financial institution perspective, the strict rules governing retail cascade issues, supplements and conflict of interests (which sometimes cannot be avoided) impose an obligation on banks and financial intermediaries to provide all relevant information and to act to protect as far as possible the investors. From the retail investors' standpoint, they now enjoy a potential protection as never before. As ever, only experience will tell whether the European legislator has been successful, but we can say that the indicators for optimism are all present.

---

92   *Ibid.*

Fraud within the banking sector

Nikolay Dobrev
University of Liverpool

1.   Introduction

Fraud within the banking sector is a serious problem that affects both individuals and corporations. The level of bank fraud is rapidly increasing. It is difficult to obtain accurate statistical data on fraud since it is often well hidden and very hard to prove, unlike robbery, for example, and financial institutions are often reluctant publicly to disclose instances of fraud, in order to preserve their reputation. Bank fraud may result in the bankruptcy of the financial institutions involved, and thus it may affect the national economy.

Generally, bank fraud is defined as a criminal offence of knowingly executing, or attempting to execute, a scheme or artifice to defraud a financial institution, or to obtain property owned by or under the control of a financial institution, by means of false or fraudulent pretences, representations or promises.[1] Fraud involves different ways of using trickery to obtain another person's or organisation's assets. Frequently, bank fraud is committed by well-educated persons with extensive knowledge of the financial and business sectors, and of banking law, so often it is not discovered for a considerable time. There are many ways of concealing bank fraud, limited only by the fraudster's ingenuity, and even well-trained investigators may find it difficult to identify some bank frauds. Effective investigation of bank fraud is essential for establishing adequate control over this widespread problem. Unless the expertise is available, fraud investigators and the police may struggle to confirm that a bank fraud has been committed, even with clear clues about possible fraudulent activities.

In recent years, fraud and bad management have been the precipitating factor in many banking crises, and although measures have been taken to minimise fraud, it is still increasing. Fraudsters are becoming more organised, which results in higher losses. Although management teams are focusing more on bank fraud, a lot remains to be done.

2.   Types of bank fraud

Bank frauds may be classified into three groups: by flow, by victims and by act.

2.1   Flow frauds

Flow frauds are described by the frequency and the value involved. They may be classified into two types:

---

[1]   Garner, BA (ed), Black's Law Dictionary (8th edn, St. Paul, MN , Thomson West Group, 2004) 685.

- smash and grab: frauds not frequently committed, but high in value over a short period; and
- drip: a large number of frauds, of small value and repeated over a long period.

2.2 Victims frauds

Victims frauds is a classification based on the people affected by loss through fraud. There are also two types:

- fraud against a company (bank): the bank is the victim of any loss incurred through the fraud; and
- fraud against outsiders: the victim of the fraud is an outsider to the company or bank, that is, a bank customer.

2.3 Fraudulent acts

Fraudulent acts are the action that takes place in cases of fraud, that is, the people involved in the act and the method or form by which they perpetrate the fraud. They could be the bank's employees, the bank's executive management board, armed robbers or outsiders, perhaps in collusion with insiders.

3. Methods by which fraud can be perpetrated

There are various methods by which fraud may be perpetrated in banks and other organisations. The list is usually not exhaustive as new methods are continuously being devised.

3.1 Advance fee fraud

Advance fee fraud has recently become one of the most profitable banking frauds, generating an impressive amount of money for its perpetrators. Although schemes of this kind appear to be simple, they are still poorly understood, which is why their victims are persuaded that they have found a 'fantastic deal'.

In most advance fee fraud scams, a potential victim is persuaded to part with a sum of money or property as a form of investment in a bogus business scheme, in anticipation of gaining a substantial benefit. It may involve an agent approaching a bank, a company or an individual with an offer to access substantial funds at below-market interest rates, often for long term. The alleged source of funds is not specifically identified, and the only way to access the funds is through the agent, who requires a commission 'in advance'. As soon as the agent collects the fee, he disappears and the facility does not materialise. Any bank desperate for funds, and especially distressed banks and banks needing significant funds to bid for foreign exchange, may fall victim to this type of fraud. The bank is expected to pay a certain amount of money in anticipation of receiving access to deposits at below-market interest rates in return. Of course, these deposits never materialise. When the deal fails and the fees paid in advance are lost, the victims are unlikely to report the losses to the police or to the authorities.

In most cases of advance fee fraud, the victims are not banks but individuals and small businesses. A common feature among the victims is that either they or their business are seeking credit and are having difficulty obtaining it. In other cases, victims are persuaded that they have the opportunity to join a business deal which is going to make them a large profit. In order to add credibility to the transaction, fraudsters usually attempt to involve banks in their schemes, and banks may inadvertently become accomplices to the fraudsters perpetrating the advance fee fraud.

There are many types of advance fee fraud, some of which are extremely complex, but in all schemes at some point the victim has to pay an advanced fee. Fraudsters approach banks in different ways, often through a bank's customer whom they have persuaded to cooperate with them and who is willing to invest in their scheme. The fraudster might persuade the customer to apply for a bank loan to obtain funds to invest. Often, such a scheme will be easily detected by more experienced bank employees, but it may be difficult to convince the customer not to invest his money. Banks are affected by advance fee fraud in a number of other ways as well. Fraudsters often enter into correspondence with a bank about deposits and remittances which they claim will be made or received at some point in the future. Junior employees may spend a lot of time answering this correspondence and making other arrangements in the mistaken belief that it concerns good business for the bank.[2]

Since Fraudsters are usually very intelligent people, often with an impressive educational background. Each detail of the fraud scheme is likely to be carefully planned in order to make it almost impossible for bank employees fully to understand what is happening. Bank employees should be trained to recognise and understand advanced fee schemes. They should be able to sense that a situation is fraudulent and to stop the financial institution getting involved by following their employer's policy. Most commonly, employees are instructed to close the account(s) and inform the police that fraud is suspected. It is good policy to refer all suspicious transactions to the bank's manager for a second opinion. Financial institutions should provide special educational programmes or seminars for their employees which will explain in detail some of the most common fraud schemes within the banking sector, including advance fee fraud.[3] Bank personnel should be aware of what they should do and how they are expected to act in the event of any type of fraud. This training is cost-effective because the better the employees are prepared, the lower the chance of a bank becoming a victim of fraud, potentially saving hundreds of thousands of dollars. It is also good practice for banks to cooperate with each other and to share information concerning fraud.

3.2 Forged cheques or cheque frauds

Cheques have been used as a financial instrument for hundreds of years.[4] Today, cheque fraud is one of the biggest challenges facing the financial system. Surveys indicate that the number and the financial value of cheque frauds against financial

---

2   Albrecht W. Steve, Albrecht Conan C., Albrecht Chad O. *Fraud Examination* (3rd Edn., Mason, OH,: South-Western, 2009)
3   *Fraud Examiners Manual* (International Edition, Association of Certified Examiners, Austin Texas, 2011)
4   The earliest evidence of deposits subject to 'cheque' dates back to medieval Italy and Catalonia. However, some experts believe that the Romans may have invented the cheque in around 352 BC.

institutions are increasing.[5] In the last few decades, forged cheques have become more popular with fraudsters, who have utilised the rapid development and sophistication of computer technology to produce high-quality, increasingly realistic counterfeit and forged cheques, which are difficult for financial institutions to detect. Cheque frauds have become one of the most common methods of defrauding victims and financial institutions, by both individuals and by organised gangs. In addition, the participation of insiders and bank employees contributes to the high rate of cheque fraud. Employee participation is most commonly connected with a lack of recognition at work, inadequate compensation or other personal issues to which the employers should pay significant attention in order to reduce the risk of insiders taking part in cheque frauds.

Today, the problem of cheque fraud is extending from banks to their customers – banks are beginning to shift the responsibility to their customers. The banking industry has been pressing for changes to the Universal Commercial Code, which establishes the laws that regulate banks and other businesses. Under the last amendments to the Uniform Commercial Code, such losses are shared between the bank and the depositor.

Some financial institutions are more vulnerable to cheque frauds than others. Bad marketing strategies, improper internal control or a certain location may draw the attention of fraudsters and make a bank an easy target. Forgers are attracted by banks that regularly allow customers to open accounts by post. Vulnerability to cheque frauds may vary depending on the geographical region. An increased number of cheque fraud complaints within an area usually indicates the presence of an active, organised group. Investigators who have been assigned to a certain region must maintain regular contact with businesses and regulators in order to prevent future losses.

Over half of all cheque frauds are committed by criminal gangs. Since the late 1980s, foreign crime rings have been responsible for the majority of cheque frauds in North America. The principal ethnic gangs involved in illegal cheque fraud schemes include Nigerian, Asian, Russian, Armenian and Mexican groups. Only a relatively small number of organised groups are caught. Usually, the groups involved in cheque fraud are loosely organised; their members often network among several organisations; and there is no set hierarchy, even though members generally have specific roles, such as leader, counterfeiter, cheque procurer and cheque passer. The leader may be well-educated, often holding a business or law degree and with expertise in the banking sector. Cheque procurers are responsible for stealing cheques and are often employed within a financial institution. Counterfeiters will duplicate corporate and payroll cheques, traveller's cheques, credit cards and so on,

---

5   The 2009 ABA American Bankers Association (ABA) study estimates there were 760,955 cases of cheque fraud in 2008, with actual losses estimated at $1.024 billion, compared with 561,306 cases and $969 million in 2005 (2006 ABA Study) and 616,469 cases and $677 million in 2002 (2003 ABA Study). Counterfeited cheques resulted in a loss of $271 million for banks in 2006, a 160% increase from three years before. One in four money centre-sized banks spent more than $20 million each in cheque fraud-related operating expenses (not including actual losses). The median expense was about $10 million for money centre banks, between $500,000 and $1 million for regional banks, between $50,000 and $250,000 for mid-size banks and about $5,000 for community banks.

as well as personal identification. Information brokers gather personal and financial information on legitimate individuals, which associates use to open new bank accounts, to pass counterfeit cheques and to secure loans which they do not repay. Cheque passers negotiate stolen and counterfeit cheques through the banking system and collect the proceeds that are later distributed to the group. They often travel throughout the country to open new accounts and transport their illicit proceeds. Typically, they negotiate only about 10% of a group's illicit cheques. The group sells the rest of the cheques to other individuals and organisations. Cheque passers have little contact or status within the hierarchy and often are the only members whose ethnic backgrounds differ from the core group.

Cheque fraud schemes across the United States range from depositing single stolen cheques to counterfeiting thousands of negotiable instruments and processing them through a number of bank accounts. It is not possible to discuss all the known cheque fraud schemes here, so a brief explanation of the techniques used to commit cheque fraud follows.

(a)   *Counterfeited cheques*

Counterfeited cheques are simply printed on non-bank paper and look exactly like genuine cheques. Usually, they are drawn on the accounts of legitimate companies. They are becoming a major problem for banks since, with technological advances, it is possible to produce counterfeit cheques that are not easily detectable, even by the experts. Simple software that does not need any special training to use is available, and the fraudster's initial investment will be quickly recouped, at a cost to banks of hundreds of thousands of dollars.

Fraudsters use high-quality printers and scanners to produce authentic-looking cheques, but there are still some pointers to recognising counterfeited cheques. The printing on the cheque should be a uniform texture and colour, with no slants. The transit number in the top right corner must match the electronically encoded number at the bottom of the cheque. The first three of the electronically encoded numbers indicate the district office of the issuer.[6] In counterfeited cheques, these numbers do not always match. The cheque number is included in the encoded serial number at the bottom. Knowing that many merchants regard cheques with low cheque numbers as suspect, forgers often attempt to add a digit. Here again, they may have difficulty matching the ink used to produce the cheque. A simple and effective method of detecting counterfeit cheques is to fan a group of cheques. Counterfeit cheques will sometimes stand out as a slightly different colour.

(b)   *Cheque theft*

There are various types of cheque theft. One of them is known as cheque washing: thieves steal a cheque, for example, from a mailbox, remove the information it and rewrite the cheque to themselves. It is easy to remove the ink on a cheque by chemical treatment, usually with common household chemicals such as acetone, which erases most inks and is a good drying agent, carbon tetrachloride, bleach and

---

benzene. These are common cleaning agents and are easy to use. Cheque washing has become widespread in the United States due to its simplicity.[7]

Recently, banks have responded to cheque washing by introducing high security cheques which react to chemicals, showing that they have been washed, and should contain at least 10 safety features. For manually written cheques, a specific type of pen is available that has an ink which will not dissolve in chemicals.

Another very common cheque theft is stealing a blank cheque stock which is already encoded with customer account information. Usually, fraudsters steal corporate cheques because they are easily cashed.

Some fraudsters may even make use of stolen cancelled cheques. By using a stolen cancelled cheque, a cheque thief can order cheques from a mail-order cheque printer and have them sent to a mail drop address. Cheques may then be written on the new stock and cashed using a false identification.

(c) *Paperhanging*

Paperhangers are fraudsters who ask for cash back when purchasing an item at a retail store and paying by cheque. The cheques used by paperhangers may either be counterfeit or be written on a closed account. A variation of this scam is to make a fraudulent deposit at a bank and ask for cash back. Often, women with crying children are used as paperhangers as they are less suspicious.

(d) *Cheque kiting*

Cheque kiting involves opening accounts at two or more banks and using the 'float time' between banks to give the impression that the fraudster has money in his accounts. The money does not exist, but it takes time for the banks to realise this. The fraudster opens several chequebook accounts and invests only a small amount of money. For example, a cheque written to the fraudster from bank A is deposited and credited to an account at bank B. Because bank B now shows a credit balance, the fraudster can withdraw enough money to deposit back into the first bank before the cheque is returned for lack of funds. In this way, the fraudster can generate a lot of money before being discovered. Today, this type of fraud is less successful since electronic technology has reduced the float time and banks are able to process payments much more quickly, and cases of cheque kiting are decreasing.

(e) *Prevention and investigation*

The variety and complexity of cheque frauds has resulted in many techniques being developed for their prevention and investigation. Law enforcement agencies view prevention measures as the internal responsibility of banks and other potential fraud victims in the financial community. The banking and investment sector stresses the concept of 'know your customer' and the performance of due diligence as keystones of its fraud prevention methodology. However, there are some special safety features which make cheques a lot more difficult to forge. Probably the most efficient safety

---

7   Albrecht W. Steve, Albrecht Conan C., Albrecht Chad O. Zimbelman *Fraud Examination* (3rd Edn. Mason, OH: South-Western, 2009)

features are true watermarks in the paper and the use of thermochromatic ink and paper or ink that is reactive to at least 15 chemicals.[8]

One measure that employers should introduce (on a mandatory basis) is to train their employees to recognise both fraudulent cheques and the schemes behind them. Financial institutions and their employees should follow the same strict cheque acceptance policy at all times. Most financial institutions require periodic training of tellers and other employees, which is essential for the effective prevention of cheque fraud. Law enforcement agencies may provide cheque fraud awareness training to financial institutions, accountants and individuals. Training sessions focus on identifying the warning signs for fraud and improving internal controls and fraud reporting procedures. The training also builds better communication between investigators and officers of victim support institutions.

Certain warning signs have been indicated by the US Federal Bureau of Investigation (FBI) and can be accepted as signals for cheque fraud. An analysis of fraudulent cheque crime in New York City by the FBI found that cheque passers commonly use the following techniques:

- customer attempts to open an account with a corporate cheque or other third-party cheque;
- customer tries to flatter, hurry or confuse the teller to draw attention away from the transaction;
- customer delays endorsing a cheque or producing identification during peak hours to frustrate the teller and speed up the transaction;
- customer presents for cash a low-numbered cheque drawn on a new account;
- customer offers foreign documentation (birth certificate, passport, visa) or non-photo identification (credit card) instead of photo identification to open an account or cash a cheque;
- customer offers altered or damaged identification to open an account or cash a cheque;
- customer attempts to cash or convert several small cheques into wire transfer, gold or other tender; and
- customer requests an exception to established rules to force the transaction.[9]

3.3 Fund diversion or fraud committed by bank employees

Insider bank fraud is perpetrated by someone who works in the bank – most commonly an employee. They have access to restricted areas or information inside the financial institution and the large number of employees who have access to such information and to the bank's money makes it difficult for banks to control their employees. A good way to prevent fraud committed by bank employees is to separate all the functions relating to loans, to reduce the possibility of an insider perpetrating a loan fraud. The segregation provides for at least one, if not several, levels of independent review to reduce external loan fraud exposure. Banks should set some

---

8   Albrecht W. Steve, Albrecht Conan C., Albrecht Chad O. *Fraud Examination* (3rd Edn., Mason, OH: South-Western, 2009)

9   FBI Financial Institution Fraud Criminal Referral Statistics for Fiscal Year 1995, September 30 1995.

standard internal control measures to assist in the detection and deterrence of fraud. Some of the common bank fraud schemes committed by inside employees are as follows:[10]

- *fraudulent loans:* occur when a bank's loan officer forges documents, creates false entities or lies about the ability of the applicant to repay in order to 'borrow' a sum of money from the bank that they never intend to repay;
- *identity theft:* a bank employee steals personal information from customers in order to sell the information or to make fraudulent purchases using the stolen identity;
- *illegal insider trading:* this occurs when an insider has the authority to make investments on behalf of the bank and engages in high-risk trades without the bank being aware of it. A series of illegal trades gone wrong can cause enough damage to put a bank out of business;
- *fraudulent institutions:* in this form of fraud an entire bank is created fraudulently. The bank is illegal and uninsured. The scam revolves around people making uninsured deposits to the bank, only to have the bank, along with their money, eventually disappear;
- *Forged documents:* a forged document claiming that a sum of money has been transferred to another account or something similar can be valuable to a fraudster who does not want the bank to notice any missing money; and
- *wire fraud:* it is common for banks to wire large sums of money on a daily basis. An insider may fraudulently wire money to a personal account at an offshore bank. It may take the bank months or even longer to notice the missing funds.

Sometimes, bank employees work with large amounts of money.

Research indicates that anyone is capable of committing a fraud, especially when there is a certain opportunity. Usually, fraudsters cannot be distinguished from other people: they are an average person who has compromised his integrity and become involved in fraud. Often, fraud perpetrators are well-educated employees in whom their employer places a lot of trust. It is practically impossible for an employer to predict which employees may become dishonest. Generally, when there is an opportunity to commit a fraud and some way to rationalise the fraud as acceptable, there is a danger that an employee will not to be able to resist to the opportunity of enriching himself through fraud.

Employee embezzlement is probably the most common type of occupational fraud. Embezzlement may be divided into direct and indirect offences.[11] Direct fraud occurs when the bank's assets go directly to the perpetrator without the involvement of a third party. Indirect employee fraud occurs when an employee accepts bribes from a third party to break their employer's rules. Here, the employee is paid by an

---

10   *Fraud Examiners Manual* (International Edition, Association of Certified Fraud Examiners, Austin Texas, 2011)

11   For more detailed analysis on occupational fraud see Wells, Joseph T, Principles of Fraud Examination (3rd edn, Hoboken, NJ: John Wiley & Sons 2011); and Kranacher, Mary-Jo, Riley, R and Wells, Joseph T, Forensic accounting and Fraud Examination (Hoboken, NJ: John Wiley & Sons, 2010).

organisation that deals with the perpetrator's employer (eg, selling the personal information of a bank's customer).

Standardising the accounting procedures within financial institutions should assist the prevention of fraud. In order to prevent fraud committed by insiders, it is essential for a bank to establish a clear organisational structure. It is less easy for employees to commit fraud in an environment where everyone knows exactly who is responsible for each activity. Often, frauds are concealed in accounting records, which are based on transaction documents. In order to cover up a fraud, paper or electronic documentation must be altered, misplaced or made fraudulent. Frauds can be discovered within the accounting records by examining transaction entries that have no support or by probing financial statement amounts that are not reasonable. The accounting system helps to distinguish fraud from unintentional mistakes.

Appropriate hiring is a critical element for creating a good control structure. Research has shown that only about 30% of employees in the United States are honest all the time. Another 30% are dishonest and about 40% are honest in certain situations but not all the time.[12] Unfortunately, when dishonest employees have been hired even the best control will fail to prevent fraud. However, effective internal audit and detection controls can help to ensure that violations are being appropriately handled.

Of course, bank fraud may be committed by outsiders without help from an inside bank employee, for example, identity theft, cheque fraud, credit card fraud and money laundering. Probably one of the biggest problems among these is identity theft, which causes many problems and may result in significant financial loss.

There are various ways in which banks can protect themselves against fraud committed by employees. As well as the standard internal control measures and separation of all functions related to loan-making and debt servicing discussed above, there are other useful practices such as having the board of directors or some other committee approve all larger and unusual transactions, for which it would be held responsible. This practice would make it more difficult for insiders to commit large-scale fraud. All transfer journal entries and orders should be reviewed regularly. Independent reviews should be performed by internal or external auditors, who will be able to offer a second opinion on loan transactions. Such reviews should be performed on a regular basis. Usually, this type of review is scheduled for loans over a specified dollar amount, most commonly $25,000 or $100,000. Officers' personal accounts should be examined routinely to prevent fraud schemes such as wire transfer fraud, embezzlement, withdrawals from dormant accounts and conflicts of interest. All employees should be trained in the proper documentation for the transactions they are handling.

3.4   Account opening fraud

Today, millions of households use online banking and hundreds of thousands of new accounts are opened every month. This enables account opening frauds and, despite

---

12   Richard Hollinger, *Dishonesty in the Workplace: A Manager's Guide to Preventing Employee Theft* (Park Ridge, IL: London House Press, 1989) 1-5.

the banks' effort to strengthen their verification systems, the environment for fraudsters is still easy. Banks' standard and security procedures appear to be easily bypassed by stolen information. A single fraudulent account opening may lead to losses of thousands of dollars. Basically, account opening fraud refers to financial identity theft. The forgers use false identification to open new personal or business accounts, which are used to obtain products and services. Personal accounts may be opened using fraudulent cheques. In one such scheme, the fraudster opens a new personal account with two forged or stolen cheques. He deposits one of the cheques and takes cash for the other, then continues to write cheques to overdraw the deposited amount.

Account opening fraud is not easy to detect, and it is not possible to establish a system that will prevent every case. However, a customer identification policy will reduce the number and should be set up. Employees should be trained to be alert for other indicators: a new account requesting immediate cash withdrawal upon deposit; large cash deposits; a request for a large number of temporary cheques. It is important to consider the customer's residence or place of business – it is uncommon for customers to open an account outside the bank's trade area.

3.5   Money transfer fraud

Money transfer services are among the most popular methods of sending money easily and rapidly, and are many fraudsters' preferred method for obtaining cash. It is difficult to recover money stolen in this way. Wire transfers of funds date back to 1940s, and their importance and frequency tends to increase every year. According to experts from the American Bankers Association, wire transfer fraud is more common in business and government accounts than in consumer accounts, because the balances are bigger. However, individuals are advised to protect themselves when banking online by installing a good anti-virus program on their computers, and using secured wireless and firewalls; and they are advised to be wary of sharing information on their bank accounts, and never to give any banking information to someone who is not a representative of a legitimate financial institution with which they already do business. Many schemes have been successfully used by fraudsters to gain money, such as the improper transfer of funds by dishonest bank employees; forged authorisations; misrepresentation of identity; and unauthorised personnel gaining access to the wire transfer room and its equipment; or the actual transmission is intercepted and altered.

Certain steps will help to prevent and detect wire transfer fraud within banks. Audits within the banking sector should include security procedures for the transfer of funds. Banks must provide customers with their own unique codes to authorise or order wire transfers and keep an up-to-date list of employees authorised to perform wire transfer transactions. Generally, banks deal with many transactions daily, and should review all wire transfer transactions at the end of each day. This will help to ensure that the original transfer instructions were executed correctly. It is good practice for bank employees to contact businesses to which the funds are transferred to confirm the authenticity of fund transfer requests. Customers should be contacted through the phone numbers they gave when opening their account, not the phone numbers provided by the callers who requested the transfers. This is a useful precaution since forgers often give different numbers. The authenticity of fax instructions for wire transfers should be confirmed in the same way. Bank employees should never disclose sensitive information over the phone until the caller's identity and authorisation have been verified with the customer information file. All accounts connected with a wire transfer should be reconciled by bank employees who were not involved with the wire process. The in-house wire operations manual must be available only to authorised personnel and must be stored securely when not in use. The possibility that office cleaning staff might access confidential information about bank clients cannot be dismissed. Other precautions include recording all incoming and outgoing calls for wire transfer instructions and screening wire transfer personnel applicants. If a wire transfer employee resigns, they should immediately be moved to another department to work out their notice. All employees involved in the transfer of funds should be required to take a regular vacation each year – refusing to take a vacation is a warning sign. All employees must be trained on proper internal controls, fraud awareness and the importance of protecting information. They should also be aware of alerts issued by government agencies and professional groups.

3.6   Letter of credit fraud

Letters of credit were originally introduced by the merchant banking system in Europe – a letter addressed by the buyer's bank to the seller's bank stating that it would pay the seller on behalf of the buyer if the buyer defaulted.

In the United States, the law governing letters of credit is found in the Uniform Commercial Code. We can define letter of credit as a legal promise of a bank addressed to a seller (beneficiary) that payment will be made if the beneficiary presents the documents stated in the credit within the proper time frames.

Letter of credit fraud is a problem where banks issue documentary credits in order to ensure payment for goods shipped in connection with international trade. This type of fraud may be perpetrated by fraudsters presenting forged documents to the issuing bank with a demand for payment. Of this type of fraud, the most common attempted against banks is providing false documentation to show that goods had been shipped when in reality no goods or inferior goods have been shipped.

3.7   Computer fraud or electronic fund transfer

Probably the simplest explanation of electronic fund transfer is the transfer of money between accounts. It is also known as electronic banking. Electronic fund transfer provides electronic payments and collections. It has gained popularity over the years as it is a cheaper system to run than paper cheque payments. Money is transferred from one bank account directly to another without any paper money changing hands, and with reduced administrative costs and increased efficiency. Electronic fund transfer services include transfers through automated teller machines, point-of-sale terminals and automated clearinghouse systems, phone bill-payment plans in which periodic or recurring transfers are contemplated, and remote banking programs.

Electronic bill presentment and payment is a process that enables bills to be created, delivered and paid over the Internet. Basically, there are there are three types of presentment models. The first is a direct model where a biller delivers the bill to customers via its own website, or via a third-party's site. This means that merchants deal with each customer individually. The second type is the consolidator model. In this type of electronic bill presentment and payment, bills from multiple billers are delivered to a single website, to be presented in aggregate to the consumer for viewing and payment. Customers subscribe only to the services of a consolidator, which will consolidate bills on behalf of its customers and allow individual subscribers to receive and pay all their bills on a single website. In the third model, billers subscribe to the services of a biller consolidator that allows its subscribers to present their bills and receive payments from customers on its Internet site. Here, there are different billers who subscribe to different consolidators, so a customer may need to enter several websites to gain access to all of his bills. Biller consolidators draw most of their revenue from the fees paid by biller subscribers.

Some of the newest fraud schemes in operation are built around the fraudulent use of stolen identities and other account information in international wire transfers. Banks or their customers may become victims of fraud, especially identity theft, if they do not carefully monitor the use of their name on the Internet. Most online banking fraud schemes involve two simple steps: the fraudster obtains a customer's account access data and then uses this information to transfer money to other accounts, from which he is able to withdraw the funds.

3.8 Automated teller machine fraud

Generally, automated teller machine (ATM) fraud schemes include counterfeit ATM cards and counterfeit ATM machines, stolen cards, and unauthorised access to PIN numbers by unauthorised persons. There are several ATM fraud prevention measures available to financial institutions. The main problem areas should be identified – location of ATMs is very important – and appropriate lighting at the ATM and surrounding area should be provided. ATMs must be inspected regularly and security cameras should be installed in high-risk areas. Banks should provide additional security information and advice to their customers.

3.9 Credit card fraud

The most common credit card frauds are using credit cards to make purchases without authorisation and counterfeiting credit cards. Other types of credit card fraud include the unauthorised use of a lost or stolen credit card, applying for a credit card in another person's name using stolen identity information, stolen card numbers, counterfeit cards, and phone and mail order fraud. Bank fraud includes misusing an existing account that belongs to the victim and opening a new account in the name of the victim, then committing unlawful acts.

Fraudsters quickly devised a resourceful response to CVV (Visa's Card Verification Value) and CVC (MasterCard's Card Validation Code) security systems used as protection for Visa and MasterCard. The CVV system uses a three-digit number embedded in the magnetic strip of the credit card which identifies it as a legitimately issued credit instrument.[13] However, fraudsters get round this by leaving the magnetic strip uncoded or making it unreadable so that merchants handling the transaction enter the credit card number manually, and the transaction never falls under the scope of the CVV system.

Most banks have already found a successful way to protect their customers from this kind of fraud. The CVV2 and CVC2 systems use a three-digit security code that is printed on the back of the cards. It is designed to validate that a genuine card is being used during a transaction. When a point-of-sale terminal reads a card's magnetic strip, Visa's CVV or MasterCard's CVC can be verified during the authorisation. The number appears in reverse italic at the top of the signature panel at the end. The CVV2 and CVC2 programs can also be used to reduce fraud in card-not-present transactions.

Many methods are used to forge credit cards. Forgers may use software programs such as Creditmaster, which allows them to produce valid credit card numbers that they can put on counterfeit cards.

Another common scheme for forging credit cards involves the use of a special device known as wedge, which can store up to 200 credit card numbers. It is mainly used when victims pay their bills in a shop or restaurant by credit card. The seller or waiter swipes the card into a wedge while conducting the legitimate transaction. Once the forger has collected enough numbers, he can easily produce his own fake cards using the stolen information.

Credit card frauds may result in substantial losses, so both the issuing banks and cardholders are interested in minimising this fraud. However, banks do not usually bear the losses related to identity theft that involves credit cards. Thus, they must keep their customers informed on how to protect themselves. There is plenty of advice on preventing credit card fraud available. First, cardholders should never give out their credit card number online unless they are certain that the website is secure. They should check that they are purchasing merchandise from a reputable source, and they should send an email to the seller to make sure the email address is active. Special precautions should be taken when dealing with foreign individuals or companies. Cardholders should review their credit card statements and immediately report any unrecognisable charges, and they must immediately report any lost or stolen cards to the card issuer.

4. Conclusion

Over the past few decades, bank fraud has become a major problem, resulting in significant losses every year. It is producing negative effects not just on individuals and financial institutions, but on national economies too.

Banks have to deal with the criminal intentions of both customers and 'insider' bank employees. Finding the right way to react against fraud can be a difficult task. An essential step for financial institutions in preventing and detecting fraud is to

---

13 *Fraud Examiners Manual* (International Edition, Association of Certified Fraud Examiners, Austin, Texas, 2011) and *Fraud Examiners Manual* (US Edition, Association of Certified Fraud Examiners, Austin Texas, 2012)

establish an effective control environment for its employees. This means measures such as good management, appropriate hiring and a clear organisational structure.

The management's role is probably the most important condition for establishing an appropriate work environment, because employees tend to copy management's behaviour. Inappropriate conduct at work is easily learned and repeated by the staff. It may encourage some employees to commit fraud and affects the performance of the whole organisation:

- The management team should set an example and provide a stable work environment and open communication with employees;
- Good and clear control procedures must be established – this is essential for preventing fraud;
- Internal control and communication between employees, the management team and the bank's customers are essential for preventing fraud;
- Staff should be kept informed on what is appropriate through regular supervisor-employees meetings and anti-fraud training, and the provision of a code of conduct (which should contain clear and easy to follow rules);
- Communication must be consistent in order to be an effective deterrent against fraud. This will help to ensure that the control procedures are followed at all times;
- Maintaining good communication between managers and employees is as essential as maintaining communication and cooperation between different banks, and between banks and their customers and shareholders; and
- Another important condition for establishing a good and controlled work environment is hiring appropriate employees.

There is no easy way to ensure that all employees are entirely honest – research conducted by the Association of Certified Fraud Examiners has shown that a very high percentage of bank employees would commit fraud if an opportunity presents itself. Banks are especially prone to fraud committed by employees since the range of personnel, such as managers, loan officers and tellers, who have access to cash on a daily basis and can easily steal, makes them vulnerable, even in a well-controlled work environment.

Clear internal regulations are an essential element in fraud prevention. Every employee should be aware of exactly who is responsible for each business activity. This makes it easier to track missing assets and make fraud more difficult. Internal audit control units that carry out random inspections can have a significant deterrent effect – this kind of control has a visible security function which makes even dishonest employees question whether they can commit fraud and what the risk is of being caught. As an additional measure, an appropriate loss prevention programme may be established to ensure that fraud is properly investigated and that violations are duly punished.

Often, the fraud is complex and difficult to prove. Without a good accounting system, it may be difficult for a bank to distinguish between fraud and unintentional errors. Generally, banks employ a lot of people, most of whom have easy access to cash and information that may easily be stolen. The control procedures must be organised such that employees' actions are compatible with the goals of the management team. Having good control procedures minimises the risk for fraud. Control activities and procedures may vary for different financial institutions. Good fraud detection and prevention efforts involve matching the most effective control procedures with the known risks for fraud.

Today, with the increasing frequency of fraud, banks are facing a variety of challenges concerning fraud prevention. There are two key areas that management teams should focus on – the creation of a culture of honesty and high ethics and the proper assessment of the risks for fraud. These will provide a base on which to develop strategies for combating fraud. The potential for fraud within the banking sector can be reduced by accurate identification and measurement of the sources of risks, implementing appropriate prevention and control measures, monitoring employees and having regular internal and external audits to provide independent checks on the bank's performance.

Banks should be aware that it is not possible to have a detection system that will prevent all instances of fraud. However, the risk of fraud in the banking sector may be minimised by developing a work environment that reduces the opportunity for employees and customers to commit fraud.

About the authors

Constance E Bagley
Professor, Yale University
connie.bagley@yale.edu

Constance E Bagley is a professor in the practice of law and management at Yale University and a senior research scholar at Yale Law School. She was previously an associate professor at the Harvard Business School and a senior lecturer at the Stanford University Graduate School of Business. Before joining the Stanford faculty, she was a corporate securities partner in the San Francisco office of Bingham McCutchen. She was also a member of the faculty of the Young Presidents' Organisation International University for Presidents in Hong Kong and the Czech Republic, and is the author of *Winning Legally* and *Managers and the Legal Environment.*

Roger Barker
Head of corporate governance, Institute of Directors
roger.barker@iod.com

Roger Barker has been head of corporate governance at the Institute of Directors (IoD) since 2008. He is senior adviser to the Board of the European Confederation of Directors' Associations (ecoDa) and the director of ecoDa's education programmes. Dr Barker is a visiting lecturer at the Said Business School (University of Oxford), the *École Supérieure des Sciences Économiques et Commerciales*, Paris, University College, London and the UK Ministry of Defence. Dr Barker's book *Corporate Governance, Competition, and Political Parties: Explaining Corporate Governance Change in Europe* was published by Oxford University Press in January 2010. He is also the author of the IoD's main guide to the role of the board, *The Effective Board: Building Individual and Board Success* (Kogan Page, 2010). During the first part of his career, Dr Barker worked as an investment banker in London and Zurich. He is the holder of a doctorate on corporate governance from Oxford University, where he was a lecturer at Merton College, and has degrees in economics, finance and political science from the universities of Cambridge, Southampton and Cardiff.

Andrew S Boutros
Assistant US attorney, US Attorney's Office for the Northern District of Illinois
asboutros@gmail.com

Andrew S Boutros is an assistant US attorney in Chicago and currently serves in the office's Financial Crimes and Special Prosecutions Section. As a federal prosecutor, Mr Boutros has conducted some of the office's most significant complex, multi-district, international fraud investigations and prosecutions of business organisations and corporate executives.

While in private practice, Mr Boutros conducted a variety of corporate investigations, litigated cases in federal court and in arbitration, and advised clients on corporate compliance matters, including the Foreign Corrupt Practices Act. Mr Boutros also represented corporations and executives in criminal and regulatory matters being investigated by the Fraud Section of the

Department of Justice, the US Attorneys' Offices, the Securities and Exchange Commission and other government agencies. Mr Boutros has significant experience in negotiating corporate deferred prosecution agreements.

Mr Boutros teaches at the University of Chicago Law School and is co-chair of the American Bar Association Global Anti-corruption Task Force. He has authored several articles on white-collar defence matters, international corruption and other related topics, and also lectures on the subject.

Marjorie Hurwitz Bremner
Human resources partner, Berg Kaprow Lewis LLP
marjorie.bremner@bkl.co.uk

Marjorie Hurwitz Bremner is a human resources (HR) partner at Berg Kaprow Lewis LLP, chartered accountants and business advisers, and heads up BKL HR Consultancy. BKL HR advises clients on all aspects of the employment lifecycle.

After graduating from Glasgow University, Ms Hurwitz Bremner studied personnel management in Edinburgh. She is a fellow of the Chartered Institute of Personnel and Development, holds a Further and Adult Teaching Certificate and is a Centre for Effective Disputes Resolution-accredited and ONC-qualified mediator.

Ms Hurwitz Bremner has worked in a range of business sectors, including charities, healthcare, retail, manufacturing, design, architecture, information technology, media and professional practice. She is chair of the UK 200 Group Forensic Accounting and Disputes Resolution Panel and a member of Resolve UK Mediation Panel.

Ms Hurwitz Bremner lectures and produces topical articles on a regular basis. She carried the Olympic Torch on July 25 2012 in recognition of her extensive voluntary work for a range of community organisations, as well as her fund-raising achievements, including completing nine marathons. Ms Hurwitz Bremner was especially privileged to be passed the flame by Gordon Banks (1966 World Cup) outside Wembley Stadium.

Ferdinando Bruno
Appointed professor, University of Lugano, Switzerland
ferdinando.bruno@usi.ch

Ferdinando Bruno is an appointed professor (*docente a contratto*) of the courses "The Law and Practice of International Capital Markets" and "International Taxation and Financial Instruments" at the University of Lugano, Switzerland.

Mr Bruno is a dual qualified as an *avvocato* in Italy and as a solicitor in England and Wales. He gained several years' experience in corporate and commercial law, insolvency law, international capital markets, international tax law, banking and finance, European and international law and international financial services law.

He graduated with a degree in law from University Federico II of Naples (Italy) and holds a PhD in economic law from University Federico II of Naples, international practice diplomas in international capital markets and loans and international mergers and acquisitions from The College of Law of England and Wales, London/International Bar Association, an LLM in international business law from the London School of Economics and Political Science, a postgraduate diploma in EU competition law from King's College, London, a certificate in banking and finance from London Guildhall University, a master's (*diploma di specializzazione*) in EU law and economy from University Federico II of Naples and a certificate in international private and public law from The Hague Academy of International Law, Netherlands. He has more than 100 articles and research books to his credit.

Jon Cooper
Partner, Bond Pearce LLP
jon.cooper@bondpearce.com

Jon Cooper is a partner and head of the health and safety team at Bond Pearce LLP.

Bond Pearce has been recognised for many

years as one of the leading UK practices in health and safety. In the current edition of the *Chambers Guide to the Legal Profession*, Mr Cooper is recognised as a "star individual".

He and his team have been involved in many of the most significant cases in health and safety in recent years, including the Buncefield prosecution, the prosecutions arising from the explosion and multiple fatalities at Corus, Port Talbot, the Channel Tunnel rail link fire and the prosecution of the Health Protection Agency for failings in relation to e-coli.

Mr Cooper sits on the editorial advisory committee of Lexis Nexis's *Health and Safety at Work* publication.

David Curran

Chief executive officer and chief legal officer, Risk Readiness Corporation
dcurran@riskreadinesscorp.com

David Curran is chief executive officer and chief legal officer of Risk Readiness Corporation, a risk technology and advisery firm focused on proactive reduction and elimination of risk and costs for complex organisations. Mr Curran has spent more than 25 years at the intersection of risk, law, business and technology. He has served as a senior legal officer with companies such as IntraLinks, Inc, Campbell Soup Company, Reader's Digest and Vertis, Inc; and as chief executive officer of three technology companies focused on compliance and risk, including Integrity Interactive Corporation and Data Communique, a part of Havas. Mr Curran has written and spoken widely about the need for transformative solutions on how organisations approach and combat risk and compliance and ethics failures.

Nikolay Dobrev

Associate professor, Sofia University Business School and Law School
Lecturer, University of Liverpool
nikolay.dobrev@my.ohecampus.com

Nikolay Dobrev is an instructor and faculty manager for the University of Liverpool/Laureate online LLM programmes. He has taught the following courses: "Aspects of Banking Law", "Commercial Contracts"; "International Financial Services Law"; "Law of the World Trade Organisation"; "International Law and Foreign Investment"; and "LLM Research Methods Training/Dissertation". As an associate professor at Sofia University Business School and Law School (Bulgaria), Dr Dobrev has delivered lectures on banking law, insurance law, financial law, international law and EU law.

Dr Dobrev is an LLM graduate of Columbia Law School, New York. He is the editor in chief of the *Bulgarian Journal of International Law.*

Dr Dobrev has had some considerable experience as a practising lawyer, including as head of legal and compliance at Citibank NA (Sofia), a legal consultant at PricewaterhouseCoopers and a lawyer at the US Agency for International Development. He has been a member of the Sofia Bar since 2005 and is managing partner of Dobrev Law Office.

Jan M Eickelberg

Professor of law, Berlin School of Economics and Law
eickelberg@gmx.de

Jan Eickelberg is a professor in civil law at the Berlin School of Economics and Law with a special focus on commercial and company law. After studying at the Universities of Bonn, Lausanne (Switzerland), Munster (PhD on gap-filling in uniform law in Germany, England and United States) and Cambridge (LLM in international law), Mr Eickelberg started his working life as a lawyer at international law firm Freshfields Bruckhaus

Deringer in Cologne. He then moved to one of the biggest insolvency administrators in Germany, Görg Lawyers, Cologne. In 2006 Professor Eickelberg was appointed associate notary in Cologne. Three years later he moved to Berlin and became managing director of the German Association of Notaries (with offices in Berlin and Brussels). In 2011 he was nominated professor in law at the Berlin School of Law and Economics. Professor Eickelberg also holds university teaching positions at the Humboldt University (Berlin) and the University of Breslau (Poland). He has published articles for numerous publications, including the *Neue Juristische Wochenschrift, Deutsche Notarzeitschrift, notar* and *Europäische Zeitschrift für Wirtschaftsrecht*. Furthermore, he is co-writer of various books on different aspects of civil and commercial law.

Rita Esen
Reader, University of Northumbria
rita.esen@northumbria.ac.uk

Rita Esen has a PhD in law and extensive experience in the legal/regulatory issues of computer investigations, ethical hacking and computer network security. She has successfully worked nationally and internationally on the legally sensitive areas of computer forensic investigations and computer data authentication/admissibility, developing a reputation for professionalism, expertise and competence which has been put to excellent use in academic and research initiatives and consultations.

Paul Feldberg
Senior associate, Willkie Farr & Gallagher LLP
pfeldberg@willkie.com

Paul Feldberg has practised for over 15 years in the areas of criminal fraud, money laundering and corruption, gaining valuable experience from his work both in the private sector and at two major fraud regulators, Her Majesty's Revenue and Customs and the Serious Fraud Office. In recent years Mr Feldberg has advised large multinational organisations on a variety of complex governance, corruption and fraud issues. He has also worked for multilateral development banks such as the European Bank for Reconstruction and Development, advising on their internal investigation and governance processes. Mr Feldberg led the Serious Fraud Office investigation into BAE System's alleged corrupt practices in Eastern Europe, working closely with both Eurojust and the US Department of Justice. He recently worked with the legal team advising Macmillan Publishers Limited in connection with its settlements with the Serious Fraud Office and the World Bank Group. His work has included leading internal investigations in Africa, conducting risk assessments in Eastern Europe and delivering anti-bribery and corruption training in a number of countries.

T Markus Funk
Partner, Perkins Coie LLP
mfunk@perkinscoie.com

T Markus Funk is a partner at Perkins Coie specialising in anti-corruption and corporate social responsibility compliance. Mr Funk, a former federal prosecutor in Chicago with 10 years' experience, from 2004 to 2006 served as the US Department of Justice resident legal adviser for Kosovo. He has the distinction of being the only person to have received both the Department of Justice's Attorney General's Award for trial performance and the State Department's Superior Honour Award.

Mr Funk, who in 2012 was named both Colorado Lawyer of the Year and the state's top corporate/compliance lawyer, has also authored a number of books, including *Child Exploitation and Human Trafficking: Examining the Global Challenges and US Responses* (co-authored with Chicago US District Judge Virginia M Kendall), *The Haiti Trial Skills Manual, Stemming the Suffering: Victims' Rights and the International Criminal Court, The Kosovo Trial Skills Handbook* and the forthcoming *Mutual*

Legal Assistance Treaty Guide for Federal Judges. His legal work has been featured by outlets such as *CNN, The Economist, MSNBC, The National Law Journal, The New York Times* and *The Wall Street Journal.* He started his legal career as a law clerk to Morris S Arnold of the US Court of Appeals for the Eighth Circuit and Chief US District Judge Catherine Perry, and as a lecturer in law at Oxford University.

Peter Giblin
Professor, Cass Business School
peter@giblin.com

Peter Giblin specialises in working with senior-level decision makers to support them as they grow their businesses by identifying, attracting, managing, developing and evaluating talented personnel. He also practised corporate and tax law in both the United States and France, and was managing director and worldwide head of finance and administration of a major British merchant bank. Mr Giblin is a visiting professor in the Faculty of Management at Cass Business School, where he is a founding member of the Centre for Research in Corporate Governance. He is a graduate of Yale University and the Columbia School of Law, and was a Fulbright scholar in Venezuela and a Hague fellow in the Netherlands. He is a member of the board of trustees of the American University in Cairo and the Audit and Risk Management Committee of the University of Essex, and a member of the British Psychological Society, where he is Level A/Level B-qualified in occupational testing.

Hazel Grant
Partner, Bristows
hazel.grant@bristows.com

Hazel Grant is an IT lawyer, specialising in IT procurements and information law. Her work regularly involves advising on commercial and procurement law issues including structuring public procurements, handling complaints and drafting agreements in line with government guidance. Her clients include government bodies, global IT service providers and national charities.

As a data protection specialist, Ms Grant advises on data protection compliance strategies (eg, planning international data transfers using EU model clauses and binding corporate rules), as well as the implementation of privacy-compliant technologies and processes. Her data protection work includes advising on cloud computing, cookie law compliance and data security breaches. Additionally, she advises on responses to freedom of information requests and handling subject access requests.

As part of her compliance work, Ms Grant advises on the implementation of the anti-bribery procedures required by the Bribery Act 2010.

Ms Grant is an editor of the *Encyclopedia of Data Protection and Privacy* and a contributing editor for the *Encyclopedia of Information Technology Law.* She is a member of the editorial board of the *Freedom of Information Journal* and of the Certification Advisory Board of the International Association of Privacy Professionals.

Lutz-Ulrich Haack
Student, German Graduate School of
Management and Law, Heilbronn
Doctoral candidate, Otto von Guericke University
lutz-ulrich.haack@hhl.de

Lutz-Ulrich Haack graduated from HHL-Leipzig Graduate School of Management as a Diplom-Kaufmann (equivalent to an MSc in business administration). He studied at Peking University and UC Berkeley Extension. Mr Haack is currently enrolled in business law at the German Graduate School of Management and Law in Heilbronn. He also is a doctoral candidate of marketing at Otto von Guericke University, Magdeburg.

Boris Georg Hallik
DekaBank, Frankfurt
borisgeorg.hallik@deka.de

Boris Hallik is a fully qualified German lawyer and worked for DekaBank for 11 years. For the past four years he has been head of the strategic sourcing department at DekaBank Frankfurt. He has seven years' experience as senior counsel in IT and e-commerce law and detailed knowledge of German IT and outsourcing law, English IT and e-commerce law, and data protection law. He is highly experienced in IT contract negotiations with major international and national IT licensors and providers.

The strategic sourcing team is responsible for controlling and reporting the annual expenses of DekaBank Group and for the permanent risk management of DekaBank's top 500 providers. In addition, Mr Hallik is in charge of governance procurement management and legal procurement procedures and directives. DekaBank's strategic sourcing department takes responsibility for commodity group strategy, supplier evaluation and development, supplier portfolio management and commodity market research.

Mr Hallik is an active member of the German Association of Law and Informatics, the Society of Computer and Law, Bristol and the German Association Materials Management Purchasing and Logistics Working Group on Banking and Finance. In 2011 and 2012 he was a main speaker at several contract management seminars.

Wolf Juergen von Kumberg
European legal director and assistant general counsel, Northrop Grumman Corporation
wolf.vonkumberg@euro.ngc.com

Wolf Juergen von Kumberg has been the European legal director and assistant general counsel to Northrop Grumman Corporation and its predecessor, Litton Industries, Inc, for over 20 years. Before that he served five years as the vice president – legal affairs for Litton Canada, after having spent several years in legal practice with a major Toronto law firm. He has received law degrees from Canadian and European universities and is qualified as a lawyer in both Canada and England.

As legal director, Mr Von Kumberg manages the European corporate staff and is responsible for the legal affairs of Northrop Grumman Corporation in Europe and several Asian locations. He has offices in both London and Zurich.

Mr Von Kumberg has been involved in many of the company's international legal conflicts and has been a keen advocate for early dispute resolution. In that context, he is a director of the International Mediation Institute, which has advocated international standards for mediators. He is in also a fellow of the Chartered Institute of Arbitrators and sits on its board of management, and is a director of the American Arbitration Association.

Ian Leist
Barrister, Fulcrum Chambers
ianleistqc@fulcrumchambers.com

Ian Leist QC is a 'silk' and a leading criminal court advocate, with expertise in terrorism cases and cases with political and human rights dimensions. He is a commercial fraud and anti-corruption specialist.

He has substantial experience in both jury and non-jury trial and appellate advocacy, including before the Court of Appeal and the Supreme Court. Between 2000 and 2010 he represented former soldiers from the Parachute Regiment on behalf of the Ministry of Defence in the Bloody Sunday inquiry. Between 2004 and 2009 he acted as independent counsel instructed by the Metropolitan Police and Her Majesty's Revenue and Customs investigating allegations of internal corruption in the London City Bond judicial inquiry.

Mr Leist is a human rights adviser to Islam Channel TV and has advised members of the Muslim community in Bosnia on matters arising from the Srebrenica massacre. He has advised on the impact of counterterrorism legislation on community relations and human rights, and has advised commonwealth and foreign governments in Africa on rule of law and governance issues, including money laundering.

Mr Leist is a director of Future Radio Africa. He writes regularly for Thomson Reuters on anti-bribery and corruption, good governance anti-terrorism and human rights.

Fang Ma
Lecturer in law, University of Hertfordshire
f.f.ma@herts.ac.uk

Fang Ma is a lecturer at the School of Law of the University of Hertfordshire. Dr Ma teaches company law and international commercial law at both undergraduate and postgraduate levels. Her research interests include Chinese and English company law, corporate governance and international trade law. Dr Ma has recently published *Company Law (Q&A)* with Pearson; in addition, she has published in leading corporate and commercial law journals such as *Company Lawyer, International Commercial and Company Law Review* and the *Journal of Business Law.*

Peter Mancusi
Executive vice president, Weber Shandwick
peter.mancusi@gmail.com

Peter Mancusi is an executive vice president in the Boston office of Weber Shandwick, one of the world's leading public relations firms, where he has counselled a broad range of corporate and institutional clients facing reputational issues. Mr Mancusi also oversees audits designed to assist corporate clients in identifying vulnerabilities and develops crisis preparedness plans that enable executive teams to communicate immediately and confidently when a crisis hits. He is also a lawyer and veteran journalist, having spent more than 20 years at *The Boston Globe* as a reporter and editor, including four years as the paper's business editor.

Richard L Narva
Founder and senior adviser, Narva & Company
rnarva@narvaandcompany.com

Richard Narva leads an interdisciplinary team of advisers helping family-controlled enterprises to preserve their values and vision while addressing organisational, strategic, governance and human capital issues. He has been a member of the Massachusetts Bar since 1975 and practised corporate law specialising in mergers and acquisitions, before succeeding his father as president of Morton Shoe Companies, Inc, becoming the third generation in his family to head this American Stock Exchange-listed firm founded in 1921. He presents frequently and is the author and editor of numerous publications on the general theme of improving governance of family-controlled enterprises. Mr Narva has been elected to the boards of directors of both public and private family-controlled businesses. He currently serves on the councils of advisers of several family-controlled companies and as a trustee of a trust for the benefit of the family shareholder group that controls an international retail company.

Robert Nothhelfer
Former head of GRC Lidl International and University of Freiburg
Robert.nothhelfer@gmx.de

Robert Nothhelfer graduated in economics and was awarded his PhD for researching on learning processes in organisations at the University of Freiburg. After working for BDO as an auditor and for Bertelsmann in corporate reporting, he joined the Schwarz Group heading the accounting and reporting. After an internal change to Lidl Germany he was responsible for all administrative processes and in 2008 he set up the new data protection system and organisation. In 2011 he started to set up the new governance, risk management, compliance department for Lidl International. Currently, he researches the most effective ways to implement compliance management systems in large organisations.

Thushara Polpitiye

Solicitor and managing director, Astute HR Ltd
thushara.polpitiye@astutehr.co.uk

Thushara Polpitiye is a solicitor specialising in human resources support and employment law advice and assistance to employers and employees operating in a wide range of sectors, for both contentious and non-contentious matters. He has helped employers and employees to deal with a variety of legal claims including unfair dismissal, discrimination, harassment, unpaid wages, Transfer of Undertakings (Protection of Employment) Regulations and numerous other types of claim. He has extensive experience in dispute resolution and strategic thinking and his experience spans public and private sector companies and employees.

Mr Polpitiye is a member of the Employment Lawyers Association.

Zabihollah Rezaee

Thompson-Hill chair of excellence and professor of accountancy, University of Memphis
zrezaee@memphis.edu

Zabihollah Rezaee is the Thompson-Hill chair of excellence and professor of accountancy at the University of Memphis and has served a two-year term on the Standing Advisory Group of the Public Company Accounting Oversight Board. He received his BS from the Iranian Institute of Advanced Accounting, his MBA from Tarleton State University, Texas and his PhD from the University of Mississippi. Professor Rezaee holds several certifications. He has also been a finalist for the SOX Institute's SOX MVP 2007, 2009 and 2010 Award.

Professor Rezaee has published over 200 articles in a variety of accounting and business journals and made more than 210 presentations at national and international conferences. He has also published numerous books – *Financial Institutions, Valuations, Mergers, and Acquisitions: The Fair Value Approach, Financial Statement Fraud: Prevention and Detection, U.S. Master Auditing Guide* (third edition), *Audit Committee Oversight Effectiveness Post-Sarbanes-Oxley Act, Corporate Governance Post-Sarbanes-Oxley: Regulations, Requirements, and Integrated Processes, Corporate Governance and Business Ethics and Financial Services Firms: Governance, Regulations, Valuations, Mergers and Acquisitions* – and has contributed to several other books. Dr Rezaee's recent book *Corporate Sustainability: Integrating Performance and Reporting*, co-authored with Ann Brockett at E&Y, won the 2013 Axiom Gold Award in the category of business ethics.

Peter Ries

Professor of corporate law
Berlin School of Economics and Law
peter.ries@hwr-berlin.de

Peter Ries is a professor of corporate and commercial law at the Berlin School of Economics and Law. In addition, he works as a judge at a Berlin court in charge of corporate law matters. From 1990 to 1995 he worked for international law firms in the United States (McGuire Woods Battle & Boothe, Washington DC) and Germany (Droste, merged with Lovells), where he specialised in M&A and corporate law. Dr Ries studied law and history in Wurzburg, Munich and at the London School of Economics and Political Science. He earned his PhD at Munich University with a thesis about antique Roman contract law. He has published articles for numerous publications and is co-writer of various books on different aspects of corporate and commercial law. In 2008 he was appointed as an expert by the German Parliament for the reform of the German Closed Corporation Act.

Mark Roellig
Executive vice president and general counsel,
Massachusetts Mutual Life Insurance Company
mroellig49@massmutual.com

Mark Roellig is the executive vice president and general counsel of Massachusetts Mutual Life Insurance Company ('MassMutual'). In this capacity Mr Roellig is responsible for the legal affairs of the company and advises management and the board of directors to ensure that MassMutual complies with corporate governance requirements and safeguards the interests of its policyholders. He is also responsible for the corporate secretary, corporate compliance, internal audit, government relations and the corporate administration and real estate and facilities departments of MassMutual. Before joining MassMutual in 2005, Mr Roellig served as general counsel and secretary to three public companies before their sales/mergers: Fisher Scientific International Inc, Storage Technology Corporation and US WEST Inc. In 2012 Mr Roellig was the recipient of the Association of Corporate Counsel Excellence in Corporate Practice Award. He has published numerous articles on corporate law department leadership and management and is the co-chair of the PLI Corporate Counsel Institute. Mr Roellig received his bachelor's degree in applied mathematics from the University of Michigan, his law degree from George Washington University and his MBA from the University of Washington.

Aaron Schildhaus
Lawyer, Law Offices of Aaron Schildhaus
schildhaus@dosins.com

Aaron Schildhaus, an international corporate and business lawyer with over 40 years' experience specialising in commercial transactions, investment, trade and finance. Mr Schildhaus provides advice and assistance to US and non-US entities and law firms on global corporate structuring, data protection matters, international money laundering, international anti-corruption, US export control issues and the design and implementation of corporate compliance programmes relative to these and other areas of global business concern. He has been a frequent speaker and writer on anti-corruption compliance matters worldwide for over 20 years.

Mr Schildhaus is past chair of the American Bar Association's Section of International Law, has been a member of its council since 2004 and serves as senior adviser to its International Anti-corruption Committee. Mr Schildhaus is an active member of the District of Columbia Bar. In March 2013 Mr Schildhaus became president/chief executive officer of D&O Supplemental (Directors and Officers Supplemental International Insurance LLC), a US company specialising in providing insurance to companies and their officers and directors to protect them personally against the high expenses of criminal investigations (www.dosins.com). He speaks English, French, German, Italian and Spanish.

Richard Smerdon
Editor, *CCH Corporate Governance Handbook*
richard.smerdon@mailbox.co.uk

Richard Smerdon is the executive editor of the Wolters Kluwer UK/CCH publication *Corporate Governance Handbook*. He is also a former rapporteur for the All-Party Parliamentary Corporate Governance Group, a guest lecturer at the *Financial Times* non-executive directors' programme "So you want to be a non-executive director?" and at the Jersey International Business School, and a contributing editor to the research paper programme of the European Corporate Governance Institute.

He is the author of books and many articles on company law and corporate governance, and was also cited as a specialist in corporate governance matters in relation to the United Kingdom in the foreword of the European Commission's 2003 report on governance codes written by Holly Gregory of US law firm Weil,

Gotschal & Manges LLP.

During his career Mr Smerdon has been a corporate finance partner with European and California law firm Osborne Clarke.

Mark Watts
Partner, Bristows
mark.watts@bristows.com

Mark Watts is an IT specialist with over 18 years' experience. He advises companies on IT legal issues such as software development, system deployment, outsourcing, e-commerce and data protection. Much of his experience was gained in house at IBM, where he held various roles.

Mr Watts has advised on many high-profile private and public sector outsourcing transactions. He advises companies deploying business-critical IT platforms and applications, as well as advising on the creation of social networking websites, cloud computing, mobile apps and online trading websites. Mr Watts has particular expertise in data protection; he was global privacy counsel at IBM for many years. He advises many multinationals companies on general international data protection compliance issues, particularly on international data transfers matters, such as binding corporate rules.

Mr Watts has particular expertise in advising companies on how to respond to data protection enforcement actions, including monetary penalty notices.

Mr Watts is on the correspondent panel of *Computer Law & Security* and is a member of the editorial board of *Privacy & Data Protection*.

Stuart Weinstein
Associate dean (research and enterprise),
University of Hertfordshire School of Law
s.weinstein@herts.ac.uk

Stuart Weinstein is associate dean (research and enterprise) at the University of Hertfordshire School of Law, Hatfield, Hertfordshire. Before joining the University of Hertfordshire School of

Law, he worked as general counsel to Korean multinational Daewoo in Seoul, Republic of Korea, and Los Angeles. Mr Weinstein is co-author with Charles Wild of *Smith & Keenan's English Law* (17th ed, Pearson 2013) and *Smith & Keenan's Company Law* (16th ed, Pearson 2013). In addition to his various research and writing projects, Mr Weinstein remains active in practice as a solicitor of the Superior Courts of England and Wales advising companies, governmental entities and non-profit organisations on aspects of legal risk management, governance and compliance. He is admitted to practise law in the US jurisdictions of California, District of Columbia and New York.

Mr Weinstein earned his BA (honours) in the history of ideas from Williams College, Williamstown, Massachusetts, his JD from Columbia Law School, New York City, where he was a Harlan Fiske Stone scholar, and an MBA with commendation from the University of Hertfordshire Business School, and he was selected to be a Fulbright scholar grantee. Mr Weinstein also serves as vice chair of the Bar Standards Board's Education and Training Committee.

Charles Wild
Professor of legal education and dean,
University of Hertfordshire School of Law
c.wild@herts.ac.uk

Charles Wild is professor of legal education and dean of the University of Hertfordshire School of Law, where he teaches company law, corporate governance and risk management. He is the co-author with Stuart Weinstein of *Smith & Keenan's English Law* (17th ed, Pearson 2013) and *Smith & Keenan's Company Law* (16th ed, Pearson 2013). Dr Wild holds a PhD in law from the University of Sheffield, an MBA (distinction) from the University of Hertfordshire Business School and an LLM in international and commercial law from the University of Sheffield (distinction), together with a number of other qualifications, including a BSc (hons) in economics from University College, London. Dr Wild is also a member of the

Education and Training (Standard Setting)
Committee at the Law Society of Scotland.